Dictionary of Literary Biography

Dictionary of Literary Biography Documentary Series

1 *Sherwood Anderson, Willa Cather, John Dos Passos, Theodore Dreiser, F. Scott Fitzgerald, Ernest Hemingway, Sinclair Lewis,* edited by Margaret A. Van Antwerp (1982)

2 *James Gould Cozzens, James T. Farrell, William Faulkner, John O'Hara, John Steinbeck, Thomas Wolfe, Richard Wright,* edited by Margaret A. Van Antwerp (1982)

3 *Saul Bellow, Jack Kerouac, Norman Mailer, Vladimir Nabokov, John Updike, Kurt Vonnegut,* edited by Mary Bruccoli (1983)

4 *Tennessee Williams,* edited by Margaret A. Van Antwerp and Sally Johns (1984)

5 *American Transcendentalists,* edited by Joel Myerson (1988)

6 *Hardboiled Mystery Writers: Raymond Chandler, Dashiell Hammett, Ross Mac-* donald, edited by Matthew J. Bruccoli and Richard Layman (1989)

7 *Modern American Poets: James Dickey, Robert Frost, Marianne Moore,* edited by Karen L. Rood (1989)

8 *The Black Aesthetic Movement,* edited by Jeffrey Louis Decker (1991)

9 *American Writers of the Vietnam War: W. D. Ehrhart, Larry Heinemann, Tim O'Brien, Walter McDonald, John M. Del Vecchio,* edited by Ronald Baughman (1991)

10 *The Bloomsbury Group,* edited by Edward L. Bishop (1992)

11 *American Proletarian Culture: The Twenties and The Thirties,* edited by Jon Christian Suggs (1993)

12 *Southern Women Writers: Flannery O'Connor, Katherine Anne Porter, Eudora Welty,* edited by Mary Ann Wimsatt and Karen L. Rood (1994)

13 *The House of Scribner, 1846–1904,* edited by John Delaney (1996)

14 *Four Women Writers for Children, 1868–1918,* edited by Caroline C. Hunt (1996)

15 *American Expatriate Writers: Paris in the Twenties,* edited by Matthew J. Bruccoli and Robert W. Trogdon (1997)

16 *The House of Scribner, 1905–1930,* edited by John Delaney (1997)

17 *The House of Scribner, 1931–1984,* edited by John Delaney (1998)

18 *British Poets of The Great War: Sassoon, Graves, Owen,* edited by Patrick Quinn (1999)

19 *James Dickey,* edited by Judith S. Baughman (1999)

See also DLB 210, 216, 219, 222, 224, 229, 237, 247, 253, 254, 263, 269, 273, 274, 280, 284, 288, 291, 294, 298, 301, 304, 308, 309

Dictionary of Literary Biography Yearbooks

1980 edited by Karen L. Rood, Jean W. Ross, and Richard Ziegfeld (1981)

1981 edited by Karen L. Rood, Jean W. Ross, and Richard Ziegfeld (1982)

1982 edited by Richard Ziegfeld; associate editors: Jean W. Ross and Lynne C. Zeigler (1983)

1983 edited by Mary Bruccoli and Jean W. Ross; associate editor Richard Ziegfeld (1984)

1984 edited by Jean W. Ross (1985)

1985 edited by Jean W. Ross (1986)

1986 edited by J. M. Brook (1987)

1987 edited by J. M. Brook (1988)

1988 edited by J. M. Brook (1989)

1989 edited by J. M. Brook (1990)

1990 edited by James W. Hipp (1991)

1991 edited by James W. Hipp (1992)

1992 edited by James W. Hipp (1993)

1993 edited by James W. Hipp, contributing editor George Garrett (1994)

1994 edited by James W. Hipp, contributing editor George Garrett (1995)

1995 edited by James W. Hipp, contributing editor George Garrett (1996)

1996 edited by Samuel W. Bruce and L. Kay Webster, contributing editor George Garrett (1997)

1997 edited by Matthew J. Bruccoli and George Garrett, with the assistance of L. Kay Webster (1998)

1998 edited by Matthew J. Bruccoli, contributing editor George Garrett, with the assistance of D. W. Thomas (1999)

1999 edited by Matthew J. Bruccoli, contributing editor George Garrett, with the assistance of D. W. Thomas (2000)

2000 edited by Matthew J. Bruccoli, contributing editor George Garrett, with the assistance of George Parker Anderson (2001)

2001 edited by Matthew J. Bruccoli, contributing editor George Garrett, with the assistance of George Parker Anderson (2002)

2002 edited by Matthew J. Bruccoli and George Garrett; George Parker Anderson, Assistant Editor (2003)

Concise Series

Concise Dictionary of American Literary Biography, 7 volumes (1988–1999): *The New Consciousness, 1941–1968; Colonization to the American Renaissance, 1640–1865; Realism, Naturalism, and Local Color, 1865–1917; The Twenties, 1917–1929; The Age of Maturity, 1929–1941; Broadening Views, 1968–1988; Supplement: Modern Writers, 1900–1998.*

Concise Dictionary of British Literary Biography, 8 volumes (1991–1992): *Writers of the Middle Ages and Renaissance Before 1660; Writers of the Restoration and Eighteenth Century, 1660–1789; Writers of the Romantic Period, 1789–1832; Victorian Writers, 1832–1890; Late-Victorian and Edwardian Writers, 1890–1914; Modern Writers, 1914–1945; Writers After World War II, 1945–1960; Contemporary Writers, 1960 to Present.*

Concise Dictionary of World Literary Biography, 4 volumes (1999–2000): *Ancient Greek and Roman Writers; German Writers; African, Caribbean, and Latin American Writers; South Slavic and Eastern European Writers.*

John Steinbeck:
A Documentary Volume

Dictionary of Literary Biography® • Volume Three Hundred Nine

John Steinbeck:
A Documentary Volume

Edited by
Luchen Li
Kettering University

A Bruccoli Clark Layman Book

THOMSON

GALE

Detroit • New York • San Francisco • San Diego • New Haven, Conn. • Waterville, Maine • London • Munich

THOMSON

★

GALE

™

Dictionary of Literary Biography
Volume 309: John Steinbeck:
A Documentary Volume
Luchen Li

Editorial Directors
Matthew J. Bruccoli and Richard Layman

LIBRARY OF CONGRESS CATALOGING-IN-PUBLICATION DATA

John Steinbeck : a documentary volume / edited by Luchen Li.
    p. cm. — (Dictionary of literary biography ; v. 309)
    "A Bruccoli Clark Layman Book."
    Includes bibliographical references and index.
    ISBN 0–7876–8127–X (alk. paper)
    1. Steinbeck, John, 1902–1968. 2. Novelists, American—20th century—Biography. I. Li, Luchen. II. Series.
    PS3537.T3234Z71549 2005
    813'.52—dc22
                                           2005000500

Printed in the United States of America
10 9 8 7 6 5 4 3 2 1

To my wife, Yan, and our children, Tengbo and Emy

Contents

Plan of the Series

The advisory board, the editors, and the publisher of the *Dictionary of Literary Biography* are joined in endorsing Mark Twain's declaration. The literature of a nation provides an inexhaustible resource of permanent worth. Our purpose is to make literature and its creators better understood and more accessible to students and the reading public, while satisfying the needs of teachers and researchers.

To meet these requirements, *literary biography* has been construed in terms of the author's achievement. The most important thing about a writer is his writing. Accordingly, the entries in *DLB* are career biographies, tracing the development of the author's canon and the evolution of his reputation.

The purpose of *DLB* is not only to provide reliable information in a usable format but also to place the figures in the larger perspective of literary history and to offer appraisals of their accomplishments by qualified scholars.

The publication plan for *DLB* resulted from two years of preparation. The project was proposed to Bruccoli Clark by Frederick G. Ruffner, president of the Gale Research Company, in November 1975. After specimen entries were prepared and typeset, an advisory board was formed to refine the entry format and develop the series rationale. In meetings held during 1976, the publisher, series editors, and advisory board approved the scheme for a comprehensive biographical dictionary of persons who contributed to literature. Editorial work on the first volume began in January 1977, and it was published in 1978. In order to make *DLB* more than a dictionary and to compile volumes that individually have claim to status as literary history, it was decided to organize volumes by topic, period, or

genre. Each of these freestanding volumes provides a biographical-bibliographical guide and overview for a particular area of literature. We are convinced that this organization—as opposed to a single alphabet method—constitutes a valuable innovation in the presentation of reference material. The volume plan necessarily requires many decisions for the placement and treatment of authors. Certain figures will be included in separate volumes, but with different entries emphasizing the aspect of his career appropriate to each volume. Ernest Hemingway, for example, is represented in *American Writers in Paris, 1920–1939* by an entry focusing on his expatriate apprenticeship; he is also in *American Novelists, 1910–1945* with an entry surveying his entire career, as well as in *American Short-Story Writers, 1910–1945, Second Series* with an entry concentrating on his short fiction. Each volume includes a cumulative index of the subject authors and articles.

Between 1981 and 2002 the series was augmented and updated by the *DLB Yearbooks*. There have also been nineteen *DLB Documentary Series* volumes, which provide illustrations, facsimiles, and biographical and critical source materials for figures, works, or groups judged to have particular interest for students. In 1999 the *Documentary Series* was incorporated into the *DLB* volume numbering system beginning with *DLB 210: Ernest Hemingway*.

We define literature as the *intellectual commerce of a nation:* not merely as belles lettres but as that ample and complex process by which ideas are generated, shaped, and transmitted. *DLB* entries are not limited to "creative writers" but extend to other figures who in their time and in their way influenced the mind of a people. Thus the series encompasses historians, journalists, publishers, book collectors, and screenwriters. By this means readers of *DLB* may be aided to perceive literature not as cult scripture in the keeping of intellectual high priests but firmly positioned at the center of a nation's life.

DLB includes the major writers appropriate to each volume and those standing in the ranks behind them. Scholarly and critical counsel has been sought in deciding which minor figures to include and how full their entries should be. Wherever possible, useful references are made to figures who do not warrant separate entries.

Each *DLB* volume has an expert volume editor responsible for planning the volume, selecting the figures for inclusion, and assigning the entries. Volume editors are also responsible for preparing, where appropriate, appendices surveying the major periodicals and literary and intellectual movements for their volumes, as well as lists of further readings. Work on the series as a whole is coordinated at the Bruccoli Clark Layman editorial center in Columbia, South Carolina, where the editorial staff is responsible for accuracy and utility of the published volumes.

One feature that distinguishes *DLB* is the illustration policy—its concern with the iconography of literature. Just as an author is influenced by his surroundings, so is the reader's understanding of the author enhanced by a knowledge of his environment. Therefore *DLB*

volumes include not only drawings, paintings, and photographs of authors, often depicting them at various stages in their careers, but also illustrations of their families and places where they lived. Title pages are regularly reproduced in facsimile along with dust jackets for modern authors. The dust jackets are a special feature of *DLB* because they often document better than anything else the way in which an author's work was perceived in its own time. Specimens of the writers' manuscripts and letters are included when feasible.

Samuel Johnson rightly decreed that "The chief glory of every people arises from its authors." The purpose of the *Dictionary of Literary Biography* is to compile literary history in the surest way available to us—by accurate and comprehensive treatment of the lives and work of those who contributed to it.

The *DLB* Advisory Board

Introduction

John Steinbeck was one of the most accomplished and widely read American authors of the twentieth century. Today his books continue to sell millions of copies every year, both in and outside the United States. His themes cover a broad range of issues—social, political, cultural, moral, global, and environmental. Throughout his career he experimented with several literary styles and wrote in various genres, including novels, short stories, screenplays, journals, essays, and newspaper and magazine articles. Although Steinbeck's works have enjoyed wide popularity, they have also been the subject of pointed criticism, and he occupies a controversial position in American literary history.

Steinbeck was among the last of the generation of American writers that included F. Scott Fitzgerald, John Dos Passos, Ernest Hemingway, and William Faulkner. Born on 27 February 1902 in Salinas, California, Steinbeck grew up in the farming country of the Salinas Valley. He began attending Stanford University in 1919 as a student of writing, literature, and marine biology but had to leave school periodically to work in various jobs. His sporadic attendance at Stanford ended when he left the university without a degree in 1925. After a short sojourn as a newspaper reporter in New York, Steinbeck returned to California in June 1926 and concentrated on writing his first book, *Cup of Gold* (1929), a fictionalized account of the life of Henry Morgan, the late-seventeenth-century Welsh buccaneer. The novel received little critical attention, but the publication of Steinbeck's first book convinced the New York literary agency of McIntosh and Otis to represent the young author for his future works.

As a representative American writer of the 1930s, Steinbeck has been highly regarded by critics and readers for his writings about the era of the Depression. During his adolescence he knew of the hardships of farmhands and migrant workers, and he gained firsthand knowledge of their situation when he did farmwork himself in his twenties. He documented the harsh lives of migrant laborers in "The Harvest Gypsies" (1936), a series of articles he wrote for *The San Francisco News,* and his understanding of their condition informs such novels as *In Dubious Battle* (1936), *Of Mice and Men* (1937), and *The Grapes of Wrath* (1939). The California landscape also shaped Steinbeck's works. His native region, the Salinas Valley and the Monterey Peninsula area, serves as the setting for many of his short stories and novels, including *Tortilla Flat* (1935) and *Of Mice and Men.*

Although Steinbeck's novels of the 1930s, particularly *The Grapes of Wrath,* made him a national figure, his writing was the target of political attacks. His reputation peaked in the late 1930s and early 1940s, but even during these peak years both radicals and conservatives treated him as an outlaw. Upon publication in 1939, *The Grapes of Wrath* drew criticism for its language and alleged factual inaccuracies; the novel was even labeled communist propaganda and denounced as obscene and sensationalistic. The controversy over the book was such that the board of education in Kansas City banned it from city libraries, and the board of the library in East St. Louis ordered the burning of the three copies owned by the library. *The Grapes of Wrath,* which won the 1940 Pulitzer Prize, was also denounced on the floor of the United States House of Representatives by Oklahoma congressman Lyle H. Boren as a "dirty, lying, filthy manuscript."

Steinbeck's fall from critical and academic favor can largely be explained by the ups and downs of political trends in American society. Even in the late 1930s readers and critics thought more highly of his sympathetic portraits of the dispossessed and his understanding of common people than they did of his artistic achievement. In evaluating Steinbeck's social novels, conservative critics charged him with political radicalism, viewing *In Dubious Battle* and *The Grapes of Wrath* as challenges to the capitalist system and as evidence of the writer's sympathy with communist ideology.

Steinbeck had a profound sympathy for those who had been cheated out of their natural birthright and dignity. Injustice drove him wild; as his older sister Beth recalled, "Even as a child John sided with the underdog." These liberal sympathies bound him emotionally to the struggles of workers, as is indicated by the strike at the center of *In Dubious Battle,* but at the same time he was regarded by communists of the 1930s as "politically unreliable." Radical critics praised Steinbeck's works for being "real" but were disappointed in the writer for his "political ambivalence."

Politically oriented criticism has treated Steinbeck's works as immediate reflections of actual social struggles, such as the Californian farmworkers' strikes and the Okies' migration. Upon publication of *The Grapes of Wrath,* there were many positive evaluations and appraisals of the novel along these lines. Critics did not hesitate to label Steinbeck a proletarian writer, a label associated with that of propagandist. In his 1979 dissertation "Twentieth-Century American Political Fiction: An Analysis of Proletarian Fiction," Calvin E. Harris quotes the novelist and critic Edwin Seaver in defining the proletarian novel: "The basic distinction of the proletarian novel is its concern with political orientation, with economic interpretation, and with a certain historical perspective, with the materialist dialectic." The conclusion drawn from Harris's categorization is that proletarian novels such as Steinbeck's have less artistic value than those with more-general literary themes.

In the 1940s Steinbeck began to explore the cinema, writing the screenplay for *The Forgotten Village* (1941), a documentary about a Mexican village. During this time he also devoted much of his attention to World War II, writing *Bombs Away: The Story of a Bomber Team* (1942) and *The Moon Is Down* (1942), the story of a town occupied by fascist forces. Later in the decade he moved away from the war theme with *Cannery Row* (1945), *The Wayward Bus* (1947), and *The Pearl* (1947). In 1948 Steinbeck, accompanied by photojournalist Robert Capa, traveled to the former Soviet Union on a cultural-exchange program, a trip that was the basis for *A Russian Journal* (1948). Following the dramatization of both *Of Mice and Men* and *The Moon Is Down,* in the 1950s Steinbeck experimented with another drama, *Burning Bright* (1950). *Pipe Dream* (1955) was a musical adaptation by Richard Rodgers and Oscar Hammerstein 2nd of Steinbeck's *Sweet Thursday* (1954), the sequel to *Cannery Row.* Steinbeck's ambitious saga of the Salinas Valley and his own family history, *East of Eden,* was published in 1952. He spent the last two decades of his career living and writing in New York and Sag Harbor, on Long Island. *Sweet Thursday, The Short Reign of Pippin IV: A Fabrication* (1957), *Once There Was a War* (1958), *The Winter of Our Discontent* (1961), *Travels with Charley: In Search of America* (1962), and *America and Americans* (1966) were all published during this time.

Steinbeck's literary reputation reached a low point in the 1960s; few critics at that time would have ranked him with the great American writers of the twentieth century. When the Swedish Academy announced him as the 1962 recipient of the Nobel Prize in literature, *The New York Times* ran an editorial with the headline "Does A Moral Vision of the Thirties Deserve the Nobel Prize?" In his acceptance speech for the prize, Steinbeck declared that literature was "our greatest hazard and our only hope." He believed that the power of writing lay in uniting people and helping them to overcome their fears and troubles. He sought "to celebrate man's proven capacity for greatness of heart and spirit."

Following Steinbeck's death on 20 December 1968, his works began to be reevaluated from new perspectives. Two important publications marking this trend were Lester Jay Marks's *Thematic Design in the Novels of John Steinbeck* (1969) and Richard Astro's *John Steinbeck and Edward F. Ricketts: The Shaping of a Novelist* (1973). Steinbeck scholars still debate the extent to which his friend Edward F. Ricketts, the marine biologist who was the model for Doc in *Cannery Row,* influenced his philosophy. In the 1980s and the 1990s scholars such as John Ditsky, Warren French, Robert DeMott, Susan Shillinglaw, and Stephen K. George wrote about Steinbeck's vision of American society.

Steinbeck's literary reputation rests largely on his novels of the Depression. While these books are familiar to many readers, his nonfiction is less well known. He published articles in a variety of magazines and newspapers throughout his career. *America and Americans,* a collection of essays written to accompany photographs of everyday American life, indicates his concerns for the environment, homelessness, moral decline, racism, and ethnicity. Steinbeck was a journalist at heart. In 1943 he served as a war correspondent for the *New York Herald Tribune,* and in the 1950s and 1960s he took several trips to Europe to write for popular magazines such as *Collier's, Holiday,* and *Esquire.* His last assignment as a journalist was to report on the Vietnam War for the Long Island paper *Newsday* in late 1966 and early 1967. Steinbeck sometimes took a skeptical view of journalism as practiced. In a 1955 letter to John P. McKnight of the United States Information Service, he wrote that journalism could be both the "greatest virtue and the greatest evil. It is the first thing the dictator controls. It is the mother of literature and the perpetrator of crap. In many cases it is the only history we have and yet it is the tool of the worst men. But over a long period of time and perhaps because it is the product of so many men, it is perhaps the purest thing we have."

As a keen observer of American society as well as the world, Steinbeck often reminded himself of the importance of the role of objective eyewitness. In a 2 April 1966 *Newsday* column he wrote,

It occurs to me to wonder and to ask how much I see or am capable of seeing. It goes without saying that our observation is conditioned by our background and experience, but do we ever observe anything objectively, do we ever see anything whole and as it is? I have always fancied myself as a fairly objective looker, but I'm beginning to wonder whether I do not miss whole categories of things. . . . And I wonder what I have missed in the wonderful trip to the south that I have just completed. Did I see only America?

Steinbeck always tried to illuminate for his readers the special nature of America. He admired Washington Irving's joy in depicting the American people—their speech, stories, and patterns of thought—and he praised writers such as Sherwood Anderson, Stephen Crane, Theodore Dreiser, Faulkner, Hemingway, Sinclair Lewis, Jack London, Frank Norris, Mark Twain, and Thomas Wolfe for their vivid portraits of American life. While Steinbeck did not make himself over in the image of his literary predecessors or contemporaries, his writing was influenced by their example.

Steinbeck experimented with different styles because he easily tired of his own technique. Learning a new craft made everything fresh for him. *Of Mice and Men* was an experiment in a new genre that he called the "play-novelette." In an article published in *Stage* (January 1938) he wrote, "*Of Mice and Men* was an attempt to write a novel that could be played from the lines, or a play that could be read." He believed that "a play written in the physical technique of the novel would have a number of advantages." *The Moon Is Down* is a similar work, written to be "played from the lines." Steinbeck returned to screenwriting with *Viva Zapata!*, a fictionalized account of the life of the Mexican agrarian reformer Emiliano Zapata, which Elia Kazan made into a successful movie in 1952.

Steinbeck valued social movements, including strikes and protests, in the name of justice, but even more, he displayed a respect for all life. His view of humanity is seen in the character Dr. Burton in *In Dubious Battle*. When asked whether the revolutionary cause is good or not, Burton sighs, "Listen to me, Mac. My senses aren't above reproach, but they're all I have. I want to see the whole picture—as nearly as I can. I don't want to put on the blinders of 'good' and 'bad,' and limit my vision. . . . I want to be able to look at the whole thing." In *The Grapes of Wrath* Steinbeck depicts the migrant workers as insects driven by huge external forces and adapting themselves to the demands of their changing environments:

> The cars of the migrant people crawled out of the side roads onto the great cross-country highway, and then took the migrant way to the West. In the daylight they scuttled like bugs to the westward; and as the dark caught them, they clustered like bugs near to shelter

and to water. . . . Thus it might be that one family camped near a spring, and another camped for the spring and for company, and a third because two families had pioneered the place and found it good.

Steinbeck's treatment of his characters reflected his firm belief that life should be considered as a whole. That is why he often drew on science in his writing. In the early 1940s he made several research trips with Ricketts in order to collect marine specimens. One such trip, made to the Gulf of California in the spring of 1940, was the subject of *Sea of Cortez: A Leisurely Journal of Travel and Research* (1941), co-authored by the two friends. Steinbeck's interest in nature imparted a profound sense of the physical world to his fiction. He spent a great deal of time with Ricketts discussing scientific subjects and believed that mankind must be conscious of its place in the scheme of creation and the larger community of all living things. Steinbeck wanted his readers to ask questions about how things are rather than how they should be. Like Ricketts, he was careful not to assume that man was the measure of all things.

Skilled in dramatic techniques, Steinbeck was able to compel his readers to identify with a particular moment of crisis. He wanted his readers to become part of the story. As he wrote to his editor, Pascal Covici, in one of the letters included in the posthumously published *Journal of a Novel: The East of Eden Letters* (1969), "I want the participation of my reader. I want him to be so involved that it will be *his* story." As he noted about his technique in writing *East of Eden*,

> after everyone is asleep there is such quiet and peace, and it is during this time that I can explore every land and trail of thinking. Conjecture. . . . I split myself into three people. I know what they look like. One speculates and one criticizes and the third tries to correlate. It usually turns out to be a fight but out of it comes the whole week's work. And it is carried on in my mind in dialogue. It's an odd experience. Under certain circumstances it might be one of those schizophrenic symptoms but as a working technique, I do not think it is bad at all.

Through this method of working, Steinbeck was able to build solid narratives out of scattered material, especially in such works as *Tortilla Flat* and *Cannery Row*.

Steinbeck's prose is not simply straightforward narrative interspersed here and there with lyrical passages; instead, it is rich in literary devices. Patterns of imagery are interwoven through his works so subtly as to escape casual notice. For example, in *The Grapes of Wrath* he uses personification and metonymy in the descriptions of a turtle struggling to cross a highway (suggestive of migrant workers' struggles to survive) and of tractors moving over farmland, representing the hostile Eastern banking interests taking over agriculture. Steinbeck also employs imagery to develop characters such as Jim Casy (in *The Grapes of Wrath*) and Samuel Hamilton (in *East of Eden*). In identifying these characters, he uses earth, animal, and vegetable imagery, either to complement or contrast with their personalities. This use of imagery gives Steinbeck's prose a kind of mysticism. For example, in *To a God Unknown* (1933) the land, an oak tree, and even rain and thunder seem to carry voices of human beings. In the final scene Joseph Wayne offers himself as a sacrifice to powerful nature. This view of the living world, often interpreted by readers as paganism, is congruent with Steinbeck's philosophy, which holds that human life is a mystery and that beauty lies in the unification of man and nature. The development of the theme—how Wayne works out his own salvation by saving the land through self-sacrifice—is strikingly reinforced by Steinbeck's use of animistic mysticism.

Symbolism and allusion held great importance for Steinbeck, who described much of his writing as deliberately symbolic. In *Tortilla Flat,* often read merely as a work of local color, the *paisanos* are undeniably a colorful people, but these "exotic" figures represent characters from Arthurian legend. The title of *East of Eden* is an allusion that is internally consistent with the plot of the novel. The great quest of Adam Trask is not to find an Eden but to learn to live east of it—in a fallen world of mortal evil. The symbolism of the novel is of a piece with Steinbeck's larger view of literary art and suggestiveness. As he writes in *Journal of a Novel,* "the craft or art of writing is the clumsy attempt to find symbols for the wordlessness. In utter loneliness the writer tries to explain the inexplicable." Steinbeck believed that "a good writer always works at the impossible."

Steinbeck was not content to be merely an observer; many of his books were products of a speculative intelligence. The writing of fiction was a means for him to build new conceptions of the world, often separate from the interests of economics and sociology. Characters such as Lee in *East of Eden,* Kino in *The Pearl,* and Danny and Pilon in *Tortilla Flat* presented American readers with the perspectives of different cultures. Because Steinbeck's understanding of the broad processes of human life gave him distinction among conventional writers, his interests also carried him squarely into central truths about the universal nature of human existence.

Although a California native, Steinbeck is not a typical Western writer, not only because he lived much of his adult life in the East but also because not all of his books have Western themes or settings. In many of his works he transcends geographical regions and crosses cultural boundaries even as he writes about the West. As Steinbeck revealed to friend and reviewer Joseph Henry Jackson in 1939, "I have set down what a large section of our people are doing and wanting, and symbolically what all people of all time are doing and wanting." There are two reasons why one writes, according to Steinbeck: "One is that writers write out of recognition of their own personal failings" in order to rectify what they see lacking in themselves. The second reason is that writers are by nature private people, in many cases insecure and incapable of relating comfortably to others. For Steinbeck, the entire act of writing was private and solitary because he believed that writers themselves should never seek celebrity.

Steinbeck never wrote an autobiography. Nevertheless, by the time of his death in 1968, he had revealed himself in sixteen novels, two short-story collections, hundreds of personal letters, two screenplays, and several nonfiction books. This sizable body of work gives a definition and voice to his experience of living, working, and traveling not only across the United States but also around the world. While readers of several generations in the United States and England have grown up reading books such as *Of Mice and Men, The Pearl,* and *The Red Pony* (1937; enlarged, 1945), readers from Cairo to Beijing and from Tokyo to Stockholm continue to read Steinbeck's books in translation. Contrary to the prediction of many influential critics that his popularity would decline after his death, in the United States more than fifty thousand copies of *The Grapes of Wrath* are sold each year. Fresh adaptations of Steinbeck's best-known works, such as *East of Eden* and *Of Mice and Men,* appear regularly on the stage and screen. According to a 2002 article in *The New York Times,* his books sell about two million copies a year. In 2002, the centenary of his birth, there were almost two hundred events in thirty-eight states honoring Steinbeck.

The letters, memoirs, articles, and illustrations in this volume trace Steinbeck's career as a writer. His statements about his own books and the works of other authors are included to illuminate the philosophies behind his writing and his ideas about art. Whenever possible, reviews of his works by other authors have been selected because the most interesting judgments are those provided by other writers.

—Luchen Li

Acknowledgments

This book was produced by Bruccoli Clark Layman, Inc. R. Bland Lawson was the in-house editor.

Production manager is Philip B. Dematteis.

Administrative support was provided by Carol A. Cheschi.

Accountant is Ann-Marie Holland.

Copyediting supervisor is Sally R. Evans. The copyediting staff includes Phyllis A. Avant, Caryl Brown, Melissa D. Hinton, Philip I. Jones, Rebecca Mayo, Nadirah Rahimah Shabazz, and Nancy E. Smith.

Pipeline manager is James F. Tidd Jr.

Editorial associates are Jessica R. Goudeau and Joshua Shaw.

In-house vetter is Catherine M. Polit.

Permissions editor is Amber L. Coker.

Layout and graphics supervisor is Janet E. Hill. The graphics staff includes Zoe R. Cook and Sydney E. Hammock.

Office manager is Kathy Lawler Merlette.

Photography editors are Mark J. McEwan and Walter W. Ross.

Digital photographic copy work was performed by Joseph M. Bruccoli.

Systems manager is Donald Kevin Starling.

Typesetting supervisor is Kathleen M. Flanagan. The typesetting staff includes Patricia Marie Flanagan and Pamela D. Norton.

Walter W. Ross is library researcher. He was assisted by the following librarians at the Thomas Cooper Library of the University of South Carolina: Elizabeth Suddeth and the rare-book department; Jo Cottingham, interlibrary loan department; circulation department head Tucker Taylor; reference department head Virginia W. Weathers; reference department staff Laurel Baker, Marilee Birchfield, Kate Boyd, Paul Cammarata, Joshua Garris, Gary Geer, Tom Marcil, Rose Marshall, and Sharon Verba; interlibrary loan department head Marna Hostetler; and interlibrary loan staff Bill Fetty, Nelson Rivera, and Cedric Rose.

Permissions

Guardian Newspapers Limited

Harold Brighouse, review of *To a God Unknown,* "Pan in California," *Manchester Guardian,* 27 March 1935, p. 7. Guardian Unlimited © Guardian Newspapers Limited 2005.

Heldref Publications

Rebecca Hinton, "Steinbeck's *The Grapes of Wrath,*" *The Explicator* (Winter 1998). Used by permission of Heldref Publications.

Henry Holt & Company, Inc.

Steinbeck to Pascal Covici, 28 January 1963, reprinted in Jay Parini, *John Steinbeck: A Biography* (New York: Holt, 1995). Illustration on p. 284. Copyright © 1995 by Henry Holt & Company, Inc. Reprinted with permission. All rights reserved.

Johns Hopkins University Press

Peter Lisca, "Journal of a Novel: The East of Eden Letters," *Modern Fiction Studies,* 16 (Winter 1970–1971). © Purdue Research Foundation. Reprinted with permission of The Johns Hopkins University Press.

Library Journal

"Coalition receives $260K for centennial programs," *Library Journal* (15 September 2001).

Limited Editions Club

Excerpt from "Why Steinbeck Wrote The Grapes of Wrath, by Joseph Henry Jackson, and Other Essays," *Booklets for Bookmen,* no. 1 (New York: Limited Editions Club, 1940). Copyright © 1940 Limited Editions Club. Reprinted with permission.

Los Angeles Times

Review of *Cup of Gold* (upon reprint of book), "Steinbeck's First," *Los Angeles Times,* 26 July 1936. J.H.C., review of *The Red Pony, Los Angeles Times,* 10 October 1937.

Luchen Li

Illustrations on pp. 8, 312.

***The Mercury News,* San Jose, California**

Paul G. Teal, review of *Cup of Gold, San Jose Mercury Herald,* 1 December 1929, p. 7. Copyright © 2005 Knight Ridder. All Rights Reserved.

Museum of Modern Art/Film Stills Archive

Illustrations on pp. 161, 179, 213, 244. Digital Images © The Museum of Modern Art, New York.

The Nation

Review of *To a God Unknown, Nation,* 137 (18 October 1933): 456. Helen Nelville, review of *Tortilla Flat, Nation,* 140 (19 June 1935). Reprinted with permission.

New Republic

Clarence Brown, "The Callus Behind the Fiction," *New Republic,* 161 (20 December 1969). Stanley Kauffman, review of *Of Mice and Men* (movie), *New Republic* (2 November 1992).

New York Post

Frederick Turner, "The Wrath, the Discontent and the Grapes," *New York Post,* 16 April 1989, p. 10. F.H.M., review of *Cup of Gold, New York Evening Post* (28 September 1929), sec. M, 7. Reprinted by permission of *New York Post.*

New York Times Co.

Martin Arnold, "Of Mice and Men and Novelists," *New York Times,* 7 February 2001. Dagoberto Gilb, "Sentimental for Steinbeck," *New York Times,* 18 March 2002. Fred T. Marsh, review of *Tortilla Flat, New York Times Book Review,* 2 June 1935, p. 5. Fred T. Marsh, review of *In Dubious Battle, New York Times Book Review,* 2 February 1936. Charles Poore, review of *Grapes of Wrath, New York Times,* 14 April 1939. Peter Monro Jack, review of *Grapes of Wrath, New York Times Book Review,* 16 April 1939. Brooks Atkinson, review of *The Moon is Down* [stage version], *New York Times,* 12 April 1942. Oriana Atkinson, review of *A Russian Journal, New York Times Book Review,* 9 May 1948. Eric F. Goldman, review of *Travels with Charley, New York Times Book Review,* 9 May 1948. John Gardner, "The Essential King Arthur, According to John Steinbeck," *New York Times Book Review,* 126 (24 October 1976). Used by permission. Copyright © The New York Times Co.

Newsday, Inc.

"Bulgarians Criticize Steinbeck," *Newsday* (23 January 1967). Copyright © Newsday, Inc.

North American Review

Grant Tracey, "Steinbeck Revisited," *North American Review* (September–October 2000).

Oregon State University Press

Illustration on p. 169.

Pacific Discovery

Joel W. Hedgpeth, review of *The Log from the Sea of Cortez, Pacific Discovery,* 6 (January–February 1953).

Reprinted with permission from *Pacific Discovery,* publication of the California Academy of Sciences.

Jay Parini

Jay Parini, "California Dreamer," *Book* (May–June 2000). Reprinted by permission of the author.

Penguin Group (USA)

Excerpts from *Steinbeck: A Life in Letters,* edited by Elaine Steinbeck and Robert Wallsten (New York: Viking, 1975). Copyright © 1975 by Viking Press, an imprint of Penguin Group (USA) and John Steinbeck. Reprinted with permission. Katherine Beswick to Steinbeck, summer 1928, reprinted in Jackson J. Benson, *The True Adventures of John Steinbeck, Writer.* Robert Capa, "A Legitimate Complaint," in Steinbeck, *A Russian Journal* (New York: Viking, 1948). Copyright © Viking Press, a division of Penguin Group (USA).

Publishers Weekly

"Recollecting Steinbeck," *Publishers Weekly* (28 January 2002).

Edward F. Ricketts Jr.

Illustrations on pp. 131, 132.

Salinas Californian

W. Max Gordon, review of *East of Eden, Salinas Californian,* 14 September 1952. Copyright © 1952 by The Salinas Californian. All rights reserved.

San Francisco Chronicle

Joseph Henry Jackson, review of *Tortilla Flat, San Francisco Chronicle,* 28 May 1935, p. 16. Jackson, review of *In Dubious Battle, San Francisco Chronicle,* 1 January 1936. Scott Newhall, review of *Sea of Cortez: A Leisurely Journal of Travel and Research, San Francisco Chronicle,* 14 December 1941. Joel W. Hedgepeth, review of *Sea of Cortez: A Leisurely Journal of Travel and Research, San Francisco Chronicle,* 14 December 1941. Brian St. Pierre, "Steinbeck's Timeless Tale of Migrant Suffering," *San Francisco Chronicle,* 26 March 1989. Reprinted with permission.

Smithsonian Magazine

Bil Gilbert, "Prince of Tides," *Smithsonian Magazine,* 32 (January 2002): 95. Copyright © 2002 *Smithsonian Magazine.*

The Spectator

Robin King, review of *The Wayward Bus, The Spectator,* 173 (19 December 1947). Reprinted with permission.

Peter Stackpole

Illustrations on pp. 38 and 90.

Stanford Daily Publishing Corporation

A.M., review of *Cup of Gold, Stanford Daily,* 30 October 1929, p. 2. Copyright © 1929 Stanford Daily Publishing Corporation.

Stanford University Archives

Illustration on p. 33.

John Steinbeck Estate/McIntosh and Otis

Robert DeMott, ed., *Your Only Weapon Is Your Work: A Letter by John Steinbeck to Dennis Murphy* (San Jose, Cal.: Steinbeck Research Center, 1985). Excerpts from *Steinbeck: A Life in Letters,* edited by Elaine Steinbeck and Robert Wallsten (New York: Viking, 1975). "Robert Capa: An Appreciation by John Steinbeck," in Capa, *Images of War* (New York: Grossman, 1964). Steinbeck, "The How, When and Where of High School," *Salinas Californian,* July 1963. Steinbeck, Nobel Prize acceptance speech, *Literature, 1901–1967,* edited by Horst Frenz, Nobel Lectures Series (Amsterdam: Elsevier, 1969). Illustrations on pp. 6, 7, 9, 13, 14, 15, 19, 21, 26, 27, 28, 29, 38, 41, 49, 54, 56, 57, 61, 112, 124, 148, 161, 163, 169, 172, 173, 174, 180, 181, 182, 183, 185, 186, 193, 196, 198, 201–203, 209, 214–215, 218, 222–224, 228, 234, 235, 237, 258, 269, 279, 280–281, 284, 288, 292, 294, 295, 298, 301, 303, 305, 306, 309, 310–311. Reproduced by permission of McIntosh and Otis on behalf of the John Steinbeck Estate.

Thomas Cooper Library, University of South Carolina

Illustrations on pp. 140, 175, 178, 205, 227, 267.

Time, Inc.

William Henry III, review of *The Grapes of Wrath* (movie), *Time* (2 April 1990). Anonymous review of *The Red Pony,* 29 (11 October 1937). Steinbeck in Sweden, *Time,* 41 (19 April 1943). Anonymous review of *A Russian Journal, Time,* 51 (26 January 1948). William Henry III, review of *The Grapes of Wrath* (movie), *Time* (2 April 1990), p. 71. Copyright © 1937, 1943, 1948, 1990, by Time, Inc.

Times Literary Supplement

"America the Beautiful," *Times Literary Supplement,* 1 December 1966, pp. 1120. Anonymous, "Looking After Number One," *Times Literary Supplement,* 7 July 1961, p. 413. Reprinted by permission of *Times Literary Supplement.*

Visva-Bharati University

Robert J. Cooke, review of *America and Americans, Visva-Bharati Quarterly,* 31 (1965–1966). Reprinted with permission.

The Washington Post Company

Harrison Smith, review of *Burning Bright: A Play in Story Form, Washington Post,* 22 October 1950. Copyright © 1950 The Washington Post Company.

Washington Times Corp.

Vincent D. Balitas, *Insight on the News,* 18 (25 March 2002). Used by permission. Copyright © 1990–2004 Washington Times Corp.

Western Literature Assocation

Robert E. Morsberger, "The Acts of King Arthur and His Noble Knights," *Western American Literature,* 12 (August 1977). Copyright © Western Literature Association. All rights reserved.

John Steinbeck:
A Documentary Volume

Steinbeck's Works

BOOKS: *Cup of Gold* (New York: McBride, 1929; London: Heinemann, 1937);

The Pastures of Heaven (New York: Brewer, Warren & Putnam, 1932; London: Philip Allan, 1933);

To a God Unknown (New York: Ballou, 1933; London: Heinemann, 1935);

Tortilla Flat (New York: Covici-Friede, 1935; London: Heinemann, 1935);

In Dubious Battle (New York: Covici-Friede, 1936; London: Heinemann, 1936);

Nothing So Monstrous: A Story (New York: Pynson, 1936);

Saint Katy the Virgin (New York: Covici-Friede, 1936);

Of Mice and Men (New York: Covici-Friede, 1937; London & Toronto: Heinemann, 1937);

Of Mice and Men: A Play in Three Acts, by Steinbeck and George S. Kaufman (New York: Covici-Friede, 1937);

The Red Pony (New York: Covici-Friede, 1937; enlarged edition, New York: Viking, 1945; London: Heinemann, 1949);

Their Blood Is Strong (San Francisco: Simon J. Lubin Society, 1938);

The Long Valley (New York: Viking, 1938; London: Heinemann, 1939); republished as *The Red Pony and Other Stories* (Cleveland: World, 1948);

The Grapes of Wrath (New York: Viking, 1939; London: Heinemann, 1939);

The Forgotten Village (New York: Viking, 1941);

Sea of Cortez: A Leisurely Journal of Travel and Research, by Steinbeck and Edward F. Ricketts (New York: Viking, 1941); republished in part, with "About Ed Ricketts," by Steinbeck, as *The Log from the Sea of Cortez* (New York: Viking, 1951; London: Heinemann, 1958);

The Moon Is Down (New York: Viking, 1942; London: Heinemann, 1942);

The Moon Is Down: A Play in Two Parts (New York: Dramatists Play Service, 1942; London: English Theatre Guild, 1943);

Bombs Away: The Story of a Bomber Team (New York: Viking, 1942);

Cannery Row (New York: Viking, 1945; London: Heinemann, 1945);

The Wayward Bus (New York: Viking, 1947; London: Heinemann, 1947);

The Pearl (New York: Viking, 1947; London: Heinemann, 1948);

The First Watch (Los Angeles: Ward Ritchie Press, 1947);

A Russian Journal (New York: Viking, 1948; London: Heinemann, 1949);

Burning Bright: A Play in Story Form (New York: Viking, 1950; London: Heinemann, 1951);

Burning Bright: Play in Three Acts (New York: Dramatists Play Service, 1951);

East of Eden (New York: Viking, 1952; London: Heinemann, 1952);

Viva Zapata! (Rome: Edizioni Filmcritica, 1953); republished as *Viva Zapata! The Original Screenplay,* edited by Robert E. Morsberger (New York: Viking, 1975);

Positano (Salerno: Ente Provinciale per il Turismo, 1954);

Sweet Thursday (New York: Viking, 1954; London: Heinemann, 1954);

Un Américain à New York et à Paris, translated into French by Jean-François Rozan (Paris: Julliard, 1956);

The Short Reign of Pippin IV: A Fabrication (New York: Viking, 1957; London: Heinemann, 1957);

Once There Was a War (New York: Viking, 1958; London: Heinemann, 1959);

The Winter of Our Discontent (New York: Viking, 1961; London: Heinemann, 1961);

Travels with Charley: In Search of America (New York: Viking, 1962; London: Heinemann, 1962);

Speech Accepting the Nobel Prize for Literature, Stockholm, December 10, 1962 (New York: Viking, [1963]);

America and Americans (New York: Viking, 1966; London: Heinemann, 1966);

The Acts of King Arthur and His Noble Knights: From the Winchester Manuscripts of Thomas Malory and Other Sources, edited by Chase Horton (New York: Farrar, Straus & Giroux, 1976);

Uncollected Stories of John Steinbeck, edited by Kiyoshi Nakayama (Tokyo: Nanún-do, 1986);

The Harvest Gypsies: On the Road to The Grapes of Wrath, introduction by Charles Wollenberg (San Bernardino, Cal.: Borgo Press, 1988);

John Steinbeck on Writing, edited by Tetsumaro Hayashi, Steinbeck Essay Series, no. 2 (Muncie, Ind.: Steinbeck Research Institute, Ball State University, 1988);

Working Days: The Journals of The Grapes of Wrath, 1938–1941, edited by Robert DeMott (New York: Viking, 1989).

Editions and Collections: *Steinbeck,* edited by Pascal Covici, Viking Portable Library (New York: Viking, 1943); revised and enlarged as *The Portable Steinbeck,* introduction by Lewis Gannett (New York: Viking, 1946); republished as *The Indispensable Steinbeck* (New York: Book Society, 1950) and as *The Steinbeck Omnibus* (London: Heinemann, 1950); 1946 edition revised and enlarged as *The Portable Steinbeck,* edited, with an introduction, by Pascal Covici Jr. (New York: Viking, 1971);

The Steinbeck Pocket Book, edited by Covici (New York: Pocket Books, 1943);

The Short Novels of John Steinbeck, introduction by Joseph Henry Jackson (New York: Viking, 1953); republished, without Jackson's introduction (London: Heinemann, 1954)—comprises *Tortilla Flat, The Red Pony, Of Mice and Men, The Moon Is Down, Cannery Row,* and *The Pearl;*

Selected Essays of John Steinbeck, edited by Kiyoshi Nakayama and H. Hirose (Tokyo: Shinozaki Shorin, 1961);

The Grapes of Wrath, edited by Peter Lisca, Viking Critical Library (New York: Viking, 1972); revised as *The Grapes of Wrath: Text and Criticism,* updated by Kevin Hearle (New York: Penguin, 1997);

Short Stories by John Steinbeck, edited, with an introduction and notes, by Yasuo Hashiguchi (Tokyo: Seibido, 1980);

The Essential Steinbeck (New York: Seafarer Books, 1994)—comprises *The Grapes of Wrath, Cannery Row, Of Mice and Men,* and *Tortilla Flat;*

Novels and Stories, 1932–1937, edited by Robert DeMott and Elaine Steinbeck (New York: Library of America, 1994);

The Grapes of Wrath and Other Writings, 1936–1941, edited by DeMott and Elaine Steinbeck (New York: Library of America, 1996);

Novels, 1942–1952, edited by DeMott (New York: Library of America, 2001);

America and Americans, and Selected Nonfiction, edited by Susan Shillinglaw and Jackson J. Benson (New York: Viking, 2002); republished as *Of Men and Their Making: The Selected Non-Fiction of John Steinbeck* (London: Allen Lane, 2002).

PLAY PRODUCTIONS: *Of Mice and Men,* New York, Music Box Theatre, 23 November 1937;

The Moon Is Down, New York, Martin Beck Theatre, 7 April 1942;

Burning Bright, New York, Broadhurst Theatre, 18 October 1950.

PRODUCED SCRIPTS: *The Forgotten Village,* motion picture, Pan-American Films, 1941;

Lifeboat, motion picture, screenplay by Jo Swerling, based on a screen treatment by Steinbeck, 20th Century-Fox, 1944;

A Medal for Benny, motion picture, screenplay by Frank Butler, based on a screen treatment by Steinbeck and Jack Wagner, Paramount, 1945;

La Perla (The Pearl), motion picture, screenplay by Steinbeck, Wagner, and Emilio Fernández, Aguila Films/RKO, 1948;

The Red Pony, motion picture, Republic, 1949;

Viva Zapata! motion picture, 20th Century-Fox, 1952.

OTHER: *Vanderbilt Clinic,* text by Steinbeck (New York: Presbyterian Hospital, 1947);

Edward F. Ricketts and Jack Calvin, *Between Pacific Tides,* revised edition, foreword by Steinbeck (Stanford, Cal.: Stanford University Press, 1948);

Adlai E. Stevenson, *Speeches,* foreword by Steinbeck (New York: Random House, 1952);

Al Capp, *The World of Li'l Abner,* introduction by Steinbeck (New York: Farrar, Straus & Young, 1953);

Edith Ronald Mirrieless, *Story Writing,* preface by Steinbeck (New York: Viking, 1962);

"A Letter from John Steinbeck Explaining Why He Could Not Write an Introduction for This Book," in *The Thinking Man's Dog,* by Ted Patrick (New York: Random House, 1964);

"Robert Capa: An Appreciation by John Steinbeck," in *Images of War,* by Robert Capa (New York: Paragraphic Books, 1966).

SELECTED PERIODICAL PUBLICATIONS—UNCOLLECTED: "Fingers of Cloud: A Satire on College Protervity," *Stanford Spectator,* 2 (February 1924): 149, 161–165;

"Adventures in Arcademy: A Journey into the Ridiculous," *Stanford Spectator,* 2 (June 1924): 279, 291;

"The Stars Point to Shafter," *Progressive Weekly* (24 December 1938);

"How Edith McGillcuddy Met Robert Louis Stevenson," *Harper's,* 183 (August 1941): 252–258;

"Miracle of Tepayac," *Collier's,* 122 (25 December 1948): 22–23;

"His Father," *Reader's Digest,* 55 (September 1949): 19–21;

"Sons of Cyrus Trask," *Collier's,* 130 (12 July 1952): 14–15;

"The Secret Weapon We Were Afraid to Use," *Collier's,* 131 (10 January 1953): 9–13;

"Jalopies I Cursed and Loved," *Holiday,* 16 (July 1954): 44–45, 89–90;

"Fishing in Paris," *Punch,* 227 (25 August 1954): 248–249;

"How to Fish in French," *Reader's Digest,* 66 (January 1955): 59–61;

"Some Thoughts on Juvenile Delinquency," *Saturday Review,* 38 (28 May 1955): 22;

"How Mr. Hogan Robbed a Bank," *Atlantic,* 197 (March 1956): 58–61.

LETTERS: *Journal of a Novel: The East of Eden Letters* (New York: Viking, 1969; London: Heinemann, 1970);

Steinbeck: A Life in Letters, edited by Elaine Steinbeck and Robert Wallsten (New York: Viking, 1975; London: Heinemann, 1975);

Letters to Elizabeth: A Selection of Letters from John Steinbeck to Elizabeth Otis, edited by Florian J. Shasky and Susan F. Riggs, introduction by Carlton A. Sheffield (San Francisco: Book Club of California, 1978);

Steinbeck and Covici: The Story of a Friendship, edited by Thomas Fensch (Middlebury, Vt.: P. S. Eriksson, 1979).

Papers:

Most of John Steinbeck's papers are at the Center for Steinbeck Studies, San Jose State University; the National Steinbeck Center, Salinas, California; and the Special Collections division of Stanford University Libraries. Other Steinbeck papers are in the Beyer Collection of Firestone Library, Princeton University; the Harry Ransom Humanities Research Center, University of Texas at Austin; Alderman Library at the University of Virginia; Bracken Library at Ball State University, Muncie, Indiana; and the John Steinbeck Library in Salinas.

Chapter One: 1902–1930

Chronology

27 February 1902	John Ernst Steinbeck is born in Salinas, California, the third of four children and the only son of John Ernst Steinbeck and Olive Hamilton Steinbeck.
9 January 1905	Steinbeck's younger sister, Mary Blanch Steinbeck, is born in Salinas.
Fall 1908	Steinbeck enters the first grade at what is known as the Salinas "Baby School."
Fall 1910	At the age of eight Steinbeck begins third grade at the West End School, near his home.
Early February 1911	The Sperry Flour Mill is shut down, putting Steinbeck's father out of work; he has been the manager at the mill since the mid 1890s, when the family settled in Salinas.
January 1912	John Steinbeck Sr. buys out Blackie's Feed Store in Salinas and starts his own business. John Jr. is given a chestnut-colored Shetland pony, Jill; like Jody Tiflin in Steinbeck's *The Red Pony* (1937), he is expected to care for her.

Steinbeck in 1907 (John Steinbeck Library, Salinas)

John Ernst Steinbeck Sr. and Olive Hamilton Steinbeck at the time of their marriage (John Steinbeck Library, Salinas;
from Jackson J. Benson, The True Adventures of John Steinbeck, Writer, *1984;*
Thomas Cooper Library, University of South Carolina)

Steinbeck's younger sister, Mary, and Steinbeck on Jill, the pony who inspired the stories of his 1937 story sequence
The Red Pony *(John Steinbeck Library, Salinas; from Jackson J. Benson,* The True Adventures of John
Steinbeck, Writer, *1984; Thomas Cooper Library, University of South Carolina)*

Fall 1912	Steinbeck is allowed to skip the fifth grade and enter the sixth grade at the West End School, making him a year younger than most of his classmates through high school.
28 July 1914	World War I begins.
Fall 1915	Steinbeck enters Salinas Union High School as a freshman.
February 1919	A general strike paralyzes Seattle.
16 June 1919	Steinbeck graduates from Salinas Union High School.
September 1919	Organized by the Industrial Workers of the World (IWW), 350,000 steelworkers in nine states walk off their jobs. Earlier in the same month, the Boston police force strikes.
1 October 1919	Steinbeck registers as a freshman at Stanford University, listing English as his major field of study. He rooms with George Mors. At some point in the fall, Steinbeck meets Carlton A. "Dook" Sheffield in a French class the two are taking, and they become close friends.
1920	Sinclair Lewis's *Main Street* and F. Scott Fitzgerald's *This Side of Paradise* are published.
5 April 1920	After a two-month leave of absence owing to a serious case of influenza, Steinbeck returns to Stanford and registers for the spring term, signing up for courses in American history, elementary economics, and English literature.

The house in which Steinbeck was born and grew up, at 132 Central Avenue, Salinas, California (photograph by Luchen Li)

EL GABILAN

and dried the dishes; then there was a secret class meeting and after that the phonograph was started again.

Just before midnight the party broke up and the school became enveloped in silent darkness once more. Never had there been such class spirit, never had there been such good eats, never had there been so much fun; so it is not surprising that everyone declared it the *best* party he had ever attended.

SENIOR PLAY.

June 13, 1919.

The Senior Class Present

Mrs. Bumpstead-Leigh

CAST OF CHARACTERS

Justin Rawson	John Steinbeck
Miss Rawson	Ynez Sargent
(Sister to Justin Rawson)	
Geoffrey Rawson	Wm. Black
(His younger son)	
Anthony Rawson	Milton Austin
(His elder son)	
Leavitt	Thomas Sherwood
Mrs. Leavitt	Lillian Winham
Peter Swallow	Edmund Silliman
Kitson	Ralph Muller
Mrs. De Salle	Orpha Teel
Mrs. Bumpstead-Leigh	Irene Hughes
(Adelaide, her elder daughter)	
Violet De Salle	Hazel Carpenter
(Adelaide's younger sister)	
Nina	Mildred Tuttle

Act I—Living room in Justin Rawson's Long Island country house, (after breakfast).
Act II—Same (1 hour later).
Act III—Same (10 minutes later).

Page sixty-three

Page from the 1919 Salinas Union High School yearbook with cast list for the senior play, in which Steinbeck performed (John Steinbeck Library, Salinas)

Early May 1920	An attack of acute appendicitis puts Steinbeck in the hospital for surgery and makes him unable to complete the remainder of the spring term at Stanford.
June–September 1920	With the help of his father, Steinbeck and Mors obtain jobs on a surveying crew and find the working conditions unbearable. After they quit, Steinbeck's father finds jobs for them with the maintenance crew at the Spreckels Sugar Company plant near Salinas.
1 October 1920	Steinbeck registers for the autumn quarter at Stanford, where he rooms again with Mors.

Late November 1920	With several uncompleted courses to make up, Steinbeck is on academic probation at Stanford. He is more interested in reading and writing than attending classes. One Sunday morning his roommate, Mors, wakes up to find Steinbeck gone and a note saying, "Gone to China. See you again sometime. Please free the chipmunk." Steinbeck goes to the San Francisco area and stays for a time with friends. He is unsuccessful in trying to get to China or finding other employment. He finally winds up as a straw boss supervising pickup crews at a Spreckels sugar-beet ranch near Chualar, about ten miles south of Salinas.
31 December 1920	Steinbeck is "officially" requested to withdraw from Stanford University.
January 1921	Steinbeck works on a dredging crew and at the same time works on his writing.
2 February 1922	James Joyce's *Ulysses* is published.
June 1922	Steinbeck returns to the Spreckels Sugar plant to work as a bench chemist. Encouraged by his parents, he decides to return to Stanford.
11 November 1922	Steinbeck applies for readmission to Stanford, submitting some letters of reference.
2 January 1923	Steinbeck registers for the winter quarter at Stanford as an English and journalism major.
26 February 1923	John Steinbeck Sr. is appointed treasurer of Monterey County by the county board of supervisors.

Steinbeck (far right) with Stanford classmate Eddie Johnson (next to Steinbeck) and two unidentified men waiting for the train to the Spreckels sugar-beet ranch in Chualar, California, 1922 (L. E. Johnson; from Jackson J. Benson, The True Adventures of John Steinbeck, Writer, *1984; Thomas Cooper Library, University of South Carolina)*

April–May 1923	Steinbeck continues his involvement with the English Club at Stanford.
19 June 1923	Steinbeck registers for the summer quarter, which is held at the Hopkins Marine Station, located near his family's summer cottage in Pacific Grove. He takes a class in zoology, which sparks an interest in nature and natural processes that later manifests itself in his writing.
September 1923	Steinbeck returns to Salinas, living with his parents and working as a bench chemist at Spreckels Sugar. At this time he begins a practice, which he carries on throughout his life, of using letters as a way of warming up for his writing.
January 1924	Steinbeck takes a class in short-story writing at Stanford with Edith Ronald Mirrielees, whose influence on his development as a writer is significant.
February 1924	Steinbeck's short story "Fingers of Cloud" is published in *The Stanford Spectator,* a campus literary magazine.
June 1924	A second short story by Steinbeck, "Adventures in Arcademy: A Journey into the Ridiculous," is published in *The Stanford Spectator.*
17 June 1925	Steinbeck leaves Stanford for the last time.
November 1925	Steinbeck sets out for New York on a freighter, the *Katrina,* which sails from Wilmington, in southern California.
December 1925	Steinbeck arrives in New York. Gene Ainsworth, the husband of his older sister Beth, helps him obtain a job as a laborer on the construction of Madison Square Garden. He works at this job for about five or six weeks but quits after a worker falls from a scaffold, landing near him. At the same time Steinbeck is writing short stories but has difficulties in finding publishers.
March 1926	Steinbeck's uncle Joe Hamilton helps him land a job as a reporter for the *New York American.*
May 1926	Steinbeck does not do well in his job as a reporter and is fired. He spends the next month trying his hand at freelance writing, but after several failed attempts at having his stories published, he decides to return to California.
Mid June 1926	Steinbeck returns to California and continues to write, supporting himself with a variety of jobs.
September 1926	Steinbeck is hired by Alice Brigham, the wealthy widow of a prominent San Francisco surgeon, as a caretaker for her summer home on the south shore of Lake Tahoe. Here Steinbeck spends most of his time writing.
October 1926	Ernest Hemingway's *The Sun Also Rises* is published.
March 1927	Steinbeck's short story "The Gifts of Iban" is published in *The Smoker's Companion* under the pseudonym John Stern.
April 1927	With the help of new acquaintance Lloyd Shebley, who works for the California Division of Fish and Game, Steinbeck obtains a part-time job at the Tallac Hatchery, south of Lake Tahoe.
May 1927	On a vacation Steinbeck returns to Salinas and takes several trips to Palo Alto and San Francisco. He becomes interested in a play that Webster "Toby" Street, a friend from Stanford, is working on. The play, "The Green Lady," later becomes the basis for Steinbeck's novel *To a God Unknown* (1933).
Mid June 1927	Steinbeck returns to the Lake Tahoe area and works for the Brigham family for the remainder of the summer, during which time he works on his first novel, *Cup of Gold* (1929).
January 1928	Steinbeck completes the manuscript of *Cup of Gold.* Katherine "Kate" Beswick, a friend from Stanford, agrees to type it up without charge. Amasa "Ted" Miller, another

Caretaker's cabin on the Brigham family property at Lake Tahoe, where Steinbeck lived while working for the Brighams off and on from 1926 to 1928 (H. R. and Katherine Ebright; from Jackson J. Benson, The True Adventures of John Steinbeck, Writer, *1984; Thomas Cooper Library, University of South Carolina)*

	Stanford friend, now in New York, agrees to act as Steinbeck's informal agent and to see if he can get the novel published.
February 1928	Steinbeck starts planning a new novel, tentatively titled "The Green Lady," after Street's play. This novel later becomes *To a God Unknown*.
May 1928	Steinbeck begins the first draft of his new novel, quits his work for the Brighams, and takes a vacation before starting a new job at the fish hatchery in Tahoe City, on the western shore of the lake.
June 1928	Steinbeck meets Carol Henning in Tahoe City.
August 1928	Shebley leaves the Tahoe City hatchery to seek a movie career in Hollywood, and Steinbeck is left alone.
September 1928	After Steinbeck and a coworker wreck the hatchery superintendent's new truck, he is laid off and returns to the family cottage in Pacific Grove; he then works as warehouseman in San Francisco but quits in late December.
January 1929	Steinbeck receives word from Miller in New York that after seven rejections, the typescript of *Cup of Gold* has been accepted for publication by Robert M. McBride and Company. At the same time, Steinbeck is hard at work on the manuscript of "The Green Lady."
July 1929	After abandoning the first version of "The Green Lady," Steinbeck is working on a second version.

August 1929	*Cup of Gold* is published by McBride. Even though the book receives little critical attention, it sells fairly well. Steinbeck, however, is not happy with the garish dust jacket, designed by his artist friend Mahlon Blaine.
29 October 1929	The New York stock market crashes, marking the beginning of the Great Depression.
November 1929	Steinbeck and Carol announce their intention to marry, and the following month they travel south to Los Angeles and stay with Sheffield and his wife.
December 1929	Steinbeck reads Hemingway's work for the first time and realizes that Hemingway's prose style is close to what he has been working toward.
14 January 1930	Steinbeck and Carol are married in Glendale, California, with Sheffield as a witness, and the couple settles in Eagle Rock, in the hills east of Los Angeles. In the following months they make several moves in the area of Glendale and Eagle Rock.
March 1930	Steinbeck changes the working title of "The Green Lady," now completed, to "To an Unknown God," a title taken from a Vedic hymn.
July 1930	Steinbeck finishes the manuscript for "Dissonant Symphony," an experimental novel, and submits it to Scribners. The publisher later turns it down.
August 1930	Steinbeck and Carol move to his family's cottage in Pacific Grove at the end of the month.
October 1930	Steinbeck meets Edward F. "Ed" Ricketts for the first time, one of the most important meetings in his life. Steinbeck hears from an old Stanford friend, Elizabeth Smith (who goes by the name John Breck, one of her writing pseudonyms), about a new literary agency in New York, McIntosh and Otis, which he later contacts.
December 1930	Steinbeck sends a murder-mystery manuscript, "Murder at Full Moon," to Miller to see if a publisher for it can be found.

The Steinbeck family reading at home in a photograph Steinbeck took using a timed shutter delay; from left, Steinbeck; his mother; his younger sister, Mary; and his father (John Steinbeck Library, Salinas; from Jackson J. Benson, The True Adventures of John Steinbeck, Writer, *1984; Thomas Cooper Library, University of South Carolina)*

John Ernst Steinbeck, the third of four children and the only son of John Ernst Steinbeck and Olive Hamilton Steinbeck, was born on 27 February 1902 in Salinas, California. He had two older sisters, Esther and Beth, and a younger, Mary. The Steinbecks were a middle-class family; Olive Steinbeck had been a schoolteacher, and John Steinbeck Sr. ended his career as treasurer of Monterey County, a position he served in until his death in 1935. Salinas is a medium-sized town in the narrow strip of agricultural land in the Salinas Valley, bounded by the Gabilan Range on the east and the Santa Lucia Range and Monterey Bay on the west. The land and people of the valley and the waterfront of Monterey Bay presented Steinbeck with much of the material for his fiction.

Steinbeck's love for nature and his thoughts about man's place in it were probably inherited from his parents. His father taught him that even the smallest things in nature are important and that human beings must practice conservation because they are part of the chain of life. Although Steinbeck usually credited his father with supporting him in his desire to become a writer, his mother planted the seed with her bedtime stories of enchanted forests. She told her children stories, read books, and

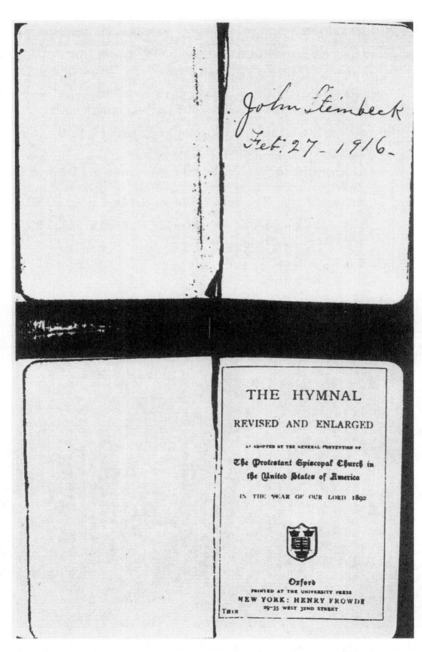

Steinbeck's copy of the Episcopal Church hymnal, signed and dated on his fourteenth birthday (John Steinbeck Library, Salinas; from Robert J. DeMott, Steinbeck's Reading, 1984; Thomas Cooper Library, University of South Carolina)

sang songs to them. Among the tales John heard from his mother or read on his own were stories by such writers as Robert Louis Stevenson, Thomas Hardy, Alexandre Dumas père, *and Sir Walter Scott. His other readings included John Bunyan's* The Pilgrim's Progress *(1678), John Milton's* Paradise Lost *(1667, 1674), and the Bible. Later, Olive Steinbeck introduced her son to the classics and then-popular writers such as James Branch Cabell and Donn Byrne. The young Steinbeck and his sisters always received books for their birthday presents. When he was nine, he received a copy of Sir Thomas Malory's* Le Morte Darthur *(1485). Malory's work stimulated his interest in language and generated his lifelong interest in the stories of King Arthur. The Arthurian legends and the various national myths of the American frontier and the West that he later read remained important to him throughout his life. Malory's stories helped to form Steinbeck's sense of right and wrong, his feelings of noblesse oblige, and his predilection for the cause of the oppressed. Several of his novels—including* Tortilla Flat *(1935), with a form and structure echoing Malory;* The Wayward Bus *(1947), Steinbeck's version of the Everyman allegory; and* In Dubious Battle *(1936)—allude to the epic struggle between good and evil.*

The family environment played an important role in Steinbeck's success through high school. He decided to become a writer sometime in 1915, when he was a freshman, after receiving encouragement from an English teacher. As Irene Hughes, editor in chief of the 1919 Salinas Union High School yearbook, El Gabilan, *recalled, no student exerted more literary effort toward its success than Steinbeck. In addition to his editing, he contributed an article titled "The How, When and Where of High School," one of the first of his writings to be published. Steinbeck was a well-rounded student and in 1919 served as senior-class president.*

After graduating from high school in 1919, Steinbeck left home for Stanford University, which he attended intermittently for five years. Between academic years, and sometimes during them, he worked at a variety of jobs as a rancher and cotton picker. A student of writing, literature, and marine biology, he attended meetings of the university's English Club and took a zoology course at the Hopkins Marine Station in Pacific Grove during the summer of 1923. In 1924 two of his short stories appeared in The Stanford Spectator. *According to Jay Parini in* John Steinbeck: A Biography *(1995), during this time Steinbeck's real university was his group of*

 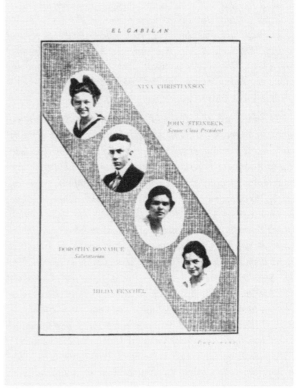

Front cover of the Salinas Union High School yearbook for 1919, the year Steinbeck graduated; page from the yearbook with Steinbeck's picture (Center for Steinbeck Studies, San Jose State University)

friends–including Carlton A. "Dook" Sheffield, Webster "Toby" Street, Carl Wilhelmson, John Breck (whose real name was Elizabeth Anderson), and Katherine "Kate" Beswick–and a few professors, such as Edith Ronald Mirrielees. With his English Club friends Steinbeck would sit around in the late evenings, arguing over the merits of Sinclair Lewis, Cabell, Willa Cather, and F. Scott Fitzgerald. After the spring quarter of 1925, Steinbeck felt that he had had all of the college he deserved and that he must face his economic situation. He left Stanford in 1925, without attempting to finish a degree program.

In 1925 Steinbeck was influenced by several important new publications of American fiction, including Fitzgerald's The Great Gatsby, Ernest Hemingway's story collection In Our Time, John Dos Passos's Manhattan Transfer, Lewis's Arrowsmith, and Sherwood Anderson's Dark Laughter. After leaving Stanford, Steinbeck traveled by freighter to New York, where he hoped to have his writing published. He worked for a time as a laborer and later, with the assistance of an uncle, Joe Hamilton, became a reporter for the New York American. Before long, he lost this job and became frustrated at his inability to sell any of the stories he had been writing. Out of funds and discouraged, he returned to the West Coast in the summer of 1926, working his way once again on a freighter. For the next two years he supported himself and his writing through a series of jobs in the Lake Tahoe area. During this time Steinbeck submitted stories to several magazines, but he did not place any work commercially until 1927, when "The Gifts of Iban" was published under the pseudonym John Stern in an obscure magazine, The Smoker's Companion.

Working in the Lake Tahoe region gave Steinbeck enough time to work on his first novel, Cup of Gold (1929), a fictionalized version of the life of Henry Morgan, the late-seventeenth-century Welsh buccaneer. Steinbeck kept up a frequent correspondence with old friends from Stanford, including Beswick, Wilhelmson, and Sheffield. Steinbeck worked consistently on Cup of Gold during the winter of 1927–1928. Drafts of chapters from the novel were sent to Street, Wilhelmson, and Beswick, each of whom responded in detail. Steinbeck followed their advice in revising the manuscript. While in New York, Steinbeck had looked up a Stanford friend, Amasa "Ted" Miller, who was starting a career in law. Because no professional literary agent had yet shown any interest in Steinbeck's writings, Miller had offered to try to place them, and Steinbeck now sent him the typescript of Cup of Gold. In the summer of 1928 he met the girl who was to become his first wife, Carol Henning, in Tahoe City, where he was working at a fish hatchery. Later that year Steinbeck moved to San Francisco, where Carol had a job. Steinbeck shared an apartment with Wilhelmson and started a new project, later to become his second novel, To a God Unknown (1933). He wrote to Beswick on 3 October 1928, "I know that Cup of Gold is a bad book, but on its shoulders I shall

climb to a good book. Critics could hurt my feelings, but they couldn't kill this ego. Something there is in me which is stronger than lust and nearly as strong as hunger." Not until late January 1929 was Miller able to wire Steinbeck from New York that he had found a publisher for Cup of Gold, Robert M. McBride and Company. The novel had been read and rejected by seven other publishers. In August 1929 Cup of Gold was published by McBride, but the book received little critical attention.

Steinbeck and Carol were married on 14 January 1930 in Glendale, California. They initially settled in Eagle Rock, east of Los Angeles, but by the end of August 1930 they had moved to the Steinbeck family cottage in Pacific Grove, on the Monterey Peninsula. While living in Eagle Rock, they had met another young writer, George Albee, with whom they exchanged frequent letters after moving north. In October, Steinbeck met Edward F. "Ed" Ricketts, a marine biologist who owned and operated Pacific Biological Laboratories on the waterfront in Monterey. He became Steinbeck's closest friend during the two decades of the novelist's most important work. Ricketts reinforced Steinbeck's interest in science and influenced his mature view of the world. So taken was Steinbeck with Ricketts and his ideas that he used the biologist as the basis for characters in several of his novels. The two men later collaborated on an important work of nonfiction, Sea of Cortez: A Leisurely Journal of Travel and Research (1941), a key to the understanding of Steinbeck's best fiction.

Education

The How, When and Where of High School (1919)
Steinbeck

In addition to editing his high-school yearbook, El Gabilan, *during his senior year, Steinbeck also contributed short pieces, such as the following selection.*

These directions may be of use to visitors, visiting; friends, friending; and most important, parents parenting.

Math Room

We will begin with the room which draws the most vivid descriptions from the lips of the students. This is the math room. Math is not a Spanish swear word, although allusions to it are often accompanied by Spanish and otherwise. Math is the science of getting the best marks possible from the least work. There is always a large class in Freshman algebra, the only conceivable reason being that the Freshmen are not given very much choice in the matter. After the first year, some are still fired with the zeal of an Archimedes (we don't know what that means, but doesn't it sound grand?) but most of the students exhibit real intelligence and avoid math.

The math room is noted for its flunks, its pencil sharpener, its pictures, which are the objects of long and studious contemplation by the students, and its teacher, who is a fine scout when she gets away from the zero exponents.

Across the hall from the math room is the office and record room. It is here that we are shown the way to right living and gently slammed back into the straight and narrow. It is in this room that the red-splotched messengers of flunks are stored.

The secretary is very popular; she can issue entrances and excuses, and she can tell the trembling Senior whether he is going to continue his acquaintance with her for another year or not. But all in all, the office is not to be compared with the English room.

English Room

The English room, which is just down the hall from the office, is the sanctuary of Shakespeare, the temple of Milton and Byron, and the terror of Freshmen. English is a kind of high brow idea of the American language. A hard job is made of nothing at all and nothing at all is made of a hard job. It is in this room

and this room alone that the English language is spoken. After taking English for four years we wish to advise Freshmen to use nothing but second hand books; they make the course much easier.

Study Hall

The study hall is a combination of all the trials described above. When we don't want to work, in fact have nothing to work on except some math, and English and maybe a little Spanish and physics, we are compelled to keep our eyes on our books while our minds are busy with a fate for the teacher which would make the Kaiser's look like a vacation at Palm Beach. Then when we are cramming for an ex. in woodwork, it is announced that we will sing. We get up, but the words which come to our lips are not those contained in the song.

Other schools besides Salinas are those of fish, of life and of the squad. With all due apologies to Voltaire, Henry VIII, K. C. B., King Cole, and any others who may have thought along this same line, "I thank you."–John Steinbeck, '19.

–reprinted in *Salinas Californian,* July 1963

* * *

San Juan Grade at the Gabilan Range foothills in Salinas Valley (from David A. Laws, Steinbeck Country:
Exploring the Settings for the Stories, *2002; Collection of Luchen Li)*

Salinas Californian, Rodeo Edition, July 1963
"Steinbeck in 1919 Annual"

Steinbeck in 1919 Annual

"English is a kind of high brow idea of the American language.

"A hard job is made of nothing at all and nothing at all is made of a hard job."

Was this philosophy expressed by John Steinbeck while attending Salinas high school one that eventually jelled into his Nobel-worthy prose?

This was the gist of John's advice to students in the 1919 El Gabilan yearbook on "The How, When and Where of High School".

John starts: "These directions may be of use to visitors, visiting; friends, friending; and most important, parents parenting.

Math Room

"We will begin with the room which draws the most vivid descriptions from the lips of the students. This is the math room. Math is not a Spanish swear word, although allusions to it are often accompanied by Spanish and otherwise. Math is the science of getting the best marks possible from the

JOHN STEINBECK
President of the 1919 senior class at Salinas union high school . . . with the class motto: "As a Man Thinketh in His Heart so Is He."

least work. There is always a large class in Freshman algebra, the only conceivable reason being that the Freshmen are not given very much choice in the matter. After the first year, some are still fired with the zeal of an Archimedes (we don't know what that means, but doesn't it sound grand?) but most of the students exhibit real intelligence and avoid math.

"The math room is noted for its flunks, its pencil sharpener, its pictures, which are the objects of long and studious contemplation by the students, and its teacher, who is a fine scout when she gets away from the zero exponents.

"Across the hall from the math room is the office and record room. It is here that we are shown the way to right living and gently slammed back into the straight and narrow. It is in this room that the red-splotched messengers of flunks are stored.

"The secretary is very popular; she can issue entrances and excuses, and she can tell the trembling Senior whether he is going to continue his acquaintance with her for another year or not. But all in all, the office is not to be compared with the English room.

English Room

"The English room, which is just down the hall from the office, is the sanctuary of Shakespeare, the temple of Milton and Byron, and the terror of Freshmen. English is a kind of high brow idea of the American language. A hard job is made of nothing at all and nothing at all is made of a hard job. It is in this room and this room alone that the English language is spoken. After taking English for four years we wish to advise Freshmen to use nothing but second hand books; they make the course much easier.

Study Hall

"The study hall is a combination of all the trials described above. When we don't want to work, in fact have nothing to work on except some math, and English and maybe a little Spanish and physics, we are compelled to keep our eyes on our books while our minds are busy with a fate for the teacher which would make the Kaiser's look like a vacation at Palm Beach. Then when we are cramming for an ex. in woodwork, it is announced that we will sing. We get up, but the words which come to our lips are not those contained in the song.

"Other schools besides Salinas are those of fish, of life and of the squad. With all due apologies to Voltaire, Henry VIII, K. C. B., King Cole, and any others who may have thought along this same line, 'I thank you.' "
—John Steinbeck, '19.

Reprint in the Salinas Californian *of Steinbeck's "The How, When and Where of High School," from the 1919 yearbook of the Salinas Union High School* (Salinas Californian)

*Newspaper reprint of the picture from the 1919 yearbook of the Salinas Union High School showing Steinbeck
(back row, far right) and other members of the track team (John Steinbeck Library, Salinas)*

Steinbeck to Carl Wilhelmson, 7 April 1924

*From Steinbeck's college days it became clear that the most
important thing in his life was literature; he read whatever he
could in an attempt to master the language for what he called
"distinguished writing." In this letter to Carl Wilhelmson, a
Stanford classmate and another would-be writer, Steinbeck
describes his struggles with one writing instructor.*

Dear Carl:

Here, on this paper, there are only you and me,
and the things that each of us tries so hard to understand, clambering up through long, long researches into
the past, and thinking ponderously and seeking, and
finding that for which we looked a glorified question
mark.

It would be desirable to be flung, unfettered by
consciousness, into the void, to sail unhindered through
eternity. Please do not think that I am riding along on
baseless words, covering threadbare thoughts with garrulous tapestries. I am not. It is the words which are
inadequate.

You know so much and I can tell you nothing,
and I don't think I can even make you feel anything
you have not felt more poignantly than I, who am a
mummer in a brocaded boudoir.

I wrote of miners' faces around a fire. Their bodies did not show in the light so that the yellow faces
seemed dangling masks against the night. And I wrote
of little voices in the glens which were the spirits of passions and desires and dreams of dead men's minds.
And Mrs. Russell [an instructor] said they were not
real, that such things could not be, and she was not
going to stand me bullying her into such claptrap nonsense. Those were not her words but her meaning, and
then she smiled out of the corner of her mouth as
nurses do when an idiot child makes blunders. And I
could not stand that, Carl, so I swore at her because I
had been out all night in the making of my pictures.
And now she is very cold, and she means to flunk me

in my course, thinking that she can hurt me thus. I wish that she could know that I do not in the least care.

And I wish you were back, because you could understand the things I try to say, and help me to say them better, and I know you would, for you did once.

John Steinbeck
—*Steinbeck: A Life in Letters,* edited by Elaine Steinbeck and Robert Wallsten (New York: Viking, 1975), pp. 6–7

* * *

Roommates at Stanford
Carlton A. Sheffield

Carlton A. "Dook" Sheffield met Steinbeck at Stanford University, and the two kept up a lifelong friendship through their correspondence. In the following excerpt from his memoir, originally published in 1983, Sheffield vividly recalls Steinbeck's days at Stanford.

Sometime in the late fall of 1919, during the beginning of my freshman year at Stanford University, I became aware of a large, quiet freshman classmate. We were enrolled in a class in elementary French, and beyond the fact that I knew his name was Steinbeck and that he seemed unhappy when called upon to recite, I knew nothing about him. We nodded when we met, and once in a while exchanged pungent views on the absurdities of French grammar and pronunciation, but that was about the extent of our acquaintanceship, though we both lived in Encina Hall, the huge old dormitory now almost exclusively occupied by administration.

He was seventeen years old, almost eighteen, then, and looked a little older. His hair was dark and curly, and the way it was clipped high and close around his temples emphasized the height of his forehead, the breadth of this face at the cheekbones and its length down to the heavy, bluntly tapering chin. He had thick lips; his ears seemed to stick out at a slight angle; his nose was large, broad, and rather shapeless. In general, his expression was serious and dignified, but when he laughed, as he often did, one suddenly noticed how blue his eyes were and what an intense sparkle they had. They seemed to dance with merriment and delight when something pleased him.

Apparently he was eager to try everything. He went out for freshman football and was tried at various positions in the line, but in spite of his six feet and 180 pounds, he soon gave up the idea, perhaps because he could not work up the required spirit during a mere scrimmage, and perhaps because he had never taken kindly to being ordered around. Also, having for some

time been larger than most of his schoolmates, he had early developed an instinctive gentleness in games requiring physical contact, lest his size and weight bring injury to his opponents or give him unfair advantage.

Within the next several months he also tried his hand at crew and while straining at the oars damaged the blood vessels of his legs, an injury from which he never fully recovered. He played polo, too, probably as a member of the ROTC unit, and that contributed a badly cracked kneecap that gave him periodic trouble for the rest of his life. It is possible that he tried still other sports. If so, he did not distinguish himself in any of them.

. . . .

In his freshman year, John had also set another precedent in inter-class rivalry, though this one was neither generally adopted nor condoned. A group of marauding sophomores hunting for frosh to bedevil shouldered their way into his room (the locking of doors was forbidden) and summarily demanded that he come with them. He had been expecting such an incursion and was prepared. From his desk drawer he pulled a long-barreled .45-caliber Smith and Wesson revolver, snapped off the safety, and invited them to come and get him. After a brief conference they decided not to and retired, muttering threats about what future actions they would take to punish such a lack of sportsmanship. As far as I can learn, he was never troubled again, though the incident did nothing to increase his popularity.

Another photograph, taken about the same time, shows him again as a non-conformist. On the broad stone steps in front of Encina most of the residents of the hall were gathered for the start of the annual Pajamarino, a mildly Rabelaisian tradition in which everyone put on his loudest pajamas or nightshirt and toured the campus in shrieking serpentine, making special point of running through the ten-existent sororities and women's halls. Instead of pajamas, John wears a violently striped shirt, a turban, and a bath towel that is several inches short of his bare knees. It is held in place by something that looks like a Sam Browns belt from which hangs a whiskbroom. Dangling from the rear is a University of California pennant. His face bears an elaborate burnt-cork moustache.

Early photographs of him, however, are extremely rare, for he consistently refused to pose before the camera. A woman to whose house I had taken him about 1924 was unpleasantly insistent on taking a snapshot of him, even after he had at first courteously and then quite brusquely refused. When she continued to focus on him, he abruptly turned and walked away down the street, leaving his coat and hat

Fingers of Cloud

A Satire on College Proterrity.

By JOHN E. STEINBACK

GERTIE swept all of the dirt to the largest crack in the floor of the porch. Several times she went back to gather up bits that had escaped the flat side of the broom. Then she very carefully edged the line of dust to the crack and tumbled it over, chuckling gaily while she swept briskly at imaginary particles.

"Last time, last time—shan't ever do it again—last time—last time." She ended with a little shriek and a vicious stab at the receiving crack. The broom sailed into the house, popped against a wall, and the door slammed after it. Gertie flounced her skirt and sat down on the top step, her voice continuing at a monotonous sing-sing.

"Ma's gone—Ma's gone—and she ain't comin' back no more," and mixed with a giggle— "This is the best fun since Pa didn't come back. Wish't Ma belonged to a lodge," and a business-like chant, "Don't have to sweep no more—don't have to wash dishes no more—don't have to do ab-so-lute-ly nothin'—no more." The "no more" was working itself into a refrain. Again she ended with a little shriek of pleasure.

The porch creaked and groaned as she got up and stretched herself, going over every muscle like a dog. Her feet landed together after the jump from the top step; she sagged suddenly and grunted, then righted herself and marched gaily out of the gate into the street, feet lifted high, head up, doing a heel and toe at every step, losing herself in the sun-sodden afternoon. On her flat, pink face there was a benign smile that seemed glued on; her hair, as white as a washed sheep's wool and nearly as curly, bobbed knowingly on the top of her head, and her pink eyes blandly regarded everything on the street, accepted houses and fences and grass plots, enjoyed them and cast them aside for new houses and picket fences and grass plots.

The street sickened, became weed filled, and died, while the hills jounced steadily toward her. At the shallow river with its yellow sand banks she pulled off her shoes and threw them to the ground; then pulling her thin dress above her waist she plunged in. Her toes dug themselves into the soft sand on the bottom and her moving legs tossed little waves over her knees. At a deep place she sank to her waist and the bottom of her dress floated for a second. On the other side she splashed out on the bank and started up a little hill which pretended to be a mountain. The slope was carpeted with the palest green of early spring. Some yellow May-flowers peeked from under their leaves and said,

"Boo! you're running away, my girl." Gertie stopped and regarded them fiercely.

"I am not running away. I guess I'm eighteen and know my own mind. Besides, I'm an orphant, and an orphant can't run away because she ain't got absolutely nothing to run away from."

She trampled the flowers into the ground and pranced o On top of the foolish, little mountain she sat down to watc the autos crawl along the highway. A faint echo of their horr came to her from below. Now and then there would be a blinc ing flash as the sun found a windshield.

The clouds had been up here when she was below. She ha rather bargained on touching them, but now they had jumpe higher than she could reach. Lying down she could better watc them hurrying along. A big grey one brushed her eyelids wit its hanging shreds until they closed; a smaller one rushed up an pressed gently, and she slept.

The sky was splitting. A cruel, crooke line of light brought Gertie to a sitting po sition. Then there was a crash as of tw giant freight cars hurtling together and th pop-pop of fragments falling on the roof o a tin warehouse. Suddenly the black ai broke to pieces, the hills sounded and re sounded, the moving air moaned, drew bac and charged buffeting and tearing at th ground. Gertie sat huddled in a heap mut tering to herself. Rain came, each drop magnified a thousand diameters, the ai was full of it, not falling but rushing for ward in the arms of the driving wind, anc all the while snakes of light quivered anc were lost.

The sleep-heavy limbs of Gertie came tc life, and she ran down the hill snatching a the wet skirt which wound around her legs and tossing her head to shake the matted hair out of her eyes. She fell and rolled, rose and tripped again From her chest between breaths came a moaning cry.

A coal fire roared in the bunkhouse of the foreign camp The Filipinos sat on the floor with their feet under them. From the outside the howling wind came through the cracks in the house and made the burlap hangings move restlessly. Burlap tacked loosely on the walls, a littered floor of dust-colored wood, a few boxes to sit on, and the fat-bellied stove, that was the lounging room of the bunkhouse. Three of the pock-marked, brown men played cards on the floor under a coal oil lamp. They threw down their cards without a word. No one was talking in the room. Ten or twelve more of the squatty figures were dumped about the room, half smiling because there would be no work in the beet fields the next day. Pedro, the boss, sat on a box near the stove, great head on chest, his palms pressing on his temples while the fingers worked busily in his tangled black hair. One of the players pointed at him derisively.

"Hee! Pedro is not so happy tonight. He loses money to-morrow. We eat and we do not work," he became mock solemn, "—but I think we will eat potatoes and rice." The others chuckled in appreciation. Pedro did not appear to hear.

(Continued on page 161)

DOUBT

A Rondeau

By K. B.

I think I'll wait; I can't be sure
That this is love. This overture
　　Of melting tenderness you play
　　May NOT be love—and yet it may.
Your stumbling phrases, half obscure,
Are sweet to hear, but immature;
And, lest they fail to grow secure,
　　　　I think I'll wait.

If this be love I now abjure
I shall regret the forfeiture;
　　I shall remember, with dismay,
　　I had it, once, to throw away. . . .
Yet, lest this thing should not endure—
　　　　I think I'll wait.

First page of Steinbeck's story, published in The Stanford Spectator *(February 1924), that was inspired by his experiences as a straw boss on a sugar-beet ranch in Chualar, California, in 1920 (John Steinbeck Collection, Stanford University Libraries)*

behind. Later, in explanation of his attitude he said, "I have a superstitious feeling about being photographed as if the camera took away a part of me I can never get back." During our college period I did manage to get two or three bad pictures of him with a Brownie, but over his protests.

His early publishers had trouble with him on the same score, and for some years the only publicity picture of him they had was a black-and-white sketch. (He liked that, he said, because it did not look a bit like him, and therefore nobody could recognize him.) Eventually, in 1935, in Pacific Grove just after *Tortilla Flat* had come out, he reluctantly permitted one "official" photograph to be taken for general use. Another, taken about the same time by Sonya Noskourak, was published in a lush interview:

> Down out of the hills he came, he said; he felt as if he had somehow always lived in them. And John Steinbeck looks as if he might have; of giant height, sunburned, with fair hair and fair moustache and eyes the blue of the Pacific on a sunny day and a deep, quiet, slow voice. He belongs to this Coast, the Monterey bay, the ranges and cliffs of the Big Sur country. . . .

The article first gave currency to the erroneous statement that he was born in Florida. He was really born on February 27, 1902, in the family home on Central Avenue in Salinas, California. Not for several years did he permit other photographs, and then only because his growing fame made it inescapable.

In the spring of 1920, or about the middle of his sophomore year, I had come to know him better, and from time to time we put on boxing gloves and sparred a few rounds in my room or the larger one which he shared with George Mors. Invariably I got the worst of it, for John had height, reach, weight, speed, and skill plus a catlike movement which made his blows unexpected and blurringly fast. On the other hand, he fought considerately, usually trying to keep his punches from being too punishing and never taking unfair advantage, though I regularly ended on the floor.

. . . .

Only once in the next two and a half years did I hear anything more about John Steinbeck—somebody reported seeing him at "Big Game" time in 1922, his coat lined with dozens of chemist's phials filled with grain alcohol, which he was sharing liberally with friends—and during that time I almost forgot him. In fact, when I next saw him on January 2, 1923, I could barely recall his name and made the monumental mistake of calling him "Steiny." (He had always resented

nicknames and viewed that one with even more distaste than "Jack" or "Johnny.") I never did it again.

Nor did I ever succeed in getting a full or coherent story of the reasons for his disappearance or of all his activities during his absence, and I have lost some of the details of what he did tell me. In brief, the reasons he gave involved an unidentified girl he had been seeing in San Francisco—one who had wounded him very deeply, and who, he felt, had intolerably abused his confidence and trust; how I can't recall. (There were other and less-romantic reasons.) Anyway, he decided to run away to sea, and China sounded like a good place. He returned to his dormitory room, collected his most essential possessions, and departed without waking George.

. . . .

In the spring of 1923, Steinbeck invited me to spend the Easter holidays at his Salinas home on Central Avenue, one block west of the main street of town. We drove down in my car.

His 1890s house was large, white, and formal. It had modified iron-and-wood gingerbread decorations, high roof with gables, a long, narrow front porch, and a relatively small but well-kept yard, where his father grew fine gladioluses. Everything emanated respectability. Several steps led up to the porch, and the glass in the front door was multi-colored.

Inside, the house was also eloquent of the turn of the century, its high ceilings and furnishings sound and well cared for. Opening from just to the left of the front door was John's mother's bedroom, and behind that was his father's. To the right was the traditional parlor with sliding doors, kept closed most of the time, rarely used by the family, which preferred the more informal living room behind it as the center of household activities. The parlor was usually kept darkened, dustless, and in perfect order, its heavy furniture carefully polished. The living room, although meticulously neat, had an air of greater comfort and appeared more lived in. Behind it was the large, somber dining room, top-heavy with massive furniture and precisely arranged glass and china cupboards. Beyond was the kitchen, large and fairly modern, with a narrow, closed-in porch for refrigerator and laundry at the rear. A utility room with mangle and pressing machine opened off the dining room. The small storage barn in the back yard had perhaps housed a horse in earlier days.

. . . .

One of the classes in which both John and I enrolled was Verse Writing (English 35), taught by William Herbert Carruth. He was grey haired, elderly—

Steinbeck writing at Stanford, circa 1924 (Carlton A. Sheffield; from Jackson J. Benson, The True Adventures
of John Steinbeck, Writer, *1984; Thomas Cooper Library, University of South Carolina)*

to our eyes—and delightfully informal. When the weather permitted, we met on the Quadrangle lawn in the shade of a huge oak tree, sitting or sprawling as he read and criticized the contributions of the group. His criticisms were kind, and I can appreciate what restraint he used when I review his written comments on some of the inept rhymes that I turned in.

On the nights before the class, John and I used to face each other across our study table, searching for inspiration or even a phrase that we could build on to fit the metrical or structural assignment. Often, after long periods of nail-biting and trading suggestions, we would go for long walks, hoping for ideas which sometimes came. For one of the meetings John produced a verse that started:

So we manned the brigantine
With Chinks and yellow Malays,
Couldn't speak the language of the Irish and the Dutch;
Had to feed them rice and things,
They wouldn't eat with faylays [pidgin English for a native
    term meaning "knives and forks"];
Take them as a people and they don't amount to much.

Professor Carruth wasn't taken in by so palpable an evasion—actually John had despaired of finding a rhyme (neither of us knew that Malay should be accented on the last syllable) and didn't want to spoil the fine sound of the lines—and merely read the word with skeptical emphasis, commenting dryly that the use of unusual foreign terms, especially in stressed position, was better avoided.

Very few examples of John's lyric talents have survived, and those that do rarely mirror the quality of his prose. The final assignment of Carruth's course was a sonnet, and John's followed a classic format, at least in its rhyme scheme.

Now and then in the next few years he lapsed into verse, usually of a lighter variety and motivated by something he had read or done. From Lake Tahoe in November, 1926, came a letter with the following disquisitions on aspects of the amusement world:

In a recent article written by the estimable Mr. Hearst, a certain chorus girl, in suing a certain Hobokenite for seventy-five thousand dollars declares that she is not interested in the money. She merely wants to show that class of men who make a practice of playing on the trustfullness [*sic*] of her sisters, that they can't get away with it any more. "Chorus girls," she says, "are the most trusting and naive creatures in the world, and I am sick of seeing them so shamefully mistreated and lead [*sic*] astray" Of course an event like this can have only one effect on me. I must break into verse.

1.

Now here is a girl who can stand
On the steps of the law and demand,
That justice be gave
To the trustful and brave
Little theatre slave
For the way men behave—
Along with some seventy grand.

2.

Some call it trustfulness and some
Would say that these chorines were not so dumb,
Who take the cash and let the credit go.
This one takes credit but the cash will come.

—John Steinbeck, the Good Companion: His Friend Dook's Memoir, edited by Terry White, introduction by Richard H. A. Blum (Berkeley, Cal.: Creative Arts, 2002), pp. 3–9, 18, 28–30

Cup of Gold (1929)

Steinbeck to Webster Street, Winter 1926

After Steinbeck returned from New York in May 1926, both spiritually and financially bankrupt, he obtained a job as caretaker on a large estate at Lake Tahoe. There, he wrote later, "It required that I be snowed in for eight months every year. My nearest neighbor was four miles away." During this time he worked on his first novel, Cup of Gold *(1929). From Lake Tahoe he wrote his Stanford friend Webster "Toby" Street.*

Dear Toby:

Do you know, one of the things that made me come here, was, as you guessed, that I am frightfully afraid of being alone. The fear of the dark is only part of it. I wanted to break that fear in the middle, because I am afraid much of my existence is going to be more or less alone, and I might as well go into training for it. It comes on me at night mostly, in little waves of panic, that constrict something in my stomach. But don't you think it is good to fight these things? Last night, some quite large animal came and sniffed under the door. I presume it was a coyote, though I do not know. The moon had not come up, and when I ran outside there was nothing to be seen. But the main thing was that I was frightened, even though I knew it could be nothing but a coyote. Don't tell any one I am afraid. I do not like to be suspected of being afraid.

As soon as you can, get to work on the Little Lady ["The Green Lady," Street's play in progress]. Keep your eye on cost of production, small and inex-

pensive scenes, few in the cast and lots of wise cracks, as racy as you think the populace will stand. Always crowd the limit. And also if you have time, try your hand on a melo drahmar, something wild, and mysterious and unexpected with characters turning out to be other people and some of them turning out to be nobody at all.

And if you can find a small but complete dictionary lying about anywhere send it to me. I have none, and apparently the Brighams [Steinbeck's employers] are so perfect in their mother tongue that they do not need one.

I shall send you some mss pretty soon if you wish. I have been working slowly but deliciously on one thing. There is something so nice about being able to put down a sentence and then look it over and then change it, sometimes taking half an hour over two lines. And it is possible here because there seems to be no reason for rush.

If, on going through Salinas, you have the time, you might look in on my folks and tell them there is little possibility of my either starving or freezing. Be as honest as you can, but picture me in a land flowing with ham and eggs, and one wherein woolen underdrawers grow on the fir trees. Tell them that I am living on the inside of a fiery furnace, or something.

It's time for me to go to the post office now, I will cease without the usual candle-like spluttering. Write to me when and as often as you get a chance. I shall depend on the mail quite a lot.

love
John
—Steinbeck: A Life in Letters, pp. 3–4

* * *

Steinbeck to Sheffield, 25 February 1928

In the following letter to Sheffield, written from Lake Tahoe, Steinbeck reports that while the manuscript of Cup of Gold *was finished, he was preparing a new work, later to become his second novel,* To a God Unknown *(1933).*

Dear Duke:

It is a long time since I have begun a letter such as I mean this to be: an unhurried dissertation in which there is no sense of duty. Perhaps I have lost the power to write such a letter. Of late it has been my habit to write one page of short, tacit observation, which might have given you the idea that I am become nervous and short. And you, of late, have been determinedly cynical. Thus our letters.

My failure to work for the last three weeks is not far to find. I finished my novel and let it stand for a while, then read it over. And it was no good. The disappointment of that was bound to have some devastating, though probably momentary effect. You see, I thought it was going to be good. Even to the last page, I thought it was going to be good. And it is not.

Why are you telling me about the things you go to? Are you ashamed or proud? Do you want me to know you attend such gatherings? I think you think I look down on Rosalind [Rosalind Shepard, a girlfriend of Sheffield's], and you want to justify her. You make fun of these things and yet they must impress you to some extent. I know they would impress me. I have always been a little afraid of a woman who wore a dress that cost more than a hundred dollars.

I have a new novel preparing but preparing very slowly. I am not quick about such things. They must roll about in my mind for an age before they can be written. I think it will take me two years to write a full length novel, counting the periods when I walk the streets and try to comb up courage enough to blow out my brains.

Isn't it a shame, Duke, that a thing which has as many indubitably fine things in it as my Cup of Gold, should be, as a whole, utterly worthless? It is a sorrowful matter to me.

As usual I have made a mess of this letter. I didn't finish it the other night. Now it is late the night before the [mail] boat, and I shall get very little written on it. Do you realize that I am twenty-six now? I don't. I don't feel twenty-six and I don't look that old, and I have done nothing to justify my years. Yet I don't regret the years. I have enjoyed them after a fashion. My sufferings have not been great nor have my pleasures been violent. I wish we might resurrect a summer out of the heap of years, but that is not possible at this time. Some other summer we will try.

Am I to be allowed to meet Rosalind, or are you afraid of me now? I should really like to. I feel none of the old antagonism toward her at any rate. I have been cutting wood violently to keep from being lonely. And I am lonely just the same. I wish you would write more often. I am on the point of joining a correspondence club if you don't.

A triumph. I am learning to chew tobacco, not the lowly Star but the lordly Boot Jack, a bit under the tongue you know and swallow the spit. I find I like it. It is snowing again. Confound it, will the winter never be over? I crave to have the solid ground under my feet. You cannot understand that craving if you have never lived in a country where every step was unstable. It is very tiresome and tiring to walk and have the ground give way under you at every step.

I am finishing the Henry ms [Cup of Gold] out of duty, but I have no hope of it any more. I shall probably pack it in Limbo balls and place it among the lost hopes in the chest of the years. Good bye, Henry. I thought you were heroic but you are only, as was said of you, a babbler of words and rather clumsy about it.

I shall make an elegy to Henry Morgan, who is a monument to my own lack of ability. I shall go ahead, but I wonder if that sharp agony of words will occur to me again. I wonder if I shall ever be drunken with rhythms any more. Duke has his Rosalind, but I have no Rosalind nor any Phryne. I am twenty-six and I am not young any more. I shall write good novels but hereafter I ride Pegasus with a saddle and martingale, for I am afraid Pegasus will rear and kick, and I am not the sure steady horseman I once was. I do not take joy in the unmanageable horse any more. I want a hackney of tried steadiness.

It is sad when the snow is falling.

love
jawn
—*Steinbeck: A Life in Letters,* pp. 10–12

* * *

Katherine Beswick to Steinbeck, summer 1928

Steinbeck met Carol Henning in Tahoe City in the summer of 1928, and the two fell in love. To share his feelings, he wrote his close friend Katherine "Kate" Beswick, who was then living in Greenwich Village, New York. The following is Beswick's response.

My dear:

I shall write this, but God knows when it can be mailed. I have no money and no stamps and the monthly remittance from the family can scarcely arrive before the 2nd of August. So be it!

Your news letter of the 26th has just come, and I am so awfully relieved to know that nothing more catastrophic than a love affair is responsible for your silence. And why, dear, should I hold it against you that you are "so damned Irish"? It is, rather, that you're so delightfully Irish. I should be infinitely disappointed in you, I think, if you failed to go on, from one love affair into the next, so long as the power is on you. It's one of those things which just must be, and which is wholly delightful and desirable. . . .

And you must have gathered that my love for you is of a somewhat peculiar brand. It would be battered and broken by double-dealing and disloyalty—but otherwise it is singularly undemanding.

Chapter One.

All afternoon the wind sifted out of the black Welsh glens
and mountain clefts crying notice that Winter was come sliding
down over the world from the Pole; and riverward there was
a faint moaning of new ice. It was a sad day, a day of grey
unrest and discontent. The horses nervously shifted their
feet in the pastures, and birds,in little cliques of four or
five , flew twittering from tree to tree and back again.
A few goats clambered to the tops of high, lone rocks and
long stared upward with their yellow eyes and sniffed the heavens.

Now it was evening, and little pellets of hard snow
came ticking on the house. The wind rustled in the dry thatch
and fled along the road with small cryings. Night grew
down,and Winter sent ambassadors ahead of his arrival.

Inside the ancient farm-house a fire was blazing on the
hearth, a kettle over it and an oven hiding in the coals. The
light glinted on the tips of pikes unused a hundred years, since
Morgans xixxxxxxi clamored in Glendower's ranks and trembled
at the flinty heroids of Iolo Goch. From its corner the booad
brass straps of the great chest of history sucked in the light
and glowed ~~noddedly~~. Papers there were in the chest and,under
them, parchments in Latin, Welsh and English--- Morgan was born,
Morgan was married, Morgan became a knight, Morgan was hanged.

Old Robert sat in his high backed chair and smiled into
the fire. His smile was perplexity and a strange, passive
defiance. He thought to make that fate,which was responsible----

First two pages of the typescript for Steinbeck's first novel, Cup of Gold, *published in 1929 (Stanford University)*

for his being and his defeats, a little ashamed of itself by smiling at it. And it was perplexing that he , who knew so much more than his neighbors, who had studied and pondered so deeply, should not xxxxxxx be even a good farmer. Sometimes he imagined that he understood too many things ever to do anything well. And so he sipped the burned ale of his own experimenting and smiled into the xxx fire. He was gloriously lazy of course. His wife whispered excuses for him to the neighbors strangers.

His aged mother was beside him, shivering to the fire as though the very wind-sounds about the house were cold to her. For many years,now, she had been practicing the second sight and taking great pride in it. And all the family knew her prophecies to be whole guesses whose shrewdness grew less sharp with her years. They listened to her with respect and awe, and asked of her the location of lost things. And if, after her closed-eyed recitation, the scissors were not under the second board of the shed floor, they pretended to find them there anyway. Thus they guarded her self-esteem with their reverence, for, had she lost the robe of augury, there would have remained only a little,wrinkled, old woman soon to die.

Mother Morgan was all about the room, pervading it with her energy. She ran back and forth with the quick, short steps of a quail-- to the kettle to peer inside-- back again to the cupboard for a spoon to stir it--(a-trip) to the table for a last look-- then paused a pause to sigh with the weariness of her activity: for she was one who labored breathlessly at keeping

Why should you have thought yourself too old to be stricken? It is not only women who "go on forever." The damned, delightful Irish male has a very similar tendency. But it is true, as you say, that one does find old age an impediment to haste. I am thrilled that you can cast it aside for a long enough time to be in love. I am afraid I can never again be capable of a violent and romantic love affair–and it is very sad. I have a disturbing tendency to look at myself and laugh–and that rather wet-blankets the more romantic aspects of an affair. . . .

However, when you are a bit calmer, I do wish you would tell me about everything–the lady herself, for instance, and the progress of the affair. I am by way of being a bit renowned for wisdom and sympathetic understanding. . . .

Personally, of course, I am a little opposed to your marrying although, as I have prophesied, I think it inevitable within the next few years. It has a tendency

Katherine "Kate" Beswick, a close friend of Steinbeck's from the Stanford English Club (from Jackson J. Benson, The True Adventures of John Steinbeck, Writer, *1984; Thomas Cooper Library, University of South Carolina)*

to spoil things a bit; one can never be quite so free with a married man. However, I leave the matter entirely in your hands. . . .

I shall get more writing done, I think, now that I am not consumed with a desire to be going places and doing things. I am unendingly grateful to you and Henry Morgan for bringing me once more to the consciousness that I really can do something. I am convinced, now, as I used to be years ago, that I shall do something good eventually. Life is a very sound investment–in other words, I am happy. . . .

I really can't think of another thing that wants saying right now. I shall go out and have adventures so that I shall have much to tell you if I am to carry on this unilateral episode for an indefinite period.

Always I love you, dear,
Katherine

–quoted in Jackson J. Benson, *The True Adventures of John Steinbeck, Writer* (New York: Viking, 1984), pp. 135–136

Steinbeck's first wife, Carol Henning Steinbeck, whom he married on 14 January 1930 (Center for Steinbeck Studies, San Jose State University; from Jay Parini, John Steinbeck: A Biography, *1995; Thomas Cooper Library, University of South Carolina)*

* * *

Cup of Gold
Will Cuppy

Will Cuppy was one of the first reviewers of Cup of Gold.

Being a life of Henry Morgan, buccaneer, with occasional references to history, and a promising stab at a novel of adventure. Strangely enough, the tale lacks the color and spirit traditional to its genre, perhaps because the author has preferred to tinker with a realistic method—or maybe it was an oversight. Mr. Steinbeck lapses into pedestrian narrative at times, but even so, enough brave names and places are bandied about to hold the interest of most fans; and Mr. Steinbeck's graceful manner lifts the

Dust jacket for Steinbeck's first novel, a fictionalized account of the life of Sir Henry Morgan, published in 1929 (from Sotheby's New York, The Maurice F. Neville Collection of Modern Literature, *November 16, 2004)*

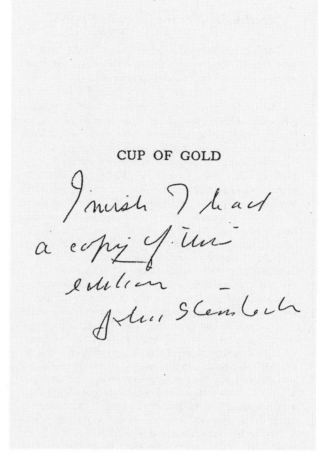

Half-title page, inscribed by Steinbeck, in a first-edition copy of his first novel (National Steinbeck Center, Salinas)

yarn above the adventure groceries of this degenerate age. The tale tells of Henry's boyhood in the Welsh glens, his sailing for the Indies at the age of fifteen, his slavery in Barbados and later triumphs on the Spanish Main, including the sack of Panama, the Cup of Gold, for love of the mysterious Ysobel, alias the Red Saint, and his respectable death years later as lieutenant governor of Jamaica.

—New York Herald Tribune, 18 August 1929; reprinted in
John Steinbeck: The Contemporary Reviews, edited by
Joseph R. McElrath Jr., Jesse S. Crisler, and
Susan Shillinglaw (Cambridge & New York:
Cambridge University Press, 1996), p. 3

* * *

"Decidedly Not for Juvenile Perusal"

The following unsigned review of Cup of Gold *labels the novel unfit for young readers because it is a bloody tale of all aspects of Morgan's life, including his romances.*

Henry Morgan, pirate, freebooter and lieutenant governor, whose greatest ambition was to sack "The Cup of Gold" in Panama, has, through the pen of John Steinbeck, presented his life story for the readers of good fiction in one of the latest books from the Robert McBride Publishing Company. While most previous stories, whether historical or fictional of Morgan's life, were written for the consumption of school boys, here is one that is decidedly not for juvenile perusal. For here is presented Morgan's complete life (including his loves) dealing with every phase, whether real or legendary, of England's most noted buccaneer. Here is seen Morgan in all his brutalness [*sic*], his ambition and his passion. One cannot help but thrill at the downright courage of the man, nor fail to sympathize with him at his disappointments. Morgan, for one of the few times in a life which has appeared many times on paper, is actually seen as a man. He was really human at times, loving all earthly pleasures and, according to the worthy Mr. Steinbeck, actually possessed ideals. He had a natural tendency for exaggeration which, one suspects, has been handed down to his most recent biographer, which is altogether excusable in as much as no claim is made to the historical accuracy of the book. *Cup of Gold* is thoroughly masculine and should find much favor with those male readers who used to delight in those bloody tales of piracy and rebellion.

—*St. Louis Star,* 1 September 1929; reprinted in *John Steinbeck: The Contemporary Reviews,* p. 3

Morgan, the Pirate, Sails Raging Main

An unsigned review in the Columbus Ohio State Journal *noted that there is "little of fact or history" in* Cup of Gold.

This is a romanticized story of Morgan, pirate, pillager, killer, lieutenant-governor of Jamaica and sacker of Panama, known to the world of that day as "the Cup of Gold." From the time when Morgan was a lad on his father's country acres until the day he died in his bed at Jamaica, the story takes him, through his slavery, his years as a buccaneer, his knighting by King Charles, and finally his death. He started with nothing save a love for far places; he took a brown-skinned slave for a mistress, and was defeated when he attempted a similar conquest of the Red Saint of Panama; finally, he married his orphan first cousin, then died like a gentleman.

There is little of fact or history here, although, as the author says, there is an occasional historical reference. The story is fiction, purely, and Morgan is perhaps a more romantic figure here than he was in real life. Some of his cruelties are softened, and under Mr. Steinbeck's pen the buccaneer is at times a strange, abstract creature who knows neither love nor sorrow; who, dying, could not recall that he had any sins to confess or to repent.

There is enough of the biographical novel here to take away the shimmer of imagination, so that the net result is a meaty, pleasing yarn wherein action sets the pace and clever writing plays the tune.

—*Ohio State Journal,* 15 September 1929; reprinted in *John Steinbeck: The Contemporary Reviews,* pp. 3–4

* * *

Morgan, Buccaneer
F.H.M.

The reviewer in the New York Evening Post *found Steinbeck's writing in* Cup of Gold *to involve a discordant blend of styles.*

This novelized "Life of Henry Morgan, Buccaneer," written "with occasional reference to history," somehow does not "come off." It seems to fall between two stools of style in considering the historical subject, the modern naturalistic and the period manner, and they do not harmonize. Yet there is much swing and movement to the narrative at times, and Henry's many undesirable qualities are not camouflaged. Morgan was a cruel, orgiastic brute. And when the author makes him philosophize in his "don't call it love" affairs with his women, Henry does not ring true. The actual record of his life shows he was no introspect. He looked into the wine when it was red, and into women's eyes when he was ready for them. It is a question whether he ever looked into his own soul. Yet Mr. Steinbeck's fantasy is enjoyable reading, with its highlighting of the sack of Panama, the West Indian "Cup of Gold," even though we find it hard to believe that Morgan died thinking he "always had some rather good end in view," in all his deviltries.

—*New York Evening Post,* 28 September 1929; reprinted in *John Steinbeck: The Contemporary Reviews,* p. 4

* * *

The Reviewer
A.M.

The reviewer in The Stanford Daily *reacted positively to Steinbeck's first novel, pointing out that "it is the vivid, complete, and truly introspective picture of Henry Morgan's life and character that make [sic] the book a thing to be remembered."*

There were once two Steinbecks, cousins. One of them [Stanford Steinbeck, born 1907] came to Stanford and became President of the student body. The other came to Stanford and became a novelist.

Cup of Gold, by John Steinbeck, is a fanciful, rather weird, and sometimes historical novel concerning the life of one Henry Morgan, buccaneer, pirate, and member of the "Brotherhood" that caused so much trouble to Spain's power on the seas during the sixteenth century. And Henry is the whole show. We see him first as a boy of fifteen, dreaming of life beyond the seas and eternally yearning for the wild adventurous life of men who did things. We leave him just as death is coming, and all the terrible deeds of his past life are passing by in bewildering confusion.

Cup of Gold is the picture of a dreamer—of a dreamer who eternally searched for some ephemeral happiness. Cities and countries richer than man ever dreamed of, fell before his armies. He had women, gold, ships, and power. But peace was not there and Henry Morgan was a lost soul looking for something he could never find. And thus he died.

All novelists have some sort of a philosophy and John Steinbeck is no exception. Says he, "All the world's great have been little boys who wanted the moon; running and climbing, they sometimes caught a firefly. But if one grow to a man's mind, that mind must see that it cannot have the moon and would not want it if it could—and so it catches no fireflies."

It is not the plot in *Cup of Gold* that makes the book interesting, for there have been many such plots. And it is not the characters, for there have been many such in the minds of all writers. It is the vivid, complete, and truly introspective picture of Henry Morgan's life and character that make [*sic*] the book a thing to be remembered. As one reads the book he feels as though he had experienced the same things in his own life. If you ever left the place in which you grew up, then you know how Henry felt that wintry morning he bid goodbye to the valleys of Cambria.

John Steinbeck is a Stanford man, a member of the class of '24. Since leaving school he has spent his time traveling abroad and in this country, writing things when time allowed. *Cup of Gold* is his first attempt in the field of novel-writing.

—*Stanford Daily,* 30 October 1929, p. 2; reprinted in *John Steinbeck: The Contemporary Reviews,* pp. 4–5

* * *

Cup of Gold
Paul G. Teal

Paul G. Teal reviewed Cup of Gold *for Carol Steinbeck's hometown newspaper, the* San Jose Mercury Herald, *praising the novel for its historical accuracy in documenting the details of Morgan's life.*

Henry Morgan, pirate of note and ruler of the Spanish main who was never defeated, as far as men knew, humiliated and repulsed by a woman, who used only a pin for a weapon.

Henry Morgan, a swashbuckler of power and might, envied by half the world, the most lonesome man that sailed the seven seas—

Henry Morgan, who chose a friend from his crew of adventurers and then killed the friend because he was afraid of his pity—

And lastly, Henry Morgan, "respected" citizen and overlord of Port Royal, who put former members of his crew to death on charges of piracy, with the excuse: "I do not hang you because you are pirates but because I am expected to hang pirates. I am sorry for you. I would like to send you to your cells with saws in your pockets, but I cannot. As long as I do what is expected of me I shall remain the Judge. When I change for whatever motive, I may myself be hanged."

Cup of Gold seems everything that a novel, a history and a book of travel should be. It impresses the reader as containing all elements of literature clamped between two cloth-bound covers. There is pathos and horror in it and nobleness and smallness. There are descriptions of cities and islands and swamps. Its people are broad and narrow, strong and weak, clever and dull and all of these virtues and vices are bound up in Henry Morgan as portrayed by John Steinbeck, who, by the way, is a Palo Alto man.

The tale follows the history of this famous pirate accurately. Not an action of his that is known or sufficiently rumored has been left out. And into this bit of history, which is far from dull even when recounted by the most drab of historians, Steinbeck has woven bits of scintillating beauty, incidents of stark horror, and has peopled all incidents with genuine human beings.

He begins with Morgan as a small boy in Scotland, merely an adventurous small boy who leaves home. Henry is indentured as a slave in Barbados, an island of the British West Indies. His master took an interest in the boy, taught him history and English and gave him access to a large library. Here the future buccaneer studied war. Everything he could find out about fights at sea he consumed—for young Henry had long determined to become a pirate. By way of assuring his future he soon became manager of his master's plantation and stole and laid aside enough money to set him up in the pirate business.

Because of his actual knowledge of sea warfare, his ability to handle men and his sagacity, Henry Morgan soon became the most successful pirate in the trade. Thousands of men flocked to his standard when he called.

The sack of Panama, the Spanish city known as the "Cup of Gold," was the high point in Morgan's career. The reason for this venture was the high point in his affairs of the heart—if he could be said to have a heart.

For Henry Morgan sacked Panama so that he might find a woman there. Her name was La Santa Roja—The Red Saint—and she was known the world over for her charm. And when Henry Morgan found The Red Saint she scorned him and jeered at him and defended herself with a pin until he left the city like a whipped cur.

Desire of The Red Saint put Henry Morgan on his way to Panama. He called for volunteers and an army of pirates responded. They knew that Morgan never failed. The destination was not announced until the pirates had landed on the beach that mouthed the swampy sloughs that led to Panama. The crew nearly revolted with dread at the thought of attacking the impregnable city. But they thought too of The Red Saint.

"There is a woman in Panama and she is lovely as the sun. They call her the Red Saint in Panama. All men kneel to her. She has stolen worship from the Blessed saints." This was the rumor of the Red Saint.

Barges were built and the army and supplies began their watery march toward Panama. Disease and fatigue harassed them but under the lash of Morgan's will they continued.

The city was taken easily and sacked. Morgan failed to find the Red Saint at first. She heard he was searching for her and came to his headquarters. He offered her marriage and she scorned him. He asked for her hand in the sweetest words he could remember.

"You forget only one thing, sir," she said. "I do not burn. You do not carry a torch for me and I hoped you did. I came this morning to see if you did. And I have heard your words so often and so often in Paris and Cordova. I am tired of these words that never change. Is there some book with which aspiring lovers instruct themselves? The Spanish men say the same things, but their gestures are a little more practiced, and so a little more convincing. You have much to learn. I wanted force—blind, unreasoning force—and love not for my soul or for some imagined beauty of my mind, but for the white fetish of my body," she told the pirate.

Her husband was soft and delicate, she said. She was tired of such men.

Morgan, thinking this his cue, tried force. But The Red Saint was not interested. She repulsed his advances by stabbing a small pin in his face. She dared him to kill her. He hadn't the nerve. He was cowed. A woman had defeated the world's greatest pirate.

Infuriated Henry Morgan killed the first man that crossed his path—an epileptic whom he despised. Half crazed he returned to the palace of the Governor and sat amidst the gold that had been looted. His only friend entered. Morgan thought of the pity and comfort his friend would have for him when he explained his failure. Morgan couldn't stand the thought of that. He shot his friend through the heart.

But, nevertheless, Morgan finished things in a business-like way in Panama. He sold The Red Saint back to her husband for a great sum. He took the treasures back to the coast, piled them aboard his ship, made all but a few men drunk, then scuttled all ships but his and sailed away with the swag. His army wakened next day to face starvation. A few escaped but most of them died.

Morgan bribed British officials with some of his fortune and was knighted instead of being jailed. The government sent him to Port Royal where he judged and hung wrong-doers until he died.

—*San Jose Mercury Herald,* 1 December 1929; reprinted in *John Steinbeck: The Contemporary Reviews,* pp. 5–7

* * *

Steinbeck to Grove Day, 5 December 1929

A few months after the publication of Cup of Gold, *Steinbeck wrote from San Francisco to Stanford friend Grove Day.*

Dear Grove:

It is a very long time since I have started a letter with any anticipation of enjoying the writing of it.

Long ago I determined that any one who appraised The Cup of Gold for what it was should be entitled to a big kiss. The book was an immature experiment written for the purpose of getting all the wise cracks (known by sophomores as epigrams) and all the autobiographical

The Stanford English Club in 1926, the year after Steinbeck left the university for the final time. In the middle row are Steinbeck's friends Grove Day, at far left; and Webster "Toby" Street, third from left (Stanford University Archives; from Jackson J. Benson, The True Adventures of John Steinbeck, Writer, *1984; Thomas Cooper Library, University of South Carolina).*

material (which hounds us until we get it said) out of my system. And I really did not intend to publish it. The book accomplished its purgative purpose. I am no more concerned with myself very much. I can write about other people. I have not the slightest desire to step into Donn Byrne's shoes. I may not have his ability with the vernacular but I have twice his head. I think I have swept all the Cabellyo-Byrneish preciousness out for good. The new book is a straightforward and simple attempt to set down some characters in a situation and nothing else. If there is any beauty in it, it is a beauty of idea. I seem to have outgrown [James Branch] Cabell. The new method is far the more difficult of the two. It reduces a single idea to a single sentence and does not allow one to write a whole chapter with it as Cabell does. I think I shall write some very good books indeed. The next one won't be good nor the next one, but about the fifth, I think will be above the average.

I don't care any more what people think of me. I'll tell you how it happened. You will remember at Stanford that I went about being different characters. I even developed a theory that one had no personality in essence, that one was a reflection of a mood plus the moods of other persons present. I wasn't pretending to be something I wasn't. For the moment I was truly the person I thought I was.

Well, I went into the mountains and stayed two years. I was snowed in eight months of the year and saw no one except my two Airedales. There were millions of fir trees and the snow was deep and it was very quiet. And there was no one to pose for any more. You can't have a show with no audience. Gradually all the poses slipped off and when I came out of the hills I didn't have any poses any more. It was rather sad, but it was far less trouble. I am happier than I have ever been in my life.

My sister [Mary] is married to Bill Dekker and has two very beautiful children. They are the only children whom I have ever liked at all. They live in Los Angeles and enjoy themselves.

I don't think I write very interesting letters any more. I have this pelican of a novel hanging about my neck and it is decomposing and bothering me about every hour of the day. I dream about it. I can't enjoy a party because it is not done. I write two pages and destroy three. It is over-ambitious I think.

I am engaged to a girl of whom I will say nothing at all because you will eventually meet her and I think you will like her because she has a mind as sharp and penetrating as your own.

I think that is all. I hope you will not let a great time pass before answering, though I realize that there is nothing to answer.

Sincerely,
John
—*Steinbeck: A Life in Letters,* pp. 17–18

To a God Unknown (1933)

Steinbeck to Day, December 1929

In another letter to Day, Steinbeck explains his theory and practice of writing.

I am answering your letter immediately.

I want to speak particularly of your theory of clean manuscripts, and spelling as correct as a collegiate stenographer, and every nasty little comma in its place and preening of itself. "Manners," you say it is, and knowing the "trade" and the "Printed Word." But I have no interest in the printed word. I would continue to write if there were no writing and no print. I put my words down for a matter of memory. They are more made to be spoken than to be read. I have the instincts of a minstrel rather than those of a scrivener. There you have it. We are not of the same trade at all and so how can your rules fit me? When my sounds are all in place, I can send them to a stenographer who knows *his* trade and he can slip the commas about until they sit comfortably and he can spell the words so that school teachers will not raise their eyebrows when they read them. Why should I bother? There are millions of people who are good stenographers but there aren't so many thousands who can make as nice sounds as I can.

I must have misinformed you about my new book. I never read Hemingway with the exception of The Killers. I have not lost the love for sound nor for pictures. Only I have tried to throw out the words that do not say anything. I don't read much when I am working because novels have a way of going right on whether you are writing or not. You'll be having dreams about it that wake you up in the night, and maybe you'll be kissing some girl the way she expects it, and all the time your mind will be saying, "I'll do the thing this way, and I'll transpose these scenes." A novel doesn't stop at all when your pen is away.

Next week maybe I'll be moving to Los Angeles with Carol and we'll have some kind of a little house on the outskirts and you can come to see us. We haven't much money but it's very cheap to live out here. Maybe you'd like to settle near to us. I don't like Stanford and never did. Prigs they are there and pretenders. Maybe you could get a part time job in the south and we could sit in front of a fire and talk, or lie on the beach and talk, or walk in the hills and talk. I'd like you to know Carol. She doesn't write or dance or play the piano and she has very little of any soul at all. But horses like her and dogs and little boys and bootblacks and laborers. But people with souls don't like her very much.

Let me hear from you as soon as you can.

john

—*Steinbeck: A Life in Letters*, pp. 19–20

* * *

Steinbeck to Wilhelmson, early 1930

Steinbeck wrote Wilhelmson from his and Carol's home in Eagle Rock, east of Los Angeles, explaining how he had arrived at a new working title, "To the Unknown God," for his novel in progress. He later revised it to "To an Unknown God," and the novel was eventually published in 1933 as To a God Unknown.

Dear Carl:

I do not know how long it is since I have written to you. Everything has been in a haze pretty much for the past three weeks. I have been working to finish this ms. and the thing took hold of me so completely that I lost track of nearly everything else. Now the thing is done. I started rewriting this week and am not going to let it rest. Also I have a title which gives me the greatest of pleasure. For my title I have taken one of the Vedic Hymns, the name of the hymn—

TO THE UNKNOWN GOD

You surely remember the hymn with its refrain at the end of each invocation "Who is the god to whom we shall offer sacrifice?" Don't you think that is a good title? I am quite enthusiastic about it.

Carol is a good influence on my work. I am putting five hours every day on the rewriting of this one and in the evenings I have started another ["Dissonant Symphony," never published]. I have the time and the energy and it gives me pleasure to work, and now I do not seem to have to fight as much reluctance to work as I used to have. The start comes much easier. The new book is just a series of short stories or sketches loosely and foolishly tied together. There are a number of little things I have wanted to write for a long time, some of them ridiculous and some of them more serious, and so I am putting them in a ridiculous fabric. It is not the series in Salinas at all. I shall not do that yet. I am too vindictive and harsh on my own people. In a few years I may have outgrown that.

The dog is growing like a weed. He is three times as big as he was when we got him. You can see him grow from day to day. It has been quite cold here for the last few days with a good deal of rain and wind. But we have a big fire place in the house and the hill side behind us is covered with dead wood so we do not suffer. Indeed we enjoy it. You know, we really do not live in a city at all. We are out on a wooded and very sparsely-settled hill side. In three minutes you can climb to the top of the hill and be above everything and away from everything. It is much better than living in a city.

Are you working, and if so on what? It must be wet as hell up there now. You have told me things about the rainy season up there and it seems to be

Carlton A. "Dook" Sheffield, Steinbeck's Stanford roommate and lifelong friend; Steinbeck's younger sister, Mary, who also attended Stanford (from Jackson J. Benson, The True Adventures of John Steinbeck, Writer, *1984; Thomas Cooper Library, University of South Carolina)*

mostly floods. Carol and I thought of taking a run up to Salinas but we got a plumbing bill for about thirty dollars and a stop was put to that.

Duke [Sheffield] is well and Maryon [Sheffield's second wife] has been slightly unwell but has recovered.

Let me know how you are and what you are working on.

Sincerely
John
—*Steinbeck: A Life in Letters,* pp. 21–22

* * *

Steinbeck to Ted Miller, 1930

To a God Unknown *originated in Steinbeck's work with Street's play "The Green Lady," and he wanted to give Street credit in a foreword to the book. From Eagle Rock, Steinbeck wrote Ted Miller, his informal agent in New York, expressing this desire.*

Dear Ted:

Herewith enclosed is the ms. ["To an Unknown God"] which has been taking up so much time in the last year and a half. I know that it will not seem worth the effort. I shall insure it heavily. Please let me hear from you immediately you receive it for I shall be anxious. There is a carbon but it is on inferior paper and is only held for a safeguard in case this is lost.

If McBride should decide to take this tell them that I want a short foreword in which some mention of Toby Street should be made. I shall write that later. He has decided that he didn't do as much on this as he at first thought he did. But such a foreword is really necessary. On the other book I asked for a dedication and they paid no attention. If the foreword is refused they can go to hell.

Sincerely
john
—*Steinbeck: A Life in Letters,* p. 23

* * *

Steinbeck to Miller, 6 August 1930

The following letter to Miller is one of the last Steinbeck wrote from Eagle Rock before he and Carol moved to his family's cottage in Pacific Grove, on the Monterey Peninsula, where they could live rent free. According to Sheffield, the Steinbecks had done "such a beautiful job of rebuilding the Eagle Rock shack that the owner evicted them and gave it to his daughter as a wedding present." Steinbeck's father gave the couple a monthly allowance of $25, and Carol contributed her earnings from various jobs. In the letter Steinbeck reacts to a publisher's rejection of "To an Unknown God."

Dear Ted:

I have received Farrar's rejection of my manuscript. It is terse and to the point. The man makes no bones about his rejection and I like that. But now that I have it, I do not know what to do next. I know nothing whatever about the market.

Aren't you getting sick of trundling this white elephant around? It is discouraging, isn't it? Nobody seems to want my work. That doesn't injure me but it must be having a definite effect on you that you are handling a dud. Let me know what you think about it.

Our house here has been sold over our heads and we are going back north to the Grove. In many ways we are glad to leave the south although we are very fond of this house. It is pretty hot down here now and my mind seems more sluggish than it usually is.

affectionately
john
—Steinbeck: A Life in Letters, p. 26

Carl Wilhelmson, a Stanford friend with whom Steinbeck shared a San Francisco apartment in late 1928 (from Jackson J. Benson, The True Adventures of John Steinbeck, Writer, *1984; Thomas Cooper Library, University of South Carolina)*

* * *

Steinbeck to Wilhelmson, late 1930

After moving back to Pacific Grove, Steinbeck was still saddened by the recent rejection of "To an Unknown God," as is indicated in this letter to Wilhelmson. John "Jack" Calvin was a writer of juvenile adventure stories whom Steinbeck met while living in Pacific Grove.

Dear Carl:

It is a gloomy day; low gray fog and a wet wind contribute to my own gloominess. Whether the fog has escaped from my soul like ectoplasm to envelope the peninsula, or whether it has seeped in through my nose and eyes to create the gloom, I don't know. Last night I read over the first forty pages of my new novel and destroyed them—the most unrelieved rot imaginable. It is very sad.

We went to a party at John Calvin's in Carmel last week. These writers of juveniles are the Jews of literature. They seem to wring the English language, to squeeze pennies out of it. They don't even pretend that there is any

dignity in craftsmanship. A conversation with them sounds like an afternoon spent with a pawnbroker. Says John Calvin, "I long ago ceased to take anything I write seriously." I retorted, "I take *everything* I write seriously; unless one does take his work seriously there is very little chance of its ever being good work." And the whole company was a little ashamed of me as though I had three legs or was an albino.

I am very anxious to see a copy of Midsummer Night [*Midsummernight*, Wilhelmson's 1930 novel]. When I can afford to, I will buy it. It was different with my own first novel. I outgrew that before I finished writing it. I very definitely didn't want you to have it just as I didn't want to have it myself. I shall be glad to arrive at an age where I don't outgrow a piece of work as children outgrow shoes.

This letter would seem to indicate that I am unhappy. Such is not the case. As long as I can work I shall be happy (except during moments of reflection) regardless of the quality of the work. That is a curious thing but true.

There was a great fire last night. The Del Monte bath house burned to the ground. We got up and went to it and stood in the light and heat and gloried in the destruction. When Cato was shouting in the Roman Senate "Carthago delenda est," I wondered whether in his mind there was not a vision of the glorious fire it would make. Precious things make beautiful flames. The pyre that Savonarola made of all lovely and profound, wise and beautiful things of northern Italy must have been the finest fire the world has seen. I believe there is an account which says that when Caesar burned the great library at Alexandria, the populace laughed and groaned in exquisite despair.

You say you are striving for tenseness in your ms. I feel increasingly that you and I are the only ones of our entire acquaintance who have retained any literary responsibility and integrity. That is worth while regardless of the badness of my work.

Modern sanity and religion are a curious delusion. Yesterday I went out in a fishing boat—out in the ocean. By looking over the side into the blue water, I could quite easily see the shell of the turtle who supports the world. I am getting more prone to madness. What a ridiculous letter this is; full of vaguenesses and unrealities. I for one and you to some extent have a great many of the basic impulses of an African witch doctor.

You know the big pine tree beside this house? I planted it when it and I were very little; I've watched it grow. It has always been known as "John's tree." Years ago, in mental playfulness I used to think of it as my brother and then later, still playfully, I thought of it as something rather closer, a kind of repository of my destiny. This was all an amusing fancy, mind you. Now the lower limbs should be cut off because they endanger the house. I must cut them soon, and I have a very powerful reluctance to do it, such a reluctance as I would have toward cutting live flesh. Furthermore if the tree should die, I am pretty sure I should be ill. This feeling I have planted in myself and quite deliberately I guess, but it is none the less strong for all that.

I shall stop before you consider me quite mad.

Sincerely,

John

—*Steinbeck: A Life in Letters,* pp. 30–31

* * *

Steinbeck to Miller, December 1930

In December 1930 Steinbeck completed a murder mystery, "Murder at Full Moon," and sent the manuscript to Miller to see

if he could find a publisher for it. In this letter Steinbeck reveals that the murder mystery was written for financial reasons. (It was never published.)

Dear Ted:

I think the manuscript enclosed in this package is self explanatory. For some time now, I have been unhappy. The reason is that I have a debt and it is making me miserable.

It is quite obvious that people do not want to buy the things I have been writing. Therefore, to make the money I need, I must write the things they want to read. In other words, I must sacrifice artistic integrity for a little while to personal integrity. Remember that when this manuscript makes you sick. And remember that it makes me a great deal sicker than it does you.

Conrad said that only two things sold, the very best and the very worst. From my recent efforts, it has been borne to me that I am not capable of writing the very best yet. I have no doubt that I shall be able to in the future, but at present, I cannot. It remains to be seen whether I can write the very worst.

I will tell you a little bit about the enclosed ms. It was written complete in nine days. It is about sixty two or three thousand words long. It took two weeks to type. In it I have included all the cheap rackets I know of, and have tried to make it stand up by giving it a slightly burlesque tone. No one but my wife and my folks know that I have written it, and no one except you will know. I see no reason why a nom de plume should not be respected and maintained. The nom de plume I have chosen is Peter Pym.

The story holds water better than most, and I think it has a fairish amount of mystery. The burlesqued bits, which were put in mostly to keep my stomach from turning every time I sat down at the typewriter, may come out.

Don't let it make you too sick. It only took nine days to write and it didn't have any effect on me whatever. I feel very badly about it, but I won't be very happy anyway unless this debt is paid. It isn't a large debt but it is worrying me.

Carol and another girl, both of wide experience, are opening a small publicity and advertising agency on the peninsula. Come west soon and be their attorney.

Let me hear from you when you can. And if you don't get either card or present from me this Christmas, you will know that I am broke. I so warn you in advance. And I hope you have a good drunken Christmas.

affectionately,

John

—*Steinbeck: A Life in Letters,* pp. 32–33

Chapter Two: 1931–1935

Chronology

January 1931	Steinbeck becomes a frequent visitor to Edward F. "Ed" Ricketts's Pacific Biological Laboratories on Cannery Row in Monterey.
April 1931	Steinbeck urges his friend Amasa "Ted" Miller, who has been acting as his informal agent in New York, to try a new literary agency, McIntosh and Otis, to place his manuscripts.
18 August 1931	After receiving a rejection for the novel with the working title "To an Unknown God," Steinbeck plans to rewrite it. He sends the experimental novel "Dissonant Symphony" to Miller to pass along to McIntosh and Otis, marking the beginning of Steinbeck's long association with Mavis McIntosh and Elizabeth Otis as his literary agents.

Edward F. "Ed" Ricketts, the marine biologist with whom Steinbeck formed a friendship in the early 1930s (photograph by Peter Stackpole; Center for Steinbeck Studies, San Jose State University; from Jay Parini, John Steinbeck, 1995; Thomas Cooper Library, University of South Carolina)

December 1931	Carol Steinbeck finishes typing up her husband's manuscript of *The Pastures of Heaven* (1932), and the typescript is sent to Miller in New York to give to McIntosh and Otis.
27 February 1932	On his thirtieth birthday Steinbeck receives a telegram from McIntosh and Otis telling him that *The Pastures of Heaven* has been accepted for publication by Jonathan Cape and Harrison Smith.
March 1932	Carol obtains a job working for Ricketts that pays her $50 a month.
May 1932	The firm of Cape and Smith goes bankrupt, and *The Pastures of Heaven* is picked up by Brewer, Warren and Putnam. Steinbeck sends another manuscript, "St. Katy the Virgin," to McIntosh and Otis, but they are unable to place it.
June 1932	Carol and comparative-mythology scholar Joseph Campbell have a brief romantic encounter, which is terminated by mutual consent when Campbell leaves with Ricketts on a specimen-collecting trip to Alaska.
July 1932	With the promise of money from *The Pastures of Heaven* and with Carol no longer working for Ricketts, the Steinbecks move back to southern California, settling in the Montrose area, just north of Eagle Rock.
October 1932	*The Pastures of Heaven* is published.
8 November 1932	Franklin Delano Roosevelt is elected president.
January 1933	The Steinbecks experience financial problems. Steinbeck asks McIntosh and Otis to withdraw his "Dissonant Symphony," and he eventually destroys the manuscript. On 3 January, Steinbeck writes to Robert O. Ballou that he will send *To a God Unknown* (1933)–the final version of the title for the novel–to him by the end of February.
11 February 1933	Steinbeck sends *To a God Unknown* to McIntosh and Otis.
Mid March 1933	Steinbeck moves into the family home in Salinas to take care of his mother, who is seriously ill. Carol works at part-time jobs in Monterey while John writes, using the dining- room table outside his mother's room as a desk.
May 1933	The U.S. Agricultural Adjustment Act is passed to lift agricultural prices to "parity" with industrial prices.
30 June 1933	Steinbeck finishes the story "The Red Pony" while taking care of his mother.
9 August 1933	Steinbeck writes to his Stanford friend Carl Wilhelmson telling him that he has been working on several stories and complaining that it is difficult to write when his parents are in bad health. Some of these stories are later incorporated into *The Red Pony* (1937) and others used in *Tortilla Flat* (1935).
September 1933	*To a God Unknown* is published by Robert O. Ballou.
November 1933	"The Red Pony" (later retitled "The Gift") is published in *The North American Review*.
December 1933	"The Great Mountains" is published in *The North American Review*. "The Gift" and "The Great Mountains" form the first two parts of *The Red Pony* and are later included in *The Long Valley* (1938).
February 1934	Steinbeck's mother, Olive Hamilton Steinbeck, dies in Salinas on 19 February as the result of a stroke. On 25 February, Steinbeck finishes the short story "The Chrysanthemums" while taking care of his father.
March 1934	Steinbeck finishes the manuscript of *Tortilla Flat* and sends it to McIntosh and Otis. The Steinbecks accompany Ricketts on a specimen-collecting trip to Laguna Beach for a week.

April 1934	Steinbeck's story "The Murder" is published in *The North American Review*. It wins a 1934 O. Henry Award.
May 1934	Steinbeck and Carol divide their time between Pacific Grove and his family's home in Salinas. In preparation for a new novel, Steinbeck begins to perform research by going on various expeditions and collecting firsthand information on migrant workers, communists, and labor organizations. During this period he works on more short stories that later appear in *The Long Valley*. "The Harness" (originally titled "The Fool"), "Flight" (originally titled "Manhunt"), "The White Quail," and "Johnny Bear" (originally titled "The Sisters") are written this summer.
August 1934	Steinbeck begins working on his strike novel, eventually published as *In Dubious Battle* (1936).
October 1934	Steinbeck's short story "The Raid" is published in *The North American Review*.
November–December 1934	Ben Abramson, a Chicago bookseller, introduces Steinbeck's writings to publisher and editor Pascal Covici, who soon becomes Steinbeck's editor and remains so for the rest of the author's life.
4 February 1935	Steinbeck completes the manuscript of *In Dubious Battle* and signs a contract with Covici-Friede to publish *Tortilla Flat*.
March 1935	Otis takes over from McIntosh to handle Steinbeck's career for the agency. His short story "The White Quail" is published in *The North American Review*.
May 1935	After a long illness, John Ernst Steinbeck Sr. dies on 23 May at the home of his daughter Esther in Watsonville, California. *Tortilla Flat* is published on 28 May and quickly becomes a best-seller.
22 June 1935	Steinbeck's short story "The Snake" is published in *The Monterey Beacon*.
August 1935	Steinbeck signs a contract with Covici-Friede for *In Dubious Battle* after it was rejected by an editor who was sitting in for Covici while he was away on a promotional trip. Covici is furious that the substitute editor rejected Steinbeck's manuscript. This same month Covici travels to San Francisco on a business trip and meets Steinbeck for the first time.
September 1935	The Steinbecks travel to Mexico in order to escape publicity.
October 1935	While in Mexico the Steinbecks receive a telegram from McIntosh and Otis reporting that Paramount Pictures has purchased the motion-picture rights to *Tortilla Flat* for $4,000.

After several rejections of "To an Unknown God" (published as To a God Unknown, *1933), Steinbeck suggested to his informal agent in New York, Amasa "Ted" Miller, that he send it to the literary agency of McIntosh and Otis. Miller convinced Mavis McIntosh and Elizabeth Otis to represent Steinbeck in 1931. Steinbeck's relationship with this firm, documented in more than six hundred letters, was to last for the rest of his life. On 27 February 1932, his thirtieth birthday, he received news that his short-story sequence* The Pastures of Heaven *(1932) had just been placed with a publisher, Jonathan Cape and Harrison Smith. At this time Carol Steinbeck was working at*

Edward F. "Ed" Ricketts's marine-research laboratory on Cannery Row in Monterey; Steinbeck frequently visited the lab, and it provided material for several of his stories and novels.

While Steinbeck was working on another rewrite of "To an Unknown God," he had several conversations with Ricketts, whose view of life was Darwinistic, animalistic, and naturalistic. The novel concerns a New England family that settles in California. Ricketts convinced Steinbeck that the protagonists should battle with the elements—the natural environment—rather than with religious myths, although the novel is rich with mythic allusions. McIntosh and Otis first convinced Robert O. Ballou of Cape and

Elizabeth Otis   7/17/71

A New York city girl, went to Vasser (MacIntosh went to Wisconsin)
who met McIntosh at a crooked literary agency.

Together they decided to start an honest agency; incorporated in
    1928 and moved to 42st street (?)

First read Pastures of Heaven--got Ballew, then Ballew failed
    (Ballew still alive--good taste, not business sense--he was
    looking for real literary quality)

    They felt that the ms (Pastures) was wonderful--the question was,
        who should we give it to?

In his first writing, knew nothing about punctuation--seemed to
    just put a comma every seven words.

Otis's impression about S's politics was that S just cared for the
    country.

Style--always wrote, from beginning to end of career, those sentenc
    that had their own distinctive rhythm.

All his life he loved words--even at the end.

First reall help from Otis with ms came with Grapes because of the
    dirty words

        Before that she did mention to him that the ending to To a
        God Unknown was vague.

Terrible two days on Grapes--if you make the changes and keep same
    rhythm, he insisted--so Otis worked on them and worked on
    them and finally he accepted the results

        When she went down to send the telegram (it had to be in
        that day--one more day and the publisher would have gone
        ahead with the original) the girl told her, "I don't hhink
        I can accept that telegram" Otis told her that hhe just
        had to send it.

Steinbeck had a tremendous ear for dialogue

During the early years, she was placing stories for $45 and $60

Otis would call him intuitive, rather than mystical.

    S's mother clairvoyant--visions--things she saw.

Tortilla Flat was not turned down as many times as legend has it.

Neither Ballew nor Covici did much editing.

When Covici was failing (before Grapes) she came into the office
    in the morning and three or four top-drawer publishing people
    where waiting.

*First page of a "resume" of her career prepared by Elizabeth Otis, who became Steinbeck's literary agent in the early 1930s
(Center for Steinbeck Studies, San Jose State University)*

Smith to sign a contract with Steinbeck for The Pastures of Heaven *and two subsequent novels. After the firm went bankrupt, Ballou took the contracts with him when he joined Brewer, Warren and Putnam, which published* The Pastures of Heaven *in 1932. After Ballou started his own firm, he agreed to publish* To a God Unknown, *which had been rejected by several publishers, with Steinbeck's agreement that he would revise the novel. Through the summer and fall of 1932, Steinbeck worked assiduously on the manuscript. After completing the revision in February 1933, he sent it to McIntosh and Otis.*

In mid March 1933 Steinbeck had to move back to Salinas because his mother was seriously ill, but he continued his writing. During this time he mainly wrote short stories, including "The Red Pony" and "The Great Mountains." In the summer, while taking care of his ailing father, Steinbeck had more time to reflect on his purpose and ambition as a writer. He and Ricketts had several long discussions about the nature and mechanics of death. Steinbeck's understanding of the whole process of life and death began to form a more concrete part of what he wanted to say in his writing. Borrowing Ricketts's interpretation, he began to see groups as "beings in themselves, entities. . . . [T]hese huge creatures, the groups, do not resemble the human atoms which compose them," he wrote his friend Carlton A. "Dook" Sheffield on 21 June 1933. Steinbeck decided that this view would provide thematic material for his future fiction.

In September 1933 To a God Unknown *was published by Ballou, and in November "The Red Pony" appeared in* The North American Review. *As Steinbeck's short stories were published, they began to draw a national audience. Late that year, he received a visitor at his house in Pacific Grove, a young, aspiring novelist named Martin Bidwell. Bidwell had read Steinbeck's first novel,* Cup of Gold *(1929), and admired his writing; he now solicited advice from the writer. As Bidwell recounted their conversation in "John Steinbeck: An Impression," published in* Prairie Schooner *in 1938, Steinbeck asked him, "What kind of trouble are you having with your novel?" When Bidwell explained that he could not sell his work because his agents wanted him to change the main character, Steinbeck responded, "Don't you realize that you're the one who should be pleased—that you're writing solely for yourself? What anybody else thinks or says about it doesn't matter. That's why you're having trouble. You're selling yourself out. You're being dishonest! . . ." With pride, Steinbeck told the young man, "My wife and I live in this house [the Steinbeck family cottage in Pacific Grove] on almost nothing. We never have any money. We can't go out to dance, or to the theater. But that isn't important. I'm writing as I know I should write. Nothing will ever stop me!"*

On 19 February 1934 Steinbeck's mother died in Salinas following a stroke, and he then had to care for his father. He also completed short stories, including "The Chrysanthemums." In March he finished the manuscript of Tortilla Flat *(1935) and sent it to McIntosh and Otis. Later in the spring and summer,*

Steinbeck completed more short stories, subsequently published in The Long Valley *(1938).*

Early in 1935 Steinbeck completed the manuscript of In Dubious Battle *(1936). In March, Otis took over from McIntosh in handling Steinbeck's contracts with the agency. Also around this time, he signed a contract with Covici-Friede to publish* Tortilla Flat. *Otis persuaded editor Pascal Covici that no matter what he thought of the controversial politics of* In Dubious Battle, *the novel would be a commercial success. The controversy over the highly political* In Dubious Battle *prompted Steinbeck to submit something different to alleviate the tension.* Tortilla Flat, *a work he had dismissed as insignificant, was published on 28 May 1935. It was illustrated with droll line drawings by Ruth Gannett, an accomplished artist and the wife of the critic Lewis Gannett. Steinbeck's only regret was that publication of the book came just a few days after the death of his father. During the summer of 1935* Tortilla Flat *reached the national best-seller list, and Steinbeck became a literary celebrity.*

Not all critics liked Tortilla Flat, *however. Some denounced the book as a callous glorification of idleness and illiteracy, while others viewed it as a failed attempt at lighthearted humor. The Monterey Chamber of Commerce issued a press release denying that there was such a place in Monterey. Despite this controversy,* Tortilla Flat *won the California Commonwealth Club's 1935 gold medal for the best book of fiction about California.*

The Pastures of Heaven (1932) and *To a God Unknown* (1933)

Steinbeck to George Albee, 1931

Steinbeck kept up a frequent correspondence with George Albee, a young writer he and Carol had met while living in Eagle Rock. In 1931 he wrote from Pacific Grove offering encouragement to Albee.

Dear George:

Your letter this morning aroused a degree of argumentativeness in me—a good sign that the great depression is about over. It strikes me that the world is not nearly as hostile as you are. You fight it so, George. I think it angers you because it pays so little attention to you.

Fine artistic things seem always to be done in the face of difficulties, and the rocky soil, which seems to give the finest flower, is contempt. Don't fool yourself, George, appreciation doesn't make artists. It ruins them. A man's best work is done when he is fighting to make himself heard, not when swooning audiences wait for his paragraphs. An elevated train two doors away can have far more to do with a fine book than advance royalties or "an eager printer's boy waiting in the hall." If you don't want to fight them you shouldn't be writing. One can force attention by making one's work superb. Only practice can do that.

Things like this hurt. My sister is staying over night. I say—"I have a new story. I wish you'd listen to it." She says, "I'd love to." The story is three weeks of thinking and working. I am proud of it. It makes me laugh because it is so funny. I can hardly read the end because it is so sad. Its characters are my own children. And after supper, my sister walks up town and buys a Saturday Evening Post. I do not read her this story. It is silly. But why should I be angry when she would rather read a story whose value is $3,000 rather than one from my ragged notebook—in first draft and unsaleable. How can I blame her when I wouldn't like to read my own first drafts if I hadn't written them? It takes a great expert to judge a story in manuscript. You must remember that before you let your feelings be hurt.

I think Carolyn would be a good wife. You don't want your wife to think you a genius. No wife ever could and it would be terrible if she did. I had a mistress once who thought I was. I was young enough to think I was too. I had to leave her in sheer boredom and disgust. It's too onerous to be a genius.

John

—*Steinbeck: A Life in Letters*, edited by Elaine Steinbeck and Robert Wallsten (New York: Viking, 1975), pp. 34–35

* * *

Steinbeck to Albee, 27 February 1931

In his next letter to Albee, Steinbeck describes his financial problems and his troubles with "To an Unknown God" (published as To a God Unknown *in 1933).*

Excuse this kind of writing. It is the only kind I am capable of just now. A visit to the dentist this morning has battered my outlook. I meant to answer your last letter before this. In my last letter I had no intention of giving you advice. Advice is not my nature anyway. I blunder terribly, George. I go through life a grazing elephant, knocking down trees I am too stupid to consider formidable. My blindness and unawareness terrify me in the few moments of light. I'm twenty-nine today, and I haven't thought enough things or done enough things to be that old. This afternoon my parents will drive over to get us and take us to dinner. Dinner at Highland or Del Monte. The check will be not less than thirty dollars, and I can't pay a dentist bill. There's

Farm field in Steinbeck's native Salinas Valley, the setting for many of his books (from Steve Crouch, Steinbeck Country, *1973; Thomas Cooper Library, University of South Carolina)*

something silly about it. I don't just know where it is, but it's crazy some way.

In a rougher age I would have been eliminated I guess. A saber tooth would have grabbed me while I looked stupidly at pond lilies.

When I was sixteen or seventeen I spent a goodly time looking in mirrors bemoaning my ugliness, turning my head to see whether some position or other wouldn't soften the coarseness of my features. None of them did. The people I admired and envied! If I could only have looked forward I wouldn't have minded so much. The beauty of the school, at thirty-two,—baldness and astigmatism and the gin which society forced him to drink, have made him look like a slender pig. The lovely girl I didn't dare speak to because my lips were thick and my nose resembled a wen, is sagging under the chin and her eyes have the worried look of half-successful people who only buy at the best markets and who will mortgage the house rather than keep a car two years.

Then after a while I stopped looking in mirrors. It was safer. I didn't see myself for a number of years, and when I finally did look again, it was a stranger I saw, and I didn't care one way or another what he looked like.

This was begun some days ago. It probably doesn't mean anything. I am having trouble with my manuscript. Most of my troubles arise in something like that. Also I have a toothache, two huge fever blisters, and the itch of departing novocaine. These are enough to disrupt any philosophy. In addition—this paper which was guaranteed to take ink, didn't very well. I feel peeled of my skin and the nerve ends quivering in the air.

I'm having a devil of a time with my new book. It just won't seem to come right. Largeness of character is difficult. Never deal with an Olympian character. I think better times will come to me pretty soon. March is a curious month for my family. Every disaster of every kind—death, sickness, financial stress, during the last two generations of my family, has occurred in March. My mother goes through the month with her teeth set, fully believing it is an evil month for us. If a March passes without evil she celebrates.

Aren't you ever coming up again? This is the grand time of the year, and you didn't even see the coast country. It is the most fantastic place. We have no car now, but I drive my folks places. They are enjoying it so much.

[unsigned]

—Steinbeck: A Life in Letters, pp. 35–36

* * *

Steinbeck to Ted Miller, 1931

After receiving several rejections for "To an Unknown God," Steinbeck wrote to Amasa "Ted" Miller in New York from Pacific Grove, asking him try a new literary agency, McIntosh and Otis, which he had learned about from Carl Wilhelmson. Miller followed the suggestion and delivered Steinbeck's unsold manuscripts to Mavis McIntosh and Elizabeth Otis. The ensuing relationship between Steinbeck and McIntosh and Otis lasted for the rest of his career.

Dear Ted:

I remembered some things I wanted to ask you. First—does McBride still hold the copyright on the Cup [*Cup of Gold* (1929)] and what arrangement did they make for the disposal of the extra copies and what is the chance of acquiring that copyright without buying it?

Second—by now you must know or have some strong conviction about the Unknown God. Do you honestly think it has the least chance in the world? Do you think it worth while to resubmit to John Day as they suggested or was that bull on their part? Wouldn't it be a load off your shoulders if you put the whole caboodle with an agent? I wouldn't mind. It must be rather disheartening to you to collect my rejection slips. Carl Wilhelmson recommends Mavis McIntosh of McIntosh & Otis at 18 East 41st Street, if

you want to unload the stuff. His name should be used.

Third—on what grounds was the murder story rejected? Was it the sloppiness of it or just that it wasn't a good enough story? Do you think there is the least chance of selling it? Are you discouraged about the whole business? Have these rejections carried any editorial interest at all?

I know it is hard to write when you don't know what I want to know. Rejection follows rejection. Haven't there ever been encouraging letters? Perhaps an agent with a thorough knowledge of markets would see that the mss. were not marketable at all and would return them on that ground. You see the haunting thought comes that perhaps I have been kidding myself all these years, myself and other people—that I have nothing to say or no art in saying nothing. It is two years since I have received the slightest encouragement and that was short lived.

I shall finish at least one novel this year. It will probably be better than the others. I am leaving the long fine book for a while to do a shorter one. The big book should take a number of years. It is a fairly original plan (the new book) and quite a vital story or really series of stories [*The Pastures of Heaven* (1932)].

I guess that's all. Will you please write and answer the questions though? You must understand how anxious I am.

Affectionately,
John

—Steinbeck: A Life in Letters, pp. 39–40

* * *

Steinbeck to Mavis McIntosh, 8 May 1931

In one of his first letters to McIntosh, Steinbeck tells her that "To an Unknown God" was conceived as a play and acknowledges his lack of familiarity with dramatic technique. "Murder at Full Moon," a murder mystery Steinbeck completed in December 1930, was never published.

Dear Miss McIntosh:

Thank you for your letter. I am sorry I must answer it from memory; Tillie Eulenspiegel, the Airedale, has puppies, as sinful a crew as ever ruined rugs. Four of them found your letter and ate all of it but the address. I should imagine they were awed by the address if I had not learned that they hold nothing in reverence. At present they are out eating each other, and I must try to remember the things I should answer.

I have no readable carbon of Murder at Full Moon. If you think it advisable, I shall have one made. The quicker I can forget the damned thing, the happier I shall be.

To An Unknown God should have been a play. It was conceived as a play and thought of and talked of as such for several years. But I have no knowledge of the theater nor any knowledge of dramatic technique. Does one find a collaborator in such a case? I didn't know the novel dragged, and I thought I was fairly aware of its faults. It is out of proportion because it was thought of as two books. The story changes tempo and style because it changes speed and spirit. I tried to fit the style to the subject, that is all. I should like to write it again.

In a few days I'll send you some short stories. They are amusing, but I'm afraid unsaleable. I wrote them to amuse myself. Perhaps it would only waste your time to send them.

The present work [The Pastures of Heaven] interests me and perhaps falls in the "aspects" theme you mention. There is, about twelve miles from Monterey, a valley in the hills called Corral de Tierra. Because I am using its people I have named it Las Pasturas del Cielo. The valley was for years known as the happy valley because of the unique harmony which existed among its twenty families. About ten years ago a new family moved in on one of the ranches. They were ordinary people, ill-educated but honest and as kindly as any. In fact, in their whole history I cannot find that they have committed a really malicious act nor an act which was not dictated by honorable expediency or out-and-out altruism. But about the Morans there was a flavor of evil. Everyone they came in contact with was injured. Every place they went dissension sprang up. There have been two murders, a suicide, many quarrels and a great deal of unhappiness in the Pastures of Heaven, and all of these things can be traced directly to the influence of the Morans. So much is true.

I am using the following method. The manuscript is made up of stories, each one complete in itself, having its rise, climax and ending. Each story deals with a family or an individual. They are tied together only by the common locality and by the contact with the Morans. Some of the stories are very short and some as long as fifteen thousand words. I thought of combining them with that thirty-thousand word ms. called Dissonant Symphony to make one volume. I wonder whether you think this is a good plan. I think the plan at least falls very definitely in the aspects of American life category. I have finished several and am working on others steadily. They should be done by this fall.

That is all I can think of. If there was more to be answered it is in the stomachs of those khaki-colored devils in the garden. They are eating the fence now. The appetite of a puppy ranks with Grand Canyon for pure stupendousness.

I am very grateful to you for your interest and to Carl Wilhelmson for his recommendation. He, by the way, is so abjectly melancholy that I imagine he is either in love or very happy about something.

Sincerely,
John Steinbeck
—*Steinbeck: A Life in Letters,* pp. 42–43

* * *

Steinbeck to McIntosh, 18 August 1931

While Steinbeck still hoped to have the experimental novel "Dissonant Symphony" published, "To an Unknown God" was more important to him.

Dear Miss McIntosh:

I think I told you in an earlier letter that the imperfections of the Unknown God had bothered me ever since I first submitted the book for publication. In consequence of this uneasiness, your announcement of the book's failure to find a publisher is neither unwelcome nor unpleasant to me. If I were sure of the book, I should put it aside and wait for some other story to gain it an entrance. But I know its faults. I know, though, that the story is good. I shall rewrite it immediately. Whether my idea of excellence coincides with editors' ideas remains to be seen. Certainly I shall make no effort to "popularize" the story.

I have a carbon of the Unknown God. It will not be necessary to return the original.

Mr. Miller will hand you a manuscript of about thirty thousand words ["Dissonant Symphony"]. It is an impossible length for marketing. I had thought perhaps it could be included under one cover with the ten stories which will make up The Pastures of Heaven. The name is bad, but that can be readily changed. Will you let me know your opinion of this plan?

The Pastures stories proceed rapidly, perhaps too rapidly. They should be ready to submit by Christmas.

Thank you for your help. I am an unprofitable client.

Sincerely,
John Steinbeck
—*Steinbeck: A Life in Letters,* pp. 45–46

* * *

Steinbeck to Albee, 1931

During a short interval between work on stories in The Pastures of Heaven, *Steinbeck replied to a letter from Albee urging him to read Thomas Wolfe's* Look Homeward, Angel *(1929). The advertising agency that Carol Steinbeck and a friend had started in late 1930 had closed by this time.*

Dear George:

This is the day between—one ms. finished yesterday and the next one not quite hatched. It will be by tomorrow though. This is a good day to write letters.

I'm pretty happy over these stories. That is because they aren't finished, I guess.

It isn't unusual that you worry about my financial future. Everyone I have ever known very well has been concerned that I would eventually starve. Probably I shall. It isn't important enough to me to be an obsession. I have starved and it isn't nearly as bad as is generally supposed. Four days and a half was my longest stretch. Maybe there are pains that come later. Personally I think terror is the painful part of starvation.

You are sanguine about my inheritance. There will be nothing, you know. I'll be lucky if I have this house. No—money is not for us. Other people get Phelan Awards [a cash award given in California for writing]. Probably because they want them badly. My one long chance was to have married money and I didn't do that. I have come to be a complete fatalist about money. Even the law of averages doesn't hold with me. Any attempt to get me any kind of an award is pre-doomed to failure. Furthermore I seriously doubt that my brand of literature will ever feed me. And I haven't sense enough to worry about it. If eventually I have to go to work digging ditches, I shall have had my chance.

I read only a page or so of Look Homeward, Angel. The pages I read seemed to be a hodgepodge of quotations. I shall read all of it sometime since you recommend it so highly. I was somewhat deterred from reading it by the overwhelming praise of Sinclair Lewis.

It is a gray day with little dusty spurts of rain. A good day for inwardness. Only I doubt that I have many guts of my own to look inward at. That is one of the great troubles with objective writing. A constant practice of it leaves one no material for introspection. If my characters are sad or happy I reflect their emotions. I have no personal nor definitive emotions of my own. Indeed, when there is no writing in progress, I feel like an uninhabited body. I think I am only truly miserable at such times.

Carol is probably going to work next week. She looks forward to it. It is not good for her to be housed here with me all day. I am too impatient of movements or noise in the house. And it is such a small house.

You see, my letters are bound to be tiresome because I can talk of nothing but the work I am doing. Monomania!

This probably sounds like a doleful letter and it shouldn't be because I don't feel at all doleful.

John
—Steinbeck: A Life in Letters, pp. 47–48

* * *

Steinbeck to Miller, 16 February 1932

The following letter to Miller indicates Steinbeck's frustration over attempts to place The Pastures of Heaven *with a publisher. Eleven days later, however, the book was accepted for publication.*

Dear Ted:

Thank you for doing all that work. It was a lot of trouble. Miss Mc. [McIntosh] dismissed the ms. by saying the form doesn't interest her, but it may interest someone else. The Pastures has begun its snaggy way. Morrow won't publish as a first novel, but will if a more closely integrated work can precede it. Publishers are afraid of short stories unless the writer of them has a tremendous name. And so I presume that the Pastures will go the way of all the others. Miss Mc. was non-committal about it. Meanwhile I work at the Unknown God. I have changed the place, characters, time, theme, and thesis and name so maybe it won't be much like the first book. It's good fun though.

I wonder you don't lose faith in my future. Everyone else does. For myself, I haven't brains enough to quit. Maybe you haven't brains enough to get out from under the wreck. Thirty years hence I'll still be working. I am very happy when I'm working.

Have McBride's relaxed their grip on that copyright?

I'm pretty damn sick of my consistent failure. Everyone says nice things and no one buys my books. Wurra—wurra. M. and O. have been kind and have expended lots of stamps on me. I wonder how soon they'll get sick of it.

Please write more often.

Affectionately,
John
—Steinbeck: A Life in Letters, pp. 53–54

* * *

Dust jacket for Steinbeck's 1932 short-story cycle (from Christie's East, Jack E. and Rachel Gindi Collection of Modern Literature, 20 April 1994; Special Collections, Thomas Cooper Library, University of South Carolina)

Steinbeck to Carlton A. Sheffield, 1932

The following note to Steinbeck's college friend Carlton A. "Dook" Sheffield was written in the pages of a ledger of journal-like entries addressed to Sheffield.

To Dook—

When I bought this book, and began to fill it with words, it occurred to me that you might like to have it when it was full. You have that instinct so highly developed in magpies, packrats and collectors. I should like you to have this book and my reasons are all sentimental and therefore, of course, unmentionable. I love you very much. I have never been able to give you a present that cost any money. It occurs to me that you might accept a present that cost me a hell of a lot of work. For I do not write easily. Three hours of writing require twenty hours of preparation. Luckily I have learned to dream about the work, which saves me some working time.

Now as always—humility and terror. Fear that the working of my pen cannot capture the grinding of my brain. It is so easy to understand why the ancients prayed for the help of a Muse. And the Muse came and stood beside them, and we, heaven help us, do not believe in Muses. We have nothing to fall back on but our craftsmanship and it, as modern literature attests, is inadequate.

May I be honest; may I be decent; may I be unaffected by the technique of hucksters. If invocation is required, let this be my invocation—may I be strong and yet gentle, tender and yet wise, wise and yet tolerant. May I for a little while, only for a little while, see with the inflamed eyes of a God.

I wonder if you know why I address this manuscript to you. You are the only person in the world who believes I can do what I set out to do. Not even I believe that all the time. And so, in a kind of gratitude, I address all my writing to you, whether or not you know it.

Now this book is finished, Dook. You will have to work on it; to help straighten out the roughness, to say where it falls short. I wish I valued it more so that it would be a better gift. It isn't nearly all I hoped it would be. I remember when I finished the earlier book of the same title. I took it to you and you said, "It is very good." And I knew you knew it was terrible, and you knew I knew you knew it. And if this one is as bad I hope you will tell me. I've worked too hard on it. I can't tell much about it.

Anyway—this is your book now. I hope you'll like to have it.

                                        love,
                                        John
                            —Steinbeck: A Life in Letters, pp. 64–65

* * *

In a Peaceful Valley
Margaret Cheney Dawson

In her review Margaret Cheney Dawson praises the "unity of feeling" in the stories of The Pastures of Heaven.

The Pastures of Heaven—*Las Pasturas del Cielo*—was the felicitous name given to a little California valley which, "by some regal accident," had escaped being ravaged both by Spanish adventurers in the old days and American adventurers in the new. As Mr. Steinbeck pictures it, still before the "development" which he suggests will one day be its fate—it holds in its gentle grip something almost unique in California, indeed in America, today: peace. It offers a very normal, friendly kind of atmosphere in which the accents of disaster and sorrow are not lacking, but which nevertheless seems dominated by a kind of magic. Whether the spell is cast by nature's beauty or the author's charming serenity of

"The Whole Sweep of the Valley"

In a review of The Pastures of Heaven *in* The New Yorker, *Robert M. Coates suggests that Steinbeck's writing bears the marks of Sherwood Anderson, George Milburn, and even O. Henry.*

The best of the novels I looked into this week is, oddly enough, hardly a novel at all, at least in the sense of having a settled cast of characters and a continuous story about them. This is *The Pastures of Heaven,* by John Steinbeck, published by Brewer, Warren & Putnam, and it has to do with the communal life of the inhabitants of a valley in California so charming and so fertile that the Spanish settlers called it by the name which now serves as the title of Mr. Steinbeck's book.

Such a story, dealing with a variety of characters and the intricacies of their relations, must almost necessarily be episodic in treatment, and the danger is that, unless some mood or central theme can be found to bind it all together, it may fall in too loose a pattern, becoming merely a sequence of short stories rather than parts of a connected whole.

It may, indeed, be said that at times Mr. Steinbeck fails to recognize this danger, and gives away [*sic*] occasionally to a leaning for a sort of O. Henry twist at the end of some of his episodes which, while surprising the reader, also has the effect of leaving him a little up in the air. And again, perhaps because this is a first novel, his debt to some of his predecessors in this field of writing—Sherwood Anderson, George Milburn, etc.—is sometimes a little too plainly evident.

But in the main his grasp of the whole sweep of the valley, and the people in it and their lives, is comprehensive and sure; and his characters—the penniless Shark Wicks, who made himself, by sheer power of imagination, a miser; T. B. Allen, the garrulous storekeeper; Miss Morgan, the school-teacher; the shiftless Bert Monroe; Tularecito, the daft little Mexican boy; and all the others—weave in and out of each other's lives casually, ironically or tragically, but always with an effect as of real life. I think you'd enjoy it.

–*New Yorker*, 8 (22 October 1932); reprinted in *John Steinbeck: The Contemporary Reviews,* edited by Joseph R. McElrath Jr., Jesse S. Crisler, and Susan Shillinglaw (Cambridge & New York: Cambridge University Press, 1996), p. 13

style the reader will probably neither know nor care, but he will feel it and believe in it.

The inhabitants of the Valley farmed the easy-yielding soil, attended school board meetings and barbecues, talked about stock prices and cake recipes. The framework was solidly conventional, but the picture itself often arrestingly vivid. Take Shark Wicks,

for instance. Shark had two treasures, his incredibly beautiful and equally stupid daughter Alice and his reputation for shrewdness. The first he guarded with suspicious vigilance and the second he enhanced by manipulating imaginary investments in a ledger until the profit column showed six-figure entries. "Shark ain't nobody's fool," the villagers would say, and Shark, throwing out a hint now and then about real estate or utility values, let the impression of his riches grow until he came to think of them as real himself. Then, in a fatal hour, one treasure canceled the other. For Shark, enraged by a whisper of gossip about Alice, rushed off with a gun and fell straightway into the hands of the law. And when the judge tried to put him under bond to keep the peace the awful truth was out: he had no money. Then the fleshly daughter absconded, in effect, with the imaginary ducats. Shark, in chagrin, left the valley.

Tularecito, also, was cast for a tragic role. Nobody knew where he came from, this "frog-child" with thick, short arms and long, dangling legs. He had been found crying in the sage bush one night by a Mexican Indian, who swore that the baby winked at him and said: "Look! I have very sharp teeth!" Whatever the truth of this report, the little "frog," far from being an intellectual prodigy, grew to have the strength of a giant but only the brain of a five-year-old child. Under one circumstance he was vicious: when any one destroyed his handiwork. It must have seemed reasonable to him that if the teacher made him draw animals on the board then no one should be allowed to erase them, and that no one should dare fill in the hole he had dug deep into the earth to find his brothers, the gnomes. But his murderous defense of these logical conclusions landed poor Tularecito in the asylum for the criminal insane.

Thus each of the chapters presents an individual or group enacting some small drama against the backdrop of Heaven's Pastures. Short stories they are really—these tales of the giggling, pious Lopez sisters who became "bad women" with the air of two little girls pretending to "get lost," and the New England patriarch who tried to found a dynasty in defiance of California's genius for restlessness, and all the others. Yet there is at least, besides the little intermingling of events and names, a binding unity of feeling that perhaps justifies the author in calling this a novel. And there is a clarity, good humor and delicacy in Mr. Steinbeck's writing that makes the book fine reading, regardless of its category.

–*New York Herald Tribune*, 23 October 1932; reprinted in *John Steinbeck: The Contemporary Reviews,* pp. 13–14

* * *

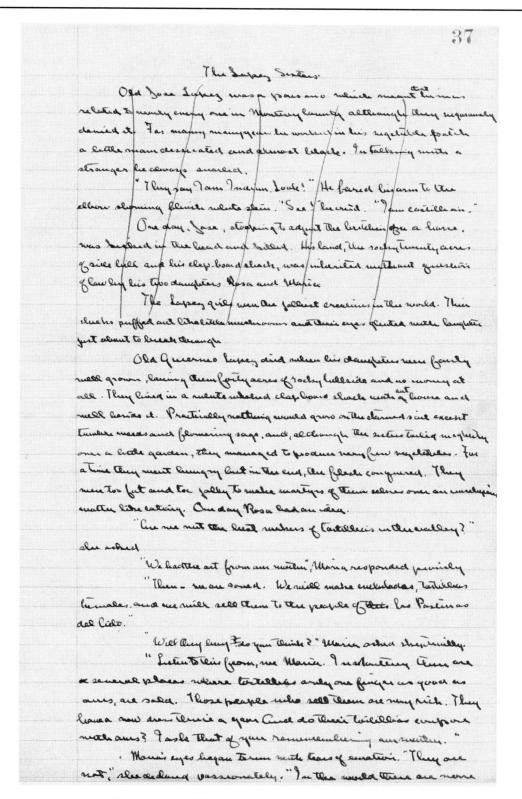

First page of Steinbeck's manuscript for "The Lopez Sisters," one of the stories from The Pastures of Heaven
(from William McPheron, John Steinbeck: From Salinas to Stockholm, *2000;
Special Collections, Thomas Cooper Library, University of South Carolina)*

Steinbeck to Robert O. Ballou, 3 January 1933

In a letter to publisher Robert O. Ballou, Steinbeck mentions the need to change the title of his next novel from "To an Unknown God" to To a God Unknown, *the title under which it was published by Ballou in 1933.*

Dear Ballou,

Your letter came this morning together with one from Mc & O [McIntosh and Otis] containing the belated check. It was a relief. Tillie, properly Tylie Eulenspiegel, was an Airedale terrier and a very beautiful one. She was beautifully trained—could point quail, retrieve ducks, bring in hares or clear a road of sheep. More important than these though, she had the most poignant capacity for interest and enjoyment in the world. It was much more important to us that she be alive than that people like Hearst and Cornelius Vanderbilt foul up the planet. *She* was house broken.

This book draws to a close. It will (if nothing happens) be ready to send before the end of February. I shall be very glad to have it done. I hope to God you'll like it. I have grave doubts. The title will be To A God Unknown. The transposition in words is necessary to a change in meaning. The unknown in this case meaning "Unexplored."

This is taken from the Vedic hymns. I want no confusion with the unknown God of St. Paul.

That's all. Thanks again for routing out the check.

John Steinbeck
—*Steinbeck: A Life in Letters,* pp. 66–67

* * *

Steinbeck to Sheffield, 21 June 1933

The following letter to Sheffield indicates Steinbeck's views on social organization. He elaborates on the qualities and power of the group as a whole but warns that this power can be destructive to the individual.

This is not a letter to read unless you have so much time that you just don't care. I just want to talk and there is no one to talk to. Out of the all encircling good came a theme finally. I knew it would. Until you can put your theme in one sentence, you haven't it in hand well enough to write a novel. The process is this (I am writing this at the risk of being boring. One can refuse to read a letter and the writer of it will never know.) The process is this—one puts down endless observations, questions and remarks. The number grows and grows. Eventually they all seem headed in one direction and then they whirl like sparks out of a bonfire. And then one day they seem to mean something.

When they do, it is the most exciting time in the world. I have three years of them and only just now have they taken a direction. Suddenly they are all of one piece. Then the problem begins of trying to find a fictional symbolism which will act as a vehicle.

Let me quote a few of the notes. The coral insect working with hundreds of billions of others, eventually creates a strange and beautiful plant-like formation. In the course of time numberless plants create the atoll. Architecturally the atoll is very beautiful and good. Certain groups in Europe at one time created the Gothic spire. They seem to have worked under a stimulus as mysterious, as powerful and as general as that which caused the coral insects to build.

Note—in nineteen seventeen this unit was in a physical and psychic condition which made it susceptible to the inroads of the influenza germ. This germ at other times was not deadly, and, when encountered now, causes discomfort but not ordinarily death. It has been shown that at the time mentioned the germ had not changed but the receptivity of the race had.

Note—in Mendocino county a whole community turned against one man and destroyed him although they had taken no harm from him. This will sound meaningless to you unless you could see the hundreds of notes that make them meaningful to me. It is quite easy for the group, acting under stimuli to viciousness, to eliminate the kindly natures of its units. When acting as a group, men do not partake of their ordinary natures at all. The group can change its nature. It can alter the birth rate, diminish the number of its units, control states of mind, alter appearance, physically and spiritually. All of the notations I have made begin to point to an end—That the group is an individual as boundaried, as diagnosable, as dependent on its units and as independent of its units' individual natures, as the human unit, or man, is dependent on his cells and yet is independent of them.

Does this begin to make sense to you? The greatest group unit, that is the whole race, has qualities which the individual lacks entirely. It remembers a time when the moon was close, when the tides were terrific. It remembers a time when the weight of the individual doubled itself every twenty-eight days, and strangely enough, it remembers every step of its climb from the single cell to the human. The human unit has none of these memories.

The nature of the groups, I said, were changeable. Usually they are formed by topographical peculiarities. Sometimes a terrible natural stimulus will create a group over night. They are of all sizes, from the camp meeting where the units pool their souls to make one yearning cry, to the whole world which fought the war. Russia is giving us a nice example of human units who are trying with a curious nostalgia to get away from their individuality and reestablish the group unit the race remembers and wishes. I am not drawing conclusions. Merely trying to see where the stream of all my notes is going.

One could easily say that man, during his hunting period, had to give up the group since all the game hunters must; and now that his food is not to be taken by stealth and precision, is going back to the group which takes its food by concerted action. That if one lives by the food of the lion he must hunt singly, if by the food of the ruminants he may live in herds and protect himself by his numbers.

It can be placed somewhat like this for the moment—as individual humans we are far superior in our functions to anything the world has born—in our groups we are not only not superior but in fact are remarkably like those most perfect groups, the ants and bees. I haven't begun to tell you this thing. I am not ready to.

Half of the cell units of my mother's body have rebelled. Neither has died, but the revolution has changed her functions. That is cruel to say. The first line on this thing came from it though. She, as a human unit, is deterred from functioning as she ordinarily did by a schism of a number of her cells.

And, when the parts of this thesis have found their places, I'll start trying to put them into the symbolism of fiction.

The fascinating thing to me is the way the group has a soul, a drive, an intent, an end, a method, a reaction and a set of tropisms which in no way resembles the same things possessed by the men who make up the group. These groups have always been considered as individuals multiplied. And they are not so. They are beings in themselves, entities. Just as a bar of iron has none of the properties of the revolving, circling, active atoms which make it up, so these huge creatures, the groups, do not resemble the human atoms which compose them.

This is muddled, Dook. I wouldn't send it to anyone else in this form. But you and I have talked so much together that we can fill in the gaps we leave. We were awfully glad to get both your letters. Write often, this is a deadly time for us. And you might put your mind on the problem I have stated. If you could help me put it into form, I probably would have less trouble finding my symbols for reproducing it. You will find the first beginning conception of it among the anthropologists, but none of them has dared to think about it yet. The subject is too huge and too terrifying. Since it splashed on me, I have been able to think of nothing else.

It is an explanation of so many mysterious things, the reasons for migrations, the desertion of localities, the

sudden diseases which wiped races out, the sudden running amok of groups. It would explain how Genghis Khan and Attila and the Goths suddenly stopped being individual herdsmen and hunters and became, almost without transition, a destroying creature obeying a single impulse. It would explain the sudden tipping over of Prohibition, and that ten years ago the constitution of the US was a thing of God and now it is abrogated with impunity. Oh! it is a gorgeous thing. Don't you think so?

I am ignorant enough to promulgate it. If I had more knowledge I wouldn't have the courage to think it out. It isn't thought out yet, but I have a start. Think of the lemmings, little gophers who live in holes and who suddenly in their millions become a unit with a single impulse to suicide. Think of the impulse which has suddenly made Germany overlook the natures of its individuals and become what it has. Hitler didn't do it. He merely speaks about it.

I'll stop before I drive you as crazy as I have become since all my wonderings have taken a stream like force. All the things I've wondered about and pondered about are seeming to make sense at last. Why the individual is incapable of understanding the nature of the group. That is why publishing is unsure, why elections are the crazy things they are. We only feel the emotions of the group beast in times of religious exaltation, in being moved by some piece of art which intoxicates us while we do not know what it is that does it. Are you as nuts as I am now?

love
john
—*Steinbeck: A Life in Letters,* pp. 74–77

* * *

Steinbeck to Albee, 1933

Steinbeck further developed his ideas on the social group through extensive reading and thinking. In the following letter to Albee, he elaborates on these ideas, which emerge in such later works as "The Leader of the People," the fourth story in The Red Pony *(1937);* In Dubious Battle *(1936); and* The Grapes of Wrath *(1939).*

Dear George:

I have your letter of this morning. Mary [Steinbeck's younger sister] just went home. We liked having her, but she brought her children which took all her time from helping, and the noise they made was out of place in this house of gloom and melancholy. They made us nervous. I like them. They are the best children. But this is no place for any child. We are taking care of a dead person. We work as hard as we can to

Inscribed free front endpaper in the first edition of The Pastures
of Heaven *(from* Christie's East, *Jack E. and Rachel Gindi*
Collection of Modern Literature, 20 April 1994;
Special Collections, Thomas Cooper Library,
University of South Carolina)

keep from thinking of it. We try all we can to keep out
of her mind.

I can answer all of your questions now. But I hesitate because of the work it entails. I shall try though,
because you need help and this will help you, not
because it is something I have discovered. I haven't discovered it. The discovery has come as all great ones
have, by a little discovery by each of a great number of
men, and finally by one man who takes all the little dis-
coveries and correlates them and gives the whole thing
a name. The thesis takes in all life, and for that part, all
matter. But you are only interested in life and so am I.

We know that with certain arrangements of
atoms we might have what we would call a bar of iron.
Certain other arrangements of atoms plus a mysterious
principle make a living cell. Now the living cell is very
sensitive to outside stimuli or tropisms. A further

arrangement of cells and a very complex one may make
a unit which we call a man. That has been our final
unit. But there have been mysterious things which
could not be explained if man is the final unit. He also
arranges himself into larger units, which I have called
the phalanx. The phalanx has its own memory–memory of the great tides when the moon was close, memory of starvations when the food of the world was
exhausted. Memory of methods when numbers of his
units had to be destroyed for the good of the whole,
memory of the history of itself. And the phalanx has
emotions of which the unit man is incapable. Emotions
of destruction, of war, of migration, of hatred, of fear.
These things have been touched on often.

Religion is a phalanx emotion and this was so
clearly understood by the church fathers that they said
the holy ghost would come when *two or three were gath-*
ered together. You have heard about the trickiness of the
MOB. Mob is simply a phalanx, but if you try to judge
a mob nature by the nature of its men units, you will
fail as surely as if you tried to understand a man by
studying one of his cells. You will say you know all this.
Of course you do. It has to be written in primer language. All tremendous things do.

During the war we had probably the greatest phalanx in the history of the world. If we could devote our
study to the greater unit, we would be capable of judging
the possible actions of the phalanx, of prophesying its variability, and the direction it might take. We can find no
man unit reason for the sudden invasion of Europe by a
race of Hun shepherds, who were transformed overnight
into a destroying force, a true phalanx, and in another generation had become shepherds again, so weak that an
invasion of Tartars overwhelmed them. We can find no
man unit reason for the sudden migration of the Mayas.
We say Attila did it or Ghenghis Khan, but they couldn't.
They were simply the spokesmen of the movement. Hitler
did not create the present phalanx in Germany, he merely
interprets it.

Now in the unconscious of the man unit there is a
keying mechanism. Jung calls it the third person. It is
the plug which when inserted into the cap of the phalanx, makes man lose his unit identity in the phalanx.
The artist is one in whom the phalanx comes closest to
the conscious. Art then is the property of the phalanx,
not of the individual. Art is the phalanx knowledge of
the nature of matter and of life.

Dr. [Walter K.] Fischer at Hopkins [Marine Station, Pacific Grove] said one day that you could find
any scientific discovery in the poetry of the preceding
generation. Democritus promulgated an accurate
atomic theory four hundred years before Christ. The
artist is simply the spokesman of the phalanx. When a
man hears great music, sees great pictures, reads great

poetry, he loses his identity in that of the phalanx. I do not need to describe the emotion caused by these things, but it is invariably a feeling of oneness with one's phalanx. For man is lonely when he is cut off. He dies. From the phalanx he takes a fluid necessary to his life. In the mountains I saw men psychologically emaciated from being alone. You can't find a reason for doing certain things. You couldn't possibly find a reason. You are dealing with a creature whose nature you cannot know intellectually, of whose emotions you are ignorant. Whose reasons, directions, means, urges, pleasures, drives, satieties, ecstasies, hungers and tropisms are not yours as an individual.

I can't give you this thing completely in a letter, George. I am going to write a whole novel with it as a theme, so how can I get it in a letter? Ed Ricketts has dug up all the scientific material and more than I need to establish the physical integrity of the thing. I have written this theme over and over and did not know what I was writing. I found at least four statements of it in the God [To a God Unknown]. Old phalanxes break up in a fine imitation of death of the man unit, new phalanxes are born under proper physical and spiritual conditions. They may be of any size from the passionate three who are necessary to receive the holy spirit, to the race which overnight develops a soul for conquest, to the phalanx which commits suicide through vice or war or disease. When your phalanx needs you it will use you, if you are the material to be used. You will know when the time comes, and when it does come, nothing you can do will let you escape.

There is no change with mother nor can there be for a long time to come. I hope this letter will give you something to chew on. Don't quibble about it with small exceptions until the whole thing has taken hold. Once it has, the exceptions will prove unimportant. Of course I am interested in it as tremendous and terrible poetry. I am neither scientist nor profound investigator. But I am experiencing an emotional vastness in working this out. The difficulty of writing the poetry is so great that I am not even contemplating it until I have absorbed and made a part of my body the thesis as a whole.

I corrected and sent back the proofs of the God this week. It reads pretty well. Ballou is rushing it so it may be out among the earliest of the Fall books. And that is all for this time.

Love to you and Anne and I do wish I could talk to you.

john
—*Steinbeck: A Life in Letters*, pp. 79–82

* * *

Steinbeck to Albee, 1933

Steinbeck and Albee corresponded frequently to share their experiences with writing and having their work published.

Dear George:

One piece of advice I can offer, and that is that you should never let any one suggest anything about your story to you. If you don't know more about your character and situation than anyone else could, then you aren't ready to write your story anyway. It is primarily a lonely craft and must be accepted as such. If you eliminate that loneliness of approach, you automatically eliminate some of the power of the effect. I don't know why that is.

I can't tell which of the endings you should use. The second sounds very Dostoievsky, and after all you never saw a prisoner flayed. You may argue that your reader never did either and so how can he tell. I don't know, but he can. You might be able to make your second ending ring true, but you would be almost unique in letters if you could. I have somehow the feeling that you will abandon this book. Not because it isn't good but because publishers are in a peculiar condition now. That you are heartily sick of the book is apparent. One thing you will have to do about your genius, though. You will have to give him some dignity and depth. You are writing about Howard Edminster, and while Howard may write superb poetry, his life and acts are those of a horse's ass and a charlatan. Meanwhile your age does not justify that you waste tears over one book. You are growing out from under it and so you can never catch it again. Put it away and, at some time when publishing changes, you will find an out for it. That isn't my advice, you know. I can't tell you how to work and how to think. My method is probably wrong for you. Certainly my outlook and vision of life is completely different from yours.

The pony story is finally finished and the second draft done. I don't know when Carol will find time to type it, but when she does, I'll send you the second draft and then you won't have to bother to send it back. It is an unpretentious story. I think the philosophic content is so buried that it will not bother anybody. Carol likes it, but I am afraid our minds are somewhat grown together so that we see with the same eyes and feel with the same emotions. You can see whether you like it at all. There never was more than a half hour of uninterrupted work put on it, and the nausea between paragraphs had to be covered up. I don't see how it can have much continuity, but Carol says it has some.

I guess that's all. There is no change here. Mother's mind gets farther and farther from its base. She is pretty much surrounded by dead relatives now.

bye
john
—*Steinbeck: A Life in Letters*, pp. 84–85

* * *

Dear Mr. Needham:

May I make this opportunity to thank you for kindness toward my work? You of all American critics who have dealt with my books, have neither applied the term mystic, nor left a loophole of escape for your self. I don't know why the word mystic should be such a term of reproach. As used by critics, of course, it implies sloppy thinking and execution. Every other critic save you, has, reviewed my books carefully. If the first paragraph praised the work, the last knocked hell out of it or vice versa. By this method the critic has made sure of being right.

I knew when I started this series of books, that I would meet opposition. The great submerged part of man, the unconscious, while in some respects, fairly charted by psychologists, had never been touched in fiction. I did not know what form the opposition would take, and, when To a God Unknown was issued, I waited with some anticipation. This volume which simply attempts to show some sense of how the unconscious impinges and in some cases crosses into the conscious, was immediately branded mystical. It had never occurred to the critic that all the devils in the world and all the mysteries and all the religious symbology in the world were children of the generalized unconscious. Can it be that such of the critics in the world are sublimely unconscious of the investigations and experiments in human psychology which are marshalling not only a new knowledge of man but a new conception of realities? You may judge then my relief on finding that you did know what I was trying to do, understood the foundations and found it valid in literature. The god unknown, that powerful fruitful and moving unconscious is likely to remain unknown to book reviewers.

Thank you again for treating with understanding, work which because it deals with an untouched field, is bound to be difficult and fumbling.

I hope I may sometime have the opportunity of meeting you and telling with you.

sincerely
John Steinbeck

Pacific Grove, California.

Letter from Steinbeck to Wilbur Needham, literary editor of The Los Angeles Times, concerning Needham's review of his 1933 novel To a God Unknown (Center for Steinbeck Studies, San Jose State University)

Symbols of Earth
Virginia Barney

Virginia Barney reviewed To a God Unknown *in* The New York Times Book Review.

The unknown god of the hero of Mr. Steinbeck's second novel is an earth god whose sole commandment is "increase and multiply." It is a heathen god, manifest wherever life is reproductive, disdainful of sterility. Joseph Wayne meets and is moved by false gods but he never yields to them. His brother Benjy seeks the god of the pleasures of the senses. Brother Burton worships the god of his Calvinist ancestors. Brother Thomas identifies himself with the pure animalism of creature feeling. Rama, wife to Thomas, symbolizes the mother of all living. The Catholic priest worships a god he can respect but cannot follow. Joseph is even drawn to the strange mortal who, living on a California cliff, has figured it out that he is the last man of the Western world to see the evening sun go down and who, therefore, at each sunset, sacrifices some live thing to the sun god.

In his wife, Elizabeth, Joseph discovers a woman who is both of earth and of aspiration. Rama is earth itself; but Elizabeth is the spirit of earth. And so when Elizabeth dies in the solitary place by the big rock; when the tree which, to Joseph, embodies the spirit of his father is killed by Burton who disapproves of it as a pagan symbol; when the lean years come and the land and the beasts that feed upon it become unproductive; when aridity, sterility and death, disease and famine come, Joseph is defeated. Taking a leaf from the eccentric cliff dweller, Joseph sacrifices a calf to the rain god. Then the truth comes to him and in the solitary place by the big rock he sacrifices himself. And even before consciousness departs the rain comes and fertility is assured.

The bare narrative, reduced from its wrappings, is very brief. Joseph Wayne leaves his revered father in Vermont to seek land of his own in California. The father dies shortly afterward, but Joseph communes with him through a tree. His brothers come to California and take up homesteads adjacent to him. Joseph woos and wins the school teacher Elizabeth, who bears him a child. Life moves on rhythmically at the ranch. A great fiesta is given. All is well. Then Benjy is killed in the arms of a jealous Mexican's wife and a whole chain of disaster follows.

This is a symbolical novel conceived in mysticism and dedicated to the soil. To this reviewer it is little more than a curious hodgepodge of vague moods and irrelevant meanings. It cannot be said to be successful even of its kind. It treads dangerous ground without a touch of that sureness and strength which characterize the very few good works of its order in modern times. The elements of realism and symbolism fail to cohere and it oversteps all the bounds of convincingness even on the mystic plane. *To a God Unknown* is a novel which attempts too much; and by any standard it achieves too little.

–*New York Times Book Review,* 1 October 1933; reprinted in *John Steinbeck: The Contemporary Reviews,* pp. 24–25

* * *

Brief Reviews of *To a God Unknown*

The following short notices express reservations about the new style in Steinbeck's second novel.

This book reads like a novelized version of a Robinson Jeffers poem, and its setting is what may be known to tourists of the future as the "Robinson Jeffers country." It is the story of a Yankee Abraham who has emigrated to California and who, in obedience to the voice of his God which is the earth and the fulness thereof, sacrifices his wife and ultimately himself on the altar of fertility. In the bas-relief of a poem, where much is taken for granted, the characterization of the story might have been adequate, but in a novel, which demands treatment in the round, it is pitifully thin and shadowy and invalidates the most ambitious effects of the book.

–*Nation,* 137 (18 October 1933); reprinted in *John Steinbeck: The Contemporary Reviews,* p. 25

It is a surprise to find Mr. Steinbeck leaping from the sharp characterization of his first book to mystic symbols of nature worship. He writes of his principal character with the fervor of a faithful apostle. Joseph had no creed, no desire to be remembered; above such human emotional indulgences as pain and sorrow, he lived like a man who, having Nature for a mistress, was willing to go through any straits to satisfy and please her. Nothing disturbed his passion except sterility, and, when that came to him in the form of a drought that ruined his lands, Joseph stretched himself on the rock which symbolized his worship and cut open his veins, exchanging his life for the life of the soil.

–*New Republic,* 77 (20 December 1933); reprinted in *John Steinbeck: The Contemporary Reviews,* p. 26

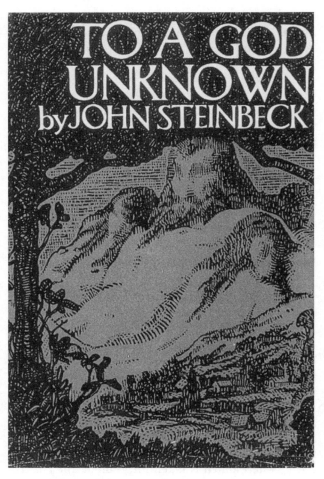

Dust jacket for Steinbeck's novel about a man's mystical attachment
to the land of the Salinas Valley (from Christie's East, Jack E.
and Rachel Gindi Collection of Modern Literature,
20 April 1994; *Special Collections, Thomas Cooper
Library, University of South Carolina*)

California's lonely valleys and giant redwoods of all but fabulous age are plausibly a haunt of Pan. Neither that nor the Indian name is given to the pastoral god who darkly moves the people of the Wayne ranch, but behind these passionate pages there is the ancient and mystical spirit of fecundity. It is two years since Mr. Steinbeck published *The Pastures of Heaven,* and there is internal besides the external evidence of deliberation in his second book. We do not deny that the Wayne brothers reach elemental bigness, but Mr. Steinbeck's earnest seeking for the terse and telling phrase has some disconcerting results. "The red wine sang," "the tyres cried on the rocks," and when Elizabeth thought "If only he had the body of a horse I might love him more" we remembered Gilbert, who almost wrote that the meaning doesn't matter if it's only idle chatter of a

D. H. Lawrence kind. This is, however, a novel built to a climax. At that climax, dealing with drought, Joseph Wayne sacrifices his own blood to the rain god, and we are unconscious of absurdity. It is action for which Mr. Steinbeck's character-drawing of Joseph has prepared us; it is a poet-novelist's victory over common sense.

–Harold Brighouse, "Pan in California," *Manchester Guardian,* 27 March 1935; reprinted in *John Steinbeck: The Contemporary Reviews,* pp. 26–27

* * *

Steinbeck to Edith Wagner, 13 June 1934

Edith Wagner, whom Steinbeck had known from childhood in Salinas, was the mother of his friend Max Wagner and the source for his story "How Edith McGillcuddy Met R.L.S." As a girl she had met the Scottish author by chance when he visited California. Coincidentally, Wagner had written her own account of the incident, which she hoped to publish, around the same time that Steinbeck wrote his, so he withdrew his story from his agents. Wagner's story was never accepted for publication, and several years later, with her permission, Steinbeck sent "How Edith McGillcuddy Met R.L.S." to his agents again. It was published in Harper's *in August 1941.*

Dear Mrs. Wagner:

I am writing to my agents today, asking them to hold up the story. It is awkward for this reason—they've had the story for at least two weeks and since they are very active, it has undoubtedly gone out. However, it can be stopped. I hope you will let me know how yours comes out, as soon as you hear. If it should happen to have been bought by the time my letter reaches New York, it can be held up. Mine, I mean.

Pacific Grove summer has set in, fog most of the day. The people who come over from the Valley love it, but I wish the sun would shine.

Well, I hope nothing untoward happens about this story. In sending it away I enclosed a note saying it had been told me by you. Plagiarism is not one of my sins. I'll write you when I hear any outcome.

Affectionately,
John
–*Steinbeck: A Life in Letters,* p. 96

Notes in Steinbeck's ledger recording his writing progress during the summer of 1934
(Center for Steinbeck Studies, San Jose State University)

Tortilla Flat (1935) and
In Dubious Battle (1936)

Steinbeck to McIntosh, 1934

In the following letter to McIntosh, Steinbeck explains the connection between Tortilla Flat *(1935) and the Arthurian legends.*

Dear Miss McIntosh:

I want to write something about Tortilla Flat and about some ideas I have about it. The book has a very definite theme. I thought it was clear enough. I have expected that the plan of the Arthurian cycle would be recognized, that my Gawaine and my Launcelot, my Arthur and Galahad would be recognized. Even the incident of the Sangreal in the search of the forest is not clear enough I guess. The form is that of the Malory version, the coming of Arthur and the mystic quality of owning a house, the forming of the round table, the adventure of the knights and finally, the mystic translation of Danny.

However, I seem not to have made any of this clear. The main issue was to present a little known and, to me, delightful people. Is not this cycle story or theme enough? Perhaps it is not enough because I have not made it clear enough. What do you think of putting in an interlocutor, who between each incident interprets the incident, morally, esthetically, historically, but in the manner of the paisanos themselves? This would give the book much of the appeal of the Gesta Romanorum, those outrageous tales with monkish morals appended, or of the Song of Solomon in the King James version, with the delightful chapter headings which go to prove that the Shulamite is in reality Christ's Church.

It would not be as sharp as this of course. But the little dialogue, if it came between the incidents would at least make clear the form of the book, its tragi-comic theme. It would also make clear and sharp the strong but different philosophic-moral system of these people. I don't intend to make the parallel of the round table more clear, but simply to show that a cycle is there. You will remember that the association forms, flowers and dies. Far from having a hard theme running through the book, one of the intents is to show that rarely does any theme in the lives of these people survive the night.

I shall be anxious to know your reaction to the Communist idea [the story idea for *In Dubious Battle*].

Thank you for your letter.

Sincerely,
John Steinbeck

—*Steinbeck: A Life in Letters*, pp. 96–97

* * *

Steinbeck to Albee, 1935

In late 1934 Ben Abramson, a book dealer in Chicago, recommended Steinbeck's works to Pascal Covici, of the publishing firm Covici-Friede. Covici later became Steinbeck's lifelong editor and friend. The following letter to Albee includes Steinbeck's first mention of Covici.

Dear George:

The book [an advance copy of Albee's 1935 novel *Not in a Day*] came this morning two days after your letter. It found us in a mad manuscript period. Carol batting out finished copy [of *In Dubious Battle*] like mad. But I'm letting her read the book first. She takes little rests and plunges into it and lets out bellows of laughter. I envy both her and you. She reads very fast and I read very slowly. She'll be through with it tonight. So I shall only start this letter and finish it when I have read Not in a Day. I don't like the dust jacket. Saving the back flap, I burned it. But I think the binding and boards and set up and printing is superb. Knopf does that sort of thing so darned well.

Yesterday I went collecting with Ed [Ricketts]. The first time I had been out in a long time. It is fine spring now and I enjoyed it a lot. Went over to Santa Cruz. Carol wouldn't go because she was typing and wouldn't take the time off. It would have done her good. But we're broke now and one hamburger was all we could afford. I had been working longer than she had so I took the day off. Today back at revising and proofreading. I'm making dumplings for dinner. I hope they're good. It's a dirty shame Carol has to work so hard. She's putting in nine hours a day at it. I wish I could do it but my typing is so very lousy.

I had a letter from Covici which sounded far from overenthusiastic. I liked it. It gave me some confidence in the man. I like restraint. Covici says, "I am interested in your work and would like to arrive at an agreement with Miss McIntosh." My estimation of him went up immediately. It is nice to know that he is more enthusiastic than that, of course. This morning I got applications on the Phelan Award sent at your request. I shall probably fill out the blank and send it in. I don't know whom to get to sponsor me but maybe I'll think of some one. That's all for now.

Now it's Monday morning. Carol has gone to work for the S.E.R.A. [State Emergency Relief Administration.] Poor kid has to put in six hours there and then come home and type ms. She has nearly two hundred pages yet to do. What a job. She is taking it awfully well as usual.

I read Not in a Day last night. Finished it about three this morning. I don't know whether it is high or low comedy but I do know it's awfully funny. My own

Dust jacket for Steinbeck's 1935 book about the lives of a group of paisanos in a poor section of Monterey (from Sotheby's New York, The Maurice F. Neville Collection of Modern Literature, November 16, 2004*)*

work seems stodgy and heavy by comparison. I hope you will read Tortilla Flat some time. That is neither heavy nor stodgy. Anyway I'm glad you wrote this book and I am convinced that it will release you from the necessities for working on fan magazines. I hope it sells a million copies. Congratulations.

I have a great deal of proof reading and correction to do and besides that I am doing the house and the cooking and bedmaking. So I'll sign off. But I am pleased with Not in a Day. Don't let it make a slave of you. I mean, if it sells well, people will want another just like it, and don't let them have it. For right at that point of capitulation is the decision whether the public is going to rule you or you your public.

I simply have to go to work. Goodbye. You have complimented me greatly by sending the book.

                                        jon
                    —*Steinbeck: A Life in Letters*, pp. 101–102

*   *   *

Steinbeck to McIntosh, 4 February 1935

In a letter to McIntosh, Steinbeck defends the use of "the speech of working men" in his strike novel, In Dubious Battle.

Dear Miss McIntosh:

Herewith the signed contracts [for *Tortilla Flat*]. They seem fine to me. Thank you. You have been very good to me.

We'll get the new book off to you about the fifteenth. Title has been slightly changed to include one more word, In Dubious Battle. Much better sound and also gives a kind of an active mood to the thing. I guess it is a brutal book, more brutal because there is no author's moral point of view. The speech of working men may seem a little bit racy to ladies' clubs, but, since ladies' clubs won't believe that such things go on anyway, it doesn't matter. I know this speech and I'm sick of working men being gelded of their natural expression until they talk with a fine Oxonian flavor.

There are curious things about the language of working men. I do not mean the local idioms, but the speech which is universal in this country among traveling workers. Nearly every man uses it individually, but it has universal rules. It is not grammatical error but a highly developed speech form. The use of the final g in ing is tricky, too. The g is put on for emphasis and often to finish a short hard sentence. It is sometimes used for purpose of elision but not always. Certain words like "something" rarely lose the final g or if they do, the word becomes "somepin" or "somepm." A man who says thinkin' will say morning if it comes on the end of a sentence. I tell you these things so you will understand why, in one sentence having two present participles, one g will be there and the other left off. This is a pretty carefully done ms. If you will read such a sentence over, aloud, you will see that it naturally falls that way.

I hardly expect you to like the book. I don't like it. It is terrible. But I hope when you finish it, in the disorder you will feel a terrible kind of order. Stories begin and wander out of the picture; faces look in and disappear and the book ends with no finish. A story of the life of a man ends with his death, but where can you end a story of man-movement that has no end? No matter where you stop there is always more to come. I have tried to indicate this by stopping on a high point but it is by no means an ending.

Pascal Covici, who became Steinbeck's editor and publisher in 1935 (Publishers' Weekly, *20 January 1940; Thomas Cooper Library, University of South Carolina*)

I hope Mr. Covici will be interested in this book. I am very tired. This has been completed quickly.

Sincerely,
John Steinbeck
—*Steinbeck: A Life in Letters,* pp. 105–106

* * *

The First Reader
Harry Hansen

In this review Harry Hansen writes that "the characters of Tortilla Flat *belong to the immortal band of vagabonds who romp through the books of all nations. . . ."*

I was having a perfectly grand time leaning back in my chair and laughing at the devices of Pablo and Pilon to get wine for themselves in *Tortilla Flat* when Miss Marx said, casually, "You know the *Russian Revolution,* by Chamberlin, is ready Tuesday, don't you?"

"Listen," I said, "Pablo and Pilon are two good-for-nothing wine guzzlers, mixed breeds, in a part of Monterey, Cal., that you don't care a rap about, but they are drinking to each other's health, and John Steinbeck, who writes the book, says this is what follows:—

"Two gallons is a great deal of wine, even for two paisanos—Spiritually the jugs may be graduated thus:—Just below the shoulder of the first bottle, serious and concentrated conversation. Two inches farther down, sweetly sad memory. Three inches more, thoughts of old and satisfactory loves. An inch, thoughts of old and bitter loves. Bottom of the first jug, general and undirected sadness.

"Shoulder of the second jug, black, unholy despondency. Two fingers down, a song of death or longing. A thumb, every other song each one knows. The graduations stop here, for the trail splits and there is no certainty. From this point on anything can happen."

I looked at Miss Marx, and she said, "You do know that the *Russian Revolution,* by William Henry Chamberlin, is published tomorrow?"

"What, again?" I said.

"In two volumes," she said, with what I take to be a look of malicious mischief.

"It will have to wait," I said. "You know what life was like last week. Four volumes of Pareto, and even if I didn't read them through I did that other unpardonable thing for reviewers—I continued reading in them after writing my review. Two volumes of the life of William Booth—a grand book, by the way, but two volumes. Don't you think I should be allowed to review a few thin pamphlets for a change?"

So I went back to *Tortilla Flat,* which happens to be the name of the place where the backwash of Monterey, Cal., lives. Danny, the chief character, is a *paisano,* a "mixture of Spanish, Indian, Mexican and assorted Caucasian bloods." A *paisano* has lived in California for a hundred or two years. He speaks English with a *paisano* accent and Spanish with a *paisano* accent. We shall have to get Professor Louise Pound to make some talking machine records of *paisano* accents.

Since the behavior of Danny and his friends is rather low-life, the things they do are not for a conference of clergymen. Danny served in the war; so did the others, and Big Joe Portagee was six months late getting his discharge because he had been sentenced to the hoosegow for striking the sergeant with a kerosene can and stealing two gallons of cooked beans. Theft was a familiar way of getting what they wanted; when Pablo and Pilon couldn't lift a few articles they adopted deceit, and Tortilla, the Italian, and various women were victims of their devices.

Big Joe Portagee had done entirely too much shoveling while in the army to be interested in Pilon's desire to look for buried treasure—he "abhorred the whole principle of shoveling." But Pilon had the naive belief, shared with other residents of Tortilla Flat, that you are apt to come upon buried treasure on St. Andrew's Eve. After a night of wandering among the pines, cautiously avoiding other forms that moved in and out among the trees on the same errand—some of whom might be the shades of the folk who had buried the treasure—Pilon and Big Joe dug up a square block of concrete with a metal plate on top of it. It was a marker sunk by the United States Geodetic Survey.

"Maybe we can take this good piece of metal and sell it," said the Portagee.

"Johnny Pom-pom found one," said Pilon sadly. "Johnny took the metal piece and tried to sell it. It is a year in jail to dig one of these up and two thousand dollar fine."

The characters of *Tortilla Flat* belong to the immortal band of vagabonds who romp through the books of all nations, combining a childlike belief with cunning and never profiting very much by their knavery. These are twilight stories, that never get into good company, that repeat anecdotes one has heard told about other louts in other localities.

In the end the author gets Danny roaring drunk and lands him at the bottom of the gulch, with injuries from which he never recovers, so that Danny becomes a legendary hero of *Tortilla Flat,* a fellow with enormous vinous capacity. He has realized Danny only partially, for the story skips back and forth between Danny and his cronies, and the tragic end of Danny seems a trifle too casual to be moving.

John Steinbeck, the author, is a native of Salinas, Cal., and 32 years old. He lives at Pacific Grove, between Monterey and Carmel, Cal. After he attended Stanford University he worked as rancher, painter and carpenter's helper, then came east and worked as a day laborer on the Madison Square Garden, then building. This is similar to the career of William Saroyan, who worked his way east a number of years ago and became a teletype operator for a telegraph company near the Washington Market. Steinbeck has written some effective short stories, and one of them we republished in the "O. Henry Prize Stories for 1934." It was called "The Murder" and had a singularly effective ending. *Tortilla Flat* has been illustrated with drawings by Ruth Gannett. . . .

—*New York World Telegram,* 28 May 1935; reprinted in
John Steinbeck: The Contemporary Reviews, pp. 31–32

***

Steinbeck to McIntosh, April 1935

Steinbeck became upset when Covici rejected In Dubious Battle *because of the communist ideology expressed in the novel.*

Dear Miss McIntosh:

I confess that I am deeply shocked at the attitude of Covici, not from pique but because it is a perfect example of the attitude which makes the situation in I. D. B. what it is. Does no one in the world want to see and judge this thing coldly? Answering the complaint that the ideology is incorrect, this is the silliest of criticism. There are as many communist systems as there are communists. It should be obvious from the book that not only is this true, but that the ideologies change to fit a situation. In this book I was making nothing up. In any statement by one of the protagonists I have simply used statements I have heard used. Answering the second criticism that the book would be attacked by both sides, I thoroughly anticipated such attack in trying to do an unbiased book. And if attack has ever hurt the sale of a book I have yet to hear of it.

That is the trouble with the damned people of both sides. They postulate either an ideal communist or a thoroughly damnable communist and neither side is willing to suspect that the communist is a human, subject to the weaknesses of humans and to the greatnesses of humans. I am not angry in the least. But the blank wall of stupid refusal even to look at the thing without colored glasses of some kind gives me a feeling of overwhelming weariness and a desire to run away and let them tear their stupid selves to pieces. If the fools would only change the name from Communist to, say, American Liberty Party, their principles would probably be embraced overnight.

I guess this is slopping over enough. I am sorry that the book cannot go through. I would do it just the same again. I suppose in the event of an English sale, the censor would clean up my carefully built American language.

As for submitting another book to Covici—you will do as you think best about that. I am so tired. I have worked for so long against opposition, first of my parents who wanted me to be a lawyer and then of publishers who want me to be anything but a writer, that I work well under opposition. If ever I had things my own way I would probably go dry. This will knock out all plans of going to Mexico I guess. I had hoped to be able to start off the big book which would take a long time and would be a very grave attempt to do a

Steinbeck's record of the stories he completed during the summer of 1934
(Center for Steinbeck Studies, San Jose State University)

first-rate piece of work. However, Covici should know saleability, and obviously I don't. Oh, the devil. We've managed to live thus far and write what we want to write. We can probably go on doing it.

Right today I am discouraged. I won't be tomorrow.

Sincerely,

John Steinbeck

—*Steinbeck: A Life in Letters*, pp. 107–108

* * *

Steinbeck to Elizabeth Otis, 13 June 1935

Immediately after publication Tortilla Flat *became a success and moved up the best-seller list in a couple of months. The following letter from Steinbeck to Elizabeth Otis indicates his surprise at the instant popularity of the book.*

Dear Miss Otis:

If you have anything of mine the New Yorker could use, fine. The only things I can think of are the short things like the Vigilante or possibly St. Katy which I would like to make someone print. I'm not being cocky but I have never written "for" a magazine and shan't start now.

One very funny thing. Hotel clerks here are being instructed to tell guests that there is no Tortilla Flat. The Chamber of Commerce does not like my poor efforts, I guess. But there is one all right, they know it.

My father's death doesn't change any plans but does give us freedom of movement for the first time in three years. I can't get used to having no illness in the family.

While I think of it—I am very much opposed to drawing money from any publisher for work that has not been done. I'd much rather have less and have it without any obligation. The idea of a salary doesn't appeal to me at all. I intend to write what I want to.

The publicity on TF [*Tortilla Flat*] is rather terrible out here and we may have to run ahead of it. Please ask CF [Covici-Friede] not to give my address to anyone. Curious that this second-rate book, written for relaxation, should cause this fuss. People are actually taking it seriously.

I had an awfully nice letter from Bob Ballou. Wish I could have stayed with him but I'm so awfully sick of not being able to have shoes half-soled.

In your dealings you need make no compromise at all for financial considerations as far as we are concerned. Too many people are trapped into promises by gaudy offers. And my father's estate, while small, will keep us for a number of years if necessary. And we've gone through too damned much trying to keep

the work honest and in a state of improvement to let it slip now in consideration of a little miserable popularity. I'm scared to death of popularity. It has ruined everyone I know. That's one of the reasons I would like In Dubious Battle printed next. Myths form quickly and I want no tag of humorist on me, nor any other kind. Besides, IDB would reduce popularity to nothing but I do think it would sell.

I suppose it is bad tactics but I am refusing the usual things—the radio talks, the autograph racket, the author's afternoons and the rest of the clutter—politely, I hope, but firmly.

Will Heinemann buy TF? I suppose To A God Unknown failed miserably in England as it did here.

By the way, the rainy season is on in Mexico now. We can't go until August I guess, if then. I'll leave this open in case anything else occurs to me.

That's all,

John Steinbeck

—*Steinbeck: A Life in Letters*, pp. 111–112

* * *

A Bookman's Notebook
Joseph Henry Jackson

In his review of Tortilla Flat, *Joseph Henry Jackson of the* San Francisco Chronicle *had high praise for Steinbeck's new book.*

This is a story of California's own Monterey, but not the kind of story you think it is.

It is no tale of the fading glories of old Spain, nor yet a tale of pioneer days in California; it is a story of today, and of a handful of *paisanos* who have, all in all, a pretty good time. What is a *paisano*? Let Mr. Steinbeck answer that himself: "He is a mixture of Spanish, Indian, Mexican and assorted Caucasian bloods. His ancestors have lived in California for a hundred or two years. He speaks English with a *paisano* accent and Spanish with a *paisano* accent. He is a *paisano*, and he lives in that uphill district in the town of Monterey known as Tortilla Flat, although it isn't a flat at all."

These, then, are the people about whom Mr. Steinbeck has written this completely charming little book. Specifically, he has written about four of them—Danny, Pilon, Pablo and Big Joe Portagee, who together form the Athos-Porthos-Aramis-and-D'Artagnan combination of Tortilla Flat.

Danny had grown up in Tortilla Flat, but he hadn't been much of a figure in the little community's life until after he came back from driving mules in Texas for the duration of the war.

When he returned, he found that he was an heir and an owner of property, no less. The *viejo*—that is, his grandfather—had died and left him two small houses on Tortilla Flat. Danny bought a gallon of red wine and went to look at the property. It wasn't long before his three friends had rallied round him. One house Danny took for himself as was his right. The other he rented to Pablo, Pilon and Big Joe. That they paid no rent was a minor detail. They were his friends, and they shared what they had with him, which was chiefly wine. Even when they burned down the house and moved in with Danny, it was all right. There was too much responsibility about owning two houses anyway.

After their move, the Tortilla Flat Musketeers grew even closer friends.

Whatever one did was a matter for all. There was the adventure of The Pirate, for instance; they were together on that, even to the extent of lending The Pirate their best clothes when it came time for him to go to the church and see with his own eyes the golden candlestick that was his vow dedicated by Father Ramon to the service of San Francisco. There was the time, too, that Danny gave the vacuum cleaner to Dolores Ramirez as a present. Dona Ramirez's house had no electric wires, but the cleaner was a present nevertheless, and a fine one, and it got Danny the lady's favors. But, though it was well enough to have Danny fooling with the ladies, too much was too much. The remaining three friends got Danny out of that by their wisdom and shrewdness, and afterward Danny was glad.

They stuck together, also, on another memorable occasion—when Teresina Cortez and his steps-and-stairs family were in danger of starving. It must never be said that Danny and Pilon and Pablo and Big Joe couldn't remedy so simple a situation as that. And there was a minor crime wave in Monterey; but nobody ever discovered who was to blame for the sacks of beans that vanished from the warehouse. Nobody ever discovered, either, which of the four had fathered Teresina's new baby. But that was not, after all, important.

Such a fine life, with a real house to live in and wine almost all the time, cannot go on forever; such things do not happen.

And that was true in this case. The four had had their day when Fate took a hand and removed Danny. That was the end of it, and it is the end of Mr. Steinbeck's book. But the day had been a good one, and it had lasted long enough to furnish the materials of this saga, for which the reader may be thankful.

The trouble with a book like this is that you can't describe it. The best you can do is to indicate it—faintly, in the sketch book manner, at best leaving out all the intangibles that really give it its quality. I can't reflect the charm, the humor, the pathos, the wit and wisdom and warm humanity which illuminate every one of Mr. Steinbeck's pages. If I could, I should be writing just the same kind of book. But I can at least urge you to read *Tortilla Flat*. Don't, please, miss it. Simple as it is, it has in it all the elements that go to make the best stories. And unless you are a very dour person indeed you will relish it as you have very few books in your experience.

—*San Francisco Chronicle*, 28 May 1935; reprinted in *John Steinbeck: The Contemporary Reviews*, pp. 32–33

* * *

Life in a California Shantytown
Fred T. Marsh

Fred T. Marsh reviewed Tortilla Flat *for* The New York Times Book Review.

Tortilla Flat is the tumbledown section of the town of Monterey in California. Here live the *paisanos*, a mixed race of Spanish, Indian, Mexican and assorted Caucasian bloods. In Mr. Steinbeck's humorous and whimsical tale they appear as a gentle race of sun- loving, heavy wine-drinking, anti-social loafers and hoodlums who work only when necessity demands and generally live by a succession of devious stratagems more or less outside the law. *Tortilla Flat* is not as sad and gentle a story as *Mrs. Wiggs of the Cabbage Patch*. It is not as raucous in its humor nor as grim in its realism as *Tobacco Road* or *God's Little Acre*. It is not as whimsical and pathetic as *One More Spring*. It comes closer, perhaps, to the novels that deal in a spirit of charm and amused sympathy with the manners and vagaries of Southern Negroes.

Mr. Steinbeck writes with affection about the group that gradually accumulates in Danny's house, the little wooden shack set in a weedy yard and half hidden by straggling pines. "The paisanos," he says, "are clean of commercialism, free of the complicated system of American business, and, having nothing that can be stolen, exploited or mortgaged, that system has not attacked them very vigorously."

Danny and his friends, most of them, did not have even a house in the early days. But Danny came back from the war to learn that his grandfather had died and left him two houses up in Tortilla Flat.

"Engaging and Moral Legends"

Lewis Gannett, whose wife, Ruth, provided the illustrations for Tortilla Flat, *reviewed the book for the* New York Herald Tribune.

Danny of Tortilla Flat behind Monterey was undoubtedly what settlement workers would call an anti-social character; and so were his friends, Pilon and Pablo, and Big Joe Portagee and Jesus Maria Corcoran. But they were among the most lovable men whom I have met for many a day; and in his book about them, *Tortilla Flat* . . . , John Steinbeck has fulfilled that promise which some of us so enthusiastically discerned three years ago in his *Pastures of Heaven.* . . .

Tortilla Flat is full of such engaging and moral legends. It includes also the stories of the Pirate who, with his five dogs, gathered pitchwood in the forest and hid his earnings in the sand; and of a little Mexican corporal who, also, for a time, lived in Danny's house, where the windows were never washed because, as Pilon pointed out, if the windows were clear the light would be better and then they would be tempted to stay indoors instead of going out into the fresh air; and of that final party for Danny which the entire Flat still remembers with reverence. But I shall not spoil the Danny saga by repeating more of it.

Mr. Steinbeck is an artist; and he tells the stories of these lovable thieves and adulterers with a gentle and poetic purity of heart and of prose that reminds one of Robert Nathan's lovely *One More Spring.* I like *Tortilla Flat,* and I do not think that I am prejudiced in its favor merely because I lived with Danny for two months before I read the book, while Ruth Gannett was drawing pictures to illustrate it. John Steinbeck is a born writing man, and *Tortilla Flat* a book to cherish. . . .

—"Books and Things," *New York Herald Tribune,* 29 May 1935; reprinted in *John Steinbeck: The Contemporary Reviews,* p. 34

The news is too much for Danny, who gets gloriously drunk, smashes a few windows and winds up in jail. Jail is a pleasant place to rest in for a few days, especially since Tito Ralph, the keeper, is an old friend. But it becomes boring after a while. So one night when he goes out with Tito to drink wine at the Torrellis he decides not to return but to go up and inspect his new property, already becoming a burden and a responsibility on his hitherto carefree soul.

On the way he runs into his old friend Pilon, Pilon the realist and the contriver. Taking possession of the first house is a thrill and Pilon decides that he, too, should become a man of property. After some dickering he strikes a bargain with Danny to rent the second house for fifteen dollars a month. The fact that Pilon has never had fifteen dollars in cash at one time in his life is forgotten in the excitement of the moment. But once Pilon is established the burden rests on his spirit. So he takes in Pablo, who is to pay him fifteen dollars a month, thus passing on the weight of his responsibility and easing his conscience.

But Pablo has no money either. And Danny, who is taking an interest in Mrs. Morales, the widow lady of substance next door, begins to hint for some money. So Pablo and Pilon rescue Jesus Maria Corcoran, a good man, from his bed in a ditch by the roadside and pass the burden on to him. All three are relieved when the little shack burns down. They have done their best. Now they can all go to live in Danny's house free of responsibility.

The further adventures of the friends in their daily search for free food and a dollar or two with which to buy wine continues through the story, interrupted by occasional flashes of drama and love making. But the policy of taking new members into their community in the hope of solving the financial problem is for the most part a mistake. In desperation they lure The Pirate, a poor half-wit of the town, from his chicken house where he had lived happily many years with his five dogs. They know The Pirate earns twenty-five cents a day collecting and selling pitch and never spends any of it, since he begs from the back doors of restaurants enough food for himself and his dogs. But when the innocent Pirate brings out his hoard, over a thousand quarters, and tells them how he is saving to buy a candlestick for St. Francis, who had spared one of his dogs from death, the brotherhood mournfully resign themselves to protecting The Pirate's money as their own.

Mr. Steinbeck tells a number of first-rate stories in his history of Danny's house. He has a gift for drollery and for turning Spanish talk and phrases into a gently mocking English. The book is as consistently amusing, we think, as *February Hill.* But we doubt if life in Tortilla Flat is as insouciant and pleasant and amusing as Mr. Steinbeck has made it seem.

—*New York Times Book Review,* 2 June 1935; reprinted in *John Steinbeck: The Contemporary Reviews,* pp. 38–39

* * *

Aristocrats without Money
Helen Neville

Helen Neville reviewed Tortilla Flat *for* The Nation.

The subject matter of *Tortilla Flat*–five men living by their wits on the thin edge of society–is surely grim enough, but Mr. Steinbeck's approach to it is wholly in the light-hearted, fantastic tradition; it suggests such novels as *Vile Bodies* and *South Wind*. Yet it is an approach somewhat justified by the temperament of the characters who manage to preserve, in the midst of their various vicissitudes, an equanimity comparable to the author's own.

Economically, these five *paisanos* living in a squalid section of Monterey, in Southern California, may occupy one of the most desperate positions in the social scheme, but in their aristocratic immunity to the problems of such a position they deserve to rank with those gay and moneyed bohemians whom we encounter in the novels of Evelyn Waugh. Such necessities as rent and food scarcely seem to trouble them; as long as they can "lift" an occasional jug of wine, or enough money to pay for one, they are completely happy. The rent problem is permanently solved when Danny, the hero, falls heir to two houses, in one of which he installs his friend Pilon. Pilon agrees to pay him fifteen dollars a month–an agreement which neither party takes very seriously, since both know that whatever money flows in Pilon's direction is sure to be spent on wine. After a night of revelry Pilon's house burns down; and he and the two friends whom he has invited to join him go to live in Danny's house, where the question of rent has not even a nominal significance. The question of food is permanently settled when they annex to their clan a genial half-wit, practiced in the art of procuring hand-outs from back kitchens. All these situations are handled in the spirit of farce–a spirit with which the men themselves would seem to be in perfect agreement. Only Danny succumbs, somewhat unconvincingly, to a fit of despair, but neither this nor his suicide, to which it ultimately leads, supplies a tragic note; they are merely occasions for getting drunk in his honor and singing bawdy songs.

Mr. Steinbeck's attempt to impose a mood of urbane and charming gaiety upon a subject which is perpetually at variance with it is graceful enough, but the odds are against him. The traditional "smart" novel–such as *Tortilla Flat* aims to be–generally deals with a stratum of society with which such a mood is wholly consistent; in doing so, it avoids a certain confusion. The theme of such a novel as *Vile Bodies* was, of course, that of utter futility; but it was the kind of futility which lent itself inevitably to satire or farce, and each of its situations, no matter how absurd or impossible it might be, was entirely convincing, since it never seemed to yield implications other than those which the author had found in it. The futility in *Tortilla Flat* is of quite a different order; its situations are rife with possibilities which, despite the amount of indifference to them manifested by Mr. Steinbeck and his characters, it is not always easy to ignore.

–*Nation,* 140 (19 June 1935); reprinted in *John Steinbeck: The Contemporary Reviews,* pp. 42–43

Chapter Three: 1936–1940

Chronology

The Los Gatos, California, home of John and Carol Steinbeck (Center for Steinbeck Studies, San Jose State University; from Jay Parini, John Steinbeck, *1995; Thomas Cooper Library, University of South Carolina)*

May–June 1936	Steinbeck meets John O'Hara, who has been hired by theatrical producer Herman Shumlin to write a play based on *In Dubious Battle*. On 11 June, Steinbeck receives the gold medal of the Commonwealth Club of California for *Tortilla Flat*.
August 1936	Steinbeck works on a series of articles on migrant workers for *The San Francisco News*. On one of his fact-finding trips he is introduced to Tom Collins, who manages a federal-government labor camp. By mid August, Steinbeck completes the second draft of *Of Mice and Men* and finishes writing the article series. Also in this month, his short story "The Leader of the People" (later included in *The Long Valley* [1938] and the 1945 edition of *The Red Pony*) is published in London in *Argosy*. His essay "The Way It Seems to John Steinbeck" appears in the fall issue of *Occident*.
12 September 1936	Steinbeck's "Dubious Battle in California," a summary of the California migrant-worker situation, is published in *The Nation*.
October 1936	Steinbeck's short story "The Lonesome Vigilante" is published in *Esquire*. His series of articles on migrant workers is published on 5–12 October in *The San Francisco News* under the alternate titles "The Harvest Gypsies" and "California's Harvest Gypsies."
November 1936	Franklin D. Roosevelt is reelected president on 3 November. Steinbeck's short story "Breakfast" is published in the 9 November issue of *Pacific Weekly*. Ed Ricketts's Pacific Biological Laboratories on Cannery Row in Monterey burns down on 25 November. Ricketts is unable to save much except for some clothing. All of his records, personal possessions, documents, and books are lost.
November–December 1936	Steinbeck begins work on a long novel with the working title "L'Affaire Lettuceberg." Some elements of it are later included in the draft of *The Grapes of Wrath* (1939). In December the story *Saint Katy the Virgin* is published in a limited edition by Covici-Friede for distribution as Christmas gifts. The story is later included in *The Long Valley*.
February 1937	The novel version of *Of Mice and Men* is published on 6 February by Covici-Friede and is chosen as a selection of the Book-of-the-Month Club. The book enters the best-seller lists almost immediately. Late in the month, Steinbeck and Carol plan a trip to Europe.
23 March 1937	The Steinbecks sail for the East Coast via the Panama Canal aboard the *Sagebrush*.
15 April 1937	The Steinbecks arrive in Philadelphia and continue by train to New York, where Steinbeck attends a dinner honoring Thomas Mann. The event makes Steinbeck miserable because he does not like publicity. During their stay in New York the Steinbecks have a fight that further weakens their marriage.
May–June 1937	The Steinbecks leave for Europe aboard the *Drottningholm* in late May and arrive in Göteborg, Sweden, in early June. They spend the first part of the month in Copenhagen and then travel on to Stockholm, where they develop a friendship with the Swedish painter Bo Beskow, whom Steinbeck met briefly in the Covici-Friede office in the winter of 1936. Beskow paints the first of three eventual portraits of Steinbeck. On 5 June the Commonwealth Club of California awards a second gold medal to Steinbeck, for *In Dubious Battle*.
July 1937	The Steinbecks travel from Sweden to Helsinki and then on to Leningrad and Moscow.
August 1937	On a small freighter the Steinbecks depart for New York, where they confer with playwright-director George S. Kaufman on the play version of *Of Mice and Men*. At Kaufman's farm in Pennsylvania, Steinbeck works intensively for a week and completes the final script. Afterward, the Steinbecks purchase a red Chevrolet in New York and depart for California via Chicago, where they visit Steinbeck's uncle Joe Hamilton and the bookseller Ben Abramson. They continue their journey following Route 66 through Oklahoma to California. Steinbeck's short story "The Prom-

	ise" (later included in the first edition of *The Red Pony* [1937] and *The Long Valley*) is published in the August issue of *Harper's*.
September 1937	Steinbeck's short story "The Ears of Johnny Bear" is published in *Esquire*.
October 1937	Steinbeck's best-known short story, "The Chrysanthemums," is published in *Harper's*. In the middle of the month he sets off on another tour of the California migrant camps to gather information and returns to Los Gatos early the following month.
23 November 1937	The play version of *Of Mice and Men* begins its run on Broadway at the Music Box Theatre. It is a success and runs for 207 performances. The play is published this year as *Of Mice and Men: A Play in Three Acts* by Covici-Friede.
12 January 1938	The play version of *Tortilla Flat,* adapted by playwright Jack Kirkland, opens in New York at Henry Miller's Theatre but runs for only four performances.
February 1938	Steinbeck resumes work on the manuscript of "L'Affaire Lettuceberg." He spends about ten days in Visalia, California, with Collins to assist migrant workers. At about this time Steinbeck meets the movie critic and documentarian Pare Lorentz, who is also involved in studying the problems of the migrant laborers.
7 March 1938	Steinbeck visits migrant-labor camps with *Life* photographer Horace Bristol.

Tom Collins, manager of the Kern County Migrant Camp, with a camp resident, 1936. Steinbeck met Collins on a fact-finding trip for his 1936 series of articles on the problems of migrant laborers, "The Harvest Gypsies" (photograph by Dorothea Lange; from Jay Parini, John Steinbeck, *1995; Thomas Cooper Library, University of South Carolina).*

Front cover of the 1938 republication of the article series originally published in 1936 in The San Francisco News
as "The Harvest Gypsies" (from William McPheron, John Steinbeck: From Salinas to Stockholm,
2000; Special Collections, Thomas Cooper Library, University of South Carolina)

April 1938	The articles comprising "The Harvest Gypsies" are republished by the Simon J. Lubin Society in San Francisco as *Their Blood Is Strong.* "Starvation Under the Orange Trees," an article on migrant labor, is published in the 15 April *Monterey Trader.*
May 1938	Steinbeck receives the New York Drama Critics Award for the play version of *Of Mice and Men.* He completes the first draft of "L'Affaire Lettuceberg." Unhappy with the manuscript, Steinbeck decides to burn it and starts work on a new version, which eventually becomes *The Grapes of Wrath.*
June 1938	Steinbeck's short story "The Harness" is published in *The Atlantic Monthly.*
Late July 1938	Publisher Pascal Covici declares bankruptcy and is hired as a senior editor at Viking Press.
September 1938	Steinbeck's second short-story collection, *The Long Valley,* is published. About this time, Carol comes up with the title for *The Grapes of Wrath.* The Steinbecks begin construction on a second home on ranch property they have acquired about five miles from Los Gatos.
Late October 1938	Steinbeck completes *The Grapes of Wrath,* and Carol finishes typing the manuscript.

January 1939	Elizabeth Otis visits the Steinbecks in Los Gatos to negotiate some changes in *The Grapes of Wrath*. She persuades Steinbeck to make some changes, but he does not agree to change much of the language or the controversial ending of the novel. Steinbeck is elected to the National Institute of Arts and Letters, an honor that he accepts gratefully.
April 1939	*The Grapes of Wrath* is published and becomes an immediate best-seller. *Between Pacific Tides*, by Ricketts and Jack Calvin, is published by Stanford University Press. On 25 April, Steinbeck travels to Chicago to help Lorentz with the making of a documentary, *The Fight for Life* (1940), and stays about a month.
May 1939	After leaving Chicago, Steinbeck makes a hurried trip to New York and Washington, D.C., and returns secretly to Los Gatos in order to avoid publicity. (He has also been warned that some Californians angered by *The Grapes of Wrath* are planning to frame him on manufactured criminal charges.)
June 1939	Steinbeck spends most of this month in Los Angeles working with Lorentz on *The Fight for Life*. A boyhood friend, Max Wagner, introduces Steinbeck to band singer Gwyndolyn "Gwyn" Conger.
August 1939	The Steinbecks' marriage continues to disintegrate; after a fight Carol returns to their home in Los Gatos, and Steinbeck returns to the ranch.
September 1939	Hitler's troops invade Poland on 1 September, provoking England and France to declare war, marking the beginning of World War II. The Steinbecks take a getaway trip, traveling to the Pacific Northwest to see sights and to visit friends. They then move on to Chicago to see Steinbeck's uncle Joe and to visit Lorentz, who is still working on *The Fight for Life*.
October–November 1939	Steinbeck spends time in Los Gatos and Pacific Grove reading, studying, and helping Ricketts. They also make several field trips together.
December 1939	Steinbeck is in Los Angeles on 15 December to view the screenings of the motion-picture adaptations of *Of Mice and Men* and *The Grapes of Wrath*. On 22 December *Of Mice and Men* opens in Hollywood. Carol becomes pregnant just after Christmas; Steinbeck persuades her to have an abortion, from which an infection develops, and she has to have a hysterectomy.
24 January 1940	The movie version of *The Grapes of Wrath* has its world premiere at the Rivoli Theatre in New York and receives overwhelming endorsements from critics.
16 February 1940	The motion-picture version of *Of Mice and Men* opens at the Roxy Theatre in New York.
11 March 1940	The Steinbecks, Ricketts, and four crew members embark on a leased boat, the *Western Flyer,* for the Gulf of California to collect specimens and take notes for an extensive book on the marine life of the area. They return to Monterey on 20 April.
May 1940	On 6 May *The Grapes of Wrath* receives the Pulitzer Prize in fiction. This month Steinbeck receives two other awards for *The Grapes of Wrath,* one from the American Booksellers Association and the other from the editors of the journal *Social Work Today*. On 23 May, Steinbeck is back in Mexico working on the screenplay for a documentary about life in a traditional Mexican village, *The Forgotten Village* (1941).
22 June 1940	On a visit to Washington, D.C., Steinbeck meets with President Roosevelt in order to present his views on how to combat Nazi propaganda.
July 1940	Steinbeck begins writing "The God in the Pipes," a play-novel that introduces some of the characters who eventually appear in *Cannery Row* (1945).
12 September 1940	Steinbeck returns to Washington, D.C., and meets with Roosevelt, urging him to institute a plan to ruin the German economy and prevent the spread of Nazism. Roosevelt is sympathetic but ignores the plan.

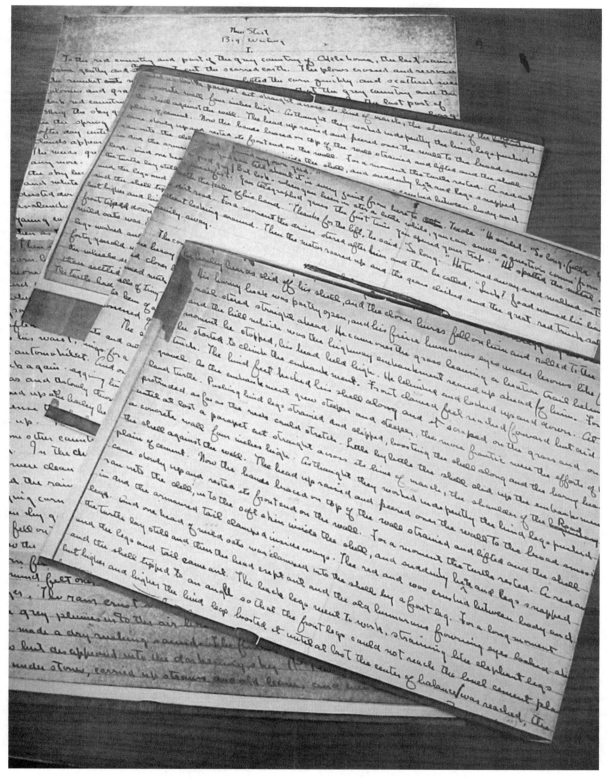

Manuscript pages from The Grapes of Wrath *(1939), Steinbeck's novel about a displaced Oklahoma family seeking farmwork in California (Alderman Library, University of Virginia)*

| Mid October 1940 | Steinbeck returns to Mexico to work on the filming of *The Forgotten Village*. |
| November 1940 | Steinbeck leaves Mexico and arrives in Hollywood to meet Gwyn; his affair with her continues as his relationship with Carol deteriorates. On 5 November, Roosevelt wins his campaign for a third term as president. |

In early January 1936 Steinbeck signed a contract with Paramount Pictures for the movie rights to Tortilla Flat *(1935). His strike novel,* In Dubious Battle, *was published by Covici-Friede that same month and sold moderately well, but* Tortilla Flat *remained a best-seller. Instead of spending much time handling publicity, Steinbeck was working on his next project, a short novel with the working title "Something That Happened," eventually published as* Of Mice and Men *(1937).*

With the income from his recent success with Tortilla Flat, *Steinbeck and Carol were able to purchase two acres of land near Los Gatos, in Santa Clara County, where he could build a home and enjoy more privacy for his work. In May or June 1936 he met the writer John O'Hara, who had been hired to write a play based on* In Dubious Battle *(a project that was never carried out).*

In the summer of 1936 Steinbeck began work on a series of articles on migrant workers for The San Francisco News, *published in October as "The Harvest Gypsies." On one of his fact-finding trips he was introduced to Tom Collins, manager of a federal migrant-worker camp. His travels to the camps and observation of the migrants' situation prompted Steinbeck to tell their stories through his writing. In November and December he began work on a long novel tentatively titled "L'Affaire Lettuceberg." Some of the writing was later incorporated into the draft of* The Grapes of Wrath *(1939).*

In February 1937 Of Mice and Men *was published by Covici-Friede and was named a selection of the Book-of-the-Month Club. It became a best-seller almost immediately. The Steinbecks planned a trip to Europe and sailed for the East coast via the Panama Canal aboard the Sagebrush. After arriving in Philadelphia on 15 April, they continued to New York, where they had a fight that revealed the extent to which their marriage had deteriorated.*

While Steinbeck was in New York, several playwrights expressed interest in dramatizing Of Mice and Men. *Annie Laurie Williams, the agent who handled movie and drama contracts for McIntosh and Otis, showed the novel to Beatrice Kaufman, Eastern representative of Goldwyn Pictures, and her husband, playwright and director George S. Kaufman. Kaufman shared his wife's enthusiasm and enlisted Sam H. Harris as producer, arranging for a fall theatrical production of* Of Mice and Men.*

The Steinbecks left for Europe in late May. In Stockholm they developed a friendship with the Swedish painter Bo Beskow, whom Steinbeck had met briefly in the Covici-Friede offices in the
winter of 1936. Beskow had just won first prize in a nationwide mural competition and was later to achieve an international reputation. In the summer of 1937 he painted the first of three portraits of Steinbeck.*

After the Steinbecks returned to their New York home in August 1937, Steinbeck met with George S. Kaufman to discuss the stage adaptation of Of Mice and Men. *At Kaufman's farm in Pennsylvania, Steinbeck worked to complete the final script. The Steinbecks then returned to California by car. From October to November, Steinbeck made more information-gathering trips to the migrant-labor camps. In the meantime,* Of Mice and Men *was being readied for its run on Broadway at the Music Box Theatre. Opening on 23 November, the play was a great success. In contrast, the stage version of* Tortilla Flat, *adapted by playwright Jack Kirkland, was a flop when it opened in New York in January 1938.*

In February 1938 Steinbeck continued work on "L'Affaire Lettuceberg" and traveled to Visalia, California, with Collins to assist the migrant workers. At about this time Steinbeck met the movie critic and documentary maker Pare Lorentz, who shared his interest in the migrant-labor situation. In March, Steinbeck toured labor camps with Life *photographer Horace Bristol. In late October, Steinbeck completed the second version of "L'Affaire Lettuceberg," and Carol suggested a new title,* The Grapes of Wrath, *taken from a line in Julia Ward Howe's "The Battle Hymn of the Republic" (1862).*

In January 1939 Elizabeth Otis, of McIntosh and Otis, visited Steinbeck in Los Gatos to suggest some changes to The Grapes of Wrath. *He agreed to some of her suggestions but refused to change much of the language or the controversial ending of the novel.* The Grapes of Wrath *became an immediate best-seller when it was published in April.*

The Grapes of Wrath *not only brought attention to the plight of the migrant workers but also raised many doubts about Steinbeck's political ideology, and he had to travel with some secrecy. He spent most of the summer of 1939 working with Lorentz on a documentary,* The Fight for Life *(1940). Around this time a boyhood friend, Max Wagner, introduced Steinbeck to band singer Gwyndolyn "Gwyn" Conger. In the meantime the Steinbecks' marriage continued to deteriorate.*

In early 1940 the motion-picture adaptations of The Grapes of Wrath *and* Of Mice and Men *premiered in New York City. Back on the West Coast, Steinbeck, Carol, Ed Ricketts, and four other crew members embarked on a sea expedition that spring to the Gulf of California to collect specimens and take* notes for a book on the marine life of the region. On 6 May The Grapes of Wrath *received the Pulitzer Prize in fiction.*

In the following months Steinbeck spent some time engaging himself in war issues. In June 1940 he traveled to Washington, D.C., and met with President Franklin D. Roosevelt to present his views on combating Nazi propaganda. He returned to visit the president in September with a plan for ruining the German economy through the distribution of counterfeit money.

In October 1940 Steinbeck returned to Mexico to continue work on a documentary about life in a Mexican village, The Forgotten Village *(1941). After returning from Mexico to Hollywood, he found his relationship with Gwyn Conger had evolved substantially; his affair with Gwyn was to bring his marriage to an end.*

A Prize for *Tortilla Flat* (1935)

Steinbeck to Joseph Henry Jackson, January 1936

The success of Tortilla Flat *(1935) was further confirmed when it won the 1935 Commonwealth Club gold medal for the best work of fiction about California. Steinbeck wrote to Joseph Henry Jackson, book reviewer for the* San Francisco Chronicle, *saying that the award really belonged to Danny, Pilon, and other characters from* Tortilla Flat.

Dear Joe:

I feel very bad about this Commonwealth Club award. I don't know who offered the book in competition. I assure you that the refusal to go isn't the small mean thing it seems. I would like you to know exactly why I can't go.

Nothing like this has ever happened to me before. The most I have had to dodge has been a literary tea or an invitation from a book shop to lecture and autograph. This is the first and God willing the last prize I shall ever win.

The whole early part of my life was poisoned with egotism, a reverse egotism, of course, beginning with self-consciousness. And then gradually I began to lose it.

In the last few books I have felt a curious richness as though my life had been multiplied through having become identified in a most real way with people who were not me. I have loved that. And I am afraid, terribly afraid, that if the bars ever go down, if I become a trade mark, I shall lose the ability to do that. When I do I shall stop working because it won't be fun any more. The work has been the means of making me feel that I am living richly, diversely, and, in a few cases and for a few moments, even heroically. All of these things are not me, for I am none of these things. But sometimes in

my own mind at least I can create something which is larger and richer than I am. In this aspect I suppose my satisfaction is much like that of a father who sees his son succeed where he has failed. Not being brave I am glad when I can make a brave person whom I believe in.

I am very glad that the book got the prize, but I want it to be the book, not me. Those people in that book were very dear to me, but I feel that if I should accept a reward which in this case belongs to Danny and Pilon and the rest, I should not only be cheating them, but cheating them should cut myself off from their society forever.

This is not clear, concise, objective thinking, but I have never been noted for any of these things. If I were a larger person I would be able to do this and come out of it untouched. But I am not.

And will you help me out of it? Will you please present the committee as much or as little explanation as you think wise or necessary? I don't know. I have no social gifts and practically no social experience.

Mean while, don't think too harshly of me for this bolt. I hate to run away but I feel that the whole future working life is tied up in this distinction between work and person. And while this whole argument may seem specious, I assure you it is heartfelt.

Regards
John

—Steinbeck: A Life in Letters, edited by Elaine Steinbeck and Robert Wallsten (New York: Viking, 1975), pp. 118–119

In Dubious Battle (1936)

Tortilla Flat Author Produces Proletarian Novel of Sound Worth

Jackson

Reviewing In Dubious Battle *(1936) for the* San Francisco Chronicle, *Jackson praised Steinbeck's "proletarian novel."*

One of the pleasant successes of last year's fiction crop was a very amusing yarn called *Tortilla Flat,* a story of a handful of carefree ragged edgers living in California's Monterey and getting along however they might, provided only that they had enough money or could develop enough schemes to get hold of a jug of wine sufficiently often. It was a gay, tenderly written little tale and it found thousands of admirers. People, indeed, went around telling other people they simply must read it, which in the end is the way best sellers are made.

Now, in this new novel, John Steinbeck has done something totally different; something as startling in its way (at least to those whose acquaintance with the author is limited to *Tortilla Flat*) as though, say, P. G. Wodehouse should have written *Germinal*. This *In Dubious Battle* is just as little like its immediate predecessor as you could very well imagine. It is a story of men on the thin edge of society, to be sure, but men who are workers rather than charming loafers, men who have to labor but want a fair return for the work they do. It is, in fact, a "proletarian novel," and a better one than most that advertise themselves as such.

Mr. Steinbeck has chosen as his central figure not so much an individual as a working principle. The hero of his book is really The Strike. Naturally he needs an individual on whom he may hang his story; his character, Jim Nolan, serves that purpose.

You meet Jim at an important moment in his life. He has made up his mind that the system has kicked him around long enough. His father was killed by a riot gun. His mother had died because she just didn't want to live any more; life had dealt too harshly with her. Jim himself had been a shipping clerk until one night he had stopped to hear a speaker in The Square. The speech had wound up in a riot and Jim, an innocent bystander, had been slugged and dumped into jail. He had tried to explain about it after he woke up. The police called his boss on the telephone. When they said he had been picked up at a "radical meeting" the boss said he had never heard of him. That was the last straw. Jim was through with the system. He would join the Party; that is, he would if they would have him. They took him and decided to train him for "field work."

His first experience in the field, as helper to a man trained in up-to-date Party methods is what makes this story. For Jim was put to work immediately with McLeod who knew the game.

Down in the apple country 2000 fruit tramps had gathered to handle the crop. The Grower's Association had waited until the pickers arrived; then they announced a pay cut. Their attitude was that since most of the pickers had to have some kind of work at any price at all, in order to keep alive, much less move on to the next crop, they would have to take the cut. There was nothing they could do about it.

That was what Mac and Jim were working to stop. It was a tremendously difficult task. Fired by Party principles, they knew what they had to do—or at least Mac did. But they had to do it blindly. They ran the chance, almost a certainty it was, that they would be hated as cordially by the pickers as by the growers. A

few pickers, maybe, would be for a strike, would be glad to have the man among them who knew how to organize. But when the shoe began to pinch, they would turn tail. They would forget principles and tomorrow and hate the man who had persuaded them to demand fair play. Nine out [of] 10 of them would take any pay they could get, in order to get away and move on. It wouldn't occur to them that if the Grower's Association succeeded in the pay cut, the growers in the next valley or in control of the next crop would follow suit.

Mac knew that he and Jim were up against this situation. But he was able to think about tomorrow, next year, the next 20 years. Not all the time; sometimes he got mad. But mostly he could bring his mind back to the principle of the thing. That was why he was such a good organizer and why Jim was sent out with him to train.

And Mr. Steinbeck's novel is the story, seen from inside, of how the strike was promoted, how it flared up, almost died, was stimulated again by the skill and strength of the man called Mac, of the methods the growers used to combat it—the whole story as it has happened again and again, not only in California but almost anywhere you like to mention.

It isn't an argument, this book; at any rate, it isn't consciously an argument. Mr. Steinbeck sits aloof as far as he can; tells the story from the mountain top looking down—though with a very powerful pair of field glasses, I should say. Just the same, it is the kind of book that should do much to make the ordinary, decently liberal citizen see two sides of the labor question.

Steinbeck is just as willing to show his reader the brutalities of the strikers as he is to show them the brutalities of the so-called "Citizens' Vigilante Committee," made up, as he very shrewdly points out, of "a bunch of fool shoe clerks and the American Legion boys trying to pretend they aren't middle aged." Certainly Legionaires may not like that description of themselves; but some of them have earned it, whether it applies to all or not. He is out to show both sides, and only a stupidly reactionary reader will be unwilling to admit that the "vigilance" idea has almost as much blood on its head—and hands—as the strike idea.

A great many people will not like what he is saying here, of course. The reader who belongs to the let-'em-eat-cake school will consider Mr. Steinbeck's eminently just presentation nothing less than subversive, wicked and revolutionary; I can see such readers—the vigilante boys who went out and broke windows and heads on no more evidence than an anonymous letter dropped into the lion's mouth—positively sweating in their haste to get Steinbeck nominated for inclusion in Mrs. [Elizabeth] Dilling's "Red Network."

But those readers may as well calm themselves. Because a good many out-and-out communists aren't going to like the book any better than they will. Plenty of extreme leftists are going to go into nice little rages at Steinbeck's failure to make his book a fine hot argument for their cause. They are going to feel very badly because Jim Nolan's first effort to serve the Party ends in his death, and because the strike he helped foment doesn't in the book prove a great success, set the growers back on their heels, and prove the match that touches off the blaze of better days for labor. They're not going to like this, either: Says Dr. Burton to Mac, "You people have an idea that if you can once establish a thing, the job'll be done. Nothing stops, Mac. If you were able to put an idea into effect tomorrow, it would start changing right away. Establish a commune and the same gradual flux will continue." Especially they won't care about this paragraph, in which Dr. Burton, on-the-fencer, expresses very much what Mr. Steinbeck himself seems to feel: "I just want to see it, Mac. I[t] might be like this: When group-man wants to move he makes a standard, 'God wills we recapture the Holy Land'; or he says, 'We fight to make the world safe for democracy'; or he says, 'We will wipe out social injustice with communism.' But the group doesn't care about the Holy Land or democracy or communism. Maybe the group simply wants to move, to fight, and uses those words simply to reassure the brains of individual men. I say, it might be like that, Mac." No; the enthusiast battling for a new social order under communism or any other banner, won't care for anything as mild as that. And he'll be disappointed in Mr. Steinbeck because he doesn't shout and wave his arms and emit war cries.

However, the reader who absorbs *In Dubious Battle* intelligently will find out these things for himself. It remains only to say that it is a splendidly written, excellently conceived and executed novel. Mr. Steinbeck writes, as always, with strength and beauty. If you find that, after 200 pages or so of magnificently realistic writing (poetically realistic writing, if you'll allow the description) he goes a trifle mystical; well, if he sees the thing that way, then that's the way he sees it. His conception, for example, of the mob, the crowd, as "not men, but a different kind of animal" is thoroughly sound. His observation, put into Mac's mouth, that "Guy after guy gets knocked into our side by a cop's nightstick" makes such good sense that it's a wonder the men who line up against labor don't see it, for their own sakes. But in the latter half of the book, Jim Nolan gets beyond me in precisely the degree that Mr. Steinbeck makes him get beyond himself. I can't follow him quite to that exalted level to which the author raises him. I can't feel him as all genuine, for instance, when

he talks about pulling the bandage off his wounded head in order to stir up the men with the sight of blood. But it may be my fault.

However, there is no question about the quality of the book as a whole. Mr. Steinbeck, as I've already said, has written a better proletarian novel than most of those that claim that distinction. He has also written a far better novel.

–*San Francisco Chronicle,* 1 January 1936; reprinted in *John Steinbeck: The Contemporary Reviews,* edited by Joseph R. McElrath Jr., Jesse S. Crisler, and Susan Shillinglaw (Cambridge & New York: Cambridge University Press, 1996), pp. 51–53

* * *

In Dubious Battle and Other Recent Works of Fiction
Fred T. Marsh

Fred T. Marsh found In Dubious Battle *to be not only a well-written proletarian novel but also "a profound psychological novel."*

You may remember *Tortilla Flat,* Mr. Steinbeck's last novel, which described with genial gusto and gentle irony the picaresque adventures of a small group of Latin-American vagabonds in a California suburban slum. That was a gay, melancholy and charming book. It did for the lotus eaters of a bum's paradise what *Penrod* did for the small boys of the middle-class suburbs of pre-war days—described them accurately, wittily, ironically, engagingly, as they would appear to bustling outsiders nostalgic for the simple amoral life. You would never know that *In Dubious Battle* was by the same John Steinbeck if the publishers did not tell you so.

It seems to me one of the most courageous and desperately honest books that has appeared in a long time. It is also, both dramatically and realistically, the best labor and strike novel to come out of our contemporary economic and social unrest. It will alienate many of Steinbeck's readers, particularly in California, where *Tortilla Flat* headed the best-seller lists for weeks and where the new story is laid. But it is not cut to any orthodox, Communist or other pattern. It is such a novel as Sinclair Lewis at his best might have done had he gone on with his projected labor novel instead of turning to the far easier, although possibly no less valuable job of striking a blow against fascism.

Steinbeck keeps himself out of the book. There is no editorializing or direct propaganda. His purpose is to describe accurately and dramatize powerfully a

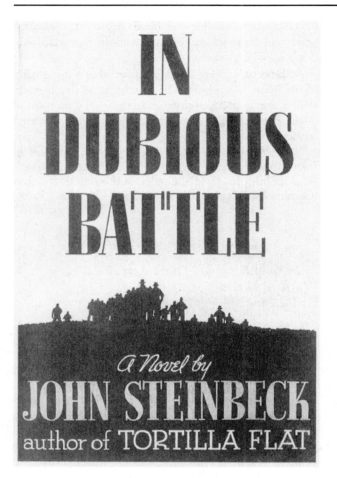

Dust jacket for Steinbeck's 1936 strike novel (from William
McPheron, John Steinbeck: From Salinas to
Stockholm, 2000; Special Collections, Thomas
Cooper Library, University of South Carolina)

small strike of migratory workers, guided by a veteran
Communist organizer, in a California fruit valley. It is
true the book is focused on strike headquarters—on
the two Communist field workers, the little doctor
who gives his services to the strikers but remains
philosophically and ironically but sympathetically
detached from the spirit of fervor, and the strikers'
natural leaders, some of whom have no use for
"Reds," but decide to strike in personal and group
rebellion against what seems to them a double-cross
on the part of the owners. But the arguments on the
other side are also given, though not without the caus-
tic commentaries and violent reactions of the workers
and the ideological counter-arguments of their Communist mentors.

All the elements of such a strike are here. The
concealed discontent and hostility emerged into the
open. The party workers succeed in winning over the
leaders to a program of united and effective action. A
small fruit-grower, at odds with the powerful interests in
the valley, is induced to give the men a camping-
ground on his place. A doctor is imported to enforce
sanitation and prevent the authorities from using the
health laws as an excuse to oust the strikers. Bribes and
promises are offered. Overtures are made and rejected.
Scabs are imported and the strike enters the stage of
violence.

First blood is drawn by "vigilantes," irresponsi-
bles of the kind which shortsighted capitalists—knowing
they cannot depend 100 per cent on the law, which,
after all, is dependent on popular support—foster and
encourage, sometimes getting more than they bargain
for. Thousands of peaceful citizens in the valley, resentful against the domination of a "big three" owning
group, sympathize with the strikers and supply them
with food. The law wavers and tries to get rid of them
peaceably before it turns against them. Violence results
in counter-violence. The strikers are doomed. But to
the irreconcilables they have won a moral victory, a
minor victory on a broad front.

But his is a story of individuals as well as one of
mass action and of mental and spiritual attitudes translated into action. Mac, the hard-boiled organizer; Jim,
the new convert, intense and brooding and passionate;
London, the born leader whom Mac and Jim succeed in
winning over and putting at the head of the little army—
these three principals are real men, who, like men in
other fields of endeavor, lead both public and private
lives; are plain human beings off guard and off duty,
but something else again as leaders in a cause or a fight.
Just so, the thousand or more men under them inte-
grate and disintegrate, now an amorphous tangle of
individuals and small groups, now an army, now a
fanatic mob moving as one, fused into a single will,
with double the strength of their numbers, only to dis-
solve again into helpless disorder. It is his extraordinarily effective and moving handling of these elements
which makes Steinbeck's book not only a powerful
labor novel of our times but a profound psychological
novel of men and leadership and masses.

In Dubious Battle will not change the opinions of
those already seated firmly in the saddle of their various faiths, opinions and prejudices. These strikers and
their leaders and their arguments and actions will, however, win the admiration and sympathy of many middle-
grounders. They will repel many others—just as do their
prototypes in real life. It's an honest book, and it is also
a swift-moving and exciting story.

—*New York Times Book Review,* 2 February 1936;
reprinted in *John Steinbeck: The Contemporary Reviews,*
pp. 59–61

* * *

John Steinbeck Comes of Age
Bernard Smith

Reviewer Bernard Smith found that while Steinbeck's personal sympathies gave him an artistic feeling for the subject of In Dubious Battle, *he was "not yet expert in his knowledge of the issues and processes which stir[red] him so deeply."*

John Steinbeck has written a proletarian novel: he tells here the story of a strike and of the making of a revolutionary, and he tells it from the standpoint of a radical sympathizer. That fact must be stated immediately and baldly in order to warn the readers of Mr. Steinbeck's previous book, *Tortilla Flat,* who thought it merely "another *February Hill"* and were "charmed" and "amused" by it and looked forward to another titillating novel by the same author. This book has neither humor, gayety nor gentleness; what it has are such painful emotional qualities as hatred and bitterness. And what it deals with are such painful physical entities as hunger, torture and death.

From the first page of cold, brief, yet strangely tense description of a lower-class rooming house to the last agonizing line of oratory, Mr. Steinbeck's narrative builds and mounts and at last soars. The dramatic movement has a cumulative power, the characters are vividly portrayed, and the dialogue is compact, natural, and in manner and flavor invariably true to type. All of this amounts to saying that Mr. Steinbeck is an artist, which he is. With material as inherently rich in sheer human interest as this, he could not help but produce a book capable of holding any but the most antagonistic reader.

But this is a story which is interesting for more reasons than that which arises out of the experiences of its characters. To begin with, it announces the enlistment of one of the most gifted writers of our younger generation into the ranks of the proletarian novelists. Mr. Steinbeck is no raw youngster coming to the radical movement to learn the elements of his craft. He comes as a mature, technically proficient writer, with a valid emotion and a remarkable intuitive understanding of people.

Another reason is what it indicates about the development of the author considered purely from the point of view of aesthetic achievement. It indicates that he has found himself, that he has integrated his sentiments with his observations and both with his art, and that there is now nothing to prevent him from doing something very big, perhaps even great. I can explain what I mean by referring to the faults of his two preceding novels, in one case a fault of conception, in the other a fault of structure. *To a God Unknown* (published in 1933) was architecturally sound, but weak and soppy inside. Invested with a beautiful feeling about the land—the soil and the things that come of it—and expressed sensitively and poetically, it petered out finally in a murky symbolism which suggested that the author was uneasy and unsure about his feelings concerning the relation of mankind to the terrible forces of nature. His search within himself led to a mystical paganism, which helped him not at all. But his next work, *Tortilla Flat,* proved that he was coming out of the clouds of introspection and landing on his feet. He was looking at men with his eyes wide open. Unfortunately, it proved also that he was seeing them in fragments, so to speak, for the book was not really a novel but a collection of character sketches and anecdotes. It lacked causality, growth and completion. In *In Dubious Battle,* however, it is clear that he has discovered a unifying idea, a vision, that enables him to see his characters whole and consistently in the light of reality. Here the drama never falters, the development and conclusion are logical and forceful, and there is no final surrender to symbolism.

Only one thing is still lacking: He has yet to make his vision so much a part of himself that his understanding of it is as near being instinctive as such things can be. If that sounds too literary, I can make it matter-of-fact by saying that he is not yet expert in his knowledge of the issues and processes which stir him so deeply. This reveals a curious situation. It was not very long ago that proletarian novels were usually written by men who were excellent students of economics and labor tactics, but indifferent writers. Now we are beginning to get proletarian novels by men who are excellent writers, but indifferent students of political theory. For example, there is the central character of Mr. Steinbeck's book. He is a labor organizer, member of a revolutionary party; he is brave and wise and magnetic, and he is consumed by a flaming devotion to his party and his ideals. But Mr. Steinbeck makes that man say things for which he could be expelled in disgrace from his party twenty times over. Specifically, this man displays a recklessness and a cold-blooded manipulation of violence which are romantic fictions of the author's imagination.

The truth is that Mr. Steinbeck is outside the movement about which he writes. His natural sympathies with the underdog together with the dramatic and heroic aspects of the revolutionary's life have aroused him to an artistic understanding of his subject, but they cannot give him a factual and intellectual understanding. It is to be hoped that further study of the grubbier everyday side of his material will subdue a little his Hemingwayish adoration of physical conflict.

We need not fear that such study will reduce the passion or impair the sensitiveness of his writing. Mr.

Steinbeck is too much an artist to be sapped by his political and social investigations. He can absorb the latter and be the better for it; he is not likely to become simply a politician. The reader of this story cannot doubt that. Embodying innumerable complexities of emotion and thought, yet simple in method, courageously direct in appeal, and combining lucidity with strength in style, it could only have come from a man who possesses a completely disciplined craft, and that means more than the ability to put the right words together in the right sequence. Focusing the reader's attention upon the broad social drama–the welding together of a mob of migratory workers in the California apple region, into a communal fighting army–he is actually giving the reader an insight into the minds of rebels: the diverse but significantly related characters that emerge from the class struggle and the motives that make such men elect a cruel and dangerous life. The impersonal epic is there–the battles with the deputies and the vigilantes, the tumult of the picket-line, the last desperate stand against destruction–but with it goes the personal epic. And when it is all done you realize that the latter has permitted you to penetrate into the psychological sources of types of personality that are too little known in American literature. And you realize, too, that Mr. Steinbeck has achieved this with a minimum of effort, with a phrase here and a line of dialogue there, and that is why you must have faith in his future.

–*New York Herald Tribune*, 2 February 1936; reprinted in *John Steinbeck: The Contemporary Reviews*, pp. 61–63

* * *

Though the Field Be Lost
Harry Thornton Moore

Harry Thornton Moore argued that In Dubious Battle *could not be dismissed as "propaganda."*

Despite his preoccupation with localized atmosphere, John Steinbeck has always written of the common people as one of them, with an intense love of their simplicity and heartiness and what might in the best sense be called their vulgarity. His leading characters have been good earthy men who have lived life in the full. But they have gone down in some form of defeat. Now Steinbeck has identified his characters with the class struggle, and although in the present novel they fight a battle whose outcome is dubious, they taste a promise of victory such as their predecessors have not known. It is a victory of integration for them and for their author as well; and the proletarian novelists have been reinforced by one of the ablest young writers in the country.

The foreground heroes of this story are two young agitators, an old hand and a greenhorn, who are control-

THIS LIMITED EDITION OF IN DUBIOUS BATTLE CONSISTS OF NINETY-NINE NUMBERED COPIES, SIGNED BY THE AUTHOR; OF WHICH THIS IS NUMBER *96*

Signed limitation page in a copy of the 1936 limited edition of Steinbeck's novel (from Sotheby's New York, The Maurice F. Neville Collection of Modern Literature, November 16, 2004)

ling a strike of fruit-pickers. They are likable and always real. Besides the struggle of keeping the strike going against crushing odds, they have fierce internal conflicts between their momentary feelings and their devotion to the long view. And through them and beyond them runs the story of the background heroes, the migratory workers who have been practically dehumanized before the start of the story. You sense the strike awaking them, restoring their humanity: another thousand men have been aroused to resistance by the wholesale sadism of hired bullies, and even though this strike is lost, with some of the strikers brutally murdered, you know the others will carry on the fight on other fronts.

Steinbeck creates a marvelously living world here, very full and vivid. You get the feel of the whole place, the zombie-men coming to life, then all the tension of resentment and opposition–you sympathize strongly and want hard to participate. Many of the surrounding characters are done in the flat–all the strikers and all the opposition–but Jim and Mac are very good people and they take you with them. Their development (that of Jim especially) is interesting to watch, and the cool way they go after things. Steinbeck sees them, he sees all of his people, sympathetically; he has a great tenderness; and he goes whole-hog, pulling none of his punches.

In Dubious Battle cannot be dismissed as a "propaganda" novel—it is another version of the eternal human fight against injustice. It is an especially good version, dramatically intense, beautifully written without being too literary for the subject matter, and its climaxes have a sweeping power. It is the real thing; it has a vigor of sheer story-telling that may sweep away many prejudices and win it the wide audience it deserves.

—*New Republic,* 86 (19 February 1936); reprinted in *John Steinbeck: The Contemporary Reviews,* pp. 63–64

* * *

Steinbeck to Louis Paul, February 1936

In Dubious Battle is often misunderstood as Steinbeck's expression of support for communists. To answer this misconception, he wrote author Louis Paul to explain his feelings about them.

Dear Louis Paul:

I don't like communists either, I mean I dislike them as people. I rather imagine the apostles had the same waspish qualities and the New Testament is proof that they had equally bad manners. But this dislike is personal. I never knew D. H. Lawrence either. The whole idea of the man turns my stomach. But he was a good writer, and some of these communist field workers are strong, pure, inhumanly virtuous men. Maybe that's another reason I personally dislike them and that does not redound to my credit. However, that's not important.

I haven't an idea what the press will do, nor do I much care. I have enough money now to live and write for three years if we are careful and I can get a hell of a lot of words down in three years.

You ask why you never see my stuff in Esquire. I guess they were never interested. I have a good many stories in New York but no one wants them. I wrote 9 short stories at one sitting recently. I thought some of them were pretty good, too, but that's as far as it got. The North American Review used to print some at 30 dollars a crack.

I have to start [writing] and am scared to death as usual—miserable sick feeling of inadequacy. I'll love it once I get down to work. Hope you'll be out before too long.

Sincerely,
John Steinbeck
—*Steinbeck: A Life in Letters,* p. 120

Cup of Gold Revisited

By 1936 critics were already noting the great differences among Steinbeck's published works. Wilbur Needham made this point in a review of Steinbeck's recently republished first novel, Cup of Gold *(1929).*

Here is a new edition of John Steinbeck's first book—practically a new book, since it is doubtful if more than a handful of people ever read its microscopically small first edition. By now, those who like Steinbeck are aware of the fact [that], as Lewis Gannett puts it [in] his preface, "no two of his books have ever fitted in the same valise." *Tortilla Flat* made him famous; but, stubbornly, he went on to write, not another amusing tale of the Monterey *paisanos,* but a dramatic labor novel, *In Dubious Battle.* His astounded readers are now treated to the spectacle of Steinbeck wallowing in gore and action, color and hard, brilliant romance.

Cup of Gold is a novelization of Sir Henry Morgan's life, from his birth in the Welsh glens to his Carib exploits and the capture of Panama and his death in Jamaica, written "with occasional reference to history." It is a gorgeous story; but you may be sure Steinbeck has not handled it in any orthodox fashion. I hope its publication may lead many to discover, with further surprise, his two really great books: *The Pastures of Heaven* and *To a God Unknown.*

—"Steinbeck's First," *Los Angeles Times,* 26 July 1936; reprinted in *John Steinbeck: The Contemporary Reviews,* p. 7

Of Mice and Men (1937): The Novel

Steinbeck to Pascal Covici, 28 February 1937

Of Mice and Men was an immediate success upon publication in early 1937; Steinbeck thanked his publisher, Pascal Covici, for the strong sales figures.

Dear Mr. Covici:

You do such nice things. The [Diego] Rivera book came and I am very grateful for it. It is a valuable thing and a beautiful job. Thank you.

You know, we've been married seven years or going on seven and one of the dreams of our marriage was that the moment we could, we would do some traveling. Well we're going to do it. My wife has never been on a ship. We're taking booking on a freighter sailing for New York about the first of April. We plan to go on to Europe from there. I'll give you the ship's name before we start. We haven't closed the booking yet. The boat is very slow, 31 days to N.Y.

Joe Jackson told me that you had sold 117,000 copies of Mice. That's a hell of a lot of books.

Anyway I'll hope to see you before very long. You couldn't arrange to sail with us, could you, train here and freighter back. That would be fine.

Anyway thank you again for everything.

John Steinbeck
—*Steinbeck: A Life in Letters,* pp. 135–136

* * *

Books and Things
Lewis Gannett

In one of his early reviews of Steinbeck's writings, Lewis Gannett commented on Steinbeck's skill at characterization in Of Mice and Men.

"Guys like us, that work on ranches," George told Lennie, "are the loneliest guys in the world. They got no family. They don't belong no place. They make a little stake and then they go into town and blow it in, and the first thing you know they're poundin' their tail on some other ranch."

"But not us," Lennie interrupted. (This is in John Steinbeck's story *Of Mice and Men* . . . which the Book-of-the-Month Club sends its members this month.) "We got a future. Some day gonna have a little house and a couple of acres an' a cow an' some pigs, an' live off the fatta the lan'—an' have rabbits! An' I get to tend the rabbits."

It was a sort of incantation with which George, a small, quick, bony-nosed man, soothed Lennie when that huge, shapeless halfwit grew restless. They had a dream, and Lennie lived for it, and George, who loved him, knew it could never come true.

"Funny how you and him string along together," said Slim, the jerkline skinner, prince of the ranch, who could drive twenty miles with a single line to the leaders. "It seems kinda funny, a cuckoo like him and a smart little guy like you travelin' together."

"It ain't so funny," George said. "Him and me was both born in Auburn. When his Aunt Clara died Lennie just come along with me out working. Got kinda used to each other after a little while. He ain't no cuckoo. He's dumb as hell, but he ain't crazy."

"He's a nice fella," said Slim. "Guy don't need no sense to be a nice fella. Seems to me sometimes it jus' works the other way around. Take a real smart guy and he ain't hardly ever a nice fella."

Danny and Big Joe Portagee and Jesus Maria Corcoran, citizens of *Tortilla Flat,* didn't have much sense either; nor did the farmers of *The Pastures of Heaven.* They talked tough, and they had no morals,

Dust jacket for Steinbeck's 1937 novel about the friendship between a pair of migrant farmworkers (Bruccoli Clark Layman Archives)

but you ended the books loving them; and you will close this strange, tragic little idyll with a vast sense of compassion for big, dumb Lennie and for George, who knew Lennie would never get to tend those rabbits, and that if he did stroke their fur with his too strong hands he would kill them. And it is, perhaps, that compassion, even more than the perfect sense of form, which marks off John Steinbeck, artist, so sharply from all the little verbal photographers who record tough talk and snarl in books which have power without pity. The most significant things John Steinbeck has to say about his characters are never put into words; they are the overtones of which the reader is never wholly conscious—and that is art.

John Steinbeck said once that when he was six an aunt—one of his string of fabulous aunts, down in the Big Sur country, south of Salinas and Carmel—gave him a copy of Malory's *Morte d'Arthur,* and that he read it through again and again. He said, too, that though his name was German his heritage was rather Irish. I think that Celtic background lives in all his sagas of the California behind the concrete roads, as well as in that first *Cup of Gold,* where Malory shone like a star behind a mountain peak. The Celts have never lost the sense of wonder; nor has Steinbeck, though to the real smart guys who are hardly ever nice fellas it vanished long ago. It gives a richness to Celtic lives and to Steinbeck's writing.

—*New York Herald Tribune,* 25 February 1937; reprinted in *John Steinbeck: The Contemporary Reviews,* pp. 73–74

* * *

Casuals of the Road
Henry Seidel Canby

Henry Seidel Canby praised Steinbeck's realistic depiction of the farmhands' working conditions in Of Mice and Men.

Mr. Steinbeck has given us *In Dubious Battle,* a proletarian novel about the rights of laboring men, which did not please the party workers because there was as much sentiment as ideology in it. He has given us *Tortilla Flat,* a loose-hung story of California Mexicans as irresponsible as children, which did not please the serious-minded because the characters found liquorous wastefulness so perfectly delightful. Now he has written a long short story which should please everybody.

It should please everybody because it has every element of good story-telling, and it must be remembered that most of our successful novels of recent years, with any substance of art to them, have succeeded by violating most of the canons of the story-teller's art in order to emphasize ideology, the stream of consciousness, or behaviorism.

Of Mice and Men is the story of a defective. His weakness is soft things, strokable things. Upon them his great fingers sooner or later close. He does "a bad thing," he kills them. But the principle in Lennie is nevertheless the principle of good. And defective though he may be, it is his longing for living things that are lovable and to be taken care of—like rabbits—that makes articulate the longing of all the rough hands at the ranch for something of their own, land, a house, animals, perhaps a wife—something different from their wandering from lousy bunks to gilt saloons, getting nowhere, owning nothing. George, Lennie's friend, who has got him out of danger before, and Crooks, the nigger hostler, and Candy, the broken-down swamper, and even Slim, who is the just and capable man in the story, all feel it. And slowly the

plan develops. "Everybody wants a little bit of land, not much. Jus' som'thin' that was his."

This is the principle of good, even in the moron, Lennie. The principle of evil is, obscurely, in the conditions of life that keep these men bummers and vagabonds. But it focuses in the boss's vicious son Curley, the ex-prizefighter, and in Curley's wife, a poor little prostitute infected by egoism because some one once told her she could go into the pictures, and held here among these men by Curley, where all she can do is to wander about like some venereal germ looking salaciously for a victim. And she finds Lennie, trying not to do a bad thing.

The story is as simple as that, but superb in its understatements, its realisms which are used, not to illustrate behavior, but for character and situation. Indeed, there has been nothing quite so good of the kind in American writing since Sherwood Anderson's early stories. It is a limited kind, but close to the heart of the whole fiction business. If you can create a character—a fresh character, belonging to his soil and shaped by a fresh set of experiences; and if (choosing sentiment rather than the other offgivings of human nature—and sentiment is quite as real as its opposite), and if you can make that character make its own story, you are closer to the job of fiction than most writers come in our time.

I question the extravagant claims for style in the jacket blurbs of this book. The excellence of Mr. Steinbeck's book is precisely that it does not make you think of style or of "soaring beauty." Its style is right for its subject matter, and that subject matter is deeply felt, richly conceived, and perfectly ordered. That is praise enough for a book.

—*Saturday Review,* 15 (27 February 1937); reprinted in *John Steinbeck: The Contemporary Reviews,* pp. 76–77

* * *

Steinbeck Touches the Sublime

An anonymous reviewer in The San Francisco Call *called* Of Mice and Men *Steinbeck's finest work.*

Through California's fertile valleys trudge "the loneliest guys in the world."

They are cattle-ranch hands, drifting from job to job.

"They got no fam'ly. They don't belong no place. . . . They ain't got nothing to look ahead to."

But George and Lennie HAVE something to look ahead to. They dream of saving a stake, of buying a few cheap

Poster for the 1939 motion-picture adaptation of Steinbeck's 1937 novel (Bruccoli Clark Layman Archives)

acres in the hills, of having their own rooftree, of raising their own fruit and chickens and pigs and rabbits. Lennie is a simple-minded Hercules. George, wiser, watches over him, snatches Lennie from the disasters into which he blunders, keeps his dear dream alive.

The dream seems ready to come true when simple Lennie runs afoul of shrewd, bullying Curley, the boss's son, and Curley's man-chasing, painted, voluptuous, tantalizing wife. Then comes tragedy, stark, utter, smashing.

It IS tragedy, pure classic, profoundly concerned with human weakness and suffering, hurtling from heights of pity to depths of agony. And all simple, direct, mincing no word, wasting not a single magnificent brush-stroke. Call it the finest published work of one of America's most gifted writers.

—*San Francisco Call,* 7 February 1937; reprinted in *John Steinbeck: The Contemporary Reviews,* p. 77

* * *

Dust jacket for the first British edition of Steinbeck's 1937 novel (from Sotheby's New York, The Maurice F. Neville Collection of Modern Literature, November 16, 2004)

"The Tragedy of Loneliness"

First Lady Eleanor Roosevelt commented on the theme of friendship in Of Mice and Men.

. . . I have just finished a little book called *Of Mice and Men* by John Steinbeck, which a fellow columnist, Mr. Heywood Broun, reviewed in his column not long ago. My admiration for Mr. Broun leads me to want to look into anything he praises, and so I sent for the book to bring it away with me. It is beautifully written and a marvelous picture of the tragedy of loneliness.

I could see the two men, one comes across their likes in many places, not only in the West described in the book but in every part of the country. When I closed *Of Mice and Men* I could not help but think how fortunate we are when we have real friends, people we can count on and turn to and who we know are always glad to see us when we are lonely.

—"My Day," *New York World-Telegram,* 16 March 1937; reprinted in *John Steinbeck: The Contemporary Reviews,* p. 90

Reading at Random
Dorothea Brande Collins

Dorothea Brande Collins found fault with the "masculine sentimentality" of Of Mice and Men.

. . . As for *Of Mice and Men*—surely no more sentimental wallowing ever passed for a novel, or had such a welcome, as this sad tale of a huge half-wit and his cowboy protector! Mr. Steinbeck this time wrings the Tears of Things from a ten-gallon hat, and reviewers who cannot bear the mawkishness of a Milne, the crudity of a Coward, or the mysticism of a Morgan were able to take the sorrowful symmetries of a Steinbeck to their hearts and write their reviews with tears running down their cheeks.

Who does not know by this time of Lennie, who loved to stroke soft furry things, but didn't know his own strength? Of Slim, with the "God-like eyes," knight *sans peur et sans reproche* of the bunkhouse? Of George, who loved Lennie well enough to shoot him? Of "Curley's wife," that wax-dummy girl who might have come straight out of the window of a chain dress-shop, so glossy, so hard, so brightly painted—and so far from ever having drawn a breath?

Mr. Steinbeck is "economical." He is, indeed. That is perhaps the secret of his charm. I feel sure that all those reviewers who cheered so hard for *Of Mice and Men* would, if they could have been caught while still sobbing over George and Lennie, have admitted that even critics are only boys at heart, for that is just the mood that Mr. Steinbeck's work induces. So perhaps again, they would admit that the secret of his success is that a certain simple type of reader feels, when he discovers that he has foreseen correctly any movement of a story, a kind of participation in the creative act of the author. Almost any critic would admit this if the book under consideration were one of the Tarzan books, or a book by Lloyd Douglas, or any one of a dozen "popular novelists" of the sort they affect to despise, but perhaps they have not noticed that the symmetry and expectedness (or, if you prefer, read "economy") of Mr. Steinbeck's work put the average pulp-writer to shame.

If Lennie kills a mouse by stroking it, you may be sure he will unintentionally kill something larger in the same way; when you hear of Curley's wife's soft hair, "like fur," you can begin to cooperate with the author by expectation of her end. When George learns that a poor old worthless smelly dog can be dispatched easily by a shot in the back of his head, you are unwarrantably guileless if you do not suspect the manner in which Lennie will meet his death. If an old man dreams of a home, peace, and security, you may be sure that a home, peace, and security are what he will most agonizingly just miss. And so forth. You can call this sort of foreshadowing "economy" if it pleases you; but if "economy" is the word you choose you should abandon the word "obvious" hereafter and forever.

It may be some time before the current vogue for Steinbeck passes. Masculine sentimentality, particularly when it masquerades as toughness, is a little longer in being seen through than the feminine or the inclusively human variety. Undoubtedly there are plenty who would deny, even today, that *The Sun Also Rises* and *What Price Glory?* are (although far more distinguished) prototypes of *Of Mice and Men*. Surely it should not be too hard to find the soft spots where the decay shows: the romantic overestimation of the role of friendship, the wax-figure women, bright, hard, treacherous, unreal—whether a Lady Brett, the French girl behind the lines, or "Curley's wife," these are all essentially hateful women, women from whom it is a virtue to flee to masculine companionship. There was certainly a sort of stag-party hysteria and uproar about the approval we have been hearing for this padded short story about underdogs and animals, bunkhouses and bathos, which has seldom risen so high since "Wait for baby!" soared over the footlights. . . . Ah, I was forgetting Mr. Chips.

—*American Review*, 9 (April 1937); reprinted in *John Steinbeck: The Contemporary Reviews*, pp. 90–91

The Red Pony (1937)

Dreams and Tragedies in Salinas Hills
J.H.C.

The Red Pony *(1937) was a sequence of three related stories, "The Gift," "The Great Mountains," and "The Promise." They were later published as part of the collection* The Long Valley *(1938) and in an expanded edition of* The Red Pony *(1945) including a fourth story, "The Leader of the People."*

If American collectors know one-tenth as much as we believe they do the entire edition of Steinbeck's *Red Pony* is exhausted. The publisher has sold out his stock, and it is to be hoped that Los Angeles admirers of this powerful California writer have not failed to secure their copies.

There are three stories printed between the elegant covers of this volume: "The Gift," "The Mountains" [*sic*], "The Promise." They are episodes in the life of Jody, a 10-year-old farm boy from up Salinas way. Jody had dreams and they quivered into life over far horizons. Then Jody got a red pony, and Billy Buck, who knew all about horses, taught him how to take care of it. But Jody's faith in Billy was shaken when, in spite of everything, the pony died; all because Billy was not a rain prophet. That tale is followed by a touching interlude concerning the fate of old men and horses. The last story shows how Jody got another pony—at a price.

Once upon a time Mr. Aristotle laid down the rules for writing masterpieces. Whether he got it out of Aristotle or not, Steinbeck knows the rules. He knows what he intends to do and does it in the simplest and most effective fashion. He knows life at both ends and the middle. He grips your heart and satisfies your mind—if you have one. If you have not, it makes no difference, he takes hold of you anyway.

—*Los Angeles Times*, 10 October 1937; reprinted in *John Steinbeck: The Contemporary Reviews*, pp. 100–101

* * *

Steinbeck Inflation

In reviewing The Red Pony *for* Time, *an anonymous reviewer commented on the high price of the limited-edition volume.*

For a parallel to the inflation that has skyrocketed the value of John Steinbeck first editions, bibliophiles must turn to the classic rise in the price of calves' liver, once given away in most butcher shops, currently selling at 85¢ a lb. Distributed free to Publisher Covici-Friede's friends last Christmas, Author Steinbeck's *St. Katy the Virgin*, a short story, is now quoted at $10. Published last fortnight in an edition limited to 699 autographed, de luxe copies, Novelist Steinbeck's latest work, *The Red Pony,* was quoted at $10 a copy, and no man knew where it would go from there.

Some readers, baffled by the famine-price set on this slim, 81-page volume (all the more remarkable in view of Steinbeck's proletarian themes), may jump to the wrong conclusion that *The Red Pony* contains erotic or esoteric matter too caviarish for the general. On the contrary, *The Red Pony* is neither scandalous nor abstruse but of an innocence that almost qualifies it for juvenile readers. It consists of three episodes based on Author Steinbeck's youth. Central character is a healthy, shy, tow-headed, 10-year-old farm boy named Jody Tiflin. Given a red pony colt by his father, coached in its training by the hired hand, Jody is in perpetual seventh heaven except when he is in school. A few days before the pony is ready to ride, it catches pneumonia, sneaks away to die in the woods, where Jody is found beside the corpse, hammering insanely on the long-since smashed head of a buzzard that was too slow to escape his wild grief.

Most tenuous, but also the most interesting in showing how the early Steinbeck twig of romanticism was bent is the second episode: Jody who feels deeply the mystery of the distant California Sierras, thinks he has the answer when he watches an old Mexican going off into the mountains to die.

Last episode relates how Jody got his second pony. In return for Jody's putting in a summer's hard work, Farmer Tiflin lays out $5 to breed their own mare Nellie. Jody dedicates himself completely to Nellie's prenatal care, to giving his father more than his five-dollars' worth. When complications develop at the delivery, the hired hand kills Nellie with a hammer, and in a gory Cesarean delivers Jody his promised colt.

California-born (1900) [*sic*], big, blond, blue-eyed, slow-spoken John Ernest [*sic*] Steinbeck has been a farm hand, hod carrier, caretaker, chemist and painter's apprentice, itinerant newspaper-man. At Stanford University off and on for six years, he treated it as a sort of public library where he read only what took his fancy: physics, biology, philosophy, history. Indifferent to most fiction, he thinks Thackeray passable, cannot stomach Proust because he "wrote his sickness, and I don't like sick writing." He is dead set against publicity, photographs, speeches, believes "they do you damage." Now living in Los Gatos, Calif., since publication of his best-selling *Of Mice and Men* (167,000 copies), Mr. Steinbeck can well afford to abandon an erstwhile $25-a-month budget which he and his tall, brunette wife Carol supplemented by fishing, not for fun, from their own launch in Monterey Bay.

    —Time, 29 (11 October 1937); reprinted in *John Steinbeck: The Contemporary Reviews,* pp. 102–103

Of Mice and Men: The Play

Of Mice and Men
Margaret Shedd

Margaret Shedd reviewed the stage version of Of Mice and Men, *which Steinbeck completed with the help of playwright-director George S. Kaufman in August 1937. After a summer run in San Francisco, the play opened on Broadway on 23 November 1937.*

San Francisco had two world premieres this summer. That both plays will be headlined fall openings in New York is not the point to be recorded here, which is, instead, the almost extravagant difference between Jean Giraudoux's *Amphitryon 38* . . . and the production with which this review is concerned: John Steinbeck's *Of Mice and Men* presented by the San Francisco Theatre Union.

Whatever the cause—ingenuousness, curiosity, lust for contemporaneousness of scene,—one expects a great deal from a play about the living, wandering men who plant crops they never see harvested, and harvest where they have not seen the planting, in a soil which refuses them roots, men who are lonely beyond our natural heritage of loneliness. All the exciting dramatic realities are in the theme, and when the curtain goes up on *Of Mice and Men* the play seems authentic: characters who demand we learn all about them, situations which we feel impelled to follow through to a consummation or an intensity of non-consummation which is the same thing. A simple background of Santa Clara hills and a nonexistent river in the orchestra pit, beside which Lennie and George lie down to sleep, give promise of evoking what is inherent in the tragic saga of the itinerant agricultural worker.

But *Of Mice and Men,* in its present form, does not tell that saga; it does no more than block in the tantalizing outlines, with too much sentimental detail of rabbits and murders and with gaping omissions. Why? Maybe the answer to that question would also answer the "why" of the whole socially-minded theatre.

The San Francisco Theatre Union's production is good! It is forthright, giving off a clear integrity not easy to overrate. The group draws its personnel from workers; rehearsal must come in their spare time. This means that several months are spent on every play, and so the actor has, perforce, a chance for slow identifications with his part. Combined with this impression of growth is a striking directness of attack which may be explained partly by the fact that bindlestiffs are familiar people to the garage repairman, milkman, store salesperson, who make up the cast; no doubt many of these actors themselves originated in agricultural communities.

The Theatre Union was justly appreciative of the opportunity to predate the rest of the world with *Of Mice and Men*. Long before the book was out the Union knew that Steinbeck was living and working in one of the agricultural areas. All intelligent Californians realize that history is being made in those centres. The Theatre Union, whose administration has been consistently clear and direct, believed it should have plays about local current history. Wellman Farley, the president, said this to John Steinbeck and forthwith Steinbeck handed him an as yet unpublished manuscript, *Of Mice and Men*.

There is something nice about that transaction; one dislikes to be querulous about the result of it. Steinbeck, I believe, made no pretense that this was a critic-proof, completed play: the six scenes are taken verbatim from the novel. So it would be unjust to criticize the play, as given in San Francisco, from a structural technical angle. Let that be done when New York sees its version. But a non-technical analysis is integral to the western production because here is an excellent left-wing group with competent actors and direction, situated in what is probably the best theatre town in America, which opens its

new playhouse with a production written by a young man whose novel on the same theme holds for months the top spot on best-selling lists and who, at the same time, is admittedly social minded. And the play is a success, favorably received by good audiences. It sounds like the dream come true of a real people's theatre. But what?

Of Mice and Men could have been a character study of eight or ten persons in relation to each other, a slow digestive process for the audience, at the end of which Lennie and Candy and Slim and all would have been absorbed, understood, pitied, loved, hated. Or it could have been essentially a study of Lennie, the pathetic, destructive village idiot, all too common and all too misunderstood. Or it could have been a high-powered tragedy on almost classical lines. That does not exhaust the list of possibilities for the play, but in any one of these forms it would have been a social document with a punch far greater than it now carries. As it stands it looks like a social document (a highly personalized one), for the negative reason that it doesn't look like anything else. And the violences, which are probably what have sold the book to a majority of its readers, appear to have been

Burgess Meredith as George and Lon Chaney Jr. as Lennie in the 1939 motion-picture adaptation of Of Mice and Men
(MOMA/Film Stills Archive; from Joseph R. Millichap, Steinbeck and Film, *1983;*
Thomas Cooper Library, University of South Carolina)

thrown in for high seasoning. The result is, to say the least, confusing.

For instance, at what appears to be the climax of the play—that is if you consider that the theme is the stiff's right to be a man—a point in Scene 3 where George, Candy and Lennie are pyramiding up their hope for a little ranch of their own, a point which has been built to a fine natural tight excitement by the audience's intense desire that these men shall be different from the other fifty thousand and really get their ranch, abruptly the tension is ruined by an extraneous remark of Candy's, apropos of his dog, that he hopes when he gets old somebody will take him out and shoot him too. The remark is not in character. Candy on the whole is excellently developed and he is well played by Carl Anderson. But no actor can compete with the author if he decides to walk into a play and interrupt him. The timing and movement of this particular scene have been meticulously rehearsed; but eternal rehearsal could never have given rhythm to it because the rhythm is not there. And that in turn is because there is no basic dramatic pattern there.

If this sounds like harsh criticism of small detail I must answer that there is no criticism too severe for an author who, through confusion of purpose, destroys epic material. Precisely this happens over and over in *Of Mice and Men*.

The question "why" repeats itself often to the audience mind, because adequate motivation is not furnished. The very core of the play, Lennie's obsession for stroking mice, is an example of the confusion and of the lack of motivation. It is widely known that many itinerants carry small animals with them on their travels—rats, dogs, rabbits: this has in it the raw element of human interest. It is also a matter of common knowledge that a great many bindlestiffs are feeble-minded; there is certainly the raw element of human tragedy in that. But for an author merely to throw together these two facts to make a curiosity is not enough. Steinbeck at no point establishes whether Lennie's destruction of the animals he strokes is a matter of abnormality or of accident. He implies it is accident, which, happening so often, is not convincing. The audience assumes it is sadism and gets a little excitement out of that. Actually there is no excuse for this confusion. If Lennie is to be any sort of universal symbol, anything more than an isolated monstrosity, and if the play is to be more than a reporter's notebook, then all questions of behavior psychology must be settled before they arise. "Strange as it seems" is no longer satisfactory predication for serious writing.

And always the "why" comes up. Why doesn't George leave Lennie to his fate? For the clumsy, pitiful fool to be pursued and killed by such a bully as Curley is the way the cards might really fall. When George shoots Lennie it needs explaining, and to watch that scene is to witness something shocking, not conclusive. One doubts that George could have done it, because his author has been to some pains to show how beaten and frustrated he is: George who abandons the plan for a home although the money for it is still available; George who, after numerous allusions to his certainty that they will get into trouble at this ranch, has still stayed on there; George who goes off of a Saturday evening and leaves Lennie alone with Curley's wife (that the murder does not happen that night is merely another of Steinbeck's vagaries). In fact most of the events seem vagrant. This should be tragedy, but it has no stature. Its authenticity lies in its small talk, not in the consistent development of a theme.

The best projected character is George, the little man, played by Sal Pizzo, who successfully suggests the unwilling wanderer's galling helplessness and at the same time his essential manliness. Wellman Farley, as Lennie, keeps the simpleton hero too much on the one note of pitiful, clumsy childishness; but that, as well as the limitations of the character of Curley's wife (which has in it the makings of a great acting part) are dictated by the author. Perhaps Farley in the one case and Alice Hult in the other do well to keep the motivation in simple channels.

The direction by Florence Hagee shows a consistent effort to organize the play into bounds of some sort, with the curious result of creating time and again an unfulfilled prediction that just around the next corner the play will solidify, take form. Mrs. Hagee's direction is, in effect, of the play as it might have been rather than as it is.

Perhaps what the proletarian theatre wants is not literature but photographic reality of scene, a factual presentation of working class life. T. K. Whipple's recent analysis, *Literature in the Doldrums,* would indicate exactly that. And yet the Theatre Union's production of *Of Mice and Men* indicates something else. I think the Union hoped it had the makings of a great play, not just another tract.

Their painstaking effort to suggest a Chekhovian texture, would show that: the magnificent weaving in of incidental background events, references to past detail which seem insignificant but which are never accidental nor wasteful.

The fifth scene of *Of Mice and Men* should have been—but is not—such a delight. Here we have Lennie, who has just fondled his puppy to death (and whom by now we know quite well) and the girl, Curley's wife, about whom we have accidentally learned a good deal. Up to this point the story of the girl has been nicely suggested: there is much tragic humor in the character of this little trollop who thinks her husband isn't a nice man, who was a natural for the movies but didn't get in them because her old lady must have stole the letter from the guy in Hollywood.

These two—both dull as to wits and with a desperate need for communication; and the only communication there can seem to be between them results in the destruction of both. The scene climaxes in the girl's murder, of course, and in its way it is an absorbing scene. It is at the same time a denunciation of its author. It becomes at once apparent that the background, as essential as the seen happenings, is only an accident. The impression given is that Steinbeck had to have a girl for Lennie to kill, and in a workmanlike desire for verisimilitude he knew the girl had to have a background, just as she had to have soft hair; so he looked in his notebook and pulled out a girl, probably an actual girl he had talked to.

But this real girl leaps out of the notebook, and the fugitive but moving events of her background completely dwarf the events we see. That she is choked to death seems beside the point.

Let the girl live and speak her real piece! Let Lennie live! Why does their author hurry to put them under the ground? Or if he must kill them let him at least not do it wantonly! He does not know what dynamite he has in those characters. Nor does the so-called left-wing theatre know what it has. And exactly because, in the case of the left-wing theatre, it does not know what it wants.

. . . The one thing the left theatre knows it wants, and gets, is "agit prop" plays. It does them well, witness *Waiting for Lefty*. But if it chooses to be anything more than a high-powered propaganda device for class consciousness it must go farther than that. It must want great plays. When they appear it may not be able to produce them adequately but it must recognize them. If it does not, no one will, because the modern great play, when it does appear, is going to break molds, be searching to express a new human consciousness.

Of Mice and Men is certainly not a great play, although, just as certainly, it has in it the raw material of one. The very fact that the San Francisco Theatre Union produced the play is an occasion for good cheer. And yet, even with clarification of its dramatic cloudiness, *Of Mice and Men* would still be only a study of men, not of classes. Is it possible that the left wing theatre really wants a play like that?

–*Theatre Arts*, 21 (October 1937); reprinted in *John Steinbeck: The Contemporary Reviews*, pp. 109–112

* * *

Theatre: A Completely Satisfying American Play

The anonymous reviewer in Literary Digest *had high praise for the stage version of* Of Mice and Men.

A great play has reached Broadway–a play of lowly, cast-off men, whose stark emotions have tamed testy critics and tired audiences into stunned reverence. It is the dramatization of John Steinbeck's best seller, *Of*

Mice and Men. The millions whom the novel hypnotized have but one question: Does the play make George and Lennie and their friends real with the mighty brutality and overpowering tenderness of the book? It does.

The hulking, stupid, well-meaning brute, Lennie, creates the situation in his first speeches. "Guys like us," he observes to George, "guys like us what work on ranches are the loneliest guys in the world. They got no family. They don't belong no place."

Then, breaking off with the look of a trusting animal, he says: "With us it ain't like that. We got a future. We got somebody who gives a damn about us. An' why? Because I got you to look after me and you got me to look after you, and that's why."

The tone is set. With that Mr. Steinbeck and his actors proceed relentlessly to unfold the tragedy of loneliness that errs unwittingly in its immense craving for affection. Lennie wants love and beauty so desperately that he takes a field mouse and the stroking of his giant hands kills it. Lennie loves the warmth of young animals, so he nestles a puppy until his caresses choke it. Lennie worships beauty in women, and it is natural to him to run his hands through a woman's silken hair. But she (the boss's son's wife, played by Claire Luce) is a harlot. When she screams, suspecting the usual thing, her screams terrify him. He tries to keep her quiet. Lennie is a big and stupid man. He doesn't know his small gesture has crushed her to death.

This is the point toward which the play drives mercilessly. George, Lennie's small, smart friend who has always cared for him and gotten him out of scrapes, has but one course. He spares Lennie a vengeful lynching by shooting him in the back while he talks happily of the rabbit farm George has promised to get them. A rock would crack at that scene.

The scenes take place in and around a California ranch. Men come when there is work, move on to the next spot when the job is done. Their language is lusty and forthright, but never obscene. In the words of Richard Watts, Jr., *New York Herald Tribune* critic, "there is no line in it that does not possess the true ring of authenticity." It is a play for adults, not for children or bigots seeking the secret thrill of naughty words.

A fair share of praise goes to the versatile and prodigious George S. Kaufman, for his directing. He has stressed every chance for realism. Wallace Ford, once of Hollywood and *The Informer*, fires George with the deep and unaccountable friendship which caused him to waste his life protecting Lennie. The robust, kindly mule skinner, the disillusioned Negro who reads books in the barn because the whites won't have him, and particularly Candy (played by John F. Hamilton) are fine and moving characterizations. Broderick Crawford, son of the famed comedienne, Helen Broderick, takes what must be the most difficult acting assignment in recent years, as Lennie, and makes it a creation of stature. There would be no play if Lennie lost the affection of the audience.

The author, John Steinbeck, is thirty-five, lives in California with his wife. As a boy he worked on ranches with these very tramp laborers. He came to New York in 1920 as a reporter, ended up carrying bricks, and went back west to be a watchman.

Of Mice and Men has been justly described as "the first completely satisfying American play of the season."
—*Literary Digest*, 124 (18 December 1937); reprinted in *John Steinbeck: The Contemporary Reviews*, pp. 121–122

* * *

Steinbeck to George S. Kaufman, November 1937

After reading reviews of Of Mice and Men, *Steinbeck wrote Kaufman from Los Gatos praising his direction of the play.*

Dear George:

As the reviews come in it becomes more and more apparent that you have done a great job. I knew you would of course but there is a curious gap between the thing in your hand and the thing set down and you've jumped that gap. It's a strange kind of humbling luck we have. Carol and I have talked of it a number of times. That we—obscure people out of a place no one ever heard of—should have our first play directed and produced by the greatest director of our time—will not bear too close inspection for fear we may catch the gods of fortune at work and catching them, anger them so they hate us. Already I have made propitiation—thrown my dear ring in the sea and I hope no big fish brings it back to me.

To say thank you is ridiculous for you can't thank a man for good work any more than you can thank him for being himself. But one can be very glad he is himself and that is what we are—very glad you are George Kaufman.

It doesn't matter a damn whether this show runs a long time. It came to life for one night anyway, and really to life, and that's more than anyone has any right to hope.

Sometimes in working, the people in my head become much realler than I am. I have had letters. It seems that for two hours you made your play far more real than its audience and only the play existed. I wish I could transport into some mathematical equation, my feeling, so that it might be a communication unmistakable and unchanging.

And that's all.
John
—*Steinbeck: A Life in Letters*, pp. 144–145

* * *

CAST OF CHARACTERS

This play was first presented by Sam H. Harris at the Music Box Theatre on the evening of November 23, 1937, with the following cast:

GEORGE .... Wallace Ford
LENNIE .... Broderick Crawford
CANDY .... John F. Hamilton
THE BOSS .... Thomas Findlay
CURLEY .... ~~Tom~~ Sam Byrd
CURLEY'S WIFE .... Claire Luce
SLIM .... Will Geer
CARLSON .... Charles Slattery
WHIT .... Walter Baldwin
CROOKS .... Leigh Whipper

Staged by George S. Kaufman
Settings by Donald Oenslager

Signed cast list for Of Mice and Men, *the Broadway production of which premiered on 23 November 1937 (from Sotheby's New York,* The Maurice F. Neville Collection of Modern Literature, *November 16, 2004)*

"Play Seems Lousier Every Reading"

Jack Kirkland, who had adapted Erskine Caldwell's novel Tobacco Road *(1932) for the stage in 1934, took out an option on* Tortilla Flat. *When he finished his dramatization of the book, he sent it to Los Gatos for Steinbeck's approval. On 8 December 1937 Steinbeck wired Annie Laurie Williams, the agent who handled movie and drama contracts for McIntosh and Otis, asking if she could get Kirkland to come out to the West to discuss the adaptation. Kirkland's version of* Tortilla Flat *opened on Broadway in January 1938 but ran for only a few performances.*

PLEASE QUERY KIRKLAND REGARDING POSSIBILITY OF COMING WEST TO DISCUSS TORTILLA STOP WILL HELP HIM TWO WEEKS IN REWRITING BETWEEN US PLAY SEEMS LOUSIER EVERY READING DIALOGUE IS OFF TONE VULGARITY CREEPS IN PLAY CHANGES TEMPO AND IN MANY CASES IS DULL BE DISCREETLY PRESSING AND PLEASE WIRE HIS ANSWER

JOHN
—*Steinbeck: A Life in Letters*, p. 149

Steinbeck to Claire Luce, 1938

After Williams reported that Claire Luce, who played Curley's wife in Of Mice and Men, *was concerned about her interpretation of her role, Steinbeck wrote the actress to explain the character.*

Dear Miss Luce:

Annie Laurie says you are worried about your playing of the part of Curley's wife although from the reviews it appears that you are playing it marvelously. I am deeply grateful to you and to the others in the cast for your feeling about the play. You have surely made it much more than it was by such a feeling.

About the girl—I don't know of course what you think about her, but perhaps if I should tell you a little about her as I know her, it might clear your feeling about her.

She grew up in an atmosphere of fighting and suspicion. Quite early she learned that she must never trust any one but she was never able to carry out what she learned. A natural trustfulness broke through constantly and every time it did, she got hurt. Her moral training was most rigid. She was told over and over that she must remain a virgin because that was the only way she could get a husband. This was harped on so often that it became a fixation. It would have been impossible to seduce her. She had only that one thing to sell and she knew it.

Now, she was trained by threat not only at home but by other kids. And any show of fear or weakness brought an instant persecution. She learned she had to be hard to cover her fright. And automatically she became hardest when she was most frightened. She is a nice, kind girl and not a floozy. No man has ever considered her as anything except a girl to try to make. She has never talked to a man except in the sexual fencing conversation. She is not highly sexed particularly but knows instinctively that if she is to be noticed at all, it will be because some one finds her sexually desirable.

As to her actual sexual life—she has had none except with Curley and there has probably been no consummation there since Curley would not consider her gratification and would probably be suspicious if she had any. Consequently she is a little starved. She knows utterly nothing about sex except the mass of misinformation girls tell one another. If anyone—a man or a woman—ever gave her a break—treated her like a person—she would be a slave to that person. Her craving for contact is immense but she, with her background, is incapable of conceiving any contact without some sexual context. With all this—if you knew her, if you could ever break down the thousand little defenses she has built up, you would find a nice person, an honest person, and you would end up by loving her. But such a thing can never happen.

I hope you won't think I'm preaching. I've known this girl and I'm just trying to tell you what she is like. She is afraid of everyone in the world. You've known girls like that, haven't you? You can see them in Central Park on a hot night. They travel in groups for protection. They pretend to be wise and hard and voluptuous.

I have a feeling that you know all this and that you are doing all this. Please forgive me if I seem to intrude on your job. I don't intend to and I am only writing this because Annie Laurie said you wondered about the girl. It's a devil of a hard part. I am very happy that you have it.
                                        Sincerely,
                                        John Steinbeck
                —Steinbeck: A Life in Letters, pp. 154–155

* * *

Drama and Dramatists
Isaac Goldberg

Reviewer Isaac Goldberg called Of Mice and Men *"one of the most important dramas to have reached our stage in many years."*

Not being of that gentry whose opinions, to them, are sacred, I can with the greater ease discuss deviations from those opinions. I am immensely interested in the differences that divide the critics in the

Claire Luce as Curley's wife and Broderick Crawford as Lennie in Of Mice and Men *(photograph by Peter Stackpole; from William McPheron,* John Steinbeck: From Salinas to Stockholm, *2000; Special Collections, Thomas Cooper Library, University of South Carolina)*

case of John Steinbeck's play, *Of Mice and Men*. Gentlemen such as Messrs. Krutch and Gassner, for example, are among those to whom I always look for stimulating discussions of the current drama. When one of them finds the Steinbeck play "literary" in the bad sense of that term and when the other finds a character such as Lennie too abnormal, too psychopathic, for the dignity of tragedy, it is to me, as a critic, interesting and even important. Agreement with one's own opinion is, naturally, flattering; moreover, it soothes. Disagreement, however, is stimulating, and by no means always in the disagreeable sense.

My feeling about *Of Mice and Men* is that it is one of the most important dramas to have reached our stage in many years. I can see, I can feel, the force of Mr. Krutch's and Mr. Gassner's respective objections. I can appreciate, from both the book and the actual production, those elements of the piece that lend themselves to sensationalism and to false emphasis. (Are these not often the same thing?) And yet (to underscore a more violent disagreement with virtually the whole sanhedrin of New York critics), as in the case of Ben Hecht's unlucky *To Quito and Back,* I feel that the faults are far outweighed by the virtues. In the case of Steinbeck's play, indeed, I feel that we have, with whatever reservations may be made, a true tragedy.

As I see it, *Of Mice and Men* is a fable of human aloneness, complicated by human incapacity and misunderstanding. There is not a truly "evil" person in the story; there is not a truly "evil" motive. All the harm that is done comes, not from human perversity, but from human ineptitude. The embrace of love becomes the embrace of strangulation. Wilde, writing his ballad in Reading Gaol, knew that fatal caress. The case of Lennie is, in its way, a pathological symbol. It reaches deep down into the human psyche, however. It has its patent reference to the sanest of us, just as the criminal in the cell has his patent reference to the most law-abiding.

For these people, even for the blusteringly self-revealing Curley and for his wife whose frustrated tenderness takes the form of an inciting snarl, one feels a sad pity. The end of the play is foreshadowed at the very beginning, not only in the structural skill with which the action is articulated, but in the impossible goal that these derelicts have all set for themselves: a goal that becomes communal in its aims as it becomes, in the end, communal in its defeat. It is not strange that Lennie's vision of a Utopia should infect the others. They all have a touch of Lennie in them. So—and this is one of the points—have you and I. It is, to me, a serious mistake to sit back from these misfits in the belief that they are too far removed from us to have relevancy. This is a cycle of human destruction—destruction of others, and of self. A theologian might say that each wanted love, but wanted it not enough, or wanted not enough of it. A psychologist might say that they feared love too much. They are at that stage in civilization when the stranger is the enemy because he has not yet proved himself the

Steinbeck's inscription to Crawford on the free front endpaper in Of Mice and Men: A Play in Three Acts, *1937 (from* Sotheby's New York, The Maurice F. Neville Collection of Modern Literature, *November 16, 2004)*

friend. It is a stage—witness Europe and Asia and the United States—that we have not yet outgrown. But surely no one who cannot forget the action of the children in Lawrence's *Sons and Lovers,* when they hasten the death of their doomed mother, should misunderstand the end of Steinbeck's tale, when George kills Lennie. It is possible to kill from love as well as from hate. George is more articulate than Lennie, but almost as confused. And every other man in the action is quite as guilty as George—just as guilty as if he, and not George, had pulled the trigger. Just as guilty, and, who knows, just as merciful.

There is, in the tale as it unfolds a healing terror, a scarifying pity. Although the play takes place upon the deceptive plane of reality, it does achieve, for many spectators, and with a cast of humble toilers, that tragic effect which the Greeks achieved with a cast of gods and almost superhuman beings. These lowly figures tread their way to a predestined doom as surely as any Oedipus, any Electra. Not since the coming of O'Neill has any American playwright so infused his drama with a seemingly inevitable catastrophe.

I am not a box-office critic, nor do I take it that one of the functions of criticism is prophecy. But my eye is upon Mr. John Steinbeck. And some of my hope.

—One Act Play, 1 (January 1938); reprinted in *John Steinbeck: The Contemporary Reviews,* pp. 122–123

New York Drama Critics' Circle Award

Upon learning that Of Mice and Men *had won the New York Drama Critics Circle Award, Steinbeck sent a telegram to the Critics' Circle on 23 April 1938.*

GENTLEMEN: I HAVE ALWAYS CONSIDERED CRITICS AS AUTHORS NATURAL ENEMIES NOW I FEEL VERY MILLENIAL [*sic*] BUT A LITTLE TIMID TO BE LYING DOWN WITH THE LION THIS DISTURBANCE OF THE NATURAL BALANCE MIGHT CAUSE A PLAGUE OF PLAYWRIGHTS I AM HIGHLY HONORED BY YOUR GOOD OPINION BUT MY EGOTISTICAL GRATIFICATION IS RUINED BY A SNEAKING SUSPICION THAT GEORGE KAUFMAN AND THE CAST DESERVE THEM MORE THAN I. I DO HOWEVER TAKE THE RESPONSIBILITY OF THANKING YOU.

JOHN STEINBECK
—Steinbeck: A Life in Letters, p. 164

The Long Valley (1938)

The Steinbeck Country
Elinor Davis

In reviewing Steinbeck's 1938 story collection, The Long Valley, *Elinor Davis singled out the three stories published the previous year in the first edition of* The Red Pony.

Steinbeck is one of the few American writers who refuse to be backseat-driven by success; he writes what he wants to write, instead of letting the expectations of his public push him into a groove. Yet in this collection of fifteen short stories there is less variety than you would expect, after his last three novels; which may be just as well. The one distinctly off-the-trail story of the lot is a burlesque hagiography, which might better have been left in private circulation. The others all deal with what will soon be known as the Steinbeck country, the regions around Monterey and Salinas, which seems to be populated by suppressed husbands, frustrated wives, brides who cheat unless you horsewhip them, old men who are no good any more, sex-starved spinsters of good family who fool around with Chinamen and then hang themselves, etc. About the only people in the book who are pointed in my direction are a couple of communists who go looking for martyrdom under orders; and even them Steinbeck regards with a faintly ironic eye.

However, if that is what he sees that is what he has to write about; and here is certainly some of the best writing of the past decade. Outside of one or two stories you won't find an ounce of fat in his style; and you could pick forty paragraphs out of this volume that would be fit to appear as models in any textbook of composition. Steinbeck makes his country live and the people live as part of it, as much a part as the horned toads or the buzzards. It is not so much the malice of man that gets them down as Nature, internal and external; the pity you feel for them is the pity you would feel for an animal trapped and doomed. But Steinbeck is not too proud to pity them himself; and if his vision is perhaps limited in scope there are no blind spots in the areas where it operates. He sees clear down through these people, and reproduces them in as many dimensions as they have.

Preferences among the fifteen stories will differ, of course; but perhaps most readers would agree that the best are the three episodes in a boy's life which have already been published, in a limited edition, as *The Red Pony.* The same boy and his grandfather, a wornout pioneer to whose repetitious reminiscences people no

Dust jacket for the first edition of Steinbeck's 1938 story collection (from Robert B. Harmon, The Collectible John Steinbeck, *1986; Thomas Cooper Library, University of South Carolina)*

longer want to listen, appears in "The Leader of the People." How much autobiography there may or may not be in all this does not matter; those stories are packed with truth, that would have been just as true in the Stone Age. Notable among the others are "The Raid"–how it feels to be beaten up by vigilantes, and to have to wait for it; "The Vigilante"–after-effects of a lynching on a member of the mob; and "Johnny Bear," in which a half-wit with a trick of reproducing over-heard conversations catalyzes both the good and evil emotion of a whole community. A collection of short stories does not always add much to the stature of a successful novelist; but *The Long Valley* leaves Steinbeck still the best prospect in American letters. . . .

–*Saturday Review,* 18 (24 September 1938); reprinted in *John Steinbeck: The Contemporary Reviews,* p. 139

The Grapes of Wrath (1939)

Steinbeck to Elizabeth Otis, 1938

When Steinbeck sent the complete manuscript of The Grapes of Wrath *(1939) to Elizabeth Otis of McIntosh and Otis, he requested that the words and music of Julia Ward Howe's "The Battle Hymn of the Republic" (1862) be included in the published book. The title of the novel is taken from the first verse of the song.*

Dear Elizabeth:

This afternoon by express we are sending you the manuscript of The Grapes of Wrath. We hope to God you like it. Will you let us know first that you received it and second what you think of it. I forgot to put the enclosed in [the words and music of "The Battle Hymn of the Republic"]. I should like the whole thing to go in as a page at the beginning. All the verses and the music. This is one of the great songs of the world, and as you

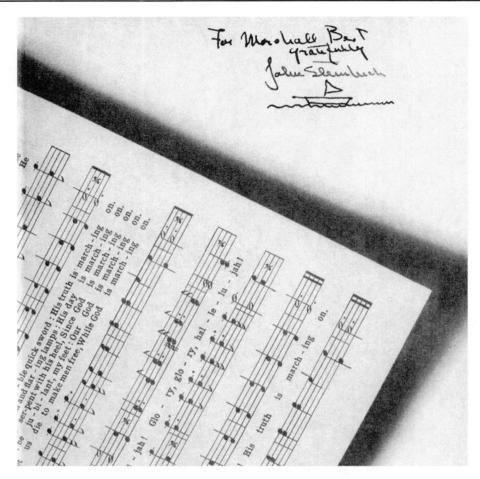

Inscribed free front endpaper from the first edition of The Grapes of Wrath, *with words and music of Julia Ward Howe's "The Battle Hymn of the Republic" (1862), the source for the title of Steinbeck's novel. The inscription is to Marshall Best, editor in chief at Viking (from Sotheby's New York,* The Maurice F. Neville Collection of Modern Literature, *November 16, 2004).*

read the book you will realize that the words have a special meaning in this book. And I should like the music to be put there in case anyone, any one forgets. The title, Battle Hymn of the Republic, in itself has a special meaning in the light of this book.

Anyway there it is, and we will be hanging on your opinions because we know so well they will be honest and untouched by publicity.

Love to all of you,

John

—Steinbeck: A Life in Letters, p. 173

* * *

Books of the Times

Charles Poore

In one of the earliest reviews of The Grapes of Wrath, *Charles Poore praised Steinbeck's remarkable sympathy with and understanding for the characters in the novel.*

Their covered wagons are antique jalopies and the gold of their Eldorado hangs on trees in California orchards. If they lived a hundred years ago—these salty, brave and enormously human wanderers of John Steinbeck's magnificent new novel, *The Grapes of Wrath*—we should call them heroic pioneers. We should admire their courageous will to survive in spite of nature's elements and man's inhumanity. We should relish their Rabelaisian candor, their shrewdness and their humor. We should undoubtedly say their spirit made this country great.

Well, we can admire those great-hearted qualities all the more, knowing that they belong to contemporary Americans, and that novelists need not go to the past to find them.

For within recent years thousands upon thousands of people like the Joads in *The Grapes of Wrath* have been rolling westward, carrying all they own in perilous cars of strange vintages, hungry, restless, the children riding on top of the tents and the blankets and the cooking pots, their desperate elders hanging on wherever they can. . . .

Out of the dramatic elementals of this great American migration (there is, by the way, an excellently illustrated article about it in this month's *Fortune)* Mr. Steinbeck has created his best novel. It is far better than *Of Mice and Men,* where the overmeticulously orchestrated theme of loneliness gave certain artificiality to the story's course. Here, his counterpoint of the general and the particular—the full sweep of the migration and the personal affairs of all the Joads—has the true air of inevitability.

Mr. Steinbeck did not have to create a world for the Joads. It is there. What he did have to do is to make you see it and feel it and understand it. And he does this in the one way a novelist can give life and truth to his story: through the creation of character. It is in Tom Joad (who learns at last what Harry Morgan learned in *To Have and Have Not,* that standing alone will do nothing much to move impressively united opponents) that the story makes Mr. Steinbeck's eloquently presented point.

But our belief depends, in great measure, upon our belief in them all—from the rare and garrulous grandfather who dies on the way, or Rose of Sharon, whose child is born much later, after her whippersnapper of a husband has deserted, or sin-haunted Uncle John, or the mother, who is the best man of the lot, or the father, who is slowly losing his grip, or Casy Strange, the ex-preacher who joins their caravan for a time, or Al, the born mechanic, or Noah, who makes his separate peace—to Ruthie and Winfield, the two most completely credible children we've seen in any recent novel.

For, as MacLeish once said in a totally different connection, out of the vigor of emotions may well come a new art: "But to mistake the art for the emotions is to perform no service to criticism. Only the art matters. The emotion lights the stove." And Mr. Steinbeck's triumph is that he has created, out of a remarkable sympathy and understanding, characters whose full and complete actuality will withstand any scrutiny.

When his characters hold the stage the story has a superb drive and force. It is only in his commentary on the migration, the chapters interleaving the story of the Joads, that he is apt to be a little too hortatory. Here, in a grave, stately prose that seems to be half Jacobean and half Hemingway, he occasionally obscures the story with the moral—which is better borne out in the lives of his characters.

One believes in them absolutely because one sees every side of their natures. And their natures are shown in every possible kind of test and confrontation, in words that can offend only the squeamish and in scenes you will never forget.

The most memorable scene is the last one. . . .

Everything in the book leads up to it. From the time when Tom Joad (who'd been in jail for killing a man who had planned to kill him) came home to the Oklahoma farm, where his family was getting ready to go in search of the land of oranges and grapes and promise, to the book's ending the march of events is as relentless as it is absorbing to read. The scenes along Route 66, the wanderer's trail, in Hoovervilles, in the government camp—where the Joads found the humanity and courtesy almost unbelievable, after what they'd been through—are wonderfully realized. You can't help believing in these people, in their courage and in their integrity.

–*New York Times,* 14 April 1939; reprinted in *John Steinbeck: The Contemporary Reviews,* pp. 153–154

* * *

Books
Clifton Fadiman

Clifton Fadiman predicted correctly that The Grapes of Wrath *would win the Pulitzer Prize in fiction.*

If only a couple of million overcomfortable people can be brought to read it, John Steinbeck's *The Grapes of Wrath* may actually effect something like a revolution in their minds and hearts. It sounds like a crazy notion, I know, but I feel this book may just possibly do for our time what *Les Misérables* did for its, *Uncle Tom's Cabin* for its, *The Jungle* for its. *The Grapes of Wrath* is the kind of art that's poured out of a crucible in which are mingled pity and indignation. It seems advisable to stress this point. A lot of readers and critics are going to abandon themselves to orgies of ohing and ahing over Steinbeck's impressive literary qualities, happy to blink at the simple fact that fundamentally his book is a social novel exposing social injustice and calling, though never explicitly, for social redress. It's going to be a great and deserved best-seller; it'll be read and praised by everyone; it will almost certainly win the Pulitzer Prize; it will be filmed and dramatized and radio-acted—but, gentle reader, amid all the excitement let's try to keep in mind what *The Grapes of Wrath* is about: to wit, the slow murder of half a million innocent and worthy American citizens.

I don't know and in truth I don't much care whether it's the "work of genius" the publishers sincerely believe it to be. What sticks with me is that here is a book, non-political, non-dogmatic, which dramatizes so that you can't forget it the terrible facts of a wholesale injustice committed by society. Here is a book about a people of old American stock, not Reds or rebels of any kind. They are dispossessed of their

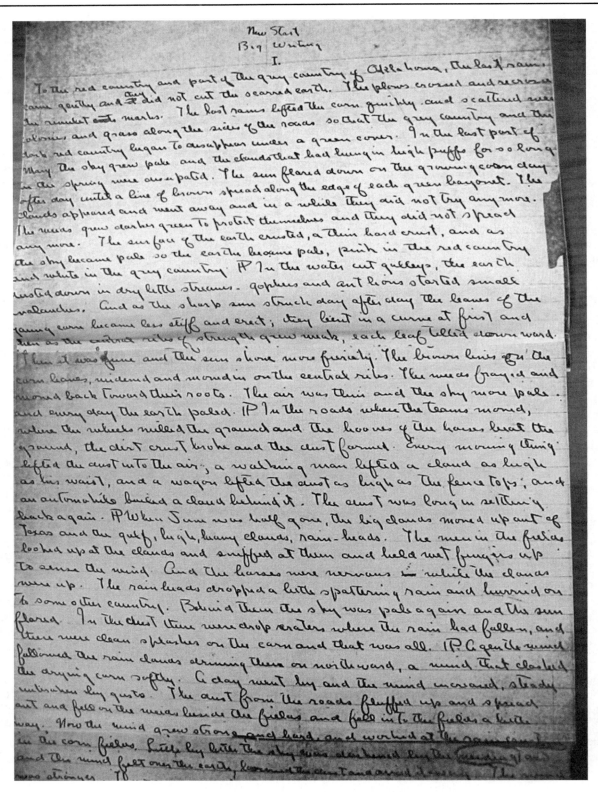

First page of Steinbeck's manuscript for The Grapes of Wrath
(Alderman Library, University of Virginia)

Dust jacket for the first edition of Steinbeck's 1939 novel (from Sotheby's New York, The Maurice F. Neville Collection of Modern Literature, *November 16, 2004)*

land, their pitiful, little homes are destroyed, they are lured to California by false hopes. When they get there, after incredible hardships, they are exploited, reduced to peonage, then to virtual slavery. If they protest, they are beaten, tortured, or their skulls are smashed in. Even if they do not protest, they are hounded, intimidated, and finally starved into defeat. The industrial and political groups that do these things know quite well what they do. Hence they cannot be forgiven.

Along Highway 66, ribboning from the Mississippi to Bakersfield, California, these disinherited, in their rickety jalopies, have been for the last five years streaming into the Far West. Driven off their farms by the drought, dust, or the juggernaut of the tractor, the small farmers and sharecroppers of half a dozen states, but mainly Oklahoma and Arkansas, have been staking their salvation on the possibility of work in California.

Steinbeck creates a family–the Joads of Oklahoma–and makes them typify a whole culture on the move. At the same time he gives us this migrant culture itself, in all its pathetic hopefulness, its self-reliance, the growing sense of unity it imparts to its people.

If ever The Great American Novel is written, it may very possibly be composed along the lines here laid out by Steinbeck. No one since the advent of Sinclair Lewis has had so exact a feeling for what is uniquely American. This feeling Steinbeck shows not only in his portrayal of the Joads themselves, in his careful notation of their folk speech, folk myths, folk obscenities, but in a thousand minor touches that add up to something major: the description of the used-car market, of the minds of truck-drivers and hash-house waitresses, of Highway 66, of the butchering and salting down of the pigs. It is this large interest in the whole lives of his Oklahoma farmers that makes *The Grapes of Wrath* more than a novel of propaganda, even though its social message is what will stick with any sensitive reader.

The book has faults. It is too detailed, particularly in the latter half. Casy, the ex-preacher, is half real, half "poetic" in the worse sense of the word. Occasionally the folk note is forced a little. And, finally, the ending (a young girl who has only a day or two before given birth to a dead child offers the milk of her breasts to a starving man) is the tawdriest kind of fake symbolism. Just occasionally Steinbeck's dramatic imagination overleaps itself and you get a piece of pure, or impure, theatre like these last pages. One should also add that his political thinking is a little mystical. The sense of unity that his migrants gradually acquire is not necessarily, as he implies, of a progressive character. It is based on an emotion that can just as easily be discharged into the channels of reaction. In other words, are not these simple, tormented Okies good Fascist meat, if the proper misleaders are found for them?

It is unlikely, however, that such misgivings will occur to you in the reading of the book. Its power and importance do not lie in its political insight but in its intense humanity, its grasp of the spirit of an entire people traversing a wilderness, its kindliness, its humor, and its bitter indignation. *The Grapes of Wrath* is the American novel of the season, probably the year, possibly the decade. . . .

–*New Yorker,* 15 (15 April 1939); reprinted in *John Steinbeck: The Contemporary Reviews,* pp. 154–155

* * *

Steinbeck's Uncovered Wagon
George Stevens

George Stevens praised Steinbeck for the understanding of the migrant workers' problems shown in The Grapes of Wrath.

It is exciting to watch the steady unfolding of a real writer's talent, to follow his development from promise to achievement, with the sense that he knows what he wants and knows what he is doing. It is particularly exciting because it is rare. Van Wyck Brooks pointed out long ago that the blighted career, the unfulfilled promise, is the rule in American writing, and his statement turned out to be as accurate in prophecy as in diagnosis. Writers who produced one or two good books; writers who abandoned literature to go to Hollywood, or to go to Spain, or to write plays, or to attend meetings, or simply to retire on their earnings; writers who exhausted their resources and kept doing the same book over and over—one after another they have left their over-excitable discoverers holding the bag: a bag full of words like "genius" and "masterpiece," to be taken three times a day, with meals.

Among the novelists of his generation, the most notable exception to this state of things is John Steinbeck. He has never yet flashed in the pan. . . . Steinbeck tore up the manuscripts of his first two novels, and retired the third. Since his first published book, *The Cup of Gold* [*sic*], each successive one has revealed a new facet of his ability. *Tortilla Flat* was the humorous and sympathetic story of some attractive and disreputable Mexicans. *In Dubious Battle* was a serious labor novel, remarkable of its kind in presenting the issues in terms of animate characters, who had the vitality to take the story over for themselves. *Of Mice and Men* was a miniature tragedy which lost none of its effectiveness for being written with an eye on the stage, which was just as poignant whether you took it straight or symbolically. Different as these novels are (and Steinbeck's variety is further manifested in the stories in *The Long Valley*), there has been a constancy of flavor which is impossible to define: something deeper than the "personality" of the author, which never intrudes; something more impalpable than "ideas"; something in the style, but in a style of which one is almost never conscious.

For these reasons Steinbeck's reputation is unique. All our reviewers, and such critics as we have among us, are pretty consciously in the "watch Steinbeck" movement. If it is turning into a bandwagon, that is not Steinbeck's fault. He has already survived some fairly indiscriminate adulation. His activities, outside of writing novels, have managed to remain his own affairs, to a remarkable degree in the great American goldfish bowl; and nothing has interfered with his serious production. The lively curiosity which Steinbeck has inspired is a

Steinbeck's 6 September 1938 note to his agent, Elizabeth Otis, asking for her response to the title of The Grapes of Wrath *(from William McPheron,* John Steinbeck: From Salinas to Stockholm, *2000; Special Collections, Thomas Cooper Library, University of South Carolina)*

legitimate curiosity about his work. Because of his variety, nobody can put him in a pigeon-hole; nobody has been able to say, "Steinbeck has done it again," but rather, "What is Steinbeck going to do next?" Since it became known that Steinbeck had a new novel for spring publication, and that it was by far his longest and most ambitious production to date, it is safe to say (for whatever it may mean) that no other book on the current lists has been so eagerly looked forward to by the reviewers.

The Grapes of Wrath is worth it, worth all the talk, all the anticipation, all the enthusiasm. Here is the epitome of everything Steinbeck has so far given us. It has the humor and earthiness of *Tortilla Flat,* the social consciousness of *In Dubious Battle,* the passionate concern for the homeless and uprooted which made *Of Mice and Men* memorable. These elements, together with a narrative that moves with excitement for its own sake, are not mixed but fused, to produce the unique quality of *The Grapes of Wrath.* That quality is an understanding of courage—courage seen with humor and bitterness and without a trace of sentimentality; courage that exists as the last affirmation of human dignity. To convey that understanding with passionate conviction, in human terms and also in terms of mature intelligence, so that we respond integrally and without reservation, is a very considerable thing for a novel to do. That is what *The Grapes of Wrath* does. It is by no means perfect, but possibly its faults (one of which is egregious) are a measure of its worth, in that it triumphantly lives them down.

The Grapes of Wrath is the story of the new American nomads, of the migrant farmers who have lost their few acres in the Oklahoma dust bowl to the onward march of tractors and foreclosures. It is in particular the story of one family, the Joads from a farm near Sallisaw. You have seen them going west through Texas and New Mexico on Route 66, or you have seen them in Resettlement Administration photographs: three generations in a second-hand truck, piled high with everything they own. Car after car, from Arkansas to California; people with no home but the road, no prospects but hope, no resources but courage: the thirty-niners in their uncovered wagons.

With this material Steinbeck has done what, according to at least one theory, cannot be done: he has made a living novel out of the news in the paper, out of contemporary social conditions. In "Land of the Free," Archibald MacLeish wrote a sound track to the Resettlement Administration's documentary stills. He looked at the pictures of the plowed-under farmers and wrote a poet's abstract statement, pared down to gaunt monosyllables, of a seemingly insoluble problem. Steinbeck has looked at the Oklahoma farmers themselves—the "Okies" in Salinas County, California, driven from camp to camp, finding no work, not allowed to settle. What he has written about them is a narrative: colorful, dramatic, subtle, coarse, comic, and tragic. For *The Grapes of Wrath* is not a social novel like most social novels. It is instead what a social novel ought to be. When you read it, you are in contact not with arguments, but with people. . . .

Others will see in it a different and more immediately sociological value. Unquestionably *The Grapes of Wrath* states the problem of the southwestern tenant farmer in a form that will bring it home to the imaginations of thousands who have hitherto looked on it with comparative unconcern. Unquestionably, also, Steinbeck sees his material both as a narrative and as a condition calling for action. At regular intervals in the book he inserts general chapters stating the problem in terms of pure non-fiction. For my own part, I found these chapters at best superfluous, occasionally sententious, and in one instance downright bad (this is a very windy passage indeed, in which the author coins the word "Manself," which I hope no one will ever use again). It is not these chapters, but the story of the Joads, that makes you want to do something about the migratory tenant farmers.

There remain one warning and one major criticism. It is only fair to say that there are conservative readers whom the language used by the Joad family will offend.

In my opinion, all the dialogue is necessary and right; Steinbeck's ear is perfect, and he lets the Joads talk with uninhibited coarseness. I think this is vital in a serious book like *The Grapes of Wrath,* and that it would be obscene to write the dialogue otherwise; but I realize that some readers will feel differently.

As for the criticism—a point on which another group of readers will disagree—I think that the last scene of the novel is bathos. It describes a physically possible but highly unusual event which even if palatable would be unconvincing; and even if Steinbeck had made it convincing, he would have added nothing to the story. The fact is that the story has no ending. We are left without knowing what happens to the characters. That is a necessary condition of writing about the immediate situation of the tenant farmers' odyssey, and we could put up with the absence of a satisfactory ending. But the final episode in the book seems to me a trick to jar the reader out of the realization that the story really does not end. It takes away a little of the effectiveness, and there will be many readers to wish Steinbeck hadn't done it.

But *The Grapes of Wrath* is good enough to live down more than this. Mrs. Roosevelt spoke recently of the need for a novelist who can interpret what is going on in this country among the kind of people of whom book readers in general know little—people like the Joads. John Steinbeck is the novelist. He knows what the country is doing to the Joads, and what goes on in their minds and emotions.

—*Saturday Review,* 19 (15 April 1939); reprinted in *John Steinbeck: The Contemporary Reviews,* pp. 157–159

* * *

John Steinbeck's New Novel Brims with Anger and Pity
Peter Monro Jack

Peter Monro Jack asserted that Steinbeck wrote The Grapes of Wrath *"with a sincerity seldom equaled."*

There are a few novelists writing as well as Steinbeck and perhaps a very few who write better; but it is most interesting to note how very much alike they are all writing. Hemingway, Caldwell, Faulkner, Dos Passos in the novel, and MacLeish in poetry are those whom we easily think of in their similarity of theme and style. Each is writing stories and scenarios of America with a curious and sudden intensity, almost as if they had never seen or understood it before. They are looking at it again with revolutionary eyes. Stirred like every other man in the street with news of foreign persecution, they turn to their own land to find seeds of the same destructive hatred. Their themes of pity and anger, their styles of sentimental elegy and scarifying denunciation may come to seem representative of our time. MacLeish's *Land of the Free,* for instance, going directly to the matter with poetry and pictures—the matter being that the land is no longer free, having been mortgaged, bought and finally bankrupted by a succession of anonymous companies, banks, politicians and courts, or, for the present instance, Steinbeck's *The Grapes of Wrath,* as pitiful and angry a novel ever to be written about America.

It is a very long novel, the longest that Steinbeck has written, and yet it reads as if it had been composed in a flash, ripped off the typewriter and delivered to the public as an ultimatum. It is a long and thoughtful novel as one thinks about it. It is a short and vivid scene as one feels it.

The opening scene is in Oklahoma, where a change in the land is taking place that no one understands, neither the single families who have pioneered it nor the great owners who have bought it over with their banks and lawyers. As plainly as it can be put, Mr. Steinbeck puts it. A man wants to build a wall, a house, a dam, and inside that a certain security to raise a family that will continue his work. But there is no security for a single family. The cotton crops have sucked out the roots of the land and the dust has overlaid it. The men from the Bank or the Company, sitting in their closed cars, try to explain to the squatting farmers what they scarcely understand

themselves: that the tenants whose grandfathers settled the land have no longer the title to it, that a tractor does more work than a single family of men, women and children put together, that their land is to be mechanically plowed under, with special instructions that their hand-built houses are to be razed to the ground.

This may read like a disquisition by Stuart Chase. There is, in fact, a series of essays on the subject running through the book, angry and abstract—like the characters, "perplexed and figuring." The essayist in Steinbeck alternates with the novelist, as it does with Caldwell and the others. The moralist is as important as the story-teller, may possibly outlast him; but the story at the moment is the important thing.

The most interesting figure of this Oklahoma family is the son who has just been released from jail. He is on his way home from prison, hitch-hiking across the state in his new cheap prison suit, picking up a preacher who had baptized him when young, and arriving to find the family setting out for California. The Bank had come "to tractorin' off the place." The house had been knocked over by the tractor making straight furrows for the cotton. The Joad family had read handbills promising work for thousands in California, orange picking. They had bought an old car, were on the point of leaving, when Tom turned up from prison with the preacher. They can scarcely wait for this promised land of fabulous oranges,

Migrant family stopping for roadside repairs in California, 1936 (photograph by Dorothea Lange; from Jay Parini,
John Steinbeck, 1995; Thomas Cooper Library, University of South Carolina)

grapes and peaches. Only one stubborn fellow remains on the land where his great-grandfather had shot Indians and built his house. The others, with Tom and the preacher, pack their belongings on the second-hand truck, set out for the new land, to start over again in California. . . . Californians are not going to like this angry novel. . . .

The beauty and fertility of California conceal human fear, hatred and violence. "Scairt" is a Western farmer's word for the inhabitants, frightened of the influx of workers eager for jobs, and when they are frightened they become vicious and cruel. This part of the story reads like the news from Nazi Germany. Families from Oklahoma are known as "Okies." While they work they live in what might as well be called concentration camps. Only a few hundred are given jobs out of the thousands who traveled West in response to the handbills. Their pay is cut from 30 cents an hour to 25, to 20. If any one objects he is a Red, an agitator, a troublemaker who had better get out of the country. Deputy sheriffs are around with guns, legally shooting or clubbing any one from the rest of the Union who questions the law of California. The Joad family find only one place of order and decency in this country of fear and violence, in a government camp, and it is a pleasure to follow the family as they take a shower bath and go to the Saturday night dances. But even here the deputy sheriffs, hired by the banks who run the Farmers Association, are poking in their guns, on the pretext of inciting to riot and the necessity of protective custody. The Joad family moves on through California, hunted by anonymous guns while they are picking peaches for 2 1/2 cents a box, hoping only for a little land free of guns and dust on which they might settle and work as they were accustomed to. The promised grapes of California have turned into grapes of wrath that might come to fruition at any moment.

How true this may be no reviewer can say. One may very easily point out that a similar message has been read by the writers mentioned above, and that Mr. Steinbeck has done the same thing before. It is easy to add that the novel comes to no conclusion, that the preacher is killed because he is a strike-breaker, that Tom disappears as a fugitive from California justice, that the novel ends on a minor and sentimental note; that the story stops after 600 pages merely because a story has to stop somewhere. All this is true enough but the real truth is that Steinbeck has written a novel from the depths of his heart with a sincerity seldom equaled. It may be an exaggeration, but it is the exaggeration of an honest and splendid writer.

—*New York Times Book Review,* 16 April 1939; reprinted in *John Steinbeck: The Contemporary Reviews,* pp. 159–161

* * *

The Finest Book John Steinbeck Has Written
Joseph Henry Jackson

Jackson, who earlier had high praise for Tortilla Flat *and* In Dubious Battle, *called* The Grapes of Wrath *a "magnificent book."*

"You never been called 'Okie' yet? 'Okie' use' ta mean you was from Oklahoma. Now it means you're scum. Don't mean nothin' itself; it's the way they say it. But I can't tell you nothin'. You got to go there. I hear there's three hundred thousan' of our people there—an' livin' like hogs, 'cause ever'thing in California is owned. They ain't nothin' left. And them people that owns it is gonna hang on to it if they got ta kill ever'body in the worl' to do it. An' they're scairt, an' that makes 'em mad. You got to see it. You got to hear it. Purtiest god-damn country you ever seen, but they ain't nice to you, them folks. They're so scairt an' worried they ain't even nice to each other.". . .

Multiply the Joads by thousands and you have a picture of the great modern migration that is the subject of this new Steinbeck novel which is far and away the finest book he has yet written. Examine the motives and the forces behind what happened to the Joads and you have a picture of the fantastic social and economic situation facing America today. Cure? Steinbeck suggests none. He puts forward no doctrine, no dogma. But he writes. "In the souls of the people the grapes of wrath are filling and growing heavy, growing heavy for the vintage." I have no doubt that Steinbeck would not enjoy being called a prophet. But this novel is something very like prophecy.

The Joads were only one family to learn that a bank was not a man. It was made up of men but it was a bigger thing and it controlled them, even though sometimes they hated to do what the bank-monster said they must. That monster moved out the Joads and other thousands. Little farms, even tenant-farming wouldn't work any more on the worn-out land. Only huge land companies and tractors could make it pay. It happened all at once, and they had to go somewhere; thousands and tens of thousands were in the same boat.

Angry and puzzled, the heads of families tried to figure. When the little handbills appeared in the lost country, they thought they saw a way out. If they sold everything, they might buy an ancient car and move to California where the handbills said there was a chance for pickers. The second-hand car dealers cheated them right and left, but they bought the rattletraps; they had to. And they took to the road, headed westward over Highway 66. . . .

What happened to the Joads is the immediate story of this novel. What happened and is happening to the thousands like them is the story behind the story; the reason Steinbeck wrote *The Grapes of Wrath.* What may hap-

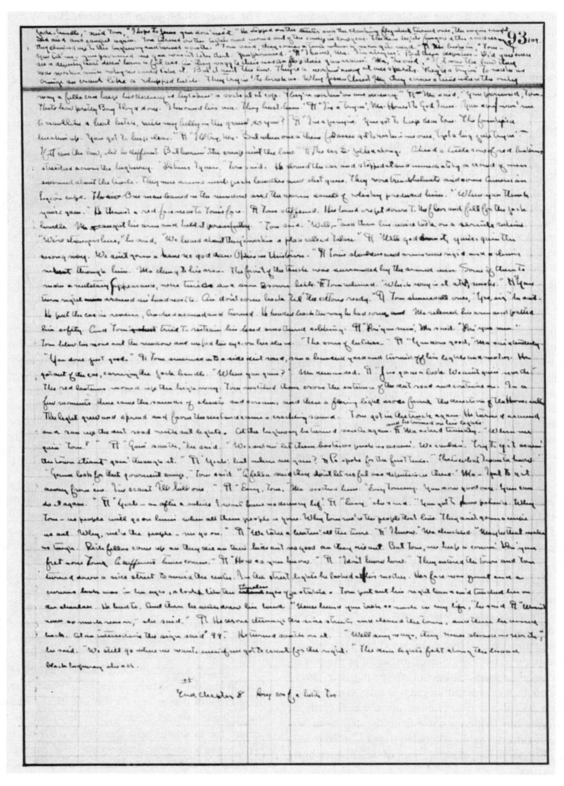

Last manuscript page of chapter 20 (numbered chapter 8 in the manuscript) of The Grapes of Wrath *(Alderman Library, University of Virginia; from Robert DeMott, ed.,* Working Days: The Journals of The Grapes of Wrath, 1938–1941, *1989; Thomas Cooper Library, University of South Carolina)*

pen—must happen, he believes—in the long run is the implication behind the book. "Whereas the wants of the Californians were nebulous and undefined, the wants of the Okies were beside the roads, lying there to be seen and coveted; the good fields with water to be dug for, earth to crumble in the hand, grass to smell. . . . And a homeless, hungry man, driving the roads with his wife behind him and his thin children in the back seat, could look at the fallow fields which might produce food but not profit, and that man could know how a fallow field is a sin and the unused land a crime against the thin children." There is the hint. And here again: "And the great owners, with eyes to read history, and to know the great fact: when property accumulates in too few hands it is taken away. And that companion fact: when a majority of people are hungry and cold they will take by force what they need. And the little screaming fact that sounds through history: repression works only to strengthen and knit the repressed." Prophecy perhaps. Certainly a warning.

For the story itself, it is completely authentic. Steinbeck knows. He went back to Oklahoma and then came West with the migrants, lived in their camps, saw their pitiful brave highway communities, the life of the itinerant beside the road. He learned what was behind the handbills. And he came back with an enormous respect for the tenacity of these dispossessed, and with the knowledge that this migration is no less a forerunner of a new way than was that migration of those earlier Americans who took California from another group of landholders who had grown too soft to hold it.

It is a rough book, yes. It is an ineffably tender book too. It is the book for which everything else that Steinbeck has written was an exercise in preparation. You'll find in it reminders of *Pastures of Heaven,* of *In Dubious Battle,* of *The Red Pony,* even of *Tortilla Flat.* But here there is no mere exploration of a field, no tentative experimenting with a theme. This is the full symphony, Steinbeck's declaration of faith. The terrible meek will inherit, he says. They will. They are on their way to their inheritance now, and not far from it. And though they are the common people, sometimes dirty people, starved and suppressed and disappointed people, yet they are good people. Steinbeck believes that too.

It is easy to grow lyrical about *The Grapes of Wrath,* to become excited about it, to be stirred to the shouting-point by it. Perhaps it is too easy to lose balance in the face of such an extraordinarily moving performance. But it is also true that the effect of the book lasts. The author's employment, for example, of occasional chapters in which the undercurrent of the book is announced, spoken as a running accompaniment to the story, with something of the effect of the sound track in Pare Lorentz's *The River—* that lasts also, stays with you, beats rhythmically in your mind long after you have put the book down. No, the

reader's instant response is more than quick enthusiasm, more than surface emotionalism. This novel of America's new disinherited is a magnificent book. It is, I think for the first time, the whole Steinbeck, the mature novelist saying something he must say and doing it with the sure touch of the great artist.

—*New York Herald Tribune,* 16 April 1939; reprinted in *John Steinbeck: The Contemporary Reviews,* pp. 161–163

* * *

A Variety of Fiction
Philip Rahv

Reviewing The Grapes of Wrath *in the leftist* Partisan Review, *Philip Rahv acknowledged Steinbeck's concern with the plight of the migrant workers but dismissed the novel as "didactic and long-winded."*

. . . From Mr. John Steinbeck—whose inspired pulp-story, *Of Mice and Men,* swept the nation like a plague—one expects nothing. It is therefore gratifying to report that in *The Grapes of Wrath* he appears in a more sympathetic light than in his previous work, not excluding *In Dubious Battle.* This writer, it can now be seen, is really fired with a passionate faith in the common man. He is the hierophant of the innocent and injured; and his new book, though it by no means deserves the ecstatic salutations it has received in the press, is an authentic and formidable example of the novel of social protest.

The book is at the same time a detailed exposure of dreadful economic conditions and a long declaration of love to the masses. It is an epic of misery—a prodigious, relentless, and often excruciating account of agrarian suffering. . . . Mr. Steinbeck spares us not a single scene, not a single sensation, that could help to implicate us emotionally. And he is so much in earnest that a number of times he interrupts his story in order to grapple directly with his thesis. Thus several chapters are devoted to outright political preaching from the standpoint of a kind of homespun revolutionary populism.

But the novel is far too didactic and long-winded. In addition to the effects that are peculiar to his own manner, Mr. Steinbeck has assembled in this one book all the familiar faults of the "proletarian" literary mode. There are the usual idealized portraits and the customary conversions, psychologically false and schematic as ever, to militant principles. Moreover, the technical cleverness displayed in *Of Mice and Men* is lacking in this novel, which should be credited with valid political observation and sincere feeling, but which fails on the test of craftsmanship. Its unconscionable length is out of all proportion to its substance; the "ornery" dialect spoken by its farmers impresses one as being less a form of human speech than a facile convention of the local-color schools; and as to problems of characterization, Mr. Steinbeck does not so much create character as he apes it. For aping, too, can be turned into a means of "re-creating" life. It would appear from this and similar novels that on a sufficiently elementary level, and so long as a uniform scheme of behavior—however simple—is imposed upon characters, all a fiction writer requires to make his people seem real is the patience to follow them everywhere, the perseverance to copy down everything they say and everything they do. . . .

—*Partisan Review*, 6 (Spring 1939); reprinted in *John Steinbeck: The Contemporary Reviews*, p. 166

* * *

American Tragedy
Malcolm Cowley

Malcolm Cowley, writing in The New Republic, *disagreed with critics who said that* The Grapes of Wrath *was the greatest novel of the decade, claiming instead that it "belongs very high in the category of the great angry books like* Uncle Tom's Cabin. . . ."*

While keeping our eyes on the cataclysms in Europe and Asia, we have lost sight of a tragedy nearer home. A hundred thousand rural households have been uprooted from the soil, robbed of their possessions—though by strictly legal methods—and turned out on the highways. Friendless, homeless and therefore voteless, with fewer rights than medieval serfs, they have wandered in search of a few days' work at miserable wages—not in Spain or the Yangtze Valley, but among the vineyards and orchards of California, in a setting too commonplace for a color story in the Sunday papers. . . . The novel, which has just appeared, is John Steinbeck's longest and angriest and most impressive work. . . .

The second half of *Grapes of Wrath*, dealing with their adventures in the Valley of California, is . . . good but somewhat less impressive [than the first]. Until that moment the Joads have been moving steadily toward their goal. Now they discover that it is not their goal after all; they must still move on, but no longer in one direction—they are harried by vigilantes, recruited as peach pickers, driven out again by a strike; they don't know where to go. Instead of being just people, as they

Dust jacket and title page for the 1940 Russian translation of The Grapes of Wrath *(from Christie's East, Jack E. and Rachel Gindi Collection of Modern Literature, 20 April 1994; Thomas Cooper Library, University of South Carolina)*

were at home, they hear themselves called Okies—"and that means you're scum," they tell each other bewilderedly. "Don't mean nothing itself, it's the way they say it." The story begins to suffer a little from their bewilderment and lack of direction.

At this point one begins to notice other faults. Interspersed among the chapters that tell what happened to the Joads, there have been other chapters dealing with the general plight of the migrants. The first half-dozen of these interludes have not only broadened the scope of the novel but have been effective in themselves, sorrowful, bitter, intensely moving. But after the Joads reach California, the interludes are spoken in a shriller voice. The author now has a thesis—that the migrants will unite and overthrow their oppressors—and he wants to argue, as if he weren't quite sure of it himself. His thesis is also embodied in one of the characters: Jim Casy, a preacher who loses his faith but unfortunately for the reader can't stop preaching. In the second half of the novel, Casy becomes a Christ-like labor leader and is killed by vigilantes. The book ends with an episode that is a mixture of allegory and melodrama. Rose of Sharon, after her baby is born dead, saves a man from starvation by suckling him at her breast—as if to symbolize the fruitfulness of these people and the bond that unites them in misfortune.

Yet one soon forgets the faults of the story. What one remembers most of all is Steinbeck's sympathy for the migrants—not pity, for that would mean he was putting himself above them; not love, for that would blind him to their faults, but rather a deep fellow feeling. It makes him notice everything that sets them apart from the rest of the world and sets one migrant apart from all the others. In the Joad family, everyone from Grampa—"Full a' piss an' vinegar," as he says of himself—down to the two brats, Ruthie and Winfield, is a distinct and living person. And the story is living too—it has the force of the headlong anger that drives ahead from the first chapter to the last, as if the whole six hundred pages were written without stopping. The author and the reader are swept along together. I can't agree with those critics who say that *The Grapes of Wrath* is the greatest novel of the last ten years; for example, it doesn't rank with the best of Hemingway or Dos Passos. But it belongs very high in the category of the great angry books like *Uncle Tom's Cabin* that have roused a people to fight against intolerable wrongs.
—*New Republic*, 98 (3 May 1939); reprinted in *John Steinbeck: The Contemporary Reviews*, pp. 166–167

* * *

Thanking Eleanor Roosevelt

In early April 1940, Eleanor Roosevelt made an inspection tour of California migrant-worker camps. She was quoted in a 3 April story in The New York Times *as having said, "I never have thought* The Grapes of Wrath *was exaggerated." Steinbeck wrote the First Lady on 24 April thanking her for her support.*

Dear Mrs. Roosevelt:

I am very sorry I was out of the country when you were last on the coast, for I have looked forward to meeting you with great pleasure. Perhaps on your next swing, I shall be here.

Meanwhile—may I thank you for your words. I have been called a liar so constantly that sometimes I wonder whether I may not have dreamed the things I saw and heard in the period of my research.

Again thank you and I hope I may not miss you again.

Sincerely yours,
John Steinbeck
—*Steinbeck: A Life in Letters,* p. 202

The Californians: Storm and Steinbeck
Edmund Wilson

Edmund Wilson's reviews of The Grapes of Wrath *and Steinbeck's other works offer a generally negative assessment. The following is from a joint review of Steinbeck and another California writer, Hans Otto Storm.*

. . . John Steinbeck is a native Californian, and he has occupied himself more with the life of the state than any of these other writers. His exploration in his novels of the Salinas Valley has been more thoroughgoing and tenacious than anything of the kind in our contemporary fiction except Faulkner's intensive cultivation of the state of Mississippi.

And what has Mr. Steinbeck found in this region he knows so well? I believe that his virtuosity in a purely technical way has tended to obscure his themes. He has published eight volumes of fiction, which represent a great variety of forms and which have therefore seemed to people to be written from a variety of points of view. *Tortilla Flat* was a comic idyll, with the simplification almost of a folk tale; *In Dubious Battle* was a strike novel, centering around Communist organizers and following a fairly conventional pattern; *Of Mice and Men* was a compact little drama, contrived with almost too much cleverness, and a parable which criticized humanity from a non-political point of view; *The Long Valley* was a series of short stories, dealing mostly with animals, in which poetic symbols were presented in realistic settings and built up with concrete detail; *The Grapes of Wrath* was a propaganda novel, full of preachments and sociological interludes, and developed on an epic scale. Thus attention has been diverted from the content of Mr. Steinbeck's work by the fact that whenever he appears, he puts on a different kind of show. He is such an accomplished performer that he has been able to hold people's interest by the story he is telling at the moment without their inquiring what is behind it.

This variability of the form itself is probably an indication that Mr. Steinbeck has never yet found the right artistic medium for what he wants to say. But there is in his fiction as a whole a substratum which does remain constant and which gives it a certain basic seriousness that that of the mere performer does not have. What is constant in Mr. Steinbeck is his preoccupation with biology. He is a biologist in the literal sense that he interests himself in biological research. The biological laboratory in the short story called "The Snake" is obviously something which he knows at first hand and for which he has a strong special feeling; and it is one of the peculiarities of his vocabulary that it runs to biological terms. But the laboratory described in "The Snake," the tight little building over the water, where the scientist feeds white rats to rattlesnakes and fertilizes starfish ova, is also one of the key images of his fiction. It is the symbol of his tendency in his stories to present life in animal terms.

Mr. Steinbeck almost always in his fiction is dealing either with the lower animals or with human beings so rudimentary that they are almost on the animal level; and the close relationship of the people with the animals equals even the zoöphilia of D. H. Lawrence and David Garnett. In *Tortilla Flat,* there are the Pirate's dogs, with which he lives in a kennel and which have caused him practically to forget human relationships. In *In Dubious Battle,* there is another character whose personality is confused with that of his dogs. In *The Grapes of Wrath,* the journey of the Joads is figured at the beginning by the progress of a turtle, and it is accompanied and parodied all the way by animals, insects and birds. When the expropriated sharecroppers are compelled to abandon their farm in Oklahoma, we get an extended picture of the invasion of the house by the bats, the weasels, the owls, the mice, and the cats that have gone back to the wild. Lennie in *Of Mice and Men* likes to carry around animal pets, toward which as well as toward human beings he has murderous animal instincts. The stories in *The Long Valley* are almost entirely about animals and plants; and Mr. Steinbeck does not have the effect, as

Lawrence or Kipling does, of romantically raising the animals to the stature of human beings, but rather of assimilating the human beings to animals. "The Chrysanthemums," "The White Quail" and "The Snake" deal with women who identify themselves with respectively chrysanthemums, a white quail and a snake. In "Flight," a young Mexican boy, who has killed a man and run away into the mountains, is finally reduced to a state so close to that of the beasts that he is taken by a mountain lion for one of themselves; and in the fantasy of "Saint Katy the Virgin," where a bad pig is made to repent and become a saint, the result is not to dignify the animal as the "Little Flowers of Saint Francis" do with the Wolf of Agubbio, for example, but to reduce human religion to absurdity.

The chief subject of Mr. Steinbeck's fiction has been thus not those aspects of humanity in which it is most thoughtful, imaginative, constructive, but rather the processes of life itself. In the natural course of nature, living organisms are continually being destroyed, and among the principal things that destroy them are the predatory appetite and the competitive instinct that are necessary for the very survival of eating and breeding things. This impulse of the killer has been preserved in a simpleton like Lennie in a form in which it is almost innocent; and yet Lennie has learned from his more highly developed friend that to yield to it is to do something "bad." In his struggle against the instinct, he loses. Is Lennie bad or good? He is betrayed as, Mr. Steinbeck implies, all our human intentions are: by the uncertainties of our animal nature.

And it is only, as a rule, on this primitive level that Mr. Steinbeck deals with moral questions: the virtues like the crimes for Mr. Steinbeck are still a part of these planless and almost aimless, of these almost unconscious, processes of life. The preacher in *The Grapes of Wrath* is disillusioned about the human moralities, and his sermon at the grave of Grampa Joad, so lecherous and mean during his lifetime, evidently gives expression to Mr. Steinbeck's point of view: "This here ol' man jus' lived a life an' jus' died out of it. I don't know whether he was good or bad, but that don't matter much. He was alive, an' that's what matters. An' now he's dead, an' that don't matter. Heard a fella tell a poem one time, an' he says 'All that lives is holy.'"

The subject of *The Grapes of Wrath,* which is supposed to deal with human society, is the same as that of "The Red Pony," which is supposed to deal with horses: loyalty to life itself. The men who feel the responsibility for having let the red pony die must retrieve themselves by sacrificing the mare in order to bring a new pony into life. And so Rose of Sharon

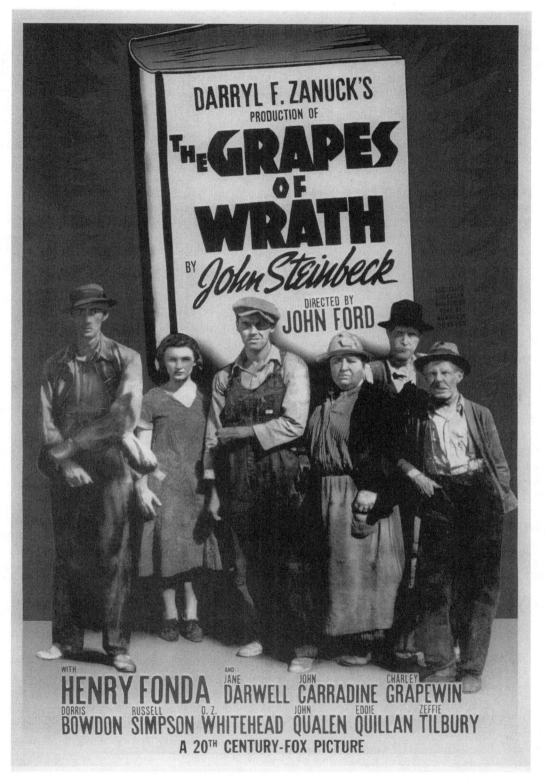

*Poster for the 1940 movie version of Steinbeck's 1939 novel. Jane Darwell, third from right, received
an Academy Award for her portrayal of Ma Joad (Bruccoli Clark Layman Archives).*

Joad, with her undernourished baby born dead, must give her milk, in the desolate barn which is all she has left for a shelter, to another wretched victim of famine and flood, on the point of death from starvation. To what good that ponies and Okies should continue to live on the earth? "And I wouldn' pray for a ol' fella that's dead," the preacher goes on to say. "He's awright. He got a job to do, but it's all laid out for 'im an' there's on'y one way to do it. But us, we got a job to do, an' they's a thousan' ways, an' we don' know which one to take. An' if I was to pray, it'd be for the folks that don't know which way to turn."

This preacher who has lost his religion does find a way to turn: he becomes a labor agitator; and this theme has already been dealt with more fully in the earlier novel, *In Dubious Battle*. But what differentiates Mr. Steinbeck's picture of a labor movement with radical leadership from most books on such subjects of its period is again the biological point of view. The strike leaders, here as in other novels, are Communists, but the book is not really based on the formulas of Communist ideology. The kind of character produced by the Communist movement and the Communist strategy in strikes (of the Communism of the day before yesterday) are *described* by Mr. Steinbeck, and they are described with a certain amount of admiration; yet the party member of *In Dubious Battle* does not talk like a Marxist of even the Stalinist revision. The cruelty of these self-immolating revolutionists is not palliated any more than the cruelty of the half-witted Lennie; and we are made to feel throughout that we are witnessing examples of human behavior from which the only conclusion that the author seems confident in drawing is that this is how life in our age is behaving. There is developed in the course of the book—especially by a fellow-traveler doctor who seems to come closer than the Communist to expressing Mr. Steinbeck's own ideas—a whole philosophy of "group-man" as an "animal." . . .

This animalizing tendency of Mr. Steinbeck's is, I believe, at the bottom of his relative unsuccess at representing human beings.

The *paisanos* of *Tortilla Flat* are really not quite human beings: they are cunning little living dolls who amuse us like pet guinea-pigs or rabbits. A special convention has been created to remove them from kinship with the author and the reader. In *The Grapes of Wrath,* on the other hand, Mr. Steinbeck has summoned all his resources to make the reader feel his human relationship with the family of dispossessed farmers; yet the effect of this, too, is not quite real. The characters of *The Grapes of Wrath* are animated and put through their paces rather than brought to life; they are like excellent character actors giving very conscientious performances in a fairly well written play. Their dialect is well done, but they talk stagy; and, in spite of Mr. Steinbeck's attempts to make them figure as heroic human symbols, you cannot help feeling that they, too, do not quite exist seriously for him as people. It is as if human sentiments and speeches had been assigned to a flock of lemmings on their way to throw themselves into the sea.

I do not mean to say, however, that this picture of human beings as lemmings hasn't its partial validity or its pertinence at the present time. In our time, Shakespeare's angry ape, drest in his little brief authority, seems to make of all the rest of mankind angry apes or cowering rodents. The one thing that was imagined with intensity in Aldous Huxley's novel of last autumn was the eighteenth-century exploiter of the slave trade degenerating into a fetal anthropoid. All the world is today full of people like the Joads deprived of the dignity of a human society, as they had previously been deprived of the dignity of human work, and made to flee from their houses like prairie-dogs driven before a prairie fire.

Huxley has a good deal to say, as our American Humanists did, about the importance of distinguishing clearly between the human and the animal levels; and, like the Humanists, he has been frightened back into one of those synthetic moral cults which do duty for our evaporated religions. The doctor in *In Dubious Battle* deprecates even those elements of religion that have entered into the labor cause; and he takes no stock in the utopianism of the Communists.

For myself, I prefer Mr. Steinbeck's naturalistic point of view toward the animal-man to Mr. Huxley's mysticism. We may conceivably learn something and get somewhere by studying humanity in a biological spirit; I am skeptical about our doing either by the methods of self-contemplation advocated by Mr. Huxley.

For the rest, Mr. Steinbeck has invention, observation, a certain color of style which for some reason does not possess what is called magic. I have not read the first three of his novels, but none of the ones that I have read seems to me precisely first-rate. *Tortilla Flat*—perhaps by reason of the very limitations of its convention—seems artistically his most successful production. Yet there is behind the journalism, the theatricalism and the tricks of most of his other books something that does seem first-rate in its seriousness, in its unpanicky questioning of life. . . .

—*New Republic*, 103 (9 December 1940); reprinted in *John Steinbeck: The Contemporary Reviews,* pp. 183–187

* * *

Steinbeck to Otis, 15 December 1939

Late in 1939 Steinbeck wrote Otis to report on screenings of the movie versions of both The Grapes of Wrath *and* Of Mice and Men. *He also mentioned plans for two trips with Ed Ricketts, one to study the coastal waters north of San Francisco for a marine-specimen handbook and the other a longer trip to the Gulf of California. The latter trip, undertaken in the spring of 1940, was the basis for* Sea of Cortez: A Leisurely Journal of Travel and Research *(1941), co-authored by Steinbeck and Ricketts.*

Dear Elizabeth:

I have so much to tell you that it will take some time. I'll go about it slowly. Your letter first. Many thanks for the $13,000. But remember the excitement when the N. American Review actually paid $90 (on The Red Pony)? Such excitement will never come again.

There is no question of a cut version of Grapes in paper covers. I should never consent to it. So that is out. C. [Covici] can get as stubborn as he wants about it.

Pictures—We went down in the afternoon and that evening saw Grapes at Twentieth-Century. Zanuck has more than kept his word. He has a hard, straight picture in which the actors are submerged so completely that it looks and feels like a documentary film and certainly it has a hard, truthful ring. No punches were pulled—in fact, with descriptive matter removed, it is a harsher thing than the book, by far. It seems unbelievable but it is true. The next afternoon we went to see Mice and it is a beautiful job. Here Milestone [director Lewis Milestone] has done a curious lyrical thing. It hangs together and is underplayed. You will like it. It opens the 22nd of December in Hollywood. As for Grapes, it opens sometime in January. There is so much hell being raised in this state that Zanuck will not release simultaneously. He'll open in N.Y. and move gradually west, letting the publicity precede it. He even, to find out, issued a statement that it would never be shown in California and got a ton of mail, literally, in protest the next day. He has hired attorneys to fight any local censorship and is trying to get Thomas Benton for the posters. All this is far beyond our hopes.

Now I come to a very curious thing. [Victor] Fleming the director and Spence Tracy have wanted to make The Red Pony. They are nuts to make it. They talked to me about it and I slept over it but didn't sleep at all. It seemed to me that these men are expensive and good men. I don't know whether anything will come out of it, but here is what I suggested. They were to make the film—no salaries. If necessary, money to make it should be collected by subscriptions. I would not only give the story for nothing but would work on the script. When finished, it would be distributed to any town or city which would guarantee to use the proceeds to endow one or more children's beds in the *local* hospitals. Tremendous prices would be asked for seats. They were very enthusiastic. Said they thought they could get not only the best people but equipment and film for nothing. Maybe this is nuts but no film has ever been made for a definite purpose. Tracy is particularly moved because his own little son had infantile paralysis which crippled it. Fleming says that such a film would not make less than $2,000,000 and that's a lot of endowed beds.

Now—the collecting. I got a truck and we are equipping it. We don't go to Mexico until March, but we have the handbook to do first and we'll go north in about a week I guess for the solstice tides. It will be a tough job and I'm not at all sure we can get it done by March. And I have a terrific job of reading to do. Ricketts is all right but I am a *popular* writer and I have to build some trust in the minds of biologists. This handbook will help to do that. The Mexican book will be interesting to a much larger audience, and there is no question that Viking can have it.

Yesterday we went to Berkeley with a design for our traveling refrigeration plant and it is being built. Also ordered a Bausch and Lomb SKW microscope. This is a beauty with a side bar and drum nose piece. Primarily a dissecting microscope. My dream for some time in the future is a research scope with an oil immersion lens, but that costs about 600 dollars and I'm not getting it right now. The SKW will be fine for the trip. But that research model, Oh boy! Oh boy! Sometime I'll have one. It may interest you to know that business at the lab is picking up. I can't tell you what all this means to me, in happiness and energy. I was washed up and now I'm alive again, with work to be done and worth doing.

I guess that's all.

Love,
John

* * *

L. M. Birkhead to Steinbeck, 2 May 1940

Steinbeck received the following letter from the director of a group called Friends of Democracy seeking to refute the notion that The Grapes of Wrath *was a work of "Jewish propaganda."*

Dear Mr. Steinbeck:

I hope that you will not think I am impertinent, but our organization has had put up to it the problem of your nationality. You may consider that it is none of our business, nor the business of anyone else in the country. However, there is a very widespread propaganda, particularly among the extreme reac-

John Carradine as Jim Casy and Henry Fonda as Tom Joad in the 1940 movie adaptation of The Grapes
of Wrath *(MOMA/Film Stills Archive; from Joseph R. Millichap,* Steinbeck and Film, *1983;*
Thomas Cooper Library, University of South Carolina)

tionary religionists of the country, that you are Jewish and that "Grapes of Wrath", is Jewish propaganda.

I wonder if you have any sort of a statement that you could send me which would clarify this issue.

I think you will be interested in the work that our organization has been doing in combatting the pro-Nazi and anti-Semitic propaganda so wide-spread throughout the country. I am sending you a copy of our most recent publication, "Father Coughlin: Self-Condemned".

Thanking you in advance, I am,

Yours sincerely,

L. M. Birkhead

—reprinted in *John Steinbeck Replies* (New York, 1940)

* * *

Steinbeck to Birkhead, 7 May 1940

Steinbeck quickly responded to Birkhead's letter.

Dear Mr. Birkhead:

I am answering your letter with a good deal of sadness. I am sad for a time when one must know a man's race before his work can be approved or disapproved. It does not seem important to me whether I am Jewish or not, and I know that a statement of mine is useless if an *interested* critic wishes to ride a preconceived thesis. I cannot see how The Grapes of Wrath can be Jewish propaganda but then I have heard it called Communist propaganda also.

It happens that I am not Jewish and have no Jewish blood but it only happens that way. I find that I do not experience any pride that it is so.

If you wish—here is my racial map although you know what an intelligent anthropologist thinks of racial theories. As you will see, I am the typical American Airedale.

My grandfather on my father's side was German, the son of a farming family which lived and still lives on a fairly large farm near Düsseldorf. My grandfather came to America in the late fifties in time to be in the Civil War. There has been little communication with the German branch since then except for a visit to Germany about four years ago by a second cousin of mine. He reports that the family still lives on the same farm and that they appear to be good citizens, intensely blond and quite able to prove the nonsensical thing the Nazis insist on. Their name and ours by the way was Grosssteinbeck but the three s's in a row were an outrage to America so my grandfather dropped the first syllable in the interest of spelling.

My German grandfather married a New England woman whose family name was Dickson who came from Leominster, Massachusetts, where her family had lived since the middle seventeenth century.

On my mother's side my blood is all north Irish, my grandfather whose name was Hamilton having come from Mulkeraugh near Londonderry and his wife whose name was Feaghan from nearby.

Anyway there it is. Use it or don't use it, print it or not. Those who wish for one reason or another to believe me Jewish will go on believing it while men of good will and good intelligence won't care one way or another.

I can prove these things of course—but when I shall have to—the American democracy will have disappeared.

Yours is only one of many letters I have received on the same subject. It is the first I have answered and I think it is the last. I fully recognize your position and do not in the least blame you for it. I am only miserable for the time and its prejudice that prompts it.

Sincerely,
John Steinbeck

P.S. On both sides and for many generations we are blond and blue-eyed to a degree to arouse the admiration and perhaps envy of the dark-complexioned Hitler.

—*Steinbeck: A Life in Letters,* pp. 203–204

* * *

The Wrath of John Steinbeck
Robert Bennett

Prompted by the publication of The Grapes of Wrath, *Robert Bennett recalled the following episode from Steinbeck's youth.*

If anyone has the temerity to trace the true history of John Steinbeck, let him first pick up the fragments and put them together. That is the beginning. Mr. Bullfinch did it nicely for the older Prometheus. All we can do is to offer a fragment for some future Bullfinch to exhume.

Now every generation has its own Prometheus. Sometimes he turns out to be a "she" with plenty of spunk; more often he is an ordinary man in your own home town. No doubt you recall Prometheus. He wasn't merely a classic myth, you know. Not at all. He was a great man who saw the need of art, warmth, cookery and security and brought these gifts to men in spite of all the gods on Olympus, especially Zeus. But for all his trouble he was seized as a radical and put in chains. Later he was delivered and ever since then has been known as one of the Immortals. Thus originated one of the earliest dramatic situations . . . deux [*sic*] ex machina!

The story hasn't changed much in four thousand years. Since Prometheus the First, many have challenged the established order of gods, governments and more often man himself to bring new and necessary benefits to society. Many have called attention to gross blunders in economics, medicine, science, religion and political economy while setting out to remedy the evils and thereby adding fresh truths by their endeavors. Of such men is John Steinbeck.

Of course there is always a handful of the young who start out to be Prometheans but most of them spill their coals by the wayside and become easy-going, noncombustible in the end. The rest trust in God when they have to; in fact they have no one to trust in but God. So there is always a good deal of talk about trusting in the Lord and a lot of worrying in silence. John Steinbeck is not one of this ilk. He is for going after things and threshing them out like they do on the Salinas ranches.

Like most Prometheans, however, we know little of his early life and anecdotes. His autobiography should be found in his works and should be enough for us. But it is not enough. Apparently we find interest and pleasure in knowing stories of his early life and just how he was regarded by his friends.

John Steinbeck, as a young man not yet twenty-one, looked like any other young man of his time except that he was normal, healthy and strong-minded. He had his own ideas about things, was curious about everything and had faith in himself. He took no stock in *"the modern girl-struck boy whose popularity is reckoned by his knowledge of spotted stories"* or so he told me while lunching one day back in 1920. He said, *"Don't think by that that I am aiming a dart at iniquity because glass houses don't thrive where there*

Page 272   Grapes of Wrath   Steinbeck

"On'y way you gonna get me to go is whup me." She moved the jack handle gently again. "An' I'll shame you, Pa. I won't take no whuppin', cryin' an' a-beggin'. I'll light into you. An' you ain't so sure you can whup me anyways. An' if ya do git me, I swear to God I'll wait till you got your back turned, or you're settin' down, an' I'll knock you belly-up with a bucket. I swear to Holy Jesus' sake I will."

Pa looked helplessly about the group. "She's sassy," he said. "I never seen her so sassy." Ruthie giggled shrilly.

The jack handle flicked hungrily back and forth in Ma's hand. "Come on," said Ma. "You made up your mind. Come on an' whup me. Jes' try it. But I ain't a-goin'; or

Page 1   John Steinbeck

To the red country and part of the gray country of Oklahoma, the last rains came gently, and they did not cut the scarred earth. The plows crossed and recrossed the rivulet marks. The last rains lifted the corn quickly and scattered weed colonies and grass along the sides of the roads so that the gray country and the dark red country began to disappear under a green cover. In the last part of May the sky grew pale and the clouds that had hung in high puffs for so long in the spring were dissipated. The sun flared down on the growing corn day after day until a line of brown spread along the edge of each green bayonet. The clouds appeared, and went away, and in a while they did not try any more. The weeds grew darker green to protect themselves, and they did not spread any more. The surface of the earth crusted, a thin hard crust, and as the sky became pale, so the earth became pale, pink in the red country and white in the gray country.

In the water-cut gullies the earth dusted down in dry little streams. Gophers and ant lions started small avalanches. And as the sharp sun struck day after day the leaves of the young corn became less stiff and erect; they bent in a curve at

Pages from the typescript of The Grapes of Wrath, *typed from Steinbeck's manuscript by his wife, Carol (Library of Congress; from Robert J. DeMott, ed.,* Working Days: The Journals of The Grapes of Wrath, 1938–1941, *1989; Thomas Cooper Library, University of South Carolina)*

are cobbles." And continuing, *"It is a weak mind, however, which can be hogtied by a woman's leg. Do we live in an age of weak minds. . . ."* He started talking to other fellows about it. They laughed. They were all hog-tied. But after that they eyed him a little differently. Here was a big fellow who was undoubtedly good football material arguing and talking like an adolescent visionary.

At that time Steinbeck was collecting rejection slips from various magazines. He said to me at the time, *"I suppose that is part of the trail which one who wishes to write must travel. I am conceited enough to think that I can write, or will be able to some day and I am going to stick to it."* Already he was beginning to realize he was playing with "fire" and liking it. He was taken with the idea of bringing down flame from heaven . . . and having it published!

Sometime later he continued in this vein: *"I have been working on a ranch down the country and, incidentally, arguing Socialism with the laborers. Do you know, Bob, nothing can kill Socialism in the minds of thinking people quicker than the arguments of the grubbers. It is so plainly a matter of getting something for nothing with a little revenge thrown in that the idea is sickening. Your arguments were logical and broad. Too broad perhaps for there can never be successful Socialism so long as such narrowness and greed, as I have seen, exist."*

Isn't it a trifle quixotic, this talk of bringing fire from heaven? He defends his Plan and explains its practicability: *"I guess I am queer and quite a few think that I am mentally turned because I have views of my own and occasionally have an idea. I figured out a theory which I have called 'Partial Immortality of the Mind' which throws out the idea of a soul and yet answers the questions of spiritualism and religion. I argued it with three ministers and beat them and then they have the nerve to spread the report that I was* eccentric. *You know how things travel in a small town. Some people have it that I am a raving maniac with infrequent lucid periods. Five hundred years ago they would have burned me at the stake for my ideas. They are just as intolerant now, but the law prohibits burning. This is a very prosaic world, Bob, in spite of Zane Grey and E. A. Poe. If we could lose our inborn hatred for change, what advances we could make!"* Well, he admitted there were obstacles to his plan but just then a coal gleamed brightly into a flame and he decided to take the risk.

I remember a Sunday of the same year. It was a few days before Christmas. John and I had been working all week in the men's haberdashery of an Oakland department store, Capwell's, I think it was. Came Saturday, we went home to spend the weekend with my parents. At breakfast the following morning my Mother startled us with the remark: "Of course you boys will want to go to church with

me this morning." Of course we didn't want to, but of course we did. So we dressed for the ordeal, putting on the new dollar neckties we had bought less the ten percent discount given us because we were employees of the Big Store.

In a little while, after having walked the blocks to the Methodist Church at the corner of 63rd and Shattuck Avenue, we were in our pew and in the throes of "How Firm A Foundation." I happened to look at John. He was singing . . . yes, he was singing . . . and firmly. The Rev. N. E. Dribbs was in the pulpit; a tall, gaunt, long-shouted expounder of the old time religion, as devout, and long-winded limb of the Lord as ever was. Words never failed him and I might add neither did his nose. It always called for a substantial wiping before and after a lengthy climax.

The text for this particular Sunday morning was culled from Luke 15:17: "And when he came to himself, he said, How many hired servants of my father's have bread enough and to spare, and I perish in hunger!" The announcements for the week over, the sick and deceased accounted for, the collection taken and blessed, the organ stilled but still ominous, the congregation reclined and resigned, the sermon was well gotten into before I became aware of misgivings in the mind of the young Fire-Bringer. An under-earth rumbling seemed to be emanating from our neophyte. But the preacher heard it not. He was too absorbed with . . . "The swine, according to Jewish opinion, is an unclean animal, not to be eaten as food, and therefore is not raised, except by those idolaters and men of no religion who live as outcasts in their country. Hence swineherding is looked upon as the lowest and most abject of all occupations. He may not enter the temple or even come near it. The swineherd in our text this morning is the Prodigal, crying out in hunger and remembering the plenty in his father's house. 'I perish with hunger!' What I propose to you is that the truth here expressed is that a life separated from God is a life of bitter hunger, or even of spiritual starvation! The soul is a creature that wants food in order to its satisfaction as truly as the body!"

The handkerchief was whisked out and the nose cared for. Meanwhile the mumblings of my friend became more audible. I believe I heard something like . . . "a lot of crap . . . if the soul is immortal, why worry about it . . . it's the body that. . . ." On my left my Mother suddenly became animated. She leaned forward to look at us, smiled quizzically and resumed her post, all attention. She had not heard. But she would later.

The sermon moved forward. The nose continued to be responsive. "Ho, every one that thirsteth, come ye to the waters: and ye that hath no money, come ye buy and eat! Wherefore do you spend money for that which is not bread, and labor for that which satisfieth not? Ho, hearken diligently unto me, eat and let your soul delight itself in fatness. Of them that have tasted, the Lord is gracious, and therefore desire the sincere milk of the Lord, that they may grow thereby."

"Yes, you all look satisfied here, while outside the world begs for a crust of bread or a chance to earn it. Feed the body and the soul will take care of itself!" You couldn't call this a mumble. It was a challenge from St. John. A few heads turned and twice as many eyes searched the faces behind them. The minister paused longer than usual this time as though settling something in his mind. My Mother was visibly disturbed. She leaned forward again, glared at us and made little clicking sounds with her tongue. John looked at the clock. I snorted. My Mother jabbed me in the ribs.

The minister continued, "There is no end to the diverse arts men practice to get some food for their souls. Ho, ye starving minds, hearken to God, God alone is the true food. . . ."

"What is this, God's free lunch? You can't satisfy real hunger on that . . . is this supposed to be a serial . . . to be continued in the next world. . . ." This time the preacher spotted his interlocutor.

"Young man," he said, "if you think you can preach a better sermon than I, come on up here and let us hear you! Or else have the courtesy to remain silent."

John didn't flutter an eyelid but returned with quiet wrath, "I don't think much of preaching. . . . Go on . . . you're getting paid for it."

The congregation sat rigid. Only the children wiggled around and ogled us with unblinking eyes. My Mother looked as though she wanted to crawl into her pocketbook. The Fire-Giver had interrupted the inspired word of God! It was unpardonable.

A few days after this, John Steinbeck said goodbye to me and went back to his home in Salinas . . . back to Tortilla Flat, the Pastures of Heaven and the Long Valley. Little did I dream that nineteen years later this young Prometheus would finally bring his fire from heaven in the flaming Grapes of Wrath!

—*The Wrath of John Steinbeck; or, St. John Goes to Church* (Los Angeles: Albertson Press/Bunster Creely, 1939)

* * *

Why Steinbeck wrote *The Grapes of Wrath*
Joseph Henry Jackson

Jackson, who reviewed several of Steinbeck's books, offered the following assessment of the significance of The Grapes of Wrath.

When a man writes an emotional, wrathful, questioning novel you can depend upon it that he has been profoundly shocked and hurt by something. Usually what has shocked him is some fresh evidence of man's cruelty, his greed, his treatment of his fellow-men. Occasionally such a book results from the novelist's perception of Nature's own violence and humanity's helplessness against it. In either case it is the artist's sensitivity to pain that pulls the trigger. "Is this just?" he cries, outraged. "Is this decent?" And he hurls the question at the world with all the force of which he is capable.

The Grapes of Wrath was written in precisely this mood. Like Zola when he saw the pitiful situation of the Belgian coal-miners, like Dickens with the debtors' prisons, like Harriet Beecher Stowe when she discovered that overseers sometimes beat slaves, Steinbeck was moved by a great wave of pity. Here was a group of workers, necessary to the State of California which must have its fruit, its cotton, its lettuce picked at exactly the right moment, yet treated with what seemed to him callous disregard of its common human rights. Moreover the problem was suddenly brought into focus by the westward movement of thousands of families blown and tractored off their overworked land in parts of Oklahoma, Nebraska and Kansas. No existing machinery could possibly have taken adequate care of these new migrants. There were too many of them; they came too fast, too recklessly, too hopefully. Yet on the other hand there was exploitation, there was cruelty, there was the kind of vicious nastiness that springs from fear. Steinbeck thinks in terms of the dispossessed; his sympathy naturally goes out to the under dog. Wherefore *The Grapes of Wrath,* no rounded presentation of the problem (which it never pretended to be) but a magnificent piece of special pleading, a novel that moved its readers—to pity, to disgust, to rage, but always moved them—and the most discussed, most significant work of fiction of its year, perhaps of its decade.

Behind the writing of *The Grapes of Wrath* was a series of circumstances with which John Steinbeck, in any positive sense, had really very little to do.

Steinbeck, first, was born and brought up in California's Salinas Valley, which is agricultural country with lettuce as its most important crop. As a

Steinbeck's friend Collins at Camp Weedpatch, a California migrant-labor camp (photograph by Dorothea Lange, courtesy of the Library of Congress; from Jackson J. Benson, Looking for Steinbeck's Ghost, *1988; Thomas Cooper Library, University of South Carolina)*

boy he worked in the fields, learned at least the motions through which the agricultural worker must go, came to understand something of the small hopes and fears and ambitions of the floating population on which California depends for fulfillment of its seasonal labor requirements. It is doubtful if he attached any serious social significance to what he saw then. Unquestionably, however, it was those years of contact with working men that sharpened his ear for the rhythm of their speech, that gave him his knowledge of their viewpoint.

In the second place, Steinbeck came of literary age at precisely the moment when migratory labor in California had seized the chance to make itself heard for the first time on a national scale—the occasion of the Salinas lettuce strike in 1936. He had four books to his credit, none of them successful, but all of them showing very clearly his preoccupation with men who had been passed over, men who had less, in one way or another, than their fellows.

Now something was happening under his very nose, in his own Salinas Valley. Men who had little were fighting back, saying loudly that they were entitled to more and that they were going to try to get it. Steinbeck's sensitiveness was ripe to react to the tragedy of the little man and his unquenchable courage in the face of calamity. When he met Tom Collins, a man who knew the ins and outs of labor troubles from long experience and was willing to show his new friend some things he had never seen, the fifth book was as good as written. It was *In Dubious Battle,* called by many the best strike novel ever to see print. Oddly enough, that novel, the first in which Steinbeck straightforwardly espoused the cause of the worker, was thoroughly disliked by the left wing, which felt that its author had failed to make it the thoroughgoing propaganda that, to the leftist, it should have been.

But the chain of circumstances was not yet complete. *In Dubious Battle* was published early in

Collins with a migrant family at Camp Weedpatch (photograph by Dorothea Lange, courtesy of the Library of Congress;
from Jackson J. Benson, The True Adventures of John Steinbeck, Writer, *1984;*
Thomas Cooper Library, University of South Carolina)

1936. By the summer of that year, the migration from the southern middle-west had begun to grow to the point where Californians were troubled about it. No one had worried much about the run-of-the-mill migratory worker; such groups were a traditional part of California's agricultural life. But the Salinas affair had brought into the open the inescapable fact that the migratory population was being rapidly augmented and that something would have to be done, (a) from the labor standpoint, and (b) from the humanitarian point of view. Nobody mentioned the specific labor problem out loud unless it was necessary; in some circumstances such matters are too hot to handle freely. But such questions as housing, hygiene, sanitation—these were reasonably safe. The San Francisco *News* commissioned the author of *In Dubious Battle* to write a series of articles on California's migratory workers.

Steinbeck, however, had learned some of the facts of life and labor when neither is organized, and some of the less pleasant truths about how far men will go when profit drives. He had not learned quite as much about the problems of the decent farmer, but nothing had slanted him that way. In any event, no artist can examine all sides of a question; the fact

that he is an artist limits him. It was the little man he had seen hurt. It was the worker, the dispossessed, the exploited, that had aroused his sympathy. His articles in the *News* considered that side of the question only. And there was plenty to consider. There were instances of vigilantism of a peculiarly unpleasant kind. There was terrorism. Men were starved and beaten, gassed and shot. Because more and more families were pouring into the State from the Southwest, wages were depressed. There was evidence that the wave of new immigration had been encouraged by printed handbills, by newspaper advertisements in the regions where the wind and the tractor were moving tenant farmers off the land. Steinbeck set it all down, asking the question which he was to present so movingly in *The Grapes of Wrath:* "What is to be done about it?"

Then two things happened. The curve of immigration into California began to rise sharply. Uncounted and uncountable thousands poured over Highway 66 and into California, the land of milk and honey, the country where there was always plenty of work. And Steinbeck met Pare Lorentz, whose pioneering work in the documentary film had begun to make him known in a field very closely related to Steinbeck's own.

The general idea of *The Grapes of Wrath* had already begun to simmer in Steinbeck's imagination. Now, under these two new pressures, it began to take definite shape. Where there had been one squatter camp beside a California highway, half a dozen sprang up. The battered car, loaded with mattresses and pots and children, that had rattled its Oklahoma license-plates up and down the Valley, became one of an endless parade. Municipal, county, even State organizations began to creak and strain under the load that had been put upon them. There was sickness and filth and starvation up and down California; even the best intentions were not enough. Nor were the intentions always of the best. In the great agricultural areas there was panic, and panic breeds viciousness and violence. Camps were burned out, loosely organized vigilante groups drove the migrants on—not to anywhere in particular, just out of the city, the county, for the next crowd of frightened, angry citizens to take care of. All of this Steinbeck saw. With a photographer he visited hundreds of migrant camps, took notes, made a pictorial record later to be printed in *Life* as evidence that the motion-picture made from *The Grapes of Wrath* had exaggerated. He talked to Pare Lorentz, too, and listened to him expound his theory of the technique of the documentary film, heard a play-back of the radio drama, *Ecce Homo!,* that Lorentz had done for the Columbia Workshop, unconsciously absorbed many of the Lorentz principles, as the merest glance at the "inter-chapters" in *The Grapes of Wrath* will show. Then he was ready. Everything added up. Steinbeck had by no means seen the whole problem, but he had seen enough to show him that there was injustice crying to be righted, that men were being hurt, that people he believed to be fundamentally decent and willing to work were being crushed by other men in the grip of a system about which nobody seemed to be able to do anything. Something had to be done. Men must not be treated like this, no matter what the reason or the excuse. He did not know the answer, nor does *The Grapes of Wrath* put forward any answer other than a kind of undefined, often mystical humanitarianism. But he could ask the question. Because he was a born novelist, he could ask it in a fashion that would arouse people to seek an answer somewhere. No one, even Steinbeck himself, dreamed that *The Grapes of Wrath* would make that question the most vital, the most discussed domestic problem of 1939 and 1940.

The Grapes of Wrath appeared in the spring of 1939 with no book-club selection to give it impetus,

merely the publisher's statement that he believed it to be an important novel.

Immediately upon its publication, *The Grapes of Wrath* touched off within California a controversy which quickly became national. Were the Joads, Steinbeck's migrant family, typical of the Oklahoma new-poor? Were the Joads' experiences typical? Was California as a whole the callous, brutal, exploiting State that the Joads found it in Steinbeck's story? There was very little discussion about *The Grapes of Wrath* as a work of fiction. From the beginning it was taken as substantial fact, debated on that ground, damned or praised as a document and not as a novel. More, a whole host of subsidiary points arose. Had Steinbeck written an obscene book? Many sincerely thought so, and Steinbeck, his publishers and reviewers the country over were deluged with letters expressing the writers' disgust with the frankness Steinbeck had employed. Had Steinbeck fairly represented the Joads themselves? Not only the farmers of California rose to deny it, but speakers for the "Okies." An Oklahoma representative caused to be inserted in the Congressional Record an "extension of remarks" in which he declared that not only had Steinbeck foully slandered the "most patriotic, most democratic and finest moral fiber in the Nation"—the Oklahoma tenant-farmers—by naming them "Okies," but that he had written a book which was "filthy, obscene, vulgar, degraded, depraved, unclean, malicious, low, damnable and lying." He added that it was "to the eternal credit of the Postal Department of the United States that it banned this obscenity from the mails." The Postal Department had done nothing of the sort. Nor had Steinbeck "labeled" these migrants "Okies"; the term was in common use for at least three years before *The Grapes of Wrath* was published. Among the migrants themselves there was disagreement, too. Letters to the newspapers from workers in the fields took both sides: Steinbeck had told the truth; Steinbeck had lied. The Associated Farmers, an organization of producers within the State, issued official and unofficial denials that Steinbeck's story was representative of conditions as they existed. Immediately the Associated Farmers were attacked by those whose sympathies were with the workers; they were in the wrong, said these sympathizers, because they had come together in a group to protect their own interests. That this was an illogical protest from people who were advocating just such organization for their interests did not seem to occur to any of them. But, logical or illogical, the wrath on both sides was the one positive thing about the reaction to Steinbeck's novel. A question that demanded answering had been dragged out into view, dramatized with extraordinary force, thrust under the public's nose. And nobody knew the answer.

The discussion did not die down. Instead, it spread beyond California, into areas that had been preoccupied with other matters. In many ways the ground had been prepared for the very question Steinbeck was asking. Lorentz's documentary pictures, *The Plow that Broke the Plains* and *The River,* had roused Americans to what was happening, had driven home the news stories and pictures of the dust-bowl tragedy. His radio play, *Ecce Homo!,* had made many a citizen uneasy as he thought of the thousands of Americans on the road, unanchored, floating, with nothing to tie to. The Federal Government's soil conservation plans, President Roosevelt's scheme for a magical belt of trees down the middle of the United States, picture-books like that by Margaret Bourke-White and Erskine Caldwell—such things had started the public thinking about what could be done, for men and soil both. *The Grapes of Wrath,* though it offered no solution, found an audience willing and anxious to debate the question it put forward. As 1939 advanced, sales soared. Announcement of the forthcoming motion-picture brought a larger group of readers. By the end of summer Steinbeck and his novel were dinner-table topics from one end of the country to the other.

Perhaps the most interesting phenomenon connected with *The Grapes of Wrath* was the number of people who were furious at what they conceived to be the obscenity in Steinbeck's story.

Not only were critics, editors, librarians and the publishers of the book flooded with complaining letters, but in several cases there were open attempts made to suppress the novel. In California these came to nothing, though there was one public burning, later hushed up because those who opposed the book on political grounds realized that efforts at suppression would merely lend color to the charges of Fascist tactics. Elsewhere librarians were cautious; some of them locked *The Grapes of Wrath* in the reserve room; many ordered so few copies that there was bound to be a safe, long waiting-list; a few refused outright to have the book on the library shelves. Most of the complaint, however, came from the reading public. In Oakland, California, one department-store buyer was threatened with a horse-whipping by an angry customer. Reviewers who had discussed the book found themselves on the receiving end of telephone calls and letters denouncing Steinbeck's "filth" in the most extravagant terms, most of them making the point that "no doubt" Steinbeck had inserted the bits to which they objected "in order to make more money." The protest was no mere crank affair, but an extraordinary and widespread revulsion against what the protestants considered to be an outrage against their conception of the decencies.

Some of this unquestionably came from readers who were politically opposed to the attitude Steinbeck took, and used the peg of "obscenity" on which to hang their opposition. Many, without doubt, were thoroughly frightened by Steinbeck's implications, his historical reminder in one of the inter-chapters that when enough men were hungry they rose and took what they needed. In such cases the fear was translated into anger which found its object in the portions of the book to which the complainants objected. But there was more than that behind the wave of protest.

The fact of the matter is that *The Grapes of Wrath* found tens of thousands of readers who had never come across a book of its kind before—readers who had never been exposed, for example, to the Jameses, Joyce and Farrell, readers who had grown up through the magazines as far as *Gone With the Wind,* perhaps, or *So Red the Rose,* and who honestly felt themselves betrayed when a best-seller turned out to harbor anything from a turtle which frankly wet the hand of the person who held it to a new mother who shockingly gave her breast to a full-grown man. Such readers did not know that a similar incident had been part of Greek legend, that Rubens had actually painted old Cimon drawing milk from the breast of Pero, or that de Maupassant had paralleled the scene in *The Idyll.* They were new readers, these people, when it came to books which concerned ideas rather than simple stories. They knew well enough that an old man sometimes accidentally fumbles his shirt-tail into sight when buttoning up his trousers, but they were shocked that a writer should say so. Old people were sweet, old people were saintly; old people might sometimes be cantankerous, but behind it all they were nice. It was a dreadful thing to take away from an old man the dignity which was the only thing left to age. Wherefore the shock was genuine; it proceeded directly from the tradition in which these readers had grown up. It was an honest shock, arising from an honest sense of betrayal. And the fact that it was so widespread is an interesting demonstration of the often unrealized lack of literary sophistication in a pridefully literate country.

The Grapes of Wrath, then, was unquestionably the best novel of 1939, will very likely prove to be the most significant of its decade. For once, a "proletarian" novel has come to life. Despite its weaknesses, the failure of the author to think his problem through, the sentimental speeches put into the mouth of ex-preacher Casy, the feeble ending (strong enough just as a stage-trick, but hollow when the reader looks back at it), the book has a surging vitality that cannot be denied. The Joads are alive; it is impossible to regard them as mere characters in a story; their agonies and hopes and fears are the reader's because Steinbeck has made them so. Which is to say that the triumph of *The Grapes of Wrath* is, in the final analysis, due to its qualities as a novel and not its effectiveness as a work of propaganda, enormously moving as it is in that sense also.

As for Steinbeck himself, the book and its aftermath have marked the most important point in his career so far. Sensibly, he has allowed his imagination a rest. Because marine zoology happens to be a hobby of his, when *The Grapes of Wrath* was finished he turned to working on a handbook of marine invertebrates in some of the Pacific gulfs and bays. He will say nothing about whatever plans he may have for fiction, excepting that he does not intend to write another book until he has something

to say. When that time comes, it is altogether possible that readers may discover a new Steinbeck, a Steinbeck who has grown on beyond *The Grapes of Wrath,* who has left behind the moments of mysticism that have persisted throughout his writing, who has whittled sentimentality down to simple sentiment, and who has emerged into the full maturity of a talent that is already head and shoulders above its contemporaries. Good evidence for this is his wise refusal to link himself with any of the sociological or political consequences of his book. Groups such as California's Simon Lubin Society have had to get along without him, sincere though they may be in their efforts to do something for the migrants, new and old. He is a novelist; that is the point. He intends to go on being a novelist.

—Why Steinbeck Wrote The Grapes of Wrath, by Joseph Henry Jackson, and Other Essays, Booklets for Bookmen, no. 1 (New York: Limited Editions Club, 1940), pp. 3–14

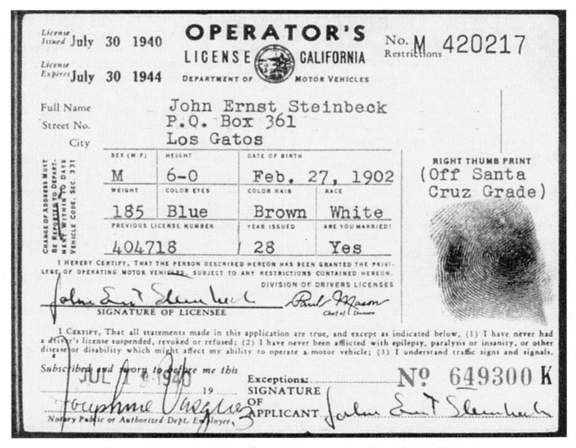

Steinbeck's California driver's license (from Sotheby's New York, The Maurice F. Neville Collection of Modern Literature, November 16, 2004*)*

Steinbeck and the President

Steinbeck to Franklin D. Roosevelt, 24 June 1940

Coming back from Mexico, where he had been working on the documentary The Forgotten Village *(1941), Steinbeck requested a meeting with President Franklin D. Roosevelt to present his plans for confronting German propaganda.*

My dear Mr. Roosevelt:

For some time I have been making a little moving picture in Mexico. In this line I have covered a great deal of country and had conversations with many people of many factions.

In the light of this experience and against a background of the international situation, I am forced to the conclusion that a crisis in the Western Hemisphere is imminent, and is to be met only by an immediate, controlled, considered, and directed method and policy.

It is probable that you have considered this situation in all its facets. However, if my observation can be of any use to you, I shall be very glad to speak with you for I am sure that this problem is one of the most important to be faced by the nation.

Respectfully yours,
John Steinbeck
—*Steinbeck: A Life in Letters,* p. 206

* * *

Steinbeck to Franklin D. Roosevelt, 13 August 1940

Two months after he proposed a strategy to combat Nazi propaganda, Steinbeck requested a meeting with the president to present a plan to sabotage the German economy. The idea was the work of Steinbeck and his friend Melvyn Knisely, an anatomy professor at the University of Chicago. According to Knisely's wife, "The idea was to scatter good counterfeit German paper money over the land, in big amounts. The then Secretary of the Treasury vetoed the idea. . . ." Steinbeck later wrote, "A friend and I took a deadly little plan to Washington and the President liked it but the money men didn't. That is, Lothian and Morgenthau. It would have worked, too, and would work most particularly in Italy."

Dear Mr. Roosevelt:

I assure you that if there were any alternative, I should not bother you with this letter. When you were kind enough to receive me I said I did not want a job. But after listening to the growing defeatism in the country, especially among business men, I find I have a job whether I want one or not.

When I spoke to you I said that the Germans were winning in propaganda matters through boldness and the use of new techniques. This has also been largely true in their military activities. At the time I had been thinking that our weapons and tactics would have to come not only from the military minds but from the laboratories.

Perhaps you have heard of Dr. Melvyn Knisely, who has the chair of Anatomy at the University of Chicago. He is a remarkable scientist and an old friend of mine. Discussing with him the problem of the growing Nazi power and possibilities for defense against it, he put forth an analysis and a psychological weapon which seem to me so simple and so effective, that I think it should be considered and very soon. I would take it to some one less busy than you if I knew one with imagination and resiliency enough to see its possibilities.

What I wish to ask of you is this—Will you see Dr. Knisely and me in a week or ten days—see us privately and listen to this plan? Within half an hour you will know that we have an easily available weapon more devastating than many battleships or you will not like it at all. Afterwards—if you agree—we will discuss it with any one you may designate on the National Defense Council.

Please forgive this informality, but frankly, I don't know anyone else in authority whom I can address informally.

May I have a yes-no reaction to this letter at your convenience?

Sincerely yours,
John Steinbeck
—*Steinbeck: A Life in Letters,* pp. 210–211

Chapter Four: 1941–1945

Chronology

Mid January 1941	Steinbeck writes the preface for a semi-autobiographical novel by Tom Collins, "They Die to Live," and the copy for a photojournalism story, to be published in *Life*, about the reality behind *Tortilla Flat* (1935). Steinbeck begins work on his part of the manuscript of *Sea of Cortez: A Leisurely Journal of Travel and Research* (1941), written with Ed Ricketts to report on their spring 1940 voyage aboard the *Western Flyer* to the Gulf of California.
February 1941	Because Steinbeck's wife, Carol, is having a difficult time recovering from the flu, which has bothered her since December, he talks her into taking a vacation in Hawaii. On 7 February she sails for Hawaii. During her absence Gwyn Conger comes to Monterey to visit Steinbeck, and he travels to Los Angeles occasionally to see her.
March 1941	Mavis McIntosh, of McIntosh and Otis, visits Steinbeck in Monterey, where he shows her around and introduces her to friends.
April 1941	Carol returns from her vacation, and Steinbeck tells her about his affair with Gwyn. He sends for Gwyn, and she comes to Monterey; a terrible confrontation ensues. Late in the month the Steinbecks separate permanently, and Steinbeck moves into a house on Eardley Street in Pacific Grove that they had purchased in January.

Steinbeck's first wife, Carol Henning Steinbeck, in 1941, the year the couple separated (National Steinbeck Center, Salinas; from Jackson J. Benson, The True Adventures of John Steinbeck, Writer, *1984; Thomas Cooper Library, University of South Carolina)*

May 1941	Steinbeck's screenplay for the documentary *The Forgotten Village* (1941) is published by Viking Press.
4 July 1941	Steinbeck completes the first draft of his portion of *Sea of Cortez* and is at work on another manuscript with the working title "God in the Pipes," which is in part the basis for *Cannery Row* (1945).
August 1941	Steinbeck's story "How Edith McGillcuddy Met Robert Louis Stevenson" is published in *Harper's*.
September 1941	Steinbeck begins the screenplay for a movie based on his story sequence *The Red Pony* (1937). Deciding to move to the East Coast, he asks Gwyn to go with him, and she agrees.
October 1941	Steinbeck flies to Washington, D.C., to attend a conference on the Foreign Information Service (FIS), established this year by President Franklin D. Roosevelt to counter Axis Powers propaganda with radio broadcasts in Europe. Steinbeck and Gwyn move into a house on a farm owned by actor Burgess Meredith near Suffern, New York. Steinbeck begins writing material for the FIS.
November 1941	Steinbeck and Gwyn move into a two-bedroom apartment in a residential hotel, the Bedford, on East Fortieth Street in Manhattan. The documentary *The Forgotten Village* runs into legal difficulties with the New York State Board of Censors because of obscenity charges. After a public hearing the ban is lifted, and the documentary is shown. Late in the month Steinbeck begins work on "The New Order," eventually published as the novel *The Moon Is Down* (1942).
December 1941	*Sea of Cortez,* by Steinbeck and Ricketts, is published by Viking Press on 5 December. Later in the month Steinbeck submits the manuscript for *The Moon Is Down* to Viking. He and Gwyn spend the Christmas and New Year holidays in writer Roark Bradford's French Quarter home in New Orleans.

Gwyn Conger in a photograph before her marriage to Steinbeck on 29 March 1943 (Center for Steinbeck Studies, San Jose State University; from Jay Parini, John Steinbeck, *1995; Thomas Cooper Library, University of South Carolina)*

January 1942	Steinbeck and Gwyn return to New York on 7 January. He is busy working on a stage version of *The Moon Is Down*.
March 1942	*The Moon Is Down* is published by Viking Press on 6 March. It sells well and becomes a Book-of-the-Month Club selection. Carol Steinbeck files papers for a divorce on grounds of mental cruelty.
7 April 1942	The play version of *The Moon Is Down* opens on Broadway and runs for nine weeks. Around this time Steinbeck is offered a permanent job with the Office of War Information (OWI), but he has to go through a security check.
May 1942	Steinbeck is offered a temporary assignment to write two books for the U.S. Army Air Forces. The motion-picture adaptation of *Tortilla Flat* opens in New York.
Late May–June 1942	Steinbeck and photographer John Swope accompany Army Air Forces trainees on a series of training trips to gather material for *Bombs Away: The Story of a Bomber Team* (1942).
27 November 1942	*Bombs Away* is published by Viking Press, with royalties donated to the Army Air Forces Aid Society Trust Fund.

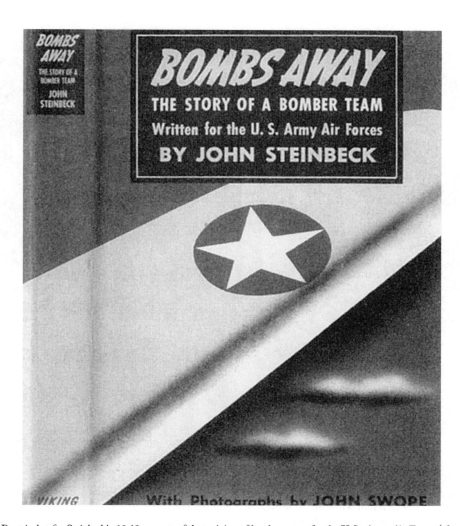

Dust jacket for Steinbeck's 1942 account of the training of bomber crews for the U.S. Army Air Forces (from William McPheron, John Steinbeck: From Salinas to Stockholm, *2000; Special Collections, Thomas Cooper Library, University of South Carolina)*

December 1942	Steinbeck begins work on a script for an Army Air Forces training movie. His childhood friend Jack Wagner approaches him with an idea for a movie, and over the next few weeks the two collaborate on the screenplay for *A Medal for Benny* (1945).
January 1943	Steinbeck finishes the screenplay for the Alfred Hitchcock motion picture *Lifeboat* (1944); he and Gwyn move to an apartment in New York.
March 1943	The movie adaptation of *The Moon Is Down* is released. Steinbeck applies for a job as a war correspondent and is hired by the *New York Herald Tribune*. On 18 March the final notice of the Steinbecks' divorce is issued. On the 29th Steinbeck and Gwyn are married in the New Orleans home of writer Lyle Saxon.
5 April 1943	Steinbeck receives word from the War Department that he has been accredited as a correspondent for the European theater.
May 1943	Steinbeck spends the month preparing for his new job as a war correspondent. Gwyn objects to his going, but he is determined to do so.
June 1943	Steinbeck leaves for England aboard a troopship on 3 June and arrives in London five days later.

Steinbeck and Max Wagner, an old friend from Salinas, in London in 1943, the year Steinbeck became a war correspondent for the New York Herald Tribune *(from Jackson J. Benson,* The True Adventures of John Steinbeck, Writer, *1984; Thomas Cooper Library, University of South Carolina)*

Steinbeck and others posing with a German Nazi flag after the capture of the island of Ventotene, off the coast of Naples,
in September 1943; top, from left: Lt. Cmdr. John Kramer, Capt. Charles Andrews, and Lt. Douglas Fairbanks Jr.;
bottom, from left: Lt. Arthur Bryant and Steinbeck (Center for Steinbeck Studies, San Jose State University;
from Jackson J. Benson, The True Adventures of John Steinbeck, Writer, *1984;*
Thomas Cooper Library, University of South Carolina)

July–October 1943	Steinbeck reports on the war from various points in England, North Africa, and Italy. On 15 October he returns to the United States in poor shape physically and emotionally.
November 1943	Steinbeck begins work on the manuscript of *Cannery Row.*
December 1943	*The Steinbeck Pocket Book,* edited and introduced by Pascal Covici, is published by Blakiston and distributed by Pocket Books. Steinbeck begins writing a novella with a Mexican setting with the working title "The Good Little Neighbor."
January 1944	While traveling in Mexico with Gwyn, Steinbeck plans *The Pearl,* a work that eventually becomes the screenplay for a 1947 movie and is published in book form that same year. Gwyn announces that she is pregnant. Steinbeck sees Hitchcock's movie *Lifeboat* and is quite unhappy about changes to the screenplay. He asks 20th Century-Fox to remove his name from the credits.
Spring 1944	Steinbeck meets Ernest Hemingway at a party in New York at Tim Costello's on Third Avenue. The meeting ends in disaster when Hemingway breaks John O'Hara's walking stick, a gift from Steinbeck.
June–July 1944	Steinbeck continues to work on *Cannery Row* in a New York office provided by Viking Press. He completes the book in six weeks.

2 August 1944	Gwyn gives birth to a boy, whom she and Steinbeck name Thomas Myles Steinbeck.
September 1944	Steinbeck envisions a new novel that is to be set in the Salinas Valley. He persuades Gwyn to move back to California so that he can be near the setting for the novel.
Early October 1944	The Steinbecks move back to California, Steinbeck traveling by car and Gwyn and the baby arriving by plane.
Late November 1944	Steinbeck begins work on *The Pearl*.
Early December 1944	Although the official publication of *Cannery Row* is not scheduled until January 1945, booksellers are already selling advance copies by the thousands.
2 January 1945	*Cannery Row* is officially published by Viking Press.
9 February 1945	Steinbeck and Gwyn arrive in Mexico City to assist in the casting, locations, and music for the movie version of *The Pearl*.
May 1945	The motion picture *A Medal for Benny* is released to mixed critical response.
August 1945	Steinbeck works with Max Wagner (Jack's brother) and Emilio "Indio" Fernández on the screenplay of *The Pearl*.
November 1945	After a brief visit to New York, Steinbeck returns to Mexico for three weeks to work on the filming of *The Pearl*.
December 1945	"The Pearl of the World," the novella that is published in book form as *The Pearl* in 1947, appears in *Woman's Home Companion*. Steinbeck returns to New York from Mexico.

Steinbeck and friends in Hollywood, circa 1945; from left, Frank Loesser, Steinbeck, Margery Hunter, Max Wagner, Howard Hunter, Gwyn Steinbeck, and Lynn Loesser (Center for Steinbeck Studies, San Jose State University; from Jackson J. Benson, The True Adventures of John Steinbeck, Writer, *1984; Thomas Cooper Library, University of South Carolina)*

In January 1941 Steinbeck returned to Hollywood to wrap up his work on the screenplay for the documentary The Forgotten Village (1941). By the end of the month he was back at his Pacific Grove cottage to work on his portion of Sea of Cortez: A Leisurely Journal of Travel and Research (1941), the book he was writing with Ed Ricketts about their spring 1940 sea expedition to the Gulf of California. Steinbeck planned to finish the draft as quickly as possible because he was always anxious to move on to something different. At the same time, his editor, Pat Covici, and his agent, Elizabeth Otis, reported that the sales of his previous books had fallen off, and they urged him to finish Sea of Cortez. He did so, writing in haste, but he understood that the book would be too philosophical for readers accustomed to his fictional works.

In the meantime, Steinbeck's marriage to Carol continued to collapse. He persuaded her to take a long vacation in Hawaii, and during this time Gwyndolyn "Gwyn" Conger came to Monterey to visit him, while he traveled to Los Angeles occasionally to work and to meet with her. When Carol learned of the affair upon her return home on 2 April 1941, she and Steinbeck had a terrible confrontation; later in the month they decided on a permanent separation.

Despite his unhappy personal life, Steinbeck remained active and productive throughout 1941. Upon completing his portion of Sea of Cortez, he began a work of fiction tentatively titled "God in the Pipes," which later developed into Cannery Row (1945). In September, Steinbeck began writing the screenplay for the motion-picture adaptation of The Red Pony (1937) and made the decision to move to the East Coast with Gwyn.

In October 1941 Steinbeck and Gwyn first moved into a house owned by actor Burgess Meredith near Suffern, New York, later moving into a two-bedroom apartment in a residential hotel, The Bedford, on East Fortieth Street in Manhattan. By late November, Steinbeck was working on "The New Order," a tale of a town occupied by a military force, which was to become The Moon Is Down (1942).

In January 1942 Steinbeck was busy with the stage version of The Moon Is Down; the novel version was published on 6 March by Viking Press and was named a Book-of-the-Month Club selection. Around this time Carol filed papers for a divorce from Steinbeck on grounds of mental cruelty. On 7 April the play The Moon Is Down opened on Broadway.

Steinbeck's enthusiasm for the war effort finally brought him an assignment. Appointed a "special civilian consultant" to the U.S. Army Air Forces, his job was to publicize the role of the air corps in the war and thereby help the War Department gain increased appropriations from Congress to expand strategic bombing capability. In May and June 1942 he traveled with photographer John Swope and Army Air Forces cadets on training missions gathering information for Bombs Away: The Story of a Bomber Team, which was published by Viking in late November of that year. In December, Steinbeck began work on the screenplay for an Army Air Forces training movie.

In March 1943 Steinbeck was hired as a war correspondent by the New York Herald Tribune, and he received the final notice of his and Carol's divorce. He and Gwyn traveled to New Orleans, where they were married on 29 March. Afterward he spent much of his time preparing for his new job. Despite objections from Gwyn, Steinbeck was determined to and left for England in June.

For the next four months Steinbeck reported on the war from various points in England, North Africa, and Italy. He tried to locate his sister Mary's husband, William Dekker, an army officer thought to be in England at the time, but as he moved with the army to North Africa, Steinbeck learned that his brother-in-law had been reported missing in action in Sicily. In England, Steinbeck also had the opportunity to meet with his childhood friend Max Wagner, who was serving as an enlisted man with the army, and found time for some casual historical research on the regions believed to be the setting for the Arthurian tales.

On 15 October 1943 Steinbeck returned to his New York home suffering from blackouts and blinding headaches. In November, following Covici's earlier suggestion that he write a novel in the style of Tortilla Flat (1935), he began working on Cannery Row. In the winter of 1944 Steinbeck cut himself off from social and domestic activities, depressed over his recent experiences covering the war.

During a long trip to Mexico in early 1944, Steinbeck's affection for that country and its culture revitalized him. He renewed his acquaintance with several people from the Mexican movie industry who had worked on The Forgotten Village and accepted a proposal to write another screenplay for a movie to be filmed in Mexico. The resulting work, The Pearl, was published in book form in 1947 and released as a movie the following year.

From June to July 1944 Steinbeck worked intensively on Cannery Row, completing it in six weeks. On 2 August the Steinbecks' first son, Thomas Myles Steinbeck, was born. Steinbeck was already thinking of his next novel, to be set in the Salinas Valley, and convinced Gwyn that they should move back to California. They moved to Monterey in October.

On 2 January 1945 Cannery Row was officially published by Viking Press, although booksellers had been selling copies before this date. The following month the Steinbecks went to Mexico City to assist in the production of the movie version of The Pearl, staying through the summer and fall. During the brief interval of their return to Monterey, Steinbeck began to realize that the community was no longer as welcoming to him as formerly. Meanwhile, Gwyn complained about his work on his new book (The Wayward Bus, published in 1947) and his long visits with Ricketts. In December 1945 the Steinbecks sold their house on the Monterey peninsula, and the family returned to New York.

The Forgotten Village (1941)

Steinbeck to Elizabeth Otis, 7 February 1941

Steinbeck wrote his agent, Elizabeth Otis, from Pacific Grove early in 1941 with news of progress on the documentary The Forgotten Village *(1941). He was angered that M-G-M had manipulated events to prevent Spencer Tracy from providing the narration for the movie, which in the end was read by Steinbeck's friend Burgess Meredith. Steinbeck also asked Otis to try to place a story he had written in the early 1930s based on a childhood experience of Edith Wagner, the mother of his friend Max Wagner. Steinbeck initially withdrew his story, "How Edith McGillcuddy Met R.L.S. [Robert Louis Stevenson]," because Wagner had written her own version of the event with hopes of publishing it. Now that she was quite old and in dire financial straits, he wanted Otis to place his story and donate the proceeds to Wagner. It was published in* Harper's *in August 1941.*

Dear Elizabeth:

Well, I am back from Hollywood and I hope for the last time. Put Carol on the boat and then word that Herb was in the hospital and that Tracy wasn't to be let to do the commentary. They wanted me down there, so I went. Got Burgess Meredith to do the commentary and he will do a good job too.

I have a good deal of anger left, that's all. The picture is good and should be sold. We got taken by M-G-M and I feel vengeful about it. Here's the story as I finally traced it down. Tracy wanted to do this commentary very much. M-G-M wanted him to do a new version of Jekyll and Hyde which he didn't want to do. So they promised him he could do the narration for me if he would do Jekyll. So he started it. Then they cut him off the narrative knowing he wouldn't stop a picture already in production. I would like to teach them not to tread on me. Mannix [Edward Mannix of M-G-M] is the man I'm after. I intend to blast their production of Tortilla Flat with everything I have. Life has asked me to do a story on the true Tortilla Flat and I may take it just to slap M-G-M. Perhaps you do not think revenge is good but I would like to teach these bastards they can't double-cross me with impunity.

To this end I wish you would read The Yearling again. Just a little boy named Jody has affection for a deer. Now I know there is no plagiarism on The Red Pony. But we are going to make The Red Pony, and two stories about a little boy in relation to animals is too much, particularly if in both cases the little boy's name is Jody. Will you see if we can't stop them from using the name and as much of the story as seems possible? If we don't want money we might easily get a court order. And I want to

plague them as much as I can. I have a dozen ways, these are just two. I'd like advice on the second.

The next is funny. Donald Friede wanted to meet me and Pat arranged it. He worked for two days on me to go into the Selznick agency—only for pictures, you understand—greatest respect for M & O but this has nothing to do with them. His offers were fantastic. He even told a girl I know he would see that she did all right if she would persuade me. I wouldn't mention this to anyone else but I do think it is funny. And of course it got exactly nowhere. The only thing I want in the world not he nor anyone else can give me but I didn't tell him that.

I have one more request to make of you. Do you remember a long time ago I wrote a story called How Edith McGillicuddy [*sic*] Met R.L.S.?

Well, she has finally released it or rather got back her rights and it was never published. Remember I had to withdraw it? Well, she is very old and crippled now and quite poor. I am sending you the story. Do you think you can sell it? It's my story and under my name. If you can sell it, maybe to a national magazine, get as much as you can for it and I will turn the money over to her. It must not be mentioned in print that she needs the money but you can tell any editor it is a true story. It would make her feel good and would ease the little time she has left if you could do this.

Had a letter from Carol but in Los Angeles. No word from her in the Islands yet but she was having a wonderful time on the boat, already just about owned it. She will have a marvelous time of it.

Good luck and all. And love to you,

John

—Steinbeck: A Life in Letters, edited by Elaine Steinbeck and Robert Wallsten (New York: Viking, 1975), pp. 225–226

* * *

Steinbeck, Not a Bit Hard-Boiled
Richard F. Crandell

Richard F. Crandell, reviewing the book version of The Forgotten Village, *praised Steinbeck's text and the stills from the movie.*

It is difficult to write on the inside of an eggshell without breaking the egg. So with a man's mind. And his heart. The shell resists men bringing the truth. If a man comes into a small village, one which is everywhere, with the truth, the shell resists and the man, be he a Steinbeck, an Ibsen, a Schick or a Noguchi, must contrive cunningly to get into the shell with the truth.

John Steinbeck tells us this story, a simple little story and one of the most important in the world, of the fight of the Mexican government to bring sanitation into the distant and superstition-ridden villages of our beautiful neighbor of the south. If it inspires only two, or even one, young American doctor to go down and help with this work, it will not have been written in vain.

First he wrote the text, drawing on his travels in untouched Mexican villages. In the little pueblo of Santiago, where the coming of babies and of the corn are the thrilling and important things of life, superstition and death lurk. The water which brings life to the corn brings death to the babies. The charms of the Wise Woman, all the snakeskins and herbs and magic, cannot drive the deadly little animals from polluted water. Children writhe with the stomach pains; their lips are dry, their breath hot. At the funerals mothers are proud and smile at the birth of a new angel, yet their bellies are full of dread.

To illustrate Steinbeck's story of this "Enemy of the People" in the torrid zone thousands of feet of motion pictures were made in the mountain towns, with Mexican Indians taking the parts. From this film 136 still pictures point up the Steinbeck text in the book. Many of them are superb. Agustin Delgado and Filipe Quintanor took the pictures under the direction of Mr. [Herbert] Kline and Alexander Hackensmid. The film itself will be released in the fall with Burgess Meredith as the "voice."

If the stills are indicative of the true merit of the film, it will have high rank in the documentary world. The cameramen for this book have brought out something in these carbon black reproductions that give full credence to the Steinbeck text.

As the camera focuses on Trini, the Wise Woman, looking with fear at the coming of the "horse-blood men," you feel the fear and suspicion of a thousand years of ignorance peering out of those heavy-lidded eyes. These actors are genuine and their sorry problems are translated to film as carefully as Steinbeck fashions his words.

Steinbeck of "the hard-boiled school" drops his guard again in this gatheringly powerful story. With his pen he has gone out to rally help for another bewildered and suffering group of the little people. Increasingly as he calls attention to the Okies, the sufferers of the flats and now the ignorant of rural Mexico, it appears that, far from being "hard-boiled," this writer is a Francis in store-clothes. The "muchas gracias!" of the overworked doctors and nurses of the Mexican rural health service for this gringo visitor and his picture entourage will be more sincere than a thousand phony good-will tours.

—*New York Herald Tribune,* 1 June 1941; reprinted in *John Steinbeck: The Contemporary Reviews,* edited by Joseph R. McElrath Jr., Jesse S. Crisler, and Susan Shillinglaw (Cambridge & New York: Cambridge University Press, 1996), pp. 195–196

Sea of Cortez (1941)

John Steinbeck's Chioppino of Biology and Philosophy
Scott Newhall

In his review of Steinbeck and Ed Ricketts's Sea of Cortez: A Leisurely Journal of Travel and Research *(1941), Scott Newhall acknowledged Steinbeck's courage in writing about something as "prosaic as voyaging to the Gulf of California" but lamented his desire to show himself as a philosopher rather than as a writer.*

John Steinbeck, of course, can write a great novel. But *Sea of Cortez* is by no means a work of fiction. Rather it is a sort of chioppino of travel, biology and philosophy.

A year and a half ago, Mr. Steinbeck, Mr. Ricketts and a crew of four—Tony, Tiny, Sparky and Tex—sailed from Monterey for the Gulf of California. For six weeks they were to collect and preserve the marine invertebrates which infest the tidal sands of the Gulf coast.

When the party returned they had collected 550 different species, they had consumed 45 cases of beer and the two leaders of the expedition each had enough information to write half a book. Mr. Ricketts was to assemble the biological information gathered during the trip; Mr. Steinbeck was to help collect and label, to observe the country, and then after speculation, to translate the meaning of the expedition for the lay mind. This review is concerned with the first half of the book, Mr. Steinbeck's.

Certainly, *Sea of Cortez* is far from Steinbeck at his ablest. This is probably because he has subordinated his very real ability as a writer to his desire to be first a philosopher, and second a naturalist. . . .

In attempting to write a book about anything so prosaic as voyaging to the Gulf of California, or so disciplined as collecting biological specimens, or so confusing as philosophical speculation, John Steinbeck accepted perhaps a far greater challenge than even he realized. He may not have lost the battle, but at least he is badly battered. He becomes inaccurate when he dogmatically states that Padre Clavigero visited the peninsula of Lower California, he is out of date when he illustrates a scientific principle by referring to the ancient decommissioned liner *Majestic* and he is simply small-boy vulgar when he reports on Tiny's collection of Phthirius pubis.

It is unfortunate that John Steinbeck should write anything but a very good book. But, of course, any great writer faces that trap. And it is only fair to report that parts of *Sea of Cortez* come much closer to what the author can really do.

Who else could so understand and admire the small fry of Mexico? Who could speculate better whether "a nation, governed by the small boys of Mexico, would not be a better, happier country than those ruled by old men, whose prejudices may or may not be conditioned by ulcerous stomachs . . ."?

Who else could have appreciated the terrible moral decay eating into the expedition, when one of the party succumbed to the perfidy of stealing slices of lemon pie and devouring them in bed after the lights were out?

It's just too bad that the whole of Mr. Steinbeck's half is not as good. That all of it is not of the same stuff as the following communiqué:

"On the beach at San Lucas there is a war between the pigs and the vultures. Sometimes one side dominates and sometimes the other. On occasion the swine feel a dynamism and demand Lebensraum, and in the pride of their species drive the vultures from the decaying offal. And again, when their thousand years of history is over, the vultures spring to arms, tear up treaties, and flap the pigs from the garbage. And on the beach there are certain skinny dogs, without any dynamisms whatsoever

and without racial pride, who nevertheless manage to get the best snacks."
—*San Francisco Chronicle,* 14 December 1941; reprinted in *John Steinbeck: The Contemporary Reviews,* pp. 207–208

* * *

The Scientific Second Half of the *Sea of Cortez*
Joel W. Hedgpeth

Joel W. Hedgpeth called Sea of Cortez *"the first large-scale attempt" to write about both the results of a scientific expedition and the human activities associated with scientific research.* Between Pacific Tides *(1939) was an earlier book by Ricketts and Jack Calvin.*

To the general reader, lured this far by the narrative part of the book, the second half of the *Sea of Cortez,* may seem a wilderness of uncouth nomenclature and meticulous minutiae, leavened somewhat by a generous

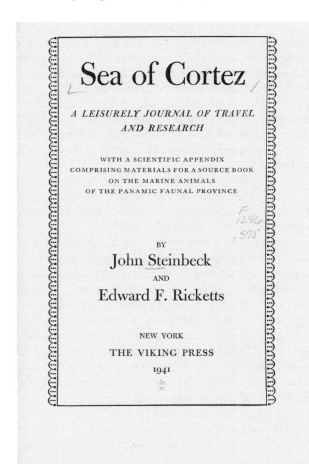

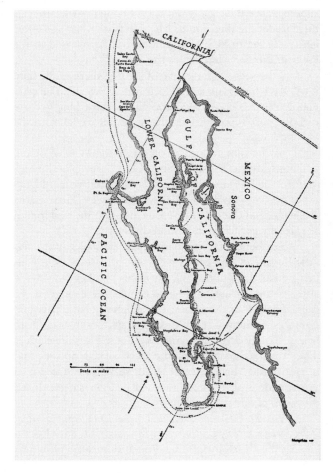

Title page for Steinbeck and Ed Ricketts's account of their spring 1940 expedition aboard the Western Flyer *to the Gulf of California, with a map showing the route of the voyage, from the 1951 republication of Steinbeck's portion of the book as* The Log from the Sea of Cortez *(Thomas Cooper Library, University of South Carolina)*

section of photographs and drawings of some of the commoner animals. To the marine biologist, however, this is the important part of the book, for these seemingly unpronounceable names and the annotated bibliographies which accompany them are signposts and traveling directions for one of the world's most interesting faunal provinces, and this appendix will hereafter be indispensable for students of the marine invertebrates of the Gulf of California.

The authors make no pretense that this annotated list is complete, but prefer to call it "a scientific appendix comprising materials for a source book on the marine animals of the Panamic faunal province." The same careful searching of the literature (as the technical papers are capriciously called) and consultations with specialists which made *Between Pacific Tides* so valuable a book are evident in this work, and it may in some ways be considered a complementary volume to *Between Pacific Tides*. Indeed, the revised edition of the latter book may include cross references to *Sea of Cortez*. It is no reflection upon the authors but upon our incomplete and haphazard knowledge of the fauna of our own backyard that the first general account of this fauna is not much more than an outline.

Although restricted principally to the littoral fauna of the Gulf of California during a period of six weeks, over 500 species of animals were collected, a far better record than that made by several more formal and handsomely endowed expeditions which have invaded the region. The echinoderms, larger mollusks and crabs are especially well represented and a fair collection of shore fishes was also made. There are omissions, inevitable because of the limitations of time and energy as well as the scarcity of good papers on certain groups. The limitation to a single short collecting season may account for the interesting failure to collect any sea spiders, as well as for other less obvious gaps in the collections. The sea anemones are omitted entirely from the appendix although frequently mentioned in the narrative, and several other groups are touched but lightly, yet on the whole the authors have succeeded in the intention of producing a source book rather than a handbook.

Popular accounts of expeditions have long been staple reading fare, but the actual results have too often been lost in the dusty tomes of libraries and museum cubbyholes. This is the first large-scale attempt to include both phases of this particular sort of human activity in one volume, and it would be interesting, if it were possible, to

The Western Flyer *returning to Monterey Bay at the end of Steinbeck and Ricketts's voyage to the Gulf of California in spring 1940 (from Katharine A. Rodger, ed.,* Renaissance Man of Cannery Row: The Life and Letters of Edward F. Ricketts, *2002; Thomas Cooper Library, University of South Carolina)*

learn what influence this book may have on the development or formation of coming generations of biologists. Certainly no reader can look at this appendix and still entertain the delusion that a scientific expedition is nothing more than an affair of moonlit nights and enraptured contemplation of new and strange animals, a delusion that Dr. [William] Beebe has done little to dispel. Not that scientific expeditions are devoid of their romantic moments, but such popularization has all too often prevented the reader from realizing the vast amount of work yet to be done to bring together and correlate the widely scattered information in order that it may assume its proper place in our knowledge. Neither John Steinbeck nor Edward Ricketts believe that the study of biology, especially the amazingly varied and complex life of the tidal regions, should be the exclusive fare of indefatigable museum drones, and that conviction is the inspiration of *Sea of Cortez*, enlivening even the remoter sections of the technical appendix.

–*San Francisco Chronicle*, 14 December 1941; reprinted in *John Steinbeck: The Contemporary Reviews*, pp. 208–209

* * *

Steinbeck to Frank Knox, 5 May 1942

After the Japanese attacked Pearl Harbor, Steinbeck took a keen interest in war issues. He wrote Secretary of the Navy Frank Knox about scientific reports on the Pacific islands then under Japanese mandate that he and Ricketts had run across in their research. These reports, he suggested, included information potentially useful for American military strategy.

Dear Mr. Secretary:

I believe that the best way to get information to its proper place is to send it to the chief. I hope you will give the following to the officer of naval intelligence most able to understand and make use of it.

It is not generally known that the most complete topographical as well as faunal information about any given area is found in the zoological and ecological reports of scientists investigating the region.

For a number of years, my partner Edward F. Ricketts and I have been charting the marine animals of the coast of North America and through this work have looked into the publications from other parts of the world, including the Japanese Mandated Islands.

Ricketts's Pacific Biological Laboratories in Monterey, 1930s (Edward F. Ricketts Jr.; from Katharine A. Rodger, ed.,
Renaissance Man of Cannery Row: The Life and Letters of Edward F. Ricketts, *2002;*
Thomas Cooper Library, University of South Carolina)

No Occidentals have been allowed to land in the Mandated Islands since they were taken under Japanese control.

The only publications or information to come from these Islands have been the reports of Japanese biologists, who are fine research men and truly pure members of the international scientific fraternity.

The reports are found to contain maps, soundings, reefs, harbors, buoys, lights and photographs of these areas. The information, if not already in the possession of Naval Intelligence, could be very valuable.

Yours truly,
John Steinbeck
—Steinbeck: A Life in Letters, p. 246

The Moon Is Down (1942)

The Will to Live and Resist
Norman Cousins

In contrast to the many negative reviews that The Moon Is Down *(1942) received, Norman Cousins commended the book version as a "unique reading experience," although he found fault with the ending.*

It would be easier to write two separate reviews of this book than to attempt the usual single account. Because when you put it down (it is a small book, a very small book, and you can read it at a single sitting), you seem to carry away two distinct sets of impressions. The first is your feeling about the book up until a dozen pages from the end. The second is your feeling about it just after you have finished it. In short, the ending, though dramatic enough, seems not of a piece with the story itself, and thereby mars as satisfying a novelette as has been published in many seasons. This is why:

This is a story whose hero is a people—the people of a small town, an honest, reasonable, slow-going people who believed that peace was the language of mankind, that one had only to speak it anywhere to be understood and respected. They believed it when the invader came, speaking the language of fascism. They learned right away that part of that language meant treachery, for they were to discover that a man they had thought to be one of themselves, the once-popular storekeeper, had proved himself the wedge which enabled the small invading force to move into the town almost unnoticed and to fasten its grip on the people so quickly and so effectively that immediate resistance was impossible.

Yet even this early lesson disturbed only slightly the unstrained quality of their mercy, nor did it inflame a bitterness measured in terms of quick violence. They had been speaking one language for centuries, and it was difficult to learn that deceit could mean deceit; and so they could not help it if they tended to see even their enemies in their own image.

Their spokesman—and he was a spokesman in the truest sense of the word—was the Mayor, a rather solid but generally inarticulate character who, seemingly, had been Mayor as far back as anyone could remember, and whose chief virtue was that his mind and the collective mind of the people were one. It wasn't that he had deep powers of insight or vision or imagination; it was that an affinity existed which enabled him to express better than any other person the public will. His job was not to create public opinion but to feel it—sometimes even before the people themselves.

Around the Mayor there were other persons as much a part of the town as the Mayor's old mansion. There was the good doctor—fireplace philosopher and friend and confidant of the Mayor; there was the Mayor's wife, a somewhat fussy and ceremonious little woman who made all the decisions except the important ones; there were the servants, a cook and a butler, both strongly individualistic, whose courage and resourcefulness seemed limitless.

But the Mayor's "palace"—once the invasion took place—also became the headquarters of the occupation forces. The Mayor stayed on in a section of the palace, and retained his nominal authority. The officers occupied another section. Off by themselves, the officers were a human and average lot, so human, in fact, that we can understand them and see them as part of a vaster tragedy. But they had been trained to speak the language of fascism, and even though some of their number realized that this language must always be unintelligible to a free people, theirs was not to question or reason, but to order. They ordered the people to obey. To work the mines. They even ordered them to be friendly.

The people are slow and they are reasonable but they are not fools. Orders spoken in the language of fascism are not reasonable orders. They will work because they have always worked but they will work out of their own free will and not because they are slaves. And when one of them strikes out and murders an officer, the others come to understand that they have a job to do: the enemy must be destroyed at any cost. This wave of resistance starts as a little stream, picks up strength and grows and broadens and becomes a flood. There is no mistaking its force or its size. This is a Niagara of resistance let loose. The people are not armed and open warfare is impossible. But in their own way they have come to understand what the language of fascism means and will have none of it. They hold back at

Poster for the 1942 movie version of Steinbeck's 1935 novel (Bruccoli Clark Layman Archives)

work. They sabotage. They communicate with Britain and get the ally to drop hundreds of sticks of dynamite by parachute.

They cannot be stopped. They cannot be stopped even when retaliation strikes back swift and deep. The Mayor is ordered to stop them, but he does not, because he knows he cannot, because he knows they are doing what he would do. But the Mayor is a symbol. He is loved and respected. The people must be punished. They must be hurt. They must pay the price of their resistance. That price is the life of the Mayor. That is the language of fascism, which twists the knife instead of withdrawing it, and yet expects the wound somehow to close. . . .

That is the rough story. As you read it, you have the sense of participation. You feel the tempo rising in you, even as it rises in the spirit of the townsfolk. You keep preparing yourself for the smashing climax. You are psychologically attuned to an ending of the proportions of *For Whom the Bell Tolls*.

But the last dozen pages do not seem to come off. It is not only that the story is not resolved—we may have to wait a long time until events themselves will justify stories such as these being resolved in the way we should like to see them resolved—but that the technique itself of the ending seems at odds with the overall pattern. The Mayor is a heroic character, certainly, but he is not the hero. And yet the hero's role is thrust upon him suddenly and a hitherto rather inarticulate old man goes off at the final curtain reciting the *Apology* from Socrates. Such a device is obviously better suited to the theatre. In fact, *The Moon Is Down* would make an even better play than it does a book. It divides itself nicely into three acts, and action is described mostly in group conversation, rather than by the direct method. Then, too, the coming and going of the characters, the development of the dramatic situations, the continuing emphasis upon strong, colorful characters—all this seems to add up to drama of the first magnitude.

But play or no play, as a book *The Moon Is Down* is a unique reading experience. Steinbeck tells his story with simplicity, force, dignity, and even beauty. I cannot recall another novel of comparable size that has achieved so much of the sense of vital suspense, so strong a feeling of reality. Steinbeck's images are strong and closely knit. Except for one or two slips, he comes as close as any author to making himself unobtrusive and leaving you free to lose yourself in the story. Which you do.

—*Saturday Review*, 25 (14 March 1942); reprinted in *John Steinbeck: The Contemporary Reviews*, pp. 223–224

* * *

John Steinbeck's Story of a Military Invasion Appears on the Stage
Brooks Atkinson

Brooks Atkinson, reviewing the stage version of The Moon Is Down *for* The New York Times, *called Steinbeck "a realist of genuine integrity."*

Take Mr. Steinbeck on his own terms. In *The Moon Is Down*, which finally turned up at the Martin Beck last week, he is making a confession of faith in a style of practicable reality. Using a small mining town as his laboratory, he has written the story of a brilliantly organized military invasion that gradually breaks down in the face of elusive resistance by free men who are ingenious and angry.

The Moon Is Down is not a rhetorical play. Using words and phrases sparingly Mr. Steinbeck underwrites his heroics. To him an ounce of conviction is worth a ton of sound and fury. But he has a talent for vivid imagery that cuts deep and stays there. "Flies conquer the flypaper," screams one of the invaders who is beginning to realize that every victory increases the hazards of conquest. "Flies capture two hundred more miles of flypaper," he laughs hysterically. Contemplating the irony of conquering a town that continues furtive resistance he bitterly exclaims: "Conquered and we are afraid. Conquered and we are surrounded." For the invaders start losing security the moment they capture the town; every step they make forward takes them two steps back. At the end of the play they are left clinging to the tail of the whirlwind they recklessly set in motion when they took over the mayor's house and started administering the town.

Mr. Steinbeck is a realist of genuine integrity. *The Moon Is Down* is a small play, deliberately. Part of the strength it has comes from the commonness of the men and women who are in it. The invaders are not supermen; they are human beings, subject to human limitations. Despite their armored swank and the omniscience of their military technique, they covet love and sociability, like any one else, and their capacity for living in a state of military correctness is not inexhaustible. The ordinary doubts of human beings weaken their bravado. Nor are the people of the town fabulous heroes. They are miners and fishermen with wives and families, subject to the usual needs. In the long run the conflict lies between character. Pit efficient inhumanity against humanity that has tasted freedom and the inhumanity finally crumbles because it is at war with the living universe. That is the theme of a quiet and sober drama that is well acted by players who are scrupulously refraining from exploiting it. To this theatregoer it is an impressive and heartening play.

Although no one doubts the high-mindedness of Mr. Steinbeck's motives, some people regard *The Moon Is Down* as a dangerous play for these times. By implication it

Dust jacket for Steinbeck's 1942 novel, about a town in Norway taken over by the Germans, that he also adapted for the stage that same year (from William McPheron, John Steinbeck: From Salinas to Stockholm, *2000; Special Collections, Thomas Cooper Library, University of South Carolina)*

is too much like passive resistance, they say. "Give the Axis powers enough rope," Mr. Steinbeck seems to think, "and they will hang themselves." As a matter of fact, Mr. Steinbeck is no ivory tower prophet. But the reception his play and novel have had poses a troublesome problem in contemporary writing. The long view toward the war and the short view are not identical.

In spite of the grave perils that surround the United Nations this year, most of us believe that the ultimate victory will be ours. That is the long-term faith; we cannot win without it. But the immediate problem is not the same. We cannot win the ultimate victory unless we are driven to action now by the fear of losing the war this year while the Axis powers are at the peak of their strength and we are barely on the threshold of our potential. In short, confidence in ultimate victory may be the sleeping dram that will lose the war before we know it. . . .

And this brings us to the character of Colonel Lanser, commanding officer of the invading detachment. Far from being a cold-blooded despot, he is tolerant and forbearing, disillusioned about the military science of conquest; and, as a veteran of the last war, he under-

stands the psychology of an invaded nation more thoroughly than the people of the town. He is a martyr to a cause in which he does not believe. Mr. Steinbeck has given his most attractive character to the enemy. Although this sympathetic characterization of a representative of tyranny violates popular expectations, it is justified by the results. For it proves that the technique of invasion fails even when it is administered humanely. Colonel Lanser's reluctance to arouse resistance in the townspeople delays sabotage, murder and reprisals. But, soon or late, the result is the same and inevitable. The town refuses to be mastered.

Take Mr. Steinbeck on his own terms. Although he is no virtuoso dramatist, he knows what he is doing. Under the casual surface of *The Moon Is Down* there is firm tension. It represents the inner serenity of a man whose mind is clear about basic things. He believes in human beings.

—New York Times, 12 April 1942; reprinted in *John Steinbeck: The Contemporary Reviews,* pp. 242–243

* * *

Two Ways to Win the War
Clifton Fadiman

Clifton Fadiman found fault with both structure and content in The Moon Is Down.

For all its qualities, John Steinbeck's *The Moon Is Down* strikes me as unsatisfactory on two counts. Its form is deceiving and its message is inadequate.

The publishers, presumably with the author's knowledge, call it a novel. At the most lavish estimate, the story hardly runs beyond forty thousand words, all quite short and simple words, too. Many current novels, it may be argued, would gain by reduction to forty thousand words, but it does not follow that forty thousand words make up a current novel. I fear *The Moon Is Down* is a novel only in a Steinbeckian sense.

The deception, however, goes deeper. The fact is that Mr. Steinbeck's book is not a narrative at all but a

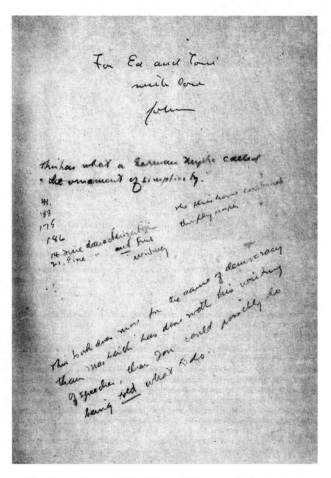

Free front endpaper of The Moon Is Down *with inscription by Steinbeck to Ricketts and Toni Jackson, Ricketts's common-law wife (from Sotheby's New York,* The Maurice F. Neville Collection of Modern Literature, *November 16, 2004)*

Sinking *Lifeboat*

Steinbeck was so upset at changes to his screenplay for Alfred Hitchcock's Lifeboat *(1944) that on 19 February 1944 he sent a telegram to Annie Laurie Williams, the agent who handled movie and drama contracts for McIntosh and Otis, requesting that his name be removed from the movie credits.*

PLEASE CONVEY THE FOLLOWING TO 20TH CENTURY FOX IN VIEW OF THE FACT THAT MY SCRIPT FOR THE PICTURE LIFE BOAT WAS DISTORTED IN PRODUCTION SO THAT ITS LINE AND INTENTION HAS BEEN CHANGED AND BECAUSE THE PICTURE SEEMS TO ME TO BE DANGEROUS TO THE AMERICAN WAR EFFORT I REQUEST MY NAME BE REMOVED FROM ANY CONNECTION WITH ANY SHOWING OF THIS FILM

JOHN STEINBECK
—*Steinbeck: A Life in Letters,* p. 267

---

play equipped with a few casual disguises. The entire construction is dramatic. The dialogue is play dialogue, not novel dialogue (and there is a sharp difference); the whole affair settles naturally into scenes and acts. It reads well but it plays much better than it reads, and you're apt to find yourself puzzled, as you turn the pages, by the absence of footlights. Indeed, I feel strongly that a dramatic critic would be far better equipped to review the book and that it has strayed into these columns through some error. Come to think of it, Mr. Steinbeck's *Of Mice and Men* was also a play disguised as a story, and was rather more effective after the false whiskers had been removed.

This lack of candor about the form of the book may not bother you at all. What may well be worrisome, though, is the inadequacy of the story's central feeling. *The Moon Is Down,* like *Of Mice and Men,* is a melodrama. It says with great dexterity things every one of us would love to believe, but for all that it remains a melodrama, which would not be to its discredit were it not obvious that Mr. Steinbeck is aiming at something loftier.

The Moon Is Down demonstrates, in terms of sound and even momentarily moving action, that the free spirit of man is unbreakable. The scene is never named (I find this annoying; others may find it an effective device), but it seems to be Norway. The invaders are not named, either, but we may as well come out with it: Mr. Steinbeck means the N-zis. The town with which the story deals is delivered up by Fifth Columnists, and the totalitarians settle down to what they call the "engineering job" of gearing it into their military-industrial economy. In the course of this effort they shoot, maim,

Spencer Tracy as Pilon, Hedy Lamarr as Sweets, and John Garfield as Danny in the motion-picture adaptation of Tortilla Flat *(MOMA/Film Stills Archive; from Joseph R. Millichap,* Steinbeck and Film, *1983; Thomas Cooper Library, University of South Carolina)*

torture, and rape, but to no avail. They are opposed by subtle sabotage, by weapons dropped into the natives' hands from English planes, by a free spirit which is so much stronger than the slave spirit of the invaders that in the end it is the conquerors who grow afraid of the conquered, it is the ruthless soldiers who grow neurotic. As the Nazi Colonel Lanser broodingly puts it, "We will shoot this man and make twenty new enemies. It's the only thing we know, the only thing we know."

Now, I submit that this is simply too easy, that it is a melodramatic simplification of the issues involved. The simplification is based on the notion that in the end good will triumph because it is good and evil will fail because it is evil. With all our hearts we would like to think this true, and that is why melodrama is a popular form of literature. But it is hardly the most elevated form.

Many of us perhaps have been wondering of late why plays such as *Candle in the Wind* (of which Mr. Steinbeck's book is a more professional version) are, for all their splendid sentiment, somehow unsatisfactory. I suppose it is because this war is bigger and more terrible than their authors seem to admit. How shall we put it? If we cease to love freedom, we are lost, but the love of freedom alone cannot win for us. That appears to be the gray truth of the matter, and it is, let us confess, not the kind of truth that inspires exciting plays and novels. Most of our imaginative anti-Fascist literature has rested upon the stirring reiteration of sentiments to which our hearts give allegiance. But it is becoming increasingly clear that this form of spiritual patriotism is not only not enough but may even impede the war effort, because it fills us with a specious satisfaction, it makes our victory seem "inevitable," it seduces us to rest on the oars of our own moral superiority.

I like a fine phrase as well as the next man. I would like to believe, with Mr. Steinbeck, that "it is always the herd men who win battles and the free men who win wars." In the long run perhaps that is true, but everybody now alive is a short runner, and it is perfectly possible for Hitler to annihilate most of us. Once we get interested in winning this war for our remote posterity, it is half lost. Why not win it for ourselves? And if we are to win it for ourselves, we will, I fear, hardly be helped by the noble message in *The Moon Is Down* and in dozens of similar works full of high intentions; we can be helped only by the blood, toil, tears, and sweat of which Mr. Churchill has spoken. We no longer need to be told we are in the right, for we know it. We wish to be told only how we may make that right prevail.

I fear this sermon has obscured the fact that *The Moon Is Down* is a tense story (or play), written with great economy and with a certain grim humor, too. Its characters we have met before in other anti-Nazi books and dramas, but here they are more sharply minted and their dialogue is recorded with precise, if limited, insight. If you read the book quickly and do not reflect upon it, it seems extraordinarily powerful. If you read it slowly and with deliberation, it seems merely extraordinarily skillful. . . .

* * *

Steinbeck's Latest Is an "Idea Novel"
Wallace Stegner

Writer Wallace Stegner commended the technical crafts-manship of The Moon Is Down *but expressed disappointment in the book as a whole.*

Undoubtedly this story of a peaceful people over-run, conquered, and eventually driven to underground resistance by an invader will receive both lavishly commendatory and inordinately harsh criticism. It deserves neither. It is neither a great book nor a bad book, though reviewers drunk on the timeliness of the theme may call it the first, and reviewers holding up *The Grapes of Wrath* as a measuring stick may call it the last. . . .

Technically the story is neat, tight, craftsmanly. Like *Of Mice and Men,* it is designed for immediate conversion to the stage, and beyond a doubt it will be a successful play. There is a good curtain line for every scene, the chapters group themselves naturally into acts, the final scene is one calculated to move almost any audience.

Yet for all that, I find *The Moon Is Down* a rather disappointing book, not because it fails to live up to *The Grapes of Wrath,* but because it fails to live up to itself. The theme of the simple courage of simple people is an old one with Steinbeck, and a perennially good one. But it doesn't come off here as it does in *The Grapes of Wrath,* in *In Dubious Battle,* or even in *Of Mice and Men.* I think there is a very sound and recognizable reason why it does not.

An embattled novelist who has produced a monumental best seller on a crucial and timely subject is in a hole. He can't go back to writing novels which are not socially-conscious, for fear of looking like a renegade. He can't repeat himself without dropping into the role of mouthpiece for reform. He must go on. But to what? He must find a problem graver and more pressing than the last one.

There is no difficulty in finding the problem. Any facet of the war problem is the automatic choice. But in choosing to write of the little people being crushed by and resisting the war, Steinbeck had to go out of his own experience. He had to fake, and he faked very well. Still, the people haven't the three-dimensional reality that his other people have had, and the horrors through which they live have been so constantly before us in the headlines and radio reports that, to put it quite

---

The Moon Is Down in Sweden

A short notice about the response to the 1943 Swedish production of The Moon Is Down *appeared in* Time.

Opening in Stockholm last month, John Steinbeck's anti-Nazi, inferentially Norwegian *The Moon Is Down* proved such a smash that it speedily moved to a bigger theater. Swedish critics, speaking of ever-growing Norwegian resistance, praised Steinbeck for prophetic insight, remarked that *The Moon Is Down is* truer today than when it was written.

Judging by reports which have sifted through, the widespread U.S. criticism that the Nazis in the play are too weak has not been voiced in Sweden.

–"Steinbeck in Sweden," *Time,* 41 (19 April 1943); reprinted in *John Steinbeck: The Contemporary Reviews,* p. 253

---

bluntly, we are calloused to that variety of pain. War can hardly move us now in the way that fiction must move us if it is to succeed. The wider the headlines stretch our sympathy for suffering humanity, the less we believe that suffering, the more we spring back into our own personal problems, the more the war becomes an abstraction.

That is the trouble with this careful, honest, skillful, and essentially true book. It deals with problems so terrible that our minds—yet—repudiate them. And I suspect that those problems are abstractions even to Mr. Steinbeck. He has never in the past evidenced any inability to move his reader, even if his reader is hard to move. But this novel will move only the easy ones. The hard ones will see even in the technique, even in the writing, signs of Mr. Steinbeck's own hesitancy.

Steinbeck is an artist, and a fine one, but he is not the infallible artist that some critics have called him, and here he makes mistakes. He uses two servants who are so plainly stock characters that they are almost ham. He cannot resist making Mayor Orden a mouthpiece of the democratic way. He is guilty of having two men on the verge of death by firing squad hold the stage for minutes quoting to each other the *Apology* of Socrates, so that the audience will know they are dying in the cause of intelligence and civilization.

The Moon Is Down is not, thank God, as talky, emotional and dishonest as Robert Sherwood's *There Shall Be No Night.* There are magnificent scenes in it, such as the one in which Lieut. Tonder of the invaders turns hysterical under the steady, silent hatred of the villagers, and the passage (unfortunately impossible on the stage) in which the inevitable growth of that hatred is recreated. But the ending seems to me false and liter-

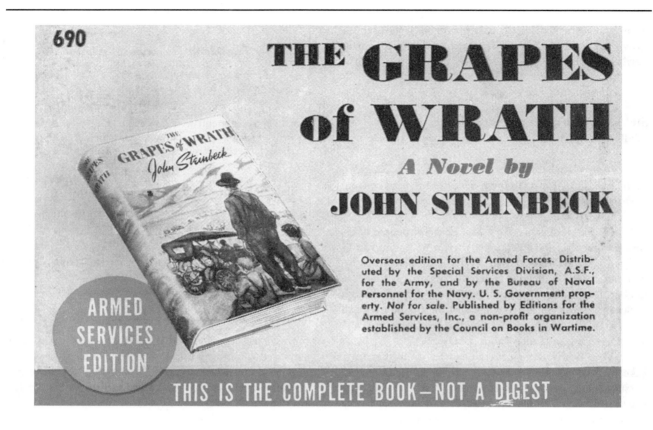

Front and back covers of the 1943 Armed Services Edition of Steinbeck's 1939 novel
(Bruccoli Collection, Thomas Cooper Library, University of South Carolina)

ary, and the people are not real enough to save the book from being exactly what it is, an idea novel, about abstractions. And this I say with some sorrow, because Steinbeck is still one of the two or three best novelists writing in America, and this book under any other name would warrant roses.

—Boston Daily Globe, 11 March 1942; reprinted in John Steinbeck: The Contemporary Reviews, pp. 221–223

Bombs Away (1942)

Books and Things
Lewis Gannett

Lewis Gannett reviewed Bombs Away: The Story of a Bomber Team *(1942), Steinbeck's account of the training missions of Army Air Forces trainees.*

John Steinbeck is half-Irish, and he has a conscience, perhaps inherited from the New England missionary who was his grandmother on his other side. When an Irishman gets mad he wants to fight, and when a New Englander gets mad he begins by preaching. Steinbeck, moreover, started out to be a biologist before he took to writing stories; in his way he is still a biologist. And he is forty years old. Put that all together and you may understand how John Steinbeck came to write *Bombs Away: The Story of a Bomber Team*. . . .

Bombs Away is the meticulously precise life-history of a bomber team: a scientifically precise account of what it is, and how it gets that way, written with passion by a man who deeply regrets that he cannot be part of one. It isn't what you would expect from the author of *Tortilla Flat,* of *Grapes of Wrath,* or even of *Sea of Cortez.* But then, nothing that Steinbeck has written has ever been just what the readers of his previous books expected of him, which is one of the things which proves that he is a writer. It isn't a story; it is at times more like a textbook, and sometimes like a sermon. Steinbeck wanted to do something about this war; *Bombs Away* is one product of that urge. . . .

I talked with John Steinbeck about this book early last summer, when the magazines were full of stories about bad morale in the training camps. "It isn't true," he said, if I remember him aright. "We've never had a better Army. I've been around a little. The officers are good; the men are good; the people making weapons are good; and they aren't excited. They are doing the job, and it is a good job. The young men of today are as good as any young men ever were—perhaps better."

This book is written in that faith, and in the further faith that the best of them are in the bomber teams, whom John Steinbeck watched training, with whom he flew over the Gulf of Mexico. It is written with a conviction that it was not to our discredit that no nation in history had ever tried more passionately or more thoughtfully to avoid fighting than we did; that it was not to the discredit of the depression generation that they did not know where they were going; that Pearl Harbor set in motion the most powerful biological drive known—that of survival; that air war is a natural channel of expression for young America; and that the nation is entitled to feel a kind of fierce joy in the experience and training of our young aviators. Wandering around the country, Steinbeck met grumblers and doubters; so he sat down, first to study, biologically, the "greatest team in the world," the American bomber team, and then to preach about it. *Bombs Away* is the result. . . .

The United States Army . . . has developed some amazing gadgets for perfecting the training of those lads. Steinbeck tells about some of them—and also about the excruciating discipline of "parachute parades" gayly imposed on the boys when they first go out of bounds. He leads you, conscientiously and patiently and proudly, through each stage of that training. He gives you an extraordinary picture of the sensation of first flight, when the little training plane seems balanced in the air, "tippy as a canoe and as dependable in the hands of a flyer," and of the mystical sense of brotherhood among flying men. (All Irishmen are part mystics, and Steinbeck is part Irish.) He says that these flying men of ours go through an experience which "has the impact of religion, and while most of them are never able to say it, never want to say it, they all understand it."

Navy flyers may feel that John Steinbeck has acquired not only a religion of flying, but a religion of Army flying, and dispute his assertions about the role of land-based bombers. But they will understand and respect the spirit in which he wrote this book. The bomber teams, to whom the book is dedicated, will not, Mr. Steinbeck thinks, want or have time to read his book, for to them it would be primer work. He wrote it as a primer for parents—and as a sermon.

—New York Herald Tribune, 27 November 1942; reprinted in John Steinbeck: The Contemporary Reviews, pp. 259–261

War Correspondent

Soon after Steinbeck married Gwyn Conger on 29 March 1943, he left to serve as a war correspondent for the New York Herald Tribune. *He wrote his new wife a series of letters, first from London and later from North Africa, commenting on his experiences.*

4 July 1943

My darling:

This is Sunday the Fourth and the streets are full of American homesickness. I have it too. I walked for hours last night and talked to so many of the soldiers. They are angry about the messes in Washington and they are homesick. The reason I have put the date at the top is that I finally have got a calendar. Bob Vining of the navy gave it to me and it is tacked to the wall and I can find out any time I want what the date is, provided of course that I know the day of the week.

I've really got a low time now. Liquor is so expensive and so bad that I do not fall back on it. I guess I've just got what the troops have. It is quite a hot day and hasn't rained in two weeks or more. Already the grass is getting brown. But it looks as though there might be some rain soon. It is getting muggy. This isn't a day to work but I must. I think I'll do a piece today about homesickness in London. That's what is happening here.

I love you and I am homesick too.

—*Steinbeck: A Life in Letters,* p. 256

* * *

July 1943

Darling, you want to know what I want of you. Many things of course but chiefly these. I want you to keep this thing we have inviolate and waiting—the person who is neither I nor you but us. It's a hard thing this separation but it is one of the millions of separations at home and many more millions here. It is one hunger in a great starvation but because it is ours it overshadows all the rest, if we let it. But keep waiting and don't let it be hurt by anything because it is the one really precious thing we have. Later we may have others but so far it is a single unit—and you have the keeping of it for a little while. You say I am busy, as though that wiped out my end, but it doesn't. You can be just as homesick and lost when you are busy. I love you beyond words, beyond containing. Remember that always when the distance seems so great and the time so long. It will not be so long, my dear.

—*Steinbeck: A Life in Letters,* pp. 256–257

* * *

8 July 1943

Dear Gwyndolyn:

The mails are terrible. Who knows, maybe a lot of letters will come over today.

It is a kind of a grey day with big clouds and the city against them is very beautiful. I have become such an assiduous worker that you wouldn't know me. The hulk that sat in the green chair day in and day out is replaced with a medium young executive, well dressed, courteous, clean, on his toes—business as usual and the chin up and nose on the grind stone. This transformation is happily not permanent. This discipline is good but I can't think what for. It is nothing I am sure that the home double bed won't cure.

The grey day is turned to rain now, a very pleasant and necessary rain.

> love to baby
> john
> —*Steinbeck: A Life in Letters,* p. 257

* * *

12 July 1943

My darling.

I wish I could go with this letter. To see you and to hold you would be so good. I know it will seem a very short time when it is over but now it seems interminable like an illness. I have small magic that I practice. When I go to bed, I build up what you look like and how you speak and some times I can almost feel you curling around my back and your breath on my neck. And sometimes it is so real that I am shocked that it isn't so.

It is raining today and coming on to the time when it will rain nearly all the time. And this morning which is Monday it fills me with gloom. I'm writing the gloom out on you and am loving it. This letter seems much closer than the others.

I love you very deeply and completely—that goes through everything and in everything. Every day I hope I will hear from you and at night I haven't. Maybe today. Some of the mail must come through. Perhaps they have held it up, needing the space. I don't know.

Good bye my darling wife. Keep writing.

I love you.

—*Steinbeck: A Life in Letters,* pp. 257–258

* * *

13 August 1943

Darling:

I haven't written for several days because I've been on the move. It seems silly to head this one "Somewhere in Africa," like saying just somewhere. Anyway this is a large city on the Mediterranean which I can't even spell [probably Algiers]. I've felt guilty about you taking all the hot weather this year but now you have your revenge. It was 140° when I landed–terrible searing heat. Up here on the sea it is only about 115° and the nights are bearable. The call came suddenly and surprised even me for I had been refused before. So I hopped it while I could. Right now I have the G. I. skitters which come to everyone and is painful but it will be gone tomorrow. Coming from cool England the heat can bowl you over.

Here I made my first error. Instead of applying for a billet from the army and getting, after hours, a cot with sixteen other men, I went up to the desk and in some of the sourest high school French asked for a room and got it. The army doesn't know how it happened. No one ever thought to try that method. I have a bath and a toilette and I am not even a general. The room itself is torn up quite a bit. Blast from bombing has loosened the wall paper. No windows nor mirrors of course. The big window is walled up with only two small holes, left open at the top. There are two small beds covered, believe it or not, with Mexican serapes.

I'm lying down to write this. It is the only way to keep from dripping on it. I shan't be here very long before I move on. Just please keep writing to London and I'll be back there probably in three weeks. This is a very crucial time. But the nearer you get to a battle front, the less news you hear. You probably know much more than I do. I'm not even going out to dinner tonight. I'll sit here and write to you and rest my stomach. Hadn't had any fruit since I left New York and of course here it is wonderful.

It's coming on to get dark and it will cool off then some. Down in the desert it was full moon and Arabs howl at the moon–a high howl that goes on for hours and sounds a little like coyotes. If you can imagine sitting in a garden and hearing American swing played on a phonograph over the background of howling Arabs, you have something.

Damned if those senators didn't arrive here about the same time as I. By now they are fighting among themselves and they are reducing American prestige to an all time low which is very, very low. We must be inspired to have made so many mistakes. Some of the reporters over here are viciously resentful of me and some are very kind. But every once in a while one of them goes out of his way to tell me how much my stuff stinks. I think they are probably right. I get very tired of it.

—*Steinbeck: A Life in Letters,* pp. 258–259

* * *

19 August 1943

My darling:

It is almost impossible to keep clean here. The water is cold and dribbles and the soap doesn't seem to take hold. I think I am getting dirtier and dirtier but it

isn't quite so noticeable since my complexion is getting darker and darker every day.

I have with me a camera man and an enlisted man and we have been jogging about the country seeing a great deal and taking some pictures. Yesterday I traveled through country that looked just like that stretch between Moss Landing and Monterey, with sand dunes and then the sea. The sea was the same blue as in Monterey and it made me very terribly homesick. And I wondered what has happened to the little house and how every one is.

I am still looking for Bill Dekker [husband of Steinbeck's younger sister, Mary] and still haven't found him. But I will in time.

I wonder what this being apart has done for us. To you, for instance, has it made you think our thing was good or do you suspect it? It has made me think it is exceptionally good and desirable. You said in one letter that you would probably have changed your whole way of life. I hope not so radically that we cannot get back to the good thing it seemed to me. The good nights with the fire going. This winter I must have the little fairy stove connected so that when we go to bed the coals can be glowing. I wonder whether you found a maid at all. I think you will agree with me from now on that we need one. I hate to wash dishes and always will. I did too damned much of it when I was a kid. And I don't like to sweep and all stuff like that. But we will try to get someone who comes in for the day rather than an in-sleeper, that is of course as long as we have an apartment.

Goodbye my darling. I would give something very large to be able to hear from you, but I don't know any way to accomplish it.

Keep good and patient for just a little while now.

—*Steinbeck: A Life in Letters,* pp. 259–260

* * *

24 August 1943

Darling:

I hope you will answer my cable because I am pretty worried about you. Six weeks it is now since I have heard.

My dear, I am very tired of being without you, very tired indeed. We shan't do this again but it was necessary this once. I get sudden fits of jealousy too that are baseless and useless but seem to come on without warning.

I think the heat is making me a little dingy. It seems to me that I cannot remember much of anything. The series of bad dreams continues. But I think everyone is having them, at least dreams that go on and on. I'm getting to the point where I half way believe that I dreamed you.

—*Steinbeck: A Life in Letters,* p. 260

* * *

25 August 1943

Dear:

Last night I went with the naval officers to a monastery in the country and in a huge dark church, the brothers were at evening prayer singing Gregorian music with only two little candles burning in the great place. I stood in the choir loft and looked down on this thing and it was very wonderful, the sound bellied up with great fullness. Afterwards we talked to the brothers and they are all nationalities. One was from Massachusetts and another a German and a third a Hollander and some French. And they were very quiet. Staying in the monastery were a few officers who have worked too hard or been under too great a nerve strain and they are there in that very quiet place just getting rest that can't be got any place else. They listen to the music and sleep and it does them a great deal of good.

It really isn't so very bad. The great trouble is the one you know, the loneliness. That I can't dissemble or disassociate. I remember best the coffee in the morning and the music at night and the dictionary sessions and the painting of chairs and where shall we eat tonight. Let's have a whale of a big Christmas and not only string popcorn but also string cranberries and also whatever tinsel we can find. Let's have a really Christmas. There won't be very much to buy for presents but we'll get some things and we'll have a goose if you can find one, a great fine goose that falls apart if you speak above a whisper. I've thought and thought and it does seem that the corner in front of the lower bathroom door is the best place for the tree. It is very funny in this heat to think of a fine cannel coal fire but I do think of it. And maybe it will be snowing. You get to dwelling on these things.

There is a theme that is beating in on me and it is the theme of Africa. It is a very strange place. It looks so like California and it is a place that has never been a nation and only a kind of a piece of loot for four thousand years and probably more. All of the time I am conscious of the many kinds of soldiers who have tramped over these roads but always to raid and to loot. You rarely find a man who says I am Algierian [*sic*]. He is French or Arab or German but never African. And yet the place has such charm and such beauty in some ways that people come back again and again to it. I know I would like to bring you here when there is peace again.

—*Steinbeck: A Life in Letters*, pp. 260–261

Cannery Row (1945)

Steinbeck to Mildred Lyman, 2 December 1944

Late in 1944 Steinbeck wrote Mildred Lyman of McIntosh and Otis with good news about the advance sales of Cannery Row *(1945). He also commented on the visit of a representative from* The Christian Science Monitor, *who was concerned that some of the girls at the Cannery Row brothel are identified as Christian Scientists. This controversy returned to haunt Steinbeck in the late 1950s, when the headmaster of his older son's school, also a Christian Scientist, made a similar complaint about the novel.*

Dear Mildred:

Beautiful cold morning. Friday night Gwyn pinned one on me. One of those fine natural binges that is not planned and is easy and natural. So last night I went to bed early and now I'm waiting for the Christian Science man.

Pat writes that advance sales on Cannery Row are beyond his expectations—60% beyond, he says. But you know Pat. Perhaps his enthusiasm exceeds his figures. Gosh, it's a beautiful day. Brilliantly sunny and clear. Some night next week Gwyn and I are going out with the sardine fleet. She has never been and it will fascinate her. It is a very spectacular thing and very exciting when they come on the fish.

I can look out at the garden from here where a little Spanish man is trimming the overgrown bushes and trees and doing a fine job of it. Sunday morning is a good time here. It's the Sundayest morning you can imagine. It lacks only chickens talking. When I was little I imagined that chickens made a very special kind of gobble talk on Sunday morning.

Well, the Xtian Science man came and he seems very nice and cagey and clever. He wondered if people wouldn't get the wrong impression. I said that some people always got the wrong impression. There wasn't much he could say without giving the impression of snobbishness. When he left, he said, "I just leave this thought with you. If they practiced prostitution *and* Christian Science, they were not good Christian Scientists." And I said, "Well, that's all right, because they weren't very good prostitutes either." So he laughed and we parted on a friendly basis. He said they would have to make a statement and I said I would be upset if they didn't.

Nurse's day off. Gwyn is making formula. And we're going to have baked beans tonight—Boston style.

Love to all,
John
—*Steinbeck: A Life in Letters*, pp. 276–277

* * *

**Steinbeck to Jack and Max Wagner,
23 January 1945**

*Steinbeck wrote Jack and Max Wagner, old friends from
his youth in Salinas, to report on the critical fortunes of the
recently published* Cannery Row *and to update them about his
progress on the screenplay for* The Pearl *(1947).*

Dear Jack and Max:

Things are lightening up a little here. The nurse was
sick and poor Gwyn has been taking care of both the baby
and the nurse. I thought Gwyn would end up in the hospital but she is all right and is getting some sleep finally.

Thom is fine and gay. Getting to be a kind of per-
sonable child. He has been very happy ever since his last
tooth came through.

And I'm in the last stretch of the Pearl. I should finish this draft in about a week. Fernandez [Emilio Fernández, director of the movie] is supposed to come up some
time around the first to the 15th of Feb. to work on
shooting script. I won't go to Mexico until I know the
cameras are rolling. I know how the delays are.

Cannery Row took a frightful pounding by the
critics and they went too far. Annie Laurie phoned to say
that her telephone rang all the time from studios wanting
to buy it and what should she do. So I told her she was
on her own—to sell or not sell—whenever she was ready.
She has a magnificent sense of timing for such things.
And she knows what we want. A lot of money, control
of the script. And this time I am going to ride herd on it.
I'll act as consultant—for a consideration. I thought the
adverse criticism would hurt the book but she says quite
the opposite. The sales are tremendous and that's what
interests the studios—not the critics.

There has been frost every day for a week. I've
never known Monterey to be like that.

I guess that's about all. I've got to go to work. The
Pearl is really in its last stages. It's a brutal story but with
flashes of beauty I think.

Let me hear from you.

John
—Steinbeck: A Life in Letters, pp. 278–279

* * *

Books
Edmund Wilson

Edmund Wilson offered grudging praise for Cannery
Row *as the most enjoyable and "least pretentious" of Steinbeck's
books.*

John Steinbeck's new novel, *Cannery Row* . . . is
one of the least pretentious of his books, but I believe
that it is the one I have most enjoyed reading. It deals
with a community a little like that of the same author's
Tortilla Flat: a cannery neighborhood in Monterey, with
a biological laboratory, a brothel, a Chinaman's general
store, and a scattering of shacks and old boilers, in
which various nondescript characters live. *Cannery Row*
is amusing and attractive in the same way as *Tortilla
Flat:* here again Mr. Steinbeck has created a sun-soaked
Californian atmosphere of laziness, naïveté, good
nature, satisfaction in the pleasures of the senses and
indifference to property rights, in which the periodical
failures and suicides hardly disturb the surface with a
momentary eruption of bubbles. But the new book is
more complex than the earlier one, in which the characters were mostly "Mexicans," "*paisanos*," all on the same
level. The characters in *Cannery Row* represent a mixture
of races and a variety of social levels. It would be

*Dust jacket for the first edition of Steinbeck's 1945 novel about
the lives of a group of ne'er-do-wells in Monterey
(Bruccoli Clark Layman Archives)*

impossible to give an account of the book by disengaging and retelling a "story": it is a series of little pictures and incidents that are often not related in any direct way. . . . But there *is* a central interest in *Cannery Row:* it is that of the relations of Doc, who runs the biological laboratory, with the other, more rudimentary members of the community. The man of science, living alone with his phonograph and his books, takes his neighbors for what they are and as they come. . . .

This is the fable: a dramatization of the point of view already implicit in most of Steinbeck's fiction. A curious and perceptive mind is situated among simple human beings and scrutinizes their activities with the same kind of interest that it finds in the habits of baby octopi, sea anemones, and hermit crabs. It is capable of sentimentalizing about them but it has difficulty con-

vincing itself or us that it accepts them on its own level. It may let them climb all over it, but it always brushes them off. Doc does, as I have said above, feel some genuine warmth of contact with his neighbors, and it may be that *Cannery Row* is Steinbeck's most satisfactory book because it attempts to objectify and exploit the author's own relation to his characters; but it is characteristic of the author as well as of his protagonist Doc that the moments when Doc feels emotion are the moments that are least well done. When Doc finds the dead girl in the surf, he can only hear imaginary music, and this music is none too well described; when the loafers and the trollops of Cannery Row give him their bang-up party, the author must rely, like Doc, on long passages of quoted verse. It is hard to put one's finger on the coarseness that tends to spoil Mr. Steinbeck as

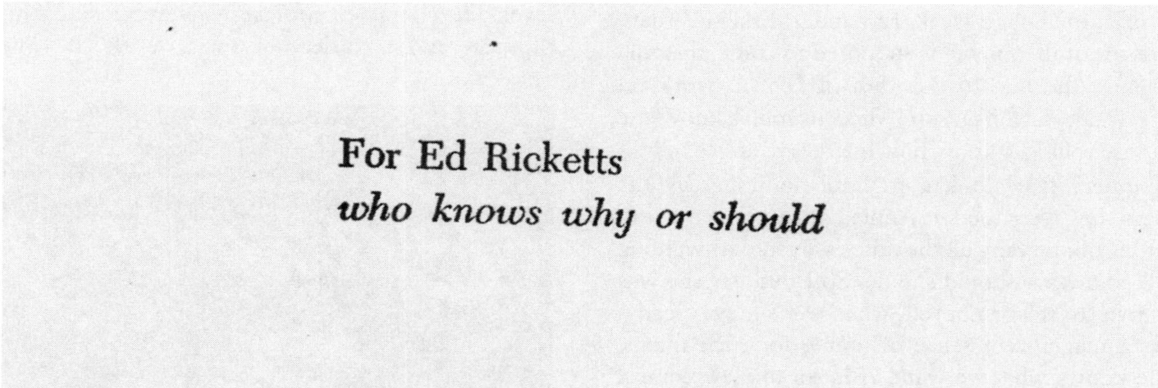

For Ed Ricketts
who knows why or should

Sept 18 · 1947

This is for the Robinsons in Carmel
· and I hope they are as much
amused by it as I was when
first I read it in galley proof

Ed. Ricketts

Dedication page from Cannery Row *inscribed by the dedicatee, Ricketts, who was the original for Doc in the novel (National Steinbeck Center, Salinas)*

an artist. When one considers the brilliance of his gifts and the philosophic cast of his mind, one keeps feeling that it should not be so. Yet it is so: when this watcher of life should exalt us to the vision of art, he simply sings "Mother Machree.". . .

—*New Yorker*, 20 (6 January 1945); reprinted in *John Steinbeck: The Contemporary Reviews,* p. 278

* * *

Who Are the Real People?
Norman Cousins

Cousins reviewed Cannery Row *for the* Saturday Review.

John Steinbeck likes to get a rise out of his readers. He likes to ruffle them and startle them with the unexpected and the bizarre. He likes to write, for example, of a brothel as a "decent, clean, honest, wholesome" place (as in *Cannery Row*), where the customers get their money's worth and where the working girls are decent, clean, honest, wholesome, etc., in contrast to the "twisted and lascivious sisterhood of married spinsters whose husbands respect the home but don't like it very much."

Our purpose here is not to take issue with Mr. Steinbeck's high regard for decent, clean, honest, wholesome persons or institutions. After all, he isn't the first to call attention to or glorify the career bed. It was

pretty much of a literary chestnut even when DeMaupassant wrote about it in "Madame Tellier's Establishment." It is pertinent only as it illustrates Mr. Steinbeck's unfailing devotion to the reverse twist under any circumstances. So much so that his unpredictableness becomes almost predictable. It is a familiar literary device having a certain effectiveness but sometimes it wears thin and shows through. When it does, it has all the charm and winsomeness of an old hangnail.

If you grant that Steinbeck's own ideas or beliefs may frequently be subordinated to the requirements of his literary devices or technique, you can avoid either the bother or the pleasure of rising to his bait; that is, you are willing to give him a liberal allowance because of his perquisites as a novelist. But there comes a point where you are certain that his technique represents an authentic and precise vehicle for his own convictions. At such a point, it is both legitimate and pertinent to ask questions.

In particular, we should like to ask questions about Mr. Steinbeck's obsession with what he likes to call "real people." It is not a solitary obsession, to be sure: other writers in what has been termed the school of modern realist writing share it. Ernest Hemingway, particularly in his novel of thugs, rum runners, and murderers, *To Have and Have Not,* and in many of his other novels and short stories, demonstrates a predilection, if not an admiration, for his own brand of real people.

But who are these real people, what are they like, that they should thus command the attention and affec-

Steinbeck, Willie (dog), son Thom, and Gwyn in the pool of their rented house in Cuernavaca, Mexico, where they lived during the filming of the movie version of The Pearl *(1947) in 1945 (Center for Steinbeck Studies, San Jose State University; from Jay Parini,* John Steinbeck, *1995; Thomas Cooper Library, University of South Carolina)*

Page from the manuscript for Cannery Row *that was omitted from the final version of the novel (Special Collections, Stanford University Library; from William McPheron,* John Steinbeck: From Salinas to Stockholm, *2000; Special Collections, Thomas Cooper Library, University of South Carolina)*

tion of these writers? In Steinbeck's case, the answers are both available and explicit in *Cannery Row*—even more, perhaps, than in its atmospheric predecessor, *Tortilla Flat*. Steinbeck's "real people" are the well-meaning, big-hearted, coarse, ignorant bums, boobs, castoffs, and misfits of both sexes. "They survive in this particular world better than other people. In a time when people tear themselves to pieces with ambition and nervousness and covetousness, they [the cast-offs, etc.] are relaxed. All of our so-called successful men are sick men, with bad stomachs, and bad souls, but Mack and the boys are healthy and curiously clean. They can do what they want. They can satisfy their appetites without calling them something else."

These "real people" of Steinbeck's are amusing enough and make good copy, but we are neither impressed nor convinced. Mr. Steinbeck has made special pets of them, and exhibits them as though they were anything but real. They are big, rough, and tough, and know how to guzzle pot likker, even if they don't know the difference between drinking and soaking. They're innocent as babes and delightfully dumb, and they have an instinct for kindness and gratitude that is as touching as it is menacing. Beware that gratitude as you would a bear-trap. The "real people" get tied into knots and they slide unsuspectingly into the gol-durndest brawls you ever saw, with split heads, bashed faces, and broken ribs as common as frogs in a pond at midnight. F'rinstance, they want to do something nice for a friend, whom they all love and respect, so they throw him a party while he is away and smash up his laboratory until the place looks like a heap of broken glass. The highspot of the evening is a "long, happy, and bloody battle that took out the front door and broke two windows."

Now this is all very stirring and refreshing. It is good to see decent, clean, honest, wholesome human beings acting in such a natural and unrepressed manner. They don't "tear themselves to pieces with ambition and nervousness and covetousness," and they know how to relax. There is no point in bringing Freud into all this, but you can't help admiring their magnificent lack of self-restraint—the real tonic for the real psyches of real people. Consider, too, their superb constitutional equipment. Contrast them with the unreal people who have stomach ulcers and various other disorders as the result of nervous living. Mr. Steinbeck's people are invariably healthy. Not an instance of cirrhosis of the liver, delirium tremens, polyneuritis, Korsakoff psychoses, or Saturday-night-paralyses in the carload. Doubtless, all his castoffs, bums, procurers, deadbeats, sporting girls, and madams die in the sublime beauty of their old age. But don't bet on it.

Apart from the ludicrous, there is something both curious and perilous about Mr. Steinbeck's preoccupation with and worship of these "real people," as distinct from all others. Curious, because he himself treats them more as phenomena than as the substance of reality; perilous, because there are inevitable concomitants of anti-culturalism and anti-intellectualism that cannot be separated from the original obsession. These by-products are more than vaguely reminiscent of a remark by an incipient hasbeen who once said that when he heard the word culture he reached for his gun. Maybe Adolf H. never actually said it; maybe it was Hermann or Little Joseph or one of the others. But whoever said it, everyone knows or should know what it meant.

We admit the urgency for a novelist to break away from the stuffy and synthetic atmosphere of penthouse cocktail parties, and to associate himself with the

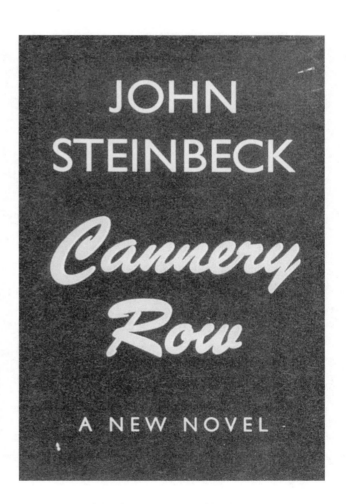

Dust jacket for the first British edition of Steinbeck's 1945 novel (from Sotheby's New York, The Maurice F. Neville Collection of Modern Literature, *November 16, 2004)*

more valid feel of large numbers of people living a less glorified life. But there is also a danger that he may lose his balance in going in the other direction—the danger that he may become patronizing and try to turn people into something special or freakish. It should be at least possible to write about the mainstream of humanity without putting a halo on the half-wit, deifying the drunk, or canonizing the castoff.

We are not saying that Mr. Steinbeck's gallery is not filled with real people. They may be real enough, but we'll be hanged if we will genuflect before them or regard them as a master race. Besides, we have devised our own test for determining whether people are real. It is infallible. You take a long, sharp pin and jab it into the arm. If blood comes out, and if the blood is red, then the person is real.

Saturday Review, 28 (17 March 1945); reprinted in *John Steinbeck: The Contemporary Reviews*, pp. 284–285

Planning for *Viva Zapata!* (1952)

Steinbeck to Annie Laurie Williams, 26 June 1945

When Steinbeck received a proposal that he write the screenplay for a biopic on Emiliano Zapata, he wrote Williams saying that he would need assurance from the Mexican government that the movie could be made with historical fidelity. Viva Zapata!, with Marlon Brando in the title role, was released in 1952.

Dear Annie Laurie:

There is a thing I want to discuss with you. I was approached the other day by an outfit that calls itself Pan-American Films with the proposition that I do a film on the life of Emiliano Zapata. Now there is no other story I would rather do. But there are certain things in the way.

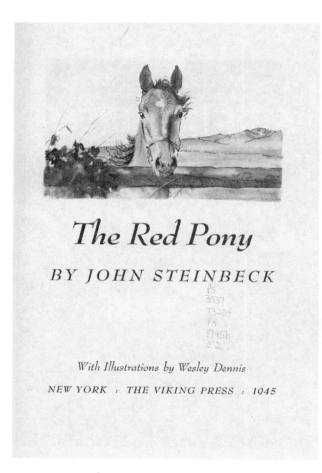

Title page for the second edition of Steinbeck's 1937 story sequence, enlarged to include a fourth story, "The Leader of the People," with the free front endpaper from a copy of the book inscribed by Steinbeck to actor Burgess Meredith in 1950 (left, Thomas Cooper Library, University of South Carolina; right, Sotheby's New York, Fine Books and Manuscripts Including Americana, June 26, 1998)

I have, as you know, work ahead for a long time to come. I would not even be ready to make a start until a year from this fall.

The difficulty of making it straight would be very great. There are still men living and in power who helped to trick and murder Zapata. I would only make it straight. I would require gov't assurance that it could be made straight historically. This will have to be an iron bound agreement because Zapata could be one of the great films of all time as by a twist or a concession it could be a complete double cross of the things Zapata lived and died for.

We're still plugging away at the shooting script. In the States I wouldn't do it but here I want to give them a tight story for the first time. It's a battle with energy because the dysentery still persists and that doesn't leave much strength.

We celebrated St. John's day with 10 dozen skyrockets and we named big ones for you and Maurice.

Love to you both,
John
—*Steinbeck: A Life in Letters,* pp. 282–283

Steinbeck and World War II

John Steinbeck, War Reporter
Christopher C. Sullivan

In a 1997 article Christopher C. Sullivan appraises Steinbeck's war journalism and The Moon Is Down.

Before Pearl Harbor, John Steinbeck was content to look at the phenomenon of armed conflict in an abstract way. War, he wrote in the 1941 book *Sea of Cortez,* could be viewed as a "diagnostic trait of Homo sapiens," comparable to the instinct of crayfish to fight as soon as they meet. "And perhaps," he added, "our species is not likely to forgo war without some psychic mutation, which at present, at least, does not seem imminent." Steinbeck relished dissecting the psychology underlying large-scale movements of people, as he had demonstrated in 1939 in *The Grapes of Wrath.* Thus, the wartime military's esprit de corps might well be lumped together with characteristics of mobs and athletic teams; war with its alternating tension and excitement, killing one day and bivouacking in the rain the next, became to the writer "one great gray dream."

Nonetheless, when Franklin Roosevelt declared global war, Steinbeck could be detached no longer, nor did he desire to be. All Americans, including this novelist at the height of his powers with an international fol-

lowing, became part of the effort to bring victory. (Only later, looking back on newswriting he produced during that period, did he use the phrase "a huge and gassy thing called the War Effort.") Thus John Steinbeck, unlikely at age forty to be called up and, anyway, under attack by his local draft board in California, among others, as a "communist" or "disloyal" because of his writings, joined up the best way he could: He picked up his duffel bag and his portable typewriter (along with four quarts of scotch) and enlisted as a writer.

During World War II, the novelist who had won the Pulitzer Prize and would later win the Nobel Prize produced journalism, working as an accredited correspondent for the New York *Herald Tribune.* Datelines on Steinbeck's dispatches included pre-D-Day London, occupied North Africa, and other parts of the Mediterranean theater of war, where he joined U.S. commando raids that were part of the Allied assault on Italy. He also wrote a government-commissioned book, *Bombs Away,* based on his experiences with American fliers in training.

At the same time, Steinbeck continued to produce fiction, notably the play-novel, *The Moon is Down,* which appeared in 1942. It is about the occupation of a town, universalized in his description but presumably Scandinavian, by an army with much in common with the Nazis, and about the townspeople's quiet but deadly effective resistance. Near the end of that book, Steinbeck puts in the mouth of the town's mayor, facing execution if the citizens' sabotage continues, a statement of the author's sociology of war. The defiant mayor tells the commander of the invading force:

The people don't like being conquered . . . and so they will not be. Free men cannot start a war, but once it is started, they can fight on in defeat. Herd men, followers of a leader, cannot do that, and so it is always the herd men who win battles and the free men who win wars.

Throughout the war years, Steinbeck continued to produce work, including some in direct support of the war effort, and in this he contrasted with Faulkner and other great writers of the era, who declined the government harness.

Yet in war, the saying goes, the "first casualty" is truth, and the statement probably has as much validity as any that becomes a cliché. In re-examining the reportage and fiction of John Steinbeck during World War II, some critics have asserted that his work, too, became such a casualty. Indeed, Steinbeck himself called his own war correspondence "untrue" when he reread it fifteen years out of context. It is not that simple.

Poster for the 1944 movie for which Steinbeck wrote the screenplay. Unhappy with the changes made to his script, he asked that his name be removed from the credits (Bruccoli Clark Layman Archives).

"Maybe the hardest thing in writing is simply to tell the truth about things as we see them," Steinbeck once observed. He is known to have discarded at least four completed manuscripts of novels because they did not meet an uncompromising standard of honesty. "Oh! the incidents all happened, but I'm not telling as much of the truth about them as I know," he explained in a letter to his publisher, referring to one of these books, a first, failed attempt to deal with the subject matter that later yielded *The Grapes of Wrath.* He went further: "I've written three books now that were dishonest because they were less than the best I could do." It is not surprising that a fourth book that he shelved was about war, produced while the fighting was still going on.

Those who knew Steinbeck say he was a personally conservative man, holding strictly to many old-fashioned values. His eagerness to pitch in on the war effort, for example, grew out of a straightforward patriotism. (This earned him considerable criticism when, during the Vietnam war, he scorned peace demonstrators. His writing during that war, in which his son was fighting, will not be addressed in this article.) Steinbeck, who had met FDR following publication of *The Grapes of Wrath,* made several suggestions to the president for defeating the Axis—from making better use of Japanese biologists' prewar maps of islands that the U.S. Navy might want to assault, to dropping tons of counterfeit marks behind German lines to drive up inflation. Ironically, Steinbeck was among those proposing creation of a wartime information service, which became the forerunner of intelligence agencies that later spied on the author himself.

In the mind of the traditionalist Steinbeck, then, honesty and duty stood out as beacons. Of the unique, ancient duty thrust upon a writer, Steinbeck said in his Nobel Prize acceptance speech:

> He is charged with exposing our many grievous faults and failures, with dredging up to the light our dark and dangerous dreams for the purpose of improvement. Furthermore, the writer is delegated to declare and to celebrate man's proven capacity for greatness of heart and spirit—for gallantry in defeat, for courage, compassion and love. In the endless war against weakness and despair, these are the bright rally flags of hope and emulation.

When deeply understood and sincerely accepted, the duties of citizen and of writer can come into wrenching conflict; this dilemma confronts journalists every day. What we see in John Steinbeck's World War II writing and his sometimes harsh self-assessment is often evidence of such conflict. At the same time, a close reading of his many kinds of writing in the crucible of war

reveals types and degrees of truth that neither he nor his critics at the time were capable of seeing. [. . .]

Besides journalism and fiction, Steinbeck's writing in World War II included what can only be called propaganda. He wrote *Bombs Away: The Story of a Bomber Group* at the request of an Army Air Corps general and turned over the book's profits to the Air Forces Aid Society Trust Fund. As propaganda, this book is worth little more than a mention here. Still, it should be noted that even in this project, Steinbeck refused to surrender entirely the writer's standard of honesty. When, after weeks of hopscotching the country, visiting Air Corps training bases and learning about fliers and their equipment, and racing to meet the military's deadlines, Steinbeck turned in his manuscript, he was asked to rewrite the ending. It should describe the young flying aces actually in battle, he was told. No, he replied, that was something he had not seen. And so, the book's concluding image, a takeoff for a training run, may have a jingoistic ring but it is not faked:

> The thundering ships took off one behind the other. At 5,000 feet they made their formation. The men sat quietly at their stations, their eyes fixed. And the deep growl of the engines shook the air, shook the world, shook the future.

Steinbeck himself departed in early 1943 to cover the war for the New York *Herald Tribune.* As later "literary journalists" have done, he immersed himself in the subject, in his case the seen-from-the-ground world of the average G.I. He succeeded so well at living the grunt's life that when he returned home later that year he had temporarily lost his hearing because of enemy shell bursts nearby and needed months to recover from other physical and emotional injuries.

Despite his fame as a fiction writer, Steinbeck took pride in his press card and in scooping more seasoned correspondents. He was free to write what he liked for the *Herald Tribune,* a fact that caused some resentment among his less footloose colleagues. He wrote feature stories, personality profiles, brief essays, almost every journalistic genre except breaking news.

An article about Dover, separated from enemy territory only by the narrow English Channel, uses fine reporting detail to show the Churchillian doggedness of average English people. German artillery pummelled the town the night before, Steinbeck writes, and everyone is cleaning up:

> In a front yard a man is standing in his garden. A flying piece of scantling has broken off a rose bush. The bud, which was about to open, is wilting on the ground. The man leans down and picks up the bud. He feels it with his fingers and carries it to his nose and smells it. He . . .

turns and looks at the French coast, where 500 men and a great tube of steel and high explosive and charts and plans, mathematical formulae, uniforms, telephones, shouted orders, are out to break a man's rose bush.

Near the end of the story, Steinbeck describes a neighbor stopping by. The two men kneel and examine the bush. "She's broke above the graft," the neighbor says. "She's not split. . . . Sometimes, when they've had a shock, they come out prettier than ever."

In a series of three dispatches appearing over a month or two, Steinbeck delightedly describes the war of Private "Big Train" Mulligan, who drives officers from town to town and finds good friends, good food, and good treatment everywhere he goes, partly by his Georgia friendliness and partly by passing out the cigarettes and other supplies he has access to because of his position. He is a man who resists promotion because he does not need the worry, a man who, as Steinbeck says, "has succeeded in making a good part of the Army work for him":

Should his officer be faint with hunger, Mulligan has a piece of chocolate to tide the captain over. What difference that the chocolate belonged to the captain in the first place and he was led to believe that it was all gone? The fact of the matter is that when he needs his own chocolate Mulligan is happy to give him half of it.

If such dispatches show journalistic qualities, the novelist in Steinbeck emerges in other reports, especially after he leaves the safe base of London and joins a fighting unit. His report of the taking of the Italian island Ventotene from German occupiers through ingenuity and bravado appeared in five consecutive dispatches in December 1943, delayed until the action was complete. It reads like a fine Steinbeck short story. It uses sharp characterization, plot development (a bluff by members of an American unit results in the surrender of a far superior German force) and other techniques of fiction to create a tale that loses none of its vividness half a century later.

Is the story true? In a strict, journalistic sense, it is not. Names are changed throughout–including the name of Douglas Fairbanks Jr., the Hollywood actor-turned-officer who led the raid but who wanted no publicity, and the name of Steinbeck himself, who carried a gun and was later recommended for a medal. (He could not receive it because he was not in the military.) Further, the novelist-correspondent left out factual material that would have muddied his plot. But does the story carry a larger truth: Something about American dash and adaptability defeating German discipline and regimentation, that goes beyond mere flag-waving? Surely

it does. The fictional sharpening helps makes [*sic*] a real-life story more focused, more memorable, more true.

One more *Herald Tribune* dispatch should be examined because it arrives at an equally complex truthfulness via an opposite approach. It is a picture of war and of the war correspondent that perfectly balances factual and insightful firsthand reporting with a clear, bitter, disturbing literary point of view: war correspondence suggestive of Norman Mailer and Michael Herr but years earlier and written on the fly.

"You can't see much of a battle," the article begins. It explains that a daily newspaper's way of communicating what goes on day-to-day in war is based largely on a general's-eye view, which the correspondent gleans from official reports. This is the skeleton of history that each day's paper tries to construct. It is a version of the truth of what happens: troops move forward or rearward a certain distance, occupy certain ground, absorb and inflict certain casualties. Steinbeck, writing from Salerno as Allied troops pushed into Italy, goes on to describe "what the correspondent really saw." He writes:

He lay on his stomach, if he had any sense, and watched ants crawling among the little sticks on the sand dune, and his nose was so close to the ants that their progress was interfered with by it. Then he saw an advance. Not straight lines of men marching into cannon fire, but little groups scuttling like crabs from bits of cover to other cover, while the high chatter of machine guns sounded, and the deep proom of shellfire.

Steinbeck, the correspondent, scuttled with them, advancing from the beachhead into town, keeping his horror in the third-person, just as journalistically factual and as shoutingly pointed as Matthew Brady's photographs of the fresh-faced dead in Civil War battles.

He [the correspondent] might have seen a small Italian girl in the street with her stomach blown out, and he might have seen an American soldier standing over a twitching body, crying. . . . He saw the wreckage of houses, with torn beds hanging like shreds out of the spilled hole in a plaster wall . . .

Stretcher-bearers walk out of step to minimize the bouncing of the bleeding wounded, while nearby a burial detail removes dog tags, "so you know that man with that Army serial number is dead and out of it." The army moves past as the correspondent pauses to eat hard-cake rations, attracting starving children–orphans?–who cry for his candy, "Caramela!" And so Steinbeck concludes the article:

Still from Lifeboat, *the Alfred Hitchcock movie with screenplay by Steinbeck (MOMA/Film Stills Archive; from Joseph R. Millichap,* Steinbeck and Film, *1983; Thomas Cooper Library, University of South Carolina)*

The correspondent will get the communique and will write your morning dispatch on his creaking, dust-filled portable: "General Clark's 5th Army advanced two kilometers against heavy artillery fire yesterday."

History owes at least a small debt to the censor who let that dispatch pass on October 6, 1943. It may represent the best kind of truth in reporting, though surely the most ironic, too: an unvarnished, accurate picture of how those charged with presenting accurate pictures cannot or must not do their jobs. Finally, as this article steps through the looking-glass of war coverage, we approach the full truth.

Why, then, did Steinbeck give such a harsh verdict when his wartime dispatches were collected in one volume fifteen years later? He wrote:

Reading them over after all these years I realize not only how much I have forgotten but that they are period pieces, the attitudes archaic, the impulses romantic, and, in the light of everything that has happened since, perhaps the whole body of work untrue and warped and one-sided.

Again, his sense of the writer's duty is haunted by the fact that his memory brings back "the other things, which also did happen and were not reported." He continues: "That they were not reported was partly a mat-

ter of orders, partly traditional, and largely because there was a huge and gassy thing called the War Effort."

There were, of course, military censors. (Steinbeck, like other correspondents, bridled under their editing. In spite, he once sent Herodotus' report of an ancient Greek battle—and it, too, was censored.) The correspondents' work was also policed back home by, as he put it, "war-minded civilians, the Noncombatant Commandos of the Stork Club." Additionally, however, there was a self-censorship by the writers, he said. Imposed from without or within, the rules were clear:

There were no cowards in the U.S. Army, and of all the brave men the private in the infantry was the bravest and noblest. . . . A second convention was that we had no cruel or ambitious or ignorant commanders. . . . A third sternly held rule was that five million perfectly normal, young, energetic, and concupiscent men and boys had for the period of the War Effort put aside their habitual preoccupation with girls.

While pointing out these and other omissions that kept the folks back home from seeing "the crazy hysterical mess" that the soldiers and correspondents saw, still Steinbeck recalls the context: "Yes, we wrote only a part of the war, but at the time we believed, fervently believed, that it was the right thing to do."

Something that Steinbeck does not say in review-ing his own war reporting may partly explain why he felt his work was "untrue." Was he, at least uncon-sciously, overcompensating in choice of subjects and wording in some articles, to present a little more evi-dence on his own behalf against those who charged him with "disloyalty" because some of his prior writing had challenged the American social and economic status quo? His letters and biographers do not say this explic-itly, and it is impossible to read a writer's mind. To an inquiring graduate student who sought to probe his thought processes, Steinbeck once said, perhaps disin-genuously, "as to what I mean by—or what my philoso-phy is—I haven't the faintest idea."

Nonetheless, Steinbeck was all too conscious of the enmity many felt for him. Once, while scouting Cal-ifornia locations for the film of *The Grapes of Wrath,* he told his companion, the director, that he could not stop "because I'd get my ass full of rock salt. They hate me around here." He was aware that J. Edgar Hoover's Red-hunting FBI was watching him. In 1942, he wrote to U.S. Attorney General Francis Biddle, asking, "Do you suppose you could ask Edgar's boys to stop step-ping on my heels? They think I am an enemy alien." Although the comment sounds flippant, Steinbeck was aware that such an attitude was what had kept him from getting any military or government job during the war. One Army report on him, based on a review of the FBI file, expressed "substantial doubt as to Subject's loyalty." Whether he colored his war writing in part to answer these whispered slurs, whether they were another brake on the truth of what he produced, no one will ever know.

The charge that hurt Steinbeck most, however, was a variant that came a year before he actually cov-ered the war. It came in response to his war novel, which he turned into a Broadway play, *The Moon is Down,* about a conquered town's resistance. The charge: That Steinbeck's book gave comfort to the Fas-cist enemy.

James Thurber, reviewing the book only four months after Pearl Harbor, ridiculed it as a "fable of War in Wonderland." But then he noted that the war could be lost and that "nothing would help more toward that end than for Americans to believe Stein-beck's version of Nazi conquest instead of the true story of hell, horror and hopelessness." Rebuttals came from many who had endured Nazi occupation, and as time passed, the most telling reply came from resistance fighters themselves, who translated and reprinted the book almost as an instruction manual. Looking through magazines in which such critiques and equally strenu-ous defenses of the author appeared, one glimpses what an all-encompassing thing the "war effort" concept was;

victory is the main or sub-theme of virtually every arti-cle, the justification for buying every ad's product. A full page for Lockheed, for example, shows a Luftwaffe bomber going down in flames, but more typical is an ad for Pepsi, showing a smiling, sweating factory worker taking a break for a patriotic drink: "American energy will win!" says the legend. Though the point of the ads and of Thurber's criticism is long moot, the context they reveal is most relevant.

Steinbeck thought he had written in *The Moon is Down* "a kind of celebration of democracy." He had deliberately universalized the story, nowhere labeling the invaders as Germans; when the play went to Broad-way the stage directions specified that the occupiers' uniforms not be identifiable as those "of any known nation." Although critics have faulted the novel-play on several grounds, some recognize that its truth could only blossom out of its own time. It is, said one, "a par-able for the future."

This was another variety of truth, which Stein-beck recognized. "You can write anything in the morn-ing paper so long as it happened," he wrote once to a friend, but added:

> The fiction writer wouldn't dare do this. What he writes must . . . not only have happened but must continue to happen. This makes it more difficult. . . . Ideally, fiction takes on a greater reality in the mind of the reader than nonfiction. Participation in *Crime and Punishment* has a greater reality to most people than any-thing that has or is likely to happen to them.

Steinbeck was tarred for making the invaders too human in *The Moon is Down.* One by one, he describes the occupying officers, each a plausible portrait of one of war's ironies: the major, an engineer who sees life in terms as mechanical as the measurements in his plans to rebuild dynamited rail lines; the ambi-tious, spit-polished captain who has "no unmilitary moments"; the green lieutenants, including one roman-tic who "sometimes spoke blank verse under his breath to imaginary dark women. He longed for death on the battlefield."

The most sympathetic officer is the leader of the occupiers, Colonel Lanser, who doubted headquarters' orders but carried them out anyway, even executions. Only he, Steinbeck says, knew what war really is in the long run:

> Lanser had been in Belgium and France twenty years before and he tried not to think what he knew—that war is treachery and hatred, the muddling of incompe-tent generals, the torture and killing and sickness and tiredness, until at last it is over and nothing has changed except for a new weariness and new hatreds.

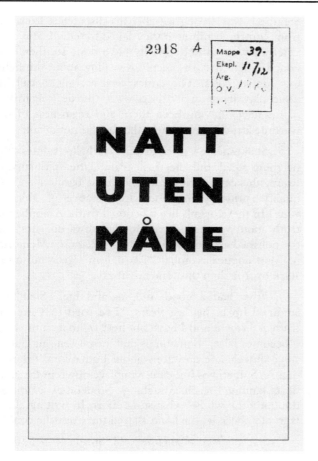

Front cover of the clandestine 1942 Norwegian edition of The Moon Is Down; *title page for the second clandestine Danish edition of the novel, published in 1943 (left, University of Oslo and Gyldendal Norsk Forlag; right, Museum of Denmark's Fight for Freedom, 1940–1945; from Donald V. Coers,* John Steinbeck as Propagandist, *1991; Thomas Cooper Library, University of South Carolina)*

Lanser told himself he was a soldier, given orders to carry out. He . . . tried to put aside the sick memories of the other war and the certainty that this would be the same. This one will be different, he said to himself fifty times a day; this one will be different.

In an extraordinary passage that follows, Steinbeck's irony about the elusiveness of war's meaning shines through:

In marching, in mobs, in football games, and in war, outlines become vague; real things become unreal and a fog creeps over the mind. Tension and excitement, weariness, movement—all merge in one great gray dream, so that when it is over, it is hard to remember how it was when you killed men or ordered them to be killed. Then other people who were not there tell you what it was like and you say vaguely, "Yes, I guess that's how it was."

Laid beside Steinbeck's nonfiction of the war years, his novel-play clearly fills in many background truths. They almost need to be read side-by-side for the complementary perspectives and insights. To take one obvious example, he has said war correspondents could not write the truth about dubious officers. Yet Steinbeck knew better than most who those officers were: he had seen many in action during his work for the War Department on *Bombs Away* and other projects. Fiction allowed him to draw at least some of the portrait, leaving it to readers, then or in the future, to decide whether it applied to their time and nation.

Laid beside Steinbeck's war correspondence, *The Moon is Down* unquestionably lacks action and life. Indeed, the book's opening lines declare: "By ten-forty-five it was all over. The town was occupied, the defenders defeated, and the war finished." More than one critic has echoed the complaint that the story's characters are "qualities masquerading as human beings." But again, perhaps Steinbeck's creation of walking representations of ideas and themes (the mayor as Democracy and Hope, and so on) was a kind of intellectual complement, almost like a cloudy mirror, to the frantic action of history that people were living at that time. For a writer of Steinbeck's facility with rich, humane characterization (it is the thing he does best), isn't it likely that this was intentional—that these universalized characters, speaking often in phrases that could be carved on monuments, were meant to reveal the unspoken ideals and philosophical doubts that the wartime world was mostly too busy, and partly too afraid, to let walk about?

If this is questionable drama, then so are the dialogues of Plato, a few lines of which provide some of the most heartrending tension in *The Moon is Down*. When the mayor, facing execution, reminisces about a schoolboy oratory performance and tries to recall the condemned Socrates' last speech, a missing word is supplied by none other than the commander of the occupying force, who has given the execution order. If the ultimate truth of this fiction is that war is a cursedly human activity, carried out by fallible and complex humans, in part because of corrupted systems of leadership invented by humans and in part because of Homo sapiens' instinct for war, could that truth be stated more forcefully than with such a tragic, yet credible, irony?

If a writer starts with the conviction that his job is to present the truth, and if he has the gift and courage to follow that quest, there are many avenues to this end and many destinations that we can correctly call truth.

Steinbeck was wrong to label his dispatches from the front "untrue"; although they failed to tell all, at a time when they could not ethically have done so, they contained much that was deeply revealing about the fighting and its costs. The critics were wrong to call his novel-play about an occupied town "untrue," regardless of his never having been there and regardless of the wartime atrocities elsewhere that he did not detail.

Shakespeare's great general, Othello, salutes "the neighing steed and the shrill trump, the spirit-stirring drum, the ear-piercing fife, the royal banner, and all quality, pride, pomp and circumstance of glorious war!" In these details lies a fictional truth. A nonfiction truth about war reflects in chiseled rows of names on the polished granite of the Vietnam Veterans Memorial in Washington: combat "journalism" gets no more stark or true than this, one might say.

"I've had a good, full, painful life," Steinbeck summed up in his last years. "I've tried to write the truth as I saw it and I have not held on to a truth when it becomes false." Sometimes that meant sending onto a stage unwelcome questions about humankind's darker nature. Sometimes it meant lying face-down in the sand of a landing beach, watching. Sometimes it meant doubting the whole exhausting effort. In writing about war, Steinbeck learned and shared the truths he could.

—Journalism History, 23 (Spring 1997): 16–22

Chapter Five: 1946–1950

Chronology

January–May 1946	Steinbeck works on the manuscript of *The Wayward Bus* (1947).
12 June 1946	Steinbeck and Gwyn's second son, John Steinbeck IV, is born.
July 1946	Steinbeck returns briefly to Mexico for postproduction work on the movie version of *The Pearl* (1947).
18 October 1946	Steinbeck and Gwyn sail for Sweden aboard the *Drottningholm,* leaving their two boys at home with a nursemaid.
15 November 1946	Steinbeck receives King Haakon's Liberty Cross from Norway for *The Moon Is Down* (1942).
Winter 1946	Swedish artist Bo Beskow paints a second portrait of Steinbeck. After a brief trip to Paris, the Steinbecks return to New York.
January 1947	Steinbeck works on a play titled "The Last Joan," based on an idea given to him by actor Burgess Meredith. Steinbeck and Gwyn continue to have marital difficulties, which they have experienced since his return from serving as a war correspondent in Europe in 1943.

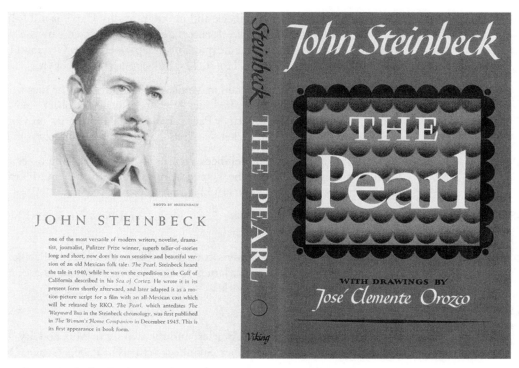

Dust jacket for Steinbeck's 1947 novelette about a Mexican pearl diver who finds a large pearl and hopes to sell it in order to procure medical treatment for his ailing son (Bruccoli Clark Layman Archives)

Early February 1947	Viking Press publishes *The Wayward Bus,* which is designated a Book-of-the-Month Club selection.
March 1947	Steinbeck discusses with noted photojournalist Robert Capa a plan for taking a trip to Russia to write articles for the *New York Herald Tribune,* which is to finance the venture.
April 1947	Steinbeck gives up on "The Last Joan" and destroys the manuscript. He spends much of his time preparing for his trip to Russia.
14 May 1947	Steinbeck's travel plans are interrupted when he suffers injuries from a fall from the second-story balcony at his New York brownstone when the railing gives way. He is hospitalized for his knee injuries.
June 1947	Steinbeck and Gwyn travel to Paris; Gwyn returns to New York on 18 July.
July–September 1947	After setting out on 21 July, Steinbeck and Capa tour the Soviet Union. Steinbeck returns to New York in late September.
November 1947	The book version of *The Pearl* is published by Viking Press, with illustrations by José Clemente Orozco.
December 1947	*The First Watch,* a pamphlet consisting of a letter from Steinbeck to a "Mr. G" dated 5 January 1938, is published by the Ward Richie Press of Los Angeles in a limited edition of sixty copies for private distribution by Marguerite and Louis Henry Cohn as Christmas gifts.
Early January 1948	Steinbeck flies to California to perform research for a planned novel about the Salinas Valley. While there, he visits old friends and does some work with Ed Ricketts.
17 February 1948	The movie version of *The Pearl* receives its American premiere at the Sutton Theatre in New York.
Mid March 1948	Steinbeck returns to New York from California.
April 1948	*A Russian Journal,* with text by Steinbeck and photographs by Capa, is published by Viking Press. Around this time, Steinbeck enters the hospital to have varicose veins removed from his legs. After leaving the hospital, he is separated from Gwyn and moves into a room at New York's Bedford Hotel. The boys remain with Gwyn.
May 1948	On 7 May, Ricketts's car is hit by a train in Monterey; four days later he dies from his injuries, before Steinbeck can reach his bedside. After the funeral Steinbeck and a close friend, George Robinson, go to Ricketts's Pacific Biological Laboratories on Cannery Row in Monterey and sort through Ricketts's effects. Steinbeck burns his letters to Ricketts.
June–July 1948	Gwyn demands a divorce when Steinbeck returns to New York. She takes the boys with her to Los Angeles, and Steinbeck spends most of his summer in Mexico working on his screenplay for *Viva Zapata!* (1952).
August 1948	Steinbeck spends his time in Mexico, Los Angeles, and New York, and his relationship with Gwyn deteriorates further.
Early September 1948	Steinbeck moves back into his family's cottage on Eleventh Street in Pacific Grove. With him is a former navy steward, James Neale, who has worked as a domestic servant with the Steinbecks in New York.
October 1948	Gwyn is granted a divorce in a Reno, Nevada, courtroom.
November 1948	Steinbeck meets Elia Kazan in Los Angeles, and the two fly to Mexico City for the filming of *Viva Zapata!* In mid November, Steinbeck returns to Pacific Grove. On the 23rd he is elected a member of the American Academy of Arts and Letters.
25 December 1948	Steinbeck's short story "Miracle of Tepayac" is published in *Collier's.*

Lobby card for the 1949 motion-picture adaptation of Steinbeck's 1937 story sequence (from William McPheron, John Steinbeck: From Salinas to Stockholm, *2000; Special Collections, Thomas Cooper Library, University of South Carolina)*

Peter Miles as Tommy Tiflin (Jody Tiflin in the book) in The Red Pony *(MOMA/Film Stills Archive; from Joseph R. Millichap,* Steinbeck and Film, *1983; Thomas Cooper Library, University of South Carolina)*

January 1949	The motion-picture adaptation of *The Red Pony* (1937) is released after a delay of seven years. Steinbeck sees the movie for the first time in Los Angeles.
Late March 1949	While working on the screenplay for *Viva Zapata!,* Steinbeck is also writing short stories and taking notes for the long novel set in the Salinas Valley that eventually becomes *East of Eden* (1952).
April–May 1949	Steinbeck finishes the first draft of the screenplay for *Viva Zapata!* He invites one of his Hollywood friends, actress Ann Sothern, to visit him on Memorial Day weekend in Pacific Grove, and Sothern brings with her a friend, Elaine Scott, a former Broadway stage manager and the wife of actor Zachary Scott. Elaine and Steinbeck fall in love at this time.
Summer 1949	Steinbeck and Elaine agree to marry if she can obtain a divorce from Scott.
August 1949	Steinbeck works on an experimental play/novelette with the working title "Everyman," later retitled "In the Forests of the Night," and finally published as *Burning Bright: A Play in Story Form* (1950). The second and final versions of the title come from William Blake's poem "The Tyger" (1794).
September 1949	Steinbeck's short story "His Father" is published in *The Reader's Digest.*
November 1949	Elaine calls Steinbeck on 1 November to tell him that she and her husband have agreed to a divorce. Late in the month Steinbeck returns to New York.
December 1949	Elaine and her daughter, Waverly Scott, travel to New York to join Steinbeck.
January 1950	Steinbeck works on the play version of *Burning Bright.* His interest in plays becomes stronger with his exposure to Elaine's circle of Broadway friends.
February 1950	Steinbeck polishes *Burning Bright* and in the meantime makes notes for a stage adaptation of *Cannery Row* (1945).
March–April 1950	Steinbeck and Elaine fly to Texas to meet her family, and they return to New York in early April.
Early August 1950	Steinbeck sets aside the dramatization of *Cannery Row* to work on a profile of Ricketts, which he submits to Viking.
18 October 1950	The play *Burning Bright* opens in New York at the Broadhurst Theatre and draws heavy criticism. It runs for only a few performances.
11 November 1950	Steinbeck lashes out at his critics in an article titled "Critics, Critics, Burning Bright," published in the *Saturday Review.*
December 1950	Elaine's divorce from Scott becomes final on 21 December. Seven days later she and Steinbeck are married in a quiet ceremony at the home of Harold Guinzburg, the president of Viking.

Steinbeck and his third wife, Elaine Scott Steinbeck, at their wedding reception, 28 December 1950 (John Steinbeck Library, Salinas; from Jackson J. Benson, The True Adventures of John Steinbeck, Writer, *1984; Thomas Cooper Library, University of South Carolina)*

In March 1946, when Steinbeck, the pregnant Gwyn, and their son, Thom, moved into their house in New York, he was depressed over the state of his marriage and anxious about his writing powers. In the years since The Grapes of Wrath (1939) he had written nothing major to satisfy his own ambitions. It was under such mixed feelings that he finished the manuscript for The Wayward Bus (1947). After the birth of the Steinbecks' second son, John Steinbeck IV, on 2 June, Steinbeck returned to Mexico briefly for some postproduction work on the movie version of The Pearl (1947).

Having completed The Wayward Bus, Steinbeck accepted an invitation from Otto Lindhardt, his Danish publisher, for him and Gwyn to visit Denmark, where he received "a hero's welcome," according to a news story in Time. One Danish newspaper ran the headline "John Steinbeck, All of Denmark Is at Your Feet." Concerned about their children at home, Gwyn convinced Steinbeck that they should return to New York. In a December 1946 letter to his friend the Swedish artist Bo Beskow, for whom he had sat for a portrait

during the recent trip, Steinbeck revealed that he was experiencing marital problems.

The Wayward Bus was published in early February 1947 to mixed reviews. Nonetheless, 600,000 copies were sold, and Viking had to print another 150,000 copies in its first trade edition, making the novel Steinbeck's most successful book. In late February, Gwyn and the two boys left for California after she had a fight with Steinbeck. Seeking a break from his domestic life, Steinbeck followed a suggestion that he do some reporting from Europe for the New York Herald Tribune. He had met photojournalist Robert Capa while covering the war in Europe in 1943, and at that time they had discussed traveling to the Soviet Union for material for a book; they now decided to carry out this plan.

When Steinbeck and Capa arrived in Moscow in July 1947, no one came to meet them at the airport, and they had to find their own way to the city, only to discover that there was no hotel room reserved for them. They survived the first few days with the help of some American correspondents. On 1

August, Steinbeck and Capa received permission to travel, first to Ukraine, then to Stalingrad and Georgia, and finally back to Moscow. They found the Ukrainians hospitable and friendly. Steinbeck and Capa left Russia in mid September, stopping in Prague and Budapest on their way back to the United States. Back in New York, Steinbeck settled down to work not only on A Russian Journal *(1948) but also on a long novel he had contemplated for years, the book eventually published as* East of Eden *(1952).*

Early in 1948 Steinbeck wrote to the editor of the Salinas Californian *requesting permission to research the newspaper files on the Salinas Valley region. Despite Gwyn's rejection of the idea of returning to California, Steinbeck flew first to Los Angeles, where he visited some friends, and then rented a Buick for the trip north. When he reached Monterey, he visited Ed Ricketts and other old friends. During the spring Steinbeck performed research for his new book, visiting the newspaper offices and going through files dating back to the 1890s. In late March he returned to New York. The coming months were to bring huge losses in his emotional life.*

Not only did Steinbeck's marriage continue to deteriorate, but he was also to lose a friend who had helped to shape his literary character, Ricketts. On the evening of 7 May 1948 Ricketts, driving down Cannery Row across the railroad tracks into downtown Monterey, collided with the Del Monte Express arriving from San Francisco. The train demolished his car and dragged him for several hundred feet along the tracks before it stopped. By the time Steinbeck had been notified and flew to Monterey, Ricketts was already dead.

Gwyn demanded a divorce when Steinbeck returned to New York, and she took the boys with her to Los Angeles. Steinbeck spent most of the summer of 1948 in Mexico working on the screenplay for Viva Zapata! *(1952). In September he moved back to his family's cottage in Pacific Grove, California; in November he learned that he had been elected a member of the American Academy of Arts and Letters.*

In early 1949 Steinbeck was working on the screenplay for Viva Zapata!, *writing short stories, and taking notes for* East of Eden. *His hope for a brighter personal life was rekindled by a new acquaintance, Elaine Scott, a former Broadway stage manager, whose marriage to actor Zachary Scott was coming to an end. For the rest of the year, Steinbeck wrote Elaine daily letters. Late in the summer they agreed to marry if Elaine could obtain a divorce from her husband.*

Around this time Steinbeck was working on an experimental play/novelette at first tentatively titled "Everyman," then "In the Forests of the Night," and finally Burning Bright *(1950), the latter two titles taken from William Blake's poem "The Tyger" (1794). At the end of 1949 Elaine joined Steinbeck in New York. His enthusiasm for drama grew with his exposure to Elaine's circle of Broadway friends, and he began work on a dramatization of* Cannery Row *(1945).*

On 18 October 1950 the stage version of Burning Bright *opened in New York at the Broadhurst Theatre; meeting with harsh criticism, the play ran for only a few performances. In response Steinbeck published an article titled "Critics, Critics, Burning Bright" in the* Saturday Review. *His personal life continued to improve, however, as Elaine's divorce from Scott became final on 21 December and Steinbeck married her on the 28th.*

End of a Marriage

Steinbeck to Bo Beskow, 16 December 1946

After returning from his recent trip to Europe, during which he sat for a second portrait by Swedish artist Bo Beskow, Steinbeck wrote Beskow to thank him. The letter hints at Steinbeck's and Gwyn's growing marital problems.

Dear Bo:

The photographs of the portrait arrived and I took one of them over to Viking Press. It has caused a great deal of enthusiasm and makes me all the more anxious to have the original as soon as possible.

Have not been feeling well. I don't know why. I am taking some vitamins to see whether it could be a food deficiency. The depression has lasted too long this time and I don't like it at all.

I have not gone back to work and that bothers me. I shouldn't take these long rests. They aren't good for my soul or whatever it is that makes you sick. I make myself think that I will go back to work right after Christmas and maybe I will. I think Gwyn and the children will go to California for a month or six weeks about the first of February to let the children see their relatives. But I will just stay here and get back to work. Marital vacations are sometimes good things. Not that we need them very much. But just as the trip to Europe made us love our house so we get to liking each other with a little time spent apart.

Relationships are very funny things. I've wondered what I would think if this one were over and I think I would only be glad that it had happened at all. I don't think I would rail at fortune, but then it is impossible to know what you would do in any given situation unless you have experienced it. It was and would be silly of me to make any sort of judgement about your difficulty because I do not know all the factors. But you'll never get out clear no matter which way you go. A man going on living gets frayed and he drags little tatters and rags of things behind him all the rest of his life and his suit is never new after he has worn it a little. I've had such a bad time the last three or four weeks. The complete and meaningless despair that happens without warning and without reason that I can figure unless there happens to be some glandular disarrangement. So I am trying to do what I can about that and to see whether the feeling will go away.

Next Sunday we have our tree decorating party. It will be a fairly large party with at least forty people but they are all nice people. In fact about the best in the city for interest. Gwyn is going to have a midnight supper and I will make a monster bowl of punch and there we will be. The idea is to decorate our Christmas tree in the course of the evening. All sorts of arguments usually develop, aesthetic ones.

It should be a very fine Christmas.

Good luck and come out from under.

[signed with a stamp of Steinbeck's trademark flying pig, "Pigasus"]

—Steinbeck: A Life in Letters, edited by Elaine Steinbeck and Robert Wallsten (New York: Viking, 1975), pp. 294–295

* * *

Steinbeck to Joseph Henry and Charlotte Jackson, 26 October 1948

Half a year after separating from Gwyn and a month after moving back to his family's Pacific Grove cottage, Steinbeck wrote San Francisco Chronicle *book critic Joseph Henry Jackson and his wife describing his new way of life. Gwyn was granted her divorce this same month.*

Dear Joe and Charlotte:

I have been meaning to write for a long time but house fixing has interfered. Strange thing, Joe—tonight I couldn't sleep and I wrote a little story that was so evil, so completely evil that when I finished it I burned it. It was effective, horribly effective. It would have made anyone who read it completely miserable. I don't mind evil if anything else is accomplished but this was unqualifiedly murderous and terrible. I wonder where it came from. It just seemed to creep in from under the door. I suppose the best thing was to write it and the next was to burn it.

It's getting cold so early. There is a nasty light of tomorrow coming through the blinds.

The wind is ashore tonight and I can hear the sea lions and the surf and the whistling buoy and the bell buoy at Point Joe and China Point respectively. China Point is now called Cabrillo Point. Phooey—

any fool knows it was China Point until certain foreigners became enamored of our almost nonexistent history. Cabrillo may or may not have first sighted this point, but them Chinks raised hell on it for fifty years, yes, and even buried their people there until the meat fell off and they could ship them cheaper to China. Mary [Steinbeck's younger sister] and I used to watch them dig up the skeletons and we stole the punks and paper flowers off the new graves too. I used to like that graveyard. It was so rocky that some of the bodies had to be slipped in almost horizontally under the big rocks. And it has just occurred to me that I'm a talkative bastard. So I'll clip off the qualifying adjectives and relax in the *now*.

love to you both
John

I've lost your home address.

—Steinbeck: A Life in Letters, pp. 336–337

* * *

Steinbeck to Pascal Covici, 22 February 1949

Writing his editor, Pascal Covici, early in 1949, Steinbeck indicated that in spite of the acrimony of his break with Gwyn, he was managing to write a great deal.

Dear Pat:

Here it is again, another year and the first one I haven't dreaded for a long time. I just finished my day's work. It is finally going like mad, or did I tell you that? And now that it is going I don't think it will take long. And as always when I am working I am gay. I'm terribly gay. I'm even gay about what I'm going to tell you. And I want you to keep this to yourself.

I'm asking Gwyn for my books. I asked for the anthologies, poetry, drama, classics etc. which I have collected over the years. Well I didn't get them. I got an absolute minimum. I wish you would please get me, if you can, complete catalogues of Everyman, Random House and the other libraries that do such things because I do want to replace the things I actually need for work. Isn't it odd that having stripped me of everything else, she also retains the tools of the trade from which she is living? A very funny girl and I think she is headed for trouble—not from me. I did get the dictionary and the encyclopedia and a few others.

I don't know what has happened but the dams are burst. Work is pouring out of me. I guess maybe I am over the illness. Who knows? But at last there seems to be some opening at the end of the street.

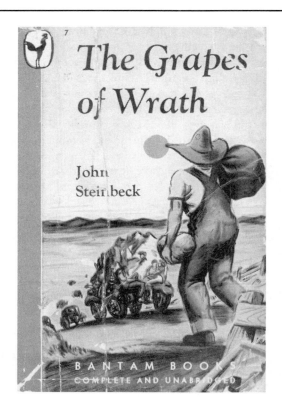

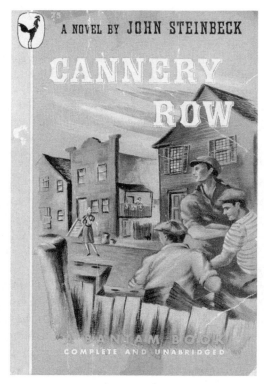

Front covers of four 1940s paperback editions of Steinbeck books (Bruccoli Clark Layman Archives)

Please let me hear from you. And don't tell any one about this book thing. I don't want to fight with Gwyn unless the children are involved and sooner or later I think they will be.

So long now
affectionately
John
—*Steinbeck: A Life in Letters*, p. 349

* * *

Steinbeck to Elaine Scott, 6 June 1949

Steinbeck met Elaine Scott, wife of actor Zachary Scott, when actress Ann Sothern brought her along on a visit over Memorial Day weekend of 1949. He and Elaine quickly fell in love and, later in the summer, agreed to marry if she could obtain a divorce from her husband.

Dear Miss West Forty-seventh Street
between Eighth and Ninth:

Am a widower with 10,000 acres in Arizona and seven cows so if you can milk I will be glad to have you give up that tinsel life of debauchery and sin and come out to God's country where we got purple sage. P. S. Can you bring a little sin and debauchery along? You can get too much purple sage but you can only get just enough sin.

I am really glad that you got some rest and that you feel somewhat restored. I guess it is that purple sage. I think I will try to bottle it.

Annie Rooney [Ann Sothern] called to say that the skirts had arrived [Chinese men's ceremonial skirts he had sent them as presents]. I would like one too but I ain't pretty enough. This has been my tragedy—with the soul to wear a scarlet-lined opera cape and small sword I have the physical misfortune always to be handed a hod. I have never quite got over this sadness. Let me know whether you want me to get another. I have been tempted to buy the whole stock because there will never be any more. The new regime is not going to approve of them I guess and they are unique as far as I know.

I was sad when you two bugs went away. Now I haven't even a half-assed reason for not working.

I am told that darling Louella tagged Annie and me last night. This will henceforth be known as The Seven Days That Shook the Pine Inn. Running naked through the woods with flowers in your hair is against the law and I told you both but you wouldn't listen.

Sometime during the summer I will drift down your way. [. . .]

Love to you and Annie.

—*Steinbeck: A Life in Letters*, pp. 357–358

* * *

Steinbeck to John O'Hara, 8 June 1949

At the time of this letter to his friend John O'Hara, O'Hara's novel A Rage to Live *had just come out.*

Dear John:

Your letter made me very happy. This is a time of most profound readjustments, emotional as well as in other directions and the reassurance of a letter like yours cannot be overestimated. Everything dried up as it is bound to, and got out of drawing and with three more mixed metaphors I will have a literary boulliabaise, or how do you spell it.

I am extremely anxious to read your new book. There are lots of reasons for this. I believe that your hatreds are distilling off and that your work is all ahead of you. Maybe the training in hatred in all of us is necessary. For hate is a completely self-conscious and personalized emotion and a deterrent to a clear view but it may be as necessary to developing ability as the adjectives we later learn to eliminate. But we must first use the adjectives before we can know how to leave them out.

I've had seven months of quiet out here to try to reduce the maelstrom to tea kettle size. For myself there are two things I cannot do without. Crudely stated they are work and women, and more gently—creative effort in all directions. Effort and love. Everything else I can do without but if those were effectively removed I would take a powder instantly.

Being alone here has allowed me to think out lots of things. There is so much yapping in the world. The coyotes are at us all the time telling us what we are, what we should do and believe. The stinking little parasitic minds that fasten screaming on us like pilot fish that fasten on a shark, they contribute only drag. I think I believe one thing powerfully—that the only creative thing our species has is the individual, lonely mind. Two people can create a child but I know of no other thing created by a group. The group ungoverned by individual thinking is a horrible destructive principle. The great change in the last 2,000 years was the Christian idea that the individual soul was very precious. Unless we can preserve and foster the principle of the preciousness of the individual mind, the world of men will either disintegrate into a screaming chaos or will go into a grey slavery. And that fostering and preservation seem to me our greatest job.

This will probably be a long and boring letter, but I need some one to talk to and good or bad for you, you are tagged.

You see I worked last year but it was all experiment and notes. I've been practicing for a book for 35 years and this is it. I don't see how it can be popular because I am inventing method and form and tone and context. And of course I am scared of it. It's a cold lonely profession and this is the coldest and loneliest because this is all I can do, and when it is done I've either done it or I never had it to do.

I've re-read your letter and this is another day. You know I was born without any sense of competition. Consequently I have never even wondered about the comparative standing of writers. I don't understand that. Writing to me is a deeply personal, even a secret function and when the product is turned loose it is cut off from me and I have no sense of its being mine. It is like a woman trying to remember what child birth is like. She never can.

Again I have re-read your letter. And you are quite right. A man is always married. I wonder though whether he can be married to the idea—with different people carrying the ball (oh Jesus!). I will know sometime maybe. Being married to me is a very hard thing. I am kind and loving and generous but there is always the rival (work) and to most women that is worse than another woman. They can kill or eliminate another woman but that rival they cannot even get close to no matter how you try to make them a part of it. And there's the necessity for being alone—that must be dreadful to a wife.

This maundering will probably go on for some time.

Now it is even more days later. I thought, after I stopped writing the other day, regarding your words about a wife. And do you remember in the Mabinogion, the ancient Welsh story of the man who made a wife entirely of flowers?

My boys will be with me in another two weeks and I will be glad. I deeply resent their growing and me not there to see. That is the only thing I resent now. The rest is all gone. But imagine if you couldn't see your daughter for months at a time when every day is a change and growth and fascination. I saw my oldest boy turn over on his back and discover the sky and in his look of wonderment I remembered when it happened to me and exactly how it was.

That's all now. But I would like and need to keep in touch.

John

—Steinbeck: A Life in Letters, pp. 359–361

Steinbeck and Ed Ricketts

Steinbeck to Edward F. Ricketts, August 1946

In the summer of 1946 Steinbeck invited Ed Ricketts to visit him in New York, but there is no record of Ricketts's having accepted the invitation. Steinbeck had recently learned about the death of Ricketts's mother.

Dear Ed:

I had your letters this morning, two of them, and I am writing immediately. The matter of death is very personal—almost like an idea—and it has to be discovered and accepted over and over again no matter what the age or the condition of the dying. And there is nothing for the outsider to do except to stand by and maybe to indicate that the person involved is not so alone as the death always makes him think he is. And that is why I am writing this letter.

The enclosed is for anything you want or need it for. It does occur to both Gwyn and me that in all of this there is some necessity of saving yourself, and I don't mean physically, and it is a thing that would occur last to you. We thought that you might like to use it to come on to see us for a couple of weeks. We thought further that a complete change of background and people for a little while might have restorative effects beyond almost anything. Perhaps we are wrong, but believe please that we would be very happy if you would do that. Think it over anyway.

I spoke to Pat [Covici] about the Guggenheim thing this morning and he suggests that you give Viking Press as one of your sponsors. He says that the interest of a publisher sometimes has some weight. So please remember that, will you?

The book sails on and I must admit that I am fascinated with it. It may be no good at all. I don't know but it holds my interest which is the most important thing.

That good Gwyn is making a lemon pie or two this afternoon than which nothing is lemoner nor nicer nor that I like more. The children are well and getting along nicely.

love to you
from both of us.
jn

—Steinbeck: A Life in Letters, p. 292

* * *

Permanent

Pacific
Biological
Laboratories

Pacific Grove, California

February 15, 1948

HPH
Here tis

Stanford University Press
Stanford University, Calif.

Gentlemen:

May we withdraw certain selected parts of "Between Pacific
Tides" which with the passing years badly need revision?
Science advances but Stanford Press does not.

There is the problem also of the impending New Ice Age.

Trillium
thats
Science too!

Sometime in the near future we should like to place our
order for one (1) copy of the forthcoming (1948, no doubt)
publication,

            "The Internal Combustion Engine, Will it Work?"

                                    Sincerely,

                                    John Steinbeck
                                    John Steinbeck

                                    Ed Ricketts
                                    Ed Ricketts

P.S. Good Luck with
      "A Brief Anatomy of the Turtle"

Letter from Steinbeck and Ed Ricketts to the Stanford University Press requesting revisions for the 1948 edition of Ricketts's and Jack Calvin's 1939 study Between Pacific Tides. *Three months after this letter was written, Ricketts died from injuries received in a Monterey railroad-crossing accident (from Richard Astro and Tetsumaro Hayashi, eds.,* Steinbeck: The Man and His Work, *1970; Thomas Cooper Library, University of South Carolina).*

Steinbeck to Ricketts, April 1948

*The following is probably Steinbeck's last letter to Ricketts, who died on 11 May 1948 from injuries sustained in an automobile accident at a railroad crossing in Monterey. Steinbeck told Ricketts that the Salinas Valley novel he was planning (*East of Eden *[1952]) would be the most ambitious book he had yet attempted.*

Dear Ed:

I am practicing for the novel very hard and I think I am getting some place. I do not want to start it until I am pretty sure that I have what I want in style and method but I am gradually getting through to the light. It is going to be bitterly resented by critics and the reader starting it may have some kind of hard going until he gets used to it but I do think that once he does, most other things might seem a little pale and bloodless. Anyway I am excited by the experiment.

It will be a hell of a long experiment though, nearly half a million words and by far the most ambitious book I have ever attempted. God help us all, we go on trying to climb that miserable mountain and it is always higher than the last rise we scrabbled onto. It seems to me that I have more than I can do and it frightens me sometimes until I think how it would be if I had less than I can do.

The circus in Madison Square Garden is sold out for the whole season. I want to take Thom. It will be the first circus when he is old enough and he is at the time now when it can be pure dream material. But there are no tickets. I am moving heaven and earth to try to get them for Saturday.

Next Tuesday I shall go into the hospital and have the varicosities in my legs removed. I will have to be in the hospital for a week because it is a large job and they don't want any of the ties to break loose. I should have had it done years ago but now finally I will complete it. The legs are not at all painful but I am told that the burst places are a lovely play ground for potential embolisms.

so long now
jn
—Steinbeck: A Life in Letters, pp. 309–310

* * *

Steinbeck to Beskow, 22 May 1948

After Ricketts's funeral Steinbeck returned to New York. His friend's death was such a blow to him that he could not concentrate on his work for a while, as he explained in a letter to his Swedish friend Beskow.

Dear Bo:

I got back from Monterey to find your letter. You see, Ed Ricketts' car was hit by a train and after fighting for his life for three days he died, and there died the greatest man I have known and the best teacher. It is going to take a long time to reorganize my thinking and my planning without him. It is good that he was killed during the very best time of his life with his work at its peak and with the best girl he ever had. I am extremely glad for that. He had just finished a plankton paper that was masterly. I will over the next few years, if I am able, edit his journals for the last fifteen years which contain his observations in every field. It is very important thinking to my mind.

Naturally this changes all of my plans about the summer and about nearly everything except my big book. You are right in your intuitions about the office and the ranch. There is nothing to do but to sit it out and that I will do, but meanwhile, if I possibly can, I will get the ranch to fall back into. As to the immediate future, I don't know. I may do a picture of the life of Emiliano Zapata if I can find someone to do it honestly. The great danger of Zanuck is that he writes and he can't but he thinks he can. I don't mean Zanuck, of course, I mean Selznick. They all sound alike. But Zanuck did a good picture for me in the Grapes of Wrath and Milestone did a good one in both the Mice and Men and the Red Pony. The last has not been released. The Pearl is a pretty good picture but I could not protect its pace. It is a little slow. I will send you a copy of the book in the next day or so. It has line drawings by Orozco. Many people do not like them but I do and it is the only book he has ever consented to illustrate and that to me is a very great compliment.

I thought for a day or so that I would run to Sweden to lick my wound and that might be a good thing too but that wouldn't be good for you and in the second place I have too much to do. There are certain responsibilities here that I can't shake off.

I haven't asked about your girl because I thought you did not want to talk about her. I have thought that men and women should never come together except in bed. There is the only place where their natural hatred of each other is not so apparent. Many animals from deer to dogs have no association between the male and the female except in the rutting season or the heat of the female. In this way they may be very biologically wise because the warfare between the unaroused male and female is constant and ferocious. Each blames the other for his loss of soul.

One pays for everything, the trick is not to pay too much of anything for anything. That was Ed Ricketts' discovery and he practiced it. He did not pay too much for a clean floor or for family or for luxuries which did not give him a really luxurious feeling. Many people disapproved of this and envied him at the same time. I among them because I am paying much too much for everything. You remember the people who bought real gold watches at country fairs and found that they were not only not gold but had no works either. This is quite a common thing in all directions.

Letters from me turn into long things. The book will be written. I have to get over a number of shocks but it will be written all right and good or bad at that. I have had the death feeling very strongly for some time now as you know but maybe this was it. I am capable sometimes of horrifying clairvoyances. They come out of the air. My mother had the second sight and so has one of my sisters, and I seem to have it a little. But I don't have the death feeling now. I know that my book has to be written, and for many reasons.

Well, I will be writing to you often now. There are times of verbosity and times of silence. And I may try to fill up one lack with you and you must not mind that. Whenever I thought of a good thought or picture—I wondered what Ed would think of it and how would he criticize it? The need is there. Maybe you who have taken part of that will have to take all of it now, at least for a while.

Let me ask you to answer to the address on this paper. Because my intellectual life is here now.

So long for now.

Jn

—Steinbeck: A Life in Letters, pp. 312–314

* * *

Steinbeck to Webster F. Street, 25 May 1948

Steinbeck wrote his Stanford friend Webster F. "Toby" Street about his friendship with Ricketts and his financial situation.

Dear Toby:

You are not the most episcotory thing in the world these days but I hope you will be able to bring me from time to time some kind of progress report of what happens out there. As you know Ed was very close to me and meant very much to me. I liked him and I would have done anything in the world for him and when ever it was possible I did what I could. The laboratory without Ed is just a run down piece of real estate and any attempt to maintain it or hold

it together is either a piece of morbid wishful thinking or an attempt to use the place simply as a place to live.

Now, there is something else that I want you to look into. I loaned Ed a thousand dollars very recently. I have his correspondence on it and he was to have signed a note for it as he indicates in his letters. This thousand was to be his share of the expenses for the book we were going to do together. That I will have to get back some how. He may have spent it on other things. I know he was pretty strapped and that his beer bill alone was more than he was making.

In spite of what people generally consider, I do not have any money. I have no savings at all and the last couple of years I have joined the great majority and gone into debt at tax time. I spend on trips and things like that only such things as are clearly and legally deductible in the carrying out of my writing. What I am getting down to is that the money must be returned because I haven't got it and I will have to borrow it next year to pay my taxes and pay interest on it. This is what I wanted to tell you.

I think you know that I put a high value on friendship. I have been kicked in the behind quite a bit on this account and that is perfectly all right and I would do it again but there are a number of reasons why I have to toughen up. I have a long book to write, a three year job. There are other situations arising which I will not go into now but that is the one firm and unalterable thing I have. That god damned book is going to get written. I'm forty-six now and if I am going to be a writer I'd better god damned well get to it. I've piddled away a great deal of my time and I haven't an awfully lot left. I don't think you can find anybody in my acquaintance to whom I have not loaned money and that is all right but now I need help in the way of indulgence and support and I am asking for the kind of support I have given to everyone else. Jim Brady used to say that it was fun to pay off if you could afford it, and so it is but I can't afford it any more. I've got trouble coming and bad trouble and I have the book to write and I am going to have to have at least the spiritual support of my friends if I have any.

affectionately

John

—Steinbeck: A Life in Letters, pp. 314–315

Periodically in the history of human observation the world of external reality has been rediscovered, reclassified and redescribed. It is difficult for us to understand the reality of Democritus, of Aristotle, of Pliny for they did not see what we see and yet we know them to have been careful observers. We must concede either that their universe was different from ours or that they warped it and to a certain extent created their realities. And if they did, there is no reason to suppose that we do not. Possibly our warp is less due to our use of many measuring devices but in the immeasurable, we probably create our worlds.

The process of rediscovery might be like this — a young inquisitive and original man might one morning find a fissure in the traditional technique of thinking. Through this fissure he might look out and find a new world about him. In his excitement a few disciples would cluster to him and look again at the world they knew and find it fresh. From this nucleus there would develope a frantic new seeing, a cult of new seers who finding some traditional knowledge incorrect, would throw out the whole structure and start again. Then, the human mind being what it is, evaluation, taxonomy, arrangement, pattern making would succeed the first excited seeing. Gradually the structure would become complete and men would go to their structure rather than to the external world until eventually something like but not identical with the earlier structure would have been built. From such structures or patterns of knowledge, disciplines, ethics even manners exude. The pattern would be set again and no one would look beyond it until one day a young inquisitive and original man might find a fissure in the pattern

Manuscript of Steinbeck's foreword to the revised 1948 edition of Ricketts's and Calvin's Between Pacific Tides. *An earlier draft had been intended to serve as the preface to a marine-specimen handbook on the San Francisco Bay area that Steinbeck and Ricketts had planned in 1939 but never written (Special Collections, Stanford University Library; from Joel W. Hedgpeth, ed.,* The Outer Shores, *1978; Thomas Cooper Library, University of South Carolina).*

and look through it and find a new world. This seems to have happened again and again in the slow history of human thought and knowledge.

There is in our community an elderly painter of sea scapes who knows the sea so well that he no longer goes to look at it while he paints. He watches intensely the work of a young painter who sets his easel on the beach and paints things his elder does not remember having seen.

Modern science, or the ~~science~~ method of Roger Bacon has attempted by measuring and checking to admit as little warp as possible, but still some warp must be there. As in many fields young inquisitive men are seeing new worlds. And from their seeing will emerge not only new patterns but new ethics, disciplines and manners. The upheaval of the present world will probably stimulate restless minds to new speculations and evaluations. The new eyes will see, will break off new facets of reality. The excitements of the chase are already felt in the fields of biochemistry, medicine and biology. The world is being broken down to be built up again and eventually the sense of the new worlds will come out of the laboratory and penetrate into the smallest living techniques and habits of the whole people.

This book of Ricketts and Calvin is designed more to stir curiosity than to answer questions. It says in effect — look at the animals, this is what we seem to know about them but it is not final and any clear eye and sharp intelligence may see something we have never seen. These things, it says, you will see but you may see much more. This is a book for laymen, for beginners and as such, its main purpose is to stimulate curiosity not to answer finally questions which are only temporarily answerable. In the laboratories fissures are appearing in the structure of our knowledge and many young men are peering excitedly through it at a new world. There are answers to the worse questions which every man must ask, in the little animals of tide pools, in their relations one to another, in their color phases, their reproducing methods. And one can live in a prefabricated world, snugly and without question or one can indulge probably the greatest human excitement that of observation to speculation to hypothesis. This is a creative process, probably the highest and most satisfying we know. If only in the process one could keep the know of humor in operation, it would be even more satisfactory. If one should keep always in mind his own contribution to the world of reality unstable built a world and we are building one. And his was a true world and ours is and the two need not meet and quarrel. His worked for him and his people and ours works for us. A great thinker built a world that operated. And given that man it would still work. We build a motor and it runs. It will always run if the principle involved is followed correctly but it is not impossible to imagine a world wherein the principle of the internal combustion engine while known would have become inoperative because it was no longer important.

This book then says — "There are good things to see in the tide pools and there are exciting and interesting thoughts to be generated from the seeing. Every new eye applied to the peep hole which looks out at the world may pull in some new beauty and some new pattern ~~~~~~ and the world of the human mind must be enriched by such fishing.

The Wayward Bus (1947)

John Steinbeck Does It Again
Harrison Smith

Harrison Smith reviewed The Wayward Bus *(1947) for the* Saturday Review.

In the new novel we have all been waiting for John Steinbeck has abandoned the familiar, odorous waterfront of Monterey with its cannery row. Gone are the doctor and the docks, the warm-hearted girls who were all whores, and the drunks and the bums who were all more delightfully human than any man could possibly be who has money in his pockets and a balance in the bank.

The setting for *The Wayward Bus* is a neat and shining little lunch room, garage, and gas station set down under a clump of lofty trees forty-two miles below San Ysidro, where the highway meets a lesser road that rambles for forty-nine miles across the farms or mountainous landscape to meet the great coastal thoroughfare. From the beginning Steinbeck creates the illusion of complete reality. The little establishment of Juan Chicoy and his wife stands four-square and solid, the battered old bus he shuttles from one highway to the other is real, the landscape is the good earth itself, the drenching rain is wet. Mr. Steinbeck had expected to have the book ready for publication many months ago, for the scene and the nine characters who play their parts have lived in his mind for several years, and have, according to Lewis Gannett, excited and stirred him as they developed.

What he has attempted and has accomplished is to present the natural man, *homo simplicimus,* and to a lesser extent the natural woman, in glaring contrast to the artificial and glazed products of middle-class civilization. This theme has fascinated writers since Rousseau and a hundred devices have been used to illustrate it: the single man or whole families cast away on desert islands, the enthronement of the noble savage, the love battle between primitive man *(homo erectus)* and sensitive, cultured woman; what else, indeed, is Tarzan but a crude attempt to glorify the vestigial animal in man, for the more extravagantly complicated civilization becomes the more we will yearn for the man creature that nature designed to walk erect and dangerous over the earth. Not that Juan Chicoy, half Irishman, half Mexican, is by any means an animal, or dangerous, except to women. He is the free man, the man who cannot be held in bonds of any sort, the man who will at any moment leave a woman who loves him too jealously, or an

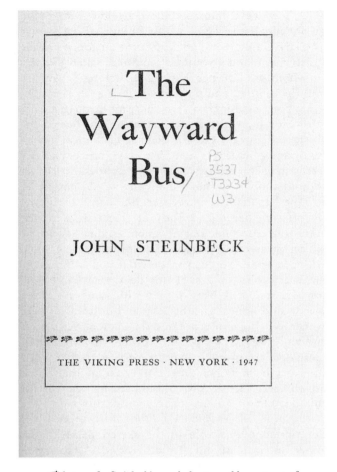

Title page for Steinbeck's novel about an odd assortment of characters traveling by bus in California (Thomas Cooper Library, University of South Carolina)

enterprise in which after toil and frugality he has succeeded, who will walk away with only the clothes on his back, to begin again anywhere else. The natural man and the free man have been constant in Steinbeck's work, from the abysmal brute in *Of Mice and Men,* to the simple and gentle heart and mind of the peasants in *Tortilla Flat,* who are as incapable of understanding what civilization is doing to them as the ape riding a bicycle in a vaudeville show.

If it has sometimes seemed possible to satirize John Steinbeck for sentimentalizing the underdog, though never so grossly or ludicrously as Saroyan, there is no trace of this weakness in *The Wayward Bus.* Juan is all man, sturdy, passionate, capable, a fine mechanic, loving and understanding people, as magnetic to women as nectar to a bee. His wife knows his virtues, but the tension under which she lives with the knowledge that she may some day lose him is a rasp to her temper and often when he is away she has to drink herself into a stupor.

Two very human underdogs live with them, an anemic, homely girl–madly in love with a picture of Clark Gable–who looks after the customers in the lunch room, and a youthful mechanic called Pimples to whom adolescence had given itching sensuality and the mottled and pustulate mask of a bad case of acne. Four customers arrive and wait through a rainstorm for Juan to drive them in the old bus to the western highway. One of them is an honest girl so luxuriantly seductive that her days are cursed by every man she meets, so that it is impossible for her to hold a job or to find a man who would not prefer to rape her than to marry her. She earns her living by offering her naked body at stag parties to the stares of respectable businessmen, ending her act by sitting in and rising from an enormous glass filled with red wine. You can make what you want of the ancient role in society of this depressed bacchante, for Mr. Steinbeck likes to play with symbols. There is a second honest girl, healthy and unfulfilled, who sometimes hopefully dreams that her parents have suddenly died. The wealthy Pritchards, with their daughter, are on their way to Mexico so that when they get back home they can boast of their little adventures. The N.A.M. should sue the author for this portrait of an American manufacturer and the Association of Women's Clubs must protest the description of his wife in the sacred name of the American woman and of motherhood. A more poisonous and mean couple have rarely been achieved in fiction. Mr. Pritchard is dirty-minded, boastful, dishonest, and hag-ridden by his wife; she has remained an aging little girl who has doubtless by immaculate conception produced a child, and who brings her family to heel by imaginary illnesses. The fourth paying customer is a sprightly little man who sells tricks, gadgets, and mildly obscene devices to amuse people with a perverse sense of humor. Perhaps he represents the pixies and malign sprites of ancient folklore among this collection of straight, twisted, or thwarted human beings.

And so eight of them wait through a rainstorm that is like a cloudburst for the bus to start. Mrs. Chicoy has to stay to look after the business, and Juan knows well that her nerves are on edge because he has been eyeing the Pritchards' daughter and knows too that she will be blind drunk when he gets back home. At the end of the journey a bridge is down so Juan recklessly takes the lumbering bus over an unused and dangerous road into the mountains. Why Juan does not abandon everyone and walk straight down into Mexico, why Mrs. Pritchard tears at her baby face with bloody nails, how her daughter finds that she loves the way a free and nat-

ural man makes love, and how Mr. Pritchard gets what is coming to him from the girl he had once seen naked, her thighs dripping with wine like purple blood, all of this must be left for the reader to discover.

The Wayward Bus cannot be coupled with any of Mr. Steinbeck's previous novels. It has not the tenderness of *The Pastures of Heaven* and *Tortilla Flat,* or the fierce brutality in *Of Mice and Men,* and it is not a novel of bitter social strife like *In Dubious Battle* and *The Grapes of Wrath.* But every page of it carries the unmistakable seal and signature of John Steinbeck's mind and style. Nor can one say that it is better or worse than this book or that book of his. It stands by itself, the work of a writer as distinctively American as Mark Twain, who has developed in power and dramatic talent for almost twenty years, and who is deeply concerned with the second greatest problem of our day, how to preserve the essential simple virtues of human beings from the catastrophe that mechanized civilization is bringing upon all of us.

–*Saturday Review,* 30 (15 February 1947); reprinted in *John Steinbeck: The Contemporary Reviews,* edited by Joseph R. McElrath Jr., Jesse S. Crisler, and Susan Shillinglaw (Cambridge & New York: Cambridge University Press, 1996), pp. 293–295

* * *

California Bus Ride
Edward Weeks

Edward Weeks reviewed The Wayward Bus *for* The Atlantic.

In *The Wayward Bus,* John Steinbeck is writing about a busload of assorted Americans who are marooned overnight at a California crossroads. The driver and his pimply mechanic patch up the rear end in the early dawn, but as day breaks and the rain comes down, the journey is further imperiled by a spring flood which deluges the San Juan valley, threatening the bridges and turning the old stagecoach road into a slithery morass.

This is Mr. Steinbeck's first full-length novel since *The Grapes of Wrath.* In the intervening eight years he served as a war correspondent with the American troops in Europe. He has been decorated by the King of Norway for the writing of his war book and play, *The Moon Is Down,* and he has published a novelette loosely tied together with the title of *Cannery Row.* But *The Wayward Bus* is a novel of

"A Surface of Flashy Cynicism"

British critic Robin King reviewed The Wayward Bus *in* The Spectator.

. . . Mr. John Steinbeck's new book comes as something of a surprise. Here again is technical brilliance of a high order; here too is excitement; here, in fact, is almost everything that made Mr. Steinbeck so popular a writer. The characters in *The Wayward Bus* come to life with a facility and an aptness that one can only admire and enjoy. . . . They are all allegedly American types and they are brought together, rather artificially and slenderly, by means of a bus. The bus is lovingly described (Mr. Steinbeck has a passion for vehicles as well as for animals and insects), and the journey these people take, each one wrapped up in his own world, sealed off from one another by their selfishness as effectively as though they were behind prison bars, can be taken as an allegory of the journey through life. Here comes the cynicism and here, I suspect, comes the flaw. Mr. Steinbeck plunges his characters into danger and boredom and he shows them at their worst. He is quite ruthless in ferreting out the despicable quality in each. In the end one hates the people in the "wayward bus," if not for the same reason that Mr. Steinbeck hates them. He despairs of human motives and he expresses his despair under a surface of flashy cynicism. "What do I care?" he seems to say. "Life is hell, people are greater hells, but there you are—there isn't much choice." All this comes to the surface when the bus breaks down. Mr. Pritchard brutally outrages his wife in a cave; Pimples assaults Norma by means of a trick appeal to her maternal sympathies; Mr. Van Brunt falls fatally ill; and Juan seduces the Pritchards' daughter Mildred. "Aren't they hell?" Mr. Steinbeck seems to say again, with a scornful laugh, and to do him justice we see that they are hell and suspect that we ourselves stand equally condemned.

—Spectator, 173 (19 December 1947); reprinted in *John Steinbeck: The Contemporary Reviews,* p. 310

much the same architecture as *The Bridge of San Luis Rey,* and to those of us who admire Mr. Steinbeck, it is refreshing to see the warm flow of vitality which surges up in his pages, and to mark such changes as have occurred in his style and in his philosophy since he wrote his great story of the Okies. . . .

Juan sets the keynote of sex, and to it Alice, his blowsy wife, and the passengers respond or recoil. The adventure of these people as they intermingle and feel each other out is told with a close perspiring intimacy which may seem repellent to nice readers, but it is only fair to suggest that with such sharp anatomical details the novelist is cutting away the gloss, the hypocrisy, the over-advertised glamour of American daily life. He is indeed using the very details which advertising stresses, but with a sharp knife instead of soft soap. He is vulgarly intent on identifying human nature for what it is. To Mr. Steinbeck feminine beauty is no deeper than the make-up. His portraits of Mildred Pritchard and Camille are a repudiation of "those bright, improbable girls with pumped-up breasts and no hips," those Hollywood visions of mediocrity.

There are five noticeable women in this book: Alice, Juan's wife, with her rage ("the uncontrolled pleasure rising in her chest and throat"), her jealousy, and her alcoholic self-pity; Bernice Pritchard ("one of the sweetest, most unselfish people you will ever meet"), as pretty and as untouchable as dry ice; Mildred, her myopic, man-hungry daughter; Norma, the pathetic infatuate of Hollywood; and, last of all, Camille, a wise, defiant tramp with her musky heritage. To Camille, as to Mrs. Pritchard, sex is repellent, though for quite opposite reasons. To the reader the intensification of this instinct among this jostled and confined company may seem forced and a little tedious. Are we all really so possessed? Would we too have caught the contagion of that bus? Is there no motive, no gratification, more compelling in a California spring? I sound like a rock-bound Puritan, but the question persists in my mind.

Very lovely, very sensuous the country is in Mr. Steinbeck's rippling prose. . . .

Very natural and funny, and at times very candid, is the talk, as when, for instance, Camille turns down Mr. Pritchard with the remark that she "is not going to be nibbled to death by ducks," or when Alice exclaims that Pimples "could eat pies standing on his head in a washtub of flat beer on Palm Sunday." But, for all this animal magnetism and photographic reality, one ends by wondering if American life is actually so empty, so devoid of meaning, so lonely for the Juans, the Pritchards, and the Camilles of today. God help us if it is.

—Atlantic, 179 (March 1947); reprinted in *John Steinbeck: The Contemporary Reviews,* pp. 300–301

The Pearl (1947)

Steinbeck's Mexican Folk-Tale

Thomas Sugrue

Thomas Sugrue reviewed the book version of The Pearl *(1947) for the* New York Herald Tribune Book Review.

In the Gnostic fragment known as the "Acts of Judas Thomas" there is a passage called the "Hymn of the Soul," which says that "If thou goest down into Egypt, and bringest the one pearl, which is in the midst of the sea, hard by the loud-breathing serpent, then shalt thou put on thy toga, which is laid over it, and with thy brother, our next in rank, thou shalt be heir in our kingdom." Among the Indians of Mexico the story is that Kino, a fisherman, found the pearl, and that Juana, his wife, and Coyotito, his infant son, were with them [him?] when the discovery was made. John Steinbeck, hearing the tale while on an expedition to the Gulf of California in 1940, decided to write it. His story was published in *The Woman's Home Companion*. It was also made into a movie, as yet unreleased, and now it is a book.

. . . Mr. Steinbeck, faithfully re-telling what he heard, left the ending as it was. Had he not done so he would be writing yet, and the incident of an Indian fisherman's surrender to the challenge of experience would be growing into the saga of man's search for a soul. As it is, the action of the story is brief, and in it, as in all folk tales, there are, as Mr. Steinbeck says, "only good and bad things and black and white things and good and evil things and no in-between anywhere."

It began one morning when a scorpion bit the baby Coyotito (the biting of the child by the scorpion, or scarab, signifies the entrance of the divine nature into the mind; the pearl of great price, the knowledge of spiritual growth, must then be found so that eventually the divine nature can be set free). The white doctor would not treat the child, so Kino and Juana and Coy-

Frontispiece and title page for Steinbeck's 1947 novelette (Thomas Cooper Library, University of South Carolina)

Pedro Armendáriz as Kino and María Elena Marqués as Juana in the 1947 movie version of The Pearl (MOMA/Film Stills Archive; from Joseph R. Millichap, Steinbeck and Film, 1983; Thomas Cooper Library, University of South Carolina)

otito got into Kino's canoe and went to the oyster bed, hoping to find a pearl that would pay for the medicine that was needed. Kino stepped into the water and let his diving rock carry him to the bottom; he filled his basket with oysters; under a lip of rock he found a very large oyster, and he carried this up in his hand. When he opened it he found that it contained the great pearl, the pearl of the world, the pearl of great price.

Almost before Kino's canoe was beached every one in the town knew of his find, and by nightfall ninety per cent of the population were scheming to get the pearl away from him. The doctor came to Kino's hut and insisted on treating Coyotito, who had been saved ten hours before by his mother, who sucked the unbearable portion of the poison from him (in the black and white of folklore Juana, or woman, is the emotion nature). Kino was attacked in the night. When he tried to sell the pearl next day prices were rigged against him. He told Juana that he would go into the mountains, to the capital, to . . . bring its true price, so that Coyotito could be sent to school (the mind must be trained and filled with wisdom).

Juana made the classic gesture of the emotion[al] nature; she tried to throw the pearl into the sea. Kino restrained her and then, after he had again been attacked, and after his house had been burned and his canoe wrecked (his assailants were nameless shadows; he recognized none of them), he set out in flight with Kino, Coyotito and the pearl. But he did not strike for the city in the hills; he did not face his dream and attempt to realize it. He followed the coast, and eventually he was found by a man on horseback; he killed the man and the two trackers who were with him, but Coyotito was shot and died. Kino and Juana returned to the town, and Kino threw the pearl into the sea.

That is the end of the story as Mr. Steinbeck heard it; the horseman is easy to identify as the Spaniard who conquered the Indian, though horsemen representing desires of the lower mind normally in folklore pursue the ego in quest of the soul. Kino, refusing the adventure of the spirit, renouncing his opportunity for realization and understanding and identity, returns to the rim of the unconscious, the primitive state wherein responsibility resides in nature and wherein man nurses, like a tree, at the breast of earth. He thought once of the city in the hills, shook briefly with the dream of the grail, then gave up in fear and ran away.

In the past Mr. Steinbeck has demonstrated an affection for this acceptance of defeat, this philosophy of rejected realization, this refusal to face up to ownership of the pearl of great price; two of his novels, *Tortilla Flat* and *Cannery Row,* were concerned with it. He has also written of those who keep the pearl and who fight for it, those who strike out for the city in the hills and who, if they are cut down on the way, fall forward. This present reversion to the theme of negation is a simple task of tale-telling, complete with

1.

When Juan Tomás had gone, Kino sat brooding on his sleeping mat. A
lethargy had settled on him and a little grey hopelessness. Every road seemed
blocked. In his head he heard only the dark music of the enemy. His senses
were hummingly alive but his mind went back to the deep participation
with all things, the gift he had from his people. He heard every little
sound of the gathering night — the sleepy complaints of settling birds,
the love agony of cats, the strike and withdrawal of little waves, and
the hiss of distance. And he could smell the sharp odor of exposed
kelp from the receding tide. The little flame of the twig fire made
the design on his sleeping mat jump before his entranced eyes.
Juana watched him with worry, but she knew him, and she
knew she could help him best by being silent and by being
near. And as though she too could hear the song of evil, she fought
it, singing softly the melody of the family, of the safety and warmth
and wholeness of the family. She held Coyotito in her arms and sang
the song to him to keep the evil out. and her voice was brave
against the threat of the dark music. Kino did not ask for his supper.
He would ask when he wanted it. His eyes were entranced, and he could
sense the wary watchful evil out side the brush house. He could
feel the dark creeping evil things waiting for him to go out into the
night. It was shadowy and dreadful. and it called to him, and threatened
him and challenged him. His hand went into his shirt and felt for
his knife. And his eyes were wide and entranced. He stood up and walked
to the door way. And Juana wanted wished she could stop him. She
raised her hand to stop him and her mouth opened with terror.
For a long moment Kino looked out into the darkness and then
he stepped out side. And Juana heard the little rush, the grunting
struggle, the blow. Juana froze with terror for a moment and then

Two pages from the manuscript of The Pearl *(John Steinbeck Library, Salinas)*

2.

her lips drew back from her teeth like a cat's lips. She set Coyotito down on the ground, she seized a stone from the fire place and rushed outside But it was one leg there / Kino lay on the ground, struggling to rise and there was no one there, only the shadows and the strike and rush of waves and the hiss of distance, but the evil was all about, hidden behind the brush fence, crouched beside the house, hovering in the air. Juana dropped her stone and she put her arms around Kino and helped him to his feet and helped him into the house. Blood oozed down from his scalp and there was a long deep cut in his cheek from ear to chin, a deep bleeding slash. Kino was only half conscious. He shook his head from side to side. His shirt was torn open and his clothes half torn off. Juana sat him down on his sleeping mat and she wiped the thick blood from his face with her skirt. She brought him pulque to drink in a little pitcher. And still he shook his head to clear out the darkness. "Who?" Juana asked. / "I don't know," Kino said. "I couldn't see — in time." Now Juana brought her clay pot of water and she washed the cut on his face while he stared dazed ahead of him. / "Kino, my husband," she cried, "and his eyes stared past her. "Kino, can you hear me? Can you understand me?. / I hear you he said cruelly. / "Kino, this pearl is evil. Let us destroy it, Kino before it destroys us. Let us break it between two stones. Let us — let us throw it back in the ocean where it belongs. Kino it is evil — it is as evil as sin." And as she spoke the light came back in Kino's eyes and they glowed fiercely. And his muscles hardened. "No," he said "I will beat this thing. I will win over it. We will have our chance. His fist pounded the sleeping mat. "No one shall take our good fortune from us." His eyes softened and he raised a gentle hand to Juana's shoulder. "Believe me, I am a man." And his face grew hard and crafty. "In the

biblical rhythms and repeated patterns of prose melody; it probably indicates, on Mr. Steinbeck's part, no more than the average man's recurrent inner wish that he had let well enough alone and never begun the lonely journey through awareness toward the crest of identity.

The Pearl, as distinguished from the Gnostic "Hymn of the Soul," is the story of a man who turned his back and walked away when his name was called and he was told to bring up out of Egypt, which is the mind of the world, the pearl whose price redeems the soul. Kino has many brothers.

—*New York Herald Tribune Book Review,* 7 December 1947; reprinted in *John Steinbeck: The Contemporary Reviews,* pp. 320–321

A Russian Journal (1948)

Steinbeck to Covici, 11 & 13 August 1947

A week after Steinbeck and Robert Capa arrived in the Soviet Union, Steinbeck wrote his editor, Covici, to share his impressions of the country and its people.

Dear Pat:

A short note anyway. We've been down here for a week and will stay until next Friday. It is beautiful country and a beautiful city but it was brutally, insanely destroyed by the Germans. The rebuilding goes on everywhere but under the great difficulty of no machinery yet. My note book is getting very full and Capa is taking very many pictures, many of them fine I think. These Ukrainians are hospitable people with a beautiful sense of humor. I am setting down whole conversations with farmers and working people for fear I might forget them. We are lucky to be able to come here. We have seen so many things.

August 13

Just came from a farm. Very good time and lots of information. We are the first foreigners who have been in the country here in many years. The children look at us in wonder for they have only heard of Americans and sometimes not too favorably. The farmers and working people are a pleasure to talk to and even the necessity of talking through interpreters does not eliminate the salt of their speech.

Thank you so much for meeting Gwyn. She was really dead tired. Those flights are exhausting. I've only had one letter but there will probably be others waiting in Moscow. I try to cable now and then to relieve her mind. I have no news of America, and it is rather nice. I couldn't change anything and it is good to be away from

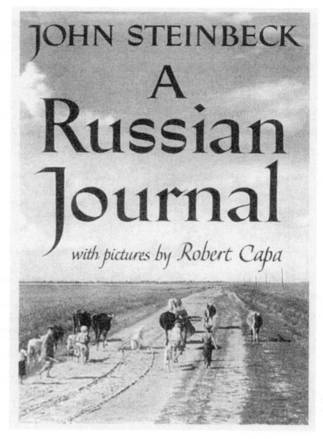

Dust jacket for Steinbeck's 1948 account of his tour of the Soviet Union with Capa (from William McPheron, John Steinbeck: From Salinas to Stockholm, 2000; Special Collections, Thomas Cooper Library, University of South Carolina)

the turmoil for a little. Why don't you drop me a note and let me know how things are going. Address c/o Joe Newman, Hotel Metropol, Moscow.

Evening is coming now. We are going to a symphony concert in the park on the cliff above the Dnieper. Playing Brahms and Prokofiev. I have a dreadful time with the spelling of Russian names and my language is limited to about 10 words, most of which have to do with drinking.

Please call Gwyn when you get this. I like her to hear from me as often as possible.

The time won't be very long until we will get home, only about six weeks. I'll be glad of a few days in Prague. I have always wanted to see that city which I have heard is very beautiful.

That's all Pat. Do drop me a line.

love

John

—*Steinbeck: A Life in Letters,* pp. 298–299

* * *

Aug 25
Moscow

Dear Elizabeth, Melissa and all: Don't let the
Swedish stamps fool you. Joe Newman is going
to Stockholm and will take these letters which
will speed their delivery by about 10 days.

Elizabeth's letter arrived this morning and
was very good to get. We just got back from
Stalingrad last night and go to Tiflis tomorrow
The jumps we are making are terrific. Should
be back from Tiflis (Georgia) by the 5th and
then except for a run to Leningrad we should
stay here in the city doing theatre, ballet etc
The 20th or thereabouts we go to Prague, guests of
the Czech gov't no less and for a couple of weeks
to Budapest as to the Hungarian gov't. We
catch a Pan American plane home in Prague and
should be back about the 1st October, just as
planned. So far the trip is going well. We
are getting what we came for and much more.
Whether we can get it written so it makes sense
is another matter. But I have voluminous
notes which I will unscramble when we get
home. Annie Laurie — I have ideas for two or
lovely moving pictures. Really!

August 1947 note from Steinbeck in Moscow to his literary agent, Elizabeth Otis, outlining the itinerary he and photojournalist Robert Capa were to follow in the Soviet Union (Special Collections, Stanford University Library; from William McPheron, John Steinbeck: From Salinas to Stockholm, 2000; Special Collections, Thomas Cooper Library, University of South Carolina)

Russian Journal

An anonymous review in Time *recounted Steinbeck's and Capa's experiences in the Soviet Union as they gathered material for* A Russian Journal *(1948).*

In London's Savoy Hotel, John Steinbeck overheard a Chicago *Tribune* man snort: "Capa, you have *absolutely no integrity!*" That wartime remark, says Steinbeck, "intrigued me–I was fascinated that anybody could get so low that a Chicago *Tribune* man could say such a thing. I investigated Capa, and I found out it was perfectly true." Photographer Robert Capa and Author Steinbeck became great friends.

Last March, in a Manhattan bar, they met again. Over two drinks they decided to go to Russia to record, not the political news, but the private life of private Russians. Last week, in the New York *Herald Tribune* (which had jumped at the chance to pay their way) and in twoscore other U.S. and foreign papers, the first chapters of their *Russian Journal* appeared. According to plan, they had brought back no headlines but an unexcited (and sometimes unexciting) report that, like any proof that the Russians are people after all, would make the brazen voice of the Kremlin all the more disheartening.

The Soviets admitted them–with some misgivings about Capa (who, in any country, talks and looks like an enemy alien) and his cameras. "The camera is one of the most frightening of modern weapons," says Steinbeck, "and a man with a camera is suspected and watched." To a polite, but suspicious young man at VOKS, the cultural relations office in Moscow, they tried to explain their mission.

"Your own most recent work," the Russian told the hulking, hearty Steinbeck, "seems to us cynical." Steinbeck explained the job of a writer was to set down his time as he understood it. He tried to make clear the unofficial standing of writers in America: "They are considered just below acrobats and just above seals." Eventually, Capa and Steinbeck were given an interpreter and approval to go to the Ukraine, Stalingrad and Georgia, where the interpreter himself needed an interpreter. They went by air, always in U.S.–built C-47s, and never found a stewardess who did anything but carry pink soda water and beer to the pilots. In restaurants, of all places, they found red tape as endless as spaghetti.

Amid the ruins of Kiev, they found German prisoners helping clear up the rubble. "One of the few justices in the world," wrote Steinbeck. "And the Ukrainian people do not look at them. They turn away. . . ." At the museum there were crowds staring wistfully at plaster models of the future Kiev. "In Russia it is always the future that is thought of. It is the crops next year . . . the clothes that will be made very soon. If ever a people took energy from hope. . . ."

Planning for *East of Eden* (1952)

On 2 January 1948 Steinbeck wrote Paul Caswell, editor of the Salinas Californian, *requesting access to the newspaper's files for research on a new novel set in the Salinas Valley, the work published in 1952 as* East of Eden. *A week after the letter was sent, Caswell replied by telegram granting Steinbeck access to the files.*

Dear Mr. Caswell:

I am gathering material for a novel, the setting of which is to be the region between San Luis Obispo and Santa Cruz, particularly the Salinas valley; the time, between 1900 and the present.

An exceedingly important part of the research necessary will involve the files of the Salinas papers; will it be possible for me to consult these files? Do you know what has happened to the files of the Index-Journal and would it be possible for you to arrange my access to them?

I expect to be in Monterey soon after January 20th; could you let me know as soon as possible (by collect wire if necessary) if these files can be thrown open to me.

I will very much appreciate your help in this project.

Very truly yours
John Steinbeck
–Steinbeck: A Life in Letters, p. 303

In the fields around shell-pocked Shevchenko, they found cheerful bands of women picking cucumbers. They were barefoot, "for shoes are still too precious to use in the fields." Everywhere, they found dogged, friendly people, willing to share their bread and cabbage, anxious to hear about America and full of misconceptions about it, instilled by the Russian press. Again and again they were asked: "Will the U.S. attack us?" Again and again they had to explain why the U.S. does not believe in controlling its press or regimenting its people.

Capa was refused permission to shoot the antlike activity at the Stalingrad tractor plant (and later had 100 of his 4,000 negatives confiscated). They came home convinced that the Soviets, who keep the permanent foreign correspondents cooped up in Moscow, have the world's worst sense of public relations. "The Embassy people and the [regular] correspondents feel alone, feel cut off. They are island people in the midst of Russia, and it is no wonder that they become lonely and bitter," Steinbeck wrote. "But if it had been part of our job to report news as they must, then . . . we too could never have left Moscow."
–Time, 51 (26 January 1948); reprinted in *John Steinbeck: The Contemporary Reviews,* pp. 329–330

*   *   *

JOHN STEINBECK

175 East Seventy-Eighth Street   New York 21, N.Y.

January 2nd
1 9 4 8

Mr. Paul Caswell
SALINAS-CALIFORNIAN
Salinas, California

Dear Mr. Caswell:

        I am gathering material for a novel, the set-
ting of which is to be the region between San Luis Obispo
and Santa Cruz, particularly the Salinas valley; the
time, between 1900 and the present.

        An exceedingly important part of the research
necessary will involve the files of the Salinas papers;
will it be possible for me to consult these files?
Do you know what has happened to the files of the INDEX-
JOURNAL and would it be possible for you to arrange my
access to them?

        I expect to be in Monterey soon after January
20th; could you let me know as soon as possible (by collect wire if necessary) if these files can be thrown
open to me.

        I will very much appreciate your help in this
project.

                                            Very truly yours

                                            John Steinbeck

JS/tr   JOHN STEINBECK

Please address my office: Room 806
                            118 E 40th St
                            New York 16, N.Y.

Steinbeck's letter to the editor of the Salinas Californian *requesting access to the newspaper's files for research on the Salinas Valley region (John Steinbeck Library, Salinas; from Robert J. DeMott,* Steinbeck's Reading, *1984; Thomas Cooper Library, University of South Carolina)*

Steinbeck reading back issues of the Salinas Californian *for the writing of* East of Eden, *published in 1952*
(from Robert J. DeMott, Steinbeck's Reading, *1984; Thomas Cooper*
Library, University of South Carolina)

The Eye of the Observer
Richard Watts Jr.

Richard Watts Jr. reviewed A Russian Journal *for* The New Republic.

It is another small but ugly symptom of the sensitive state of Russian-American relations that John Steinbeck's sympathetic account of his recent travels in the Soviet Union should be denounced so violently by Moscow commentators. *A Russian Journal . . .* certainly is not rhapsodic about the USSR; some of its criticisms of the censorship, bureaucracy, inefficiency and the regimenting of writers are sharp and outspoken.

Steinbeck frankly prefers the unregulated confusion of American life to the austere and moralistic Russian planning. But he is a warm and friendly man, as well as a charming writer, and he loved the exuberance and vitality, the expansive hospitality and the hopeful dreams of the Russian people. His book is filled with genuine, if far from uncritical, affection for them and a complete belief in their essential goodwill and desire for peace.

In a world less filled with passions, his travel record would be liked in both the US and the USSR. As it is, he has already been justified in his melancholy foresight that "this journal will not be satisfactory either to the ecclesiastical Left, nor the lumpen Right. The first will say it is anti-Russian, and the second that it is pro-Russian. Surely it is superficial, and how could it be otherwise? We have no conclusions to draw, except that Russian people are like all other people in the world. Some bad ones there are surely, but by far the greater number are very good." It does not seem a sensational statement to make, but, in the current state of violent tempers, it could well be one.

The need for a greater understanding of the Russian people being what it is, it may not be the highest praise to say that the outstanding quality of *A Russian Journal* is its friendliness and its refusal to take itself too seriously. It happens, however, that these qualities arise, not from any triviality or determined jocularity on Steinbeck's part, but from a frank and cheerful admission of his limitations of opportunity and personal equipment.

He set down what he observed and no more, and he admitted his own shortcomings as a commentator. Steinbeck had been in Moscow only once before, for a few days in 1936–he notes that the physical improvements since then have been tremendous–and his traveling companion, the brilliant Robert Capa, who took the superb photographs which accompany the text, had never been in Russia at all. They did not speak the language, although Capa speaks almost every language in some form or other, and their visit was a brief one which took them only to Moscow, Stalingrad, the Ukraine and down into ideally beautiful Georgia.

They might have pretended to the omniscience which comes so easily to travelers in the Soviet Union, no matter how brief their sojourn. *A Russian Journal* is the more interesting as reading and the more valuable as a report because they did not. It is clearly of the first importance today to understand the Russians emotionally, to see them as human beings not very different from ourselves, and the Steinbeck book, in its modest way, makes a definite contribution to just that sort of understanding.

In setting down the reasons why *A Russian Journal* offers no startling inside revelations or new material, it should be stated immediately that Soviet guile and deception are not responsible. If there was anything Steinbeck and Capa failed to see, it was not because Kremlin agents were keeping it from them or were deceiving them by elaborate window-dressing.

Steinbeck found that the Russians are the worst propagandists in the world and the people the least skilled at the art of window-dressing. The travelers saw good things, friendly people and the hope of a peaceful future in the USSR, because they were there to be seen. It was the individual Soviet citizen, in Moscow, Stalingrad, Tiflis, Batum and the collective farms of the Ukraine who convinced them that the Russians "had a hatred of war, they wanted the same things all people want–good lives, increased comfort, security and peace."

Like all travelers in the USSR, Steinbeck and Capa found that they were happier outside of Moscow and in the Russian countryside. Moscow seemed to them a somber city, with a sense of strain about it and even the jokes were sharp and critical, with no warmth in them. In the Ukraine and in Georgia they found gayety and high spirits. They were least comfortable with the intellectuals, whom they found indi-

vidually engaging, but as a group excessively earnest and intense.

The Russian literary man may be, as Stalin desired, the architect of the soul, and his contribution to the task of building the new Soviet society has been a tremendous one; but it was made at the sacrifice of his racial high spirits and his creative independence. Steinbeck did not like the extreme artistic conservatism which caused the abstractionists and experimenters to be regarded with disdain and moved their girl interpreter in Moscow to say that Picasso "nauseated her." The author found a prevailing puritanism, which made him at times almost suspect that the Russians, despite cheering evidence to the contrary, were becoming a "stuffy, non-alcoholic, non-lecherous people." Nor was he happy about the virtual worship of Stalin that he found everywhere.

As such comments suggest, *A Russian Journal* does not flatter the Soviet Union and its people. The important thing is that the criticisms are made without the captious and snarling scorn characteristic of books on Russia by hostile observers. If Steinbeck sees great flaws in the Soviet picture, it is not in contrast to an ideal and dreamy US, which never existed, but against the reasonable background of the suffering, the struggles and the triumphs of a great, once backward, essentially friendly people, who have made amazing progress against vast odds in a brief period of history. And even in the short time they stayed in the USSR, they noted signs of physical progress in the achievement of a better life for a land that had suffered to an unparalleled degree from the ravages of war.

–New Republic, 118 (19 April 1948); reprinted in *John Steinbeck: The Contemporary Reviews,* pp. 332–334

***

John Steinbeck and Robert Capa Record a Russian Journey
Oriana Atkinson

Reviewing A Russian Journal *in* The New York Times Book Review, *Oriana Atkinson called Steinbeck's descriptions of the Ukrainians "illuminating and extremely interesting."*

John Steinbeck, author of *The Grapes of Wrath, The Red Pony, Of Mice and Men,* and a number of other stories and novels which have become American classics, met the famous photographer, Robert Capa, in a bar one day. After a few drinks, they decided to collaborate on a book on Russia. . . . The result of the collaboration is *A Russian Journal.* Pic-

Steinbeck, Gwyn, and Capa in a Paris hotel, 1947 (Center for Steinbeck Studies, San Jose State University; from Jackson J. Benson, The True Adventures of John Steinbeck, Writer, *1984; Thomas Cooper Library, University of South Carolina)*

tures and text were originally published in the New York *Herald Tribune* and elsewhere.

As a reporting job the book is superb. What they saw, they have presented simply and honestly. Nobody can say that they carried chips on their shoulders. But they did find it a little difficult always to remain calm when they met simon-pure examples of Russian bureaucracy; and before they left the U.S.S.R., like everybody else who gets the opportunity, they visited the Kremlin.

This book could only have been written by an American. Although it bears throughout the stamp of Mr. Steinbeck's sincerity, he sometimes breaks into the irrepressible American nonsense that always baffles the Russians. And it is nice to know that even so high-minded an observer as Mr. Steinbeck found some of the aspects of Moscow life as comic and difficult as other Americans [. . .]

[Mr. Steinbeck's] descriptions of the Ukraine and the Ukrainian people are illuminating and extremely interesting. They visited Kiev, mother of Russian cities, and saw life and hope struggling up through the appalling ruins. They visited two collective farms there, Svenchenko 1 and Svenchenko 2, and found the workers well fed and well housed. Although there is a pitiful lack of farm machinery, the work goes on, the harvests are garnered.

"They are not a sad people," Mr. Steinbeck says. "They are full of laughter, jokes and songs." Mr. Capa's photographs bear him out. The farm people look sturdy, merry and determined. . . .

Everywhere they went the Americans were asked whether they thought there would be another war. "Will the United States attack us?" the Russians asked. "Will we have to defend ourselves again in our lifetime?" At Svenchenko 1, Mr. Steinbeck found: "They knew no more about their foreign policy than we know about ours. There was no animosity in their questions, only wonder. . . . Our host said, 'Somewhere in all of this there must be an answer and there must be an answer quickly. Let us drink to the hope that an answer may be found, for the world needs peace, needs peace very badly.'"

Since Mr. Steinbeck did not meet any members of the Politburo, he naturally does not record their opinion on this subject. As Mr. Steinbeck himself would say, "This we do not know.". . .

Misery, despair, degradation of the human spirit? The author of *The Grapes of Wrath* saw none of these. Within the narrow circumference of his journey, no political prisoners, no slave laborers, no fear, no poverty-stricken people broken on the wheel of totalitarianism made him pause and reflect. Careful analysis of the trip brings the thoughtful reader to one inescapable conclusion: The farther one gets from Moscow, even within the U.S.S.R., the freer the people, the brighter the outlook.

As far as this book goes, it is forthright, simple and direct. There is, however, a reverse side to the medal which Mr. Steinbeck did not examine. And just as he traveled in accustomed paths while in Russia, so, since his return, has he been accorded the usual, automatic treatment by the Russian press. He has been denounced as bourgeois, and he has been accused of misrepresentation, with free use of the usual odorous adjectives always applied to foreign observers. Except, of course, the Dean of Canterbury.

As for Mr. Capa's part in the collaboration, he took "thousands of flash bulbs, hundreds of rolls of film, masses of cameras and a tangle of flashlight wires," with him from America. It would seem that these supplies, plus the virgin territory of Soviet Russia, plus Mr. Capa, would produce more distinguished pictures. However, since all the film had to be developed in Moscow by unloving hands before being granted clearance, no doubt Mr. Capa thinks so, too.

—New York Times Book Review, 9 May 1948; reprinted in *John Steinbeck: The Contemporary Reviews,* pp. 335–336

* * *

A Legitimate Complaint
Robert Capa

The following essay by Capa was included in the text of A Russian Journal.

I am not happy at all. Ten years ago when I began to make my living by taking pictures of people being bombed by airplanes with little swastikas on them, I saw a few small planes with little red stars shooting down the swastika ones. This was in

---

American Academy of Arts and Letters

In November 1948 Steinbeck learned that he had been elected a member of the American Academy of Arts and Letters. On 3 December he wrote back to the academy's spokesman to express his appreciation of the honor.

My dear Mr. Brooks:

I am extremely sensible of the honor paid me by the Academy in making me a member. Having been blackballed from everything from the Boy Scouts to the United States Army, this election is not only a great experience but for me a unique one. My most profound thanks.

Yours sincerely,
John Steinbeck
—Steinbeck: A Life in Letters, p. 344

Madrid during the Civil War, and this made me very happy. I decided then that I wanted to go and see the place where the snub-nose planes and pilots came from. I wanted to visit and take pictures in the Soviet Union. I made my first application then. During these last ten years my Russian friends were often irritating and impossible, but when the shooting became serious they somehow ended up on the side where I was plugging, and I made a great many other applications. The applications were never answered.

Last spring the Russians succeeded in becoming spectacularly unpopular with my side, and considerable plugging was going on to make us shoot this time at each other. Flying saucers and atomic bombs are very unphotogenic, so I decided to make one more application, before it was too late. This time I found a certain support in a man of wide reputation, considerable thirst, and gentle understanding for the gay underdog. His name is John Steinbeck, and his preparations for our trip were very original. First he told the Russians that it was a great mistake to regard him as a pillar of the world proletariat, indeed he could rather be described as a representative of Western decadence, indeed as far west as the lowest dives in California. Also he committed himself to write only the truth, and when he was asked politely what truth was, he answered, "This I do not know." After this promising beginning he jumped out of a window and broke his knee.

That was months ago. Now it is very late at night, and I am sitting in the middle of an extremely gloomy hotel room, surrounded with a hundred and ninety million Russians, four cameras, a few dozen exposed and many more unexposed films, and one sleeping Steinbeck, and I am not happy at all. The hundred and ninety million Russians are against me. They are not holding wild meetings on street corners, do not practice spectacular free love, do not have any kind of new look, they are very righteous, moral, hard-working people, for a photographer as dull as apple pie. Also they seem to like the Russian way of living, and dislike being photographed. My four cameras, used to wars and revolutions, are disgusted, and every time I click them something goes wrong. Also I have three Steinbecks instead of one.

My days are long, and I begin with the morning Steinbeck. When I wake up, I open my eyes carefully, and I see him sitting before the desk. His big notebook is open, and he is imitating work. In reality he is just waiting and watching for my first move. He is terribly hungry. But the morning Steinbeck is a very shy man, absolutely unable to pick up the telephone and make the smallest attempt toward articulate conversation with Russian waitresses. So I give up and get up, pick up the phone, and order breakfast in English, French, and Russian. This revives his spirits and makes him rather cocky. He puts an expression of an overpaid village philosopher on his face and says, "I have a few questions for you this morning." He has obviously spent his three hours of hunger figuring out the damn things, which range from the old Greek table habits to the sex life of the fishes. I behave like a good American, and although I could answer these questions simply and clearly, I stand on my civil rights, refuse to answer, and let the thing go to the Supreme Court. He doesn't give up easily, keeps on bragging about his universal knowledge, tries to provoke me with help and education, and I have to go into exile. I take refuge in the bathroom, which place I simply detest, and I force myself to stay in the sandpaper-lined bathtub filled with cold water till breakfast arrives. This sometimes takes considerable time. After breakfast I get help. Chmarsky arrives. There are no morning and evening phases in Chmarsky's character, he is pretty bad all the time.

During our day, I have to fight with the hundred and ninety millions who don't want their pictures taken, with Mr. Chmarsky who snobs photography, and with the morning Steinbeck who is so goddam innocent that all questions posed by the curious and hero-worshiping Russian population are answered by a friendly grunt, "This I do not know." After this momentous statement he is exhausted, shuts up like a clam, and big drops of perspiration break out on his fair-sized Cyrano face. Instead of taking pictures, I have to translate Mr. Steinbeck's

strange silence into intelligent and evasive sentences, and somehow we finish the day, get rid of Chmarsky, and get home again.

After a short mental strip-tease the evening Steinbeck begins. This new character is perfectly able to pick up the telephone and pronounce words like vodka or beer, understandable to the dumbest waiter. After a certain amount of fluid, he is articulate, fluent, and has many and definite opinions about everything. This goes on till we find a few Americans who have acceptable wives, cigarettes, and native drinks, and still don't refuse to see us. By now he could be described as a rather gay character. If there is any pretty girl in a party, he is definitely ready to protect me and chooses his place right between the girl and me. Around this time he is already able to talk to other people, and if I try to save the innocent girl by inviting her to dance, no broken leg will stop him from cutting in almost immediately.

After midnight his innocence gets coupled with strength. This he demonstrates with one finger. He asks innocent husbands if they know anything about the finger game. The two gentlemen sit down, facing each other across a table, put their elbows firmly on the tablecloth, and clinch their middle fingers. After a certain amount of twisting, Mr. Steinbeck usually gets the husband's fingers down on the table-cloth, and excuses himself volubly. Sometimes, late at night, he tries the game on anybody. Once even on a Russian gent who looked obviously like a general to everybody else but him.

After a certain amount of gentle coaxing, and a long dissertation about dignity, we get home. Now it is past three in the morning. The evening Steinbeck is metamorphosed into his late night version. He is on his bed, holding firmly a thick volume of poetry from two thousand years ago, called *The Knight in the Tiger Skin*. His face is fully relaxed, his mouth is open, and the man with the quiet low voice snores without restraint or inhibitions.

I fortunately borrowed a mystery story from Ed Gilmore, just because I knew that I would be unable to sleep, and would have to read till the morning.

I leave you, gentle American readers, and have to assure your Russian counterparts that everything that Mr. Chmarsky will write about us in Pravda is absolutely true.

END OF COMPLAINT

—A Russian Journal (New York: Viking, 1948), pp. 146–149

* * *

Steinbeck to Beskow, July 1950

In this letter to Beskow, Steinbeck reflects on the grim situation in the Soviet Union as he witnessed it during his trip to gather material for A Russian Journal. *The "second play" referred to is a project he later abandoned.*

Dear Bo:

I was greatly relieved to get your letter. I am so glad you have broken the old slavery. I never liked the other one and I never knew why. But it was something basic; something maybe of odor beyond the conscious range. I am delighted that you have found a girl who delights you. Mine delights me.

I have my boys in the country with me about an hour out of New York in the rich green and little streams of Rockland County. It is rough and comfortable and we are having a good summer and I am getting work done too. What more can you wish? My boys are fine and brown. They are pretty good. I don't think I should want them more good than they are.

My first play [*Burning Bright* (1950)] goes into rehearsal on Sept. 5th and the second one probably in October. I am all finished with the Zapata script and with a biography of Ed Ricketts for a new edition of Sea of Cortez. The second play not finished yet but should be next month. So you can see that work has been coming out of me. I shall be done and ready to start on my long novel in October.

I have been horrified at the creeping paralysis that is coming out of the Kremlin, the death of art and thought, the death of individuals and the only creative thing in the world is the individual. When I was in Russia a couple of years ago I could see no creative thing. The intellectuals parroted articles they had read in safe magazines. It makes me more than sorry, it makes me nauseated. And of all the books required and sent to Russians who asked for them, not one arrived, and even the warm sweater and mittens for a girl, and a doll for a little girl—not even these were permitted to arrive. I can't think that wars can solve things but something must stop this thing or the world is done and gone into a black chaos that makes the dark ages shine. If that is what we are headed for, I hope I do not live to see it and I won't because I will fight it. God knows you and we are far from perfect but we are far better than that. We can make a noise even if not many people listen.

Shostakovich denounced me as a cannibal the other day. Of course he must—any man who can say

that his work, written in honesty, was not true, was wrong because a committee says it was—is a liar and must have a very bad artistic conscience. He can say it was inept, badly executed, childish or immature but no artist is *wrong*. I suppose we have many people who would like to curb thought too but they have not succeeded and they must not succeed. If I seem vehement about this, it is because I saw it and see it. Here, I may not be liked for what I say but I can write it and people can read it and do and that's all I ask. And I wonder (since our species is a creative one) about the hidden artists in Russia who paint behind drawn curtains, and sing music under their breaths and write poetry and burn it or hide it. I do not think any system which uses such force can survive for long but while it does—it can ruin and maim for such a long time to come. This is a tirade isn't it?

My Elaine is a wonderful girl. I can write with her sitting in the room with me and that's the best that can be said about her calmness and benignity. It is the first peace I have had with a woman. She has great style and great kindness. She doesn't want to hurt anyone for anything. I guess, in other words, she is a well adjusted girl. So that is that and I hope it is good and will be all right. I have lots of work to do and I should for once like to do it in peace. I have not had that before.

My oldest boy will be six on August 2nd. I am going in to New York tomorrow to get him some little presents. I don't know what to get him. He wants an automobile and a horse neither of which is practical. He will have to go back to his mother in October. I hope he does not have to go too many more times.

A long winter of hard work and then we will break free and if the world will let us, we will go out into it. So many people are shuddering in a planless lymph because they are afraid the world is falling apart. I do not believe that. It is changing surely but it cannot eliminate us completely. Some part of us—you in your windows and I perhaps in a sentence or two—will outwit them and go on.

Please write to me more often. I shall want to know how you are getting on.

and affection to you
and your girl
John
—Steinbeck: A Life in Letters, pp. 402–404

Revising *Viva Zapata!* (1952)

In the summer of 1950, after hearing parts of his screenplay for
Viva Zapata! *(1952) read aloud, Steinbeck wrote to Elia Kazan,
the director of the movie, requesting some changes.*

Dear Gadg:

Last night Elaine read me parts of the script. She liked it
very much and I must say I did too. It is a little double
action jewel of a script. But I was glad to hear it again
because before it is mouthed by actors, I want to go over
the dialogue once more for very small changes. Things
like—"For that matter." "As a matter of fact"—in other
words all filler wants to come out. There isn't much but
there is some. I'll want no word in dialogue that has not
some definite reference to the story. You said once that
you would like this to be a kind of monument. By the
same token I would like it to be as tight and terse as possible. It is awfully good but it can be better. Just dialogue—I
heard a dozen places where I can clean it and sharpen it.
But outside of that I am very much pleased with it. I truly
believe it is a classic example of good film writing. So we'll
make it perfect.

Let me know what happens. After Labor Day I will be
in town most of the time.

Molly [Kazan's wife] left her hat here.

Love to you both—

John

—*Steinbeck: A Life in Letters,* p. 407

Burning Bright (1950)

A New Form of Literature
Harrison Smith

One of the first reviewers of Burning Bright: A Play
in Story Form *(1950), the published version of the play, called
readers' attention to the new literary form suggested by the subti-
tle.*

Burning Bright is a drama published concurrently
with its opening in New York. For the reading public,
Steinbeck has presented it as a novelette in three acts.

"It is a combination of many old forms," he
writes in his prologue, "a play that is easy to read or a
short novel that can be played simply by lifting out the
dialogue." It is true that the average man finds it difficult to read a play; the brief descriptions of scenes and
characters intended for the guidance of producer and
actor, the hints of changes in the mood or action,
require an imaginative awareness that the reader may
be incapable of giving, so that unless the dialogue is
commanding and brilliant it is like finding a path
through a dark field.

After reading *Burning Bright,* it would appear that
there is also something lacking and unsatisfactory in the
play-novelette, or at least in this particular attempt at a
new form of literature. The characters are more vivid,
the scenes sharper, but on the whole the book is a failure
because the reader is often bewildered, as if Mr. Steinbeck's four characters were puppets moved by strings,
using words put into their mouths by a ventriloquist.

If the author were writing as a novelist and not primarily as a playwright, you might sense the background
for the motives of his people; you would certainly know
them better, for the novelist is compelled to tell you a
great deal more about them, how they live, where they
came from, what their families and friends are like, something of their childhood and of their habits and tastes.

There is a feeling of unreality in *Burning Bright*
that may come from his method of handling the story
itself. The four characters in the first act are circus people, three men and a woman, who are seen in the dressing room tent of Joe Saul and his beautiful young wife,
Mordeen. In the second act the same characters are
farmers in a Midwestern farmhouse; in the third act
they are in the captain's cabin of a cargo ship docked in
New York Harbor.

During these three incarnations of the same people, they do not change their way of speaking to suit the
scene; they never speak as would sailors, farmers or,
doubtless, circus performers. The book is literally a
morality play, and the characters can be labeled as if
they were symbols of human virtues and vices, a device
that Mr. Steinbeck has used frequently in his later novels. . . .

Symbolism in his characters and his plots may be
vital to the growth or the decline of Mr. Steinbeck as a
creative writer, but his rudimentary philosophy, his
feverish climaxes and the story as he has told it, in
whole or in part, are neither credible to the reader nor
successful as the elements of a short novel.

—*Washington Post,* 22 October 1950; reprinted in *John
Steinbeck: The Contemporary Reviews,* pp. 347–348

* * *

Hemingway and Steinbeck
Norman Cousins

Reviewer Norman Cousins reviewed Burning Bright: A
Play in Story Form *with Ernest Hemingway's* Across the
River and Into the Trees *(1950).*

. . . John Steinbeck's new book, *Burning Bright,*
seems to have been written almost in direct refutation
of Hemingway. It, too, is a philosophical summation,
but it shows pluses where Hemingway shows minuses.

Elia Kazan and Steinbeck at the Ritz Hotel in Boston during the tryouts for the stage version of Burning Bright, *October 1950 (John Steinbeck Collection, Stanford University Libraries; from Jackson J. Benson,* The True Adventures of John Steinbeck, Writer, *1984; Thomas Cooper Library, University of South Carolina)*

It reveals moral values where Hemingway reveals monomaniac meanderings. It tries to meet deep inner conflicts instead of pampering them.

The truculent, arrogant, prize-fight-conscious, sperm-ridden, perennial soldier-boy of Hemingway's book dies a heroic and glamorous death. The man who meets death in Steinbeck's book is also a pompous and self-willed brute, but there is nothing heroic about him or his death. He is a pathetic and oafish stud whose typically twisted ego makes it impossible for him to understand that virility alone does not automatically entitle him to the love of a desirable and understanding woman. No man is a real man, says Steinbeck, unless he is first of all a real human being.

Joe Saul, in *Burning Bright,* becomes this real human being. He discovers that love has higher dimensions than he had realized, and that identification with the human family is purpose and fulfillment in life. He can look at a child–any child–and feel the pride of a father relationship. He has, in short, broken through the limitations of mechanical masculinity. What he eats, whom he sleeps with, and how he punches are of less consequence than what he does to justify the gift of compassion and conscience.

But it is unfair to Mr. Steinbeck to cite aspects of his book before describing his full stage. *Burning Bright* is a play-novelette: it can be used directly as a playscript but the story is handled descriptively. Instead of chapters, the book is divided into three acts, each one of which is set against a contrasting background. The book is not to be read, nor is the play to be seen, as a conventional or specific plot with conventional or specific characters. The story, for example, is not to be regarded a tragedy because one of the central charac-

---

"The Critics Murdered Us"

On 21 October 1950 Steinbeck wrote Eugene Solow, author of the screenplay for the 1939 movie adaptation of Of Mice and Men *(1937), voicing his concerns over critics' harsh response to the stage version of* Burning Bright, *which had opened on Broadway three days earlier.*

Dear Gene:

The critics murdered us. I don't know how long we can stay open but I would not think it would be long. But there you are. I've had it before and I will survive. But a book can wait around and a play can't. We are disappointed but undestroyed.

Now I'll get to work again. One good thing about these things—they keep you from getting out of hand but they promote no humility in me. I'll not change my address.

I wish you could have seen the play because it is a good play. I think it will do well in Europe where people are neither afraid of the theme nor the language. The sterility theme may have had something to do with the violence of the criticism. Our critics are not very fecund. Then, the universal, mildly poetic language seemed to enrage them. Garland [Robert Garland, drama critic for the *New York World-Telegram*]—never quite balanced—wrote a notice of unmixed gibberish. Simply nuts.

Well—there it is anyway. It can happen to anyone— and does.

John

—Steinbeck: A Life in Letters, pp. 412–413

ters is murdered. The murder is non-violent in its symbolic presentation. In fact, the characters, story, and setting are used as part of a symbolic whole.

Steinbeck is dealing with universal types and universal situations and makes no effort to invest his people with individual color or substance. To accentuate this purpose his story unwinds through three separate and contrasting backgrounds. The characters and their story names remain constant though they are seen as circus folk in the first act, as farmers in the second, and as mariners in the third.

What does all this symbolism lead up to? It is far from obscure; what it tries to do is to penetrate through to the anchored positions of the human ego, and to release them. It tries to emancipate men from the tyranny of the personal self. It tries to develop an aspect of man's nature, too often hidden, which hungers truly for larger understanding and mutuality in life. It demolishes the supposed importance of a continuing biological

immortality, revealing the blazing truth that so long as human beings exist anywhere every man is immortal.

All this has been said before. The greatest literature in all languages has reflected the fundamental reality that all men are brothers. But it hasn't been said with any real skill or frequency in American literature in recent years. Too many of our writers, like Hemingway in his current book, have written thinly of life precisely because they have been too close to the ego and not close enough to the human heart. Too many of them have been engaged in thematic trivia instead of with great ideas and the struggle for higher values.

Steinbeck himself, in many of his earlier books, has been victimized by this obsession with marginal themes. For a long time, it appeared that he had lost or abandoned the gift of inspiration—which comes close to being the worst that can happen to a writer. But in *Burning Bright,* he is restored to his full stature as a major American novelist. He has written his most mature book, a book which, if carefully and slowly read, can be as rewarding a literary experience as any of us is likely to have for a long time. As a vital corrective to the new Hemingway book, it couldn't have been better timed.

—Saturday Review, 33 (28 October 1950); reprinted in *John Steinbeck: The Contemporary Reviews,* pp. 350–351

* * *

Burning Bright

An anonymous reviewer in Theatre Arts *called the play version of* Burning Bright *a "modern morality play."*

John Steinbeck has taken the title of his play from *The Tyger,* William Blake's moving poem of awesome wonder at the great mystery of the creation. Like Blake, he has pondered on man's finiteness in a boundless universe and found his answer in the creative richness of love; in man's capacity for good. *Burning Bright* is an affirmation of faith in the human race, an avowal of belief in the dignity of man stated with unmistakable sincerity.

Burning Bright is a modern morality play, a parable told through four symbolic characters; husband, wife, friend and intruder. The story moves continuously against backgrounds that change in each act—the first is in a circus, the second on a farm, and the third on board ship—a device which is intended to emphasize the universality of the play's theme. The effect is artificial; one regrets its use since the basic theme, valid in any setting, gained nothing from the theatrical trick. Similarly, Mr. Steinbeck's use of highly stylized language is awkward rather than poetic and does him a disservice.

However one must rejoice at what Mr. Steinbeck has to say, even while regretting that he did not say it better, for he is the very antithesis of the dramatists of despair, the delineators of disintegration. The noblest function of the art of drama is to show life as it might be; to serve, in Shaw's phrase "as a temple to the ascent of Man." This has been Mr. Steinbeck's aim; it commands respect.

Unaware that he is sterile, Joe Saul passionately desires a child to carry on the "blood line" in which he has fierce pride. Mordeen, his young wife, realizes Joe Saul's desperate need to perpetuate himself through a son and, out of selfless love for her husband she conceives a child with another man. Just before the child is born Joe Saul discovers the deception. Basic and base human emotions of love, jealousy, pride, self-pity, and self-sacrifice are encompassed in this human situation. Joe Saul's triumph is his comprehension that all men are father to all children, and every child must have all men as father. William Blake said it this way:

. . . for Man is Love
As God is Love; every kindness is a little death
In the Divine Image, nor can Man exist but by Brotherhood.

–*Theatre Arts,* 34 (December 1950); reprinted in *John Steinbeck: The Contemporary Reviews,* pp. 365–366

Chapter Six: 1951–1955

Chronology

January 1951	Steinbeck and Elaine begin the New Year with a honeymoon in Bermuda. They then spend time in Hollywood for Steinbeck's work on *Viva Zapata!* (1952) and visit with family and friends in Northern California. They return to New York late in the month.
February 1951	Steinbeck begins work on a novel with the working title "The Salinas Valley," which eventually becomes *East of Eden* (1952). He also begins keeping a journal in the form of letters to his editor, Pat Covici, related to the writing of the novel.
Late April 1951	Steinbeck has finished about one-fourth of the manuscript of "The Salinas Valley."
June 1951	While reading Genesis 4:1–16, Steinbeck decides that a better title for his new novel would be *East of Eden.*

Steinbeck with Thom and John IV, his sons by his second wife, Gwyn, at Nantucket, summer 1951 (John Steinbeck Library, Salinas; from Jackson J. Benson, The True Adventures of John Steinbeck, Writer, *1984; Thomas Cooper Library, University of South Carolina)*

Mid July 1951	Steinbeck has written more than 135,000 words of *East of Eden.* He makes a lined box for the manuscript as a present for Pat Covici with the Hebrew word *timshel* on the lid. (According to Steinbeck's research, *timshel* means "thou mayest.")
September 1951	Steinbeck's portion of his and Ed Ricketts's *Sea of Cortez: A Leisurely Journal of Travel and Research* (1941) is republished by Viking as *The Log from the Sea of Cortez,* with an introductory essay by Steinbeck, "About Ed Ricketts."
Early November 1951	Steinbeck completes the first draft of *East of Eden.*
January 1952	Steinbeck begins revising *East of Eden,* a project that takes him a few months.
7 February 1952	*Viva Zapata!* premieres at the Rivoli Theatre in New York and is an immediate commercial success.

Marlon Brando as the title character in Viva Zapata! *(1952), directed by Elia Kazan, for which Steinbeck wrote the screenplay*
(from Robert E. Morsberger, ed., Viva Zapata!: The Original Screenplay, *1975;*
Thomas Cooper Library, University of South Carolina)

March 1952	The Steinbecks leave New York on a freighter bound for Genoa and Greece. The ship changes its destination, stopping first at Casablanca in North Africa, and then continues to Algiers. The Steinbecks then take a boat to Marseilles, where they rent a car and drive down the eastern coast of Spain.
May 1952	While in Paris, Steinbeck starts writing travel articles for *Collier's.*
June–July 1952	The Steinbecks travel to various cities in Italy. In June, Steinbeck is criticized by Italian communists for his political views. The Steinbecks return to Paris and then travel to England and Ireland, where they visit the ancestral home of Steinbeck's mother's family, the Hamiltons.
August 1952	Steinbeck's articles "Duel Without Pistols" and "The Soul and Guts of France" are published in the 23 and 30 August issues of *Collier's,* respectively. The Steinbecks fly back to New York from Paris on 31 August.
September 1952	*East of Eden* is published by Viking Press, and it soon becomes a best-seller.

September–October 1952	The Steinbecks work for the presidential campaign of the Democratic Party candidate, Adlai Stevenson.
4 November 1952	Dwight D. Eisenhower is elected president.
January 1953	Steinbeck's travel articles "The Secret Weapon We Were Afraid to Use" and "I Go Back to Ireland" are published in the 10 and 31 January issues of *Collier's,* respectively. Steinbeck and Elaine go to the Virgin Islands for a winter vacation.
March–May 1953	Steinbeck sets aside a plan to write a musical based on *Cannery Row* (1945).
June–July 1953	In New York, Steinbeck works on a novel with the working title "Bear Flag," published the following year as *Sweet Thursday,* the sequel to *Cannery Row.*
September 1953	*The Short Novels of John Steinbeck,* with an introduction by Joseph Henry Jackson, is published by Viking Press. The first draft of *Sweet Thursday* is completed.
Mid October 1953	Steinbeck enters New York's Lenox Hill Hospital with a mysterious illness after returning from Long Island, where he has rented a house for a month. It turns out to be depression. Later in the year he consults with psychologist Gertrudis Brenner to get himself out of depression.
January 1954	While on vacation at Caneel Bay on the island of St. John, Steinbeck meets the economist John Kenneth Galbraith, with whom he becomes good friends.
Early February 1954	The Steinbecks plan an extensive trip to Europe.
March 1954	The Steinbecks sail for Europe in mid March. On the 26th they arrive in Lisbon and rent a car. They tour Spain and then head for Paris.

The Steinbeck family in Paris, 1954; from rear, Steinbeck, Elaine, Thom, and John IV (John Steinbeck Library,
Salinas; from Jackson J. Benson, The True Adventures of John Steinbeck, Writer, *1984;*
Thomas Cooper Library, University of South Carolina)

27 May 1954	While in Europe, Steinbeck receives word that Robert Capa has been killed in Vietnam by a land mine.
June 1954	Viking Press publishes *Sweet Thursday*. Still in Paris, Steinbeck begins contributing short weekly articles to *Le Figaro littéraire*.
Early July 1954	The Steinbecks travel to Munich at the request of Radio Free Europe. While there, Steinbeck records a statement of his position as a writer, which is broadcast over Radio Free Europe.
October–November 1954	After spending two weeks in London, the Steinbecks return to Paris, close up their rental house, and move on to Florence, Rome, Athens, and Naples.
Late December 1954	The Steinbecks return to New York aboard the *Andrea Doria*, arriving just before Christmas.
January 1955	Steinbeck meets William Faulkner for the first time.
March 1955	The motion-picture adaptation of *East of Eden*, starring James Dean, is released, and Steinbeck attends the opening at the Astor Theatre in New York on 9 March. The movie receives mixed reviews. Steinbeck's "How to Tell Good Guys from Bad Guys" is published in the 10 March issue of *The Reporter*.
April–May 1955	Steinbeck's short story "The Affair at 7, Rue de M—" is published in the April *Harper's Bazaar*. He begins his long association with the *Saturday Review*, to which he contributes editorials and articles.
June 1955	The Steinbecks move into a house at Sag Harbor on Long Island that they purchased the preceding winter.
September 1955	*Pipe Dream*, a musical-comedy adaptation of *Sweet Thursday* by Richard Rodgers and Oscar Hammerstein 2nd, goes into production.
24 October 1955	*Pipe Dream* opens for tryouts in New Haven.
30 November 1955	*Pipe Dream* opens on Broadway at the Shubert Theatre.

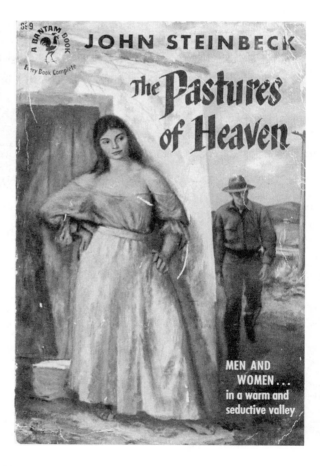

Front covers of the 1951 paperback editions of Steinbeck's 1950 novel that was also produced as a drama and his first story collection, originally published in 1932 (Bruccoli Clark Layman Archives)

1st piece

1.

An American in Paris.

At first intemperate thought it seems presumptuous for an American to write about Paris. So it did seem to me until I reversed the positions. How would I feel about a Frenchman writing about America. Then I remember that the very best account we have of America of the late 18th century was written by a travelling frenchman. He set down details of life of that time so usual to Americans that they did not bother to record them and now the french report is the only way we know what people ate and how they conducted themselves. You do not record what everybody knows and in a few years no one knows it.

But one thinks beyond history. I think of foreigners in America who ~~have~~ painted out beauties we ~~have become~~ are blind to through being too close, who ask questions which make us re inspect our selves, who remark nonsense we consider wise and discover vertues we did not know we possessed. There is a pleasure to us in that. The uninstructed eye sees things the expert does not notice.

Mine is a completely naive eye on Paris — but it is an eye of delight. I find that I should like to write about Paris to Parisians. Perhaps I can learn something by ~~so~~ so doing. Maybe a question may find an answer from some one who reads. And in these pieces I do not intend to write as an expert but only as a tourist. I do not want, as so many do, to find the obscure, the unusual, or the exotic but rather to see the common, the normal, the

Manuscript for Steinbeck's first article in his column "One American in Paris," which ran in Le Figaro littéraire *from 12 June to 18 September 1954 (Center for Steinbeck Studies, San Jose State University)*

2

usual— the way of food in the markets, the way of children at the Carosels, the sweet way of people walking in the evening. This seems good to me to set down and to inspect. Perhaps sometimes such a way may cause a comparison with my own country where there is difference and at other times, it may find a sameness that unites us. I believe that peoples are not different in ends but only in methods and techniques.

With me there can be no disappearance into the scene — no anonymity. I am recognisably American. Near the Madelein at least four men to every block try to sell me dirty pictures. My french should be a matter for international good will since whenever I try to speak it, my hearers burst into delighted laughter. ~~Recently, returning to my house from the American Express Company~~ Yesterday I went to the American Express Company and returned carrying a paper bag of money. And three young women offered me their love. I imagine that they can see through paper and had discovered that I was attractive. No, I am obviously Tourist and obviously American and since I am truly both, I see no reason to be either sad nor proud about it. It is simply a matter of fact.

For such a venture as the one I am proposing I am triply fortunate. My two young sons are coming to spend the summer in Paris with me. Thus I will have two extra pairs of eyes to see with and two extra minds to help me to inspect and discover and the eyes of children are wonderful.

Thus I hope my readers, if I have any, will understand my premise. I will offer you Paris, perhaps not as it is, but as I see it. I will make no pronouncements and if I am notably wrong about anything I will hope that some one among my readers will set me right. And if I ask a question may I hope to have an answer.

I have a lonely room in which to write, a small panelled room with books to the ceiling. My desk is in front of a window and I look out on the sun fired chestnut blossoms. The birds are crazy with excitement for the nests are finished and the eggs are laid and very soon there will be a new generation of Paris birds. And around the corner playing violently in the morning sun there is a whole, fresh, bursting generation of new Paris humans. Vitality does not go out of the world while these – birds and children exist. If we the older, impose our sadness and our cynicism, that is our fault, not theirs. I have often thought how much better it would be, if children could grow up without the stupid whips of our experience – experience for which we have learned so little.

Well – there is my plan. Now we shall see what I can carry it out, and whether it is interesting. It is a challenge to me. To write of Paris for Parisians. I hope I will not fail too miserably. II

Back in New York in late January 1951, following a Bermuda honeymoon with Elaine and a stint in Hollywood working on the screenplay for Viva Zapata! *(1952), Steinbeck began work on "The Salinas Valley," the ambitious novel eventually published as* East of Eden *(1952). He developed a distinctive writing pattern, keeping a journal in the form of letters to his editor, Pat Covici, which was published posthumously as* Journal of a Novel: The East of Eden Letters *(1969). By late April 1951 Steinbeck had finished about a quarter of the projected novel, and by mid July he had written more than 135,000 words.*

In September 1951 The Log from the Sea of Cortez, *consisting of Steinbeck's portion of his and Ed Ricketts's* Sea of Cortez: A Leisurely Journal of Travel and Research *(1941), was published after a legal delay. Covici had argued that Ricketts's name on the dust jacket would not help sales, but the Ricketts estate insisted that both authors of the original volume be credited. After consulting with Ricketts's son, Ed Ricketts Jr., Steinbeck unwillingly removed his late friend's name from the volume. In the meantime, he worked steadily, if slowly, on* East of Eden. *By early November he had completed the first draft, and he spent the first few months of 1952 revising the manuscript. While on an extended trip to Europe that began in late March 1952, Steinbeck began contributing travel articles to* Collier's.

In September 1952 East of Eden *was published by Viking Press, and it soon became a best-seller. More than one hundred thousand copies of the book had been ordered in advance by the previous April, but the Book-of-the-Month Club declined to name it a club selection because of the descriptions of whorehouses in the novel. At about the same time Ernest Hemingway's* The Old Man and the Sea *was also published. While keeping track of criticism of his own new book, Steinbeck found time to read Hemingway's short novel. During September and October, Steinbeck and Elaine worked for the campaign of Adlai Stevenson, the Democratic Party presidential candidate. According to Jackson J. Benson in* The True Adventures of John Steinbeck, Writer *(1984), Steinbeck was an admirer of the Republican candidate, Dwight D. Eisenhower, but after reading Stevenson's speeches, he switched his allegiance, defining himself as a "Stevenson Democrat."*

Early in 1953 Steinbeck was at work on a musical play that was to be a sort of extension of Cannery Row *(1945) and was to be produced by the Broadway production team of Cy Feuer and Ernest Martin. That summer Martin found the Steinbecks a rental house in Sag Harbor, on Long Island; Steinbeck was attracted to the village, finding it an East Coast equivalent of the Monterey Peninsula. He eventually set aside his plan for the musical and worked instead on a sequel to* Cannery Row *in the form of a novel. It had the working title "Bear Flag" and was published in 1954 as* Sweet Thursday. *Steinbeck had completed the first draft by September 1953. The following month he entered New York's Lenox Hill Hospital with a mysterious illness, which turned out to be depression. Later in the year he consulted with psychologist Gertrudis Brenner.*

In March 1954 the Steinbecks began an extensive trip in Europe. While in Paris, Steinbeck began contributing a short weekly article to Le Figaro littéraire. *The series, titled "One American in Paris," ran from 12 June to 18 September. Early in July, at the request of Radio Free Europe, the Steinbecks went to Munich, where Steinbeck recorded a statement of his position as a writer, which was broadcast over the radio network. In a letter to his agent, Elizabeth Otis, written from England on 17 September, he stated that he was going "to dump [his] technique, to tear it right down to the ground and to start all over."*

After returning to New York from Europe at the end of 1954, Steinbeck met William Faulkner in January 1955. According to Elaine's recollection, this meeting was quite unpleasant because of Faulkner's drinking that night. The two writers met again some months later at a literary function, where they laughed over their earlier meeting. In February the Steinbecks bought a house at Sag Harbor, which was to become their summer home. Steinbeck also purchased a boat and busied himself around the house that spring.

On 9 March 1955 the motion-picture adaptation of East of Eden *premiered at the Astor Theatre in New York and drew mixed reviews. Near the end of the month the Steinbecks attended the opening of Tennessee Williams's* Cat on a Hot Tin Roof. *Steinbeck had ambivalent feelings about the play and later referred to Williams and Faulkner as part of "the neurosis belt of the South," although he admired Williams's ability to bring a lyrical quality of speech to the stage in a natural way. That spring, as a result of his experience writing for* Le Figaro littéraire, *Steinbeck began his long association with the* Saturday Review, *contributing guest editorials and other articles. For the rest of the season the Steinbecks spent every other week in their Sag Harbor home; when he was in the city, Steinbeck used Elia Kazan's office on Times Square, writing for the* Saturday Review *and* Punch. *At this time Steinbeck was also working with Richard Rodgers and Oscar Hammerstein 2nd on* Pipe Dream, *a musical-comedy adaptation of* Sweet Thursday. *The play opened in New Haven for tryouts on 24 October 1955, and on 30 November it opened on Broadway at the Shubert Theatre. Although it ran through June of the following year,* Pipe Dream *was generally considered a failure because Rodgers and Hammerstein had watered down and sentimentalized the plot of* Sweet Thursday.

The Log from the Sea of Cortez (1951)

Sea of Cortez Revisited, or *Cannery Row* Revised
Joel W. Hedgpeth

Marine biologist Joel W. Hedgpeth, who reviewed The Log from the Sea of Cortez *(1951) for* Pacific Discovery, *had known Ed Ricketts and revised the 1952 edition of Ricketts's* Between Pacific Tides *(1939).*

Toward the end of 1941 a well-known novelist by the name of John Steinbeck, and Edward F. Ricketts, a marine biologist of less renown to the world at large, presented to the somewhat bewildered world of letters a thick book about a collecting trip to the Gulf of California, under the title: *Sea of Cortez.* . . . To the critics who were convinced that something was wrong with Steinbeck as a writer, this "sort of choppino [*sic*] of travel, biology and philosophy" was full of clues and material for essays, and in recent years three such essays have appeared in the *Pacific Spectator* alone.

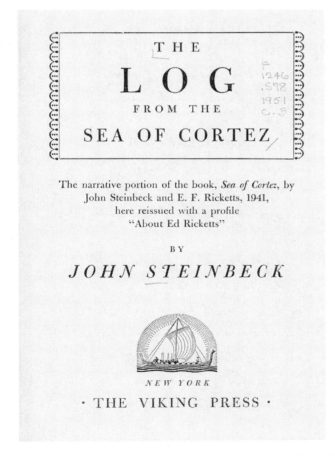

THE

LOG

FROM THE

SEA OF CORTEZ

The narrative portion of the book, *Sea of Cortez,* by John Steinbeck and E. F. Ricketts, 1941, here reissued with a profile "About Ed Ricketts"

BY

JOHN STEINBECK

NEW YORK

· THE VIKING PRESS ·

Title page for the 1951 republication of Steinbeck's portion of his and Ed Ricketts's Sea of Cortez, *published ten years earlier (Thomas Cooper Library, University of South Carolina)*

At least one well known reviewer of nature books somewhat innocently thought that the "colleagues of the learned Mr. Ricketts" would be surprised to learn that he drank great quantities of beer, and "wrote, or concurred in" certain bawdy speculations. He did not, however, miss the fundamental point that the book was the joint effort of two authors, who had a lot of fun putting it together.

That was ten years ago. Steinbeck and Ricketts had such a good time with this enterprise that they planned another—northward, this time—at first, to the Aleutians, then, more realistically, to the Queen Charlottes; and Ricketts began to develop a scheme to interlock his *Between Pacific Tides* with *Sea of Cortez* and the new book, *The Outer Shores,* which was to be in part the result of this northern expedition. He had an elaborate set of cards in two sizes and several colors printed to record all this information, with spaces for cross references to the other books. In the meanwhile, Ed Ricketts had become the Doc of *Cannery Row* and the legend was beginning to grow. Then one day in 1948 Ed forgot about the afternoon train to Pacific Grove and drove his car into its path. It was not a pleasant or an easy way to die, and the manner of it increased our sense of loss. For many of us, the heart has gone out of Cannery Row now, and only the curious passers-by go down to look at the shack that was once the "Pacific Biological Laboratories." Steinbeck was the hardest hit, because Ed was perhaps the only friend who was not in the least awed by his reputation as a writer and treated him first as a human being. When you become a famous writer, it is something like being rich: it is not easy to be sure that your friends are really your friends. He could never have any doubts like that about Ed Ricketts.

It is for the sake of saying what he had to say about his friend that Steinbeck has published this edition of *Sea of Cortez*. It consists of the narrative portion of the original book, up to page 271, with this long preface or "profile.". . .

Usually a preface to a new edition is not given much space by reviewers, but this 67-page "profile" will be approached by critics as further source material for the "Steinbeck problem," while friends of Ed Ricketts will read it to learn how Steinbeck knew him: "As I have said, no one who knew Ed will be satisfied with this account. They will have known innumerable other Eds. I imagine that there were as many Eds as there were friends of Ed." With such a disclaimer, we are left without too much to say about this portrait by Steinbeck, and are invited, in effect, to write our own, if we are not satisfied. In writing about Ed Ricketts, John Steinbeck has attempted one of the hardest writing jobs he has ever set himself to do. In a way, he has succeeded—at least, the history of this interesting friendship, and something of the personality which has had such an influence on one of our major writers has been set down. But as one who knew Ed as a fellow biologist, and didn't care how he managed his private life, I find some curious gaps in this "profile.". . .

The most conspicuous oversight in Steinbeck's profile is the failure to mention that Ed wrote another

10

"I'm John Steinbeck. Does it hurt?"
"Not much. I've heard of you."
"I've heard of you, too. Let's have a drink."
That was the first time I ever saw him. I had heard that there was an interesting man in town who ran a commercial laboratory, had a library of good music and interests WIDER than invertebratology. I had wanted to come across him for some time.

We did not think of ourselves as poor then. We simply had no money. Our food was fairly plentiful what with fishing and planning and a minimum of theft. Entertainment had to be improvised without benefit of currency. Our pleasures consisted in conversation, walks, games, and parties with people of our own financial non-existence. A real party was dressed with a gallon of forty-nine cent wine and we could have a hell of a time on that. We did not know any rich people and for that reason we did not like them and were proud and glad we didn't live that way.

We had been timid about meeting Ed Ricketts because he was rich people by OUR standards. This meant that he could depend on a hundred to a hundred and fifty dollars a month and he had an automobile. To us this was fancy and we didn't see how any one could go through that kind of money. But we

Page from the manuscript of Steinbeck's "About Ed Ricketts," published in 1951 as the introduction to The Log from the Sea of Cortez *(from Christie's New York,* Printed Books and Manuscripts, 5 December 1997; *Bruccoli Clark Layman Archives)*

book—which began as a collaboration between him and his friend Jack Calvin (who now runs a printing business in Sitka, Alaska), and which is an enduring contribution to the literature of seashore biology: *Between Pacific Tides.* It was probably the publisher's doing that the listing of this title has been removed from this reissue of *Sea of Cortez;* it should be restored in further printings. This little detail and the general tone of Steinbeck's memoir may leave the impression among uninformed readers that the narrative part of *Sea of Cortez* is even more Steinbeck's doing than it was. . . .

To say that Ed was holistic in his thinking is simply to say that he was by temperament a naturalist, devoted to achieving some synthesis of the world about him. As William Morton Wheeler once observed, such people usually become hard-boiled Aristotelians, but Ed was a soft-boiled one, unable to exorcise his inherent mysticism. He lacked the toughness of mind to adhere to an established intellectual discipline, either as a biologist or a philosopher; he lived and thought as he pleased. Those of us who had to knuckle down to conventions and circumstances envied him at times. Yet he was not always as happy in this manner of living as we who envied or admired him might imagine that we could be in similar circumstances. As Steinbeck says, he was looking for something—most often in love, but in music and in the tidepools as well—that he did not find.

On one plane he was the archetype of the Steinbeck hero (out of the clinically detailed pages of a book for men only), on another, a lost soul. Well, we are all lost souls, seeking salvation of some sort or another, but it is characteristic of Steinbeck that he does not come to grips with this aspect of Ed's character—perhaps he will in some future writing, at least by indirection. Although his critics do not use these words, they do agree that the flaw in Steinbeck's writing is his failure to meet this problem of salvation—like Ed, he is contented to take things as he finds them.

Certainly one does not try to reform one's friends, especially after they are dead, and least of all, to censure them for their faults, whether they be those of glandular imbalance or lack of philosophical discipline. It would be unkind, and not quite true, to say that this profile is simply *Cannery Row* in a new key—it is a portrait of a friend, written in kindness and love. I wish I knew how to say things as well, yet enough has been said, indeed, to demonstrate that he was a rare and lovable personality.

As for his eccentricities, they are all true enough—how many times have we been asked if there really was a beer milk shake, I wonder; he was gravely polite to dogs yet a competent embalmer of cats, and in his attire a veritable wedding guest in mufti. His easygoing attire was the cause of an unpleasant little incident in the library of a certain research foundation, but he got his revenge by making critical remarks about the rich man in science in *Sea of Cortez.* Things happen to—and around—people like

Ed, and even Steinbeck, with his love for a good story, has hardly scratched the surface of the store of anecdotes.

But it must be said again that Steinbeck has not said enough about one of the most enduring labors of Ed's life, of how for these last ten or twelve years students of marine biology have found, in the book he started to write for his friends out of the background of those years of hours in the tidepools, their introduction to the seashore of the Pacific Coast. Certainly *Between Pacific Tides* proved that Ed was one of [W. C.] Allee's finest students, and the professor may well remember him as a "sometimes disturbing, but always stimulating" student, "one of a group of Ishmaelites."

—*Pacific Discover,* 6 (January–February 1953); reprinted in *John Steinbeck: The Contemporary Reviews,* edited by Joseph R. McElrath Jr., Jesse S. Crisler, and Susan Shillinglaw (Cambridge & New York: Cambridge University Press, 1996), pp. 375–377

East of Eden (1952)

Steinbeck to Pascal Covici, December 1951

When Steinbeck finished the manuscript of East of Eden *(1952), he sent it to his editor, Pat Covici, in a mahogany box that he had carved in Nantucket the previous summer. The following letter sent with the box and manuscript later served as the dedication to the novel (omitting the words "Do you remember" from the beginning of the letter).*

Dear Pat—

Do you remember you came upon me carving some kind of little figure out of wood and you said—

"Why don't you make something for me?"

I asked you what you wanted and you said—

"A box."

"What for?"

"To put things in."

"What things?"

"Whatever you have," you said.

Well here's your box. Nearly everything I have is in it and it is not full. All pain and excitement is in it and feeling good or bad and evil thoughts and good thoughts—the pleasure of design and some despair and the indescribable joy of creation.

And on top of these are all the gratitude and love I bear for you.

And still the box is not full.

John

—*Steinbeck: A Life in Letters,* edited by Elaine Steinbeck and Robert Wallsten (New York: Viking, 1975), p. 433

* * *

Dust jacket for Steinbeck's epic 1952 novel about a family that settles in the Salinas Valley (Bruccoli Clark Layman Archives)

American Academy of Arts and Letters

Felicia Geffen of the American Academy of Arts and Letters had written Steinbeck on 25 April 1951 asking for his support in Archibald MacLeish's nomination of E. E. Cummings and Wallace Stevens for membership in the academy. Steinbeck replied, with his own suggestions for nominations, in May.

I am happy to join Archy in his nominations. Do I have the right to propose members for the institute? If I do have, I wish to propose Richard Rodgers and John O'Hara. Will you let me know? Archy could second for O'Hara and Deems Taylor can carry out the second in music. It is ridiculous that these two are not members. Will you please let me hear what comes of this?

Yours

John Steinbeck

—Steinbeck: A Life in Letters, p. 420

Steinbeck to Covici, 1952

Not long after completing East of Eden, *Steinbeck wrote Covici anticipating the criticism the book was about to receive.*

Dear Pat:

I have been going over the years in my mind, remembering all the things pre-publication critics have asked me to take out, things they would now be horrified at if I had.

One of the most dangerous things of all is the suggestion that something or other is not in good taste. Now good taste is a codification of manners and attitudes of the past. The very fact of originality is per se bad taste. I might even go so far as to believe that any writer who produced a book of unquestioned good taste has written a tasteless book, a flavorless book, a book of no excitement and surely of no originality. There is no taste in life nor in nature. It is simply the way it is. And in the rearrangement of life called literature, the writer is the less valuable and interesting in direct relation to his goodness of taste. There is shocking bad taste in the Old Testament, abominable taste in Homer, and execrable taste in Shakespeare.

Thinking about it, I believe that the following may be true. When a book is finished but not yet printed there is a well-intentioned urge, particularly in non-creative people, to help, to be part of it, and this urge takes itself out in suggestions for its improvement. It would not occur to me to make such suggestions to another writer because I know he must have a reason for everything in his book. But also I do not need the free creative ride. As I said, these impulses are kindly meant and they are almost invariably wrong.

And so you and I will do what we have done—listen with respect, correct the errors, weigh the criticism and then go about our business. I do not think that all the things in my books are good but all the things in my book are me. There is no quicker way to ruin any book than to permit collaborations. Then it becomes a nothing and a bad something has a way of being superior to a good nothing. The second-hand bookstalls are loaded with good taste. No. We know this story. We've been through it together so many times.

We'll do fine.

Yours,

John

That was damn good pie

—Steinbeck: A Life in Letters, pp. 436–437

* * *

Steinbeck's New Book, *East of Eden,* Tells of "His People" in Our Valley
W. Max Gordon

W. Max Gordon reviewed East of Eden *for Steinbeck's hometown newspaper, the* Salinas Californian.

There is nothing truly evil except what is within us, and it is man's own decision whether or not he shall rule over sin. This in essence, we think, is the theme of John Steinbeck's new book, "East of Eden," which goes on sale today here and throughout the nation.

Mr. Steinbeck has taken some 600 pages to chronicle the story of "his people" and that of an imaginary character, Adam Trask. Much of the story is laid in the Salinas valley. Many will recognize the real and imaginary people he weaves into his long story.

Steinbeck is never dull and, even if you miss his message, you'll not be bored. There is only one Steinbeck and no one writes about "his people" as well.

"His people" in this case are members of his own family. His grandfather, Samuel Hamilton, an easy-going and impractical inventor, tried to eke a living from a poor ranch near King City. He wasn't too successful, but he raised a wonderful family and the impact of his goodness and understanding was immeasurable.

"His people" also are the workmen, the ranchers, the ranch hands, the mechanics and even "the girls." He understands them, knows how they think and how they react.

Cain and Abel Theme

Steinbeck's book is heavily allegorical. He carries the Cain and Abel theme through from the first to the last. Adam Trask's brother, Charles, tried to kill him. Later in an accident Charles' forehead is

Brando as Zapata in the 1952 movie Viva Zapata! *(Center for Steinbeck Studies, San Jose State University)*

scarred, perhaps "the mark of Cain." Adam's two sons are Caleb and Aron, easily changed to Cain and Abel. In fact, Caleb, who admits he does "evil things," is responsible for his brother's enlistment in the army. Aron is killed in France in the first world war and Caleb feels he is responsible.

And in Kate, the mother of the twins, Caleb and Aron, Steinbeck has created a thoroughly vicious character. You'll not forget Kate. She kills her own parents. She marries Adam as she recovers from a beating administered by her manager in the business of sin. After the twins are born near King City she wounds Adam, deserts the children, and becomes an inmate of one of the "houses" in Salinas. She kills her benefactor, Faye, and takes over the "house."

Lee Is Strong Character

Lee, the Chinese handyman who works for Adam, is one of the strongest characters in the book. He's a philosopher and it is during his discussions with Samuel Hamilton and Adam that the theme of the book is set. Lee takes exception to the quotation in the King James version of the Bible that says "thou shalt rule over him (sin)." This appears in the story of Cain and Abel. He finds another version written "do thou rule over him." With the aid of Chinese scholars he decides it should read "thou mayest" rule over him.

"Don't you see," Lee says, "the American Standard translation orders men to triumph over sin, and you can call sin ignorance. The King James version makes a promise 'thou shalt,' meaning that men will surely triumph over sin. But in the Hebrew word 'timshel,' 'thou mayest' gives the choice. It might be the most important word in the world. That says the way is open. That throws it right back on man. For if 'thou mayest'—it is also true that 'thou mayest not.'"

Thoroughly Steinbeck

Steinbeck and his publishers say this is his greatest book. Certainly, it is thoroughly Steinbeck, whose characters talk like such characters should and do. It has many fine passages, one of which is the description of a trip with his favorite uncle. We think the public will like it, and, of course it's a "must" for Monterey county people.

—*Salinas Californian,* 14 September 1952, p. 4

* * *

Steinbeck to Nelson Valjean, 13 March 1953

Steinbeck wrote his former Stanford classmate Nelson Valjean indicating that he was not expecting a positive reaction to East of Eden *from his hometown because the people of Salinas had denounced some of his previous books.*

Dear Val:

It was a very nice thing to get your letter and I am glad you like the work. I surely moved around with a manure fork, I suppose, in doing it, and I was amazed at how much I was able to remember and I suppose I didn't remember a great deal.

I have had no reaction from Salinas regarding the book, but I have had previous experience which would indicate to me that the Salinas reaction would not be good. When I wrote Tortilla Flat, for instance, the Monterey Chamber of Commerce issued a statement that it was a damned lie and that no such place or people existed. Later, they began running buses to the place where they thought it might be.

When I did Cannery Row, I had not only a charge from the Monterey Chamber of Commerce, but from the Fish Canners Association which came to the defense of Cannery Row people with a knightly intensity. They later reversed themselves, too. So I should imagine Salinas is waiting to find out what the reaction of the rest of the country is before they decide whether they will approve of me or disapprove of me. I do not think they approve of me very highly.

It occurs to me that probably the most heartbreaking title in the world is Tom Wolfe's "You Can't Go Home Again"—it's literally true. They want no part of me except in a pine box.

I am terribly interested in what you say about my father and mother. I think no one ever had more loyalty than I had from my parents. This was—or must have been—particularly painful to them, in that I was doing something that the town considered nuts and bad taste. Being intelligent people, my parents knew that my chances of making a living at writing were about one in a million—horse racing is a sure thing compared to it. A couple of years ago I came across a story about my father which I think might interest you. When my first book came out, I didn't know it, but he apparently tried to get a few of my townspeople to buy a copy or so of it. They were not very much interested in so doing, but, as you know, we lived in Pacific Grove part of the time, and my father went to Mr. Holman of Holman's Store, and asked him if he wouldn't lay in a few copies of it—the book was called Cup of Gold. Mr. Holman said that if people wanted it and ordered it, he would certainly send for it, but he didn't think that he could go out on a limb and put any in stock, and so he did not. Well—many years later, Mrs. Holman began collecting my work, and she had to pay $78.00 for a copy of the book which, remaindered, could have been bought for 2c. or 3c. a copy. She blamed Mr. Holman for not having literary taste and she resents very much having to pay such a premium. It was a surprise to me that my father had tried to sell books for me. He did not succeed, but I honor him for having tried.

There is nothing I would rather do than to stop by and drink some of your grappa. Do you make it yourself? I wonder if I could still have the stomach for it. I remember we used to drink it out in Alisal and it had a distinct kerosene taste and the rule was then not to light a match within three minutes of having had a drink of it.

Thank you for writing. It's good to hear from you.

Yours very sincerely,
John
—*Steinbeck: A Life in Letters*, pp. 467–468

* * *

Out of the New-Born Sun
Harvey Curtis Webster

Reviewer Harvey Curtis Webster called East of Eden *a "long parable expertly told."*

Perhaps *East of Eden* isn't a great novel according to the strict conventions of formal purity so widely accepted today, but it will take almost equal quantities of pride and stupidity to deny that it is one of the best novels of the past ten years and the best book John Steinbeck has written since *The Grapes of Wrath*. Most people will like it and many will buy it. They should, for it is to be doubted if any American novel has better chronicled our last hundred years, our trek from East to West to discover an Eden that always somehow escapes us and that we as a people yet continue to hope for and believe in.

East of Eden is not a compact novel like *Of Mice and Men*, not brilliant sociological fiction like *The Grapes of Wrath* and *In Dubious Battle*, not a temperately ironical tale of the disreputable who are more lovable than the respectable like *Tortilla Flat*. It belongs really in the tradition of the novels Fielding wrote and Thackeray tried to. It jangles, yet is full of vitality; reading it you realize that Steinbeck has never learned or cared to learn the lesson of Henry James, but that doesn't seem to matter as you are carried forward by a narrative flow that encompasses vulgarity, sensibility, hideousness, and beauty.

In another sense, *East of Eden* can be taken as a long parable expertly told. Mostly it centers about Adam Trask, appropriately and Biblically named. He is a fallible, gullible intelligent man who thinks he has found his earthly paradise in the Salinas Valley, is seduced by his Eve, and comes out of the moral wilderness this sends him into to achieve belief in himself and in the world he must learn to live in.

But as its length of six hundred pages suggests, this parable is as full of incidents and people who deviate from the main line of narrative as *Tom Jones*. Some of the episodes, like the compact and highly interesting story of Cyrus Trask who never forgot the Civil War or learned gentleness, seem at first to be largely irrelevant. One feels that Steinbeck spends altogether too much time on the whores Adam's wife ultimately controls, too much loving description on the Salinas Valley, that he overcrowds his canvas with characters. Yet in the end the reader must conclude that there is little real irrelevance and that even the actual irrelevance is so full of vitality that he is glad Steinbeck did not do a sterner job of pruning.

The novel marks a definite advance in Steinbeck's thinking which has been defined by Edmund Wilson as too barely naturalistic. In his earlier novels, men approach the condition of animals with a uniformity that sometimes becomes monotonous. In *East of Eden*, the ani-

Poster for the 1955 movie adaptation of Steinbeck's 1952 novel (Bruccoli Clark Layman Archives)

James Dean as Cal Trask and Raymond Massey as Adam Trask in the 1955 motion-picture adaptation of East of Eden, *directed by Elia Kazan (MOMA/Film Stills Archive; from Joseph R. Millichap,* Steinbeck and Film, *1983; Thomas Cooper Library, University of South Carolina)*

mality is still there but it is joined to a sense of human dignity and what it may achieve. There is none of the sentimentality about the outcast you find in *Cannery Row*, none of the unconvincing mysticism of *The Wayward Bus*. The main characters are good-and-bad, good, and bad; and one always has a sense that they are endowed with a freedom of choice that permits them to change their moral category. . . .

. . . These focal characters who bring meaning and focus into what superficially seems a sprawling narrative full of unguided life are Steinbeck's artful instruments in a novel that convincingly demonstrates that he is still one of the most important writers of our time.
—*Saturday Review*, 35 (20 September 1952); reprinted in *John Steinbeck: The Contemporary Reviews*, pp. 386–387

* * *

California Moonshine
Anthony West

Anthony West found the moralizing in East of Eden *"puerile."*

Mr. John Steinbeck has placed the telling of his new novel, *East of Eden*, . . . in the hands of a narrator related to many of the characters. There is nothing especially outrageous about this device, but in this case the choice of instrument is unfortunate. When he

wishes to inform us that he nearly died of pleural pneumonia, he chooses to say that he "went down and down, until the wing tips of the angels brushed my eyes." When he is not rolling verbal syrup of this kind around his mouth, he is liable to be toying with phrases that resemble metaphors but in which something bordering on a genius for dissociation may be discerned. When Adam Trask, the hero of the novel, is working hard to clear a neglected ranch that he has just bought near Salinas, we are told that "Adam sat like a contented cat on his land." A little later, with work on the homestead going forward nicely, his happiness is increased by the knowledge that he is to become a father, and his manner grows livelier: "Adam fluttered like a bewildered bee confused by too many flowers." A certain exaltation in an expectant father is only right and proper, but since Adam has served two five-year hitches in the United States Cavalry, fought in the Indian Wars, rubbed elbows with I.W.W. stalwarts in hobo jungles, and done a twelve-month stretch on a Tallahassee chain gang, it is permissible to suggest that the delicacy of his condition is overstressed. The narrator's efforts to transform Trask into a marshmallow of a man, all sponginess, purity, and softness, are at war with Mr. Steinbeck's intentions, which are apparently to get a good man in a tough spot that will test his moral fibre.

The pregnant lady responsible for Adam's flutterings is not altogether a credit to her sex. When she is what is known in the garment trade as a sub-teen, a

[1952]

Hassler Hotel, Rome June 17   file

Dear Elizabeth: We arrived here last night tired , hot and miserable.
General Ridgeway also arrived here that day and is staying in this
hotel so that it took us over an hour fo get to the hotel through
traffic such as I have never seen. We were completely pooped when w
got here and got our clothes off. It is very hot and we have no
hot weather glothes. This is a predicament we mu st rectify very
quickly bec use the city is scorching and we have nothing but wool
clothes.

        Today Mondidori insisted that I was going to lunch and I insisted
that I was not. This took some shouting over the phone . I told
him that I would have lunch tomorrow but not today. He had invited
some people. But how could he when he was not sure when we would get
in. The sudden heat has given us both a kind of dysentery which is
unpleasant and lunch did not help.

        We are getting off the Jura piece to day. If they want to
use any of the dog pictures I will get the negatives. But they were
not taken by Elaine so we do not have the negatives.

        The collection of mail here was enommous. It came from every
place and got me a little confused. The topper was Mr. Chaplins from
colliers. A little squib taken out of context and printed in a paris
column. I will not dignify it by answering him. You might remeind
him that two years ago I was going to Marry Paulette Goddard.
This was just a couple of paragraphs out of a long evening of talk.
I am ashamed of the old lady attitude. Short and ugly words leap
to my mind. If he thinks I am going to be careful of what I say to
any one for the sake of Collier's not too unspotty position,
he is nuts. I don't want to qusrrel with them but I'll be goddamned
if I will live a colliers type life for them. I will do the best
I can to fulfill my contract and I will but I don't have to go to
bed with them. Please tell Mr. Chaplin that I have disciplined Mr.
Buckwald of the Paris Tribune but I cannot fire him. And incidently
isn't this the same man who refused to pay the money? I guess it
is, the heat Elizabeth but it makes me feel waspish.

        Miss Drudi's secretary called this moring and ask d when she
could give a cocktail party for us. I said I hated them and she said
But it would be so good for our agency. I'll see what compromise I
can make about this.

        There was a full page attack on me in the communist
peoper here yesterday with a head line. An open letter to me.
I don't know what it says exactly because I do not read Italian well

*Letter from Steinbeck to his agent, Elizabeth Otis, written from Rome during his and Elaine's European tour in
the spring and summer of 1952 (John Steinbeck Collection, Stanford University Libraries)*

".2

Then The American Embassy called me and asked if I would like b
answer the smear. I said I would have b know what it said first.
So they are going to send me a translation and I will send it on
to you. I can get the sense of it and it is in the usual communist
terms. But when I can, I will send it to you.

Next-- Al Capp whom I love wired me that he is having a hard
cover book printed by Farrar Strauss and Young and asked me if
I would do a two thoßsand word introduction. I wired yes and
asked for the deadline. I would love to do it and will. Hope they
don't rush me. But I can do it in a very short time because I have
thought of him a lot and I will do it. You can call and find out
about the book and what their plans are, if you will.

There were three delighted and busy letters from Pat here.
He told about the sales meeting and made it wound like high mass
at St. Peters. He sounds very sanguine about the books chances.

Next, Gadge Kazan called from Paris this morning. He is very
much excited about the book. Wants to make it and will talk to
Annie Laurie as soon as he gets back. He has an excellent idea
how to make it. He said over the phone to me that Zapata has already
grossed three million dollars and he intends the next one East of
Eden shall belong or at least a part of it to us so that we can share
in the mfm fixx profits.

Next-- We think you did exactly right about Waverly and
the key. We would not like her locked out but we do not want her
to spend a night. I don't thin she will ever come down from
Westport myself nor does Elaine, but Elaine says to tell you she
agrees with you completely.

I do hope you will like the Jura piece a little. This is
a very hard job. Harder than I could have imagined and not made east
.ier by the shifting sands of Colliers. I hope they will settle
down pretty soon. I am going to try to get some work done here in
Rome. I feel that there is a good political story here if I can only
get to it. And I think I can. I think we will be here in Rome
between ten days to two weeks. Then go to Naples and then drive up
the west caost and through Cannes to Paris. Then to England
and Ireland. And after that we will see what the month is.
I anticipate at least two and maybe three Italian stories. Perhaps
and English one and surely an Irish one. And that's as far as I have
thought right now. And in this heat my thinking is not too good.
I am going to write to Annie Laurie now

                    love to all
                    john

baroque quality in her romping gets two of her boy friends sent off to reform school. In her first year at high school, she drives her Latin teacher to suicide with her offbeat fancies, and two years later, hitting her stride, she cracks the safe of her father's tannery and commits arson, patricide, and matricide. This sixteen-year-old voluptuary then takes off to slake her appetite for the rarer forms of fun in the New England sporting houses. While advancing her professional career, she encounters a big-time procurer with a circuit embracing thirty-three towns and wins his simple heart. When he finds out what sort of girl he has fallen in love with, his reactions are the uncomplex ones of a deeply passionate man; he takes the lady into a rural section of upstate Connecticut and tries to beat her head in with a rock. The shady back road on which she is left for dead passes by the Trask homestead, and before long she is in bed there, being lovingly nursed by Adam Trask and cordially detested by his half brother Charles. In no time at all, the lady is married to Adam, but it is clear from the first that the young people are not made for each other. On the wedding night, the new Mrs. Trask gives her husband a Mickey Finn and tiptoes off to Charles' room. Even before Adam moves out West to the ranch near Salinas, his wife is none too keen on the farming game, and sitting around pregnant while her land-hungry husband ambles about the place with water diviners cures her of it for good. She dislikes breeding just as much as she dislikes farming, so as soon as the twins are born and she is on her feet again, she plugs Adam in the shoulder with a Colt .44 and makes for the nearest bordello. She is a career girl and a hard worker, and before long she is in a position to poison the madam and take over. Her peculiar talents give the place an uncommon atmosphere, and it is soon as widely known throughout the Golden West as that Parisian establishment called "the Enigmatic Miss Floggy's" was known in Europe during the thirties. Adam, who has no idea where she is or what she is doing, settles into a sullen grief in which the reader may well share, as all this takes us only to about page 300 and there are another three hundred pages to go. Mr. Steinbeck and his narrator, however, have got Adam to the focal tough spot of the story, and the point of it all is in sight.

Adam is for a long time unable to bring himself even to name the twins, or to pay them any other attention. The task of caring for them falls upon his Chinese cook, who at last insists they must have names—the least a child can expect of its father. A neighbor naturally suggests Cain and Abel, but Adam compromises with Caleb and Aron. In due course, the boys grow up, the family moves off the ranch into Salinas, and Caleb—to the astonishment of no perceptive reader—finds out what Mama is. In a moment of pique at his father's disapproval of his successful gambling on futures in the bean market, he takes his brother to one of the bizarre exhibitions that are a feature of her establishment. In disgust, Aron joins the Army and goes off to get himself killed in the First World War. Caleb, it becomes clear, is indeed Cain, and the book, it becomes clear, is about the riddle presented by Genesis 4:1–8, an extremely bewildering episode.

Mr. Steinbeck sees this story, which is concerned with the primitive religion of a people halfway between a nomadic and a pastoral life, through a haze of modern psychology, which is almost entirely concerned with the world of experience of the urban middle class. Cain was unhappy because his love was rejected; this made him mean, and his meanness made him feel guilty. To break his feeling of guilt, he became murderous, and thus more guilty, and so on. According to Mr. Steinbeck, this is the story of all mankind and the reason man is the only guilty animal. If this were all, the outlook for the human race would be a glum one, and Adam Trask, perversely depressed more by his wife's departure than by the manner of it, is inclined to take the dim view. His Chinese cook, aided by a philosophic neighbor, argues him out of it. The cook, a Bible student, belongs to a highgrade discussion group run by a San Francisco tong. His master's problems have persuaded him to an attentive study of the Cain and Abel story, and he has put it up to the group for clarification. They produce startling new information about the obscure sentence "And unto thee shall be his desire, and thou shalt rule over him." "Thou shalt," it appears, is a mistranslation of "*timshel*," which really means "thou mayest," and "him" refers to sin. So the last part of the sentence should read, "Thou mayest rule over sin." This calls for a new deal all round with a new deck. Spiritually armed by this knowledge, Adam goes off to the brothel to face his wife as she really is, a meeting from which he emerges unscathed, and released at last from the feeling that some vileness of his has driven the delicate creature of his illusions away. In his exaltation, he makes the perfect gesture of a mystic in an industrial society and buys himself a new Ford. The liberation is not simply a passing mood, either, and when the final crisis of the book comes, and his son stands before him stained with his war profits of seven and a half cents a pound on beans and his brother's blood, he is morally strong enough to lift the burden of guilt from the boy by murmuring, "*Timshel.*"

"The subject," Mr. Steinbeck declares, "is the only one man has ever used as his theme—the existence, the balance, the battle, and the victory in the permanent war between wisdom and ignorance, light and darkness–good and evil." It is true that this has been the single theme of a certain kind of literature. Mr. Steinbeck has written the precise equivalent of those nineteenth-century melodramas in which the villains could always be recognized because they waxed their mustaches and in which the conflict between good and evil operated like a well-run series of professional tennis matches. Experience would suggest that the conflict is in fact quite different and vastly more interesting, for the forces are not in balance and victory is not guaranteed to the side of the angels. Be that as it may, there is nothing more puerile than a discussion of the subject conducted in terms so naive that evil is identified with sexual aberration. Compared with the evil that sits smiling in the family group or mingles with the guests at a wedding in a neat suit, the evil that hides behind shutters in the red-light district is neither very deadly nor very interesting.

–*New Yorker,* 28 (20 September 1952); reprinted in *John Steinbeck: The Contemporary Reviews,* pp. 387–389

* * *

Steinbeck to Carlton A. Sheffield, 16 October 1952

Steinbeck was perplexed by West's negative review of East of Eden *in* The New Yorker *but noted in this letter to his old friend Carlton A. "Dook" Sheffield that the novel was selling quite well.*

Dear Dook:

Thank you for your good letter. It warmed me and it remembered me of very many things. I guess it was the things we disagreed about that kept us together. Only when we began to agree did we get into trouble. I'm glad you like the book. The Book–it's been capitalized in my mind for so long that it was a kind of a person. And when the last line was finished that person was dead. Rewriting and cutting was like dressing a corpse for a real nice funeral. Remembering the book now is like remembering Ed Ricketts. I remember nice things about both but a finished book and a dead man can never surprise you nor delight you any more. They aren't going any place.

I guess–what may happen is what keeps us alive. We want to see tomorrow. Criticism of the book by critics has been cautious, as it should be. They, after all, must see whether it has a life of its own and the only proof of that is whether people accept it as their own. That's why most critics do not like my present book but love the former one which formerly they denounced. I have felt for some time that criticism has one great value to a writer. With the exception of extreme invention in method or idea (generally disliked by critics because nothing to measure them against) the critic can tell a writer what *not* to do. If he could tell him what *to* do, he'd be a writer himself. What *to* do is the soul and heart of the book. What *not* to do is how well or badly you did it.

I am interested in Anthony West's review in the New Yorker. I wonder what made him so angry–and it was a very angry piece. I should like to meet him to find out why he hated and feared this book so much.

The book seems to be selling enormously. I am getting flocks of letters and oddly enough, most of them have the sense of possession just as you do. People write as though it were their book. I'll speak of Cathy for a moment and then forget the book. You won't believe her, many people don't. I don't know whether I believe her either but I know she exists. I don't believe in Napoleon, Joan of Arc, Jack the Ripper, the man who stands on one finger in the circus. I don't believe Jesus Christ, Alexander the Great, Leonardo. I don't believe them but they exist. I don't believe them because they aren't like me. You say you only believe her at the end. Ah! but that's when, through fear, she became like us. This was very carefully planned. All of the book was very carefully planned. And I'm forgetting it so soon.

I'm going to do a job that sounds very amusing. Frank Loesser and I are going to make a musical comedy of Cannery Row. It will be a madhouse but getting such a thing together should be great fun.

It is very good to be writing to you again. I hope we can keep it up. I think I'm changed in some ways, more calm, maybe more adult, perhaps more tolerant. But still restless. I'll never get over that I guess–still nervous, still going from my high ups to very low downs–just short of a manic depressive, I guess. I have more confidence in myself now, which makes me less arrogant. And Elaine has taught me not to be afraid of people (strangers) so that I am kinder and better mannered I think.

I think I am without ambition. It isn't that I've got so much but that I want less. And I do have the great pleasure in work–*while it is being done.* Nothing equals that to me and I never get used to it. My marriage is good in all ways and my powers in that direction are less frantic but not less frequent. This seems to be my golden age. I wouldn't go back or ahead a week.

In some things I think I more nearly resemble you than I did. I hope that isn't wishful thinking. I've always admired your ability to take stock of your assets, your wishes and your liabilities and out of them make a life that contains more elements good for you than any other. You used to have a little nagging conscience about contributing to some great world of thought or art. Maybe you have that without knowing it. Thoreau didn't know either. And you are more nearly like him than anyone I know. Elaine asked what you were like and instead I told her how and where you lived. She said you must be very wise. I don't think you are terribly wise—but I do think you have used your life well. I am caught up in the world and full of its frenzies but you are perfectly placed to be a quiet, thoughtful, appraiser of your time. You used to have a crippling self-consciousness—as bad as mine. Mine made me jump in where yours made you stay out. But just as my aches have eased, so must yours have done.

The cards for you and for me have been down a long time. The thing that's natural for you, you drift towards. You drift toward peace and contemplation, and I drift toward restlessness and violence. If either of us forces toward the opposite, it doesn't last long. And we don't learn—at least I don't. I mean learn lessons applicable to myself. I am fully capable of making exactly the same mistake today I did at 16 even though I know better. That's funny isn't it? I need glasses to read now, and I can't even learn to keep track of them.

It's a grey day here. My working room is on the third floor overlooking 72nd Street which is a nice street. And I guess, by count—two-thirds of my working time is looking out the window at people going by. Didn't we used to do that in your car? But then we only looked at girls. Now I look at anyone but I still like to look at girls.

And always I feel that I am living in a dream and that I will awaken to something quite different. It's very unreal but then everything always has been to me. Maybe I never saw anything real. That's what Marge Bailey [one

of Steinbeck's professors at Stanford] said about me once very long ago. I do go on, don't I? But it's fun.

We lead a very quiet life. Once a week or so we go out to dinner or to the theatre. Once a month or thereabouts people come in. It's much quieter than living in a small town. Very strange but true. People in the city never drop in. They always call first—a manners pattern small towns could well learn.

A fine old bum just went by as he does every day about this time. Apparently he gets drunk every night. Wakes about 3 in the afternoon and goes by eating an enormous piece of bread. I wonder where he gets the money to get drunk. He looks like death. I wonder how he stays alive or why.

I love the winters here. It gets quite cold and people are much more cheerful when it is cold. The first snow is like a holiday. Very good. We have a nice little library with a red rug and big chairs. In winter we build a coal fire in the fire-place and it is a very nice room to be in. I seem to be just flowing out words. But as I said before—it feels good to be writing to you.

I'd better wrap this up I guess. It looks as though it would go on interminably.

So long
John
—*Steinbeck: A Life in Letters,* pp. 458–461

* * *

James Dean as Cal Trask, Richard Davalos as Aron Trask, and Julie Harris as Abra in East of Eden
(National Steinbeck Center, Salinas)

John Steinbeck's Dramatic Tale of
Three Generations
Joseph Wood Krutch

Joseph Wood Krutch reviewed East of Eden *for the* New York Herald Tribune Book Review.

Mr. Steinbeck's new novel is described as his most ambitious effort since *The Grapes of Wrath*. That is inevitable, but it is also entirely inadequate because *East of Eden* is a novel planned on the grandest possible scale. In some of his recent books the author may have seemed to be letting himself off easy, but in this he spares nothing. Here is one of those occasions when a writer has aimed high and then summoned every ounce of energy, talent, seriousness and passion of which he was capable. The most unfriendly critic could hardly fail to grant that *East of Eden* is the best as well as the most ambitious book Mr. Steinbeck could write at this moment.

The scene is mostly the Salinas valley in California; the action mostly events in the lives of three generations of two families. In each generation two brothers in one of the families play the leading roles and in each case there is some sort of Cain-Abel relationship between them. Obviously the action is intended to be significant on three levels. In addition to being the story of certain individuals it is a story supposed to illustrate and typify certain phases in the cultural development of America. But that is not all or even the most important intention. Besides being individuals first and types second the characters are also something else—they are also symbols.

Here, so we are being told, is not only the story of certain families and the story of a frontier, but also the story of mankind. Mr. Steinbeck is not, either as man or writer, very much like Thomas Mann, but one thinks of *The Magic Mountain* as the most obvious example of another modern novel which operates upon the same three levels. And like Thomas Mann, Mr. Steinbeck employs almost the whole repertory of novelistic devices. Besides highly dramatized scenes there are panoramic descriptions, philosophic dialogues and interpolated disquisitions in which the author, speaking in his own person, discourses ironically upon such subjects as the whore house as a social institution or what goes on when women meet at the village dressmaker's.

Leaving aside for a moment the question of symbolic meaning, the first thing to be said is that the whole ramifying narrative holds the attention to an extraordinary degree throughout the six hundred long pages. Quiet, almost idyllic, passages alternate with scenes of extravagant violence. There are sadis-

tic beatings, a rape, murders and even worse horrors almost too numerous to count. But considered at least as separate self-contained episodes they nearly always come off because Mr. Steinbeck's talents seem to be under that disciplined, self-critical control too often absent in his lesser works, which often degenerated into sentimental melodrama. The violent scenes are, moreover, thrown into high relief by the consequences of the fact that Mr. Steinbeck seems to know when, as narrator, to participate in the hysteria of the scene, when to withdraw into the detached, faintly ironical spectator. Never, I think, not even in *The Grapes of Wrath,* has he exhibited such a grip upon himself and upon his material. If one has sometimes been tempted to dismiss him as merely a routine manipulator of the more obvious tricks of the tough-tender, hardboiled-softboiled school, he cannot be so dismissed here. There is seriousness as well as violence; passion rather than sentimentality. He is also, when the occasion requires, master of a quietly and humorously deft little phrase of description or comment which strikes precisely that note of serenity necessary to highlight the violence. When a wet year came to the Salinas valley "the land would shout with grass." Samuel Hamilton's Irish wife was "a tight hard little woman humorless as a chicken."

What is most likely to disturb a reader, at least during the first third of the book, is the tendency of the characters to turn suddenly at certain moments into obviously symbolic figures as abstract almost as the dramatis personae in a morality play. This awkwardness—and awkward it certainly is—becomes less and less noticeable as the story proceeds. Whether that is because Mr. Steinbeck learns better how to fuse the individual and the symbol or because the reader comes to accept his method I am not quite sure. But in any event it is not because the symbolic intention becomes any less clear or important. In each generation the Abel-Cain relationship is symbolized by a childish gift offered by each brother to the father and always in one case seemingly rejected. And in each generation one of the pair carries a scar on his forehead. Indeed, Mr. Steinbeck states explicitly as one of his theses: "The greatest terror a child can have is that he is not loved, and rejection is the hell he fears. I think every one in the world to a large or small extent has felt rejection. And with rejection comes anger, and with anger some kind of revenge for rejection, and with the crime, guilt—and there is the story of mankind." Furthermore, the central character in the whole story, a son in the second generation, is named Adam despite the fact that he is also Abel, and his wife (intended perhaps as Lilith) is

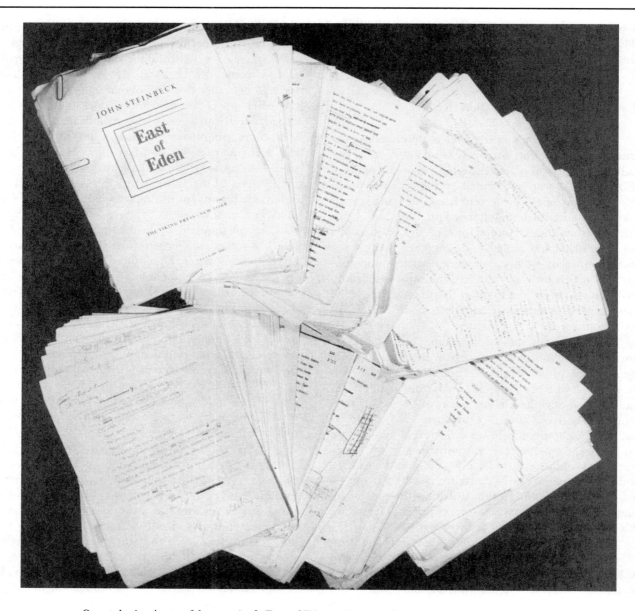

Corrected printer's copy of the typescript for East of Eden, *with corrected manuscript and typescript portions*
from an earlier draft (from Seventy: The World of Books Arts and Letters
circa 1455–1968, *1969; Bruccoli Clark Layman Archives)*

a figure of pure evil outside the reach of all good human impulses. She was a whore and murderess before she married Adam and she leaves him to become both again.

Mr. Steinbeck does not stop with this attempt to embody a meaningful myth in the chronicle history of a modern family. He goes on to draw a further moral and to pronounce a further thesis. Stated in the barest and most abstract terms this thesis is, first, that Good and Evil are absolute not relative things and, second, that in making a choice between them man is a free agent, not the victim of his heredity, his environment, or of anything else.

This thesis is first announced parenthetically, casually, and without any hint of its importance on page twelve, where it is remarked in passing that the first settlers survived their trials because they were more self-reliant than most people seem to be today, "because they trusted themselves and respected themselves as individuals, because they knew beyond doubt that they were valuable and potentially moral units." Nearly three hundred pages later it receives its most explicit discussion in a dialogue between two of the characters concerning the meaning of a phrase in the Cain-Abel story which refers, apparently, to "sin."

In the King James version the phrase reads "and thou shalt rule over him"; in the American Standard Bible it appears as "Do thou rule over him." But according at least to one of Mr. Steinbeck's characters, the crucial Hebrew word is *timshel* and it means "thou mayest." "'Don't you see?' he cried. 'The American Standard translation *orders* men to triumph over sin, and you can call sin ignorance. The King James translation makes a promise in "thou shalt," meaning that men will surely triumph over sin. But the Hebrew word, the word *timshel*—"Thou mayest"—that gives a choice. It might be the most important word in the world.'" And lest we might possibly fail to see that upon this point the whole meaning of the book is intended to depend, its last sentences are: "Adam looked up with sick weariness.—His whispered word seemed to hang in the air: '*Timshel!*' His eyes closed and he slept."

Moral relativism and some sort of deterministic philosophy have commonly seemed to be implied in the writings of that school of hard-boiled realists with which Mr. Steinbeck has sometimes been loosely associated. It is difficult to imagine how any novel could more explicitly reject both than they are rejected in *East of Eden*. The author, who was acclaimed as a social critic in *The Grapes of Wrath* and sometimes abused as a mere writer of sensational melodrama in some subsequent books, plainly announces here that it is as a moralist that he wants to be taken.

The merits of so ambitious and absorbing a book are sure to be widely and hotly debated. The final verdict will not, I think, depend upon the validity of the thesis which is part of a debate almost as old as human thought or upon any possible doubt concerning the vividness of Mr. Steinbeck's storytelling. On the highest level, the question is this: Does the fable really carry the thesis; is the moral implicit in or merely imposed upon the story; has the author recreated a myth or merely moralized a tale? There is no question that Mr. Steinbeck has written an intensely interesting and impressive book.

—*New York Herald Tribune Book Review,* 21 September 1952; reprinted in *John Steinbeck: The Contemporary Reviews,* pp. 393–395

Writing for *Collier's*

Steinbeck to Covici, 18 April 1952

With East of Eden *completed, Steinbeck and Elaine left the country in March 1952 for Europe, where he was to write travel articles for* Collier's *and she was to take photographs to accompany the articles. The following month he wrote Covici from Madrid.*

Dear Pat:

We've been nearly a week in Madrid now and go back to Seville for the great fiesta on Monday.

We have been seeing many pictures—at The Prado and today at Toledo to see the many fine Grecos. So many impressions. Maybe too many. Hard to take in in a short time, a little stunning in fact. Come in dog tired.

We did not have mail forwarded so haven't heard much of anything. Letter from Kazan saying he had testified [before the House Committee on Un-American Activities]. He had told me he was going to a long time ago. I wonder whether it made a sensation. He sent us a copy of his statement which I thought good. It must be a very hard decision to make. He is a good and honest man. I hope the Communists and the second raters don't cut him to pieces now. But they can't hurt him very much.

I haven't written anything. Going through a fallow time, which, as usual, bothers me. Actually so much coming in there hasn't been time for much to go out. And my pen has gone rusty.

I'll try to write more often.

love to all
John
—*Steinbeck: A Life in Letters,* pp. 443–444

* * *

Steinbeck to Elizabeth Otis, 26 May 1952

Steinbeck's relationship with Collier's *got off to a rocky start, as is indicated by this letter to his agent, Elizabeth Otis, written from Paris.*

Dear Elizabeth:

Your letter this morning with Colliers' reaction to the first piece. This first piece was written to order. I won't make that mistake again. I enclose the wire specifying the kind of piece required. If you can see how I could have covered all of these fields in a whole nation in 5,000 words by any other method I'll eat it. Maybe I could have done better but not much different. It may turn out that they don't want my stuff at all but Colliers stuff with my name on it. As for its not being my kind of stuff, that's balderdash. One wants Tortilla Flat and another Grapes of

2nd Piece.

American in Paris.

My friend Robert Capa was killed in Northern Viet Nam by a land mine. A part of the world fell out from under me. I have worked and travelled with Capa. I was with him in the war. He was a gallant man and a dear friend. My life has lost a brightness.

When the news came I felt the need to walk. I did not know where I walked — through streets and parks, over bridges. I saw nothing except diffused light with unreal figures moving through.

Whether it was accident or not I do not know. I found myself at the Arch of Triumph standing by the inextinguishable fiery heart of France — I think perhaps I was unconsciously drawn there where my sorrow could join with everybody's sorrow — and so merge and take some courage in the rivers of human continuity where despair is invariably defeated by hope. I have often thought that human greatness might be ascribed as the consistent victory of hope over memory.

There were many people standing under the arch looking at the flame. Some were there from curiosity but it seemed to me that there were others who had come for the same reason I had.

I was in war with my friend Capa — I know something of fighting — that final admission that we as peoples do not from intelligence. And because I knew something of fighting ; mind left Capa and went to the men of the Fortress — the weight of numbers pressing in on them. Being good

The manuscript for a tribute to war photojournalist Robert Capa, killed by a land mine in Vietnam in May 1954, that Steinbeck wrote as the second piece in his 1954 column "One American in Paris" (Center for Steinbeck Studies, San Jose State University)

2.

soldiers they did their duty as their training taught them to do. They did not ask to go there. They were sent. And they must have felt that help would come. All they had to do was to hold on until help came. And always the enemy crept closer and closer. The soldiers had their pride, their unity and only the necessity for holding on. They could not know — indeed I do not think they would permit themselves to know that the outside world from which their help must come, was arguing, bickering over who should do what and how and when. I think the soldiers might have been impatient with us if they had known. And when their bravery could not match numbers, and rain and the weight of ~~armament~~ weapons, — what then — what do they think of us now. What do their mothers, their brothers and sisters think of us now.

I do not ~~know~~ understand enough about world politics to know how they might have been saved. I only know they should have been saved — and that no blame attaches to them — only to us.

The flame under the arch gutters and flares in the breeze fed by french blood and french bravery. ~~Isn't~~ It is an unhappy thing that we, in our comfort and security, lost the fortress, not the men who defended it. Standing at the flame I found myself angry at myself and the other millions of complacent men mis' mit

I looked at the people who had come to be warmed and comforted and reassured by the little flame — over it the ~~quet~~ the arched stone record of France's greatness and under it the breeze whipped fiery flag. And I did take comfort from

3

it as those others did. In the hugeness of our stupidity and cowardice we must always come to ~~the little flame~~ warm our souls at the little fire of human beauty and greatness and to add our prayer that it may never go out. And I thought how again the flame has been given new fuel of ~~the~~ blood. I wish the ~~men~~ soldiers – those who are living could know it still burns. They ~~may~~ must be wondering now. And I wish the men of party and the men of power who make the decisions or fail to – would go to the arch and warm their souls at the blood fed fire. It couldn't do them any harm and they might catch a little greatness from it.

My friend Capa was a good and a brave man. I will go to the flame often now because he too has given it a little fuel to keep it burning. Now and then this summer I will take a few ~~time~~ flowers to the Arch – not for the soldiers but for myself because since I am one of the living, I ~~am~~ also am guilty of the past and responsible to the future.

I saw a little boy sent to buy bread and he carried the long loaf ~~over~~ on his shoulder. Then I saw him stiffen~~t~~ and start to march. His bread had become a rifle and he was a soldier of France. Under his breath he muttered ta–ra–ta–ra–ta–ra. He marched past the entrance to the Palace of the President of France. And as he passed, the guard in full dress uniform, saluted him and he returned the salute with ~~great~~ dignity.

⧺

Wrath. I write all kinds of stuff. I will not again follow their rules. They can accept or reject, but I will not work it over and over until it sounds like Quent Reynolds. I will send many pieces. No two will be alike. They understood this or said they did. I'm not a bit upset by this. In fact I anticipated it. They will have plenty to choose from but they will have to choose, not create. If they reject, we'll try to sell it elsewhere and if no one wants it we'll throw it away.

It is certain that we have changed our plans. We changed them to match conditions we didn't know about in advance. Pat [Covici] writes saying I should go to Israel, Manning [Gordon Manning, a *Collier's* editor] thinks I should go to the Slovak border. I am going to the Jura. If they think I am hanging around Paris too long—let them. I have been gathering a sense of Europe here. I know where to go now and what for. I could not have known without coming here. This is not a city desk assignment. This is no quarrel—only a restatement of an understanding.

I don't know whether the second piece I just sent off will be acceptable to Colliers either, nor the piece on the Jura but I'll do them anyway. Elaine is working hard with the camera but there is no way for her to learn. They want her to send in the undeveloped film and she never hears how it comes out. There is no way to correct a mistake if you don't know what it is. This sounds like a beefing letter and in a way it is, but now it is over.

We took a trial run in the little car yesterday (named "*Aux Armes O Citroën*") and it is very good.

We feel pretty good. There is a kind of weariness from seeing too much and trying to take in too much. But there's not any help for that.

I hope you had fun in Maine.

I'm sending a box of things for Catbird on his birthday but I'll try to send them by hand so he will surely get them.

Love and kisses to everyone,
John
—*Steinbeck: A Life in Letters*, pp. 445–446

* * *

Steinbeck to Otis, 2 June 1952

Steinbeck wrote Otis from Geneva in June with a lively account of his and Elaine's travel experiences.

Dear Elizabeth:

Now how did it get to be that date? I have the old duality—time has flown and at the same time we have been away forever.

We drove out of Paris in the little car Aux Armes. It behaves beautifully. Stayed the first night in Dijon where the streets are not paved with mustard. The second day we drove to Poligny in the Jura. Do you remember Louis Gibry to whom you once sent fruit trees? Well they are all

growing and their branches are being used to graft other trees so that the original trees you sent are spreading all over. He lives in a little old house in a peasant street, no plumbing, no inside toilet, three little girls, two hunting dogs, flies, crumbs, bees from the hives in the yard, shouting of neighbors and birds, street full of cows, a fine dust of manure over everything. He would not hear of our going to a hotel. We had his guest room. We went into the wine caves, visited every one and were visited by everyone. If you didn't watch carefully the dogs got your dinner—the whole place crawling with children. Wines were brought in from the bottoms of cellars. We went to tiny towns famous for wines and drank the best and ate cheese and loaves of bread as long as ourselves. We heard much talk. Elaine took many pictures.

Yesterday we pried ourselves loose against protest and proceeded to Geneva. We were filthy—we do not know how to keep clean with bowl and pitcher and cold water. We and the car were deep in cow manure. And we landed in this sweet and immaculate country. In Paris we met Faye Emerson and she had just come from here. She said, "Remember how you always heard of a place where you could eat off the floor? Well, I've just seen it." As for us, we had just come from the Jura where you can barely eat off the table. We got in and began taking baths, one after another. I finally have the odor of cheese, cows, people, dogs and wine caves off me and all my clothes are being cleaned.

We both suddenly became homesick last week. It is the proper time for it. It usually happens at three months. I think it was all the children in Louis Gibry's house that did it. It surely was not the backyard toilet. However, we will get over that.

Later: We have been walking all over Geneva all day and our feet are tired and hot and now we are about to dip into a martini which is a specific for tired feet. There is one very nice thing about this city—absolutely nothing of a lively nature to do at night. The result is that we are getting some sleep. I ordered a double martini of course—half for each foot.

My French gets worse every day as it gets more fluent. A man in a shop today after listening to me a while said in well-modulated English, "What in hell are you trying to say?" I guess I was being too subtle.

In Paris we knew every second person we saw. Here we have not seen a soul of our acquaintance. What a joy it is, at least for a change.

I know there is no great need to keep in touch. But it does bother me. I guess it is largely the constant and never-changing sense of impending tragedy concerning the boys. I wish I could lose that. But I never have.

Last night we had a lovely dinner on the terrace of this hotel which practically hangs over the lake. It was incredibly beautiful and the evening went on for hours.

John
—*Steinbeck: A Life in Letters*, pp. 448–451

Remembering Robert Capa

Photojournalist Robert Capa was killed in 1954 while on assignment in Vietnam. Steinbeck wrote this tribute to his friend and Russian Journal *(1948) collaborator, which was published in a posthumous collection of Capa's work,* Images of War *(1964).*

I know nothing about photography. What I have to say about Capa's is strictly from the point of view of a layman, and the specialists must bear with me. It does seem to me that Capa has proved beyond all doubt that the camera need not be a cold mechanical device. Like the pen, it is as good as the man who uses it. It can be the extension of mind and heart.

Capa's pictures were made in his brain—the camera only completed them. You can no more mistake his work than you can the canvas of a fine painter. Capa knew what to look for and what to do with it when he found it. He knew, for example, that you cannot photograph war because it is largely an emotion. But he did photograph that emotion by shooting beside it. He could show the horror of a whole people in the face of a child. His camera caught and held emotion.

Capa's work is itself the picture of a great heart and an overwhelming compassion. No one can take his place. No one can take the place of any fine artist, but we are fortunate to have in his pictures the quality of the man.

I worked and traveled with Capa a great deal. He may have had closer friends but he had none who loved him more. It was his pleasure to seem casual and careless about his work. He was not. His pictures are not accidents. The emotion in them did not come by chance. He could photograph motion and gaiety and heartbreak. He could photograph thought. He made a world and it was Capa's world.

The greatness of Capa is twofold. We have his pictures, a true and vital record of our time—ugly and beautiful, set down by the mind of an artist. But Capa had another work which may be even more important. He gathered young men about him, encouraged, instructed, even fed and clothed them; but, best, he taught them respect for their art and integrity in its performance. He proved to them that a man can live by this medium and still be true to himself. And never once did he try to get them to take his kind of picture. Thus the effect of Capa will be found in the men who worked with him. They will carry a little part of Capa all their lives and perhaps hand him on to their young men.

It is very hard to think of being without Capa. I don't think I have accepted that fact yet. But I suppose we should be thankful that there is so much of him with us still.

—"Robert Capa: An Appreciation by John Steinbeck," in Capa, *Images of War* (New York: Grossman, 1964), p. 7

Sweet Thursday (1954)

A Narrow-Gauge Dickens
Hugh Holman

Hugh Holman reviewed Sweet Thursday *(1954), the sequel to* Cannery Row *(1945), for* The New Republic.

John Steinbeck's latest novel, *Sweet Thursday,* is both a sequel to *Cannery Row* and an implicit comment on Steinbeck's career—a career which has been one of the most baffling in recent literary history. He has appeared to be a naturalist of the Biological Determination persuasion and a celebrator of the simple joys of life; the author of effective social propaganda and of mystically symbolic and wryly comic parables. Certainly a fair portion of those who read him as a social critic in the 1930's are not among the still large numbers who read him as a writer of picaresque comedy or of romantic parables.

Among the fifteen volumes of his prose fiction that preceded *Sweet Thursday,* Steinbeck has produced an impressive strike novel *(In Dubious Battle),* a powerfully effective propaganda novel *(The Grapes of Wrath),* three stylized experiments with plays in novel form *(Of Mice and Men, The Moon Is Down,* and *Burning Bright),* a volume of distinguished short stories *(The Long Valley),* an "epic" prose poem of too great length *(East of Eden),* and a group of picaresque, comic novels on the delights of poverty and lawlessness *(The Pastures of Heaven, Tortilla Flat, Cannery Row,* and *The Wayward Bus).*

The ideas which help to shape these books are as diverse as the books themselves. They include a pervasive and informed interest in marine biology, a fund of late transcendental mysticism, a Rousseauistic belief in the innate goodness of man and the inherent evil of social systems, a faith in social progress through better social structures, and an anti-intellectualism so intense that it is most likely to find truth in the mouths of half-wits and the demented.

These ideas, together with remnants of Steinbeck's earlier interests are discernible in *Sweet Thursday,* together with an added concern about writing and an attack on current standards of criticism. The novel is the account of the return of Doc, the marine biologist, to Cannery Row in Monterey after the war, his attempt to deal with his loneli-

JOHN STEINBECK

Sweet
Thursday

PS
3537
T3334
.S8
1

1954

THE VIKING PRESS · NEW YORK

Title page for Steinbeck's sequel to Cannery Row, *published in 1945 (Thomas Cooper Library, University of South Carolina)*

ness through scientific experiment and the writing of an article, and the way that Mack and the boys from the Palace Flophouse and the girls from the Bear Flag brothel, through the inspired instrumentality of the half-wit Hazel, bring together Doc and Suzy, a hustler from the Bear Flag. This plot is certainly older than the soil on which it is laid; the basic tone of the novel is the charmingly picaresque folksiness for which *Cannery Row* has prepared us, and the optimism about man's basic nature is consistently that which Doc expresses when he tells an insane but suggestively Christ-like "seer," "I'm surprised they don't lock you up—a reasonable man. It's one of the symptoms of our time to find danger in men like you who don't worry and rush about. Particularly dangerous are men who don't think the world's coming to an end."

These elements entitle us to dismiss *Sweet Thursday* as a minor episode in an erratic career. But the biologist Doc often seems suggestive of his author in his interests, his dilemma, and his statements about life; and the comments on writing are too consistent to be casual; while the tone of half-disparaging banter often seems directed against the author himself. These qualities encourage us to look at the book as one in which Steinbeck has taken a trial balance on his career—implicitly if not explicitly.

Steinbeck apparently cares little for much of our contemporary fiction, and he criticizes it for a quality he was once thought to have—that of blood, darkness, and symbolic evil. Joe Elegant, the cook at Bear Flag, is writing a modern symbolic novel, *The Pi Root of Oedipus,* filled with myth, Freudian symbols, and a grandmother who "stands for guilt . . . the reality below the reality."

Doc is tormented by the question: "What has my life meant so far, and what can it mean in the time left to me?" He is haunted by a sense of debt: "Men seem to be born with a debt they can never pay no matter how hard they try. It piles up ahead of them. Man owes something to man." He declares this to be his objective, a goal which his creator seems to share: "I want to take everything I've seen and thought and learned and reduce them and relate them and refine them until I have something of meaning, something of use." His attempt to do this through scientific writing appears doomed to failure, but the efforts of his friends force him into realizing it through action and human relationship. Yet the answer, when he finally arrives at it, seems to be:

> "What did Bach have that I am hungry for to the point of starvation? Wasn't it gallantry? And isn't gallantry the great art of the soul? Is there any more noble quality in the human than gallantry? . . . Everyone has something. And what has Suzy got? Absolutely nothing in the world but guts. She's taken on an atomic world with a slingshot, and, by God, she's going to win! If she doesn't win there's no point in living any more."

Set briefly against Cannery Row is Prairie Grove, a typical bourgeois community, against which Steinbeck levels two chapters of obvious satire which tend to spoil the tone of the book at the same time that they point up with unconscious irony the extent to which Steinbeck's characters develop bourgeois patterns for their own lives. The whores from the Bear Flag cherish and cultivate the middle class virtues however much they may depart from middle class ideas of morality. Mack and the boys from the Palace Flophouse, in their sense of social structure and social obligation, seem to differ from the unhappy people of Prairie Grove most in that they are warm, loving, and happy; so that these social and economic grotesques serve finally not to condemn the total social structure (as one feels that they were intended to do) but to criticize its failures through the examples they yield of success.

This book, however thin and unconvincing its central situation is, does make an emphatic and clear-cut statement of Steinbeck's greatest single theme: the common bonds of humanity and love which make goodness and happiness possible. The Christ-like seer declares, "There are some things a man can't do alone. I wouldn't think of trying anything so big . . . without love."

W. H. Frohock has pointed out that Steinbeck's characters are all essentially the same good, improvident, and gentle folk, and that they are happy, as in *Cannery Row,* or miserable, as in *The Grapes of Wrath,* depending upon the degree of external pressure exerted upon them. The point is valid. Steinbeck seems to see man as basically noble, with a gentle goodness like that pictured in *Sweet Thursday.* Without the pressure of social indignation he writes of such men in idyls of pastoral happiness. He can, too, portray with fury the distortions of this goodness and the piteous suffering which society can inflict. But he shares with Charles Dickens the failure to subject his people under either situation to an organized and logically consistent philosophy. Louis Cazamian has called Dickens' solution *"une forme vague et sentimentale du socialisme chrétien,"* which was rooted in human love and sympathy on the individual level. Steinbeck's solution may well be called *"socialisme chrétien"* too.

The comparison with Dickens is more than casual. Steinbeck is a modern Dickens, limited in range and theme, a narrow-gauge Dickens, but properly in the tradition of sentimental social criticism of which Dickens is the greatest master. The parallels between the men are interesting. Both are notoriously tender-spirited, sensitive to suffering, easily moved to pity, forgiving of weakness and failure, the fascinated and marvelously successful portrayers of children and child-like states of mind. Both have made sympathetic use of the wisdom of the demented.

Hazel in *Sweet Thursday* with his fear of having to be President has striking parallels to Mr. Dick and his King Charles' head. Both writers are keenly sensitive to social and economic injustice, without maintaining any really consistent framework within which to judge it. The failure to recognize or to follow the party-line in Steinbeck strike novel, *In Dubious Battle,* a failure he justified by saying of men such as his characters, "They don't believe in ideologies . . . They do what they can under the circumstances," is comparable to the "plague on all your systems" attitude in Dickens' fictional social tract, *The Chimes.*

Steinbeck shares with Dickens, too, a tendency to picture eccentrics and grotesques, a fascination with the abnormal in people, and a delight in folk speech. *Sweet Thursday* consists almost exclusively of grotesques: Fauna, who left a Mission to become madam of the Bear Flag (her real name was Flora); Joseph and Mary Rivas, a Mexican in the rogue tradition; Mack, who recites snatches from Shakespeare, Tennyson, and the Bible; the "seer," who can't resist candy bars; Hazel, the half-wit who worries because his horoscope says he will be President. Every one of them moves with Dickensian extravagance; everyone is presented with Dickensian verve; not one, I hazard a guess, would Dickens have scorned.

Dickens' two most effective novels for contemporary readers are probably *Bleak House,* with its passionate indictment of social injustice through the imbittered [sic] examination of one institution, and *David Copperfield,*

Steinbeck and Elaine in Rome, fall 1954 (John Steinbeck Collection, Stanford University Library; from Jackson J. Benson,
The True Adventures of John Steinbeck, Writer, *1984; Thomas Cooper Library, University of South Carolina)*

wherein goodness and warmth and humanity, particularly among the lowly and the simple, are celebrated. And always the imperishable but unreal glow of transcendent goodness gleams through Dickens' Christmas books. Steinbeck's *The Grapes of Wrath* is comparable to *Bleak House* both in its indictment of society and in its lack of a solution. *Tortilla Flat* and *The Long Valley* echo the nostalgic charm of *David Copperfield*. It is probably coincidence that both men were fascinated by the drama in their middle years, but I believe it is no coincidence that *Cannery Row* and *Sweet Thursday* belong in the same world of bright dreams that Dickens' Christmas books belong in: they are beautiful to contemplate, they are inspiriting, but they are not dependable indices to any actuality we may ever meet.

I think we have been wrong about Steinbeck. We have let his social indignation, his verisimilitude of language, his interest in marine biology lead us to judge him as a naturalist. Judged by the standards of logical consistency which naturalism demands, his best books are weak and his poorer books are hopeless. Steinbeck is more nearly a twentieth century Dickens of California, a social critic with more sentiment than science or system, warm, human, inconsistent, occasionally angry but more often delighted with the joys that life on its lowest levels presents. I think *Sweet Thursday* implicitly asks its readers to take its author on such terms. If these terms are less than we thought we had reason to hope for from *The Grapes of Wrath*, they are still worthy of respect.

—*New Republic*, 130 (7 June 1954); reprinted in *John Steinbeck: The Contemporary Reviews*, pp. 407–410

* * *

Steinbeck to Oscar Hammerstein 2nd, October 1955

Pipe Dream, the musical adaptation of Sweet Thursday *by Richard Rodgers and Oscar Hammerstein 2nd, opened for tryouts in New Haven on 24 October 1955, but initial enthusiasm for the play soon began to fade. After at first restraining himself, Steinbeck wrote Rodgers and Hammerstein (who also produced the show) a series of long letters with suggestions for improvement. After the Boston opening, which met with disappointing notices, he wrote Hammerstein.*

Dear Oscar:

The day after we opened in New Haven I wrote a kind of a report for you, but it wasn't the proper time. You were heavily preoccupied with getting the show open at all. Now it does seem to me to be the proper time. If changes are to be made, they must be in the works.

There are many very excellent things in Pipe Dream. If I do not dwell on them it is because you hear them everywhere and this letter purports to be a working document and not either a criticism or a flattery. I do not think this is a time to spare feelings nor to mince words. Compliments for the good things have sunk many works

including my own late lamented play *[Burning Bright]* which you will remember with a certain horror. Good people came to me after it had closed and told me what should have been done, and working on it by myself I only discovered completely what was wrong a year and a half later. And the crazy thing was that audiences were telling us all the time. And audiences are telling us now. We should listen! Your face is very well known so it may be that conversations stop when you are near. But mine isn't. They don't stop talking when I go by.

Norton [Boston critic Eliot Norton] used the word *conventional* to describe his uneasiness. I have heard others describe the same thing as sweetness, loss of toughness, lack of definition, whatever people say when they feel they are being let down. And believe me, Oscar, this is the way audiences feel. What emerges now is an old fashioned love story. And that is not good enough to people who have looked forward to this show based on you and me and Dick. When Oklahoma came out it violated every conventional rule of Musical Comedy. You were out on a limb. They loved it and were for you. South Pacific made a great jump. And even more you were ordered to go ahead. But Oscar, time has moved. The form has moved. You can't stand still. That's the price you have to pay for being Rodgers and Hammerstein.

Dust jacket for the 1956 edition of the book and lyrics for the 1955 musical adaptation of Steinbeck's sequel to Cannery Row *(from Robert B. Harmon,* The Collectible John Steinbeck, *1986; Thomas Cooper Library, University of South Carolina)*

The only thing this story has, besides some curious characters, is the almost tragic situation that a man of high mind and background and culture takes to his breast an ignorant, ill-tempered little hooker who isn't even very good at that. He has to take her, knowing that a great part of it is going to be misery, and she has to take him knowing she will have to live the loneliness of not even knowing what he is talking about if the subject gets above the belt, and yet each of them knows that the worse hell is the penalty of separation.

I have suggestions for changing every one of the things attacked in this letter, Oscar. I think they are important or I would not go out on a limb for them. Will you think about them and then perhaps submit them to some outside person who is not too close to the show, someone like Josh [Joshua Logan] or maybe Lillian Hellman, or maybe Norton, anyone who knows theatre, whom you respect and whose word you can trust. I hope you will do this. I think we are in danger, not of failure but of pale and half-assed success which to me would be worse than failure. In a word we are in grave danger of mediocrity.

Should I run for the hills now?

yours in the faith

John

—Steinbeck: A Life in Letters, pp. 516–517

Steinbeck on Other Writers

Steinbeck to Sheffield, 10 September 1952

In the following letter to his old friend Sheffield, Steinbeck indicates that he has read Ernest Hemingway's The Old Man and the Sea *(1952).*

Dear Dook:

Did I answer your card written last Feb? I think I did but I have come to put little faith in those things I think I did.

Fifty is a good age. The hair recedes, the paunch grows a little, the face—rarely inspected, looks the same to us but not to others. The little inabilities grow so gradually that we don't even know it. My hangovers are less bad maybe because I drink better liquor. But enough of this 50 talk.

We had the grand tour—six months of it and I liked it very well. I'm glad to be back. We have a pretty little house here and every day is full. Very nice and time races by. When you really live in New York, it is more rural than country. Your district is a village and you go to Times Square as once you went to San Francisco. I do pretty much work and as always—90 percent of it is thrown out. I cut more deeply than I used to which means that I overwrite more than I used to. I cut 90,000

words out of my most recent book [East of Eden] but I think it's a pretty good book. It was a hard one. But they're all hard. And if I want to know I'm fifty, all I have to do is look at my titles—so god-damned many of them. I'll ask Pat [Covici] to send you a copy of the last one. To see if you like it or not.

In Paris I wrote a picture script based on an early play of Ibsen's called The Vikings at Helgoland—not very well known—a roaring melodrama, cluttered and verbose but with the great dramatic construction and character relationships he later cleaned up. Anyway—I shook out the clutter and I think it will make a good picture.

Have three more articles to complete for Colliers to finish my agreement with them. Then I want to learn something about plays, so I'm going to try to plunge into that form this winter. You may look for some colossal flops. But I do maintain that gigantic stupidity that will let me try it.

Your life sounds good to me. I have the indolence for it but have never been able to practice it. Too jittery and nervous. And yet every instinct aims toward just such a life. I guess I inherited from my mother the desire to do four things at once.

I am gradually accumulating a library which would delight you I think. It's a library of words—all dictionaries—12 vol. Oxford, all of Mencken, folklore, Americanisms, dic. of slang—many—and then all books and monographs on words. I find I love words very much. And gradually I am getting a series of dictionaries of modern languages. The crazy thing about all this is that I don't use a great variety of words in my work at all. I just love them for themselves. The long and specialized words are not very interesting because they have no history and no family. But a word like claw or land or host or foist—goes back and back and has relatives in all directions. A negro scholar is completing a volume on all the African words in the American language. He has about 10,000 so far, some of them unchanged in meaning or form from their Zulu or Gold Coast sources. I must write to him and try to get a copy.

Just read Hemingway's new book. A very fine performance. I am so glad. The obscene joy with which people trampled him on the last one was disgusting. Now they are falling too far the other way almost in shame. The same thing is going to happen to me with my new book. It is the best work I've done but a lot of silly things are going to be said about it. Unthoughtful flattery is, if anything, more insulting than denunciation.

This has gone on quite a long time now.

Anyway, let me know what you think of the new work.

So long,

J

—Steinbeck: A Life in Letters, pp. 456–457

* * *

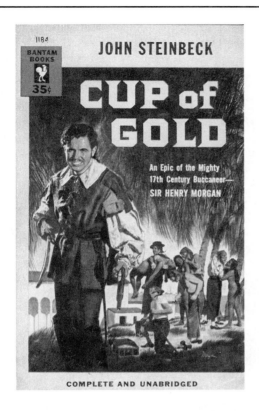

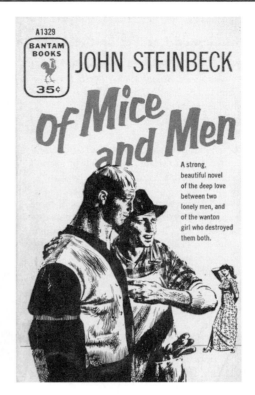

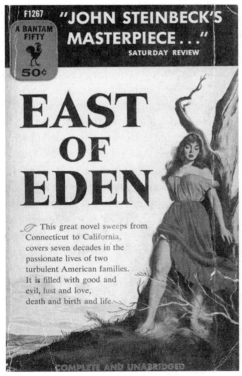

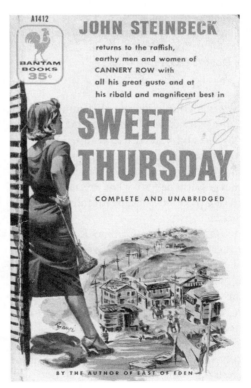

Front covers of Steinbeck paperback editions published in the mid 1950s (Bruccoli Clark Layman Archives)

"Stupid Untalented Leeches on the Arts"

When his friend John O'Hara's The Farmers Hotel *(1951) received poor reviews, Steinbeck wrote on 26 November 1951 to cheer him up. Steinbeck also noted that he faced a daunting task ahead in revising* East of Eden.

Dear John:

Don't let these neat, dry, cautious, stupid untalented leeches on the arts get you down. It's a hell of a good book. I wrote a letter to the Times differing with Miss Janeway.

They just won't forgive originality and you'll have to get used to that. Have you found too that the same people who kicked the hell out of Appointment [*Appointment in Samarra* (1934)] when it came out–now want you to write it over and over?

Hoch der Christmas

love to Belle,

John

I've got one hell of a rewrite job to do.

—Steinbeck: A Life in Letters, p. 432

Steinbeck to Richard Watts Jr., 7 April 1953

In an unusual letter, Steinbeck wrote Richard Watts Jr., drama critic of the New York Post, *to defend Tennessee Williams's* Camino Real *(1953).*

Dear Dick:

I disagree with your criticism of Tennessee Williams' show Camino Real, but I don't intend to let that interfere with an old and valued friendship. There's no reason why you should like a play; there's no reason why I should not like the same play. I found in this one clarity and beauty. I listened to what seemed to me a courageous and fine piece of work, beautifully produced, and filled with excitement.

But apart from the fate of Camino Real, I think a more serious matter is involved. At least twice a year, every critic, during the dead period, writes a piece bemoaning the lack of courage, of imagination, of innovation in the American theatre. This being so, it is my opinion that when a play of courage, imagination and invention comes along, the critics should draw this to the attention of the theatre-goer. It becomes clear that when innovation and invention automatically draw bad notices, any backer will be cautious of investment, and furthermore will not playwrights stop experimenting if their plays will not be produced?

The democracy of art does not require universal acclaim. In fact instant acceptance is often a diagnostic of inferiority.

I hope you will find it in your heart to print this letter. I am not an investor, nor am I involved in the production but both you and I are amply involved in the survival and growth of the American Theatre.

See you soon, I hope. Yours in continued friendship and admiration.

John Steinbeck
—Steinbeck: A Life in Letters, p. 471

* * *

Steinbeck to Otis, 21 April 1954

During his and Elaine's tour of Spain in the spring of 1954, Steinbeck was particularly interested in Miguel de Cervantes, an interest that might have influenced his later writing of Travels with Charley: In Search of America *(1962). He wrote his agent Elizabeth Otis from Seville, where Cervantes once lived.*

Dear Elizabeth:

Can't seem to stay awake very much. But when luncheon is at 2:30 and dinner doesn't start until 10, it kind of cuts the day wrong for my training.

A few quotes for your pleasure. Written with black chalk on a wall–"Luisa, he who writes this is leaving you forever." On hotel porch an American woman and her little boy. Spaniard asked, "Do you like the bull fight?" Woman–"We haven't seen them but I'm sure we will like them. You see my husband is a doctor so we are used to all that." Wouldn't you like to go to her husband for an office call? Over the horns with a scalpel. A new dicho or at least one I had never heard regarding drinking strong liquor. "El primero con agua, la segunda sin agua, el tercero como agua." The first with water, the second without water, the third like water. And it's true.

Am rereading Cervantes. He lived here and was in prison here and the city has not greatly changed. The little square where we drink beer and eat shrimps he mentions many times. The prison where he served was about a block from the bull ring and his window looked out on the Tower of Gold which is still there.

Also the habits of the gypsies have not changed. This morning I was sitting on a wall by the river when a gypsy asked to shine my shoes for a peseta. As he finished he caught his cloth under my rubber heel and ripped it off. It was a good trick. He then put on a new heel for 20 pesetas. Then he asked if I would like a new heel on the other shoe. It had taken me a long time to catch on. I told him one was a lesson but two would be an insult. I told him that for the first heel he would get 20 pesetas but for the second 20 days in jail. We ended good friends. In a way I love the gypsies. They are so uncompromisingly dishonest. Never for a moment do they fall into probity.

THE PIERPONT MORGAN LIBRARY
29 East 36th Street
New York 16, N. Y.

Dec. 20 1956

To the Director,

Sir:

I have read the rules established by the Trustees for the use of the Library and its collections, and in accordance with them, I hereby apply for reader's privileges in the Library.

Name _John Steinbeck_

Permanent address _206 E. 72._

New York address _New York City_

School, business or other affiliation _____

Purpose for which reader's privileges are requested (be specific) _Inspection of Malory ms and any other material pertinent to Arthurian cycle including microfilm_

Date or period for which admission is requested (not to exceed one year) _One year_

References (with supporting letter)
Viking Press, New York.

Signature _John Steinbeck_

Staff approval _____

Steinbeck's application for reader's privileges at the Pierpont Morgan Library, New York (courtesy of the Pierpont Morgan Library; from Robert J. DeMott, Steinbeck's Reading: A Catalogue of Books Owned and Borrowed, *1984; Thomas Cooper Library, University of South Carolina)*

The weather continues wonderful and we are getting a little afraid it will rain for the Feria. It did last year and completely washed it out. That would be a shame.

I'm going to the Archives of the Indies tomorrow and try to get a look at the Columbian documents. They are all here. The bones of the old boy are supposed to be in the Cathedral, in a great bronze casket carried on the shoulders of bronze kings and bishops. But then, said bones are supposed to be in lots of places.

I wonder what's the matter with me? I want to sleep all the time.

Love to all,
John
—*Steinbeck: A Life in Letters,* pp. 475–476

Chapter Seven: 1956–1962

Chronology

Early February 1956	Steinbeck and Elaine return to Sag Harbor after a winter vacation in Trinidad, and Steinbeck works on an experimental novel he calls "Pi Root."
March 1956	Steinbeck's short story "How Mr. Hogan Robbed a Bank" is published in *The Atlantic*. He is writing a satirical work, published the following year as *The Short Reign of Pippin IV: A Fabrication*.
April 1956	Steinbeck agrees to cover the year's national political conventions for the Louisville *Courier-Journal*.
May 1956	In Louisville to attend the Kentucky Derby, Steinbeck is introduced to Alicia Patterson Guggenheim and her husband, Harry F. Guggenheim, at the home of the publisher of the *Courier-Journal*. This meeting leads to Steinbeck's writing for the Long Island newspaper *Newsday* in the mid 1960s.
14 July 1956	Waverly Scott, Elaine's daughter from her first marriage, is married to Frank Skinner.
August 1956	"The Mail I've Seen" is published in the 4 August *Saturday Review*. In this article Steinbeck discourages teachers from having their students write authors for comments on their work. He and Elaine attend the Democratic National Convention so that he can report on it for the *Courier-Journal*. He confers with the eventual nominee, Adlai Stevenson. Later in the month the Steinbecks attend the Republican National Convention in San Francisco. Afterward Steinbeck sends speech material to the Stevenson campaign.
September 1956	During the election campaign Steinbeck writes speeches and broadcast programs for Radio Free Europe and the United States Information Agency.

Steinbeck, Elaine, Thom, and Shirley Fisher, a Long Island neighbor and agent with McIntosh and Otis, circa 1961
(from Jackson J. Benson, The True Adventures of John Steinbeck, Writer, *1984;*
Thomas Cooper Library, University of South Carolina)

October 1956	Steinbeck becomes involved with the Dwight D. Eisenhower administration's People to People program. As a member of a writer's committee, Steinbeck helps in drafting statements about world conditions.
November 1956	After finishing *The Short Reign of Pippin IV,* Steinbeck decides to work on recasting Sir Thomas Malory's *Le Morte Darthur* (1485) in simple, modern prose without altering the original stories. On 6 November, Eisenhower is reelected president.
January 1957	The Steinbecks plan a trip to Europe for research on the Malory project. The journey will be financed by Steinbeck's writing articles for the *Courier-Journal.*
March–April 1957	Steinbeck, Elaine, and his younger sister, Mary Steinbeck Dekker, sail for Naples aboard the *Saturnia* on 25 March. During visits to Florence and Rome, Steinbeck gathers material on Malory while Elaine takes photographs for a projected *Holiday* article on Florentine craftsmanship. Viking Press publishes *The Short Reign of Pippin IV* in April, and it is named a Book-of-the-Month Club selection. Steinbeck's article "A Game of Hospitality" is published in the 20 April *Saturday Review.* In it he criticizes American immigration officials who will not allow foreign writers into the country because their work is considered leftist. Late in April, Steinbeck meets Robert Wallsten, an actor turned writer whom he had first met at the opening of *Burning Bright* (1950), in Florence.

Steinbeck's sister Mary Steinbeck Dekker, Steinbeck, and Elaine aboard the Saturnia *celebrating Mary's birthday, 1957 (John Steinbeck Library, Salinas; from Jackson J. Benson,* The True Adventures of John Steinbeck, Writer, *1984; Thomas Cooper Library, University of South Carolina)*

June 1957	The Steinbecks travel to Paris and then on to London for a week before continuing to Denmark and Sweden. In Stockholm they visit Dag Hammarskjöld and the artist Bo Beskow, who paints a third portrait of Steinbeck. They then return to England, where Steinbeck meets Eugène Vinaver, a professor of French language and literature at the University of Manchester and the world's leading authority on Malory. The two become friends, and Vinaver agrees to help Steinbeck with his Malory project.
July 1957	The Steinbecks tour Malory country, taking notes and photographs. On the 25th they sail for home on the *Queen Elizabeth*.
September 1957	Steinbeck flies to Tokyo to attend a meeting of PEN International, where he gives a brief speech and catches the flu, delaying his return to the United States. Late in the month he returns to Sag Harbor and resumes his work on Malory.
November 1957	The Steinbecks move into a house on Seventy-second Street in New York, where Steinbeck continues his work on Malory's *Le Morte Darthur*.
June 1958	The Steinbecks fly to England and spend a month searching for physical traces of Malory's life before returning to Sag Harbor.
23 August 1958	Steinbeck's "The Easiest Way to Die" is published in the *Saturday Review*.
September 1958	Steinbeck sends the completed Malory project to his agent, Elizabeth Otis, and Chase Horton, Otis's friend and owner of the Washington Square Bookshop in New York, who had originally suggested the project to Steinbeck. Their response is lukewarm. Viking Press publishes *Once There Was a War,* a collection of Steinbeck's World War II dispatches written in Europe and North Africa.
October 1958	Steinbeck decides to set aside the Malory book and starts work on what he calls a modern Western with the working title "Don Keehan."
November–December 1958	Steinbeck works on "Don Keehan" but becomes dissatisfied with the first draft. He tries to rewrite it several times but finally gives up on the entire work, deciding instead to resume his Malory project with another research trip to England.
February 1959	The Steinbecks set out for England. During the trip they meet writer Erskine Caldwell and his wife, Virginia.
Summer 1959	During their stay in England the Steinbecks receive guests such as Elia Kazan, Stevenson, Dekker, and Wallsten and his wife, Cynthia.
Mid October 1959	The Steinbecks return from Somerset, in southwestern England, to their New York home, and Steinbeck comes down with a kidney infection.
3 December 1959	Steinbeck suffers a stroke and is hospitalized for two weeks.
January 1960	Steinbeck and Elaine spend two weeks at Caneel Bay, on the island of St. John, for his recovery.
February 1960	Steinbeck completes several essays for the *Saturday Review*.
March 1960	Steinbeck again puts aside the Malory project and begins work on what is to be his last novel, *The Winter of Our Discontent* (1961).
June 1960	Steinbeck has a truck specially modified as a camper for a planned cross-country trip. He names the vehicle *Rocinante,* in honor of Don Quixote's horse.
Mid July 1960	Steinbeck completes the manuscript of *The Winter of Our Discontent*.
September–October 1960	Steinbeck sets out on his journey in *Rocinante* on 23 September with his and Elaine's poodle, Charley. He starts out in the northeast and continues to the Midwest, gathering

	material for an account of the trip that is published as *Travels with Charley: In Search of America* in 1962.
8 November 1960	John F. Kennedy is elected president.
January 1961	From the Midwest, Steinbeck travels to the western states and then on to the West Coast, where he meets Elaine in Seattle. They then travel down the coast before Elaine flies on to Texas, where Steinbeck joins her later. After brief stays in New Orleans and Alabama, the Steinbecks head back home to New York. On 20 January they attend Kennedy's inauguration.
February 1961	The Steinbecks vacation in the Caribbean and Barbados. Steinbeck begins work on the manuscript for *Travels with Charley*.
March 1961	Steinbeck leaves for San Diego to serve as an historian for Project Mohole, a scientific expedition to explore the boundary between the earth's crust and the mantle by means of a hole drilled in the seafloor off the coast of Mexico.
April 1961	Steinbeck has to leave Project Mohole and return home, where he is hospitalized for surgery to repair a hernia. *The Winter of Our Discontent* is published by Viking Press and is named a Book-of-the-Month Club selection.
1 September 1961	Steinbeck completes the manuscript for *Travels with Charley*.
October 1961	The Steinbecks travel to Paris, where Elaine is injured in an automobile accident.
25 November 1961	The Steinbecks take a train to Milan, where Steinbeck suffers a heart attack.
December 1961	The Steinbecks travel to Rome, where they spend Christmas. On Christmas Eve they have an audience with Pope John XXIII.

Elaine, Terrence McNally (tutor for the Steinbeck boys and future playwright), Steinbeck, John IV, and Thom sailing for Europe on the Rotterdam, *1961 (from Jackson J. Benson,* The True Adventures of John Steinbeck, Writer, *1984; Thomas Cooper Library, University of South Carolina)*

January–March 1962	Steinbeck continues his European tour even though he is still recovering from his heart attack. He spends much time reading and reflecting.
April 1962	With Steinbeck's health restored, he and Elaine travel extensively in Italy and Greece.
28 May 1962	Steinbeck writes to Otis from his hotel in Mykonos, Greece, telling her that the trip is over and that they are returning to the United States.
June 1962	Viking Press publishes *Travels with Charley,* which receives positive reviews and becomes a Book-of-the-Month Club selection.
October 1962	On this morning of 25 October at their Sag Harbor home, the Steinbecks turn on their television and hear that Steinbeck has been awarded the Nobel Prize in literature. He sends a cable to Anders Österling, secretary of the Swedish Academy, to express his gratitude and makes plans to go to Stockholm. In a 30 October letter to Beskow, Steinbeck reports that he has been overwhelmed with attention from the media, meeting seventy-five reporters and photographers at one time in New York.
November 1962	Steinbeck is busy answering congratulatory messages, which arrive at the rate of hundreds a day. Among his responses are those to his old Stanford friend Carlton A. "Dook" Sheffield, writer John O'Hara, Vinaver, Princess Grace of Monaco, Stevenson, Otis, and Natalya "Tal" Lovejoy, an old friend from Pacific Grove whom he asks for help in finding the address and present name of his first wife, Carol.
December 1962	On 8 December the Steinbecks fly to Stockholm for the Nobel Prize ceremony, held on the 10th. A few days later they fly to London.

With the arrival of the New Year of 1956, Steinbeck was in a jocular mood. He wrote a teasing poem for his wife, Elaine, contrasting her with the Elaine of Arthurian legend:

Now my Miss Elaine got a new-style set,
She a high-breasted deep-breathing growed-up brunette.
She tuck her behind in and she walk real proud,
Got a B flat baritone C sharp loud.
Say, "Listen, you rounders, and you'll agree,
I got me a man and he got me."
She rustle up her bustle and the folks concur,
That she branded her a wrangler and he ear-notched her.

The couple took a winter vacation in Trinidad and returned in early February to Sag Harbor, where Steinbeck resumed work on an experimental novel that he called "Pi Root." Around this time, however, according to Jay Parini in John Steinbeck: A Biography *(1995), he was losing interest in the literary profession that he had been practicing for so long. Nonetheless, Steinbeck kept experimenting with his writing and began a work published the following year as* The Short Reign of Pippin IV: A Fabrication *(1957).*

In New York in April 1956, Steinbeck met with Mark Ethridge, publisher of the Louisville Courier-Journal, *whom he had first met on a return voyage from Europe aboard the* Andrea Doria *two years earlier. Steinbeck agreed to cover the year's national political-party conventions for Ethridge's newspaper. Later in the month, Ethridge arranged for the*

Steinbecks to visit Louisville during the Kentucky Derby. There Steinbeck met Harry F. and Alicia Patterson Guggenheim, the publishers of Newsday, *the Long Island newspaper that he had been reading on a regular basis while living in Sag Harbor. Their friendship later led to Steinbeck's working as a columnist for the paper during the Vietnam War.*

On 10 August 1956 the Steinbecks flew to Chicago for the Democratic National Convention, where Steinbeck met Adlai Stevenson in person for the first time. In the fall Steinbeck had to live up to a promise to write some speeches for the Stevenson campaign. In late November, Steinbeck joined a program called People to People, organized by the Dwight D. Eisenhower administration. The idea was to have prominent Americans make contact with private citizens and prominent people in the countries behind the Iron Curtain. Among the writers on the committee were Faulkner, Edna Ferber, William Carlos Williams, Donald Hall, Robert Hillyer, and Saul Bellow. Steinbeck joined with some reluctance, because in fact the committee had little to do with the Cold War, but he helped draft some proposals. One of the issues discussed was the freeing of Ezra Pound, the poet confined in St. Elizabeth's Hospital in Washington, D.C., for having given aid and support to the enemy while living in Italy during World War II. Concerned about the American public's reaction, Steinbeck argued with Faulkner, chairman of the committee, against the idea of releasing Pound. One issue that Steinbeck did want to discuss was the failure of the United States to aid the refugees from the 1956 Russian invasion of Hungary.

By the time Steinbeck had finished the manuscript of The Short Reign of Pippin IV, *he had decided to work on a simple, modern prose adaptation of Sir Thomas Malory's* Le Morte Darthur *(1485). During a trip to Europe in the spring and summer of 1957 he became concerned with playwright Arthur Miller's indictment for his refusal to testify before the House Committee on Un-American Activities (HUAC). On 16 May, Steinbeck wrote his editor, Pat Covici, expressing his concerns about the fate of writers such as Miller. Later that month the American embassy in Rome held a dinner for about fifty people in Steinbeck's honor, where he met several Italian writers, including Alberto Moravia, who later commented that "Steinbeck seemed to us, somehow, very serious. He was political and philosophical, in his own way. I went to dinner with him at the embassy, and I was impressed. He was grave, but his eyes were very gentle. He didn't say much, but he had courage and dignity."*

From Italy the Steinbecks traveled on to Stockholm, where Steinbeck was introduced to Mikhail Aleksandrovich Sholokhov, the Russian author of The Silent Don *(1928–1940). Steinbeck saw his old friend the painter Bo Beskow and sat for another portrait. He also found time for a long dinner with the writer and diplomat Dag Hammarskjöld, whom he had met several times on previous trips to Sweden and in New York. In England for research on Malory, the Steinbecks met Eugène Vinaver, professor of French language and literature at the University of Manchester. In July the Steinbecks toured Malory country, taking notes and photographs, before returning to the United States.*

Although regretting that he had accepted an invitation to attend a meeting of PEN International in Tokyo, Steinbeck could not think of a way to back out. Seeking advice, he wrote Faulkner, who assured him that all he needed to know was the Japanese custom of gift giving. On 31 August 1957 he left for Tokyo with the writers John Hersey and John Dos Passos. Steinbeck gave a brief speech at the meeting, but his return to the United States was delayed by a case of the flu.

In the spring of 1958 Steinbeck continued his research on Malory and planned another trip to England. In October, however, he set aside the Malory project to begin a "modern Western" titled "Don Keehan." He worked on the manuscript in November and December but finally gave up on the book. In February 1959 the Steinbecks went back to England, spending much of their time in Bruton, Somerset, and returning to New York in October. Steinbeck's work on Le Morte Darthur *was never easy. The frustration came from both his physical health and his too-complicated inten-*

tions for the project. Back in Sag Harbor, he developed a kidney infection and on 3 December suffered a stroke.

In early 1960 Steinbeck put aside the Malory manuscript again to work on several essays for the Saturday Review. *In March he began what was to be his last novel,* The Winter of Our Discontent *(1961). By the summer Steinbeck's mind had become fixed on the idea of a cross-country American trip. In this election year he wanted to travel extensively in order to take the national pulse. In June he had a truck modified as a camper, which he named* Rocinante, *after Don Quixote's horse. On 23 September 1963 he set off in the truck with Charley, his and Elaine's poodle. He headed north through Vermont and up to Maine, filling his notebook with historical reflections, philosophical musings, and narratives about his experiences. He traveled through Pennsylvania and Michigan and then through Illinois, Wisconsin, and Minnesota. After a quick trip to Montana and Washington he turned south to Oregon and California. From there Steinbeck headed east, arriving in Texas, where he met Elaine right before Thanksgiving. He and Charley then continued to New Orleans. Throughout the trip Steinbeck avoided national parks and public monuments, instead choosing places with special significance to him, such as the birthplace of Sinclair Lewis in Sauk Centre, Minnesota, and examining issues such as racial conflict in New Orleans. He completed the entire journey in about eleven weeks, exhausted but pleased that the trip had taught him much about his country and its people.*

The Steinbecks were invited to attend John F. Kennedy's inauguration and did so on 20 January 1961. After a Caribbean vacation Steinbeck began work on the manuscript of Travels with Charley: In Search of America *(1962). In April,* The Winter of Our Discontent *was published by Viking Press and was designated a Book-of-the-Month Club selection. By 1 September, Steinbeck had completed* Travels with Charley. *He and Elaine began another European trip in the fall; in Milan he suffered a heart attack. But the couple continued to Rome, where they planned to spend Christmas. On Christmas Eve they met with Pope John XXIII. Although Steinbeck was still recovering from his heart attack, he and Elaine continued to travel through March 1962.*

On the morning of 25 October 1962 at their Sag Harbor home, the Steinbecks turned on their television for the news and learned that Steinbeck had been awarded the Nobel Prize in literature. He began to receive an enormous amount of media attention and tried to answer as many congratulatory messages as he could. On 8 December the Steinbecks flew to Stockholm for the ceremony, held on the 10th. A few days later they flew to London to spend their Christmas there.

Steinbeck on Writing

Steinbeck to James S. Pope, 16 May 1956

When Steinbeck's friend James S. Pope, editor in chief of the Louisville Courier-Journal, *was asked to deliver the commencement speech for graduation at Emory University, Steinbeck wrote him a letter with a mock address for him to give. He also commented on an interview with William Faulkner that he had recently read. "The Lillymaid" is a reference to Elaine, who was helping her daughter from her first marriage, Waverly Scott, prepare for her upcoming wedding. "Alicia" is Alicia Patterson Guggenheim, publisher of* Newsday.

Dear Jim:

The Lillymaid has gone to Astolat for a couple of days to do for her daughter what her daughter had better pretty soon learn to do for herself or this marriage isn't for eternity. Also she has a yen to get her hair washed. Ain't she a doll? I *like* that dame. But being left alone, this mouse got to playing and wrote twenty-five pages of dialogue today. It was raining anyway.

A letter from Alicia today enclosed an interview with Bill Faulkner which turns my stomach. When those old writing boys get to talking about The Artist, meaning themselves, I want to leave the profession. I don't know whether the Nobel Prize does it or not, but if it does, thank God I have not been so honored. They really get to living up to themselves, wrapped and shellacked. Apparently they can't have any human intercourse again. Bill said he only read Homer and Cervantes, never his contemporaries, and then, by God, in answer to the next question he stole a paragraph from an article I wrote for the Saturday Review eight months ago. Hell, he's better than Homer. Homer couldn't either read or write and the old son of a gun was blind. And Cervantes was broke, a thing Bill never let happen to him while he could go to Hollywood and turn out the Egyptian. THE ARTIST—my ass! Sure he's a good writer but he's turning into a god damned phoney. I guess that got rid of my nastiness and Elaine wouldn't approve of my saying it. That will teach her not to go away.

It's late but I'm not sleepy so I might as well write you a commencement speech, what the hell! Of course if I had to do it myself I'd cut my throat.

I see you sitting in the front row, robed in academic splendor. It is pretty hot and you are sweating under that cape. You sat on your back tassel and pulled it off and shoved it in your pocket and that got your robe caught in your pocket and you can't get it out so you yank at it and out come your keys and a handful of small change. You keep thinking the tassel of your mor-

tarboard is a fly and you swat at it every time it swings in front of your eyes. You wish you hadn't worn nylon drawers. You itch.

Then you hear the President announce.

"And now, I have the honor to present our honored guest, William D. Pope, who has consented to address you."

As you stand up you try to work the nylon drawers out of your crevice by dragging against the little hard chair but it sticks. So you say to yourself, "The hell with it," and you try to get your notes out of your pocket under all the harness you are wearing and you realize that if you did manage to dig them out, you would have to throw your skirts over your head. So what do you do? You advance to the front of the stage and deliver the address I am about to write for you.

COMMENCEMENT ADDRESS BY JAMES S. BISHOP

"President Onassis," you begin. "Honorable Regents, members of the Faculty, without whose loving care this day could not happen (laughter), ladies and gentlemen:"

(Now draw a big deep breath because it is the last one you are going to get as you become caught up in the fire and thunder of your address. And you don't really have to go to the bathroom. It is just your imagination.)

"I suppose you think I am going to give you one of those 'You are going out into the world' speeches.["] (Laughter and cries of 'Hear, Hear.')

"Well, you are perfectly right. You are going out into the world and it is a mess, a frightened, neurotic, gibbering mess. And there isn't anyone out there to help you because all the people who are already out there are in a worse state than you are, because they have been there longer and a good number of them have given up.

"Yes, my young friends, you are going to take your bright and shining faces into a jungle, but a jungle where all the animals are insane. You are going from delinquency to desuetude without even an interlude of healthy vice. You haven't the strength for vice. That takes energy, and all the energy of this time is needed for fear. That takes energy too. And what energy is left over is needed for running down the rabbit holes of hatred, to avoid thought. The rich hate the poor and taxes. The young hate the draft. The Democrats hate the Republicans and everybody hates the Russians. Children are shooting their parents and parents are drowning their children when they think they can get away with it. No one can plan one day ahead because all certainties are gone. War is now generally admitted to be not only unwinnable but actually suicidal and so we think of war and plan for war, and design war and drain our nations of every extra penny of treasure to make the weapons which we admit will destroy us. Generals argue with Secretaries about how much *they*'ve got and how much *we*'ve got to fight the war that is admitted will be the end of all of us.

"And meanwhile there is no money for the dams and the schools and the highways and the housing and the streets for our clotted and festering traffic. That's what you are going out to. Going out? Hell you've been in it for years. And you have to scrape the bottom to avoid thinking. Some of us hate niggers and some of us hate the people who hate niggers and it is all the same thing, anything to keep from thinking. Make money! Spend all of your time trying to avoid taxes, taxes for the 60,000,000,000 dollars for the weapons for the war that is unthinkable.

"Let's face it. We are using this war and this rumor of war to avoid thought. But if you work very hard and are lucky and have a good tax-man, then when you are fifty, if your heart permits, you and your sagging wife can make a tired and bored but first-class trip to Europe to stare at the works of dead people who were not afraid. But you won't see it. You'll be too anxious to get home to your worrying. You'll want to get your blown prostate home in time for your thrombosis. The only exciting thing you can look forward to is a heart attack. And while you have been in Athens on the Acropolis not seeing the Parthenon, you have missed two murders and the nasty divorce of two people you do not know and are not likely to, but you hate to miss it.

"These are your lives, my darlings, if you avoid cancer, plane crashes and automobile accidents. Your lives! Love? A nervous ejaculation while drunk. Romance? An attempt to be mentioned in a column for having accompanied the Carrot Queen to a slaughter house. Fun? Electric canes at a convention. Art? A deep seated wish to crash the Book-of-the-Month-Club. Sport? A television set and a bottle of the proper beer. Ambition? A new automobile every year. Work? A slot in a corporate chain of command. Religion? A private verbal contract with a Deity you don't believe in and a public front pew in your superior's church. Children? Maybe a psychiatrist can keep them out of the detention home.

"Am I boring you, you nervous sons of bitches? Am I keeping you from your mouldy pleasures? And you, President Booker T. Talmadge, are you restless to get to your rare roast beef? Regents, are you lusting for the urinal? And you, Professors—are you cooking up some academic skullduggery for the Faculty Club?

"Now, you say hopelessly, he is going to give us his science lecture. And you are right again, but it is the last time you will be right.

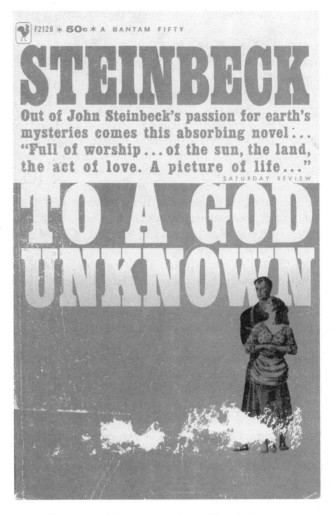

Front cover of the 1960 paperback edition of Steinbeck's 1933 novel (Bruccoli Clark Layman Archives)

"Your professors will squabble about how many milleniums ago it was when a man picked up fire and it burned him, and he picked it up again and it burned a forest and he brought it home and it burned his shelter and he threw it on a pile of bones and learned to cook and he found a piece of shining metal under a bonfire and wore it for a while and then hammered it to a cutting edge. It took him hundreds of thousands of years to get used to fire. The very concept of fire so frightened him that he refused to think about it. He called it a god or the property of a god, and gradually over hundreds of thousands of years he reluctantly evolved a set of rules and techniques and mores for thinking about fire. Then he loved it finally and it was first lord of the hearth, the center of his being, the symbol of his ease and safety. Many more people got warm than got burned and so he gradually inspected this extension of himself, this power and found what made it do the things it does. But that was the end of the process, not the beginning. And meanwhile there must have been a good number of men who seeing a forest burning shrieked out that this devil would destroy the world.

"Do you know what is wrong with you? It isn't niggers or Democrats or Russians. The Quantum Theory tumbled your convictions about order, so you refused to think about it. The Expanding Universe blasted your homocentric galaxy, and then the fissionable atom ripped the last of your fire-minded world to ribbons. For the first time you have unlimited power and an unlimited future, the great drama of magic and alchemy. And are you glad? No, you go groveling to analysts to find out what is the matter with you. You will not inspect the new world that is upon you.

"Wouldn't it be wonderful if you could look at your world and say, and hear yourself–'This was once true but it is no longer true. We must make new rules about this and this. We must abandon our dear war, which once had a purpose, and our hates which once served us.'

"You won't do it. It will have to slip up on you in the course of the generations. But wouldn't it be wonderful if you could greet the most wonderful time in the history of our world with wonder rather than with despair?"

Now you bow coldly and try to get out alive. The audience is silent and as you walk up the aisle working at your suffering crotch you hear whispered comments. "The old fart. Who does he think he is?" "Nigger lover." "Did you hear him say those Communists weren't dangerous? He must be one."

Say–I like that! I may make that speech myself–from a helicopter. But you may borrow it if you like. And invite me to hear you deliver it. I'll cover your exit and bring a few of the boys.

Oh, Elaine will be so mad at me!

yours

John

I told you I was a spastic writer–

–Steinbeck: A Life in Letters, edited by Elaine Steinbeck and Robert Wallsten (New York: Viking, 1975), pp. 528–533

* * *

Steinbeck to Pascal Covici Jr., 13 April 1956

Pascal Covici Jr., the son of Steinbeck's editor, was a student at Harvard University in 1956. He wanted to try his hand at critical writing and had sent Steinbeck some samples of his work. In his response Steinbeck shared details from his own experiences as a writer and mused on what it would mean to win the Nobel Prize in literature, which he was to receive six years later.

Dear Pascal:

We're running to Washington this morning. Haven't been there since the war. I do hope they have cleared the rubble.

I had your letter yesterday and that is exactly what I mean. But say it as roughly as you have in the letter. Make your point and make it angrily. I think of a number of pieces which should be done but that I as a novelist can't or should not do. One would be on the ridiculous preoccupation of my great contemporaries, and I mean Faulkner and Hemingway, with their own immortality. It is almost as though they were fighting for billing on a tombstone.

Another thing I could not write and you can is about the Nobel Prize. I should be scared to death to receive it, I don't care how coveted it is. But I can't say that because I have not received it. But it has seemed to me that the receivers never do a good nor courageous piece of work afterwards. It kind of retires them. I don't know whether this is because their work was over anyway or because they try to live up to the prize and lose their daring or what. But it would be a tough hazard to overcome and most of them don't. Maybe it makes them respectable and a writer can't dare to be respectable. Anyway it might be a very interesting little essay. The same thing goes for any kind of honorary degrees and decorations. A man's writing becomes less good with the numbers of his honors. It might be that fear in me that has made me refuse those L.L.D.'s that are constantly being put out by colleges. It may also be the reason why I have never been near the Academy even though I was elected to it. It may also be the reason I gave my Pulitzer Prize money away. I think you might well make a good piece of it.

It is usual that the moment you write for publication–I mean one of course–one stiffens in exactly the same way one does when one is being photographed. The simplest way to overcome this is to write it *to* someone, like me. Write it as a letter aimed at one person. This removes the vague terror of addressing the large and faceless audience and it also, you will find, will give a sense of freedom and a lack of self-consciousness.

Consider also writing some criticisms of critics. The few pieces I have written against critics have been gobbled up. And it is not considered sporting for a novelist to attack his critics. But it would be perfectly valid for you to do it.

I am in a rush but I did want to get this off because your letter was very good.

Love to you all

jn

–Steinbeck: A Life in Letters, pp. 527–528

* * *

Steinbeck to Roland Dickey, 7 December 1956

Steinbeck wrote Roland Dickey, director of the University of New Mexico Press, regarding the book Steinbeck and His Critics: A Record of Twenty-five Years, *to be published in 1957. Edited by E. W. Tedlock Jr. and C. V. Wicker, the book was a collection of representative reviews and critical essays on Steinbeck. This letter was included in the book.*

Dear Mr. Dickey:

I have read with very much interest the book, Steinbeck and His Critics, particularly since I have not seen most of the material before.

It is always astonishing to read a critique of one's work. In my own case, it didn't come out that way but emerged little by little, staggering and struggling, each part alone and separated from the others. And then, after the fact—long after—a pattern is discernible, a clear and fairly consistent pattern, even in the failures. It gives me the pleased but uneasy feeling of reading my own epitaph.

So many of the judgments and arguments in this book of opinions seem to me to be true. I only wonder why I didn't think of them myself. I guess I was so lost in the books I couldn't see the long structure. Of course, in this river of opinion there are special pleaders—men who were backing their own particular horses—but also there seem to me to be many accuracies.

This book does make me aware of how long I have been at it. Good God, I must have been writing for hundreds of years. But I must assure you that it fails to make me feel old or finished or fixed. Perhaps my new book falls into the pattern, and perhaps the two books in process will drift in the inevitable stream—but to me they are new and unique in the world and I am as scared and boastful and humble about them as I was a thousand years ago when I began the first one. And it is just as hard and I am just as excited as I was. The approach to a horizon makes the horizon leap away. And the more one learns about writing, the more unbelievably difficult it becomes. I wish to God I knew as much about my craft, or whatever it is, as I did when I was 19 years old. But with every new attempt, frightening though it may be, is the wonder and the hope and the delight. As the angels said in Petrarca, "Che luce è questa e qual nova beltate?"

Yours sincerely,

John Steinbeck

—Steinbeck: *A Life in Letters*, pp. 542–543

* * *

Your Only Weapon Is Your Work: **Preface**
Robert DeMott

In 1985, when he was serving as the director of the Steinbeck Research Center (now the Center for Steinbeck Studies) at San Jose State University, Robert DeMott published a February 1957 letter from Steinbeck to Dennis Murphy, son of a childhood friend of Steinbeck from Salinas, John Murphy. The younger Murphy was a promising writer. The following is DeMott's preface to his edition of the letter, titled Your Only Weapon Is Your Work.

According to legend, which John Steinbeck rarely did anything to discourage, he showed no interest at all [. . .] in encouraging the talents of young and unknown writers. In fact, as with so many myths about his life, nothing could be further from the truth. Steinbeck not only followed developments in twentieth-century fiction more closely than he readily admitted in public, but he was actually instrumental in the careers of a number of beginning writers. Steinbeck's aesthetic taste and judgment—what he once called his "eye for fiction"—changed markedly during his career, yet his willingness to aid writers whom he considered worthy remained a fairly constant (and seldomly [*sic*] recognized) aspect of his achievement.

During the span of three decades, from the early 1930s through the 1960s, Steinbeck offered support, advice, comfort and understanding to several apprentice writers. George Albee, Louis Paul, John Hargrave, Ritch Lovejoy, Nathaniel Benchley, and members of Budd Schulberg's Watts Writers' Workshop all received various kinds of assistance from Steinbeck (including, on a couple of occasions, offers of financial aid). Not everyone received the same attention, however. Steinbeck encouraged each writer's creativity, of course, but where he might boldly advise one person on potential fictional subjects, he would confine his relationship with another to reading, editing, or criticizing the manuscript or galley proof at hand. Sometimes, in the case of Louis Paul and later of Isak Dinesen (who was then relatively unknown in America), Steinbeck recommended writers to McIntosh and Otis, his own literary agents. At other times he agreed to provide a blurb for the dust jacket or cover of a writer's book: John Hargrave, Clyde Brion Davis, Ernie Pyle, Fred Allen, and Elia Kazan each benefitted from this form of Steinbeck's attentiveness.

That Steinbeck performed nearly all of these tasks on Dennis Murphy's behalf indicates the special feeling he held for him, and the esteem with which he regarded the Murphy family. Dennis' grandfather, Dr. H. C. Murphy, a well-known Salinas physician, was memorably portrayed in *East of Eden*. Dennis' father, John Murphy, a prominent Salinas attorney, was one of Steinbeck's closest boyhood friends. And Dennis himself, whom Steinbeck had known since he was a child (there was a persistent rumor, now discounted, that Dennis and his brother Michael were the "models" for Cal and Aron Trask in *East of Eden*), grew up thoroughly conversant and deeply impressed with Steinbeck's novels. In fact, at a very precocious age, Murphy once announced to Steinbeck that he preferred his novels to Hemingway's and Faulkner's, all of which he had read closely. It seemed quite fitting, then, in May of 1956, for John Murphy—dismayed by his son's desire to become a writer—to solicit Steinbeck's opinion about one of Dennis' unpublished stories. Immediately moved by the integrity and quality of his writing, Steinbeck took the liberty of submitting the story to McIntosh and Otis, who he hoped would accept Murphy as a client. Mindful, too, of Dennis' struggle with his father over his chosen vocation, Steinbeck defended the young man's decision, and later, in a wonderfully humorous and sympathetic letter, counselled John and Marie Murphy not to judge their son by ordinary rules of conduct. Dennis, he added, was "not only a writer but I am dreadfully afraid a very good one" (February 21, 1957).

Steinbeck's support of Dennis Murphy was not, then, simply a matter of long-standing family connections. Naturally, Steinbeck recognized that, despite thirty years' difference in their ages, he shared with Dennis some strong common bonds. They both drew [*sic*] up and attended public schools in the conservative atmosphere of the Salinas Valley; they both left that setting for Stanford University; they both felt at an early age that sense of being marked out, by sensibility and temperament, for some distinct achievement (for Steinbeck that special achievement was always associated with his becoming a writer; for Murphy, it began with his prodigal talent as a child pianist, then later found expression as a novelist, and still later, as a writer of filmscripts); and they both exhibited a propensity to forge their own identities. Most importantly, however, Steinbeck's advocacy stemmed from his belief that Murphy possessed "definite ability" as a writer. Steinbeck's readiness to serve as a guide through the mysteries of the authorial process, pointing out wherever necessary the psychological traps Murphy should avoid (Steinbeck was especially adamant about the corrosive effects of success), demonstrates the genuine admiration he had for the skill displayed in Murphy's early fiction, especially his first (and only) novel, *The Sergeant,* published by Viking Press in March, 1958.

Like Steinbeck, who occupied an influential position in his life, Murphy, too, was restless and quit college several times to experience the world first-hand. Between stints at Stanford, he travelled widely in Europe and North Africa, and served a hitch with the Army in post-war France. In the mid-1950s he returned to California to enroll in the Creative Writing Program at Stanford; then, already accepted as a client by McIntosh and Otis, he struck out on his own in the summer of 1956 for Big Sur where he devoted full attention to his novel. By late summer of that year the novel was well under way when the Steinbecks, en route to Hollywood from the Democratic National Convention in San Francisco, stopped to visit Murphy and his new bride, Pokey, at their home in Big Sur. Steinbeck refrained from reading the manuscript, reluctant to intimidate Murphy by treading across the "door step" of his "creativeness." Based on his assessment of some earlier stories, however, and steadfastly convinced of Murphy's "great ability and developing talent," Steinbeck later recommended a section of the novel-in-progress for the newly established Joseph Henry Jackson Award, which it won. (Another interesting connection—until his death in 1955, Jackson was one of the few literary critics whose judgment and companionship Steinbeck appreciated.)

Dan Dailey as Ernest Horton and Jayne Mansfield as Camille Oaks in the 1957 motion-picture adaptation of Steinbeck's 1947 novel The Wayward Bus *(MOMA/Film Stills Archive; from Joseph R. Millichap,* Steinbeck and Film, *1983; Thomas Cooper Library, University of South Carolina)*

If Steinbeck lacked a firm conception about Murphy's novel in its preliminary stages (he told the administrators of the Jackson Award that he did not even know the novel's title), that quickly changed when he studied the galleys which Viking Press provided. In *The Sergeant,* Steinbeck discovered vivid characterization, realistic subject matter, and a critical sensibility that impressed him as being not only praise-worthy, but in fact compatible with his own best work. Murphy's experience as an American GI formed the basis for his novel, a taut (but overly rhetorical) account of a naive private's struggle to achieve personal and sexual freedom. The protagonist, Tom Swanson, learns to steer a clear course toward Solange, a lovely and understanding French girl, even though he is compellingly drawn to the advances of his superior officer, Sergeant Callan, who is portrayed as a domineering and calculating homosexual. If the astringent, controlled voice of the omniscient narrator recalls Hemingway, the theme—one could say the novel's true subject—is the individual soul's battle with good and evil, clearly reminiscent of *East of Eden.* It was an achievement not lost on Steinbeck: "It's a good book—better than you have any right to expect with your first book," he informed Murphy on November 4, 1957. And indeed *The Sergeant* is a much stronger novel than Steinbeck's first, *Cup of Gold*—a comparative judgment alluded to in this encomium, which appeared prominently on the front cover of the novel's dust jacket (and which now makes the book a desirable collector's item):

> . . . *a remarkable book. It has none of the faults of a young first novelist, faults which took me many years to overcome because I thought they were virtues. I mean verbosity, ornamentation, and a lack of compactness. This book starts in one place and goes directly to its end without being distracted. I think this boy may well be a very important writer . . . Most impressive is his ability to put believable people on paper and then to relate them in scenes which happen. There is a great deal of truth and beauty in this book.*

Steinbeck's endorsement joined statements by Mark Schorer and Wallace Stegner (Murphy's creative writing teacher at Stanford). All three echoed in one way or another Viking's editorial staff: "The publishers of this first novel are deeply convinced that it marks the beginning of what will be a major American career."

Murphy's career never became "major," but as Steinbeck had predicted, *The Sergeant* sold extremely well for a first novel. It went into a third printing in cloth, appeared a year later, in May of 1959, as a Crest paperback (complete with a titillating cover design, and a portion of Steinbeck's encomium reproduced on the back), and was later made into a motion picture starring Rod Steiger. The novel also received favorable, if somewhat mixed, reviews. Critics for the *Pittsburgh Press, Newsday,* and the *San Francisco Chronicle* were especially enthusiastic, comparing Murphy to Mann, Faulkner and Hemingway, while David Dempsey, striking a more balanced note in the *New York Times,* called *The Sergeant* a "very good" first novel, but one which was not "completely realized."

Privately, Steinbeck too had one reservation, which he did not hesitate to tell Murphy. The denouement of the novel occurs when Sergeant Callan unexpectedly kills himself. "Suicide wasn't good enough and also I don't quite believe it," Steinbeck cautioned, because it was a "curtain rather than a climax," the "only *device*" in an otherwise "terse and true" novel. Anyone who remembers the death of Kate in *East of Eden* will find ammunition for the charge that established writers don't always practice what they preach, although in every other regard, Steinbeck's appraisal of the novel, as well as his continuing advice to Murphy about the singular demands of the writer's duties, are perceptive, reliable, and hard-earned.

Steinbeck's letter of February, 1957, published here for the first time, greets Dennis Murphy at the threshold of his professional career, that charmed moment when Elizabeth Otis, the head of his literary agency, had leveled her judgment on the novel, and would, shortly afterwards, submit the manuscript of *The Sergeant* to Viking Press. In a sense, then, while Dennis Murphy was part of Steinbeck's Salinas "family," part of the historical actuality of his birthplace and his formative past, Murphy also quickly became part of Steinbeck's personal and creative present, part of his connection with the "family" of Elizabeth Otis, Shirley Fisher (who became Murphy's agent), and Viking Press. With Dennis Murphy's emergence as a writer, Steinbeck sensed that a circle had closed, a bright hope had been christened. Monterey County, he confessed to Elizabeth Otis, was not "his" country any longer—"that is for Dennis Murphy now." The pietistic act—almost Medieval in its purity—of transmitting the keys of the novelist's sacred kingdom to an initiate, accounts in large part for Steinbeck's paternal tone in this letter, the felt quality and candor of his advice, as well as the sage humor of his anecdotes and the energetic elevation of his mood.

All of Steinbeck's correspondence with Murphy, which covered a five year period from 1956 to 1961, is similarly generous and enthusiastic (though it grew somewhat more tendentious toward the end). It was an enthusiasm motivated by nothing less than Steinbeck's selfless interest in Murphy's future as a writer, and one which extended to their personal relationship, especially in England where Murphy lived briefly in late 1959 near the Steinbecks at Somerset. Unfortunately, after the accidental death of his wife in 1959, Murphy's life took a turn no amount of enthusiasm, generosity, or advocacy on Steinbeck's part could alter. The "weapon" of Murphy's work proved inadequate against the demands placed on him to raise their children alone. Murphy's resolute decision to care for the children himself, even though it meant abandoning his fiction, was regrettably an attitude Steinbeck neither fully accepted nor condoned. (He always had a somewhat abstract notion of child-rearing; his real children, he once said, were his words.) Although they subsequently became estranged, for a privileged moment in the late 1950s Steinbeck stood witness as the mantle of the novelist passed successfully back home to a younger writer, whose reverence for the "pure magic" of words promised to continue an artistic tradition Steinbeck himself had started.

  —Your Only Weapon Is Your Work (San Jose: Steinbeck Research Center, 1985)

* * *

Steinbeck to Dennis Murphy, February 1957

  The following is the text of the letter published by DeMott in 1985.

Dear Dennis:

  Since writing this (sic) I have talked to Elizabeth Otis. She says your book is good and you are a writer. And that's as high praise as you are ever likely to get and in my estimation from the best critical mind in the country. I'm very glad. Now all you have to do is forty years of writing. I guess you don't have any choice. That time is over. And now you can start getting mad at critics. The University of New Mexico Press has just issued a book on my work and its criticisms over 25 years. It's very interesting, to me anyway and possibly would be to you in the sense that you must not pay any more attention to critics than you can help.

  My own new little comedy *[The Short Reign of Pippin IV]* comes out in March. Just a fun book and I think it rather for a limited audience. And then the Book of the Month Club took it which shakes my faith. It's no great compliment but it makes us a little bit solvent. But I just don't see how it can be a popular book. Everything is screwy. I'll see if Viking will send you a copy. We'll be gone when it comes out. We're sailing March 25th for Naples. We have a flat in Florence for April and May. Then we'll go to England and Scandinavia getting back in July. The address in Florence is #3 Via Torbaluoni if you care to write it down. Then in September we're going to Japan where I have never been. The heat is on me from State Dept. and the Japanese Gov't to go to a P.E.N. Congress—the first ever held in the far east. I've never been to a congress before either.

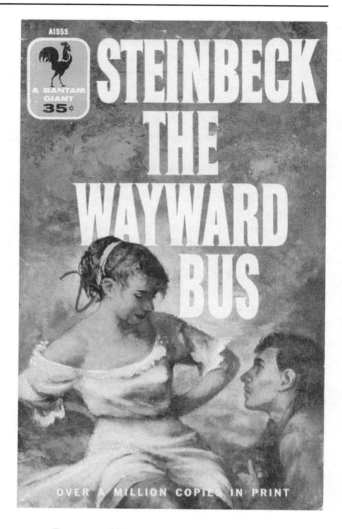

Front cover of the 1957 paperback edition of Steinbeck's 1947 novel (Bruccoli Clark Layman Archives)

Makes me feel kind of old—but what the hell. Maybe I am old. My list of titles indicates it. Only my appetites and lecheries seem unimpaired. And my appetite for work continues whatever all that means. But so many things now sound hollowly like epitaphs and I have too much I want to do. I'm about a thousand pages along in a real rendering of Malory's Morte d'Arthur in modern English. With essays and biography it will probably be 2500 pages or several volumes. And it may take several years. But I've always wanted to do it—ever since I was 10 years old. There never has been a good translation. Hell—that was the reason I started Anglo-Saxon and Old and Middle English. And now at 55 (next week) I finally get to it. And it is wonderful to be doing. And it might be my last contribution. I think I've always been a medievalist. It shows up everywhere. We don't understand them now. They are the most vital people in history—kind of crazy creative children but with great feeling. I have to do a lot of research in England. So much I want to do. I can't afford to be 55. But [Bernard] Berenson is still operating at 90–if that's any reassurance. I'll see him in Florence. And I still have more fun than almost any body and I also still cry havoc and panic and destruction more than most. And I still don't know my limitations. Maybe that's when you're old– when you know that your life is going to be from then on a slow pig slide to death. I've always liked Lucifer better than the good steady archangels. In Salinas I see people I think of as boys and by God they're old men– they not only look old, they *are* old. Not that I'm fighting age. It has compensations unbelievable–but that's not what I'm talking about. Miguel Covarrubias' father when he was 85 was dying. He had always hated the church but his old lady relatives sat like harpies around his bed–waiting. Finally he went into unconsciousness and they hustled a priest in from the next room to give him ghostly consolation. Well the holy water brought him to and he jumped up and chased the priest out of the house and he died in the middle of the street in his long night gown. Now there's a proper death for you! And Miguel said that he winged the priest with a brass spittoon as he flew out the door.

I haven't meant to write all this. I guess I just got excited after talking to Elizabeth.

You have a harder fight now than you have ever had. It is tough to battle opposition and disapproval but that's easy compared to the subtle attack of approval and flattery. There's nothing so nice as a compliment and if it can be true it's even nicer but also there is nothing more weakening. You've done well against failure. Now let's see how you defend yourself against success. Your only weapon is your work. Take everything you can but keep your work pure and innocent and fierce. And always remember that no one did it but you and consequently no one can tell you what to do or how to do it. I have belabored you with lots of advice but I have never put foot over the door step of your creativeness. And don't let anyone else do it either and that's an order. After you have finished let the sons of bitches have it but *while* you are doing it for God's sake, keep your holy loneliness. And now I guess I have indulged myself to the limit. But I do wish I could burn these things into you with a soldering iron. There's very little creativeness in the world. You have a good share of that precious stuff. See that you respect it.

So long–

John

–Your Only Weapon Is Your Work (San Jose: Steinbeck Research Center, 1985)

* * *

Steinbeck to Robert Wallsten, 19 February 1960

Steinbeck saw therapeutic value in writing verse, as is indicated in this letter to his friend Robert Wallsten, an actor turned writer who had complained about having trouble writing.

Dear Robert:

I hear via a couple of attractive grapevines, that you are having trouble writing. God! I know this feeling so well. I think it is never coming back–but it does–one morning, there it is again.

About a year ago, [playwright] Bob Anderson asked me for help in the same problem. I told him to write poetry–not for selling–not even for seeing– poetry to throw away. For poetry is the mathematics of writing and closely kin to music. And it is also the best therapy because sometimes the troubles come tumbling out.

Well, he did. For six months he did. And I have three joyous letters from him saying it worked. Just poetry–anything and not designed for a reader. It's a great and valuable privacy.

I only offer this if your dryness goes on too long and makes you too miserable. You may come out of it any day. I have. The words are fighting each other to get out.

Can I help in any way? I know the pain and bewilderment of the thing.

love to you
John
–Steinbeck: A Life in Letters, p. 661

* * *

Steinbeck to Wallsten, 13–14 February 1962

When Wallsten wrote Steinbeck in early 1962 complaining about difficulties in beginning a biography of the actress Dame Judith Anderson, Steinbeck, then traveling with Elaine in Europe, replied from Capri with an encouraging letter.

Dear Robert:

Your bedridden letter came a couple of days ago and the parts about your book, I think, need an answer. By the way, Elaine has a better title than mine. Hers is–There is Nothing Like a Broad, by Dame Judith Anderson.

Now let me give you the benefit of my experience in facing 400 pages of blank stock–the appalling stuff that must be filled. I know that no one really wants the benefit of anyone's experience which is probably why it is so freely offered. But the following are some of the things I have had to do to keep from going nuts.

1. Abandon the idea that you are ever going to finish. Lose track of the 400 pages and write just one page for each day, it helps. Then when it gets finished, you are always surprised.

2. Write freely and as rapidly as possible and throw the whole thing on paper. Never correct or rewrite until the whole thing is down. Rewrite in process is usually found to be an excuse for not going on. It also interferes with flow and rhythm which can only come from a kind of unconscious association with the material.

3. Forget your generalized audience. In the first place, the nameless, faceless audience will scare you to death and in the second place, unlike the theatre, it doesn't exist. In writing, your audience is one single reader. I have found that sometimes it helps to pick out one person—a real person you know, or an imagined person and write to that one.

4. If a scene or a section gets the better of you and you still think you want it—bypass it and go on. When you have finished the whole you can come back to it and then you may find that the reason it gave trouble is because it didn't belong there.

5. Beware of a scene that becomes too dear to you, dearer than the rest. It will usually be found that it is out of drawing.

6. If you are using dialogue—say it aloud as you write it. Only then will it have the sound of speech.

Well, actually that's about all.

I know that no two people have the same methods. However, these mostly work for me.

There's a great big wind storm blowing. No boats in today. The seas are white. Elaine came in blue with cold. Part of the island has no electricity but we have been lucky so far. When Jove puts on a storm, he does it well.

Oh! it's a lovely storm. And we're cooking beans and watching it through our big windows. We're sheltered by the cliff but we can see the trees whipping and the sea churning white down far below us. Life is very good at this moment.

love to all there
John
—*Steinbeck: A Life in Letters*, pp. 736–737

The Short Reign of Pippin IV (1957)

Steinbeck's Extravaganza
Dick Wickenden

Dick Wickenden reviewed The Short Reign of Pippin IV: A Fabrication *(1957) for the* New York Herald Tribune Book Review.

A few years from now, things in France will come to such a pass that the twelve squabbling political parties of that splendid but sorely troubled nation will be reduced to restoring the monarchy. The man destined to be crowned Pippin IV, in a rather confused ceremony at Rheims, is a charming gentleman in his early fifties, M. Pippin Arnulf Héristal. . . .

Such, at any rate, is the glimpse of the future provided by this small and amusing book. The author's

Dust jacket for Steinbeck's 1957 satirical work about a man who is made king of France when monarchy is restored to end a constitutional crisis brought on by squabbling political parties (from Robert B. Harmon, The Collectible John Steinbeck, *1986; Thomas Cooper Library, University of South Carolina)*

name is Steinbeck and his effervescent "fabrication" is an April choice of the Book-of-the-Month Club. Although new to the field of amiably satirical extravaganza he seems happily at home in it. He maintains a firm control over material that might easily have got out of hand; his inventions are never outrageous or his humorous flourishes arch, and his style is cleverly contrived so as to sound, for the most part, like an adroit translation from the French. The climax, though it might have been more incisive and tumultuous, is altogether appropriate.

The Short Reign of Pippin IV probably arises out of a deep if sometimes exasperated affection for France and the French and for the foolish race of man in general. It was clearly a great deal of fun to write, and many thousands of readers, infected by John Steinbeck's high spirits, are going to have at least as much fun reading it.

—*New York Herald Tribune Book Review*, 14 April 1957; reprinted in *John Steinbeck: The Contemporary Reviews*, edited by Joseph R. McElrath Jr., Jesse S. Crisler, and Susan Shillinglaw (Cambridge & New York: Cambridge University Press, 1996), p. 432

Steinbeck and Sir Thomas Malory's *Le Morte Darthur* (1485)

Steinbeck to Elizabeth Otis, 3 January 1957

Throughout the late 1950s Steinbeck worked on his modern prose adaptation of Sir Thomas Malory's Le Morte Darthur *(1485), reading and researching a great amount of material for the project.*

Dear Elizabeth:

Just reading and reading and reading and it's like hearing remembered music. The bay is nearly all frozen over with just a few patches of open water and as the tide rises and falls the crushing ice makes a strange singing sound. I've moved my card table to the front window with the telescope beside it so if anything goes on I can tompeep it. Two seagulls right now trying to walk on the ice and falling through every few steps and then looking around to see if anyone noticed. I have a feeling that seagulls hate to be laughed at. Well, who doesn't, for that matter?

Remarkable things in the books. Little meanings that peek out for a moment, and a few scholars who make observations and then almost in fright withdraw or qualify what they have said. Somewhere there's a piece missing in the jigsaw and it is a piece which ties the whole thing together. So many scholars have spent so much time trying to establish whether Arthur existed at all that they have lost track of the single truth that he exists over and over.

It is very easy to see how Malory, steeped as he must have been in the church, could unconsciously pattern the brotherhood after the twelve apostles. That was what people understood. Twelve was the normal number for any group of followers of a man or a principle. The symbolism was inevitable. And whether the Grail was the cup from Golgotha or the Gaelic cauldron later used by Shakespeare doesn't in the least matter since the principle of both was everlasting or rather ever-renewed life. All such things fall into place inevitably but it is the connective, the continuing line with the piece missing in the middle that fascinates me.

Another beautiful thing is how the straggling sentences, the confused characters and events of the early parts smooth out as he goes along so that his sentences become more fluid and his dialogue gets a sting of truth and his characters become more human than symbolic even though he tries hard to keep the symbol, and this I am sure is because he was learning to write as he went along. He became a master and you can see it happening. And in any work I do on this thing I am not going to try to change that. I'll go along with his growing perfection and who knows, I may learn myself. It's a lovely job if I can only lose the sense of hurry that has been growing in me for so long.

Last night when I could neither sleep nor channel my attention on my reading, my nerve ends got to whipping like the whitecaps on the bay and darkness seemed to come close and then to recede and then come close again. This was not only nonsense but fatuous nonsense. And it occurred to me that what was good for squirrels and bears might be good for me so I went out to walk and the cold got through my skin and then through my meat and then right into the center of my bones, and do you know it worked? A soothing and a quieting it was. It was about six above zero and the deep freeze acted like an anaesthetic as of course I knew it must. When I was cold clear through I could come back and read again. I think these squirrels and bears have something. I don't know whether it was fortunate or unfortunate that I didn't find a hollow log and crawl in for the winter.

Charley is having a wonderful time trying to walk on the ice. He falls through at every step and looks puzzled every time. One day soon it will support him and then he'll give those seagulls hell.

That's all for now. I'll get back to my Legend and I'll bet it turns out that it isn't a Legend at all any more than any dream is.

Love

John

—*Steinbeck: A Life in Letters*, pp. 543–545

* * *

Steinbeck to Alexander Frere, 18 January 1957

Planning a trip to Europe for his Malory research, Steinbeck wrote Alexander Frere of Heinemann, his publisher in England.

Dear Frere and Frau:

Your letter arrived with its charming news that we can lay down our heads at the Dorchester.

First, I and later we have been to Sag Harbor. I've been doing some concentrated reading–a lovely thing–and not done by me in recent years. To read and read in one direction night and day; to pull an area and a climate of thinking over one's head like a space helmet–what a joy that is! No telephones, no neighbors, no decisions except great ones–that is a good way to live for a time.

Working on the Malory is a thing of great joy to me, like coming home. I am having a wonderful time. The Morgan Library has opened its arms and its great manuscripts to me, and I can touch and feel, put a microscope on the vellum. I think I will write a small essay on what one finds on a monkish manuscript under a powerful glass. I am convinced that with practice I could tell when the copyist had a hangover. Every sharpening of the quill is apparent and since cleanliness was not a monkish virtue, the pages are rich–even racy–with fingerprints and smudges and evidences of pork pasty on fingers hastily wiped on nut-brown robes. It is fascinating and some of the scholars down there are a little puzzled and aghast at my own inspection with a sixty-power glass, but they are fascinated too. I haven't yet dared ask permission to take scrapings for analysis, but maybe later when they find I am not a crank, they may permit it.

I am having the time of my life with the work, and although I have a fairly good background, I am learning much in supplemental reading.

My love to your darling wife and whatever you can get for yourself.

Yours,
John
–Steinbeck: A Life in Letters, pp. 548–549

* * *

Steinbeck to Otis and Chase Horton, 26 April 1957

From Rome, Steinbeck wrote Otis and Chase Horton to report on his progress with the Malory project. Horton, Otis's friend and owner of the Washington Square Bookshop in New York, had originally suggested the project to Steinbeck.

Dear Elizabeth and Chase:

I have been reading all of the scholarly appraisals of the Morte, and all the time there has been a bother-

some thought in my brain knocking about just out of reach, something I knew that was wrong in all of the inspection and yet I couldn't put my finger on it. Why did Launcelot fail in his quest and why did Galahad succeed? What is the feeling about sin, the feeling about Gwynevere? How about the rescue from the stake? How about the relationship between Arthur and Launcelot?

Then this morning I awakened about five o'clock fully awake but with the feeling that some tremendous task had been completed. I got up and looked out at the sun coming up over Rome and suddenly it came back whole and in one piece. And I think it answers my nagging doubt. It can't be a theory because it won't subject itself to proof. I'm afraid it has to be completely intuitive and because of this it will never be very seriously considered by scholars.

Malory has been studied as a translator, as a soldier, as a rebel, as a religious, as an expert in courtesy, as nearly everything you can think of except one, and that is what he was–a novelist. The Morte is the first and one of the greatest of novels in the English language. And only a novelist could think it. A novelist not only puts down a story but he is the story. He is each one of the characters in a greater or a less degree. And because he is usually a moral man in intention and honest in his approach, he sets things down as truly as he can.

A novel may be said to be the man who writes it. Now it is nearly always true that a novelist, perhaps unconsciously, identifies himself with one chief or central character in his novel. Into this character he puts not only what he thinks he is but what he hopes to be. We can call this spokesman the self-character. You will find one in every one of my books and in the novels of everyone I can remember. It is most simple and near the surface in Hemingway's novels. The soldier, romantic, always maimed in some sense, hand–testicles. These are the symbols of his limitations. I suppose my own symbol character has my dream wish of wisdom and acceptance.

Now it seems to me that Malory's self-character would be Launcelot. All of the perfections he knew went into this character, all of the things of which he thought himself capable. But, being an honest man he found faults in himself, faults of vanity, faults of violence, faults even of disloyalty and these would naturally find their way into his dream character. Oh, don't forget that the novelist may arrange or rearrange events so that they are more nearly what he hoped they might have been.

For example, if Malory had been at Rouen and had seen the cynical trial, the brutal indictment and the horrible burning, might he not be tempted in his novel to right

Steinbeck's agent, Elizabeth Otis, and Elaine (Special Collections, Bracken Library, Ball State University; from Jackson J. Benson,
The True Adventures of John Steinbeck, Writer, *1984; Thomas Cooper Library, University of South Carolina)*

a wrong by dreaming he had done it differently? If he were affected by the burning of Joan and even more by his failure to save her or even to protest, would he not be likely to have his self-character save Gwynevere from the flames? In a sense he would by this means have protested against the killing of the falsely accused but he would also in a sense have cured it.

And now we come to the Grail, the Quest. I think it is true that any man, novelist or not, when he comes to maturity has a very deep sense that he will not win the quest. He knows his failings, his shortcomings and particularly his memories of sins, sins of cruelty, of thoughtlessness, of disloyalty, of adultery, and these will not permit him to win the Grail. And so his self-character must suffer the same terrible sense of failure as his author. Launcelot could not see the Grail because of the faults and sins of Malory himself. He knows he has fallen short and all his excellences, his courage, his courtesy, in his own mind cannot balance his vices and errors, his stupidities.

I think this happens to every man who has ever lived but it is set down largely by novelists. But there is an answer ready to hand. The self-character cannot win the Quest, but his son can, his spotless son, the son of his seed and his blood who has his virtues but has not his faults. And so Galahad is able to win the Quest, the dear son, the unsoiled son, and because he is the seed of Launcelot and the seed of Malory, Malory-Launcelot has in a sense won the quest and in his issue broken through to the glory which his own faults have forbidden him.

Now this is so. I know it as surely as I can know anything. God knows I have done it myself often enough. And this can for me wipe out all the inconsistencies and obscurities scholars have found in the story. And if the Morte is uneven and changeable it is because the author was changeable. Sometimes there is a flash of fire, sometimes a moody dream, sometimes an anger. For a novelist is a rearranger of nature so that it makes an understandable pattern, and a novelist is also a teacher, but a novelist is primarily a man and subject to all of a man's faults and virtues, fears and braveries. And I have seen no treatise which has ever considered that the story of the Morte is the story of Sir Thomas Malory and his times and the story of his dreams of goodness and his wish that the story may come out well and only molded by the essential honesty which will not allow him to lie.

Well, that was the problem and that was the settlement and it came sweetly out with the morning sun on the brown walls of Rome. And I should like to know whether you two find it valid at all. In my heart and in my mind I find it true and I do not know how in the world I can prove it except by saying it as clearly as I can so that a reader may say–"Of course, that's how it had to be. Whatever else could be the explanation?"

Please let me know what you think of this dizzying inductive leap. Does it possibly seem as deeply true to you as it does to me?

I shall dearly like to know what you think.

Love to all there,
John
—*Steinbeck: A Life in Letters,* pp. 552–554

* * *

Steinbeck to Eugène and Betty Vinaver, 20 July 1957

Steinbeck met Eugène Vinaver, a professor of medieval literature at the University of Manchester and a leading authority on Malory, during his and Elaine's trip to Europe in the spring and summer of 1957. Shortly before returning to the United States, Steinbeck wrote Vinaver to express his pleasure in their meeting.

My dear Professor and Madame Vinaver:

I cannot tell you what pleasure and stimulation I had in meeting and talking with you. I carry a glow from it in the mind as well as well-defined gratitude for your hospitality which was princely. Just as Launcelot was always glad and returned to find that a good fighting man was also a king's son, so I am gratified to know that the top of the Arthurian pyramid is royal. Having read you with admiration, I could not have believed it to be otherwise for I have been fortunate in meeting a number of great men and it has been my invariable experience that in addition to eminence, superiority has two other qualities or rather three–simplicity, clarity and generosity.

It could not be otherwise with you and is not. There is a final ingredient in the recipe for greatness–enthusiasm–which you have to a superlative degree. I shall carry this glow for a long time.

I hope you will not be bored with me if I write to you occasionally and, if I know myself, at great length, and even presume to ask questions both of fact and of intuition.

Elaine joins me in compliments and gratefulness. Nothing would give us greater pleasure than to be allowed to entertain you in our own querencia.

Finally, my deep thanks for your kindness, your hospitality and your encouragement. It provides a noble pediment for work which I dearly hope will not embarrass you.

Yours in pleasure
John Steinbeck
—*Steinbeck: A Life in Letters,* p. 557

* * *

Steinbeck to Eugène and Betty Vinaver, 27 June 1958

In this letter to Vinaver and his wife, Steinbeck compares people of modern times with the characters from Arthurian legend.

Dear Eugène and Betty:

Back in Londunium after a successful queste. The defeated should begin trooping in to pray you mercy at any moment now. First to Chester and circumambulated the walls–extra, super et intra, walked in the Rows and peered into crevices and holes, a noble and strange city captured between the warp and woof of Roman and medieval patterns with only a patina of sterling area. Then on by car to the dragon lake and found there our old friend Ingrid Bergman making a Chinese film, a different kind of dragon surely and it did seem odd that neither she nor any member of the company knew that they were living where the dragons fought. Then on to Caernarvon and again the walls and towers and trying with all of my might to rip off the dust-covers of time. It is not hard to do. Then on to Conway and there took our rest until next day at howre of prime. Then across Englonde and to Durham to bend knee to St. Cuthbert and to bow respect to the bones of Bede, and to shudder a little at that mailed and military bishopric, a See of iron. Then back to Alnwick with the sweet meadows behind, sheep in the moat and cows in the bailey, and then finally to the end and the proper end to Bambrugh. The rain was black and then it opened like a torn curtain and the streaks of sun exploded on the battlements as though the original Ina the flame-bearer had come back. In all of these it is necessary to see into and under and around as one must the beast in Peer Gynt. Of course I think I can but that may be self-delusion.

I, as a novelist, am a product not only of my own time but of all the flags and tatters, the myth and prejudice, the faith and filth that preceded me. I must believe that it was the same with Malory. And to understand his stories and his figures, I must, as much as is humanly possible, subject myself to his pattern and background, in all directions. A novelist is a kind of flypaper to which everything adheres. His job then is to try to reassemble life into some kind of order.

To people of our time, unable or unwilling to project into the past, a castle is a kind of lovely dream and armour the clothing of a pageant. But in Malory's time armour and castles had one major purpose, to protect lives and to serve as a base for counter-attack. The sword was not an ornament. It was designed to kill people. If the towers and curtain walls are beautiful, it is because strength with economy and purpose usually turn out to be beautiful. We do not know it now, because like purposes are involved, but the shape and line of the guided missile will be found to be lovely. It does seem to me that our time has more parallels with the fifteenth century than, let us say, the nineteenth century did, so that we may be able to understand it more nearly accurately than the Pre-Raphaelite guardsmen of the Victorian round table. For we are as unconsciously savage and as realistically self-seeking as the people of the Middle Ages.

We got back at three this morning and I have a great packet of things to remember.

I forgot to hand you some of the vellum we bought. I shall enclose it with some books I have ordered to be sent to you.

I tried soaking some of it in detergent and found the ink comes out readily. I suppose that it should then be ironed dry with a warm iron or boned to smoothness. I am taking some sheets home with me and will experiment with it to recover its original surface.

I hope in the many months to come when this work comes borning that you will not mind my asking for advice and criticism. That is the time when it has value, in the process.

And again our thanks for being so good to us.

yours,
John
—*Steinbeck: A Life in Letters,* pp. 591–592

* * *

Steinbeck to Horton, 21 October 1958

Back in Sag Harbor after another trip to Europe for research on Malory, Steinbeck wrote Horton in the fall of 1958, offering an analysis of his approach to writing the adaptation of Le Morte Darthur.

Dear Chase:

I realize that after all of our months of work together, for me to cut myself off as I have must seem on the prima donna side. And I haven't been able to explain it simply, not even to myself. Kind of like an engine that is missing fire in several cylinders and I don't know quite what is causing it. The only thing that will be applicable to you is that the engine doesn't run. The whole thing must be a little insulting to you and I don't want it to be. It grows out of my own uncertainties.

You will remember that, being dissatisfied with my own work because it had become glib, I stopped working for over a year in an attempt to allow the glibness to die out, hoping then to start fresh with what might feel to me like a new language. Well, when I started in again it wasn't a new language at all. It was a pale imitation of the old language only it wasn't as good because I had grown rusty and the writing muscles were atrophied. So I picked at it and worried at it because I wanted desperately for this work to be the best I had ever done. My own ineptness and sluggishness set me back on my heels. Finally I decided to back off and to try to get the muscles strong on something else—a short thing, perhaps even a slight thing although I know there are no slight things. And that didn't work either. I wrote seventy-five pages on the new thing, read them and threw them away. Then I wrote fifty pages and threw them away. And then it came to me in a quick flash what that language was. It had been lying around all the time ready at hand and nobody had ever used it as literature. My "slight thing" was about present day America. Why not write it in American? This is a highly complicated and hugely communicative language. It has been used in dialogues, in cuteness and perhaps by a few sports writers. It has also been used by a first person telling a story but I don't think it has been used as a legitimate literary language. As I thought about it I could hear it in my ears. And then I tried it and it seemed right to me and it started to flow along. It isn't easy but I think it is good. For me. And suddenly I felt as Chaucer must have felt when he found he could write the language he had all around him and nobody would put him in jail—or Dante when he raised to poetic dignity the dog Florentine that people spoke but wouldn't dare to write. I admit I am getting a little beyond my peers in those two samples but a cat may surely look at a Chaucer.

And that is what I am working with and that is why I have times of great happiness as well as times of struggle and despair. But it is a creative despair.

Love to you and
to Elizabeth,
John
—*Steinbeck: A Life in Letters,* pp. 598–599

* * *

*Front cover of the 1959 paperback edition of Steinbeck's
1935 novel (Bruccoli Clark Layman Archives)*

Steinbeck to Eugène Vinaver, 23 March 1959

*Back in England for further research on Malory in early
1959, Steinbeck shared more information and views with Professor Vinaver.*

Dear Eugène:

Good letters from you and from Betty this morning. What a fine related feeling to get them. Now the
work seems to begin to churn. "Hit befel in the dayes of
Uther Pendragon when he was Kynge of all England—"
And my little room looks out over the meadows and
forests of the England he was kynge of. And the pace
hasn't changed much here. Never any manufacturing.
Still cows and pigs and some sheep. The Somerset
speech is Anglo-Saxon with a lacing of Celtic—it is even
pronounced in that way. For right here the two met and

fought and later mingled. The Norman never really
took hold here. I feel at home here and why—? My
mother was of pure Celtic stock if there is any such and
my name Steinbeck is not German in the modern sense.
The two bloods meet in me just as they met here in the
Pennine Hills and so there is every reason for me to feel
that I have come home.

I brought very few source books. For the moment
I have read all I can take in. But words I need. I have
sent to London for dictionaries—lots of them. I didn't
bring them. They are too heavy. Dictionaries of old and
transition English, of later—classical and medieval, of
Welsh, Cornish, of Anglo-Saxon and of Old Norsk—
Words are very important to me now. A Somerset man
in Bruton said disparagingly of another—"'E be mean-
like. 'E be 'thout worship." Still the word "worship"
and used in its oldest sense. And the Anglo-Saxon sylla-
bles are all pronounced here. Great is said gre-at, meat
is me-at. I am learning much and there is so much to
learn. But the earth is full of it. Last night the moon
through the mist on our meadow—and time had disappeared—and night birds whirring so that past and
present and future were one. In the Vale of Avalon, the
waters have receded, but in these Mendip Hills nothing
has changed. The hill forts are still there and the oaks
and the hedges.

We have mastered the cottage as I knew we could.
I keep the fires. Elaine runs the house and it is warm
and cozy and the dreams float about. This is right. This
is good. Yesterday I cut dandelions in the meadow and
we cooked them for dinner last night—delicious. And
there's cress in the springs on the hill. But mainly
there's peace—and a sense of enough time and a shuck-
ing off of the hurry to get to the moon. I don't want to
get to the moon—do you?

I am very anxious to see your new book. It takes
years to publish. Is there any chance that I can see it in
manuscript?

I have no suggestions for change of method in
your new edition of the great Malory. But I would be
interested to know what new thoughts and findings had
come to you since the first edition. Oh! wouldn't it be
fine if another ms. should turn up? Two isn't enough
for any scientific approach. I wonder whether I could
put a bomb under the Duchess of Buccleuch—to turn
out her libraries. Not that she would read anything, but
they must have book men in their holdings. And if the
history of Prince Arthur could hide in Winchester,
think what might be lurking in the ducal bookshelves.
I'm going to give it a try.

I am so anxious to see you both. As soon as my
foot is in the door, and the full spring comes—maybe
you can come down here and walk our Camelot with
us. That would be a good thing—

It is not cold now. The moment the wind switched to the west, the sweet warm air of the Gulf Stream came in. Today is gloriously sunny.

I am very glad to be here. Very glad.

As always,

John

—*Steinbeck: A Life in Letters,* pp. 619–620

* * *

Steinbeck to Elia Kazan, 1 April 1959

Steinbeck wrote his friend the movie director Elia Kazan from the cottage in southwest England where he was performing his research on Malory. Kazan took him up on the invitation to visit, arriving that summer.

Dear Gadg:

I have your letter this morning and I shall start this, although when it may be finished I do not know. A typewriter stands between me and the word, a tool that has never become an appendage, but a pencil is almost like an umbilical connection between me and the borning letters.

You ask, parenthetically, why I should be interested in your soul. I shall put aside the implications in the fact of your asking. I do not even use the usual reasons, although they are true—that you are valuable, that you are the one continuing triumph of our species, the creative man. No, the reason I am implicated with your soul is that it helps relate me to my own. We must constantly check our evaluations against those of our peers. And I have very few peers and you are one of them. What happens to and in your soul is a kind of map of the countryside of mine.

You say that success is like a candy—quickly eaten. But the analogy is closer. The first piece is wonderful, the second less so. The fifth has little taste and after the 10th, our mouths long for a pickle to clear the sweet cloy away. When people ask me if I am not proud to have written certain things, I reply that I am when the truth is that I am not at all. I don't even remember them very well and very deeply. Now here comes your soul again, because it parallels mine. Two years ago, as you will remember, I discovered that writing had become a habit with me and more than that, a pattern. I had lost the flavor of trial, of discovery, of excitement. My life had become dusty in my mouth. What I did was not worth doing because it gave me no delight. And you remember that I stopped writing. It was very hard to do because I had become a conditioned animal and it was easier to follow the road of my habit than to set off into the bewildering brush country of what is called idleness. Because Elaine's mind deals only with

healthy exactnesses, with faces and names, she would say, "What are you doing?" And I would say "working." "No you aren't," she said. "I know when you are working." But even she can be wrong because it was some of the hardest work I ever did, sitting still in a busy world, aching for nothingness or the meaning that could only grow out of nonparticipation. Here still we are parallel.

Now hear me out because I must go into figures of speech to try to explain. Externality is a mirror that reflects back to our mind the world our mind has created of the raw materials. But a mirror is a piece of silvered glass. There is a back to it. If you scratch off the silvering, you can see through the mirror to the other worlds on the other side. I know that many people do not want to break through. I do, passionately, hungrily. I think you do also.

I wanted peace from the small and to me old or repetitious tensions—the day's breakage in the house to be repaired, the crystal system, very like the solar system, of friendships, responsibilities, associations, mores, duties, empathies all revolving and held in orbit by me, by the fact that I existed, but all of these orbiting at different rates, at different speeds and with no two parabolas the same. And what I wished was to be relieved of this power, this *me*—to sit apart, untroubled with satellites and watch and see and perhaps to understand a world which had blinded and dizzied me. You say you are not tired. Neither am I—only bewildered.

Then there is another place where you and I are very alike. We are blindingly clever. We can twist up a ball of colored yarn, put glass beads in it, hang it from a string, and whirl it so that it seems a real world to many people. Sometimes we even get to believing it ourselves, but not for long. For cleverness is simply a way of avoiding thought. Do you see now why your soul is important to me? It is a pattern of my own.

I had to make a physical sacrifice, a bodily symbol of change and revolt against what was killing me, or rather smothering and turning me down like the damper of a stove. And so I prepared to go away from everything I know and by that means to try to find my way home. When Elaine would say with compassion—"I know you are miserable. What do you want to do?" I could not say the truth which was that I wanted nothing, and wanted to want nothing. That would have made no sense to her. Nothing is an horror to her. Odd that two people could be so different because I thirst for nothing, but because I cannot have that yet I must substitute understanding for a little while. But understanding was warped all out of shape by those rotations of a thousand satellites I spoke of.

And so I came here, to the hills near Glastonbury which has been a holy place since people first came to it maybe forty thousand years ago. Maybe I am telling you this because it seems to be beginning to work. The seed is swelling and the tip is turning green. I feel more at home here than I have ever felt in my life in any place. I perceive things that truly pass all understanding. Sixty to seventy generations have been born and lived, suffered, had fun and died in these walls. The flagstones on the lower floor are smoothed and hollowed by feet. And all of those generations were exactly like me—had hands and eyes, hunger, pain, anxiety and now and then ecstasy. Under my feet there is a great stack of men and women and I am sitting on the top of it, a tiny living organism on a high skeletal base, like the fringe of living coral on the mountain of dead coral rising from the sea bottom. Thus I have the fine integrity of sixty generations under me and the firm and fragrant sense that I shall join that pediment and support another living fringe and we will all be one. I've never known this sweet emulsion of mortality and continuum before.

At about six in the morning a bird calls me awake. I don't even know what kind of bird but his voice rises and falls with the insistence of a bugle in the morning so that I want to answer, "I hear and I obey!" Then I get up, shake down the coal in the stove, make coffee and for an hour look out at the meadows and the trees. I hear and smell and see and feel the earth and I think—nothing. This is the most wonderful time. Elaine sleeps later and I am alone—the largest aloneness 1 have ever known, mystic and wonderful.

Everyone is related to the world through something. I through words—perhaps inordinately but there it is. But before I stopped writing, words had become treacherous and untrustworthy to me. And then, without announcement they began assembling quietly and they slipped down my pencil to the paper—not the tricky, clever, lying, infected words—but simpler, stately, beautiful, old with dignity and fresh and young as that bird who wakes me with a song as old as the world, and announces every day as a new thing in creation. My love and respect and homage for my language is coming back. Here are proud words and sharp words and words as dainty as little girls and stone words needing no adjectives as crutches. And they join hands and dance beauty on the paper.

This is true—as true as I can think and if you do not believe me, or think this is an effusion you can go fuck yourself. But if you do believe it or feel that it is so, because we are related, you and I—then you will know that somewhere you will find your home also. That does not mean you must remain in it. Finding it, feeling it and knowing it is there—is more than you can conceive and is enough.

If I could influence you I would tell you to go to Greece or Turkey—to Delphi, Argos, Epidaurus, Lesbos—go alone and see if that is your home. But go alone, so that when the eagles of Zeus fly out from the cliffs above Delphi, they fly for you. I am alone here. Elaine quickly builds a life of neighbors, children, tradesmen, household duties and pleasures and despairs—of friendly, unpoisoned gossip and of endless talk and talk and talk. And because I love her and do not want always to be alone, we meet and associate and enjoy and then each goes to his private home again without anger nor jealousy.

Lift up your mind to the hills, Gadg. Criticize nothing, evaluate nothing. Just let the Thing come thundering in—accept and enjoy. It will be chaos for a while but gradually order will appear and an order you did not know. No one survives in other people more than two weeks after his death unless he leaves something he has much more lasting than himself.

This is a long letter of talk. What difference? I can afford the time and even the possibility of boring you. Your soul? I've been talking about mine and it is the same as yours—not identical but like.

And I watch the words of my translation go down and god damn, I think they are good. They are clean, hard, accentless English prose, exquisitely chosen and arranged and I am overwhelmed with joy because something in me has let go and the clear blue flame of my creativeness is released. I am uplifted but not humbled because I have paid for this with the currency of confusion and little sufferings and it is mine, sealed and registered. And on that whole stack under me, no one could do it as I am doing it. It makes me want to scream with a kind of orgiastic triumph.

Go to Greece, but come by here on your way. The shield of Achilles was made of bronze compounded from the tin mined in the hills of which the diggings are still visible. The Camelot of King Arthur is only four miles from here—a great and frowning fort built thousands of years before there could have been an Arthur, and there are stone rings hereabouts which like Stonehenge bear the crossed axes which prove that the builders came from your own native Anatolia wherefrom the mysterious genius of the Hittite people spread out over the world.

Come to visit me in the place I have come home to. I will not go away from here until Thanksgiving at the earliest. That is a secret between us. I suppose most of this letter is secret between us but largely because who else would understand it? I have spoken to you as I would talk to my own heart.

Yours
John
—Steinbeck: A Life in Letters, pp. 624–628

* * *

Steinbeck to Shirley Fisher, 10 August 1959

Shirley Fisher was a Long Island neighbor of the Steinbecks and an agent with McIntosh and Otis. Steinbeck wrote her from his Somerset cottage reporting on his Malory research. He and Elaine had recently visited spots in Wales, including Usk, where they sent Fisher a birthday telegram: "Happy Birthday to Yousk from Usk."

Dear Shirley Elfinheimer:

We couldn't resist sending the wire from Usk and were afraid some one would correct it on the way. But once bitten with the silly joke, we were committed. It was like with Erskine Caldwell. I couldn't resist addressing him at Claridges as Erskine Caldwell, Ersk. Who could?

I don't know whether you have read my first book of Lancelot. I hope so. It's a crazy thing but mine own. You see I *like* Lancelot. I recognize him because in some ways he is me—corny and fallible. Then consider Guinevere. No one has ever made the point that you had to like a guy pretty much to be unfaithful with him because if you got caught, you got burnt and you knew it. The danger wasn't getting divorced or pregnant, it was getting up on a bonfire. It took some courage, did infidelity.

But it's a hard story because you have to believe the enchantments or it is all nonsense. You had to believe it as much as we believe psychiatry and much the same way. I'm trying to write it so that the reader doesn't question necromancy. It is an every day matter. Then you take treason against the king. To Lancelot—that wasn't a crime, it was a sin—the worst a man could commit. When he feels bad toward Arthur it is because he has committed the dirtiest sin he can conceive.

You know, perhaps it is your inspiration but I have been practicing on the harmonica very hard. I could always pick out a tune but not really play. Now I'm trying to learn to play and it's fun. When I get back I'm going to hunt Larry Adler out and ask him to give me some instruction about control of tones.

On the way home from the Wye Valley, we stopped at Berkeley Castle where Edward II was murdered. This is not National Trust but just the Berkeley family. No guides, you are free to walk about but there is a sign asking visitors to respect the property and it ends up with a line I like. It says—"It is the duty of a host to make a guest feel at home. It is the duty of a guest not to." Isn't that fine? The moment a guest feels at home the host has lost his property.

I hope you had a fine birthday and we are waiting to hear about it. If you are around a music store, will you see whether there is a compendium on harmonica playing?

love
John
—Steinbeck: A Life in Letters, pp. 647–648

The Public Steinbeck

Steinbeck to Arthur Larson, 12 January 1957

Steinbeck wrote to Arthur Larson, director of the United States Information Agency, regarding news that he had heard about President Dwight D. Eisenhower's plan for the program that became known as People to People. Steinbeck proposed the use of literature in the program and later became involved in the program himself.

Dear Mr. Larson:

The following notes arise out of a genuine concern about our communications with our neighbors.

Recently the President asked William Faulkner, perhaps the dean of American writers, to form a committee to recommend techniques for what Mr. Eisenhower tellingly called "a People to People program."

It has been our misfortune to dangle our freedom in front of our neighbors and then to refuse them even the simplest hospitality. Our closed and suspicious borders have not reassured our friends and have given our enemies magnificent propaganda fuel.

Our refusal of a passport to Paul Robeson, for example, was stupid. An intelligent move would have been to let him travel and to send Jackie Robinson with him.

The second item grows out of our uneasiness that we are constantly re-converting our friends who do not need it, and ignoring our enemies who do. In this, of course, we are driven by our hysteria about security.

I believe that commerce is not only the mother of civilization, but the teacher of understanding and the god of peace. And I mean all kinds of commerce—movement of goods and movement of ideas. The first act of a dictator is to close the borders to travel, goods and ideas. It is always a matter of sadness, and of suspicion to me, when we close our borders to any of these.

In 1936, I went as a tourist to Russia and what were then called the Balkans. In 1947, with Robert Capa, I toured Russia and some of the satellites for the Herald-Tribune. We asked many people who had been kind to us what we could send them. The invariable answer was "books." On returning, we sent books. They never arrived. We sent them again—and again they failed to arrive.

Next—I have had a number of letters from East German students who crossed into West Germany, ostensibly to take part in Communist rallies. These letters asked for books, gave Berlin addresses to which they should be sent, and guaranteed wide distribution. One student said, "I can assure you that at least a thousand people will read each book you send." Naturally, I sent the books—not only my own books, but many others.

Now—My conclusion is that the book is revered. The book is somehow true, where propaganda is suspected. Denial of the right to read whatever they want to is one of the most bitterly resented of all of the Soviet's tyrannies.

You will remember the Army editions of books sent to troops during the last war. They were small, compact—designed to fit in the shirt pocket. They were distributed by the millions. Publishers and authors contributed their services. Where are those plates? Could they be reprinted? They could be moved over borders in various ways—by Underground, as the East German students suggested, by balloons as Radio Free Europe has flown pamphlets, and by the inevitable movements across borders, no matter how closed they are. A packet of books thrown over the barbwire fence and picked up by a border guard *might* be burned, but I swear it is more likely that the books would be hidden, treasured

Front cover of the 1956 collection of Steinbeck's weekly articles (written in English and translated into French) that were originally published in Le Figaro littéraire *from 12 June to 18 September 1954 (from William McPheron,* John Steinbeck: From Salinas to Stockholm, *2000; Special Collections, Thomas Cooper Library, University of South Carolina)*

Steinbeck, Reporter

Around the time of this April 1956 letter to the Syndicated Newspaper Editors, Steinbeck agreed to cover the year's national political conventions for the Louisville Courier-Journal.

Thank you for accepting my convention copy sight unseen, but I think I owe you an explanation and an out. I have never been to a National Convention. That is my main reason for wanting to go.

When I first suggested that I go conventioning I was told that I had no training as a political reporter. This was true and I began to study the techniques of my prospective colleagues who were so trained. I was particularly interested in the analysis of one paragraph of a Presidential news conference by four politically trained reporters. Each one experted it differently. Walter Lippmann, the Alsops and David Lawrence have nothing to fear from me.

I have no sources—dependable or otherwise. If I should make a prediction, it will probably be assembled out of information from the wife of the alternate delegate from San José, California, plus whispers from the bell-hop who has just delivered a bucket of ice to "usually dependable sources."

A new political phrase is "running scared." This is presumed to be good because it means the candidate is running hard. Well, I'm writing scared. A good writer always writes scared.

I have promised to give you printable copy. I think I can, but if this boast should turn out to be so much grass roots, I don't think you should take the rap. I shall write what I see and hear and what I find amusing or illuminating. If you do not find it so, all bets are off. If on the other hand I succeed in interesting you and your subscribers, I shall insist, in addition to the simple money agreed on, that I be given honorary police, military, social, civic and tree planting honors.

Yours very truly,
John Steinbeck
—Steinbeck: A Life in Letters, pp. 525–526

---

and distributed. During the German occupation of Norway and Denmark, my own books were mimeographed on scraps of paper and distributed.

Now—What kind of books?

Any kind. Poetry, essays, novels, plays—these are the things desired and begged for. Pictures of how it is in America—good and bad. The moment it is all good, it is automatically propaganda and will be disbelieved.

These are some of the conclusions of the best writers in our country, and they are offered out of a simple desire to help in your very difficult task.

Yours very sincerely,
John Steinbeck
—Steinbeck: A Life in Letters, pp. 546–548

* * *

Steinbeck to Pascal Covici, 16 May 1957

When playwright Arthur Miller refused to testify before the House Committee on Un-American Activities (HUAC) and was cited for contempt of Congress, Steinbeck wrote an article in his defense that was published in the June 1957 Esquire. This letter from Steinbeck to his editor, Pascal Covici, provides background information on his position.

Dear Pat:

Spring has finally come, and late spring at that. The rains have stopped and the sunshine is beautiful, almost painfully beautiful so that in the morning you look out and take a quick breath as you do when you are quickly, sharply hurt. This afternoon I walked for quite a long time by the Arno and repeopled it. And I can now. I know what the people used to wear and to some extent how they thought, at least in so far as any age can get near another. But I told you I felt that I understood.

Thanks for sending Atkinson's letter on to me. [Brooks Atkinson, drama critic of *The New York Times*.] I have answered it.

I feel deeply that writers like me and actors and painters are in difficulty because of their own cowardice or perhaps failure to notice. When Artie told me that not one writer had come to his defense, it gave me a lonely sorrow and a shame that I waited so long and it seemed to me also that if we had fought back from the beginning instead of running away, perhaps these things would not be happening now. These committee men are neither very brave nor very intelligent. They would not attack an organism which defended itself. But they have been quite brave in pursuing rabbits and in effect we have been like rabbits. [Senator Joseph] McCarthy went down not because Eisenhower faced him. That is a god damned lie. Eisenhower was scared of him. It took one brave man, Ed Murrow, to stand up to him to show that he had no strength. And Artie may be serving all of us. Please give him my respect and more than that, my love. You see, we have had all along the sharpest weapons of all, words, and we did not use them, and I for one am ashamed. I don't think I was frightened but truly, I was careless.

Only two more days in Florence. I've had a large and good time here with too much work perhaps but very valuable.

love to all there,
john
—Steinbeck: A Life in Letters, pp. 555–556

* * *

William Faulkner to Steinbeck, 1957

Having been invited to attend the PEN International meeting in Tokyo in September 1957, Steinbeck wrote Faulkner for advice about Japanese society and received the following reply.

The thing to watch for is their formality, their excessive prolongation of mannerly behavior; I had to watch myself to keep from getting fretted, impatient, or at least from showing it, with the prolonged parade of social behavior, ritual behavior, in even the most unimportant and unscheduled social contacts. They make a ritual of gift-giving—little things, intrinsically nothing. I was always careful to accept each one as if it were a jade Buddha or ivory fan, and return in kind, I mean with the same formality, giving the same importance not to the gift but to the giving, the act.

That's all you need remember. A culture whose surface manners is important to them; a people already sold in our favor; they will know your work by the time you get there much better than you will ever know theirs. They will really make you believe that being a writer, an artist, a literary man, is very important. Probably the nicest gift you can give is an inscribed book of your own.

—Steinbeck: A Life in Letters, pp. 564–565

* * *

A Blade for Arthur Miller

Steinbeck's fondness for Arthur Miller is seen in a 1956 letter to Annie Laurie Williams, the agent who handled movie and drama contracts for McIntosh and Otis.

Did you ever hear the poem I wrote for Artie Miller? I guess he is the most peaceful man in the world and one of the gentlest. Anyway one time when I was going into Mexico, he asked me to bring him a machete. You know in Oaxaca they make the most beautiful in this hemisphere. The makers are in fact direct descendants of the sword makers who went from Damascus to Toledo in Spain and then brought their secrets to Mexico. They make the great blades which can be tied in a knot and then spring back straight. Arthur wanted the machete, not for murder but to cut brush on his country place. Anyway I bought a beauty and since most of these have some noble statement etched on them I had etched on this blade the following poem which I think is funny, if you know Artie:

Who dares raise war 'gainst Arthur Miller,
Destroys the Lamb, Creates the killer.
Then Leap, Sweet Steel, release the flood,
Until the insult drowns in Blood.

Artie loved it and perhaps even once or twice got to believing it.

—Steinbeck: A Life in Letters, p. 556

Steinbeck to Faulkner, 20 February 1957

Steinbeck wrote Faulkner to thank him for his advice on the trip to Tokyo.

Dear Bill:

Thank you very much for your advice.

I think possibly I knew these things but it is good to have them underlined. I know what you mean about the continued formality, and it makes me itch a little bit, but I think I will get by with it.

I am particularly glad about the advice about taking books. I get so damned sick of them before they are out that giving them to someone seems a poor present. But if that's what they want, that's what they'll get.

I read in the papers that you are considering going to Greece. I hope you do. Nothing has ever given me the emotional impact like that little country—an earthquake feeling of coming home, a recognition of everything. And the light makes it seem that you can look into the surfaces of things and see them in depth. I have never been quite so moved as I was by my first experience in Greece, and it doesn't get any less moving. They are wild, crazy, disrespectful, independent people and I think you'll love them.

I was asking the brother of the Queen something about peasants and he told me a story of walking with the King in the countryside and stopping where a man was tilling a field. They asked him what kind of fertilizer he was using. The man straightened up, looked in the face of his sovereign and said: "You stick to your kinging and let me stick to my farming."

Again, thanks for your advice. I shall try not to disgrace us and if I succeed in doing that, it will be a success.

Yours,
John Steinbeck
—*Steinbeck: A Life in Letters*, pp. 565–566

* * *

Steinbeck to Annie Laurie Williams, 28 August 1957

Steinbeck wrote Williams with comments on a musical stage adaptation of Of Mice and Men *(1937), produced Off-Broadway in 1957, by Ira J. Bilowit, Wilson Lehr, and Alfred Brooks.*

Dear Annie Laurie:

With reference to the Mice and Men music and plans we heard the night before last—I would not presume to give advice to creative people, which means of course, that I will inundate them with advice.

Steinbeck on Boris Pasternak

The decision to give the 1958 Nobel Prize in literature to Boris Pasternak was harshly condemned in the Soviet Union. In a 6 November 1958 letter to Stuart L. Hannon of Radio Free Europe, Steinbeck expressed dismay at the official Soviet response.

Dear Mr. Hannon:

Thank you for your very kind letter. You may use any part of the following statement you wish or all of it.

The Award of the Nobel Prize to Pasternak and the Soviet outcry against it makes me sad but not for Pasternak. He has fulfilled his obligation as a writer, has seen his world, described it and made his comment. That the product of his art has found response everywhere in the world where it has been permitted to be seen must be a satisfaction to him.

He is not to be pitied however, no matter how cruelly he may be treated. My sadness is for the poor official writers sitting in judgment on a book they are not allowed to read. They are the grounded vultures of art who having helped to clip their own wings are righteously outraged at Flight and contemptuous of Eagles. These are the sad ones at last, the crippled and distorted ones, and it is quite natural that they should be hostile toward one who under equal pressures did not succumb and did not fail. They are the pallbearers of Soviet Literature, and they must now be aware of the weight of the corpse.

No matter how they may quote Pasternak in his absence, no matter what groveling may be reported, his book is here to refute them now and always. The real traitors to literature are Pasternak's judges, and they will be punished as were the judges of Socrates—their names forgotten and only their stupidities remembered.

Yours,
John Steinbeck
—*Steinbeck: A Life in Letters*, p. 602

The company must add a freshness to my play which may well suffer from a kind of mustiness.

First, I like what I heard. I know the pressure they are under and they did it very well and I am grateful. There was freshness and force in what they did. M & M may seem to be unrelieved tragedy, but it is not. A careful reading will show that while the audience knows, against its hopes, that the dream will not come true, the protagonists must, during the play, become convinced that it will come true. Everyone in the world has a dream he knows can't come off but he spends his life hoping it may. This is at once the sadness, the greatness and the triumph of our species. And this belief on stage must go from skepticism to possibility to probability before it is nipped off by whatever the modern word for fate is. And in hopelessness–George is able to rise to greatness–to kill his friend to save him. George is a hero and only heroes are worth writing about. Boileau said that a long time ago and it is still true.

The other night the word "corn" came up and I said not to be afraid of corn. I want to amend that now. In an otherwise lovely song the words occur "It wasn't meant to be." To me this is fake corn. It implies a teleology not inherent in this play. You will find any number of things were not "meant to be" in a lot of successful plays and songs and I hate every pea-picking, Elvis Presley moment of them.

On the other hand a sense of fate expressed as I have heard it "Everything in life is 7 to 5 against"–is good corn. If the protagonists leave a feeling that they never had much of a chance–and in this play that is perfectly true–let them sing that the deck was stacked, the dice shaved, the track muddy, there was too much grease on the pig–corn, sure, but make it corn in the vernacular. I like the idea of a little party when the girl comes to her new home. Let it almost work! Almost! and let the audience feel that it might.

I like the idea that George might get the girl or at least that he might want to get the girl. This would enrich. And also you might let the girl feel that she might want George–all good and all possible.

Now let me finally speak of music. I am pleased with the freshness and unhackneyed tone. I like the hint of the blues. Remember, please, though that music can pull the guts out of an audience. Consider then–hinting at the known–the square dance, the ballad, the ode, again the blues, even the Moody and Sankey hymn form. These are part of all of us and we rise like trout to mayflies to them. Hint at them–because after all this is a ranch. Let your audience *almost* recognize something familiar and out of that go to your freshness.

My friend Abe Burrows told me a very wise thing once about theatre and I believe him. He said–"Your audience is usually ahead of the play. They get impatient if you tell them something they have already got. Give them a signal and let them do it." My own plays, most of which have failed, have failed because I told audiences things rather than let them move along. A good mule skinner simply indicates to his lead pair what he wants by a twitch of the jerk line. And the mules do it.

Now finally–I am pleased and excited with this project. I think it can have stature as well as uniqueness. I know the old feeling about never letting the author backstage but I think you will find me a different kind of author. I have no wish to protect my "immortal lines," I want a play and I'll go along with anything that works–and help with it too. Just let's keep it hard and

clean and very, very sparse. The emotion is in the situation. Let the audience emote and let the players simply twitch the jerk line.

And there is the advice I said I wouldn't presume to give you. Believe me please when I say that if I were not stimulated by what you have done–I wouldn't bother.

Good luck and thanks–

John Steinbeck
–*Steinbeck: A Life in Letters*, pp. 562–564

* * *

Steinbeck to John Forman, 3 June 1958

Steinbeck encountered a public-relations problem when the headmaster of his son Thom's school, John Forman, wrote with concerns about Cannery Row *(1945). Forman, a Christian Scientist, had received an anonymous letter pointing out that some of the girls at the Cannery Row brothel are identified as Christian Scientists.*

My dear Mr. Forman:

Your letter of May 31st arrived this morning and I have considered it very slowly trying to understand both what it says and what is perhaps implied. In this response I hope to leave no room for interpretations.

When I visited the Forman School and enjoyed your hospitality I was quite well aware that you and Mrs. Forman were Christian Scientists. And surely your feeling that there was no hostility was keen and accurate. Indeed the opposite was true, for it seemed to me that we were in agreement that the Christian fabric is a strong and ancient tree out of which a number of branches grew, and that one must know the tree before one is capable of climbing to his own personal branch. I wish my son to know the tree. The branch he chooses will be what his feeling, his thought and his nature make desirable and necessary. In this I think we agreed and I still believe that to be so. But I would no more interfere with his choice than I would rob him of any other freedom so long, a least, as his choice is not dictated by fear or ignorance, or social or economic gain. However, he must have the tools of choice–knowledge, understanding, humility and contemplation.

I have never felt or uttered contempt for any religion. On the other hand, in religion as in politics I have attacked corruption and hypocrisy and I think in this I have the indisputable example of Jesus, if authority be needed.

Let me now go to Page 17 of Cannery Row. I dearly hope that neither you nor your friend read it out of context. The statement that a number of the girls were Christian Scientists was neither contempt nor satire but simply a statement of fact. For eighteen years I lived and worked in that laboratory. The book is only fiction in form and style. I do not know what the organized church felt about it but these girls took comfort and safety in their faith and I cannot conceive of any Christian organization rejecting them. There is no possible alternative interpretation of Jesus' instructions concerning Mary Magdalene. His contempt was reserved for the stone throwers.

Cannery Row was written in compassion rather than contempt, and a bartender who reads Science and Health (and he did) seems to me no ill thing. Few heroes and fewer saints have sprung into being full blown.

In only one book have I tried to formalize my own personal branch of the ancient tree. That was East of Eden, and while it is long, it is precise.

Finally, I am content that you can and will help my son in the always agonizing search for himself, for I felt that the tone and the overtone of the school were good. And while I am not inclined to be critical, I do feel saddened by the man who, calling himself FBI, used as a weapon a misinterpretation of one sentence of a lifetime of work. It seems to me that it was an unkindly and therefore unChristian impulse.

John Steinbeck
—*Steinbeck: A Life in Letters*, pp. 584–585

* * *

Correspondent Steinbeck
Herbert Kupferberg

Herbert Kupferberg reviewed Once There Was a War *(1958), a collection of Steinbeck's World War II journalism.*

Once there was a war and John Steinbeck went to cover it. It was the New York *Herald Tribune* which sent him there, as a matter of fact, and the year was 1943. Some of those dispatches which appeared in this newspaper have now been collected in book form and fitted out with an introduction in which Mr. Steinbeck sets down his memories of soldiers, censors and war correspondents. He resisted the impulse to turn his dispatches into a book at the time, he says, because he felt that "unless the stories had validity twenty years in the future they should stay on the yellowing pages of dead newspaper files."

Well, it has been only fifteen years. But these samples of Steinbeck's journalism decidedly do have validity, both as memory joggers and as artistically wrought pictures of the war that are often quite moving.

It so happens that 1943 was one of those in-between years of the war; the year after the invasion of North Africa and the year before the invasion of France. So although Steinbeck's itinerary covered England, North

Africa and Italy, his stories for the most part deal with the everyday war, the less spectacular but more typical aspects of a soldier's life. Those are accounts of what it was like to cross the Atlantic in a silent, darkened troopship (something which nearly every soldier remembers vividly); what it was like in London during the bombings; what it was like at an American bomber base in England; what it was like when the kids asked for chewing gum and oranges; what it was like when an Italian village fell all over itself trying to surrender.

Scenes such as these retain a surprising immediacy in Steinbeck's recountings, perhaps because after fifteen years of gnawing worldwide struggle one feels almost an acute nostalgia for the days when joyous Sicilians garlanded the G.I.s with grapes, and "Lilli Marlene" wafted its haunting melody between the opposing lines. "It would be amusing if, after all the fuss and heiling, all the marching and indoctrination, the only contribution to the world by the Nazis was 'Lilli Marlene,'" wrote the Steinbeck of fifteen years ago, and he wasn't far wrong.

Unlike some correspondents, Steinbeck saw the war less in terms of military strategy and political objectives than of the people involved in it either purposefully or accidentally. In them, he found, was the stuff of life and of legend. There are both a-plenty in this warm and truthful book.

—*New York Herald Tribune Book Review*, 8 February 1959; reprinted in *John Steinbeck: The Contemporary Reviews*, p. 446

* * *

Steinbeck to John F. Kennedy, 23 January 1961

After hearing John F. Kennedy's inaugural address, Steinbeck was so moved that he wrote the following letter to the president, marking the start of a close friendship. In his reply Kennedy wrote, "I only regret that it was not possible for me to meet personally with you and other distinguished artists who were kind enough to be in Washington," adding the handwritten statement, "No President was ever prayed over with such fervor. Evidently they felt that the country or I needed it—probably both."

My dear Mr. President:

I thank you for inviting me to your inauguration. I was profoundly moved by this ceremony which I had never seen before and even more moved by your following speech which was not only nobly conceived and excellently written and delivered, but also had that magic undertone of truth which cannot be simulated.

Personally, of course, I am honored to have been invited, but much more sharply felt is my gratification that through me you have recognized the many good members of my profession as existing at all. A nation may be moved by its statesmen and defended

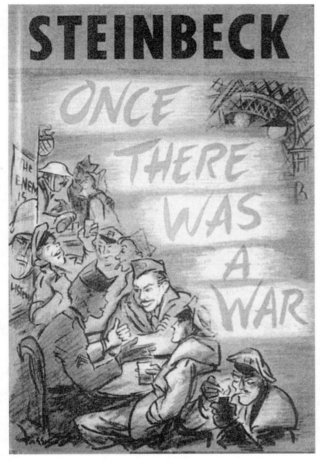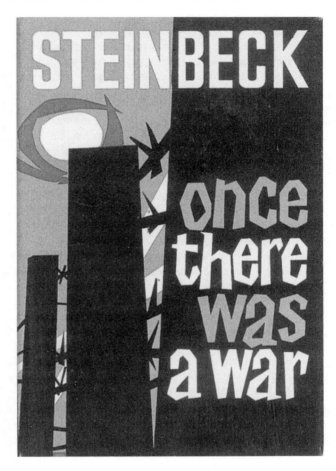

*Dust jacket for the 1958 Viking edition of Steinbeck's collected World War II journalism and the front cover of the 1959
British edition (left, from Robert B. Harmon,* The Collectible John Steinbeck, *1986; Thomas Cooper Library,
University of South Carolina; right, from Christie's East, Jack E. and Rachel Gindi Collection of Modern
Literature, 20 April 1994; Special Collections, Thomas Cooper Library, University of South Carolina)*

by its military but it is usually remembered for its artists. It does seem to me that you, sir, have discovered
or rather rediscovered this lost truth.

Again my thanks, my pledge and my passionate
hope that your words may become history. And I
believe they will!

Yours gratefully,
John Steinbeck
—Steinbeck: A Life in Letters, pp. 690–691

* * *

Steinbeck to Covici, July 1961

*After learning of Ernest Hemingway's death, Steinbeck
wrote Covici a frank letter expressing his feelings about the novelist. Steinbeck felt that Hemingway "never changed style, theme
nor story. He made no experiments in thinking nor in emotion."*

Dear Pat:

Before I am tempted into civility, let's get one thing
straight. It made me proud to see how here at New Discove
you resisted rushing to cut the lawn and plunge your arms
into the soil. Marvelous example of self-control. I could see
your knuckles pressed white on your Vodka glass while
your whole being cried out for hard physical labor.

The first thing we heard of Ernest Hemingway's
death was a call from the London Daily Mail, asking me to
comment on it. And quite privately, although something of
this sort might have been expected, I find it shocking. He
had only one theme—only one. A man contends with the
forces of the world, called fate, and meets them with courage. Surely a man has a right to remove his own life but
you'll find no such possibility in any of H's heros. The sad
thing is that I think he would have hated accident much
more than suicide. He was an incredibly vain man. An accident while cleaning a gun would have violated everything
he was vain about. To shoot yourself with a shot gun in the

head is almost impossible unless it is planned. Most such deaths happen when a gun falls, and then the wound is usually in the abdomen. A practiced man does not load a gun while cleaning it. Indeed a hunting man would never have a loaded gun in the house. There are shot guns over my mantle but the shells are standing on the shelf below. The guns are cleaned when they are brought in and you have to unload a gun to clean it. H. had a contempt for mugs. And only a mug would have such an accident. On the other hand, from what I've read, he seems to have undergone a personality change in the last year or so. Certainly his last summer in Spain and the resulting reporting in Life were not in his old manner. Perhaps, as Paul de Kruif told me, he had had a series of strokes. That would account for the change.

But apart from all that—he has had the most profound effect on writing—more than anyone I can think of. He has not a vestige of humor. It's a strange life. Always he tried to prove something. And you only try to prove what you aren't sure of. He was the critics' darling because he never changed style, theme nor story. He made no experiments in thinking nor in emotion. A little like Capa, he created an ideal image of himself and then tried to live it. I am saddened at his death. I never knew him well, met him a very few times and he was always pleasant and kind to me although I am told that privately he spoke very disparagingly of my efforts. But then he thought of other living writers, not as contemporaries but as antagonists. He really cared about his immortality as though he weren't sure of it. And there's little doubt that he has it.

One thing interests me very much. For a number of years he has talked about a big book he was writing and then about several books written and put away for future publication. I have never believed these books exist and will be astonished if they do. A writer's first impulse is to let someone read it. Of course I may be wrong and he may be the exception. For the London Daily Express, I have two lines by a better writer than either of us. When they call this morning, Elaine will dictate them over the cable. They go—

He was a man, take him all in all,
I shall not look upon his like again.

And since he was called Papa—the lines are doubly applicable.

That's all today. I got up at five. Now it's time to work.

And I did work and got a goodly part of a thing done. So I will send this.

Prosit
John
—*Steinbeck: A Life in Letters*, pp. 703–705

The Winter of Our Discontent (1961)

Steinbeck to Frank and Jo Loesser, 25 May 1960

Lyricist and composer Frank Loesser had recently married his second wife, Broadway actress Jo Sullivan, when Steinbeck wrote with news of his novel in progress, The Winter of Our Discontent *(1961). Steinbeck also alluded to his planned cross-country journey for the fall of 1960, the trip that was the basis for* Travels with Charley: In Search of America *(1962). All the nicknames in the letter refer to Jo.*

Dear Frank and Fatima:

Soraya's letter arrived and about time. I wanted to have intercourse with you, i.e., communication, but somebody gets screwed. Somehow I can't imagine the toy Brunhild in a yashmak. Yes, I do know Marrakech. I spent some disreputable time there during the war. The smell of piss of a thousand years plus a thousand years of saffron that has passed through the Arab body can be smelled deep in the Atlas—but isn't that city wall in the sunset something to see?

I have been in wonder at the word Frank—First a javelin, then a German, then a Christian, then a Western person, once a sty where pigs are fattened, then fat, then pure or good like frankincense, then open, honest, outspoken, bold—in a word Franc or Frank. And now the name describes a little, mean, crooked, evil-eyed, devious, conniving, dark-browed gnome of Jewish extraction. Grimm's law of language mutation will not take care of this situation.

I am delighted that your pocket Valkyrie is loving the trip. And if in the future a bunch of Ayrabs come up with a Middlewestern accent, I wouldn't be surprised.

My new book is known to no one except Elaine. I have told only the title, a great one, I think. The Winter of Our Discontent. It's a strange book that is taking its own pace—part Kafka and part Booth Tarkington with a soup-song of me. It's writing along and I am following mostly amazed. I hope to finish it this summer.

In the fall—right after Labor Day—I'm going to learn about my own country. I've lost the flavor and taste and sound of it. It's been years since I have seen it. Sooo! I'm buying a pick-up truck with a small apartment on it, kind of like the cabin of a small boat, bed, stove, desk, icebox, toilet—not a trailer—what's called a coach. I'm going alone, out toward the West by the northern way but zigzagging through the Middle West and the mountain states. I'll avoid cities, hit small towns and farms and ranches, sit in bars and hamburger stands and on Sunday go to church. I'll go down the coast from Washington and Oregon and then back through the Southwest and South and up the East Coast but always zigzagging. Elaine will join me occasionally but mostly I have to go alone, and I shall go unknown. l just want to look and listen. What I'll get I need badly–a re-knowledge of my own country, of its speeches, its views, its attitudes and its changes. It's long overdue–very long. New York is not America. I am very excited about doing this. It will be a kind of a rebirth. Do you like the idea? I'm not worried about being recognized. I have a great gift for anonymity.

Frank, when you are in Paris, please show your bride John's Elysée. After that I won't even mind if you take her to the Tour F.L.

And a belated congratulation on M.H.F. [*The Most Happy Fella,* Loesser's 1956 musical]. We hear from Londoners that it is terrific and a wild crazy smash. Isn't that a hell of a way to refer to a damn fine piece of work?

Anyway, have fun and write if you don't get work.

Love to you both,
John
–Steinbeck: A Life in Letters, pp. 666–667

* * *

Steinbeck's Fables
Peter Harcourt

Peter Harcourt's review of The Winter of Our Discontent *included an overview of Steinbeck's earlier works.*

For over 25 years now, John Steinbeck has been a prolific and unpredictable novelist. The first of his works to attract attention were *Tortilla Flat,* and *To a God Unknown,* both published in 1935. Already in these early works, Steinbeck revealed what we now think of as his most characteristic qualities: his warmth, his whimsy, his sense of fun, his mistrust of organized society, his belief in the validity of the simple pleasures of simple people, and if indeed his sentimentality, also his reverence for life of all kinds, for all things that grow. Like so many American writers, Steinbeck is at heart a fablist; and both these novels have all the directness and simplicity of a fable. *To a God Unknown* is undisguisedly a celebration of the forgotten mysteries of a pagan world, of the gods of the earth and the sky, with a blood sacrifice at the end that brings on the required rain. And in *Tortilla Flat*–as some ten years later in *Cannery Row* and its sequels–if the solemnity in the face of the mysterious gods of the earth has disappeared, the simple sense of wonder remains.

The world of the Salinas Valley in California–the world of Monterey that in *Tortilla Flat* produced Danny and Danny's friends and in *Cannery Row,* Doc, Mack, and the boys–is a world virtually untouched by the hustling way of life of the great American continent. In *Tortilla Flat* and in *Cannery Row* the values both praised and embodied are above all loyalty and friendship; then indolence,

drunkenness, a playful violence, cheerful drabbing with androgynous whores, and general high spirits and affection. In this world of Steinbeck's fancy, there is nothing so intense or personal as love, because love would involve complexity and tension and the whole of his characters' personalities, while the layabouts of Monterey are all just generalised warmth and good-will. They have the single dimension and immediate appeal of characters in a fairy tale. To drink wine with one's friends, to wiggle one's toes in the sun–this is the core of life and its wisdom. And however unreal this rose-coloured world may appear to us, it is difficult not to respond to these books that have been so warmly, so generously conceived.

But beneath the whimsy and unreality of these particular novels, there lies a serious social concern; and from this concern as again from the Salinas Valley came Steinbeck's two greatest works–*Of Mice and Men* and *The Grapes of Wrath.* These two books can also be seen as fables, but this time the characters have the accent and manners of real people. In *Of Mice and Men,* Lennie is a simpleton, a kind, loving creature who delights in bright colours and in the texture of soft things, but who possesses the strength of a giant. Lennie epitomises all of Steinbeck's characters who are underprivileged in some way. There is simply no place for such creatures in our society, no place for people who are inescapably different. They engender mistrust and suspicion. Lennie's strength is his undoing, and–like the old dog in the middle of the story–Lennie has to be destroyed. There is simply no other way.

The Grapes of Wrath exhibits Steinbeck's most hostile criticism of American society, a society of unchecked technological expansion and exploitation. It is the struggle of the common people to survive starvation in the face of the wasteful abundance of the privately-owned fruit farms of California; and like the turtle at the opening of the book, no matter how many set-backs they experience, they carry on in the same direction. In this book, there is faith in abundance and an affirmative anger: "We've got a bad thing made by men, and by God that's something we can change." And at the close, when Rose of Sharon gives the life in her breast to the starving man in the barn, we realise that this is not only offered as a final indication of how the poor will look after one another, but also we get the sense that Rose of Sharon's baby was not lost completely in vain: as at the end of *To a God Unknown,* Steinbeck seems to be saying, through the loss of some lives, others may continue. Once more we have a kind of sacrifice and then the sense of life going on.

But I began with a reference to the unpredictability of Steinbeck as a novelist, for he has not always assumed the dungarees of an uneducated country people. The list of his complete works is a long one and contains books that are too various both in their treatment and in their success to encourage confident generalisation. *The Moon Is Down,* for instance, is the war-time story of an unspecified occupied country and of the quiet determination of the occupied people to resist the invader. Thematically, it is not unlike *The Grapes of Wrath,* but in manner, completely different. The whole thing is seen at a distance, with none of the immediacy of the world of the Salinas Valley. The tone is measured, cool and exact; and though it achieves a quiet impressiveness by the time we get to the end, the novel as a whole seems rather less than the sum of its individually persuasive moments.

Many readers will make a similar complaint about his most recent novel, *The Winter of our Discontent.* It is the story of a New England gentleman who, through his honesty and goodwill, has come down in the world and who sees a chance, by abandoning his honesty, to regain his fortune and thus the trappings of his social position and self-respect. In the process, of course, something inside him begins to corrode and the corrosion spills over and begins to spoil the lives of the people around him. Like *The Moon Is Down,* the whole thing is seen as if from a long way off, but this time the feeling of distance is largely the result of the discrepancy between the factitiousness of the plot—the clever way it is all made to fit together at the end like a thriller—and the warm humanity and inconsequential humour that enlivens each individual page and which serves to bring his characters so vividly to life.

And yet, although the manner is so different, the perennial Steinbeck concerns are there: the validity of the affections, of decency, even of small talk endlessly indulged in as a valuable transmitter of warmth and goodwill from one person to another. There is the same power of language, the proof of his own sensitive and sensuous response to experience, the ability to compel us not only to see what he is describing but to love it as much as Steinbeck does himself:

> No one in the world can rise to a party or a plateau of celebration like my Mary. It isn't what she contributes but what she receives that makes her glow like a jewel. Her eyes shine, her smiling mouth underlines, her quick laughter builds strength into a sickly joke. With Mary in the doorway of a party everyone feels more attractive and clever than he was, and so he actually becomes. Beyond this Mary does not and need not contribute.

And finally, there is the central recognition (so laboriously worked out, I feel, in *East of Eden*) that in some ultimate sense a man *is* his brother's keeper.

But most curiously of all in this novel, there is the pervasive feeling of something intangible, joined with a mistrust of the intellect, a feeling that there is something in life that governs our actions which is much deeper than thought. It is at times close to superstition and is as

implicit in this particular novel as it was overt in *To a God Unknown.* It is as if Steinbeck wishes to suggest that in our materialistic pursuits we have lost something meaningful, something perhaps magical, that is able to give life more than a merely day-to-day significance. He doesn't know exactly what it is, or at least, he can't say directly; but he writes about it in such a way that we are made to feel the reality of his sense of loss.

The Winter of our Discontent is a curious book and a strangely moving one, the product of a veteran novelist who throughout his career has managed to retain his faith that out of goodness and simple feelings, more goodness can flow and, as at the end of the novel, the light of life can continue burning.

> –*Time and Tide,* 41 (6 June 1961); reprinted in *John Steinbeck: The Contemporary Reviews,* pp. 453–455

* * *

John Steinbeck's Modern Morality Tale
Virgilia Peterson

In her review Virgilia Peterson called The Winter of Our Discontent *a novel worth scrutiny simply because of Steinbeck's previous books, but she noted that it compared unfavorably to his best work.*

We have come to think of John Steinbeck as a writer with two literary faces, the one gleeful, the other outraged, but both startlingly and memorably alive. It is the angry face, however, the face of the moralist, that commands, *ipso facto,* the more attention, and this is the one that looks out from the pages of his latest novel, *The Winter of Our Discontent.*

Deserting, for the new book, the exuberant California scene he has so often tenanted for his readers, Mr. Steinbeck now takes a sleepy-looking Long Island village named New Baytown for his setting. By-passed by modern industrial development, New Baytown still bears the marks, beyond the new municipal pier, of its Old Harbor, where deep-hulled whalers used to dock, and on its tree-lined streets the facades of Colonial houses still keep vigil among the functional buildings of today. The people in New Baytown know each other's habits, as, too, they know each other's place. The policeman keeps the same beat; the town drunk still begs money for a drink at the same hour of the night; the bank president arrives at the bank at the precise same moment in the morning; the red setter on Elm Street knows whom to salute with his tail. The ground New Baytown stands on has never shifted, you would swear, since its earliest settlers set foot on it. But, according to Mr. Steinbeck, you would be wrong. The real, the moral ground on which New Baytown stands today has cracked and shifted, perhaps irreparably.

The protagonist of this Steinbeck novel is Ethan Allen Hawley, descendant of New England whaling captains, but now, at the threshold of his middle age, reduced, by misfortune, mismanagement, and the chicanery of an earlier generation, to working for his family as a grocer's clerk. . . . Until the moment when the author presents him, he has been resigned to failure. How, at the cost of conscience, he almost achieves money, power, and success, and what happens to make them slip from his grasp, is the burden of this story.

It is on Good Friday—a day that Ethan has always held in awe and dread—that a wholesale grocery drummer offers him a five per cent cash bribe to obtain his employer's business and leaves behind him on the counter a shiny leather billfold with twenty dollars in it. And it is some three months later, on the Fourth of July week-end, that Ethan reaps the whirlwind he has meanwhile been sowing. In that brief span, Mr. Steinbeck undertakes to prove how easy it is to make out of a lamb a shark.

No one who has attempted to breast the tides of our affluent society would dare deny that its waters are shark-infested, nor fail to notice that it is to the victorious shark that the spoils usually go. Even the sharks themselves could scarcely quarrel with the thesis that today in America honesty is losing its reputation. But it takes more than an incontrovertible thesis to make a novel. No matter how right the author is, how fine his wrath, he will not disturb his readers' sleep or trouble their complacency unless he has filled the arteries of his characters with blood. But how much can we believe in this Ethan who makes such sophisticated jokes when in bed with his Boston-Irish wife and who sees through the maneuvers of one of Steinbeck's least probable huntresses, yet has never heard, till the day we meet him, of the bribe? How far can we believe in a man of innocence and principle who finds it so ridiculously easy to outshark the sharks? And if Ethan himself is hard to accept, the rest of the characters—with the exception of Ethan's tender, womanly, foolish wife—are all drawn quite casually from stock.

When serious, John Steinbeck is one of the most serious American writers of our time. Inescapably, therefore, whatever he writes is exposed to a fiercer scrutiny than is given to most of his contemporaries. With each new Steinbeck play or novel, there springs up the question: Is this as good as his best? In the case of *The Winter of Our Discontent*, the answer is, unfortunately, no.
—*New York Herald Tribune Book Review*, 25 June 1961; reprinted in *John Steinbeck: The Contemporary Reviews*, pp. 462–463

* * *

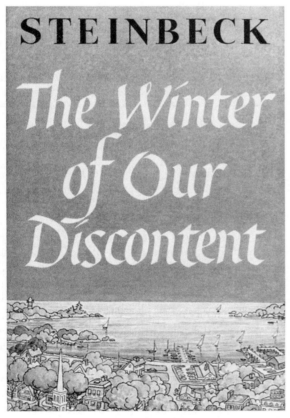

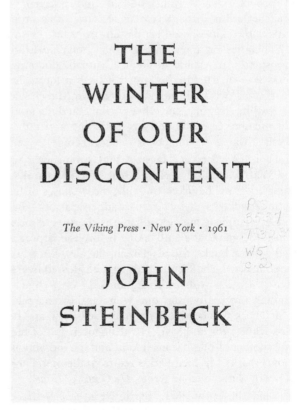

Dust jacket and title page for Steinbeck's last novel, about a middle-aged Long Island grocery clerk who yields to the temptation to engage in shady business practices (left, Sotheby's New York, The Maurice F. Neville Collection of Modern Literature, *November 16, 2004; right, Thomas Cooper Library, University of South Carolina)*

Yankee Luck
Edward Weeks

Edward Weeks reviewed The Winter of Our Discontent *for* The Atlantic.

In *The Winter of Our Discontent* . . . John Steinbeck turns for the first time in his versatile career to the East Coast for his setting and character. Bay Hampton, where on Good Friday morning his new story begins, could be any small seaport on Long Island or on the coast between New York and Boston. It is a village once famous for its Yankee skippers and sea-plucked fortunes, now being run by the new blood from Ireland and Italy. Ethan Allen Hawley, whose name echoes the past, is a gay, unaggressive spirit working as a clerk for Alfio Marullo; like his father before him, Ethan has lost the acquisitiveness of his forebears, and with it what remained of the family fortune. At the age of thirty-six all he has left is the old Hawley place, a couple of frankly envious children, and the nest egg of $6500 which his patient, pretty Irish wife, Mary, inherited from her brother.

The meaning of Good Friday was burned into Ethan as a boy, and it is ironic that on this day a series of small provocations—a bribe offered and rejected, a fortuneteller at her cards, a remark of Mary's that prodded under the skin—should startle him from his rut and even launch him on a new career. Ethan lends himself to the conspiracy of events in such a human, doubting-Thomas way that before he knows it he is in up to his knees. He has two charming accomplices in Margie and Mary, the one tempting, the other pushing, and the gradual debasement of his honesty is absorbing and rather shocking to watch. It all happens so effortlessly.

That his years at Harvard and his prowess in World War II should have left Ethan so feckless and so incompetent must be taken on faith; these phases of his career are touched so lightly as to be superficial, but what is genuine, familiar, and identifiable is the way Americans beat the game: the land-taking before the airport is built, the quick bucks, the plagiarism, the abuse of trust, the near theft, which, if it succeeds, can be glossed over—these are the guilts with which Ethan will have to live in his coming prosperity, and one wonders how happily. John Steinbeck was born to write of the sea coast, and he does so with savor and love. His dialogue is full of life, the entrapment of Ethan is ingenious, and the morality in this novel marks Mr. Steinbeck's return to the mood and the concern with which he wrote *The Grapes of Wrath.*

–*Atlantic,* 208 (July 1961); reprinted in *John Steinbeck: The Contemporary Reviews,* pp. 469–470

* * *

"Steinbeck in Holiday Mood"

British reviewer Eric Keown focused on the whimsy of The Winter of Our Discontent.

A man from the moon trying to learn about America from its current fiction would easily get the impression that all its thinking is done in small, cheerfully backward coastal communities, as untouched by progress as, say, East Anglia in 1914.

This significant retreat from the mainstream of American life is part of the new respect for the social courage of the beachcomber and the bum, and I dare say is healthy escapism. Such a forgotten port, left behind in the march of the big machines, is the scene of John Steinbeck's *The Winter of Our Discontent.* This is a study of an innocent whose character is corrupted by the discovery that graft is easy. The descendant of prosperous shipowners who have frittered their money away, he has been to Harvard and is now a grocery-clerk, happily married with two ruthless children. He has odd habits. He makes speeches to his bottles of tomato sauce and pickles, and calls his long-suffering wife by a fresh pet-name every time he addresses her. This is Steinbeck in holiday mood. One gets to know everyone in the town, even the dogs, and all their secret springs; the children come to life with alarming reality, and much of it is entertaining, but the odour of whimsy is strong, and one senses that only a part of Steinbeck's feeling was engaged. I was unprepared for the melodrama of the ending.

–"New Novels," *Punch,* 241 (5 July 1961); reprinted in *John Steinbeck: The Contemporary Reviews,* p. 470

Looking after Number One

An anonymous reviewer in The Times Literary Supplement *(TLS) found fault with the sentimentality of* The Winter of Our Discontent.

Mr. Steinbeck is a versatile novelist and he has achieved several different kinds of success. Now he has written a morality. His tempted Everyman is a grocery clerk in a small New England town. The tempters are his friends and neighbours, who, he suddenly discovers, have no morality or scruples where business and the dollar are concerned and consider him rather a fool for not looking after number one. This apparently contented, whimsically minded and unenvious man thereupon defrauds his employer, drives his best friend to suicide and ably double crosses the bank manager, who is as bad as himself. Armed with his popularity and his reputation for scrupulous, stick-in-the-mud honesty, he finds it all quite easy to do; and of course, in the end, he finds it does not pay in an ultimate sense. He cannot confide in

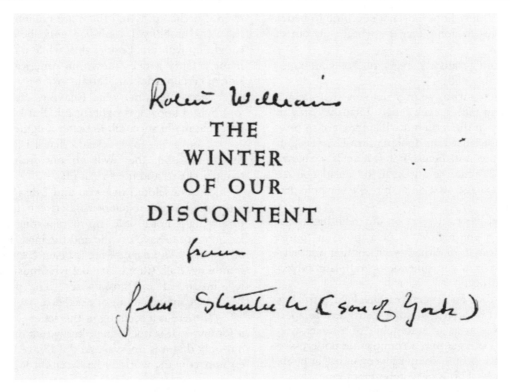

Inscribed half-title page of Steinbeck's 1961 novel (National Steinbeck Center, Salinas)

his wife and seems to be about to slip into the arms of another woman for the sole reason that she understands what he is up to. His son fools a television company in a schoolboy essay contest and he contemplates suicide.

Crime does not pay: the point is a rather obvious one and the book is, indeed, sentimental and rather trivial at heart. The hero is to begin with too good to be true and in the end too wicked. The perfect marriage with which he starts is described with that sentimental impudicity which is a feature of so many fictional happy families; the small town setting and characters seem right out of stock; we scarcely need to be told how it will all end, even to the fact that the hero will remain in possession of the considerable swag. Some of the things he gets up to—the bank robbery that he plans, for example—are quite unbelievable; and the reader could well have been spared, if not some of his conversations with his wife, at least some of his conversations with the groceries. Yet it must be said that Mr. Steinbeck has one or two good comic scenes (the one with the man from the television company, worried about another scandal on top of the payola and the quizzes, for instance) and, when he is not being embarrassing, a sort of affable, relaxed charm.

—*Times Literary Supplement,* 7 July 1961; reprinted in *John Steinbeck: The Contemporary Reviews,* pp. 470–471

Travels with Charley (1962)

Steinbeck to Otis, June 1960

Although Otis had encouraged Steinbeck's idea of traveling around the United States in order to write a book about the experience, she had reservations about his plan to make the trip alone in a truck modified as a camper. Steinbeck wrote her defending his plan. The journey, undertaken in the fall of 1960, was the basis for Travels with Charley: In Search of America *(1962).*

Dear Elizabeth:

I've put off answering your other letter about Operation America until last. I have thought of little else all weekend or since I got it. So I will try to tell you what I think about it.

Frequently, of late, I have felt that my time is over and that I should bow out. And one of the main reasons for this feeling is that—being convinced in myself of a direction, a method or a cause, I am easily talked out of it and fall into an ensuing weariness very close to resignation. Once I was sure I was right in certain directions and that very surety made it more likely to be right. But now my malleableness makes it more likely that I am wrong, and one does not fight very hard for a wrongness. Now, concerning my projected trip, I am pretty sure I am right. I only hope I do not succumb to better judgments, and in so doing tear the whole guts out of the project.

I can of course answer every one of your arguments and probably will.

Let me start with your statement that people travel by bus and talk to each other. That they stay in motels. So many of them do but while they are so traveling they are not what I am looking for. They are not *home* and they are not themselves. There is a change that takes place in a man or a woman in transit. You see this at its most exaggerated on a ship when whole personalities change.

Motels and bus routes are on the main highways. One cannot leave the highways. At a motel or tourist house you have made an inroad—your coming is noted—your name registered, your intentions and plans subject to question or curiosity.

I chose a truck for several reasons. First, a truck is a respectable and respected working instrument as apart from a station wagon or an automobile or a trailer. Second—in a truck I can get into a countryside not crossed by buses. I can see people not in movement but at home in their own places. This is very important to me.

Now my reason for wanting to be self-contained is that I also will be at home. I can invite a man to have a beer in my home, thereby forcing an invitation from him.

Next—Any stranger in a rural community is suspect until his purpose is understood. There is one purpose that is never questioned, never inspected and that causes instant recognition and sympathy—that is hunting and fishing. If in my truck I have two fishing rods, two rifles and a shotgun, there will never be any question of my purpose.

Next, I would like it fairly comfortable, if you call a bunk, a butane stove and an ice-box comfortable. If you are driving 10 or 12 thousand miles, it is no sin not to want to break down. I moved about the Okie camps in an old bakery truck with a mattress in it but that was a matter of four counties, not many states.

Next, I do not want to take a sampling of certain states as you suggest—I want the thing in context against its own background—one place in relation to another. My clothing will be khaki hunting clothes, a mackinaw and a Stetson hat. This is a uniform that will get me anywhere.

In your letter you say I should not go as J.S. novelist or journalist but as J.S. American. What I really hope for and believe I can do is to go as nobody, as a wandering car and eye. And the means I have chosen is designed to make it unnecessary for anyone to ask my name. The people I want to listen to are not the high school principal nor the Chamber of Commerce, but the man in a field who isn't likely to know my name

even if he heard it, and there are millions of those. By the very mobility I could be gone before my name caught up with me. Besides this, while it is true that my name is fairly widely known, in America it is not, outside of certain cities and certain groups.

Now I feel that what I have written here is true and right. I know it is right for me. But I fear the weariness that might succumb to better judgment.

I am trying to say clearly that if I don't stoke my fires and soon, they will go out from leaving the damper closed and the air cut off.

It is so seldom that you and I disagree that I am astonished when it happens. Between us—what I am proposing is not a little trip or reporting, but a frantic last attempt to save my life and the integrity of my creative pulse. An image of me is being created which is a humbling, dull, stupid, lazy oaf who must be protected, led, instructed and hospitalized. The play will have been stage managed out of existence.

If there is a seething in this letter—do not mistake it for anger. It is not. I don't know that my way is right but only that it is my way. And if I have had the slightest impact in the world, it has been through my way.

> The stilling mind
> Cries like a kestrel in the window crack.
> The house layered with shining cleanliness
> Is set and baited for new guests,
> And the sloven heart of the king in name
> Is dusty as a beaten rug in its beating.
> How much is required! How little needed!

Love,
John
—*Steinbeck: A Life in Letters*, pp. 668–670

* * *

Steinbeck to Covici, 20 June 1960

Steinbeck reported to Covici on the status of his planned trip in the camper, which he named Rocinante, *after Don Quixote's horse.*

Dear Pat:

Nearly every one I know feels, whether he or she admits it or not, that neglect in favor of my work is a kind of unfaithfulness. I think you are one of the very few exceptions. I think my work to you is me.

I haven't written because I have been writing. Now there's a sentence that could only be said in English.

Winter progresses, often becoming so much more real than any daily life that I seem only to be awake at my desk.

My truck is ordered for the trip I spoke of about the country. It will come in the middle of August. I plan to leave after Labor Day. I know you approve of the trip and know how necessary it is to me but there are others who find it so Quixotic that I am calling it Operation Windmills and have named my truck Rocinante. But regardless of advice, I shall go. Sure I want to go and am excited about it, but more than that–I have to go. And only I can judge that necessity. I know you understand this. I don't know what I shall find nor feel about what I shall find. For that reason I am making no literary plans in advance to warp what I see. As again in the Sea of Cortez–a trip is a thing in itself and must be kept so.

There are people who would like to contract for writing about it in advance. But since I don't know what it will be, I think any agreement might have a governing effect and I should want to see and hear what is there, not what I expect to be there. I nearly always write–just as I nearly always breathe. So there will be writing in it but I don't know what. That's one of the

reasons I am so excited about it. I will not shape it. It must make its own form.

It is still very early in the morning. I get up at dawn, make a thermos of coffee and come out to my little work house on the point where I stay until I am finished. I never answer the phone and rarely answer a letter.

One thing is so–I must finish Winter [*The Winter of Our Discontent* (1961)] before I start on Windmills. That is fixed. And I will, barring the unforseen.

That's all, Pat. I'm not good nor thoughtful but I do work and am working.

love
John
–*Steinbeck: A Life in Letters,* pp. 671–672

* * *

Steinbeck to Elaine Steinbeck, 11 October 1960

While on the road in Rocinante, *Steinbeck wrote Elaine with reports on his experiences.*

Dear Monsoon:

Seems impossible that you went yesterday morning. It seems very much longer ago than that. I've been through so many kinds of country. I'm camped in a row of great cattle trailers–longer than box cars. Got to talking to the man at the gas pump and he invited me to stay. These big trailers have taken it away from the railroads. This is also turkey country. Just below this hill the earth is black with them. There must be ten thousand turkeys in the one flock.

I guess Wisconsin is the prettiest state I ever saw–more kinds of country–hills and groves like Somerset, and the Dells a strange place of water and odd mushroom-shaped rocks. Lousy with tourist places but nearly all closed now with signs saying–"See you next spring." Then I got into St. Paul and Minneapolis. There must be some way to avoid them but I didn't make it. Crawling with traffic. Took a good time to get out of that. So I've been in Minnesota all afternoon and now am not far from the North Dakota border. At breakfast a trucker told me how women drove the big trucks during the war. I said, "My god, they must have been Amazons," and he replied, "I don't know. I never fought one." I've talked to lots of people today. Stopped quite a lot. One argument– did you know if you bake a doughnut, it will float? I'm just repeating what I heard. And I heard that Dag Hammarskjöld could easy [*sic*] be President. When I suggested that he was a Swede the reply was–"What of it?" I think I'll write that to him.

I know you think just because I'm away from you and you can't check on me, that I make up things. I'll just

Dust jacket for Steinbeck's 1962 account of his cross-country trip with his poodle, Charley, in the fall of 1960 (from Superior Galleries *Auction of Autographs, Manuscripts & Select Books, Beverly Hills, California, November 7, 1992)*

have to ask you to believe there is Swiss cheese candy. No, I didn't taste it, I just saw the sign. Also that the largest collection of Sea Shells in the world is on Route 12 in Wisconsin. Who could make up things like that? Who would want to?

I know E.O. wouldn't approve of the speed with which I am covering ground but I'm sure seeing lots and hearing lots. People don't talk about issues. They talk about how you bake a doughnut and it will float. There's lots of local politics talked but I can't see much interest in the national. But plenty in the U.N. Washington is so far away. A man today looked at my license plates and said, "Clear from New York." But mostly it's hunting and stories about hunting. The bombardment against ducks starts at dawn.

I went from maple country which is flame red to birch which is flame yellow. You would have oohed quite a lot, aahed some. I stopped at a sign that said "home made sausages," and bought some. I'm cooking it now and it smells really wonderful. And at another place I got apples that just explode with juice when you bite them. There's no doubt that frost does something to them. But it's stopping like this that gets talk going. Everyone wants to see the inside of the truck. I even do the floors with Lestoil and I keep the stove shined. When they see the guns they say, "Oh, going hunting!" and never ask another question. Because of the cap and beard they usually take me for a retired sailor and make jokes about do I get car sick. I say I sure do. On the Duluth and Minneapolis radio there is a great block of advertising for Florida real estate. I listened carefully and all it promises is that it is in Florida.

I'll go through Fargo tomorrow morning and by the time I call you tomorrow night I'll be deep in North Dakota. From now on there will be long stretches less populated. In two days I'll be climbing toward the Rockies.

Well, I had the sausage and it was just as good as it smelled. And I didn't even splash grease on this letter.

They're loading cattle outside with floodlights. Must get out to see that. The truckers are a set-apart bunch of men. The long distance ones are exactly like sailors. I suppose they have homes but they live on the road and stop to sleep.

Well, I watched. Two truckloads of yearlings. Going south to be fed—but bull calves. The beefers are kept for milk. There is too Swiss cheese candy.

I miss you already. Time gets all out of kilter.

Good night my love.

Tobit

—Steinbeck: A Life in Letters, pp. 686–688

* * *

Steinbeck to Otis, 7 December 1961

After completing the manuscript of Travels with Charley *in September 1961, Steinbeck set out with Elaine and his sons on an extended overseas trip. Accompanying the boys as a tutor was Terrence McNally, later an award-winning playwright. Steinbeck wrote Otis from Florence, shortly after he had suffered a heart attack in Milan. He addressed the concerns of Viking Press about an episode in* Travels with Charley *in which he quoted the obscenities shouted by segregationists at a black child in New Orleans. "Tom G." is Thomas Guinzburg, who succeeded his father, Harold Guinzburg, as head of Viking.*

Dear Elizabeth:

I'm afraid I scared Elaine and maybe she scared you. I can't explain it. My energy just seemed to run out, like pulling the plug of a bath tub. I'm perfectly all right now. And never did show anything in tests. It's just like an overpowering weariness. These ten days in Florence should pick me up.

I'm glad you got along with Tom G. I've always liked him. And as for the use or non use of the words in New Orleans, I don't really care. I think I protected the thing pretty well but I also don't think you can get a sense of the complete ugliness of the scene without the exact words. But then we have protected ourselves from this kind of experience for so long. No, I really don't care much—and that's a bad sign. You were very right not to send on the galleys of the last section. It's a thousand years behind me now.

This afternoon Elaine and I are going over to look at David. Just that one. I can only see one thing at a time but that's not new. It has always been that way. We had a card from Terrence saying Thom had decided to live his life in Venice. He fell madly in love with the city.

I seem to have stopped there in a kind of tiredness and now it is the 9th of December. My mind is lazy and doesn't seem to want to work for me much. Then a few minutes ago your letters came and I have to stir myself. The boys came back yesterday and I think some big change has happened. They are suddenly full of enthusiasm. It makes up for my sluggishness. They've been out all morning sniffing the city like morning dogs. The sun is bright. Elaine has rushed out to pictures. I'm perfectly all right and not weak or anything, only very lazy.

I'm going to get this off right away. Sorry we alarmed you. Everything is all right now. I'll be fine as soon as energy comes back and it always does.

Love to all there,

John

—Steinbeck: A Life in Letters, pp. 726–727

* * *

Steinbeck Rediscovers His Land and People
Fanny Butcher

Fanny Butcher praised Steinbeck's depictions of American cities and rural areas in Travels with Charley: In Search of America.

John Steinbeck, who has cut deep into the heart of America more than once with his novels (will you ever forget *The Grapes of Wrath?*), decided he wanted to see what had happened to his native country and fellow Americans since he last had had intimate contact with them across the land. He would make a journey around the world of the United States, he decided, and he would come closest to the American good earth and the American people if he went by truck, avoiding main highways as much as possible.

He bought a three-quarter ton pickup truck, had "a little house built like the cabin of a small boat" constructed on it, equipped it with "a heater, refrigerator and lights operated on butane gas, and a chemical toilet." He called it his "turtle shell" and named the conveyance Rocinante in memory of Don Quixote's steed.

He took shotguns and fishing equipment. "If a man is going hunting or fishing his purpose is understood, even applauded," but, "I no longer kill or catch anything I cannot get into a frying pan." These preparations for making talking to strangers easier proved unnecessary.

Charley, who shared Steinbeck's three months, 10,000 mile trip, was born in France, a "very big French poodle who knows a little poodle English, responds quickly only to commands in French . . . a born diplomat, a good watchdog, who roars like a lion."

Charley was not only companion but stage setting, too. For, says Steinbeck, "A dog, particularly an exotic like Charley, is a bond between strangers. Many conversations en route began with 'What degree of dog is that?'" The best way of all of opening a conversation, however, he found was to be lost.

The trip began at Sag Harbor, Long Island, just after Labor Day in 1960. His course went to the tip of Maine, across the northern United States to California, back thru Texas, New Orleans, and the south.

If the reader expects to find here a travel guide to the United States, he will be disappointed. If he hopes to find trenchant observations about life in general and about our country, occasional glowing descriptions of nature, some wonderful, revealing scraps of conversation, a penetrating insight into American mores, searching thoughts on loneliness, all

recorded by a master of the writing craft, he will be delighted with *Travels with Charley.*

"Americans are a restless people," says the author, reminding us that this country was settled by people who "hungered to move." "But just moving has obsessed many Americans," he observes, and he wonders wryly if "one goes not so much to see as to tell afterwards."

One thing he noticed about American cities all over the country is that they "are like badger holes, ringed with trash"—all of them "surrounded by piles of wrecked and rusting automobiles and almost smothered by rubbish." He saw divergent tendencies thruout the country, in northern Maine and New England, villages giving way to cities and wild life taking over, in the midwest and the far west, a population explosion and "progress" everywhere. And he says, "I wonder why progress so often looks like destruction?"

"When we get these thruways across the whole country as we will and must, it will be possible to drive from New York to California without seeing a thing," he asserts. He used other roads whenever possible and confesses, "I was born lost and take no pleasure in being found, nor much identification from shapes which symbolize continents and states."

Some of his descriptions of nature are thrilling. Of autumn in New England he writes, "It isn't only color, but a glowing. . . . There's a quality of fire in these colors." The Wisconsin fall enchanted him. "The air was rich with butter-colored sunlight, not fuzzy, but crisp and clear, so that every frost-gay tree was set off. . . . There was a penetration of the light into solid substances, so that I seemed to see into things, deep in, and I've seen that kind of light only in Greece."

Steinbeck often was asked if he was traveling for pleasure, and he could always answer yes until he went to New Orleans. There he saw a group of women called "cheerleaders" applauded by crowds as they shouted obscenities at two small Negro children entering and leaving a previously all-white school. "They were neither women nor mothers," he says, in what they were doing, and it made him sick at heart. He left the south saying sadly to himself, "I know that the solution when it arrives will not be easy or simple."

His words about his traveling companion (and the human race) are ironic: "Charley doesn't belong to a species clever enough to split the atom, but not clever enough to live in peace with itself."

–*Chicago Sunday Tribune Magazine of Books,* 29 July 1962; reprinted in *John Steinbeck: The Contemporary Reviews,* pp. 482–484

* * *

From Coast to Coast, He Met No Strangers
Lewis Gannett

Critic Lewis Gannett, whose wife had illustrated the first edition of Steinbeck's Tortilla Flat *(1935), stressed that* Travels with Charley *was unlike any of Steinbeck's previous works.*

After twenty-five years in Manhattan and Hollywood, Sag Harbor, London, Paris and points East, John Steinbeck decided that it was time for him to go back and feel America, hear its changing speech, look at its hills and water, smell its grass and trees and sewage. So he equipped himself with a three-quarter-ton pickup truck, a "camper" atop it, and set out, accompanied only by Charley. Charley is a French-born blue poodle, companionable and friendly, except for bears.

Now John Steinbeck, as readers know, is a born story-teller with a rumbling chuckle in his way of speech, and a great gift of friendship, particularly for dogs, but also for truck-drivers, bartenders and lonely wayfarers. He was, to be sure, his own bartender on most of his journey, but a small bar in a "camper" is almost as good an invitation to confidences as a dog, and Mr. Steinbeck had still another gadget for making friends along the way. He has, he says, a talent for getting lost, and a lost driver brings out the best in human nature, even in New York City policemen.

The resulting book is unlike anything Mr. Steinbeck ever wrote before, and utterly unlike the usual pseudo-sociological observations on what's wrong with America. Mr. Steinbeck set out in a benign mood, just escaping the hurricane Donna, and he claims that from start to finish he met no "strangers." Even the guardians of absentee-owned estates, who began by questioning Mr. Steinbeck's right to park and camp, quickly turned into friends. The only people Mr. Steinbeck saw that he didn't like were the screeching ninnies, locally known as "cheerleaders," who were shouting obscenities at integrated school children when he passed through New Orleans. Of course, Charley helped. Charley liked people, and people liked Charley on sight, and the friendship quickly extended to include Charley's travelling companion.

New England a little baffled Mr. Steinbeck, who is California-born and accustomed to conversation at breakfast. Breakfast with truckers was one of his delights in state after state. Truckers, forever on the move, are the kind of people who particularly appeal to Mr. Steinbeck's restless soul. But in Maine he discovered that "the natural New England taciturnity reaches its glorious perfection at breakfast." An early morning waitress who condescended to say "Yep" to an out-of-state visitor was, in Mr. Steinbeck's experience, relatively garrulous. In the midwest he found people

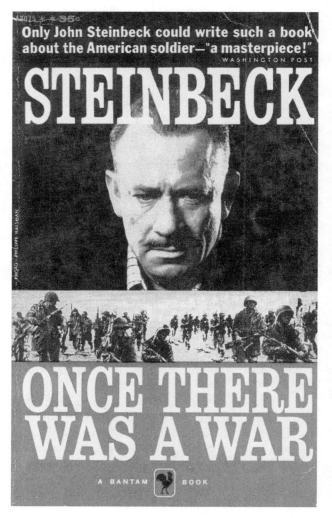

Front cover of the 1960 paperback edition of Steinbeck's 1958 collection of war journalism (Bruccoli Clark Layman Archives)

friendlier. He was startled by the sheer beauty of the Wisconsin countryside, and with the whole state of Montana he fell wildly in love. Sometimes he passed the night in trailer camps, where he discovered the friendly company of the great fraternity who live on wheels. They have no roots, he says, but they all have dogs.

In Chicago Mr. Steinbeck had a good time figuring out the history of the previous occupant of a hotel room whose wastebasket had not yet been emptied: that's one story. The trailer-travelling actor he met on a North Dakota roadside is another. So is the unbelievably co-operative Sunday garage owner on a mud road in Oregon. And so's Thanksgiving dinner with Mr. Steinbeck's wife's friends in Texas. For sheer emotion, though, try Steinbeck on the big trees of his native state, or the story of his return to Johnny Garcia's bar in

Monterey, complete with the whole cast of characters from *Tortilla Flat,* including the "American dogs."

It's a happy, relaxed book, devoid of the bitterness and violence of some of the middle-period Steinbeck. But Steinbeck is still Steinbeck—no Pollyanna he. He thinks America, putting cleanliness first, has lost the sense of taste. He doesn't like sprawling cities—always gets lost in them, for one thing, and besides, they lack dogs. The books and magazines on sale along the way, and the local radio stations he listened to, were as tasteless as the food. Mr. Steinbeck is pretty dogmatic about his thesis that Americans are a new breed, whether of Chinese, British or Negro descent, more like each other than a Lowland Scot is like a Highlander. This, he says, "is an exact and provable thing," but he didn't stop to prove it. He and Charley just kept moving along, and moving along with Steinbeck in this mood is a very pleasant experience.

—*New York Herald Tribune Book Review,* 29 July 1962; reprinted in *John Steinbeck: The Contemporary Reviews,* pp. 484–485

* * *

Steinbeck's America, Twenty Years After
Eric F. Goldman

Eric F. Goldman reviewed Travels with Charley *for* The New York Times Book Review.

There are some men, John Steinbeck says, who are born wanderers; when the winds of restlessness seize them, there is nothing for them to do but go. They find reasons for everything, including the need for the trip. In Steinbeck's case, the justification was easy enough. Here he was an American writer, writing about America, but for some twenty years he had known little of the country at first-hand. Shortly after Labor Day, 1960, Steinbeck left his Long Island home for a swing around the United States.

Three months and 10,000 miles later the 58-year-old novelist was back, physically and emotionally exhausted. But it was all decidedly worth the effort. The resulting book is pure delight, a pungent potpourri of places and people interspersed with bittersweet essays on everything from the emotional difficulties of growing old to the reasons why giant Sequoias arouse such awe. . . .

The swing into the Middle West brought out the old agrarian in Steinbeck. He deplored the superhighways and he abhorred the mammoth cities. He noted too that the road signs were shifting in tone. The New York State signs had shouted at him. The New England ones had a kind of laconic precision. In the Middle West the signs were "more benign. . . . The earth was generous and outgoing here in the heartland, and perhaps the people took a cue from it."

Once past Chicago, Steinbeck's prose takes on a new lift. This was his kind of country, and the Pacific, his Pacific, was nearing. By the time he reached Montana, he was engaged in an unabashed love affair with nature. The calm of the mountains and grasslands, he was sure, had seeped into the inhabitants. Out here even the casual conversation, in Steinbeck's glowing reportage, has an earthy sagacity. It was beyond Chicago that he talked with a crossroads storekeeper and raised the question that was beginning to bother him. Why didn't Americans argue violently about public affairs any more? . . .

On to Seattle and then down into northern California. Naturally the clash between old and new produced the sharpest twinges in the area of Steinbeck's boyhood and of his novels. In Monterey, Johnny Garcia stood behind his bar and went on and on about what a homecoming this was and Steinbeck sat on the stool thinking about the Carmel Valley when he could shoot his rifle where he pleased without disturbing anything but frogs. Suddenly he was on his feet, bolting for the door. "I was on Alvarado Street, slashed with neon light—and around me it was nothing but strangers."

Texas undid Steinbeck. He was determined not to go along with the usually easy denunciations of the state, and in this chapter he leans backward so far that at times he tumbles into saccharinity and even near incomprehensibility. But no one can doubt his meaning as he reached New Orleans and "Cheerleaders" scream at a tiny Negro girl making her terrified way into a desegregated school. Here is the most powerful writing in the book, stinging with the cold lash of outraged decency. . . .

Of one thing Steinbeck became quite sure. For all the stubborn regionalism of the United States, for all the ethnic range of its people, "we are a nation, a new breed. . . . The American identity is an exact and provable thing." But just what was this exact and provable thing? Steinbeck would try to lay hold of it and more and more he came back to the drive for change in the American character. In a whole series of mullings, he speculated on the exact cause and nature of this characteristic.

Increasingly in his travels Steinbeck caught himself when he wanted to lash out at the most fundamental result of that drive, the rampant industrialization. "It is the nature of man as he grows older to protest against change. . . . The sad ones are those who waste their energy in trying to hold it back, for they can only feel bitterness in loss and no joy in gain."

For such talk Charley had no comment at all. A wise dog does not try to top wisdom.
—*New York Times Book Review,* 29 July 1962; reprinted in *John Steinbeck: The Contemporary Reviews,* pp. 485–486

* * *

Travels with Charley
Francis J. Thompson

Francis J. Thompson, reviewing Travels with Charley *for* The Florida Historical Quarterly, *commented on Steinbeck's depiction of the South and Southerners.*

Comparison of our Nobel Prize winners, though odious, may be instructive. John Steinbeck, for example, is more akin to Pearl Buck than to either William Faulkner or Ernest Hemingway.

Steinbeck's latest book, a beatnik grand tour of the United States, starts out with an exciting account of "Donna" walloping his Sag Harbor, Long Island, cottage. The hurricane did extensive damage in the peninsula state, too, but this doesn't fit into his picture. In fact, when he gets his gear stowed away after the blow, he embarks for Bangor musing about how much he prefers autumn sight-seeing in exciting, chilly Maine to October in uneventful, warm Florida. The horrible vision of "sitting on a nylon-and-aluminum chair out on a changelessly green lawn slapping mosquitoes in the evening" hurts him until he drinks a tumbler of vodka and forgets it.

As long as he follows the Canadian border towards the occident, Steinbeck's reactions are eager, and interested, but when he turns from Seattle, he begins to yawn. Later, still, levanting from Salinas to Texas, he transmits his boredom by repeating tiresome, old jokes about the size of the lone star state, its cowboy boots, chauvinism, and so on.

Reviving as he approaches Louisiana, he gradually works himself into such a rage at the puerility of some segregationists that he appears willing to turn Dixieland over to the Black Moslems. The outward and visible signs of his agitation attract public attention. So on the edge of New Orleans he warily parks Rocinante, his mobile home, and Charley, his pet poodle, where they will be relatively safe from suspicious white tribesmen and takes a taxi to within a block of the school where the disturbances have been taking place. There he is able to spy on the natives without being detected until, outraged beyond endurance by the naughty war cries of some pale-face "cheerladies," he scurries away to safety north of the Mason-Dixon line.

Some twenty-odd years ago Edmund Wilson spoke disapprovingly of "Mr. Steinbeck's tendency to present human life in animal terms." In *Travels with*

Charley, the pooch and Rocinante, his "three-quarter-ton pickup truck equipped with miniature ship's cabin," are closer to *genus homo* than his representative Southerners are, and more *simpatico* than any bipeds observed during the journey.

En fin, just as Pearl Buck took us to China to see the truth about mankind as she knew it, so Steinbeck would have us go to canines and cars, consider their ways, and be wise. Hemingway and Faulkner on the other hand chose daring Americans for their heroes although there is evidence that the Nobel Prize was awarded the Mississippian in the mistaken belief that he, too, hated the South.
—*Florida Historical Quarterly,* 42 (July 1963); reprinted in *John Steinbeck: The Contemporary Reviews,* pp. 494–495

Nobel Prize

Steinbeck to John O'Hara, October 1962

On the morning of 25 October 1962, during the tense period of the Cuban missile crisis, the Steinbecks turned on their television set at Sag Harbor for the news and learned that Steinbeck had won the Nobel Prize in literature. His true reaction to winning the prize can probably be found in his short but plain-spoken messages to friends such as John O'Hara, the Swedish artist Bo Beskow, and Carlton A. "Dook" Sheffield.

Dear John:
Well, I'll tell you this. It wouldn't have been nearly as good without your greeting. Not nearly.
Thanks, John. The thing is meaningless alone. But if my friends like it—suddenly it has some dignity and desirability.

Yours
John
—*Steinbeck: A Life in Letters,* p. 745

* * *

Steinbeck to Bo Beskow, 30 October 1962

Dear Bo and Greta:
Thank you for your wire. It found us in complete confusion. At first I thought I could keep up but now it is like one of those old-fashioned comedies when the character gets deeper and deeper into wet plaster. You will know that I will do what must be done and then retire to the old life. You know, I have always handled things myself and without a secretary but now we must call in help. The mail is coming in sacks. There is utterly no way to take care of it.

Anyway, we will go to Stockholm. Perhaps there will be no escaping to one of our old-fashioned singing and wine-drinking parties but I wish we could. We will not stay very long. Four or five days at the most. Where would you suggest that we stay. The Grand as before? I'm going to ask Bonniers [Steinbeck's Swedish publisher] to get someone to handle telephones, people etc. If this sounds overweening, it is because I have seen what happens here. When we went in to New York we were met by 75 reporters and cameramen and that was the worst day of the Cuban Crisis. This prize is a monster in some ways. I have always been afraid of it. Now I must handle it. I shall rely on you for advice.

Sunday night we saw you on "I remember Dag Hammarskjöld." I thought it well done and that you were very good.

Anyway, we will be in touch. Do you mind if I ask that you be included in a luncheon at our Embassy?

Isn't all this silly? We'll laugh about it soon but right now it seems insufferable.

Love to you both

John

—Steinbeck: A Life in Letters, p. 743

* * *

Steinbeck to Carlton A. Sheffield, 1 November 1962

Dear Dook:

When this literary bull-running is over, I can complete some kind of communication, castrated of self-consciousness.

One thing does occur to me. This prize is more negotiable than the America's Cup although both are the product of wind. Meanwhile pray for me some. I've always been afraid of such things. They can be corrosive. This is many times harder to resist than poverty.

love

John

—Steinbeck: A Life in Letters, p. 744

* * *

Steinbeck to Eugène and Betty Vinaver, 6 November 1962

In this letter to the Vinavers, Steinbeck wrote that the Nobel Prize, although an honor, could also be "a dangerous and engulfing thing."

Dear Betty and Eugène:

We have just dug ourselves out from under an avalanche of communications but I put your cable at the very last because I liked it so much. So often in the last week I have wished to be with Eugène to discuss and to turn over leaves of thinking. And I am sure I could have found not refuge but enlightenment.

This prize is a good prize—good in intent and valuable if properly used. But it can be a dangerous and engulfing thing. To many within my memory it has been an epitaph and to others a muffling cloaklike vestment that smothers and warps. This would be good if I were ready to die or if I were material for a priesthood or if I could believe what I am expected to believe. However, none of these things is so. I have work to do. I think I am near to ready for not the Morte but for the Acts. And that is a task into which one must be born fresh and new and very humble. It is a job so precious to me that I cannot permit any academy nor any dynamite-maker to look over my shoulder. It would be far better to be in prison as Malory was because there he was free from expectation. Perhaps I am taking this too hard but I have seen it happen to people. My sign at the top [Steinbeck's trademark flying pig, "Pigasus"] is still my sign and in a very short time I shall hope to settle back into the anonymity which is required.

Don't worry about my gloom. But the danger is a very real danger. Only perhaps an awareness may pull its fangs. Again thanks for your wire. I want the [Glastonbury] thorn to bloom but really to bloom. To that end please help me to plunge my walking staff into a hospitable earth.

Love to you both,

John

—Steinbeck: A Life in Letters, pp. 748–749

* * *

Steinbeck to Sheffield, 28 November 1962

In this letter to Sheffield, Steinbeck enclosed the draft of his Nobel Prize speech.

Dear Dook:

I would like to talk to you about the nature of the award. In some way it has gathered to itself a mystique and I don't know how. What it is is a money prize awarded geographically and sometimes politically. The Swedish Academy of 17 members lay the finger on and presto—everything is changed. I think I've talked to you about this before.

I've always been afraid of it because of what it does to people. For one thing I don't remember anyone doing any work after getting it save maybe Shaw. This last book of Faulkner's was written long ago. Hemingway went into a kind of hysterical haze. Red [Sinclair]

Lewis just collapsed into alcoholism and angers. It has in effect amounted to an epitaph. Maybe I'm being over-optimistic but I wouldn't have accepted it if I hadn't thought I could beat the rap. I have more work to do and I intend to do it.

A couple of days fell in on me so that I come back to this letter with a sense of relief. I wrote the damned speech at least 20 times. I, being a foreigner in Sweden, tried to make it suave and diplomatic and it was a bunch of crap. Last night I got mad and wrote exactly what I wanted to say. I don't know whether or not it's good but at least it's me. I even put some of it in the vernacular. Hell, that's the way I write. Now they can take it or leave it. Only I hope I get the money first. They might have second thoughts after hearing my vocal efforts. I have one advantage. I mumble, so no one is likely to hear it. But it says what I want it to at last.

I can see interruptions coming. So I'd better put this away for a while. It's nice to come back to.

Next day—This letter goes on forever. Now to get back to the speech here enclosed. Elaine says I must set it. That's theatre for freeze it. But I'm not theatre and I know I will be picking at it. But it says what I want to say and in as few words as I can make it. It may sound highflown but I think the time and the place require that. I don't know whether or not it is good but it's as good as I can make it. Please don't let anyone see it before I make it on Dec. 10. It would please me to know whether or not it comes over to you but not before I do it. I have to have confidence in it or I couldn't say it.

Hearing from you and writing to you have given me a good sense of rest and continuity.

love

John

—*Steinbeck: A Life in Letters,* pp. 757–758

* * *

"Grateful and Honored"

On 25 October 1962, after learning that he had won the Nobel Prize, Steinbeck wired his thanks to Anders Österling of the Swedish Academy.

AM GRATEFUL AND HONORED AT THE NOBEL AWARD STOP I SHALL BE PLEASED TO GO TO STOCKHOLM

JOHN STEINBECK

—*Steinbeck: A Life in Letters,* p. 742

The Nobel Prize in Literature 1962: Presentation Speech
Anders Österling

The presentation speech by Anders Österling, permanent secretary of the Swedish Academy, was given at the Nobel banquet at City Hall in Stockholm on 10 December 1962. Österling summarized Steinbeck's experiences as an aspiring writer and a mature author and stated that Steinbeck received the Nobel Prize "for his realistic as well as imaginative writings, distinguished by a sympathetic humour and a keen social perception."

John Steinbeck, the author awarded this year's Nobel Prize in Literature, was born in the little town of Salinas, California, a few miles from the Pacific coast near the fertile Salinas Valley. This locality forms the background for many of his descriptions of the common man's everyday life. He was raised in moderate circumstances, yet he was on equal terms with the workers' families in this rather diversified area. While studying at Stanford University, he often had to earn his living by working on the ranches. He left Stanford without graduating and, in 1925, went to New York as a freelance writer. After bitter years of struggling to exist, he returned to California, where he found a home in a lonely cottage by the sea. There he continued his writing.

Although he had already written several books by 1935, he achieved his first popular success in that year with *Tortilla Flat.* He offered his readers spicy and comic tales about a gang of *paisanos,* asocial individuals who, in their wild revels, are almost caricatures of King Arthur's Knights of the Round Table. It has been said that in the United States this book came as a welcome antidote to the gloom of the then prevailing depression. The laugh was now on Steinbeck's side.

But he had no mind to be an unoffending comforter and entertainer. The topics he chose were serious and denunciatory, as for example the bitter strikes on California's fruit and cotton plantations which he depicted in his novel *In Dubious Battle* (1936). The power of his literary style increased steadily during these years. The little masterpiece *Of Mice and Men* (1937), which is the story of Lennie, the imbecile giant who, out of tenderness, alone squeezes the life out of every living creature that comes into his hands, was followed by those incomparable short stories which he collected in the volume *The Long Valley* (1938). The way had now been paved for the great work that is principally associated with Steinbeck's name, the epic chronicle *The Grapes of Wrath* (1939). This is the story of the emigration to California which was forced upon a group of people from Oklahoma through unemployment and abuse of power. This tragic episode in the

Steinbeck delivering his Nobel Prize acceptance speech, 10 December 1962 (John Steinbeck Library, Salinas; from Jackson J. Benson, The True Adventures of John Steinbeck, Writer, *1984; Thomas Cooper Library, University of South Carolina)*

social history of the United States inspired in Steinbeck a poignant description of the experiences of one particular farmer and his family during their endless, heartbreaking journey to a new home.

In this brief presentation it is not possible to dwell at any length on individual works which Steinbeck later produced. If at times the critics have seemed to note certain signs of flagging powers, of repetitions that might point to a decrease in vitality, Steinbeck belied their fears most emphatically with *The Winter of Our Discontent* (1961), a novel published last year. Here he attained the same standard which he set in *The Grapes of Wrath*. Again he holds his position as an independent expounder of the truth with an unbiased instinct for what is genuinely American, be it good or bad.

In this recent novel, the central figure is the head of a family who has come down in the world. After serving in the war, he fails at whatever he tries until at last he is employed in the simple work of a grocery store clerk in the New England town of his forefathers. He is an honest man and he does not complain without due cause, although he is constantly exposed to temptation when he sees the means by which material success must be purchased. However, such means require both hard scrupulousness and moral obduracy, qualities he cannot muster without risking his personal integrity.

Tellingly displayed in his sensitive conscience, irradiated like a prism, is a whole body of questions which bear on the nation's welfare problems. This is done without any theorizing, using concrete, or even trivial, everyday situations, which are nonetheless convincing when described with all of Steinbeck's vigorous and realistic verve. Even with his insistence on the factual, there are harmonic tones of daydreaming, fumbling speculations around the eternal theme of life and death.

Steinbeck's latest book is an account of his experiences during a three-month tour of forty American states (*Travels with Charley,* 1962). He travelled in a small truck equipped with a cabin where he slept and kept his stores. He travelled incognito, his only companion being a black poodle. We see here what a very experienced observer and *raisonneur* he is. In a series of admirable explorations into local colour, he rediscovers his country and its people. In its informal way this book is also a forceful criticism of society. The traveller in Rosinante [*sic*]—the name which he gave his truck—shows a slight tendency to praise the old at the expense of the new, even though it is quite obvious that he is on guard against the temptation. "I wonder why progress so often looks like destruction," he says in one place when he sees the bulldozers flattening out the verdant forest of Seattle to make room for the feverishly

1

YOUR MAJESTIES, YOUR ROYAL HIGHNESSES, MIN VAKRA FRU, LADIES AND GENTLEMEN:----------

I THANK THE SWEDISH ACADEMY FOR FINDING MY WORK WORTHY OF THIS HIGHEST HONOR. IN MY HEART THERE MAY BE DOUBT THAT I DESERVE THE NOBEL AWARD OVER OTHER MEN OF LETTERS WHOM I HOLD IN RESPECT AND REVERENCE-----BUT THERE IS NO QUESTION OF MY PLEASURE AND PRIDE IN HAVING IT FOR MYSELF.

IT IS CUSTOMARY FOR THE RECIPIENT OF THIS AWARD TO OFFER SCHOLARLY OR PERSONAL COMMENT ON THE NATURE AND THE DIRECTION OF LITERATURE. HOWEVER, I THINK IT WOULD BE WELL TO CONSIDER THE HIGH DUTIES AND THE RESPONSIBILITIES OF THE MAKERS OF LITERATURE.

SUCH IS THE PRESTIGE OF THE NOBEL AWARD AND OF THIS PLACE WHERE I STAND THAT I AM IMPELLED NOT TO SQUEAK LIKE A GRATEFUL AND APOLOGETIC MOUSE, BUT TO ROAR LIKE A LION OUT OF PRIDE IN MY PROFESSION AND IN THE GREAT AND GOOD MEN WHO HAVE PRACTICED IT THROUGH THE AGES.

LITERATURE WAS NOT PROMULGATED BY A PALE AND EMASCULATED CRITICAL PRIESTHOOD SINGING THEIR LITANIES IN EMPTY CHURCHES---- NOR IS IT A GAME FOR THE CLOISTERED ELECT, THE TIN-HORN MENDICANTS OF LOW CALORY DESPAIR.

LITERATURE IS AS OLD AS SPEECH. IT GREW OUT OF HUMAN NEED FOR IT, AND IT HAS NOT CHANGED EXCEPT TO BECOME MORE NEEDED.

THE SKALDS, THE BARDS, THE WRITERS ARE NOT SEPARATE AND EXCLUSIVE. THEIR FUNCTIONS AND DUTIES HAVE BEEN DECREED BY OUR SPECIES. THEIR RESPONSIBILITIES HAVE ONLY CHANGED INBECOMING GREATER.

WE HAVE BEEN PASSING THROUGH A GRAY AND DESOLATE TIME OF CONFUSION. MY GREAT PREDECESSOR, WILLIAM FAULKNER, STANDING HERE, REFERRED TO IT AS A TRAGEDY OF UNIVERSAL PHYSICAL FEAR, SO LONG SUSTAINED THAT THERE WERE NO LONGER PROBLEMS OF THE SPIRIT, SO THAT ONLY THE HUMAN HEART IN CONFLICT WITH ITSELF SEEMED WORTH WRITING ABOUT. FAULKNER, MORE THAN MOST MEN, WAS AWARE OF HUMAN STRENGTH AS WELL AS HUMAN WEAKNESS. HE KNEW THAT THE UNDERSTANDING AND RESOLUTIONOF FEAR HAVE ALWAYS BEEN A LARGE PART OF THE WRITER'S REASON FOR BEING.

THIS IS NOT NEW. THE ANCIENT COMMISSION OF THE WRITER IS UNCHANGED. HE IS CHARGED WITH EXPOSING OUR MANY GRIEVOUS FAULTS AND FAILURES, WITH DREDGING UP TO THE LIGHT OUR DARK AND DANGEROUS DREAMS FOR THE PURPOSE OF IMPROVEMENT. FURTHERMORE, THE WRITER MUST DECLARE AND CELEBRATE MAN'S PROVEN CAPACITY FOR COURAGE, COMPASSION AND LOVE, FOR GALLANTRY IN DEFEAT, FOR GREATNESS OF HEART AND SPIRIT. THESE HE MUST FLY AS RALLY FLAGS FOR HOPE AND FOR IMITATION. I HOLD THAT A WRITER WHO DOES NOT PASSIONATELY BELIEVE IN THE PERFECTABILITY OF MAN HAS NO DEDICATION NOR ANY MEMBERSHIP IN LITERATURE.

THE UNIVERSAL FEAR IS THE RESULT OF A FORWARD SURGE IN OUR KNOWLEGE AND MANIPULATION OF THE PHYSICAL WORLD. IT IS TRUE THAT OTHER PHASES OF UNDERSTANDING HAVE NOT YET CAUGHT UP WITH THIS GREAT STEP, BUT THERE IS NO REASON TO PRESUME THAT THEY CAN NOT OR WILL NOT DRAW ABREAST. INDEED, IT IS A PART OF THE WRITER'S RESPONSIBILITY TO MAKE SURE THAT THEY DO. WITH OUR LONG PROUD HISTORY OF STANDING FIRM IN THE FACE OF ALMOST CERTAIN DEFEAT EVEN OF EXTINCTION, WE WOULD BE NOT ONLY COWARDLY BUT STUPID TO LEAVE

Carbon-copy typescript of Steinbeck's Nobel Prize acceptance speech, inscribed to his sister Esther Steinbeck Rodgers
(from William McPheron, John Steinbeck: From Salinas to Stockholm, *2000;*
Special Collections, Thomas Cooper Library, University of South Carolina)

2

~~thex~~
THE FIELD ON THE EVE OF VICTORY.

      UNDERSTANDABLY, I HAVE BEEN READING THE LIFE OF ALFRED NOBEL: A SOLITARY MAN, THE BOOKS SAY, A THOUGHTFUL MAN. HE PERFECTED THE RELEASE OF EXPLOSIVE FORCES CAPABLE OF CREATIVE GOOD OR OF DESTRUCTIVE EVIL BUT LACKING CHOICE, UNGOVERNED BY CONSCIENCE OR JUDGEMENT. NOBEL SAW SOME OF THE CRUEL AND BLOODY MISUSES OF HIS INVENTIONS. HE MAY EVEN HAVE FORSEEN THE END RESULT OF HIS PROBING----ACCESS OF ULTIMATE VIOLENCE----TO FINAL DESTRUCTION.

      SOME SAY THAT HE BECAME CYNICAL, BUT I DO NOT BELIEVE THIS. I THINK HE STROVE TO INVENT A CONTROL, A SAFETY VALVE AND THAT HE FOUND IT ONLY IN THE MIND AND SPIRIT OF MAN. TO ME HIS THINKING IS CLEARLY INDICATED IN THE CATAGORIES OF THESE AWARDS.

      THEY ARE OFFERED FOR INCREASED AND CONTINUING KNOWLEGE OF MAN AND OF HIS ~~~~ WORLD ----FOR COMMUNICATION AND UNDERSTANDING WHICH ARE THE FUNCTIONS OF LITERATURE. AND THEY ARE OFFERED FOR DEMONSTRATIONS OF THE CAPACITY FOR PEACE---- THE CULMINATION OF ALL THE OTHERS.

      LESS THAN FIFTY YEARS AFTER HIS DEATH, THE DOOR OF NATURE WAS UNLOCKED AND WE WERE OFFERED THE TERRIBLE BURDEN OF CHOICE. WE HAVE USURPED MANY OF THE POWERS WE ONCE ASCRIBED TO GOD. FEARFUL AND UNPREPARED, WE HAVE ASSUMED LORDSHIP OVER THE LIFE AND DEATH OF THE WHOLE WORLD AND OF ALL LIVING THINGS.

      THE DANGER, THE GLORY AND THE CHOICE REST FINALLY IN MAN. THE TEST OF HIS PERFECTABILITY IS AT HAND.

      HAVING TAKEN GOD-LIKE POWER, WE MUST SEEK IN OURSELVES FOR THE RESPONSIBILITY AND THE WISDOM WE ONCE PRAYED SOME DIETY MIGHT HAVE.

      FOR MAN HIMSELF IS NOW OUR GREATEST HAZARD AND OUR ONLY HOPE--------SO THAT TODAY ST. JOHN THE APOSTLE MAY WELL BE PARAPHRASED----- IN THE END IS THE WORD, AND THE WORD IS MAN, AND THE WORD IS WITH----MEN.

             John Steinbeck   Stockholm December 10, 1962

Dear Elling:

This is a true copy of my one and only speech.

love

John

p.s. The Swedish at the beginning means "my beloved wife". Caused a sensation. No one had ever done that before.

expanding residential areas and the skyscrapers. It is, in any case, a most topical reflection, valid also outside America.

Among the masters of modern American literature who have already been awarded this Prize—from Sinclair Lewis to Ernest Hemingway—Steinbeck more than holds his own, independent in position and achievement. There is in him a strain of grim humour which, to some extent, redeems his often cruel and crude motif. His sympathies always go out to the oppressed, to the misfits and the distressed; he likes to contrast the simple joy of life with the brutal and cynical craving for money. But in him we find the American temperament also in his great feeling for nature, for the tilled soil, the wasteland, the mountains, and the ocean coasts, all an inexhaustible source of inspiration to Steinbeck in the midst of, and beyond, the world of human beings.

The Swedish Academy's reason for awarding the prize to John Steinbeck reads, "for his realistic as well as imaginative writings, distinguished by a sympathetic humour and a keen social perception."

Dear Mr. Steinbeck—You are not a stranger to the Swedish public any more than to that of your own country and of the whole world. With your most distinctive works you have become a teacher of good will and charity, a defender of human values, which can well be said to correspond to the proper idea of the Nobel Prize. In expressing the congratulations of the Swedish Academy, I now ask you to receive this year's Nobel Prize in Literature from the hands of His Majesty the King.

—*Literature, 1901–1967*, edited by Horst Frenz, Nobel Lectures Series (Amsterdam: Elsevier, 1969), pp. 572–574

* * *

Nobel Prize Acceptance Speech
Steinbeck

After Österling's presentation speech, Steinbeck delivered his acceptance speech.

I thank the Swedish Academy for finding my work worthy of this highest honor.

In my heart there may be doubt that I deserve the Nobel award over other men of letters whom I hold in respect and reverence—but there is no question of my pleasure and pride in having it for myself.

It is customary for the recipient of this award to offer personal or scholarly comment on the nature and the direction of literature. At this particular time, how-

ever, I think it would be well to consider the high duties and the responsibilities of the makers of literature.

Such is the prestige of the Nobel award and of this place where I stand that I am impelled, not to squeak like a grateful and apologetic mouse, but to roar like a lion out of pride in my profession and in the great and good men who have practiced it through the ages.

Literature was not promulgated by a pale and emasculated critical priesthood singing their litanies in empty churches—nor is it a game for the cloistered elect, the tinhorn mendicants of low calorie despair.

Literature is as old as speech. It grew out of human need for it, and it has not changed except to become more needed.

The skalds, the bards, the writers are not separate and exclusive. From the beginning, their functions, their duties, their responsibilities have been decreed by our species.

Humanity has been passing through a gray and desolate time of confusion. My great predecessor, William Faulkner, speaking here, referred to it as a tragedy of universal fear so long sustained that there were no longer problems of the spirit, so that only the human heart in conflict with itself seemed worth writing about.

Faulkner, more than most men, was aware of human strength as well as of human weakness. He knew that the understanding and the resolution of fear are a large part of the writer's reason for being.

This is not new. The ancient commission of the writer has not changed. He is charged with exposing our many grievous faults and failures, with dredging up to the light our dark and dangerous dreams for the purpose of improvement.

Furthermore, the writer is delegated to declare and to celebrate man's proven capacity for greatness of heart and spirit—for gallantry in defeat—for courage, compassion and love. In the endless war against weakness and despair, these are the bright rally-flags of hope and of emulation.

I hold that a writer who does not passionately believe in the perfectibility of man, has no dedication nor any membership in literature.

The present universal fear has been the result of a forward surge in our knowledge and manipulation of certain dangerous factors in the physical world.

It is true that other phases of understanding have not yet caught up with this great step, but there is no reason to presume that they cannot or will not draw abreast. Indeed it is a part of the writer's responsibility to make sure that they do.

With humanity's long proud history of standing firm against natural enemies, sometimes in the face of almost certain defeat and extinction, we would be cowardly and stupid to leave the field on the eve of our greatest potential victory.

Understandably, I have been reading the life of Alfred Nobel—a solitary man, the books say, a thoughtful man. He perfected the release of explosive forces, capable of creative good or of destructive evil, but lacking choice, ungoverned by conscience or judgment.

Nobel saw some of the cruel and bloody misuses of his inventions. He may even have foreseen the end result of his probing—access to ultimate violence—to final destruction. Some say that he became cynical, but I do not believe this. I think he strove to invent a control, a safety valve. I think he found it finally only in the human mind and the human spirit. To me, his thinking is clearly indicated in the categories of these awards.

They are offered for increased and continuing knowledge of man and of his world—for understanding and communication, which are the functions of literature. And they are offered for demonstrations of the capacity for peace—the culmination of all the others.

Less than fifty years after his death, the door of nature was unlocked and we were offered the dreadful burden of choice.

We have usurped many of the powers we once ascribed to God.

Fearful and unprepared, we have assumed lordship over the life or death of the whole world—of all living things.

The danger and the glory and the choice rest finally in man. The test of his perfectibility is at hand.

Having taken Godlike power, we must seek in ourselves for the responsibility and the wisdom we once prayed some deity might have.

Man himself has become our greatest hazard and our only hope.

So that today, St. John the apostle may well be paraphrased: In the end is the Word, and the Word is Man—and the Word is with Men.

—Literature, 1901–1967, pp. 575–577

Chapter Eight: 1963–1968

Chronology

Spring 1963	Steinbeck meets with President John F. Kennedy several times. He is invited by Leslie Brady, cultural attaché to the American Embassy in Moscow and later deputy commissioner of the United States Information Agency, to visit the Soviet Union under the auspices of the State Department's cultural-exchange program.
13 May 1963	Steinbeck writes to Brady suggesting that the playwright Edward Albee should be invited to accompany him on his trip to Russia.
Late June 1963	One morning Steinbeck awakes to find that he cannot see out of one of his eyes. The diagnosis is a detached retina, and surgery is performed at Long Island's Southampton Hospital on 24 June.
September 1963	The Steinbecks and Albee attend a series of briefings at the State Department in Washington, D.C., in preparation for their trip to the Soviet Union.
October 1963	Steinbeck and Elaine arrive in Helsinki, the first destination of their cultural-exchange trip, on 11 October. They later join Albee in the Soviet Union and meet with various Soviet authors and officials.
November 1963	On 15 November the Steinbecks fly to Warsaw, where, seven days later, they learn of Kennedy's assassination. They decide to continue the job that the president had given them to do, traveling on to Vienna to rest and attend a service held there for Kennedy. They then visit Budapest, Prague, and West Berlin.

Steinbeck and his wife, Elaine, in Eastern Europe, fall 1963 (from Jay Parini, John Steinbeck, *1995; Thomas Cooper Library, University of South Carolina)*

December 1963	The Steinbecks return to the United States early in the month. On 17 December they go to Washington, D.C., for three days of debriefing by the State Department and are invited to a private dinner at the White House on their last evening in the capital.
February 1964	Steinbeck meets with Jacqueline Kennedy following her request that he write a biography of the slain president. For various reasons this project is never undertaken.
April 1964	Steinbeck and Elaine travel to Rome for Easter and return for a trial in New York Family Court regarding a request by his second wife, Gwyn, for an increase in alimony and child-support payments. The judge grants only a slight increase, angering Gwyn.
Early June 1964	Steinbeck and Elaine move back to Sag Harbor, where he resumes work on a project to recast Sir Thomas Malory's *Le Morte Darthur* (1485) in modern prose.
August 1964	Thomas H. Guinzburg, who has taken over after his father's death as head of Viking Press, approaches Steinbeck with a collection of photographs taken throughout the nation, requesting that he provide text to accompany them. The resulting volume is published in 1966 as *America and Americans*.
14 September 1964	Steinbeck receives the Presidential Medal of Freedom at the White House.
October 1964	Pascal Covici, Steinbeck's longtime friend and editor, dies on 14 October. Following Covici's funeral, the Steinbecks fly to California for a family reunion in Watsonville.
December 1964	The Steinbecks spend Christmas with motion-picture director John Huston at his home in Ireland.
January 1965	The Steinbecks travel to London from Ireland and then on to Paris. On 23 January, Steinbeck's younger sister, Mary Steinbeck Dekker, dies of cancer in Carmel, California.
April 1965	Steinbeck works on the essays for *America and Americans;* he and Elaine are invited to the White House to spend a weekend with President Lyndon B. Johnson and his wife, Lady Bird Johnson.
Late Summer 1965	Steinbeck receives an offer from Harry F. Guggenheim, the publisher of *Newsday* on Long Island, to write a column on topics of his choosing. The column, titled "Letters to Alicia" (a reference to Guggenheim's late wife, Alicia Patterson Guggenheim), runs in *Newsday* from November 1965 through May 1967, averaging about four articles a month.
December 1965	The Steinbecks fly to London, arriving around the first of December, to search private libraries for Malory materials. At Alnwick Castle, near the Scottish border, Steinbeck and Malory scholar Eugène Vinaver discover what they believe to be a previously unknown manuscript relating to Arthurian legend. Later in the month, the Steinbecks go to Ireland to spend another Christmas with Huston. After the holiday they tour Ireland.
January 1966	The John Steinbeck Society of America is founded at Kent State University by Tetsumaro Hayashi and Preston Beyer.
April 1966	President Johnson appoints Steinbeck to the council of the National Endowment for the Arts. Steinbeck's younger son, John IV, finishes his basic training in the army and requests assignment to Vietnam.
May 1966	Steinbeck abandons his Malory project around this time.
June–August 1966	Steinbeck has a battle of words with the Russian poet Yevgeny Yevtushenko over his views on the Vietnam War, which Steinbeck seems to support at this time.
September 1966	Steinbeck's article "Let's Go After the Neglected Treasures Beneath the Seas" is published in *Popular Science*.

| October 1966 | Viking Press publishes *America and Americans*. Steinbeck and Elaine are accredited as correspondents for *Newsday* and leave for Vietnam. They stop in California to see Steinbeck's older son, Thom, who is in basic training at Fort Ord, near Monterey, and other family members. From there the Steinbecks fly to Hawaii, to Guam, and on to Vietnam. |

Steinbeck in the door seat of a Huey helicopter accompanying a combat patrol during his stint as a Newsday *war correspondent, December 1966 (©1983, Lt. Col. Sam M. Gipson Jr., USMC, Ret.; from Jackson J. Benson,* The True Adventures of John Steinbeck, Writer, *1984; Thomas Cooper Library, University of South Carolina)*

November–December 1966	The Steinbecks are busy covering the Vietnam War as correspondents.
January–February 1967	Steinbeck continues to report on combat missions in Vietnam until the third week of January. He and Elaine then leave Vietnam, flying to Bangkok and from there to Laos. They return to Bangkok briefly to meet with the king and queen of Thailand and then travel by train down the Malay Peninsula to the island of Penang, where they rest and work on the articles for *Newsday*.
April 1967	The Steinbecks visit Singapore and Jakarta and continue on to Hong Kong. While there, Steinbeck injures his back. Later he and Elaine travel to Tokyo for a visit with his son John. They return to New York on the third weekend of April.
May 1967	The Steinbecks are invited by the Johnsons to a weekend stay at the White House. Steinbeck experiences a great deal of physical discomfort from bursitis in his right shoulder and arm and cannot write. On Memorial Day he and Elaine are back in Sag Harbor when his back gives out again.
23 October 1967	Steinbeck undergoes five-hour surgery to repair a ruptured spinal disk. The operation is successful.

November 1967	Steinbeck learns to walk again and begins swimming therapy.
December 1967	Steinbeck and Elaine fly to the island of Grenada to continue his recuperation.
January 1968	The Steinbecks spend most of the month in Grenada before returning to Sag Harbor.
March 1968	The *Steinbeck Newsletter* (later the *Steinbeck Quarterly*) begins publication under the editorship of Hayashi at Ball State University.
May 1968	On Memorial Day weekend, while eating at a Sag Harbor restaurant, Steinbeck suffers a small stroke and is hospitalized for a week.
July 1968	Early in the month, Steinbeck suffers an episode of heart failure and is again hospitalized. On 17 July he is transferred to New York Hospital, and his condition worsens. His doctors consider bypass surgery but decide against it.
21 August 1968	Steinbeck returns to Sag Harbor.
November 1968	Steinbeck's condition becomes so severe that he has to move to his New York apartment, where treatment is more readily available.
December 1968	Steinbeck dies on 20 December at 5:30 P.M. in New York. His funeral service is held three days later at St. James' Episcopal Church on Madison Avenue. On Christmas Eve, Elaine and Thom take Steinbeck's ashes to California. Steinbeck's older sisters arrange a small family service on Point Lobos, and his ashes are buried in the family plot in the Garden of Memories Cemetery in Salinas.

Steinbeck's receipt of the 1962 Nobel Prize in literature stirred a new wave of national interest in him. Critics such as Arthur Mizener and Alfred Kazin wrote articles casting doubt on the prize committee's selection. Time, Newsweek, *and* The Washington Post *all questioned the wisdom of awarding Steinbeck the prize.* The New York Times *also ran an editorial on 26 October 1962 (the day after the award was announced) expressing similar sentiments, stating that*

the international character of the award and the weight attached to it raise questions about the mechanics of selection and how close the Nobel committee is to the main currents of American writing. Without detracting in the least from Mr. Steinbeck's accomplishments, we think it interesting that the laurel was not awarded to a writer—perhaps a poet or critic or historian—whose significance, influence and sheer body of work had already made a more profound impression on the literature of our age.

Although many friends and readers congratulated him on the award, the attacks made a strong impact on Steinbeck and even forced him to review his writing plans. Back at his Sag Harbor home in January 1963, Steinbeck was planning to begin a new project, but he was now more interested in plays than in fiction. In a long letter to his editor, Pat Covici, he meditated on the growing preference of his readers for nonfiction over fiction.

In the spring of 1963 Steinbeck was asked, at the suggestion of President John F. Kennedy, to visit the Soviet Union as part of a cultural-exchange program in which the poet Robert Frost had recently participated. Steinbeck agreed to join the program but requested that his wife, Elaine, be included. He met with Kennedy several times that spring and later suggested that the playwright Edward Albee be invited to join him on the trip to Russia because he thought that any cultural exchange should involve young writers. Steinbeck also believed that a younger writer such as Albee would have a better chance of mingling with dissidents and outsiders.

After an initial stop in Helsinki, the Steinbecks joined Albee in Moscow in October 1963. They traveled widely, meeting with groups of Russian writers and visiting schools; one of the writers they met was the poet Yevgeny Yevtushenko. They even had the opportunity to see a performance of Steinbeck's play The Moon Is Down *(1942) in Russian one night. Erskine Caldwell and his wife, Virginia, happened to be in Moscow at this time, and the Steinbecks joined them one night for dinner in their suite at the National Hotel on Red Square.*

On 15 November 1963 the Steinbecks left the Soviet Union for Warsaw, touring Poland and meeting with writers and journalists. The tragic news of Kennedy's assassination on 22 November cut their trip short. A few days later, the Steinbecks arrived in Vienna to attend a service honoring the president. From there they traveled to Budapest for a few days, where hundreds of people crowded a bookstore to meet Steinbeck and receive his autograph. After two months of travel behind the Iron Curtain, the Steinbecks returned to the United States via Prague and West Germany. On 17 December they flew to Washington, D.C., for a debriefing by the State Department and met with President Lyndon B. Johnson in the White House.

Steinbeck in Helsinki addressing an audience of booksellers, October 1963 (Center for Steinbeck Studies, San Jose State University; from Jay Parini, John Steinbeck, *1995; Thomas Cooper Library, University of South Carolina)*

In February 1964 Steinbeck was approached by Jacqueline Kennedy, who asked him to write a biography of her late husband, but he never pursued this project. Instead, he planned to resume his work, begun in 1956, on an adaptation of Sir Thomas Malory's Le Morte Darthur *(1485). At this time, however, Steinbeck found writing difficult because of troubles with his second wife, Gwyn, who had filed a lawsuit seeking more alimony and child support. As a temporary escape, he and Elaine traveled to Rome for Easter. That summer Steinbeck returned to Sag Harbor and tried to write as much as he could on the Malory adaptation, but an August visit by Thomas H. Guinzburg, head of Viking Press, changed his course. Guinzburg brought with him a collection of pictures for which he wanted Steinbeck to provide captions. Steinbeck's contribution grew into a set of essays, published in 1966 as* America and Americans.

Steinbeck's friendship with President Johnson brought him closer to national politics. On 14 September 1964 he received the Presidential Medal of Freedom at the White House. His connection with Johnson continued to strengthen, and in April 1965 he and Elaine were invited to spend a weekend at the White House.

In 1965 Steinbeck oscillated between efforts to complete his Malory book and new challenges from other areas. Late in the sum-

mer he was invited by Harry F. Guggenheim, the publisher of the Long Island newspaper Newsday, *to write a column. Steinbeck chose to write the articles in the form of letters to Guggenheim's late wife, Alicia Patterson Guggenheim, whom he had met in 1956. Titled "Letters to Alicia," the column ran from November 1965 through May 1967. In December 1965 the Steinbecks flew to England to search private libraries for Malory materials.*

The year 1966 was a monumental but perplexing time for Steinbeck. His status as a famous living writer was secured. In January the John Steinbeck Society of America was founded at Kent State University by Tetsumaro Hayashi and Preston Beyer. In April, Steinbeck was appointed by President Johnson to the council of the National Endowment for the Arts. Nevertheless, Steinbeck understood that his country was in a troubled period as the Vietnam crisis worsened. The previous spring, the president had invited him to the White House for a dinner at which the subject of Vietnam was raised. To Steinbeck, it was a troublesome issue, but when his younger son, John IV, requested assignment to Vietnam after completing army basic training, Steinbeck gave up his antiwar sentiments. In May 1966 the president met with him and his son before the latter's departure for Vietnam. In the summer Johnson suggested that Steinbeck go to Vietnam to report on the war. Steinbeck's personal, almost protective relationship with the president is reflected in letters to close friends. To many of his friends and intimates his attitude toward the Vietnam War seemed to indicate a change of heart and an abandonment of everything he had stood for.

Because of Steinbeck's support for the Vietnam War, the Russian literary establishment dragged him into a dispute with Yevtushenko in the summer of 1966. Early in July, Yevtushenko published a poem in the Moscow newspaper Literaturnaya Gazeta *criticizing Steinbeck for failing to oppose American involvement in Vietnam. Steinbeck wrote a letter to the Russian poet and had it released to the media through* Newsday.

In October 1966 Steinbeck and Elaine were accredited as correspondents for Newsday *and left for Vietnam to report on the war. Steinbeck continued to report on combat missions in Vietnam until the third week of January 1967. Following a period of travel throughout Southeast Asia, they returned to New York after stopping in Tokyo for a brief visit with John IV. In mid May the Steinbecks were invited to spend a weekend at the White House. When they returned to Sag Harbor, Steinbeck was experiencing much physical discomfort from bursitis in his right shoulder and arm and found it difficult to write. On 23 October he underwent five-hour surgery to repair a ruptured spinal disk. For the last two months of 1967 Steinbeck recuperated in New York and in Grenada.*

The Steinbecks returned to Sag Harbor at the end of January 1968, but Steinbeck's health continued to deteriorate. In May, on Memorial Day weekend, while eating in a Sag Harbor restaurant, Steinbeck suffered a small stroke and was hospitalized for a week. Following an episode of heart failure in early July, he was hospitalized again. On 21 August he returned to his Sag Harbor home but later had to move to his apartment in New York in order to be closer to medical facilities.

Steinbeck's final days were spent at University Hospital in Manhattan. On the afternoon of 20 December he was in bed, listening as Elaine read to him. At one point they reminisced about the best times that they had had in their marriage. At 5:30 P.M., just as his agent, Elizabeth Otis, and Shirley Fisher, a Long Island neighbor and also an agent with Otis's firm, arrived for a visit, Steinbeck died peacefully with Elaine at his side.

Steinbeck's funeral service was held on 23 December at St. James' Episcopal Church on Madison Avenue in New York. At the service, Henry Fonda, who had starred in the 1940 movie adaptation of The Grapes of Wrath *(1939), read aloud from Petrarch's sonnets to Laura, Alfred Tennyson's "Ulysses" (1842), and the following lines from a lyric in Robert Louis Stevenson's* Songs of Travel and Other Verses *(1896):*

> *Bright is the ring of words*
> *When the right man rings them,*
> *Fair the fall of songs*
> *When the singer sings them.*
> *Still they are carolled and said—*
> *On wings they are carried—*
> *After the singer is dead*
> *And the maker buried.*

Cultural Ambassador

Steinbeck to Leslie Brady, 13 May 1963

At the suggestion of President John F. Kennedy, Leslie Brady, cultural attaché to the American Embassy in Moscow, invited Steinbeck to visit the Soviet Union under the auspices of the State Department's cultural-exchange program. In this letter to Brady, Steinbeck suggested that the trip to Russia should include playwright Edward Albee.

Dear Lee:

That was a very good session we had last week, although we covered lightly a very un-light situation. The subject, of course, is the possibility of my going to Russia in the fall.

Incidentally, although this is a personal letter to you, you may show all or any part of it to Ed [Edward R. Murrow, director of the United States Information Agency], if you wish.

In the light of the Birmingham episodes [of racial violence] it seemed to me that I couldn't, or would be reluctant to, try to explain that situation to people whose minds would be automatically closed to explanation. Then too, K's [Nikita Khrushchev's] apparent switch back to the old party line might well make me "persona non grata." Maybe I am getting old, too. A kind of grey weariness creeps over me.

And yet, I want to go. I should go. And at least now the young and the experimenters are not as cowed as they once were. This is only one of many changes since 1947. Another would be the re-building and a new generation coming along who will not remember the war, nor the deep blight of Stalin. For my own sake, I should go.

My thinking continued this way. We have always been a shy and apologetic people. Sure we have Birmingham, but we are doing something about it. Now is the time to go—not to apologize nor to beat our breasts, but to bring some fierceness into it—the kind of fierceness the Negroes are using. I don't know that I could do it, but I could try.

Very well—if I could go—would there be any way for Elaine to go with me? She is a much better ambassador than I am and the two of us work together very well. I hope it might be arranged.

You remember that when we discussed this quite a time ago, we thought it might be good if [Elia] Kazan went along. I have telephoned him, but can't get him. He is very busy on the new theatre project.

Then, I had another idea, I wish you would take in mind. Edward Albee, our newest and perhaps most promising young playwright came to see me last week. I have known him for some time. I told him of this discussion, and he showed great enthusiasm for going. He might be a better choice. He is another generation—under 35. I think he would have an enormous impact on the younger Russians. He would be very happy to go with us, and between us we might be more effective than either one alone. He is coming on while I am leaving the scene—at least, so it is thought. His problem is that he opens a new play in early autumn—an adaptation of The Ballad of the Sad Café, but he would be free to go when he gets it opened. As for me, I have no time limitation and could make my time match his. Does this seem like a good idea? Think it over and let us discuss it.

In considering this, think also of Poland, where I have never been and Finland, where I have. My work is well known in both places.

I hope you would remember that I will not *speak,* but will discuss anything with anyone or any number. That's always better for me, since it is an exchange, rather than a telling.

That's all, except that it was a darned good dinner and a good evening. And we love the new Mrs. Brady. She and Elaine are very much alike in many ways.

I hope to hear from you soon.

Yours,

John

—Steinbeck: A Life in Letters, edited by Elaine Steinbeck and Robert Wallsten (New York: Viking, 1975), pp. 768–770

* * *

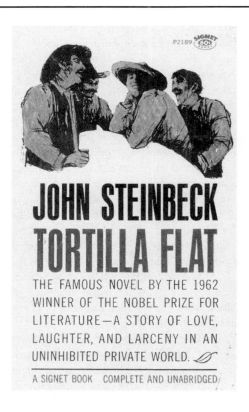

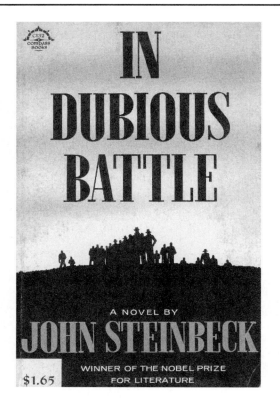

Front covers of three 1960s paperback editions of Steinbeck books originally published in the 1930s
(Bruccoli Clark Layman Archives)

Steinbeck to William A. Gilfry, 13 August 1963

Something of a celebrity after he won the 1962 Nobel Prize in literature, Steinbeck occasionally received letters from complete strangers. The following is his reply to a letter from a Winston Salem, North Carolina, man.

Dear Mr. Gilfry:

Please forgive this writing method. I am wearing prism glasses following eye surgery and have some difficulty seeing the page.

Thank you for your kind letter of August 8. It's not the interest of letters—No, it's the sheer weight that finally drives a writer to cover. You ask about the amount. It varies. This last year for various reasons it must have been thirty to forty thousand. Now it has settled down to between twenty five and fifty letters a day. Nearly all of these should be answered because they are kindly and are written in good faith. But it is simply physically impossible. If I spent every waking hour answering I could not keep up and this is leaving no time for my own work. When I came out of the hospital there were over a thousand letters to answer. How would *you* handle it?

Writing is not easy for me. It takes every bit of strength and concentration I can muster, and interruptions have a feeling like that of being hit with a stick of stove wood.

I am answering your interesting letter at length perhaps to take the place of all those I am going to have to eliminate. And I hope all of this does not sound like complaint. It isn't. This is something that happened which I didn't expect, and I can't cope with it. I didn't expect the Nobel Prize either and receiving it shocked me rather deeply. And I am still far from knowing whether I approve of it.

I was interested in your speculation about money and poets. I didn't know Robert Frost had $240,000 and I wonder whether he knew it. I didn't know him so I have no idea. My own financial image is equally obscure to me. For many years I lived a few days' rations from nothing but I did manage to stay out of debt. The books that are selling now did not sell then, although they are the same books. I presume money is coming in. It goes to a pool out of which taxes, charities, families, dependent requests are paid. Out of this pool a kind of salary is deposited to my account monthly for me to live on. I live well but not wealthily. I eat one meal a day, have a four-room cottage with a bunk house for my sons and a second-hand twenty-foot fishing boat. I drive a Ford Falcon station wagon which is getting pretty ratty. Also I

have an apartment in New York because it is more handy and cheaper than going to hotels. I travel quite a lot but always as a matter of work and research. Please don't think I am shouting "poor mouth." I'm not. I live this way because I like to live this way. I don't know how Frost felt about money but I know I have utterly no interest in it as long as there is some. I know from the poverty years that when you have no money your interest in it quickens.

You say, "How could a poet permit himself to accumulate $240,000?" What should he have done? Throw it away, refuse royalties on his books which people wanted to buy? During the war I gave a book to the Air Force Aid Society, proceeds to be given to families of casualties. It cost me well over a thousand dollars in lawyers' fees to get permission of the tax division to give it away and everyone—even the Air Force—thought I was nuts. You can't give money to friends without losing them. No, the pool is right for me. I never know what is there or who gets it. It also protects one from feeling bountiful which is as ugly an emotion as I know.

When Charley died we planted a willow tree over him; sentimental, but who isn't? Then I had to go to town and when I came back someone had planted flowers all around the tree. I don't know who did it. I don't want to know.

I haven't got another dog yet. I am torn between a white English bull terrier and my first loves which were Airedales. I will want a very young dog to raise and train with care so that independence survives obedience. I should not want to remove the ability to fight from a white terrier but I would try to make it unnecessary. I never knew a truly good fighter who picked quarrels. That is for the unsure.

I know the Bostons you speak of. I had one when I was a boy and he was a fine dog with a great deal of humor. What has happened to the breed is what I detest. They are small, pop-eyed, asthmatic, with weak stomachs and an inability to find their way home.

All of the dogs I have had have been natural dogs. I could learn from them as much or more than I could teach them.

I must be coming to an end. I shall not speak of your poems. Poetry is as private and personal as nerves.

Now I have used you as a scapegoat. The next twenty-five letters I shall not answer and my guilt will be on you. Perhaps this might be a solution to the whole problem.

Steinbeck (left) with playwright Edward Albee (right) and an unidentified third man in Prague, fall 1963
(John Steinbeck Collection, Stanford University Library; from Jackson J. Benson, The True
Adventures of John Steinbeck, Writer, *1984; Thomas Cooper Library,*
University of South Carolina)

I am glad you like the Sea of Cortez. It was little noticed when it appeared but it seems to grow on people. Such a book can't be sold. It has to creep by itself.

Now I am done. Except for one thing. What you call Great Basin in Santa Cruz County, California, is really called Big Basin, unless they have changed the name recently. I grew up among the sequoia semper virens on the coast. Big Basin was my first and very deep experiment with gigantia. And I was seven years old at the time and we went in a buckboard with feed and food and a tent in the box. No one was there and it was wonderful with hazelnuts and ferns in the dimpsy. That's a Somerset word for the twilight under trees.

So long, Scapegoat—
John Steinbeck

—*Steinbeck: A Life in Letters*, pp. 773–776

* * *

**Steinbeck to Mikhail Aleksandrovich Sholokhov,
19 September 1963**

In the fall of 1963 Steinbeck wrote to various Soviet writers he knew announcing the plan for his upcoming trip. The following letter is to the novelist Mikhail Aleksandrovich Sholokhov, whom Steinbeck had met earlier in Stockholm.

Dear Michael Sholokhov:

I hope you will remember an afternoon we spent together in Stockholm. At that time, you promised my wife and me caviar from your own river Don. She has never been quite satisfied since.

We shall be in Moscow about October 15th for a visit of about a month, and it would give us great pleasure to anticipate meeting you again.

I'm sorry I can't write to you in Russian, but there it is—I can't.

Yours very sincerely,
John Steinbeck
—*Steinbeck: A Life in Letters*, p. 778

* * *

**Steinbeck to Konstantin Simonov,
19 September 1963**

Steinbeck also wrote Russian poet Konstantin Simonov with news of his impending visit.

Dear Konstantin Simonov:

May I remind you that very long ago, I had the pleasure of meeting you and that you extended to me and to my late friend, Robert Capa, great courtesy and hospitality. I remember an evening of laughter near a spiral staircase in a time when laughter was a rare commodity.

My wife and I will be in Moscow about October 15th and it would give me great comfort to believe that I might see you again to renew an acquaintance I have valued.

Yours very sincerely,
John Steinbeck
—Steinbeck: A Life in Letters, pp. 778–779

* * *

Steinbeck to Elizabeth Otis, 18–19 October 1963

After arriving in the Soviet Union early in his cultural-exchange trip, Steinbeck wrote his agent, Elizabeth Otis, reporting that his novel The Winter of Our Discontent *(1961) was popular with Russians and was even being staged in a dramatic version.*

Dear Elizabeth:

Very little time is left for anything except sleeping. We left London a week ago and it seems months. In Helsinki they had arranged a program which nearly killed us. Can you imagine seeing 900 booksellers at 9 o'clock on Sunday morning? Well, we did. Our ambassador there [Carl Rowan] is a fine man and we got to know him and his wife quite well. Then on to Moscow where some old friends met us including Sweet Lana [Svetlana, Steinbeck's Moscow guide in 1947]. We go pretty hard here but I have demanded periods of rest. The paper Isvestia which printed Winter serially gave us 500 rubles yesterday. Today we go to the publishers who are to give us money. A number of books have come out. Winter, they say, was a great success and even Charley is being translated. A young man from the Embassy [Peter Bridges of the Political Section] is our interpreter and he is excellent. We go south to Kiev on Monday night and then to Tbilisi in Georgia, and he and his wife will go with us.

Moscow is greatly changed. Miles of new apartment houses stretching out almost into infinity, and, since land has no private value, each has lots of room and gardens around it. People are much better dressed than the last time and not so tired. In fact not tired at all. It is I who am tired.

People here are very kind to us. Our hotel is what they call Stalin neogothic—all grandeur and marble and a huge suite with great chandeliers, very different from the old Savoy with the stuffed bear, where Capa and I stayed. As we knew she would, Elaine makes an enormous hit and is greatly loved and courted.

I find I am not doing any writing, but must tell you the thaw is very definite. You can feel it everywhere. I am more than good now. It has come full circle. I asked a writer why Winter is so popular here and he said, perhaps because the problem is not unknown here. Please tell Annie Laurie [Williams] that a play version of Winter is going into rehearsal at the Moscow Art Theatre. Might be fun to have it translated and try it in New York. That would be a switch, wouldn't it?

The car hasn't come for us yet so I go on with this letter until it does. One nice thing here. They don't get moving before noon. The Finns got us up at 8. And they stayed up just as late—too. [. . .]

Well, yesterday was a strange day—First to one publishing house which had printed Winter. I am told the edition was 300,000 and was sold out immediately. After quite a talk they gave me 1,000 rubles. The strange double talk that went on we will carry engraved on our hearts where it won't do us much good either. I gave it to Elaine, new name Sonya Goldenarm, a famous Russian pickpocketess. As nearly as I can make out, payments to a foreign writer have no relation to the number of books sold. It seems that all books are sold out immediately but are not reprinted. Thus it is possible for a book of an edition of half a million to become a collector's item within twenty-four hours of its issue.

At 2 we went to Ehrenburgs' apartment for lunch. A fine lunch with lots of good talk. There is no question that the thaw is on—people—at least intellectuals—speak quite freely on almost any subject but of course they, from having no experience with the outside world, are fairly limited in some of their estimates.

We are trying to keep the appointments down and to have nothing early in the morning. Last night after the ballet, which ended at 10, we went to McGrady of Newsweek where we met American and Russian news people and had a very good time.

Now I am going to close this and send it by the first courier.

Love to all there,
John
—Steinbeck: A Life in Letters, pp. 780–781

* * *

Steinbeck signing books in a Budapest bookstore during his fall 1963 cultural-exchange tour behind the Iron Curtain (John Steinbeck Library, Salinas; from Jackson J. Benson, The True Adventures of John Steinbeck, Writer, *1984; Thomas Cooper Library, University of South Carolina)*

Steinbeck to the Writers' Union of Kiev, 15 January 1964

After returning to the United States, Steinbeck wrote the Writers' Union of Kiev and the Writers' Union of Tbilisi expressing his thanks for their hospitality during his cultural-exchange trip.

Dear Friends:

I am addressing this letter through the Writers' Union to all of my old and new friends in Ukrania. The tough old guard whom I knew as soldiers when Kiev lay ruined in its own streets will know in what high regard I hold them. But I want to address my thanks also to the young, strong ones who grew up as the city grew back to greatness. I want to thank them for coming to greet my wife and me and for making us welcome.

It pleased me greatly, but did not make me vain, to discover that I was remembered in Kiev. That gave me a good feeling like that of coming home.

What I want to say to my friends is that although we differed and argued and bickered over small things, in the great things, we agreed.

Lastly, I ask you to believe that when I disagreed, I did it there with you and faced your answers. For I do despise a guest who flatters his host and goes away to attack him.

What I have to remember and to tell my people of is the kindness and the courtesy and the hospitality we were offered. These alone constituted a great experience.

Yours,
John Steinbeck
—*Steinbeck: A Life in Letters,* pp. 790–791

* * *

Steinbeck to the Writers' Union of Tbilisi, 15 January 1964

Dear Friends:

When we left you and flew away to the north, it was my noble and misguided intention to write a separate and personal letter to every man and woman who had made our visit a special memory. I feel no shame in admitting that I can't do that. It would take the rest of my life and even then, I would leave many out, and how would I write to those whose hands I touched, whose eyes I looked into, whose health I drank and whose names I do not know? Failing in my resolve, it is with some shyness that I address this letter to all the people of Tbilisi, to the singers, the writers, the flute players, the people who served us and gave us pleasure, who listened to us and talked to us—yes—and argued with us. That was good, too.

This letter is addressed to the pretty girls swinging their skirts along the street, and to the old gentleman in his garden of the mind, to the men squeezing the heart-blood from the grapes, and to the cellar men who dug deep in the casks to dredge up for us the maturing wine. I address the good dinner companions who sang country songs in four-part harmony, and raising their glasses toasted us with such compliments that we wished we could find the heart to believe we were as good and beautiful as they said we were.

And so, I address this letter to the city itself, to the high cliffs and girdles of pines, to the chattering river which gnawed a gateway between two worlds, to the clean sharp distances dancing over foothills and up to the mountains that edge the earth surely. And this letter is addressed to the quiet and permanent wedding in Tbilisi of the ancient and the new. The people in the street look out of old, old eyes on a fresh world which they, themselves, have made. Is it any wonder then that the greatest crop in Georgia is poetry?

I know the history and the pre-history of that gate between two worlds and how it drew the wolves from everywhere, looking with steel eyes for greener lands or set to slam the gate and hold the pass.

It seems, and is to be fervently wished, that by a favor of time and processes, the wolves are caged and the gates are opening all over the world. This is my prayerful desire, and if I could choose a mission for my own, that would be it—to help cage wolves and open doors.

I have probably left out many things in this attempt of a letter—but then, I never wrote a letter to a city before. Clinging in our memory as tight as a burr on a sheep's belly are light and gaiety and kindness, and strength to protect them and these against a background of the sun-brown city and the talking river of the Gateway of the World. Keep it open, I pray you.

Yours,
John Steinbeck
—*Steinbeck: A Life in Letters,* pp. 789–790

Steinbeck (fourth from left) with Hunton Downs (to Steinbeck's right), director of Berlin's America House, at the Berlin Wall, 11 December 1963 (John Steinbeck Library, Salinas; from Jackson J. Benson, The True Adventures of John Steinbeck, Writer, *1984; Thomas Cooper Library, University of South Carolina)*

Death of John F. Kennedy

Steinbeck to Lyndon B. Johnson, 24 November 1963

Still on his cultural-exchange tour at the time of President John F. Kennedy's assassination, Steinbeck wrote to newly sworn-in President Lyndon B. Johnson from Warsaw expressing his and Elaine's sorrow.

Dear Mr. President:

May I offer my profound respect and loyalty to you in the hard days ahead. Our shock and sorrow are very great but we know the office is in strong, trained and competent hands. Our hearts are with you.

At the request of President Kennedy my wife and I have been moving about behind the Iron Curtain, talking with writers and with students. Being non-diplomatic, we have been able to observe many things not ordinarily available. And if these experiences can be of value to you, they are freely offered. Some of them are highly unorthodox.

I have never met you but I have a curious tie with you. When my wife was in college in Austin, one of her classmates was a boy named John Connally who said, "Go on into the theatre in New York but as for me, I'm going into politics. There is a man named Lyndon Johnson and I'm going along with him. He's going places." I wonder whether he would remember. Her name was Elaine Anderson–later Mrs. Zachary Scott, now Mrs. John Steinbeck.

We think it best to go on with the plan laid down although our hearts are heavy, but we hasten to offer anything we have to our President.

Yours very sincerely,
John Steinbeck
–Steinbeck: A Life in Letters, pp. 787–788

* * *

Steinbeck to Jacqueline Kennedy, 25 February 1964

After returning from his cultural-exchange tour, Steinbeck wrote the widowed Jacqueline Kennedy a long letter. He was never able to write the biography of the late president that she had suggested he undertake.

Dear Mrs. Kennedy:

I have your letter, which most astonishes me that we could make so many contacts of understanding in so many directions and so quickly. But such things do happen, wherefor I do wonder at those people who deny the existence of magick or try to minimize it through formulas.

I would like to do the writing we spoke of but as always, in undertaking something which moves me deeply, I am terrified of it. If I am not satisfied with its truth and beauty it will see no light. Meanwhile, as it was with those brave and humble Greeks, I shall make sacrifice to those powers which cultivate the heart and mind and punish the mean, the small, the boastful and the selfish.

You bridled, I think, when I used the word Myth. It is a warped word now carrying a connotation of untruth. Actually the Mythos as I see it and feel it is the doubly true, and more than that, it is drawn out of exact experience only when it is greatly needed.

Since I was nine years old, when my beautiful Aunt Molly gave me a copy of the Morte d'Arthur in Middle English, I have been working and studying this recurring cycle. The 15th century and our own have so much in common–Loss of authority, loss of gods, loss of heroes, and loss of lovely pride. When such a hopeless muddled need occurs, it does seem to me that the hungry hearts of men distill their best and truest essence, and that essence becomes a man, and that man a hero so that all men can be reassured that such things are possible. The fact that all of these words–hero, myth, pride, even victory, have been muddied and sicklied by the confusion and pessimism of the times only describes the times. The words and the concepts are permanent, only they must be brought out and verified by the Hero. And this

---

Mourning the President

Steinbeck and Elaine wrote Jacqueline Kennedy from Warsaw on 24 November 1963 offering their condolences and reporting on the sorrow of the Polish people at the death of President Kennedy.

Dear Mrs. Kennedy:

Our sorrow is for you but for us–for us–

We are in Warsaw as culture mongers at your husband's request which to us was an order. This is Sunday after black Friday. I wish you could see our Embassy here. In the great hall is a photograph and beside it a bust made by a young Pole who asked to bring it in. Since early morning yesterday there has been a long line of people–all kinds but mostly poor people. They move slowly past the picture, place flowers (chrysanthemums are a dollar apiece), and they write their names and feelings in a book. Numbers of volumes have been filled and today the line is longer than ever. It went on all night last night, silent and slow. I have never seen anything like this respect and this reverence. And if we weep, seeing it, it is all right because they are weeping. That's all–Our hearts are with you and we love you–all of us.

John and
Elaine Steinbeck
–Steinbeck: A Life in Letters, p. 787

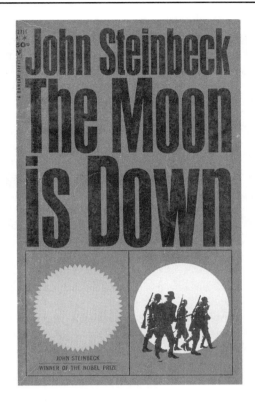

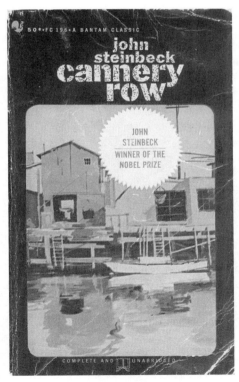

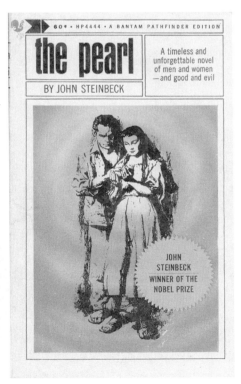

Front covers of four 1960s paperback editions of Steinbeck books originally published in the 1940s
(Bruccoli Clark Layman Archives)

thesis is demonstrable over the ages—Buddha, Jove, Jesus, Apollo, Baldur, Arthur—these were men one time who answered a call and so became the sprits'ls of direction and hope. There was and is an Arthur as surely as there was and is a need for him. And meanwhile, all the legends say, he sleeps—waiting for the call.

I have not really wandered away from the theme. At our best we live by the legend. And when our belief gets pale and weak, there comes a man out of our need who puts on the shining armor and everyone living reflects a little of that light, yes, and stores some up against the time when he is gone—the shining stays and the light is needed—the fierce and penetrating light.

Remember? We spoke of sorrow. (So many things we spoke of.) And also anger, good healthy anger. The sorrow and the anger are a kind of remembering. I know there is a cult of dismal, Joblike acceptance, a mewing "Everything that happens is good." Well that is *not* so and to say it is is to be not only stupid but hopeless. That same cult of acceptance would have left us living in trees.

You see, my dear, how huge and universal the theme is and how one might well be afraid of it. But in our time of meager souls, of mole-like burrowing into a status quo which never existed, the banner of the Legend is the great vocation.

The Western world has invented only one thing of the spirit and that is gallantry. You won't find it in any Eastern or Oriental concept. And I guess gallantry is that quality which, when faced with overwhelming odds, fights on as though it could win and by that very token sometimes does.

I shall try to find a form for this theme. Meanwhile, if you should have a feeling for talking or reminiscing or speculating, I shall be available. I shall come to you at your request or, if you would care to think without physical reminders, please come to us. Our house is one of love and courtesy and we hope of gallantry. I am sending you a version of the Morte. Meanwhile I enclose as promised, Sir Ector's lament over the body of Sir Launcelot, in the Maiden's Castle in Northumberland.

> Yours,
> John Steinbeck

It may take a swatch of time to find the clothing for the Legend. And it is possible that I never can, but I will try my best.

> J.S.

—Steinbeck: A Life in Letters, pp. 792–794

Irene and James Roosevelt, Steinbeck, Elaine, and President Lyndon B. Johnson flying on Air Force One to Adlai Stevenson's funeral, July 1965 (John Steinbeck Collection, Stanford University Library; from Jackson J. Benson, The True Adventures of John Steinbeck, Writer, *1984; Thomas Cooper Library, University of South Carolina)*

Steinbeck and Lyndon B. Johnson

Steinbeck to Johnson, 17 March 1965

In praising a speech that President Johnson delivered before the Congress, Steinbeck philosophized about the power of words. The president replied, "Thousands of letters have come to me since my speech to the Congress. But none touched me or affected me to the degree yours did. Thank you, my dear friend. Thank you for your trust and your affection."

Dear Mr. President:

Always there have been men who had contempt for the "word" although words have survived better than any other man-made things. St. John says, "In the beginning was the Word, and the Word was God." When you have finished using a weapon, someone is dead or injured, but the product of the word can be life and hope and survival. All of the greatness of our species rests on words—Socrates to his judges—the Sermon on the Mount, the introduction to Wyclif's Bible, later taken by Lincoln for the Gettysburg Address. And all of these great and irretrievable words have the bravery of fear and hope in them. There must have been a fierce but hollow feeling in the members of the Continental Congress when the clerk first read the words, "When in the course of human events–." Lincoln must have dwelt with loneliness when he wrote the order of mobilization.

In our history there have been not more than five or six moments when the word and the determination mapped the course of the future. Such a moment was your speech, Sir, to the Congress two nights ago. Our people will be living by phrases from that speech when all the concrete and steel have long been displaced or destroyed. It was a time of no turning back, and in my mind as well as in many others,

---

Presidential Medal of Freedom

Upon learning that he was to receive the Presidential Medal of Freedom for his service to the nation, Steinbeck sent a telegram of thanks to President Johnson on 1 July 1964.

DEAR MR PRESIDENT I AM DEEPLY MOVED PLEASED AND PROUD TO LEARN THAT I WILL RECEIVE THE PRESIDENTIAL MEDAL OF FREEDOM. WARMEST GREETINGS

JOHN STEINBECK

—Steinbeck: A Life in Letters, p. 801

---

you have placed your name among the great ones of history.

And I take great pride in the fact that you are my President.

Yours in admiration,
John Steinbeck
—Steinbeck: A Life in Letters, p. 817

* * *

Steinbeck to Martin Luther King Jr., 31 March 1965

Steinbeck's growing public role, arising out of his association with President Johnson, drew him into the debate over civil rights, as is seen in this response to a letter from Martin Luther King Jr.

Dear Dr. King:

I am answering your letter, which came last night by special delivery, at once.

May I say first I think the events leading up to the march from Selma to Montgomery may well be one of the great and important things in our country's history. It was flawless in its conception and in its execution. Even the accidents which could not have been foreseen, tragic though they were, wove themselves into the pattern of this fabric of the future.

But it is your letter of March 29, concerning the proposed boycott of Alabama, and your request that I sponsor it, that gives me pause. Believe me, Dr. King, if I were convinced that a general boycott would bring Alabama to its senses, I would be behind it with everything I have. However, I think the demand for general boycott is like the demand for unconditional surrender.

I have seen more than I have wanted to of war, from the school yard to combat in Europe, and I know full well that an enemy driven into a corner with no chance to escape, becomes triply dangerous because he has nothing to gain. If he is offered an escape corridor, or the slightest consideration for his pride, he will surrender more readily.

In this morning's Times, you are quoted as having said that you might advocate a selective boycott. Now this makes sense to me. Many white people in the South would come over to our side if they dared. Many others would come over if it were profitable or even non-ruinous to do so. I think that every person against whom a boycott would be dangerous should be allowed to say openly, "I am for you," or "I am against you." If the answer is "against," then I would back the boycott with every bit of influence I could bring to bear. So that is my

JUL 27 1964

JOHN STEINBECK · Box 1017, Sag Harbor, Long Island, New York

July 22, 1964

Dear Reverend King:

I have had some correspondence with you in the past at the time of your injury by a demented woman in New York. I was impressed with your tolerant understanding of the causes of that accident. And I am writing to you now perhaps only to reiterate some matters I am sure must have been in your mind, but I am deeply concerned as you must be with the recent outbreaks of violence as you must be.

When you were stabbed, you were quick to comprehend the probable causes of the attack but you were still stabbed, immobilized and in a hospital. So now, we may understand the reasons for the series of outbreaks but we are still in trouble. Forgive me if I go on at some length. Perhaps I do it to clear my own mind.

When one man outrages another he must justify it to himself with the conviction that his victim was evil, unworthy or inferior. This has always been so. The mental safety of slave owners was achieved in the feeling that the slave was an inferior animal, and after a few generations of experience of force, illiteracy and hopelessness, the slave did indeed become inferior as of the moment.. This is easy to understand since a man can never quite lose his fear of another he has injured. Access by the slave to the techiniques of the white owner would have made the slave even more dangerous than he was. I think it was the Spartans who decreed a death penalty for anyone who taught a Helot to read or write. On the other hand , the Athenians went the other way with the result that after a time most of their thinking and negotiating and even governing was done by slaves.

In America a myth was built generation by generation. A conception that the negro was lazy, shiftless, immoral and, without white guidance and discipline,incapable of self control either individually or in groups. And for a long time, with certain exceptions of course that was at least apparently true.

Do you realize (of course you do) the thrill of terror that ran through the souls of the myth bearers when you engineered the Birm ingham bus strike? The conduct and self control of the negros contradicted the whole foundation of the myth. After that there followed the whole series of civil protests within the law, and this has been going on for quite a long time now. It has created another myth which suggests that negros rather than having less self control than whites, have more. The sympathetic white has gone to the negro to learn rather than to teach.

This feeling had become almost an article of faith and it was the most terrifying manefestation to those people who were for the denial of equality to the negros.

at some kind of program. I do prayerfully hope something may be worked out because continued or inwreased violence endangers all of the gains that have been made.. I wish I could help.

Let me close with a small story. Here in this little town we have an increasing negro population. One day I was speaking to an old timer here who had the usual unthoughtful and traditional attitude toward any change." They're a danger to the whole community." he said. "What do you mean danger?" I asked. Are they presenting an increasing police problem?" He looked at me in amazement. Well, no, he said.."Come to think of it, they're policing themselves betterthan we are." I'm sorry to take your time. But I am deeply concerned.

Yours in faith and hope

John Steinbeck

Letter from Steinbeck to Martin Luther King Jr. (from Superior Galleries Auction of Autographs, Manuscripts & Select Books, *Beverly Hills, California, November 7, 1992; Bruccoli Clark Layman Archives)*

answer, Sir. I am for a selective boycott but not a blind one.

As for Governor Wallace, he is safe from impeachment in the bosom of a legislature hand-picked and exactly like himself. I have thought, however, and have suggested to friends in the government, that Wallace's statement that he could not keep the peace constitutes an abdication of which the Federal government might well take cognizance. I have further suggested and I suggest to you, that the governors' oath in all states includes the promise to defend and carry out the intention of the Constitution of the United States. In his failure to defend the Constitution and indeed in his defiance of the amendments, it seems to me that he could be considered to be in rebellion against his country. Wallace seems to forget that a war was fought on this issue, a war incidentally which people like himself lost. And I do not think that position is so far-fetched.

Finally in the recent sadness at Selma I think Wallace is as guilty of the brutality and of the murders as if he held the clubs in his own hands or pulled the triggers with his own finger.

That is all now. God bless you and keep you and particularly the cause of your devotion.

your friend,
John Steinbeck
—Steinbeck: A Life in Letters, pp. 818–819

Steinbeck and his younger son, John IV, meeting with President Johnson at the White House in May 1966, prior to John's tour of duty in Vietnam (Center for Steinbeck Studies, San Jose State University; from Jay Parini, John Steinbeck, *1995; Thomas Cooper Library, University of South Carolina)*

Steinbeck and the Vietnam War

Steinbeck to Johnson, 28 May 1966

Before Steinbeck's younger son, John IV, left for a tour of duty with the army in Vietnam, father and son met with President Johnson at the White House. Steinbeck wrote the president following the meeting.

Dear Mr. President:

I am grateful to you for receiving my son and me. It meant a great deal to both of us and I am sure that seeing you reassured him that responsibility is behind him and backing him. He had never been to Washington before. From the plane I took him first to the Lincoln Memorial. He stood for a long time looking up at that huge and quiet figure and then he said, "Oh! Lord! We had better be great."

You will understand that I am pleased with this boy and proud. He knows what he wants and must do. He is thoroughly trained to do it. He is proud of his uniform and proud of his country. He goes very soon now, and as you must know, my heart goes with

---

"John, You're an Old Wolf"

In July 1966 Russian poet Yevgeny Yevtushenko published a poem in the Moscow newspaper Literaturnaya Gazeta *criticizing Steinbeck for his support of American involvement in Vietnam. In the poem, later translated and published in* The New York Times, *Yevtushenko alludes to his meeting with Steinbeck in Moscow in 1963. Steinbeck had challenged young Russian writers to denounce the injustices of Soviet society, saying, "Well, young wolves, show me your teeth."*

Understand
These lines are not a provocative trick,
But I cannot remain silent and isolated.
Yes, we are little wolves.
But John, you're an old wolf.
So show your teeth,
The teeth of John.

—*quoted in Jackson J. Benson,* The True Adventures of John Steinbeck, Writer *(New York: Viking, 1984), pp. 992–993*

him. And I will ask you, Sir, to remember your promise to pray for him.

I know that you must be disturbed by the demonstrations against policy in Vietnam. But please remember that there have always been people who insisted on their right to choose the war in which they would fight to defend their country. There were many who would have no part of Mr. Adams' and George Washington's war. We call them Tories. There were many also who called General Jackson a butcher. Some of these showed their disapproval by selling beef to the British. Then there were the very many who denounced and even impeded Mr. Lincoln's war. We call them Copperheads. I remind you of these things, Mr. President, because sometimes, the shrill squeaking of people who simply do not wish to be disturbed must be saddening to you. I assure you that only mediocrity escapes criticism.

Again my thanks to you, Sir. You gave my boy a pediment of pride, and that a good soldier must have.

As always, faithfully,

John Steinbeck

—Steinbeck: A Life in Letters, pp. 831–832

* * *

Steinbeck to Harry F. Guggenheim, 4 January 1967

While serving as a Newsday *correspondent in Vietnam, Steinbeck wrote from Saigon to Harry F. Guggenheim, the publisher of the newspaper, with details of his experiences.*

Dear Harry:

I have asked you for some very unusual things during our association. Now I want to ask about a possibility. I've been out in the really hairy boondocks, in the waist-deep paddies where your boots suck in mud that holds like glue. The patrols go on at night now down in the Delta area and are really ambushes set up against the V.C. There are caches of weapons everywhere and very few of them are found. All a running V.C. has to do is to sink his weapons in a ditch or in a flooded paddy and later return and retrieve them.

Yesterday, I was out with a really good bunch of men. We climbed out of ditches, went through houses, questioned people. We came on one cache of weapons and ammunition in the bottom of a ditch. They smear grease on the guns and seal the shells in jugs. Every house in the area is surrounded by water—in fact the raised place where the house and its garden stand are made by dredging up the mud in baskets and piling it up to dry to a platform. Our men were moving slowly along in the water feeling for weapons on the muddy bottom—a slow and very fallible method.

The C. O. is a Lt. Col. Hyatt, fine fellow, young and intelligent. I told him about something I use on my dock at Sag Harbor. It is a five-pound Alnico horseshoe-shaped magnet that will lift about a hundred pounds. If anything metallic falls off the dock I tie a line to the magnet and drop it to the bottom. I've brought up everything from a pair of pliers to an outboard motor with it. Dragged along these ditches and paddies, it would locate arms that are now missed. But such ideas submitted to the high command rarely get implemented. And surely Col. Hyatt knew it. So I engaged to try to get him a magnet to try out. Of course, if it brings up anything, he can then requisition them.

The other thing is more serious and more sensitive. As you must know, the V.C. are tough and secret. When one is taken he refuses to talk at all. And it's on information that our lives depend, where are the rest hidden, how many are there—what weapons, what plan of attack, where are the claymore mines set, where are the booby traps? Answers to these questions could save a great many of our kids' lives.

Yesterday I remembered something from the past. Did you ever see scopolamine used, Harry? I have. First it was called twilight sleep and later truth serum. It doesn't make a man or woman tell the truth, but it makes him a compulsive talker. He just can't shut up. It relaxes the inhibitions, causes boastful thinking and everything comes out. Now Col. Hyatt says if he had access to such an injection he thinks he could cut his casualties at least 50 percent. And I have no compunction about using any method whatever to that end.

I am marking this private and very personal but of course Bill Moyers [soon to become publisher of *Newsday*] can see it. But I wouldn't let it go farther.

Please let me hear from you.

Yours,

John

—Steinbeck: A Life in Letters, pp. 840–842

* * *

Bulgarians Criticize Steinbeck

Steinbeck's support for the Vietnam War angered not only the Soviets but also other Eastern-bloc nations. The following article was published in the 23 January 1967 Newsday.

Vienna (UPI)—A Bulgarian weekly political magazine Saturday devoted 21 of its 40 pages to a denunciation of author John Steinbeck, charging that his dispatches from Vietnam amounted to "propaganda for U.S. aggression" there.

The magazine Po Sveta (Around the World) also criticized New York Times Saigon correspondent Charles Mohr and other newsmen.

Steinbeck's dispatches from Vietnam have been carried by Newsday under the heading "Letters to Alicia." The open letter said of Steinbeck:

". . . You have taken upon yourself the defense of barbarity, the barbarity of an army and of a policy which are doomed . . . You proved to be a man without conscience." Po Sveta is affiliated with the official Communist Bulgarian news agency BTA.

"Mr. Steinbeck," the open letter said, "as far as we know, your addressee, Mrs. Alicia, died in 1963. In that sense you are sending your letters to a corpse. The New York cemetery—this is the mail box for your 'truth' about Vietnam. There is something symbolic in that fact. Unlike the living, the dead cannot voice their indignation. They are indifferent to everything. Even to a lie. This is especially convenient for those to [who] have no courage to unmask the evil. Your letters to Alicia, the skeleton, are availing themselves of this convenience."

(The "Alicia" to whom the letters are inscribed refers to Alicia Patterson Guggenheim, late wife of Harry F. Guggenheim, editor and publisher of Newsday. Miss Patterson was the first editor and publisher of Newsday, from its founding by Guggenheim in 1940 until her death July 2, 1963.

(Steinbeck's letters from Vietnam are a continuation of the series he wrote for Newsday from Europe and the Middle East, starting in November, 1965. Before his departure on that assignment, Steinbeck wrote to Guggenheim explaining why his letters would be addressed to Alicia Patterson, for whom he had great admiration. "It is not mawkish nor sentimental," Steinbeck wrote. "The letters would not be to someone who is dead, but rather to a living mind and a huge curiosity. That is why she was a great newspaperwoman. She wanted to know—everything . . . If I write these letters intending to amuse, inform and illuminate Alicia, they will do the same to great numbers of people.")

In Moscow, a Russian poet accused Steinbeck yesterday of betraying his humane principles by accompanying U.S. troops to Vietnam. The poet, Vladimir Fedorov, published an 88-line poem in Sovetskaya Rossiya, or Soviet Russia, a Moscow newspaper. "John Steinbeck, look down below," the poem said. "Whose blood has dyed the ripe rice? Who will reap this bloody rice?"

—Newsday, 23 January 1967, p. 59

Steinbeck accompanying a combat patrol in Vietnam, late 1966 (from Jackson J. Benson, The True Adventures of John Steinbeck, Writer, *1984; Thomas Cooper Library, University of South Carolina)*

America and Americans (1966)

America the Beautiful

An anonymous reviewer in the Times Literary Supplement *said that although the photographs in* America and Americans *(1966) were impressive, "it is the text that matters."*

From one point of view, this is a picture book, an excellent picture book but rather conventional in that it stresses too much America the Beautiful. But it is a picture book whose accompanying text is not a rivulet but a river and the text is by that famous and idiosyncratic author (and Nobel Prizeman), John Steinbeck.

The pictures, adroitly chosen, are by some of the most famous American cameramen and some are dazzlingly beautiful and some have special kinds of fascination. But it is the text that matters. Mr. Steinbeck still thinks of the United States as "the last, best hope of earth" but in some ways, this brief commentary is as disconcerting for the 100 per cent American as was *The Grapes of Wrath*. Mr. Steinbeck has no sacred cows. Indeed, he dares attack a cow more sacred even than Mom, the rule by what he calls the "paedarchy." The "alienation of youth" does not impress him, although it does depress him.

The reign of terror, which is actually a paedarchy, increases every day, and the open warfare between adults and teenagers becomes constantly more bitter. . . . I do not blame the youth; no one has ever told him that his tricks are obvious, his thoughts puerile, his goals uncooperative and selfish, his art ridiculous. Psychoanalysts constantly remind their little patients that they must find the real "me." The real "me" inevitably turns out to be a savage, self-seeking little beast.

Mr. Steinbeck notes the importance of the fact that the Americans have always been, to quote from Professor David Potter, "a People of Plenty." He knows the importance of the forest, the *antiqua silva* that dazzled Pastorius in the late seventeenth century. Mr. Steinbeck is worried by "the Negro question." He tells us of the quick and prudent reaction of a Negro who might have been accused of rape. And of his reply to Mr. Steinbeck's congratulations—"I've been practising to be a Negro for a long time."

Mr. Steinbeck has his quirks. The longbow was a Welsh, not an English invention. The Japanese in California are taller and heavier than their parents were, but so are the Japanese in Japan. The *Nisei* no doubt "look American," but it is not a matter of features but of a score of ways of behaving that marks all Americans, white, black, yellow. The Cornish-speaking miners Mr. Steinbeck met ought to be shipped back to the Duchy, to teach the modern Cornishmen their ancestral tongue.

The pictures are brilliant, but not representative. The Middle West is nearly neglected. The antiques and ruins that Americans are so good at building are excessively represented. There is an almost total absence of academic scenes. Why not a picture of a midwestern college with a fine site like Marietta? Why, if we are to have Vanderbilt chateaux, not Biltmore rather than The Breakers? Why not some rural slums like the decayed mining villages of Pennsylvania and West Virginia or decayed textile towns like that New Hampshire town that proudly boasts it is the original of Peyton Place? But it is a pleasure to see some of the great natural sights, to realize that the power of wonder New York once had is not exhausted, to recognize a fine restaurant in San Francisco by the wallpaper and to see a member of the (Boston) Athenaeum holed up in his natural habitat. This is an expensive book but it is worth the money.

—*Times Literary Supplement,* 1 December 1966; reprinted in *John Steinbeck: The Contemporary Reviews,* edited by Joseph R. McElrath Jr., Jesse S. Crisler, and Susan Shillinglaw (Cambridge & New York: Cambridge University Press, 1996), pp. 500–501

* * *

Books
Robert J. Cooke

Reviewer Robert J. Cooke found America and Americans *"disappointing."*

A good picture book is very seldom the victim of a cleaning off of shelves—its detail is infinite and its appeal is timeless. One returns to a picture book because it makes no demands, its message is emotional rather than intellectual, yet it fills the spaces left after reading printed words. . . .

John Steinbeck's *America and Americans* is clearly a labor of love and he describes his work as "a book of opinions, unashamed and individual." The pictures are rather ordinary (with one or two notable exceptions such as "Schoolgirl" by Declan Haun on page 65) and most of them have been seen before in *Life* or *Time* or some such magazine. The almost book-length text is, indeed, Steinbeck opinion; whimsical, superficial, idle observations such as "Sometimes we seem to be a nation of public Puritans and private profligates," or "But we are an exuberant people, careless and destructive as active children." The book is disappointing. Steinbeck, like Dos Passos, grows older. . . .

—*Social Education,* 3 (December 1966); reprinted in *John Steinbeck: The Contemporary Reviews,* p. 500

* * *

America and Americans
Tetsumaro Hayashi

Tetsumaro Hayashi reviewed America and Americans *for* The Visva-bharati Quarterly. *Hayashi cofounded the John Steinbeck Society of America in January 1966.*

John Steinbeck, a Nobel Prize winner, one of the greatest living American authors, recently spoke out again forcefully in his *America and Americans,* a collection of informally written essays of serious nature about his beloved country and people. His essays are illustrated by beautiful, selected photographs of American people and typical American festivals, events, and scenes.

Like his *Travels with Charley in Search of America* (1962), this book attempts to recapture the diversified images of America and her people and to tell Americans how they stand and look to others. To a great extent, however, what he discusses seems to be an assimilation of what many sociologists, psychologists, theologians, and philosophers have argued in the past. Therefore, this book will not shock the reader, nor will it impress you with strikingly new ideas and interpretations. Yet it is the straightforwardness and honesty with which Steinbeck talks about the realistic human condition in the United States that make the work significant and captivating.

He is, for instance, unashamed when he praises his country for her greatness. At the same time, he is equally unrestrained when he points out the evils and hypocrisies of his country and people. It is this honesty and boldness as well as this fairness and insight in his critical appraisal that makes this book worth reading, for the conscience of America is revealed in the person of John Steinbeck throughout this book.

Steinbeck sees America as a country full of contradictions, conflicts, tensions, and paradoxes. Thus he dares, though sympathetically, to discuss various problems and subjects in their intricate and mysterious dichotomies: good and evil; pride and shame; hope and despair; virtue and sin; conflict and harmony; and promise and pitfalls. America is, as he sees her, a mecca of freedom, and yet she is also a home of inequality, segregation, and injustice. Americans are, implies Steinbeck, the kindest and the friendliest people on earth, but they can be as mean, cruel, and rude to their own brothers as some savages in the jungle. They love their president, and yet they crucify him, laments the patriotic writer. In "Paradox and Dream" Steinbeck states, in a positive tone, one of the self-contradictory dichotomies of the United States. "We are complacent in our possessions, in our homes, in our education; but it is hard to find a man or woman who does not want something better for the next generation." Throughout the book he points out this kind of dichotomy again and again, hoping that a better America and greater country may someday be created out of such complex characters. The reader will not always agree with Steinbeck, but he will certainly respect the author's passionate love and grave concern for his country and her future, because his love and concern are directed not merely toward America and Americans but also toward all nations and all mankind.

The truths of America and Americans he discovers and discusses in this book is [*sic*] by and large the truths of all nations and peoples on earth. It is truly due to this universal identity that the reader will find Steinbeck's message appealing. In this respect this is a book of prophecy written by a man of mission and vision, a man who loves his country and people so much that he cannot help worrying about their problems, faults, and dilemmas, a man who cannot help telling his people what is wrong with them. After Adlai Stevenson is gone, . . . America's conscience is now represented by Steinbeck who

Steinbeck at Bluff Point, near his Sag Harbor home, August 1966 (from Jackson J. Benson, The True Adventures of John Steinbeck, Writer, *1984; Thomas Cooper Library, University of South Carolina)*

denies a fairy tale of the United States but sees through chaos and confusion a really truthful picture of his country and people.

The author maintains in the concluding chapter that America's hope lies in her insatiable desire, a desire to be rebellious, angry, searching, and dissatisfied with the status quo, for the desire and dissatisfaction are an energy to be greater. In the darkness and despair John Steinbeck finds shining light for America and her people. It is not only America's hope but a hope for all mankind.

—*Visva-bharati Quarterly,* 31 (1965–1966); reprinted in *John Steinbeck: The Contemporary Reviews,* pp. 501–503

* * *

[New York City]

Wednesday
3/4/64

Dear Elizl:

Before I forget it, here is the letter we discussed the other evening. It is a little thing but could turn unpleasant. Read the letter carefully and see whether you think it is effective. If it isn't, I'll do another one.

We had such a good time the other night. I'm sorry to be so willy-nilly these last months. It's almost as though I had run out of drive. I get such a dreadful sense of repetition when I try to go to work. It's as though I had said everything I have to say. Maybe that is so, but then in the night the dragons stirs a little. I guess the thing that bothers me more than anything is that I am technically considered dead. Whatever I may write can only be considered in the light of what I have written and that often ill remembered. I understand very well why Mark Twain wanted to use a pseudonym. At least then the boys could look at it with a new eye.

Oh! I guess before long I'll stop brooding. I sit over these pads long hours every day and throw page after page away. But it has always been this way, as you will know. But the trouble is that now I don't know when I am repeating myself.

Anyway —
love
John

Letter from Steinbeck to his agent, Elizabeth Otis, expressing the sense of futility he often felt as a writer in the years following his receipt of the 1962 Nobel Prize (Center for Steinbeck Studies, San Jose State University)

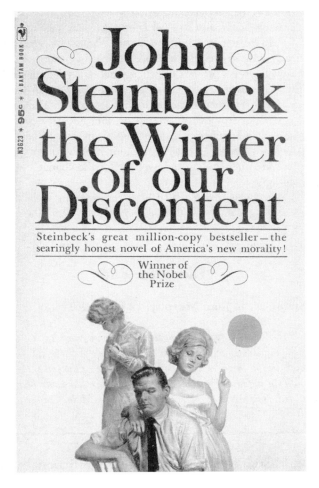

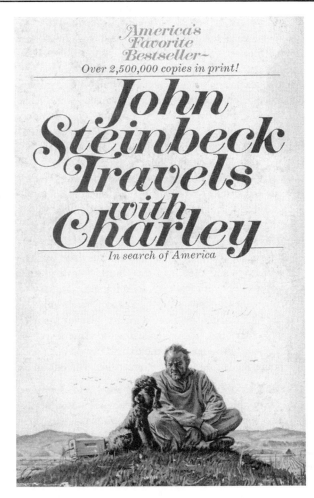

*Front cover of the 1967 paperback edition of Steinbeck's last novel, originally published in 1961; front cover
of the 1968 paperback edition of his 1962 travel book (Bruccoli Clark Layman Archives)*

America and Americans
Ted Atkinson

*Ted Atkinson reviewed the 1968 Bantam paperback edition
of* America and Americans *for the* Steinbeck Quarterly.

For the literary scholar I must assume that the text is
more important than the pictures of *America and Americans*.
If one is granted this assumption, then it follows that the
Bantam edition of *America and Americans* (1968) is as valuable to the scholar as the Viking Press edition of 1966.
The text for both editions is the same; it is only the size
and placement of pictures that differ. If, however, one considers the pictures to be of great significance, then the
Viking edition (due to its larger size and clearer reproduc-
tion of the pictures) is certainly the superior volume.

America and Americans is a highly subjective work; the
author does not claim to be objective. Since the volume is
admittedly subjective (Steinbeck states in the "Foreword"
that such is the case), we have what amounts to the

author's casual reflections on American culture. One of
the major strengths of such a work is that the author
reveals as much about himself as he does about the American tradition. It becomes quite apparent then that such a
volume is valuable to the student or scholar searching for
a compendium of Steinbeck's political, social, and economic views.

One of the most striking features about this volume is that its casual style is at once interesting and
informative. Personal anecdotes, such as the Tallac
hatchery encounter with Jim, heighten the reader's
interest and clearly illustrate points of discussion. Steinbeck's personal experience at the hatchery illustrates
well "the way the tribesmen can slip back and forth
between their two realities and between one culture and
another." Other personal observations—the old lady at
Third Avenue with her city life and trappings of a rural
dream and Mr. Kirk with his haunted house and
intriguing characters—also serve to entertain and
instruct the reader.

Aside from the power of Steinbeck's style and apart from the value of the subjective revelations, *America and Americans* is interesting because of the tension developed by honestly expressed ideas. "*E Pluribus Unum*," the first section of the text, is a discussion concerning the complex fusion of geography, climate, and ethnic anarchy that fashioned America and "made us Americans." In "Paradox and Dream," Steinbeck continues his analysis of the American identity by discussing the uniquely American dichotomies that most Americans accept as commonplace. The author states that "we are able to believe that our government is weak, stupid, overbearing, dishonest, and inefficient, and at the same time we are deeply convinced that it is the best government in the world, and we like to impose it upon everyone else." The many paradoxes of American life are further explored as Steinbeck indicates that Americans live in cities and dream of the country, earn money only to give it away, and restlessly long for security, only to be deprived of it by restlessness. The many paradoxes of American culture are again developed in "Government of the People." Here the author discusses the American attitudes toward the President and the many "inviolable, deepseated" political customs like the nominating conventions.

In the next two sections of *America and Americans*, "Created Equal" and "Genus Americanus," Steinbeck's main concern is with race and class prejudice. In the first of these sections the author labors long and well to trace the origins of racial prejudice in America. In the process he attempts to dispel illusions and establish facts. The process is continued in "Genus Americanus" as Steinbeck considers how "members of a classless society . . . work out changes in status levels without violating their belief that there are no such levels." This consideration touches upon the old notions of aristocracy, the new notions of capitalism, the strange structures of the corporation, and the curious need for "orders, lodges, and encampments." The cultural paradoxes explored in the preceding two chapters are further exploited in "The Pursuit of Happiness." In this section problems that occur from childhood to old age are considered within the bewildering American culture that was revealed in the earlier chapters. "Americans and the Land" is a rather tiresome discussion of the American's [*sic*] treatment of their landscape. From the early wanton destruction of forests to the present inadvertent pollution of water and air, the author reveals the means by which the landscape has been victimized by innumerable abuses. The slight value of this section is, however, well offset by "Americans and the World." Here the focus changes from Americans looking at Europeans and Europeans looking at Americans, to Americans looking at themselves and finally creating an American literature. After discussing the American journalist and literary artist, Steinbeck pays a tribute to the historical value of *Huckle-*

berry Finn, An American Tragedy, Winesburg, Ohio, Main Street, The Great Gatsby, and *As I Lay Dying.*

In "Americans and the Future," Steinbeck seems to clearly indicate that the tensions present in American culture will always provide the energy necessary for survival. This idea figures strongly throughout *America and Americans,* but it is particularly clear in this last section. The paradoxes and ironies of American life are successfully resolved in Steinbeck's concluding affirmation of faith in America's future: "I believe that our history, our experiences in America, has endowed us for the change that is coming."

—*Steinbeck Quarterly,* 2 (Fall 1969); reprinted in *John Steinbeck: The Contemporary Reviews,* pp. 504–506

Facing the End

Steinbeck to John Murphy, 12 June 1961

Although the following letter to John Murphy, a friend from childhood, was written in 1961, seven years before Steinbeck died, it provides a sense of the writer facing the end of his life with an unfinished mission, one that he felt could never be completed. The work he had in mind was his Malory project, left

---

Steinbeck on Fiction and Nonfiction

The following is from a long, introspective letter written on 28 January 1963 to Pat Covici, Steinbeck's longtime editor.

Fiction, it seems to me, in its inception was an attempt to put experience in a form and direction so that it could be understood. Not that fiction could be understood but that reality could. Now perhaps that has changed. Perhaps people can no longer find themselves and their neighbors in fiction and so go searching in non-fiction for some likeness of experience.

There is one difficulty in this. Writers of fiction are usually better writers than writers of fact. This was not always true. But perhaps fiction writers are no longer fastened to reality. Maybe their "schools" have taken them away from their source. Are the Greek myths fiction? Are the Sagas fiction? Not in the sense that is understood today. Ideally—the fiction writer must be much closer to reality because he does not have the corroborations as proof that the non-fiction writer has. You can write anything in the morning paper so long as it happened. The fiction writer wouldn't dare do this. What he writes must . . . not only happen *but continue to happen.*

—quoted in Jay Parini, *John Steinbeck: A Biography* (New York: Holt, 1995), p. 449

unfinished at his death on 20 December 1968 and published posthumously as The Acts of King Arthur and His Noble Knights *(1976).*

Dear John:

All my life has been aimed at one book and I haven't started it yet. The rest has all been practice. Do you remember the Arthurian legend well enough to raise in your mind the symbols of Launcelot and his son Galahad? You see, Launcelot was imperfect and so he never got to see the Holy Grail. So it is with all of us. The Grail is always one generation ahead of us. But it is there and so we can go on bearing sons who will bear sons who may see the Grail. This is a most profound set of symbols.

The setting down of words is only the final process. It is possible, through accident, that the words for my book may never be set down but I have been working and studying toward it for over forty years. Only the last of the process waits to be done—and it scares the hell out of me. Once the words go down—you are alone and committed. It's as final as a plea in court from which there is

no retracting. That's the lonely time. Nine tenths of a writer's life do not admit of any companion nor friend nor associate. And until one makes peace with loneliness and accepts it as a part of the profession, as celibacy is a part of priesthood, until then there are times of dreadful dread. I am just as terrified of my next book as I was of my first. It doesn't get easier. It gets harder and more heartbreaking and finally, it must be that one must accept the failure which is the end of every writer's life no matter what stir he may have made. In himself he must fail as Launcelot failed—for the Grail is not a cup. It's a promise that skips ahead—it's a carrot on a stick and it never fails to draw us on. So it is that I would greatly prefer to die in the middle of a sentence in the middle of a book and so leave it as all life must be—unfinished. That's the law, the great law. Principles of notoriety or publicity or even public acceptance do not apply. Greatness is not shared by a man who is great. And by the same token—if he should want it—he can't possibly get near it.

Yours,
John
—*Steinbeck: A Life in Letters,* pp. 859–860

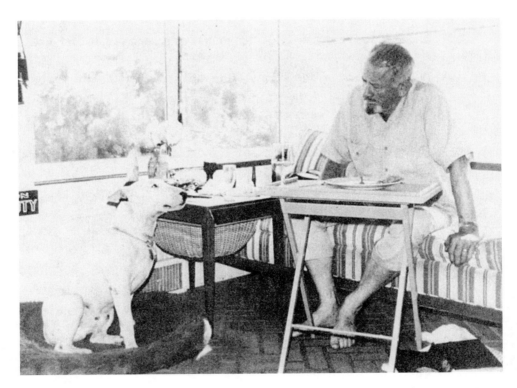

Steinbeck at his Sag Harbor home on 14 July 1968, five months before his death, with his dog, Angel (from Jackson J. Benson,
The True Adventures of John Steinbeck, Writer, *1984; Thomas Cooper Library, University of South Carolina)*

Page 1

1

~~ARTHUR~~

When Uther Pendragon was king of all England,

~~there was~~ a mighty duke in Cornwall ~~who made war against~~ defied him.

~~him.~~ ~~The duke was~~ (called the Duke of Tintagil. After

a ~~long~~ time, King Uther sent for the duke and charged him

to bring his wife with him, for she was known as a fair

and a wise lady, and her name was Igraine. ¶ When the duke

Uther

and his wife came to ~~the king,~~ he gave them great honor

and

and entertained them ~~both.~~ The king loved the Lady Igraine

and ~~he~~ desired her, ~~b~~ut she was a good woman and would

¶

not consent to the king. She told the duke her husband,

believe

"I ~~suppose~~ we were sent for that I should be dishonored;

in haste

wherefore, my husband, let us depart and ride ~~secretly~~ ~~into~~

the night to our own castle." So they departed secretly.

learned

When King Uther ~~knew~~ of their escape, he was angry.

He called his privy council and told them what had happened.

The council advised the king to order the duke and his

First two pages of the typescript for Steinbeck's adaptation of Sir Thomas Malory's Le Morte Darthur *(1485), which he worked on sporadically for the last twelve years of his life and was published posthumously in 1976 as* The Acts of King Arthur and His Noble Knights *(Center for Steinbeck Studies, San Jose State University)*

- 2 -

wife to return. They said, "If he will not come at your

summons, then you will have cause to make war upon him."

The messengers rode and brought the answer back. The

answer was that neither the duke nor his wife would come.

Then the king was furious. He sent ~~hard word again and told~~ an angry message

telling the duke to get ready to defend himself, for within forty

days ~~he~~ The king would fetch him out of the biggest castle he had.

When the duke had this warning, he prepared two

strong castles for defense, the castle of Tintagil and

the Castle Terrabil. Igraine, he put in the Castle Tinta-

gil, and himself went to defend the castle of Terrabil.

And King Uther marched with a great army and laid

siege to the Castle Terrabil. He pitched his tents before

it and attacked the walls so that many people on both sides

were killed. Then from anger and ~~for great love of~~ from longing for

Igraine, King Uther fell ~~sick~~. despondent.

At this time, Sir Ulfius a noble knight, came to

Chapter Nine: 1969–2002

Chronology

December 1969
Journal of a Novel: The East of Eden Letters, a collection of letters that Steinbeck wrote to his editor, Pascal Covici, recording his progress on *East of Eden* (1952), is published by Viking Press.

1971
A revised and enlarged edition of *The Portable Steinbeck,* edited and introduced by Pascal Covici Jr., is published by Viking.

1973
Steinbeck's "New York: The Burdens and the Glories . . . and Just Yesterday, Men Who Loved It So" is published in the 5 May edition of *The New York Times.*

1975
Viking publishes *Steinbeck: A Life in Letters,* edited by Steinbeck's widow, Elaine, and his friend Robert Wallsten, and *Viva Zapata! The Original Screenplay,* edited by Robert E. Morsberger.

The John Steinbeck Library in Salinas (photograph by Luchen Li)

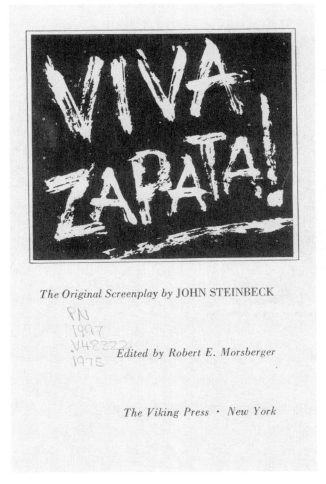

Title page for the 1975 edition of Steinbeck's screenplay for the 1952 movie about the life of Emiliano Zapata
(Thomas Cooper Library, University of South Carolina)

1976	Steinbeck's unfinished adaptation from the works of Sir Thomas Malory is published by Farrar, Straus and Giroux as *The Acts of King Arthur and His Noble Knights: From the Winchester Manuscripts of Thomas Malory and Other Sources.* The volume is edited by Chase Horton, the New York bookseller who originally proposed the project to Steinbeck. In August the First International Steinbeck Congress is held at Kyushu University in Fukuoka City, Japan.
1978	*Letters to Elizabeth: A Selection of Letters from John Steinbeck to Elizabeth Otis,* edited by Florian J. Shasky and Susan F. Riggs, is published by the Book Club of California.
1979	Thomas Kiernan's *The Intricate Music: A Biography of John Steinbeck,* the first extensive biography of the writer, is published by Little, Brown. Thomas Fensch's *Steinbeck and Covici: The Story of a Friendship* is published by Paul S. Eriksson.
1984	The most extensive Steinbeck biography, Jackson J. Benson's *The True Adventures of John Steinbeck, Writer,* is published by Viking. Robert DeMott's *Steinbeck's Reading: A Catalogue of Books Owned and Borrowed* is published by Garland. The Second International Steinbeck Congress is held in Salinas in August.
Fall 1987	*Steinbeck,* a newsletter edited by Susan Shillinglaw of the Steinbeck Research Center (now the Center for Steinbeck Studies) at San Jose State University, begins publication.

First issue of the Steinbeck commemorative stamp, postmarked on his birthday (National Steinbeck Center, Salinas)

1988	*Conversations with John Steinbeck,* edited by Fensch, is published by the University Press of Mississippi.
1989	*Working Days: The Journals of The Grapes of Wrath, 1938–1941,* edited by DeMott, is published by Viking.
1990	The Third International Steinbeck Congress is held in Honolulu on 27–30 May.
1992	A new motion-picture adaptation of *Of Mice and Men* (1937) is released, starring John Malkovich as Lennie and Gary Sinise as George.
1994	The first Library of America volume of Steinbeck's works, *Novels and Stories, 1932–1937,* is published. Edited by DeMott and Elaine Steinbeck, it comprises *The Pastures of Heaven* (1932), *To a God Unknown* (1933), *Tortilla Flat* (1935), *In Dubious Battle* (1936), and *Of Mice and Men.*
1995	Jay Parini's *John Steinbeck: A Biography* is published by Henry Holt.
1996	The second Library of America volume of Steinbeck's works, *The Grapes of Wrath and Other Writings, 1936–1941,* is published. Edited by DeMott and Elaine Steinbeck, it comprises *The Long Valley, The Grapes of Wrath* (1939), *The Log from the Sea of Cortez* (1951; first published as part of *Sea of Cortez,* 1941), and *The Harvest Gypsies* (1936).
1997	The Fourth International Steinbeck Congress is held on 19–23 March at San Jose State University, Salinas, and Monterey.
1998	The $12 million National Steinbeck Center is constructed and opened at the head of Main Street in Steinbeck's hometown, Salinas.
2001	While many academic institutions, public libraries, and Steinbeck-related organizations prepare to celebrate the upcoming Steinbeck centennial on 27 February 2002, a coalition of twenty-six nonprofit cultural organizations headed up by the Center for Steinbeck

Studies and the Mercantile Library of New York receives a $260,000 grant from the National Endowment for the Humanities to commemorate the centennial. The third Library of America volume of Steinbeck's works, *Novels, 1942–1952,* is published. Edited by DeMott, it comprises *The Moon Is Down* (1942), *Cannery Row* (1945), *The Pearl* (1947), and *East of Eden*. Starting with its Winter 2001 issue, the newsletter *Steinbeck* becomes *Steinbeck Studies*.

2002   In January the John Steinbeck Centennial Edition, a six-volume boxed set, is published by Penguin. The titles in the edition are *The Grapes of Wrath, Of Mice and Men, East of Eden, The Pearl, Cannery Row,* and *Travels With Charley. John Steinbeck: America and Americans and Selected Nonfiction,* edited by Shillinglaw and Benson, is published by Viking. "John Steinbeck's Americas: A Centennial Conference," sponsored by Hofstra University, the Center for Steinbeck Studies, and the Steinbeck Society of Japan, is held at Hofstra University on 20–23 March.

By the time Steinbeck died on 20 December 1968, many critics had concluded that he was not a major modern American author. Despite the fact that he was a Nobel laureate, his reputation had never fared well with the literary establishment. Even more troubling was the last phase of his career, during the Vietnam War. His sympathy for the war effort and his later presence on the battlefield as a war correspondent opened him up to critical attack.

The state of Steinbeck criticism in 1969 reflected a decline in his popularity. Only a few serious scholars were diligently reading and exploring his works. There were some significant publications, however. In March 1968 the Steinbeck Newsletter *(later the* Steinbeck Quarterly*) had begun publication under the editorship of Tetsumaro Hayashi, one of the founders of the John Steinbeck Society of America. In December 1969 a collection of letters from Steinbeck to his editor, Pascal Covici, concerning his progress on* East of Eden *(1952) was published by Viking Press as* Journal of a Novel: The East of Eden Letters. *This volume shed new light on Steinbeck as a serious artist. A revised and enlarged edition of* The Portable Steinbeck, *originally published in 1943, came out in 1971 under the editorship of Pascal Covici Jr. An important collection of letters,* Steinbeck: A Life in Letters, *edited by Steinbeck's widow, Elaine, and his friend Robert Wallsten, appeared in 1975. That same year, Robert E. Morsberger edited* Viva Zapata! The Original Screenplay, *a volume comprising Steinbeck's script for a 1952 biopic on Emiliano Zapata.*

Although some early Steinbeck studies were shortsighted and incomplete, Richard Astro performed extensive research and investigation for John Steinbeck and Edward F. Ricketts: The Shaping of a Novelist *(1973). Astro's book not only provides detailed information about how Steinbeck and Ed Ricketts collaborated on* Sea of Cortez *(1941) but also analyzes Ricketts's worldview and explains how it was represented in Steinbeck's fiction. Astro's emphasis on his-*

torical facts in Steinbeck studies triggered similar scholarly work in the coming years.

In 1976 Steinbeck's adaptation of the works of Sir Thomas Malory into modern prose, which he had labored on for several years and left unfinished at his death, was published as The Acts of King Arthur and His Noble Knights: From the Winchester Manuscripts of Thomas Malory and Other Sources. *Two years later a volume of letters from Steinbeck to his longtime agent was published as* Letters to Elizabeth: A Selection of Letters from John Steinbeck to Elizabeth Otis. *Two substantial biographical works were published in 1979: Thomas Kiernan's* The Intricate Music: A Biography of John Steinbeck *and Thomas Fensch's* Steinbeck and Covici: The Story of a Friendship.

In 1984 the most extensive biography, Jackson J. Benson's *The True Adventures of John Steinbeck, Writer, was published. Robert DeMott's* Steinbeck's Reading: A Catalogue of Books Owned and Borrowed *(1984) provides a wonderful perspective on Steinbeck's training and his relation to writers of the past. Many scholars came to realize that the flawed assessments of earlier critics placed his works in the constricted framework of literary forms and traditions that he hardly cared about; Steinbeck always experimented with new styles, different forms, and contrasting themes. Critics paid increasing attention to his insights in the fields of marine biology, sociology, history, politics, and cultural studies.*

Several studies published later in the 1980s, including Conversations with John Steinbeck *(1988), edited by Fensch, prepared the way for consideration of Steinbeck as a modernist. In the fall of 1987* Steinbeck, *a newsletter under the editorship of Susan Shillinglaw at San Jose State University, began publication. The 1980s closed with an important contribution to Steinbeck studies:* Working Days: The

Journals of The Grapes of Wrath, 1938–1941 (1989), edited by DeMott.

In a sign of continued public interest in Steinbeck, a new motion-picture adaptation of Of Mice and Men (1937) was released in 1992. Another extensive biography, Jay Parini's John Steinbeck: A Biography, was published in 1995.

The Fourth International Steinbeck Congress was held on 19–23 March 1997 at San Jose State University, with concurrent events in Salinas and Monterey. Hundreds of Steinbeck scholars from around the world gathered in California to celebrate the writer's literary accomplishments under the theme "Beyond Boundaries: Steinbeck and the World." Most of the presentations examined his enduring worldwide impact.

In 1998 the $12 million National Steinbeck Center opened on Main Street in Steinbeck's hometown of Salinas. The center celebrates Steinbeck's life, writings, and characters, as well as the Salinas region, the setting for much of his fiction, through dioramas, interactive exhibits, videos, events, and festivals. Since its opening, the center has received visitors of all kinds and from all over the world.

As the twenty-first century opened, preparations for the upcoming Steinbeck centennial were under way. In the winter of 2001 the newsletter Steinbeck changed its name to Steinbeck Studies. Early in the centennial year of 2002 the Fifth International Steinbeck Congress was held at Hofstra University on Long Island. Publications that year included the collection John Steinbeck: America and Americans and Selected Nonfiction, edited by Shillinglaw and Benson. Steinbeck has not only had a large public readership and interested many scholars but has also influenced several modern writers. This influence is recalled by the authors who contributed to John Steinbeck: Centennial Reflections by American Writers (2002), edited by Shillinglaw. Contributors included Norman Mailer, Arthur Miller, Richard Wilbur, and Harper Lee.

The National Steinbeck Center, built in Steinbeck's hometown of Salinas in 1998 (from Donnë Florence, John Steinbeck: America's Author, 2000; Richland County Public Library)

Journal of a Novel (1969)

The Callus behind the Fiction
Clarence Brown

Steinbeck wrote the letters that make up Journal of a Novel: The East of Eden Letters *(1969) as a working log reporting his progress on* East of Eden *(1952) to his editor, Pascal Covici. The daily entries are an important source for understanding the ideas behind the novel. Clarence Brown reviewed* Journal of a Novel *for* The New Republic.

Steinbeck thought that every man had one book in him and that *East of Eden* was his. This naturally made him nervous. It made him, when he finally brought himself to try the book, turn to a kind of athlete's compulsive checking and record-keeping and not a little voodoo to ward off the demons that impede creation: telephones, depression, doorbells, children, advice, and bad pencils. In a large ledger that his editor, Pascal Covici, had given him he wrote letters to Covici on the left-hand page at the start of each working day and the novel on the right. He began at the end of January 1951 and wrote straight through the year deep into the fall. Then the novel, except for some revision, was finished. Just before starting, Steinbeck had emerged from the writer's peculiar hell of a long dry spell and the general hell of a divorce that had deprived him of two sons. But he had remarried, this time to a woman who gave him a buoyant serenity that is evident throughout his journal, and the novel started to come.

East of Eden, as it chances, is the story of two sons who turn up in several guises but always with indelible traces of their models, Cain and Abel. It is also explicitly the story of Steinbeck's own family narrated by himself in his own name and person. Little wonder that he saw it as his one book, for it is his own primal story and the primal story of Man. He read the latter with all the emotional intensity that informs his best pages, the result being that he gradually identified it with the former. When he had settled into his new room and his new chair, before his new drafting table and his new ledger, one part of Steinbeck's mind was anxiously prodding, taunting and encouraging the other. It proposed paradoxes. In the journal the paradox is that a man might arrange himself ever so comfortably, his bowels and soul in some celestial harmony, and still be unable to write. But the paradox of the novel is the supreme, the biblical, paradox of good and evil, of the murderer's *freedom* to triumph over his sin. For passionate analysis, whatever it may lack in scholarship, there must be nothing in all the annals of hermeneutics to match Steinbeck's pages on the single Hebrew verb *timshel.* So the novel is infinitely the greater book, but its greatness confers a remarkable distinction upon the journal.

The journal, never meant for publication, is repetitious and contradictory, but these qualities are not faults, for they provide precious insights into a writer's hesitant awareness of what he was doing. The faults of the book belong chiefly to Steinbeck's anonymous editors, or perhaps just to circumstance. The journal is meaningless without a fresh reading of the novel from which, in a strictly physical sense, it was excised; but even with such reading you are not always sure just which passage is being referred to, and the editors' help on this point is haphazard. But incomparably the greatest lack of all is that of Pascal Covici.

Covici was clearly the kind of editor that every writer longs for, or ought to. His relationship is not that of Maxwell Perkins to Thomas Wolfe, whose ungovernable creativity Perkins brought under some kind of control. If Covici took a hand in Steinbeck's novel, he did it simply by being the one perfect reader of it. In the first draft, parts of the novel had the form of letters to Steinbeck's two boys. But this was abandoned, and I think the reason is clear: the novel itself was never really addressed to anyone but Covici. From 1934, when his editor discovered him—three novels had done poorly and a fourth, *Tortilla Flat,* was being rejected by all publishers—until 1964, when Covici died, he was the writer's confidant, goad, quartermaster and—in Steinbeck's consciousness, I think—his single auditor. Eliot said that writing comes from talking—to oneself, to one other, or to God. For Steinbeck, Covici was the "one other." *East of Eden* was dedicated to him. So, incidentally, was Saul Bellow's *Herzog.* And so was Charles A. Madison's *Book Publishing in America* (McGraw-Hill 1966), which I had to unearth from the British Museum for such information on Covici as one might reasonably expect to find in a preface to Steinbeck's journal. Madison quotes something that Steinbeck said after Covici's death: "Pat Covici was much more than my friend. He was my editor. . . . He demanded of me more than I had and thereby caused me to be more than I should have been without him." And from Covici, in 1941: "In my little life, which is about three-quarters done, you are my rarest experience. . . ." It was that sense of being at least one man's rarest experience that banished from Steinbeck's mind the clouds of depression, the sick fear of rejection and failure, certain frightening impulses in his own soul (all plentifully attested to) and enabled him to write.

The question how Steinbeck or any artist can fuse the dark night of the soul with the radiance of love for wife, sons, and friend into the alchemical product of art is beyond my competence, but I am convinced that this journal will provide material for part of the answer. He was obsessive about the daily production quota. One day, early on in the journal, he perversely declines to work (though he wrote the letter). He will have his hair cut. He might "go farther and get a little sweet-smelling tonic rubbed on. This is a real festive day for me with garlands. And you, old word-Scrooge, will curse and mutter because I am wasting time. Well, I defy you." That is an extraordinary tone of voice, as extraordinary as his non-feasance, and it is uncomfortably somewhere between flirt and bitch. Where does it come from? The answer is elsewhere in the passage, for Steinbeck is preparing to introduce Cathy, whose warped malignancy runs through the novel like the stain of Man's first disobedience. I think he was discovering her in himself, though it was much later in the journal that he explicitly realized his greater kinship with her than with any other character in the book.

I treasure his testimony concerning the physical side of writing. The writing callus on his middle finger grew to bothersome proportions. When he cut his thumb carving something out of wood, the writing suffered. Earlier the slant of his table had seemed wrong, and when he changed it, improving his posture, the work went easier. There was a glare on the light wood of the table, so he painted it black, which was a bad idea, so he put down a restful, green blotter. But all this is mere frippery when compared to the question of pencils. I should like to propose that Steinbeck's numerous comments on the basic instruments of authorship be made into a syllabus for the first course in "creative writing." I am not in the employ of Eberhard Faber, but I regard it as a duty to set down his devotion to the Blackwing ("Half the Pressure Twice the Speed") and, for other moods and stages of inspiration, the Mongol 480 No. 2⅜ F round.

Writers alone will understand that they can use no other information in the book. His comments on character, pace, construction, and so on, are professionally worthless, since if Steinbeck has any message at all, it is that practically nothing can be learned from predecessors, and the little that can must be painfully disremembered. A novel is oneself or it is nothing. He wrote a novel of two families against a background of history with an explicitly moral purpose and an explicitly present author. His method was sharp juxtaposition. But he was not building on Tolstoy: he was reinventing him. That his reinvention lagged behind the original is not so bad when you recall that mere imitation would have been unreadable.

—*New Republic,* 161 (20 December 1969); reprinted in *John Steinbeck: The Contemporary Reviews,* edited by Joseph R. McElrath Jr., Jesse S. Crisler, and Susan Shillinglaw (Cambridge & New York: Cambridge University Press, 1996), pp. 510–512

* * *

Journal of a Novel
Richard Astro

Richard Astro, a prominent early Steinbeck scholar, doubted that the general reading public would be interested in Journal of a Novel, *but he called it an "indispensable" work for Steinbeck critics.*

It is difficult to know how to assess properly the Viking Press's recent publication of John Steinbeck's *Journal of a Novel,* the series of "letters" Steinbeck wrote to his close friend and editor, Pascal Covici, during the composition of *East of Eden.* At first glance, these "letters," written every working day between January 29 and November 1, 1951, in a large notebook across from the text of Steinbeck's grandly conceived but largely unsuccessful novel, seem to display the last remains of a defeated novelist whose deteriorating literary talents had finally struck bottom. And even upon closer inspection, part of this initial reaction remains.

Put simply, much of *Journal of a Novel* is trivial, and despite the fact that these dispatches were not written to be published, their very existence suggests something rather pathetic about the general quality of Steinbeck's thinking in 1951. It is, in short, rather discouraging to find the author of *In Dubious Battle* and *The Grapes of Wrath* absorbed with such matters as the size of writing pencils, the operation of an electric pencil sharpener, eye doctors, the weather on Nantucket Island, and General MacArthur. And even the uncritical Steinbeck reader can find it difficult not to become annoyed at the forced sense of method and control which the novelist states he imposed on the actual writing of *East of Eden.*

Besides being repetitious, full of irrelevancies, and often just plain dull, *Journal of a Novel* shatters the myth that has often surrounded the novelist as a person. For the Steinbeck of these "letters" appears as a detached, somewhat self-indulgent, comfort-loving member of the New York literati who hardly resembles the Steinbeck that we, in our delusive simplicity, like to imagine fighting the battles of the dispossessed Joads or envision stealing vegetables for the communal stews on Cannery Row.

To the reader genuinely concerned with Steinbeck and his work, however, *Journal of a Novel* is an interesting and highly valuable book for a number of reasons. First, it is a sincere testament of Steinbeck's affection for and trust in Pat Covici who, after the death of Ed Ricketts in 1948, became Steinbeck's closest friend and professional confidant.

Further, the "letters" are highly valuable to the Steinbeck scholar in that they enlarge the critical understanding of *East of Eden* since they contain explicit state-

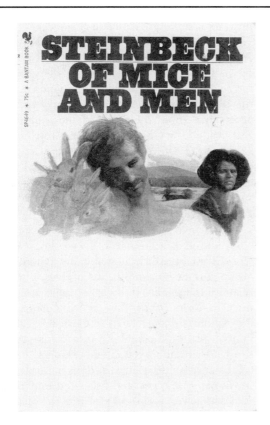

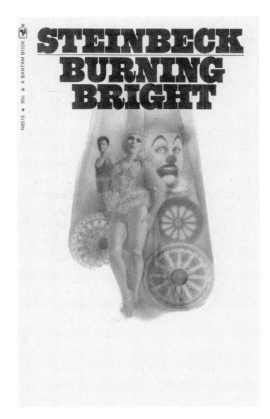

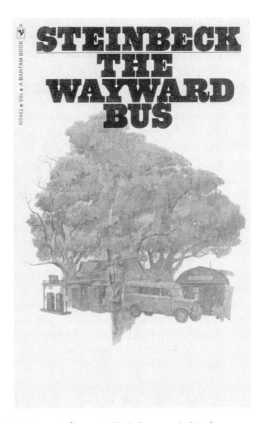

Front covers of four 1970s paperback editions of Steinbeck novels (Bruccoli Clark Layman Archives)

ments of Steinbeck's intentions in the novel. For example, one learns that Steinbeck regarded *East of Eden* as his "big novel" into which he attempted to pour "every bit of technique I have learned consciously." From the standpoint of Steinbeck's thematic concerns in *East of Eden,* the "letters" to Covici are highly important in that they contain the novelist's insistence that his main concern in *East of Eden* is with people and that he willingly subordinated his usual interest in description and setting to achieve that end. And in talking about people who are to appear in his novel, it becomes apparent that Steinbeck is more concerned with the character of Cathy Ames (Trask) than with any other single figure in the book. Calling her a monster born "with a malformed soul," Steinbeck states his desire to show that Cathy "is a little piece of the monster in all of us."

Also of importance in *Journal of a Novel* are Steinbeck's remarks about the Hamilton stories in *East of Eden.* These "letters" show, for instance, Steinbeck's fondness for the memory of his maternal grandfather, Samuel Hamilton, whom the novelist remembers "surrounded with all manner of birds and beasts and qualities of light" and whom he wants to portray in his novel "in a kind of golden light, the way such a man should be remembered." In addition, Steinbeck explains why he included the strange and very personal episode of Tom and Dessie Hamilton, why he describes the character of Abra as "the strong female principle of good as opposed to Cathy," and accounts for the character of Lee Trask's philosopher-cook, who is in the book "because I need him."

Most importantly, the "letters" to Covici, when taken as a whole, suggest that while Steinbeck consistently maintained that *East of Eden* was "not a story about the Trasks but about the whole Valley," the book was gradually transformed into a sprawling study of good and evil in the world through a symbolic representation of the Cain-Abel story (Steinbeck states that his characters are "symbol people") and an affirmation of free will (the Timshel symbol) by which each individual can maintain his integrity and purposefully assert his creative impulse. In short, *Journal of a Novel* clearly shows that in the process of writing *East of Eden,* Steinbeck's increasing absorption with the theme of good versus evil led to his preoccupation with the story of the Trask family, and the result is less a series of "contrasts and balances" as Steinbeck hoped, but rather a long, incohesive and highly episodic work which reflects the novelist's inability to weave several diverse threads into a coherent fabric.

In addition to the importance of *Journal of a Novel* in illuminating Steinbeck's intentions in *East of Eden* and indirectly accounting for the novel's failures, the "letters" are even more significant in that they clearly demonstrate a shifting balance in Steinbeck's overall world view. In short, the Steinbeck who appears in *Journal of a Novel* is not the writer who, in his best books, extolled the natural beauty of the Salinas Valley, who celebrated the ecological unity of all life, and who could champion the plight of homeless migrants or write with loving acceptance about the antics of the *paisanos* on Tortilla Flat. Rather the Covici dispatches show him as a novelist driven to affirm, at the expense of everything else, the basic humanity of the human animal which, in his earlier fiction, he had accepted *a priori;* his desperate struggle to prove that "although *East of Eden* is not Eden, it is not insuperably far away."

Viewed in retrospect, however, Steinbeck's real contribution as a thinker in his writing is his ecological world view by which he maintains that all living things are important not only in themselves, but also as they relate to the totality of their environment. "Man," says the novelist in *The Log from the Sea of Cortez,* "is related to the whole thing, related inextricably to all reality, known and unknowable." And in his greatest essays, short stories and novels, Steinbeck presents this ecological, balanced view of man and his natural environment. In *Journal of a Novel* (and by stated intention in *East of Eden*), however, Steinbeck discards or at least minimizes his interest in the natural environment, telling Covici he only wants to give "an impression of the valley" since "this book is not about geography but about people." Under most circumstances, such a one-directional and selective approach in a novel written on an epic scale would be hazardous, but to a writer like Steinbeck it is disastrous.

In one of the last letters to Covici, Steinbeck notes that most reviewers, fearing and hating ideas and speculations unclothed with flesh, will misread *East of Eden* which "is full of such things." And while this critic's objection is not that Steinbeck introduces ideas and speculations into his fiction, but simply that in *East of Eden* he does it to the exclusion of everything else, what we are ultimately left with is Steinbeck's final remark in the original dedication to Covici which appears at the end of the journal: "God damn it. This is my book. . . . My book is about good and evil. Maybe the theme got into the execution. Do you want to publish it or not?"

In no way can Steinbeck's collection of "letters" to Covici be called a significant literary landmark. Nevertheless, it presents an important portrait of John Steinbeck attempting the impossible task of "putting down the Salinas Valley from a country man's viewpoint" in a New York apartment while a MacArthur Day parade goes on below his window. It shows an already famous writer, with his greatest work behind him, trying methodically and unsuccessfully to do it all over again. No, *Journal of a Novel* is not a good book and to most readers is probably not worth the purchase price, but to the Steinbeck critic interested in what Ed Ricketts once called "the toto-picture," it is indispensable in that it clearly illuminates a highly important chapter in Steinbeck's life and career as a writer.

—*Steinbeck Quarterly*, 3 (Fall 1970); reprinted in *John Steinbeck: The Contemporary Reviews*, pp. 517–519

* * *

Journal of a Novel: The East of Eden Letters
Peter Lisca

Peter Lisca, another pioneering Steinbeck scholar in the 1970s and 1980s, reviewed Journal of a Novel *for* Modern Fiction Studies.

When Pascal Covici, Steinbeck's editor at the Viking Press, died in 1964, Steinbeck wrote, "For thirty years Pat was my collaborator and my conscience. He demanded of me more than I had and thereby caused me to be more than I should have been without him." Although it is clear in the present volume and elsewhere that Steinbeck resisted strongly any "collaboration," his use of that term in this tribute is a measure of his love and friendship. Their closeness was no secret, and Charles Madison *(Book Publishing in America)* calls their relationship "the happiest in publishing history." *Journal of a Novel* consists of a series of unmailed letters to Covici written every working day that Steinbeck spent on the first draft of *East of Eden*. So absorbed was he in the writing of that novel that between January 29 and November 1, 1951, start and finish, there is a letter for every weekday except perhaps half a dozen, and there are some Saturday and Sunday letters to make up for them when he could not stay away from his book. These letters were used as warm-up exercises—"like a pitcher warming up to pitch"—for the actual writing stint of a carefully controlled, almost invariable quota of about 1500 words. Several letters themselves run to that length, although they vary down to just a few lines, their variation reflecting the difficulty or ease with which Steinbeck was able to pick up the novel from where he had left off.

The content of these letters is varied, from personal problems or ecstasies to general philosophical speculation; and from complex problems of structuring the novel's action to the shape, size, hardness, color, sharpness, and number of pencils on hand—at least some dozen passages on pencils and almost as many on the physical properties of desk and paper.

What emerges of Steinbeck's personal life is not particularly valuable to the scholar. But it is interesting to note how much pleasure he got from working with his hands at the practical tasks of homemaking—building shelves and doors, painting walls, and at woodcarving and little practi-

cal inventions of the moment. Like a good craftsman, he loved good tools. Although the editor of this journal (an unnamed member of the Viking staff) found it necessary to delete a few lines relating to persons still living, those remaining passages show a rich personal life, full of love for his wife Elaine and her daughter, his own two sons by his previous marriage, and a variety of friends.

Although his health was excellent during this period, he seemed often concerned that he be allowed to live long enough to finish his novel, which he thought of as the high point of his career—"everything else I have written has been, in a sense, practice for this." Yet, paradoxically, he so identified his daily life with the writing of the novel that he hated to see the approaching last chapters, and these are the cause of his longest delays.

Despite the much-quoted excerpt about it being "the duty of a writer to lift up, to extend, to encourage . . ." there were other days when he thought his craft a "silly business" and even a "horse's ass business," particularly when he was reminded of critics and reviewers, whom he had once called "lice" and now "curious sucker fish who live with joyous vicariousness on other men's work and discipline with dreary words the thing that feeds them." He anticipated that the great themes, moral earnestness, and technical accomplishments of *East of Eden* would not be appreciated. In fact, his original four-page "Dedication" for the book consisted of an imaginary free-for-all on the book among himself, editor, proofreader, sales department, and reader.

Whatever the justification for Steinbeck's harshness toward the critics in 1951, and it was ample, certainly the five books and a bibliography on his work in the last eleven years, innumerable articles, three conferences of scholars in the last three years (and several books now in preparation) have done much to change that situation. In fact, his frequent insistence in these letters that the current novel's themes and symbols might remain forever inaccessible to the critics seems incredibly naive in the face of that novel's obviousness.

Except for rare passages, these letters have little critical value. As the working notes are about the book's first draft, they are sometimes not clear in terms of the published version, and this edition's scope did not allow the editor to make the kind of extended correlation that might have been interesting. Surely, with a more scholarly and complete re-editing of the journal and access to this first draft of the novel, some valuable observations might be made; but in its present form the journal has little more than a gossip interest.

—*Modern Fiction Studies*, 16 (Winter 1970–1971); reprinted in *John Steinbeck: The Contemporary Reviews*, pp. 520–521

The Acts of King Arthur and His Noble Knights (1976)

The Essential King Arthur, according to John Steinbeck
John Gardner

Steinbeck's unfinished project to recast Sir Thomas Malory's version of the Arthurian legends into modern prose was published in 1976 as The Acts of King Arthur and His Noble Knights: From the Winchester Manuscripts of Thomas Malory and Other Sources. *John Gardner reviewed the book for* The New York Times Book Review.

When John Steinbeck was at work on his *The Acts of King Arthur and His Noble Knights* in the middle and late 1950's, he hoped it would be "the best work of my life and the most satisfying." Even in its original form, the project was enormous—translation of the complete *Morte d'Arthur* of Sir Thomas Malory; and the project soon became still more difficult, not translation but a complete retelling—rethinking—of the myth. Steinbeck finished only some 293 uncorrected, unedited pages, perhaps one-tenth of the original. Even so, the book Steinbeck's friend and editor Chase Horton has put together is large and important. It is in fact two books, Steinbeck's mythic fiction on King Arthur's court, and a fat, rich collection of letters exchanged between Steinbeck, Horton and Elizabeth Otis, Steinbeck's agent. The first is an incomplete but impressive work of art; the second, the complete story of a literary tragedy—how Steinbeck found his way, step by step, from the idea of doing a "translation" for boys to the idea of writing fabulist fiction, in the mid-1950's, when realism was still king. . . .

Steinbeck's Arthurian fiction is, indeed, "strange and different," as he put it. The fact that he lacked the heart to finish the book, or even put what he did complete into one style and tone, is exactly the kind of petty modern tragedy he hated. The idea was magnificent—so is much of the writing—though we see both the idea and the writing changing as they go. In the early pages he follows Malory fairly closely, merely simplifying and here and there adding explanation for the modern young reader.

As he warms to his work, Steinbeck uses Malory more freely, cutting deeply, expanding generously. In the passage on Merlin's defeat by Nyneve he writes like a man retelling a story from his childhood, interpreting as he pleases and echoing hardly a line. Merlin tells King Arthur what he must guard against and says he, Merlin, must go to his doom. Arthur is astonished that the wizard would go to his doom willingly, but Merlin

JOHN STEINBECK · · the acts of king arthur and his noble knights · · · ·

FROM THE WINCHESTER MSS. OF THOMAS MALORY AND OTHER SOURCES · ·

· · · · EDITED BY CHASE HORTON · FARRAR, STRAUS AND GIROUX · NEW YORK

Title page for Steinbeck's adaptation from the works of Sir Thomas Malory, published in 1976 (from John Steinbeck: The Contemporary Reviews, *1996; Thomas Cooper Library, University of South Carolina)*

does so nonetheless, because, as he says, "in the combat between wisdom and feeling, wisdom never wins" (Steinbeck's addition). He travels off with the young woman he loves, fated and knowing it. With only an occasional glance at his source—sixteen cool lines (in tight modern English they could be written in three)—but keeping the formal old sound, for the most part, Steinbeck writes:

"Nyneve was bored and restless and she left Ban's court with Merlin panting after her, begging her to lie with him and stanch his yearning, but she was weary of him, and impatient with an old man as a damsel must be, and also she was afraid of him because he was said to be the Devil's son, but she could not be rid of him, for he followed her, pleading and whimpering."

"Then Nyneve, with the inborn craft of maidens, began to question Merlin about his magic arts, half promising to trade her favors for his knowledge. And

Merlin, with the inborn helplessness of men, even though he foresaw her purpose, could not forbear to teach her. And as they crossed back to England and rode slowly from the coast of Cornwall, Merlin showed her many wonders, and when at last he found that he interested her, he showed her how the magic was accomplished and put in her hands the tools of enchantment, gave her the antidotes of magic, and finally, in his aged folly, taught her those spells which cannot be broken by any means. And when she clapped her hands in maidenly joy, the old man, to please her, created a room of unbelievable wonders under a great rock cliff, and with his crafts he furnished it with comfort and richness and beauty to be the glorious apartment for the consummation of their love. And they two went through a passage in the rock to the room of wonders, hung with gold and lighted with many candles. Merlin stepped in to show it to her, but Nyneve leaped back and cast the awful spell that cannot be broken by any means, and the passage closed and Merlin was trapped inside for all time to come."

Here there are still Malorian elements—sentences beginning with "Then" and "And," formulaic repetitions, archaic diction—but all the rest is modern. For instance, it is novelistic, not mythic, to speak of Merlin's "panting," "pleading and whimpering," or of "the inborn craft of maidens" and "the inborn helplessness of men," novelistic to speak of riding *slowly* from the coast of Cornwall (a quick touch of verisimilitude), novelistic to show Nyneve clapping her hands with pleasure, or later, leaping back. By the time Steinbeck reached "The Noble Tale of Sir Lancelot of the Lake," he had his method in full control. He makes authorial comments of a sort only a novelist would risk, cuts pages by the fistful, and at the same time embellishes Malory's spare legend with a richness of detail that transforms the vision, makes it no one but Steinbeck's. Here is a passage with no real source in the original:

"A man like Lancelot, tempered in soldiery, seasoned and tanned by perils, lays up supplies of sleep as he does food or water, knowing its lack will reduce his strength and dull his mind. And although he had slept away part of the day, the knight retired from cold and darkness and the unknown morrow and entered a dreamless rest and remained in it until a soft light began to grow in his cell of naked stone. Then he awakened and wrung his muscles free of cold cramp and again embraced his knees for warmth. He could see no source of light. It came equally from everywhere as dawn does before the rise of the sun. He saw the mortared stones of his cell stenciled with patches of dark slime. And as he looked, designs formed on the walls: formal rounded trees covered with golden fruit and curling vines with flowers as frankly invented as are

those of an illuminated book, a benign sheltering tree, and under it a unicorn glowing white, with horn and neck lowered in salute to a maiden of bright needlework who embraced the unicorn, thus proving her maidenhood. Then a broad soft bed shivered and grew substantial in the corner of the cell. . . ."

There is nothing at all like this in Malory. What we have here is myth newly imagined, revitalized, charged with contemporary meaning, the kind of thing we expect of the best so-called post-modernists, writers like John Barth. Steinbeck creates a lifelike Lancelot, a veteran soldier who knows his business (how to grab sleep when you can and so on); shows, in quick realistic strokes, how the soldier wakes up, wrings his muscles against cold and cramp; and how magic starts to happen to this cool, middle-aged realist. The falsity of the magic is emphatic—"as frankly invented as [the designs] in an illuminated book."

The paragraph encapsulates Steinbeck's whole purpose at this stage—a purpose close to Malory's yet utterly transformed—to show in the manner of a fabulator how plain reality is transformed by magic, by the lure of visions that ennoble though they ultimately betray. It's a theme we've encountered before in Steinbeck, but a theme that has here the simplicity and power of myth.

The Acts of King Arthur and His Noble Knights is unfortunately not Steinbeck's greatest book, but as Steinbeck knew, until doubt overcame him, it was getting there.

—*New York Times Book Review,* 126 (24 October 1976); reprinted in *John Steinbeck: The Contemporary Reviews,* pp. 526–528

* * *

The Acts of King Arthur and His Noble Knights
Robert E. Morsberger

Robert E. Morsberger, who edited Steinbeck's screenplay for Viva Zapata! *(1952) for republication in 1975, reviewed* The Acts of King Arthur and His Noble Knights *for* Western American Literature.

Sir Thomas Malory's *Le Morte d'Arthur,* published in 1485, is a watershed in the literature of the Western world. It is the culmination of the Arthurian romances, the Matter of Britain, from Gildas through Layamon, Geoffrey of Monmouth, Chrétien de Troyes, and other "Frensshe" books, anonymous alliterative poets, Gottfried von Strassburg; in turn, it profoundly influenced subsequent literature. Milton contemplated writing an Arthurian epic, and Tennyson tried to do so. Matthew Arnold, Swinburne, E. A. Robinson and T. H. White wrote Arthurian material, Mark Twain burlesqued it,

Prince Valiant borrowed it for the comics, and Hollywood adapted it for the movies.

John Steinbeck had a lifelong love affair with Malory's tales of the Round Table and claimed that the fellowship of *paisanos* in *Tortilla Flat* was a version of them. Finally, in November, 1956, he decided to work with the original and render Malory into English for modern readers, so that they could share his enthusiasm. He was also fascinated by the problem of dictation and style: "I intend to translate into a modern English, keeping, or rather trying to recreate, a rhythm and tone which to the modern ear will have the same effect as the Middle English did on the fifteenth-century ear."

But first, he put in a year and a half of formidable research—a case of overkill so far as translation is concerned, but a labor of love and in some ways a putting off of the actual chore of writing. To obtain background, he made three trips to England and one to Italy, visited Armando Sapori and Bernard Berenson and became good friends with Eugène Vinaver, the world's leading Malory expert, who was impressed with a sample of rough translation and offered any help possible. Steinbeck decided to work with the Winchester manuscript discovered in 1936 rather than with Caxton, and he made microfilm copies of each. Though he read hundreds of books on the Middle Ages, he continued to feel that there were gaps in his reading, scholarship, and the "feel and look" of locations. He felt that the work required him to "know the countryside in which Malory lived and operated. . . . I had to go from one end of England to the other to get a sense of topography, color of soil, marsh, moor, forest, and particularly relationships of one place to another. . . . This is destined to be the largest and I hope the most important work I have ever undertaken." With his wife making a photographic record, Steinbeck roamed all over Somerset, Cornwall, Wiltshire, and Wales. "Building a background for this book has been a long and arduous job," and an expensive one, he added, "but

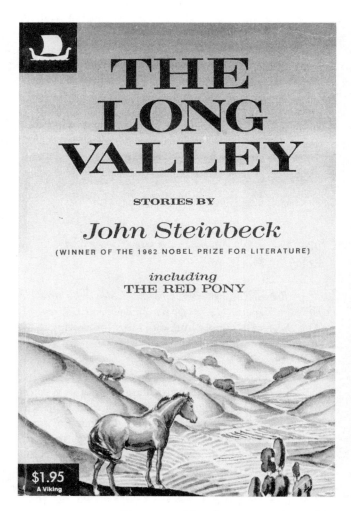

Front covers of the 1970 paperback editions of Steinbeck's 1938 story collection and his 1954 sequel to
Cannery Row *(Bruccoli Clark Layman Archives)*

highly rewarding." He began by predicting that the work would go very fast but later thought it might take 10 years. "Why has it been necessary to read so much–most of which will probably not be used? I think it necessary for me to know everything I can about what Malory knew and how he might have felt, but it is also necessary for me to be aware of what he did not know, could not have known, and could not feel," in order to avoid the error of thinking Malory was like a modern man.

Finally, he began writing, working mainly in Somerset, from July, 1958, to October, 1959. He tried for "a close-reined, taut, economical English, unaccented and unlocalized." He succeeded rather well; the prose is vigorous and clear but necessarily a hybrid that is modern in diction but retains an archaic formality. As he got into the material, he took increasing liberties with the text, not only making cuts but additions and elaborations. "I have eliminated a number of the more obscure adventures in Malory, but others I have greatly expanded in a way that might deeply shock the master." The book of Balin, The Knight with Two Swords, is a faithful rendering, extremely well done. On the other hand, Steinbeck expands three and a half pages of the adventures of Sir Ywain to 30 pages of his own, with such interpolations as a lengthy discussion of how the longbow, by destroying knighthood, would revolutionize institutions and lead to government by commoners. Thus long passages are not Malory at all but original Steinbeck in the manner of Malory.

This may explain why the project was aborted. After three years of enthusiasm, he confessed, "The work doesn't jell," and put it aside for *The Winter of Our Discontent*. In 1965, he briefly returned to Malory, but completed only seven of the adventures. These are self-contained and among the best, so that readers will find the volume satisfying and perhaps wish for more.

In addition, there are 68 pages of letters from Steinbeck to his agent Elizabeth Otis and his friend Chase Horton. Some of these are in *Steinbeck: A Life in Letters*, but many are printed for the first time. (There are additional letters on Malory to Vinaver, Pascal Covici and others in the *Life in Letters*.) But since both collections of letters are edited and excerpted, we sometimes have different parts of the same letter in the same two books. The letters deal not only with Steinbeck's research on Malory and his problems with translation and adaptation but with reflections on art and the artist, on language and style, on medieval life and thought, and on the heroic vs. modern anti-heroes. As such, they are revealing both to students of Steinbeck and of Malory and the Middle Ages.

–*Western American Literature*, 12 (August 1977); reprinted in *John Steinbeck: The Contemporary Reviews*, pp. 534–535

Working Days (1989)

The Wrath, the Discontent and the Grapes
Frederick Turner

Frederick Turner, reviewing Working Days: The Journals of The Grapes of Wrath, 1938–1941 *(1989) for the* New York Post, *found "something noble" in the journal.*

Almost half a century ago at the apex of his popularity John Steinbeck saw himself dismissed by Edmund Wilson as a crude artificer unable to breathe life into his fictional characters. When Alfred Kazin repeated and amplified this attack in his path-breaking *On Native Grounds* (1942) the charge stuck. There Kazin wrote of the apprenticelike quality of Steinbeck's work, of his primitiveness, his "slow curiosity," "simplicity of spirit" and "simple indignation" at the suffering of migrant workers in California. The Joad family of *The Grapes of Wrath*, Kazin said, could hardly fail to interest American readers since there was so much of the national experience represented in these characters. But the Joads were, after all, only "symbolic marionettes."

Through the ensuing 20 years Steinbeck's stature with readers remained high as did the sales of his books, and in 1962 he was anointed by the international literary establishment with the Nobel Prize. If readers applauded the award as much-deserved and long overdue, Steinbeck's American critics remained unconvinced and were as baffled by this Nobel as by that earlier given Pearl Buck. When Steinbeck died in 1968 his critical reputation was low and rested on a single novel that many critics refused to consider a novel at all, choosing to regard *The Grapes of Wrath* instead as a sociological phenomenon that had summed up the bygone decade of the '30s. Now, precisely a half-century since its publication, here is *The Grapes of Wrath* again in a handsome anniversary edition and accompanied by the journal Steinbeck kept while working on the novel. The occasion tells us that whether novel, tract or sociological phenomenon, *The Grapes of Wrath* remains a part of our image of ourselves as a people.

Robert DeMott, who has so carefully edited the journal now called *Working Days*, uses his introduction to chart the stages of Steinbeck's thinking during the two years of work on what DeMott calls the "matter of the migrants." First there were Steinbeck's research trips into the fields and camps beginning in 1936, during which he made contact with Tom Collins, the Farm Security Administration manager who provided him with so much crucial material. Also in 1936 there was Steinbeck's seven-part newspaper report on migrant conditions, "The Harvest Gypsies." He followed this with a fictional treatment he was calling "The Oklahomans," but abandoned it early in 1938. Immediately afterward he tried again, this time with a venomous satire, "L'Affaire Lettuceberg," which he also abandoned. But what he had experienced in the fields and camps had so impressed itself on him that it would give him no rest, and so within 10 days of the abandonment of the satire he was back at his desk and at work on the "big book" he felt the subject demanded. Here is where the journal begins.

As with his other "big book," *East of Eden* (1952), Steinbeck used the journal as a warm-up exercise, beginning each day with a few lines in which he confided his hopes and his characteristic self-doubts. And as with the later journal *Working Days* is an oddly vacant-seeming volume. It contains few insights into the author's actual method of composition. Yet in a way that is tellingly replicated in the novel itself, there is something noble here. Paralleling the Joad family's flight along Route 66 through Oklahoma, New Mexico, Arizona and into California is the writer's struggle through the summer and early fall of 1938 to be equal to the tragedy of the story he was evoking. And once he has the Joads in California his struggle is theirs, too, for he has to fight against his own destructive rage at the violence and greed of the local agricultural organizations and their goons. June 18th's entry is typical: "This is a huge job. . . . If only I could do this book properly it would be one of the really fine books and a truly American book. But I am assailed with my own ignorance and inability. If I can keep my honesty it is all I can expect of my poor brain. . . . If I can do that it will be all my lack of genius can produce. . . ."

By early September he thought he saw himself finishing about the middle of the next month. "Europe," he noted, "still tense. Hitler waiting for heaven to speak. Maybe war but I don't think so." By Oct. 14, he was in fact so close his hand was shaking. He finished Oct. 26 and felt it was not "the great book I had hoped it would be."

Maybe not. Steinbeck habitually wrecked perfectly good characters and plots by forcing them to carry monstrous allegorical burdens. This is what ruins *East of Eden* and it is what undermines the aesthetic quality of *The Grapes of Wrath*—but not its force, its enduring claim on us.

—*New York Post,* 16 April 1989; reprinted in *John Steinbeck: The Contemporary Reviews,* pp. 545–546

* * *

Struggling to a Classic
Pascal Covici Jr.

Pascal Covici Jr., son of Steinbeck's longtime editor, reviewed Working Days *for* The Dallas Morning News. *Covici called editor Robert DeMott's notes for the volume "superb."*

"My laziness is overwhelming," lamented John Steinbeck as he approached the final chapters of his American epic. "I only hope it is some good. I have very grave doubts sometimes."

"My mind doesn't want to work–hates to work in fact, but I'll make it."

If nothing else–and there's a great deal else–Robert DeMott has given us an opportunity to know directly and poignantly, and sometimes painfully, the struggles of will buried behind the seemingly pre-determined procession of words that make great literary art.

How could John Steinbeck have done it? With house problems and money problems, health problems and marriage problems, with problems political, social and even of friendship plaguing the writer, how could *The Grapes of Wrath* ever have been written? Here is the revelation of just how searing that experience of authorship turned out to be.

Mr. DeMott's introduction, uncovering with sure and sensitive knowledge what John Steinbeck did, how he worked and thought, and even how he felt, sets the scene for *Working Days.* This day-by-day account of the book's progress, and of the writer's frustrations, will fascinate a variety of readers.

First of all, those interested in social issues will recognize the tensions in the kind of involvement necessary for a writer to commit himself to what Mr. DeMott calls the "Matter of the Migrants." For over three years, Mr. Steinbeck worked for the dispossessed and oppressed working migrants from Oklahoma in their struggle simply to live despite the Associated Farmers of California and their banking allies.

But then he had to distance himself from demands and invasions that would have made writing the book impossible. Because he had acquired notoriety as author of *In Dubious Battle* (1936) and *Of Mice and Men* (1937), he received countless appeals. Down-and-outers–the people whose stories he had told in articles and whose lives he would transform into art in *The Grapes of Wrath*–wanted money from him because they thought that he had both money and luck. The money had not yet arrived. As for his "luck," his "success," Mr. Steinbeck considered it more a matter of his "destruction." "The Greeks," he wrote in *The Journals,* thinking especially of Homer and of Sophocles,

Written Under Duress

Brian St. Pierre reviewed Working Days: The Journals of The Grapes of Wrath, 1938–1941 *for the* San Francisco Chronicle.

. . . From *Working Days,* the journals Steinbeck kept while writing *The Grapes of Wrath,* comes the astonishing fact that he wrote this dense and complex novel in 100 days, by hand, under a fair amount of duress: His publisher was going bankrupt, a noisy housing project was being built next door, he and his wife Carol were ill at times, and he was plagued to the point of depression by doubts about his talent. No wonder he wrote, "I am ready to go to work and I am glad to get into other lives and escape from mine for a while."

Steinbeck undertook this journal to make himself accountable ("If a day is skipped it will show glaringly on this record"), and as editor Robert DeMott notes, it is a "hermetic—even claustrophobic" diary of the making of a book as well as its attendant terrors and distractions.

Many of the entries are rambling and banal, as many of anyone's days would be, but the earnest, die hard effort of writing and the importance of the task have great cumulative power: "I grew again to love and admire the people who are so much stronger and purer and braver than I am," he wrote of the migrants.

DeMott has surrounded the journal entries with a biographical introduction, commentary and illuminating notes, building a good book onto a narrow foundation. While not intended for general readers, the book will be important to anyone seeking a deeper understanding of Steinbeck and his work. . . .

—"Steinbeck's Timeless Tale of Migrant Suffering,"
San Francisco Chronicle, 26 March 1989; reprinted
in *John Steinbeck: The Contemporary Reviews,*
p. 545

advertising and then exploited, the lucky ones found themselves compelled to work for any wage at all, or else watch their children starve. The less fortunate died.

After the telling, Mr. Steinbeck found himself alienated from his own neighbors. Not only the FBI, but the local folks of Salinas, too, were out to get him. "Don't stay in a hotel room alone," a friendly undersheriff of Santa Clara County told him. "The boys got a rape case set for you. You get alone in a hotel and a dame will come in, tear off her clothes, scratch her face and scream and you try to talk your way out of that one. They won't touch your book, but there's easier ways."

In an earlier *Journals* entry, he had written: "All the growth of the fascist tendency is heart breaking. Nothing seems to work against its stupidity and one gets very tired. . . . I'll probably be framed before very long."

One wonders how he kept his faith in America and in democracy. This edition of *The Journals,* with

*Dust jacket for the 1989 edition of the journal Steinbeck kept
while writing his 1939 novel (Richland
County Public Library)*

"seem to have known about this dark relationship between luck and destruction." Mr. Steinbeck felt it strongly.

So there is nourishment here for the reader who wonders about writing and for the reader who wonders about success in America. Throughout his life, John Steinbeck could never see himself as the accomplished writer that he was. Success meant mostly that he felt obliged to do more and better than he saw himself as able to do.

The Grapes of Wrath did indeed make him rich, but it also made him a target for the California that he had so greatly offended. He told the truth about the banks, the Associated Farmers, the utilities and their treatment of the dust-bowl victims. Lured west by fraudulent

Mr. DeMott's superb—and superbly documented—notes, demonstrates heart-liftingly that he did. And when a writer's life is as filled with incident as John Steinbeck's, the documentation, the gossip, and the record become, at a distance, an odyssey of delight. The agony of the writer here becomes a reader's informed pleasure.

—*Dallas Morning News,* 14 May 1989; reprinted in *John Steinbeck: The Contemporary Reviews,* pp. 547–548

* * *

Book Reviews
Kenneth S. Lynn

Kenneth S. Lynn claimed that Working Days *made both* The Grapes of Wrath *and Steinbeck "more complex and more interesting."*

John Steinbeck's first lengthy examination of the Dust Bowl migrants—a series of investigative reports that were published, alongside photos of the migrants by the Farm Security Administration's Dorothea Lange, in the pro-labor *San Francisco News* in the fall of 1936—made only passing allusions to their trek westward from Oklahoma and concentrated instead on the gypsy-like existence they were reduced to in agriculturally feudal California. Subsequently, he tried and failed to write a novel called *The Oklahomans,* in which, apparently, he zeroed in once again on the California scene. His third attempt to deal with the migrants was inspired by a bloody clash between workers and growers in a lettuce strike in Salinas, California, his birthplace. But *L'Affaire Lettuceberg,* as he dubbed the manuscript he produced, was nothing more, he eventually realized, than a "vulgar" tract, and in mid-May 1938, he destroyed it. With that dark act he might have lapsed into despair—except that it was immediately followed by the mightiest outburst of imaginative energy he would ever experience.

Across a span of no more than ten days, between May 15 and 25, the entire scheme of *The Grapes of Wrath* was envisioned by Steinbeck, beginning with the grand outlines of the Joad family's journey across the country, but also including the symphonic structure of the story, with its alternating modes of exposition and narrative, and the dramatic events of individual scenes, all the way down to Rose of Sharon's gesture at the close of offering her milky breast to a starving man. He also established a writing schedule of 2,000 words a day that would enable him—that did enable him—to complete the novel by the following October. Finally, he decided that he would make a map of his literary progress by keeping a journal. Thanks to Robert

DeMott, a professor of English at Ohio University and a recognized authority on Steinbeck, that journal has now been published, with useful notes by Professor DeMott, under the title *Working Days.*

It is a harrowing document. For while *Working Days* testifies to Steinbeck's continuing grasp of his organizational plan for *The Grapes of Wrath,* as well as to his dogged determination to meet his per diem quota of words, it is also a record of doubts of his literary adequacy, of anger at being interrupted by friends and strangers, of disgust with himself about his drinking, cigarette smoking, and general lack of self-discipline, and of fears of nervous collapse and insanity. Here are some representative comments:

"Irritated today. People want to come to see me next Monday. Can't be. Just want to sit. Day not propitious. Have a loose feeling that makes me nervous . . . I get nuts if not protected from all the outside stuff" (June 3). "My whole nervous system is battered. Don't know why. I hope I am not headed for a nervous breakdown" (June 6). "Last night . . . drank a great deal of champagne [and] . . . am not in the dead sober state I could wish . . . I must not be weak. . . . The failure of will even for one day has a devastating effect" (June 13). ". . . once this book is done I won't care how soon I die, because my major work will be over" (July 11). "Drank lots of whiskey . . . and now home with a little stomach ache that doesn't come from the stomach. Terrible feeling of lostness and loneliness" (July 18). "Demoralization complete and seemingly unbeatable" (August 16). "My nerves are going fast. Getting into confusion of many particles—each one beatable, but in company pretty formidable. And I get a little crazy with all of them" (August 24). "This place has become an absolute madhouse . . . I don't know what to do. I wish—Jesus!" (August 26). "Have to cut down smoking or something. I'm afraid this book is going to pieces. If it does, I do too" (September 7). "This book has become a misery to me because of my inadequacy" (September 26). "The disintegration lately has been terrible" (October 4).

Gradually, the struggling novelist became aware that keeping the diary had a therapeutic effect upon him. "Now at last I am getting calm," he wrote on August 2. "This diary is a marvelous method of calming me down every day." And on September 26 he noted that his stomach and nerves were "screaming hell in protest," but that he had written an exceptionally long entry in order "to calm myself." His self-understanding, however, never grew beyond this point. Thus in 1952 he declared that when he wrote *The Grapes of Wrath,* "I was filled . . . with certain angers . . . at people who were doing injustices to other people." No doubt he was—but as the diary demonstrates, he also brought to his writing desk

FOR IMMEDIATE RELEASE

NEWS *from* VIKING

VIKING PENGUIN INC. 40 WEST 23RD STREET, NEW YORK, N.Y. 10010   212-337-5200

VIKING TO CELEBRATE THE 50TH ANNIVERSARY
OF THE PUBLICATION OF *THE GRAPES OF WRATH*

JOHN STEINBECK

THE GRAPES OF WRATH

Introduction by
STUDS TERKEL

WORKING DAYS

THE JOURNALS
OF
THE GRAPES
OF WRATH

EDITED BY
ROBERT DEMOTT

"It is 1988. We could see the face on the six o'clock news. It could be a Walker Evans face or a Dorothea Lange shot, but that's 50 years off. It is a face of despair, of an Iowa farm, fourth generation, facing foreclosure. I've seen this face before. It is the face of Pa Joad, Muley Graves and all their lost neighbors, tractored out by the cats."

"This anniversary edition is more than a golden anniversary celebration of an enduring book. It is as contemporary as the 1988 drought, astonishingly so..."

—Studs Terkel, from the introduction to the 50th
anniversary edition of *The Grapes of Wrath*

*Viking Press release announcing the publication of the fiftieth-anniversary edition of Steinbeck's 1939 novel and the journal
he kept while working on the novel (Collection of Robert J. DeMott)*

each day a variety of violent emotions that had nothing to do with objective social circumstances and everything to do with the personal life and psychic nature of John Steinbeck. What the diary forces us to reconsider is the relationship of the novelist to his fictive materials.

One of the odd things about the hero of the novel, Tom Joad, is his lack of interest in sex. From the time we meet him in Chapter Two, hitchhiking home to his parents' place after being released from prison in McAlester, Oklahoma, until his disappearance into the darkness of a California night near the end of the story, he is never shown in pursuit of a woman, in contrast to his younger brother, Al, who is constantly scratching a sexual itch. The explanation of Tom's conduct lies not in the novel but in the diary. By 1938, Steinbeck's relations with his wife, Carol, were frequently strained, even hostile, and the tension between them was heightened during the period when he was writing *The Grapes of Wrath* by his abstinence from sexual intercourse with her. Not until October 7, as he was nearing the end of his creative labors, did he feel "a change . . . coming over me—a goatish sexuality. The summer has just been the opposite—very low." So intense was Steinbeck's identification with his fictional hero that, whether consciously or unconsciously, he reduced Tom's sex drive to the same level as his own.

An even greater oddity about the good-guy hero of *The Grapes of Wrath* is defined by his homicidal outbursts. Tom not only has done time at McAlester for killing a man in a social quarrel, but before the novel is over he will kill another in a labor dispute. His sidekick, Jim Casy, the ex-preacher who has the same initials as Christ, is politically radicalized in the course of the novel, and after Casy's symbolic crucifixion Tom consecrates his own life to the cause of social justice. In a secular world, he will be Jim Casy's self-sacrificing disciple. But the question that Steinbeck fails to examine is whether Tom's intentions, as outlined in a farewell speech to his mother, are not an ambiguous mixture of altruism and intoxication with violence for its own sake. "I'll be all aroun' in the dark," he assures Ma Joad. "I'll be ever'where—wherever you look. Wherever they's a fight so hungry people can eat, I'll be there. Wherever they's a cop beatin' up a guy, I'll be there. . . . I'll be in the way guys yell when they're mad an'—I'll be in the way kids laugh when they're hungry an' they know supper's ready. An' when our folks eat the stuff they raise an' live in the houses they build—why, I'll be there. See?" The diarist who but slenderly understood his own raw emotions ("My whole nervous system is battered. Don't know why.") was correspondingly incapable of plumbing the mysteries of his alter ego's.

The emergence of Ma Joad as a far stronger person than her husband and the other older men in the Joad family is another notable aspect of the novel on which the diary bears. "Carol does so much," Steinbeck said of his wife in the entry of August 2. Indeed she did. Although Carol Henning was a fairly talented poet, prose writer, and painter, as well as being more deeply involved in radical politics than Steinbeck ever was, she gave up her career when she got married. In addition to assuming all the domestic duties of the household, the strong-willed, tough-minded Carol did her best to shield her shy and easily stampeded husband from intrusions on his privacy: oversaw his business relations with his agents; typed and edited his manuscripts; and, in the case of *The Grapes of Wrath,* made critical comments on the manuscript and found the perfect title for it in Julia Ward Howe's "The Battle Hymn of the Republic." On the dedication page of the novel Steinbeck wrote, "To Carol, who willed this book." Just as weakness of the senior male Joads can be linked to Steinbeck's sense of his own weakness and to memories of his weak father, whose mismanagement of a store ended in bankruptcy (the diarist wrote on June 16: "I dreamed a confused mess made up of Dad and his failures and me and my failures"), so Ma Joad's indomitability was a reincarnation of Carol's.

Working Days also contains a section called "Aftermath," which is composed of the diary entries that Steinbeck continued to make in the two years following the publication of *The Grapes of Wrath.* As Professor DeMott aptly observes, the motif of self-doubt is still prominent in these entries, but is compounded by guilt and tempered by foreshadowing, as though Steinbeck felt himself to be hovering on the brink of some enormous catastrophe. If the intimations of dark fatality are not fully articulated, it is because Steinbeck was fearful that the watchful Carol would discover the secret of his love affair with a 20-year-old showgirl named Gwyndolyn Conger, whom he began seeing in the summer of 1939 and whom he would marry in 1943. Was he already dreaming of betraying Carol while he was still writing *The Grapes of Wrath*—and did that dream, too, get into the novel? Quite conceivably. For the weakest link in the Joad family chain is Rose of Sharon's youthful husband, the androgynously named Connie, who, when the Joads finally reach California, deserts his drastically pregnant wife and disappears. An author given to sexual guilt and paranoia might well have created such a character as Connie, out of a terrible premonition of how he intended to reward the woman who had done so much to bring his greatest book into being.

Working Days serves, in sum, to make *The Grapes of Wrath* and its author more complex and more interesting. [. . .]

—*American Spectator,* 41 (August 1989); reprinted in *John Steinbeck: The Contemporary Reviews,* pp. 550–552

Stage and Screen Adaptations

Of Mice and Men
Stanley Kauffmann

Stanley Kauffmann reviewed the 1992 movie adaptation of Of Mice and Men *(1937) for* The New Republic.

In one way John Steinbeck's *Of Mice and Men* (M-G-M) is like John Berryman's poetry: it's more powerful than, aesthetically speaking, it has a right to be. I saw the first production of Steinbeck's play in 1937 (well directed by, of all people, George S. Kaufman, the ultraurban smartcracker, who reportedly had helped Steinbeck to dramatize his novel), the first film in 1939, the Broadway revival in 1975, and now I've seen the new film. The first experience was overwhelming; with later viewings, though the story was still moving, the mechanics became plainer.

For instance, in the opening scene Lenny [*sic*] implores George to repeat the daydream about the place with the rabbits that they'll have one day. Then George tells Lenny that, if he gets into trouble at the ranch they're going to, he is to come to this place and hide. Then the dead mouse in Lenny's pocket foretells more deaths (and justifies the Burns allusion in the title). Click, click, click, the pieces fall into place. Soon, Curley, son of the ranch owner, is set up as one kind of provocateur, Curley's wife as another. The putting away of Candy's old dog is not only a shivery prophecy for old Candy himself, it foreshadows another killing.

But, just as Berryman enthralls despite his limitations, so Steinbeck's work rolls on, rolls over us, like the well-constructed engine that it is. The power begins with the characters of the two protagonists: George, spryly competent, always grumbling at the burden of Lenny, always fiercely protective of him; Lenny, with the strength of an ox and the mind of a child, an absolutely innocent wrongdoer. Part of the power also comes from the inevitability of the ending. One of the reasons we hear about their dream place at the beginning is to inform us that they will never have it. And part of the power is in an old-fashioned bucolic feeling touched with the sordid—Currier and Ives with killings.

Story reminder: George and Lenny are California migrant workers in the 1930s. They travel together. George knew Lenny's aunt, who had taken care of the retarded man; when the aunt died, George took over. At the story's start, Lenny unintentionally frightens a girl in the town where they are working, and the two men have to flee.

They find work on another place farther south, where the boss's cockerel son has just married a sexy wife who is already restless. One day in the barn she teases Lenny, getting him to stroke her hair; and he doesn't want to stop. She gets scared and screams; he puts his hand over her mouth and, in his giant's fright, accidentally breaks her neck. He flees to the appointed place of refuge; George finds him there ahead of the posse that's in pursuit and shoots his best friend before the others can tear him apart.

Gary Sinise, who directed, plays George, and his performance is the worthiest element in the film. He has taciturn strength and a gift for conveying unexpressed feeling. He has played the role on stage, I've read, with John Malkovich as Lenny. Malkovich is again the Lenny here, and is quite disappointing. First, his hands. They never seem the hands of a burly, manual worker, hands of potential menace. Second, his speech. Certainly I can't rule that no retarded person speaks that way: I'm talking only of dramatic aptness. Malkovich sounds like a stock party imitation of a mental defective, done for laughs. This was not his intent, of course, but compared with Broderick Crawford, Lon Chaney Jr., and James Earl Jones in the role, Malkovich lacks entirely the aura of an earnest, bewildered giant.

Other roles, too, are poorly cast. Ray Walston's only qualification for Candy, the maimed old swamper, is that he is grizzled: he doesn't sound "country," and he lays on the pathos. Casey Siemaszko as Curley is a zero, and Sherilyn Fenn as his wife is negligible. A key role, Slim, the ranch foreman, was given to John Terry, who is good-looking and not much else.

Still, the fault doesn't lie entirely with the last three actors. Horton Foote's screenplay has whittled down all their parts, to the film's detriment. Foote even eliminates the penultimate scene in which Slim, a mature and compassionate man, guesses where Lenny is hiding and leaves, so that George can do what needs to be done, alone with his friend. The loss of this scene is a detriment, too.

Sinise as director is no great shakes. The easy stuff comes off well enough—the pastoral landscapes, the great barley fields with the harvesting teams at work—but he wobbles in the intimate moments. Candy's appeal for his dog is handled heavily, and to weight it further, Sinise finishes the sequence with a long shot of Candy standing outside the bunkhouse all alone. The moment is not exactly subtle. After Lenny kills Curley's wife in the barn, Sinise puts in a high overhead shot of the two, one live and one dead—intrusive cinematics that fracture the grip of awful irreversible error. At the finish, when George shoots the kneeling Lenny, Sinise uses a long shot to show the two men. Again, too explicit. A medium close-up of George, more or less facing us, speaking to an invisible Lenny, with the shot and Lenny's crumpling invisible, is what, consciously or not, most of us might be hoping for. The drama, not the data.

The music by Mark Isham is even more coarse. Particularly in the pursuit sequences, it's Saturday-afternoon-serial stuff. Yet despite the various hob-

Cover of the 1993 video release of the 1992 motion-picture remake of Steinbeck's 1937 novel (Richland County Public Library)

Critical Assessments

Steinbeck's *The Grapes of Wrath*
Rebecca Hinton

Rebecca Hinton discusses the concept of family in The Grapes of Wrath.

John Steinbeck's *The Grapes of Wrath* (1939) is a novel of transition. Like thousands of families in the rural southwest, the Joads leave the land their people have farmed for generations and head for California, supposedly a place of hope and prosperity. Unfortunately, they find only poverty and despair. Formerly tenant farmers with relative security and independence, they soon become migrant laborers at the mercy of the rich, struggling to maintain their pride.

These outer changes accompany a change in the concept of family. Through the altering perceptions of the representative Joads, Steinbeck implies that in times of social upheaval, the family cannot remain a self-contained conjugal unit; it must expand to include members related by plight as well as by blood and focus on the needs of the many rather than those of the few.

Steinbeck first posits the problem of family in chapter 5, through a dialogue between an anonymous tenant farmer and a tractor driver who is plowing the fields. When the driver boasts that his wages enable him to feed his family well, the tenant reminds him that because of his wages and the work producing them, hundreds of other families are denied food and shelter. To this observation, the driver replies, "Can't think of that. Got to feed my own kids." From this man's viewpoint, the family consists only of the children he has begotten, and he cares not that in maintaining them at the expense of others, he contributes to a growing subculture of poverty and unrest.

The Joads, however, exhibit a more altruistic mentality. By the time they start for California, they have already added a nonbiological family member– Jim Casy, the preacher–although their truck is loaded to its limit. When Pa queries whether they can afford to carry an extra person, Ma counters with, "It ain't kin we? It's will we?"

As they travel westward, the family continues to expand and fluctuate. In chapter 13, for example, they meet the Wilsons, who share in the intimate family ritual of Grandpa's burial by supplying a quilt and a piece of paper. Later, in chapter 20, Ma responds to the hunger of the Hooverville children, even though her own family has barely enough to eat. Significantly, expansions of the family often follow the demise of a biological member. Grandpa's death precipitates the

blings and hamperings in the film's making, despite Steinbeck's all-too-patent blueprint, the essence prevails. Perhaps *Of Mice and Men* is still affecting because of the authentic sweetness that George sees in Lenny and that he knows is doomed. Perhaps it's because the work can be taken as a monodrama, really about one individual, with the ego combating a kind of guileless id, finally suppressing it but with the knowledge of a certain prelapsarian loss. The ending moves us not to tears but to acceptance. [. . .]

–*New Republic,* 207 (2 November 1992): 24–25

John Steinbeck was haunted by the almost biblical travail of the Dust Bowl farmers, uprooted from their homesteads by bank foreclosures, trekking by the tens of thousands to the promised land of California, only to face brute exploitation as field hands. After two failed novels, he finally got it right on his third try, and after two years of developmental productions, Chicago's Steppenwolf troupe has finally succeeded in adapting his epic tale for the stage. The best measure of this portrait of a family in agony and dissolution is that it is actually better—less sentimental and truer—than the landmark 1940 film version.

The clearest instances of this newfound grit are the two most famous speeches. When Lois Smith, giving the finest performance of a great stage career, says as Ma Joad that she knows "the people" will endure, she offers none of the reassuring faith of Jane Darwell in the film. Her words are instead the hollow attempt of a frightened peasant to calm herself and to reassure a son she expects never to see again. When Gary Sinise as Tom Joad tells her that wherever people are organizing for freedom and a better day, he will be there, he does not ooze nature's-aristocrat nobility like Henry Fonda on celluloid. His is the tough, nervy attempt of a frightened man facing imprisonment or death to assert that his struggle has had some meaning.

Despite the grimness, director-adapter Frank Galati finds many small moments of decency, charity, humor and hope. He moves the 35 performers with cinematic grace and achieves great variety during a middle hour consisting largely of moving a rattletrap truck back and forth. The ordeal of the Joads remains evocative of its era, yet Steinbeck's themes prove contemporary: the vulnerability of unskilled labor, the soul-destroying impact of poverty and homelessness, the ease with which the rich and powerful subvert law enforcement to their own ends. The Joads pride themselves on being scrappers, but in this conflict they never have a chance.

—William Henry III, "*The Grapes of Wrath*," *Time*, 135 (2 April 1990): 71

relationship with the Wilsons, and Grandma dies just before the Joads arrive at the Hooverville camp.

The Joads' fellow migrants exhibit the same generosity. An example occurs in chapter 19, when a group of squatters pinch coins from their pockets to ensure a decent burial for a child who has died of malnutrition. In short, the people on the road realize that in such precarious times, one's family consists of all those in need.

The Joad family changes not only in its membership, but also in its governmental structure. Prior to their exodus, the Joads are patriarchal. When they convene for a family council in chapter 10, the men—the decision makers—squat in a circle, while each woman stands behind her husband in a supportive role. As the family's lifestyle changes, however, Ma gradually assumes leadership. She asserts herself most colorfully when confronting a deputy with a skillet (chapter 18) and Pa with a jack handle (chapter 16), but she also exhibits her decisiveness in quieter, less-dramatic ways. It is Ma, for example, who determines that the starving children must be fed, the scarcity of food notwithstanding; she who insists that the Joads cannot remain in the government camp despite the conveniences ("Well, we can't eat no toilets"); and she who declares in the final chapter that she will remove her children to higher, dry ground even if Pa chooses to remain behind.

Nevertheless, Ma represents the old order of matriarchy, for her primary concentration is still on the material needs of her own brood. When Al asks his mother in chapter 13 whether she is anxious about the future in California, Ma replies that she can live only one day at a time, attending to basic and prosaic matters:

> Up ahead they's a thousan' lives we might live, but when it comes, it'll be only one. If I go ahead on all of 'em, it's too much. You got to live ahead 'cause you're so young, but—it's just the road goin' by for me. An' it's just how soon they gonna wanta eat some more pork bones. . . . That's all I can do. I can't do no more. And the rest'd get upset if I done any more'n that. They all depen' on me jus' thinkin' about that.

Through Ma's oldest daughter, Rose of Sharon, Steinbeck appeals to young people to step beyond the traditions of their parents and reach out to meet the demands of a changing society. When the novel begins, Rose of Sharon seems to be following in Ma's footsteps, fulfilling the expectations of her background. Married in her teens to a boy from a neighboring family, she focuses all her energy on safeguarding her unborn child, fearful lest any emotional shock might harm the fetus. Aside from her family, she seems to have no interests. As time passes, however, circumstances strip away the comforting and familiar aspects of Rose of Sharon's life, forcing her to open her eyes to the larger world around her. Connie, her husband, deserts her, and the baby dies. Bereft of husband and child, Rose of Sharon is now called on to extend her love and nurturing to others in need. She shows her acceptance of this call in the final chapter by giving the milk in her breasts to a starving stranger. Her name itself suggests that she (and other young women) are to reach beyond the conjugal family, regarding all people in need as their chil-

Poster for the 1982 motion-picture remake of Steinbeck's 1945 novel (Bruccoli Clark Layman Archives)

dren. ("Rose of Sharon" is a title for Mary, whom Christians revere as the Blessed Mother.)

The changing concept of family is closely allied to Steinbeck's allusions to socialism and unionism, allusions which run throughout the novel. The author seems to say that disfranchised people such as the new migrants can survive only by pulling together, assuming authority when necessary, and regarding each other as kin.

–*Explicator*, 56 (Winter 1998): 101–103

* * *

Steinbeck Revisited
Grant Tracey

In 2000 Grant Tracey made the following assessment of Steinbeck's second story collection, The Long Valley *(1938), which had been republished by Penguin in 1995, with an introduction and notes by John H. Timmerman, and reprinted in 2000.*

A few years ago at an English department meeting my esteemed colleague John Wilson Swope stated that the two most studied writers in the nation's secondary school curriculum are William Shakespeare (naturally) and John Steinbeck. After Swope cited Steinbeck's popularity, the room thudded with percussive laughter. Why?

I've always been a Steinbeck fan. And imagine my surprise when I became Fiction Editor for the *North American Review* and discovered that in the 1930s we had published some of Steinbeck's most famous stories, including the first two installments of *The Red Pony,* and the underrated but brilliant "The Raid." I'm proud to be a part of such a publishing legacy. Several of Steinbeck's NAR stories were later collected in *The Long Valley* (1938), and have recently reappeared in a new edition. Steinbeck is always worth rereading, and if NAR readers and future contributors are looking to gauge my aesthetic preferences, pick up this book!

What I admire about Steinbeck is his dignity. He always respected the characters that he wrote about, and few were better at capturing the conflicting confusions of childhood and adolescence. In "The Gift," the first part to *The Red Pony,* Steinbeck weaves lush descriptions of the Salinas Valley with a striking story about a boy coming to knowledge. Jody begins irresponsibly, shirking his chores. But once his father gives him Gabilan the pony as a gift, he becomes responsible, feeding it, combing its mane, and finishing his farm chores on time. The gift also eventually makes him realize that people are fallible. Jody has always admired Billy Buck, the farm hand who knows all about horses. But after Billy recommends leaving Gabilan out in the sun, and the horse catches a cold and pneumonia because it had rained while Jody was at school, the youngster no longer sees Billy as perfect.

But interestingly Steinbeck doesn't judge Billy. Instead, through narrative insight, we're made to feel compassion for the ranch hand because of the pain and guilt he feels over his poor advice and letting Jody down: "Billy looked away. 'It's hard to tell, this time of year,' he said, but his excuse was lame. He had no right to be fallible, and he knew it." And Billy works diligently to try to save the pony–he drains pus out of the pony's throat, gives it steam blankets, and even performs a type of tracheotomy to help it breathe. The story is well balanced, and the conclusion packs a real punch, bringing Jody and Billy together through their shared understanding.

Jody, frustrated and unable to articulate his feelings, lashes out at a group of buzzards spiraling over the dead pony. He snags one in the air, and "He struck again and again, until the buzzard lay dead, until its head was a red pulp. He was still beating the dead bird when Billy Buck pulled him off and held him tightly to calm his shaking." Emotional tension rides this scene and Steinbeck's language–the repetitions of the actions, the stark image of the "red pulp," and Billy's comforting of Jody–all resonate a kind of muted epiphany, one that hasn't fully emerged yet. But the story does close with empathy. Jody's father, Carl Tiflin, fails to understand his son's anguish, and tells him, "[T]he buzzard didn't kill the pony. Don't you know that?" Billy, upset over his complicity in the pony's death and identifying with Jody, snaps, "Course he knows it . . . Jesus Christ! man, can't you see how he'd feel about it?"

Perhaps my colleagues laughed at Steinbeck's popularity because his stories seem too simple. One rap against Steinbeck has been that he often overdetermines his stories with heavy-handed symbols. Instead of letting symbols grow naturally out of the story's details, Steinbeck has a tendency to force his themes into a symbol. No doubt this is true in some of his work, but often Steinbeck's symbols are deceptive, open to multiple interpretations. I'm reminded of a teacher in high school who once said that the flowers in Steinbeck's "Chrysanthemums" represented Elisa Allen's desire for respect, appreciation, and freedom. This interpretation works, but is it not also possible to open the flowers and see yet another reading? Elisa's chrysanthemums are part of a self-deception, an attempt on her part to retreat from her husband's world into a false world of dreams. Henry suggests as much when he half-praises her, "You've got a gift with things . . . Some of those yellow chrysanthemums you had this year were ten inches across. I wish you'd work out in the orchard and raise some apples that big." Henry would like her help in the field, but she's self-absorbed with her garden. The traveling fix-it man, then, doesn't necessarily reinforce her lack of appreciation, but instead brutally makes Elisa realize her own illusions. "The Harness" is another story with a symbol that is ambiguous. If the harness represents Peter Randall's enslavement, then what literally enslaves him?

Despite this ambiguity in some of his symbolism, I guess I like Steinbeck's overall accessibility, the directness and ease with which he writes. And I especially like his hard-hitting working-class stories that take place in one setting in a short time span. "The Raid" is perhaps one of the most intriguing stories in *The Long Valley.* Two members of the communist party–Dick and Root, the old hand and the young novice–arrive at a small town and try to organize migrant workers to fight for their rights.

An early exploration of themes Steinbeck would address with *In Dubious Battle,* "The Raid" crams a lot of dignity in the two men's personalities. They know that they're going to be beaten for "agitating" but they stand and refuse to run. No matter what your politics might be, one can't help but admire men who believe in something so strongly that they're willing to get hurt for it. And as in many of Steinbeck's best works this story is about coming to knowledge, as the young Root ends the story no longer the pupil but the teacher. As they lie in the hospital recovering from their wounds, Root recalls Jesus's moment on the cross when he asked God to forgive those who know not what they've done. Dick, raised on a bastardized version of Karl Marx, tells him to knock off that crucifixion stuff since it's the "opium" of the masses. Root, however, insists on using whatever sources, including the Bible, [to] help him to understand the world. He refuses to follow the party line. "Sure I know . . . But there wasn't no religion to it. It was just–I felt like saying that. It was just kind of the way I felt."

And I guess Root couldn't have made for a finer epitaph for this collection of Steinbeck stories. People may want to laugh at Steinbeck's proliferation in the secondary schools or at my own "retro" admiration for his craft, but, hey, that's just kind of the way I feel.

–North American Review, 285 (September–October 2000): 44–45

Steinbeck Centennial

Prince of Tides
Bil Gilbert

In a Smithsonian *article published the month before the Steinbeck centennial, Bil Gilbert wrote about the novelist's environmental concerns.*

On the occasion of the 100th anniversary of his birth next month, John Steinbeck will be justly celebrated as a major American writer. Between 1929 and his death in 1968, Steinbeck published nearly 30 books. His masterpiece, *The Grapes of Wrath,* still sells about 200,000 copies a year. There are students of our cultural affairs who think this account of dispossessed Oklahoma farmers in the dust bowl years and *Uncle Tom's Cabin* are the two novels that most affected the American conscience.

But Steinbeck's powerful social realism is by no means his only claim to greatness. He has also significantly influenced the way we see and think about the environment, an accomplishment for which he seldom receives the recognition he deserves. Not that Steinbeck or his fictional characters were green activists, passionately concerned with issues like water quality and clean air. Yet well before ecology was a subject of much public interest, Steinbeck was artfully introducing readers to ideas about all life-forms–most definitely including our own–being interdependent parts of an organic whole.

He explained this belief most directly in the *Sea of Cortez*–written nearly 30 years before the first Earth Day–an account of what he and some companions did and thought about while they were collecting small marine animals in the Gulf of California. Many believe this was Steinbeck's best work of nonfiction and one of the most important nature books of the 20th century.

It's not clear whether Steinbeck's thinking influenced Aldo Leopold, Rachel Carson and the other natural scientists and philosophers who formulated the now-prevailing environmental dogma. But the we-are-all-in-this-together theme was a distinctive one in some of his strongest work. And Steinbeck's definition of "we," which included everything from sea slugs to the stars, anticipated ideas about the web of life, the rights of rocks and other tenets of current holistic ecology.

Steinbeck came rather late to his interest in the biological sciences. Born and raised in Salinas, California, he was part of a rather bookish, never very affluent, white-collar family. Contemporaries remembered him as something of a loner and an avid reader of romantic allegories and legends, particularly those having to do with King Arthur. He and his younger sister, Mary, sometimes dressed up and played at being residents of Camelot. But like small-town kids everywhere always looking for something to do, he often got out into the surrounding countryside. Alone or with pals, Steinbeck roamed the long Salinas Valley and the shores of the Monterey Peninsula, where his family had a summer cottage.

There's ample evidence in much of what he later wrote that Steinbeck was deeply stirred by those surroundings and was a sharp, accurate observer of common natural detail. Consider this, for example, from *The Grapes of Wrath.* "Beside the road, a scrawny, dusty willow tree cast a speckled shade . . . its poor branches curving over the way, its load of leaves tattered and scraggly as a molting chicken. . . . He knew there would be shade, at least one hard bar of absolute shade thrown by the trunk, since the sun had passed the zenith. . . . He could not see the base of the tree, for it grew out of a little swale that held water longer than the level places."

After enrolling at Stanford University in 1919, Steinbeck dropped in and out (because he was broke or bored) for six years, working between stints as a ranch hand, a radio salesman and on surveying and dredging crews. He showed no interest in earning a degree and, for the most part, attended only classes whose subjects engaged him at the time: journalism, literature and creative writing, among others. In the summer of 1923, he took a course in field zoology offered at the Hopkins Marine Station, a Stanford branch in Pacific Grove. The class, a survey of animal life on the shore of Monterey Bay, introduced Steinbeck to the belief that everything in nature was connected to everything else.

In 1925 Steinbeck went to New York to establish himself as a serious writer of fiction. After several disheartening months, he returned to California where he kept on writing, married Carol Henning, the first of his three wives and, in 1930, met a biologist named Ed Ricketts, who became his best friend and profoundly influenced his intellectual outlook. Ricketts had grown up in Chicago and attended the university there, where he was a disciple of W. C. Allee, another prominent early ecologist. He went to the Monterey Peninsula to establish the Pacific Biological Laboratory, which he eventually moved to Cannery Row, along the waterfront. Ricketts earned a living by supplying slides and specimens of marine animals for classroom use. That business provided him with sufficient means and leisure to pursue his true passion: studying the "good, kind, sane little animals" who inhabited intertidal zones along the northern Pacific coast.

Ricketts was a firm believer in "non-teleological" or "is" thinking. Such an approach, he said, "concerns

itself primarily not with what should be, or could be, or might be, but rather with what actually 'is.'" It was the extent to which Ricketts practiced his beliefs that impressed Steinbeck. Ricketts accepted people as they were, flaws and all. Steinbeck was so intrigued that in many of his novels he created characters somewhat modeled on Ricketts—the kind, ruminative Preachers and Docs seeking what is.

First and last a storyteller, Steinbeck often gave the impression that he and Ricketts spent most of the 1930s carousing and speculating about metaphysics. In fact, during the decade after they met (Ricketts was killed in 1948 when his car was hit by a train), Steinbeck wrote the six books upon which his reputation as a novelist still rests: *Tortilla Flat, In Dubious Battle, Of Mice and Men, The Red Pony, The Long Valley* and *The Grapes of Wrath.* The last appeared in 1939, the same year Ricketts published his own masterwork, *Between Pacific Tides,* an ecological reference still highly regarded by marine biologists today.

Early in 1939, Steinbeck and Ricketts chartered a trawler, the *Western Flyer,* hired a crew and set off for the Gulf of California, also known as the Sea of Cortez. They spent six weeks observing and collecting along the Baja California shore. Part of the *Sea of Cortez,* which was published in 1941, is a listing of specimens and their habitats. But the catalog is preceded by a vivid narrative that contains many observations of the coastal people and animals they encountered.

On one occasion, Steinbeck writes about the local residents asking him why he always went about picking up and pickling little animals. "We could have said, 'We wish to fill in certain gaps in the knowledge of the Gulf fauna.' . . . [but] the meaningless words of science and philosophy, are walls that topple before a bewildered little 'why.' Finally we learned to know why we did these things. The animals were very beautiful. Here was life from which we borrowed life and excitement. In other words, we did these things because it was pleasant to do them."

At another point, after a day spent working the tide pools, Steinbeck muses: "It seems apparent that species are only commas in a sentence, that each species is at once the point and the base of a pyramid. . . . One [species] merges in another, groups melt into ecological groups until the time when what we know as life meets and enters what we think of as non-life: barnacle and rock, rock and earth, earth and tree, tree and rain and air . . . most of the feeling we call religious, most of the mystical outcrying which is one of the most prized and used and desired reactions of our species, is really the understanding and the attempt to say that man is related to the whole thing."

Steinbeck's most vivid works are mainly about people such as Ma Joad, who intuitively understands this interconnectedness, or Tom Joad, who discovers it. One of the most entertaining of these pilgrims is Junius Maltby of *The Pastures of Heaven* (1932). "The laziest and most ruminative of men," Maltby drifts into the valley and marries a widow who owns a good farm. After she dies in childbirth, leaving him the farm and a son, Robbie, Maltby lets fences fall and weeds overrun the property as he spends time educating Robbie in a surreal homeschooling program. Together they poke about the fields and thickets, wade in the stream and sit in a favorite sycamore tree talking about such things as water. "Water," Junius Maltby explains to Robbie, "is the seed of life. Of the three elements, water is the sperm, earth the womb and sunshine the mold of growth."

So instructed, Robbie becomes a knowledgeable and curious child. Nevertheless, neighbors regard Maltby as a foolish father and failed farmer. "Sometimes they hated him with the loathing busy people have for lazy ones. . . . No one in the valley ever realized that he was happy."

In *The Red Pony,* which came out in 1937, a colt is lovingly raised by Jody Tiflin, a rancher's young son. The little horse sickens, and early one morning Jody finds him down and dying in a pasture. Vultures have already begun to tear at his eyes. In a paroxysm of grief and rage, the boy catches one of the slow-moving scavengers by a wing. He picks up a stone and begins to beat it to a pulp. But "the red fearless eyes [of the vulture] still looked at him, impersonal and unafraid and detached."

Jody's father runs to the pasture and tries to comfort his son with reason. "Jody, the buzzard didn't kill the pony. Don't you know that?"

"I know it," Jody says wearily.

In *The Long Valley,* issued a year later, Mary Teller finds a piece of empty land on which she imagines in minute detail a house and, more importantly for her, a perfect garden. After five years, she meets Harry Teller, a man of sufficient means and, she thinks, patience, to allow her to do as she wants with the property. They are married, and after a time Mary does indeed create her dream garden. The centerpiece is a shallow ornamental pool to which, as Mary imagined they would, many birds come to drink. Watching them in the twilight of an evening, Mary is astonished and delighted to see a pure-white quail come to the pool. "She must be the queen of the quail," Mary reflects. "She makes every lovely thing that ever happened to me one thing."

During the past year or so, I have asked a number of Steinbeck readers about their favorite passages and episodes. I was surprised that several mentioned my own favorites:

"Over the grass at the roadside a land turtle crawled, turning aside for nothing. . . . His hard legs and yellow-nailed feet threshed slowly. . . . The barley beards slid off his shell, and the clover burrs fell on him and rolled to the ground. His horny beak was partly open, and his fierce, humorous eyes, under brows like fingernails, stared straight ahead."

Paroled from state prison, Tom Joad is walking home to the farm where his family sharecrops. Seeing the turtle, he picks it up. Later, meeting Jim Casy, a wandering preacher who has lost the Spirit, Joad explains that the turtle is a present for his younger brother.

When they get to the farm, they find it abandoned and partially destroyed. While wondering what to do next, Joad decides to release the turtle. Then he and the preacher watch it crawl away. "Where the hell you s'pose he's goin'?" said Joad. "I seen turtles all my life. They're always goin' someplace. They always seem to want to get there."

For me and, it turns out, for at least some others, that turtle keeps crawling along through John Steinbeck's whole shebang.

    —Smithsonian, 32 (January 2002): 95–98

* * *

California Dreamer
Jay Parini

Jay Parini, author of the 1995 biography John Steinbeck, *wrote the following article marking the centennial of Steinbeck's birth.*

The masterpiece *The Grapes of Wrath* appeared in 1939, when the Depression had dragged on for nearly a decade and seemed to stretch endlessly ahead. Thousands of families had been dislodged from small farms in the Southwest, their plight exacerbated by drought conditions and a moribund economy. Like the Joads of John Steinbeck's novel, these distraught families piled into old jalopies and headed west, to California, hoping for work and a better life. When they arrived, they discovered that Californians didn't need them or even want them. They were herded into dismal government "sanitary camps," where illness and hunger were pervasive.

Steinbeck was sent by a newspaper to report on the migrant situation. Notebook in hand, he toured the camps in an old bakery truck, driving up and down California's Central Valley, an area that he knew well from his childhood. In one of his first newspaper arti-

STEINBECK

SAN JOSE STATE UNIVERSITY · THE STEINBECK NEWSLETTER · FALL 1995

Cannery Row Fiftieth Anniversary Edition

498

"The God in the Pipes": An Early Version of *Cannery Row*

Roy Simmonds

On 16 October 1939, a year less ten days after he had finished writing *The Grapes of Wrath*, John Steinbeck observed in his journal: "Now I am battered with uncertainties. That part of my life that made the *Grapes* is over. I have one little job to do for the government, and then I can be born again. Must be. I have to go to new sources and find new roots" (*Working Days* 106). Two days later, he was wondering if he could write what he referred to as "That pipe play," something that "might be fun" and "break this damned posterity thing that is being put on me by my contemporaries" by being "the broadest kind of satire of nearly everything" (*Working Days* 107).

Other projects intervened, however: involvement with independent documentary film-makers Pare Lorentz and Herbert Kline; biological expeditions with Ed Ricketts to Tomales Point and Duxbury Reef, later to the Gulf of California; several visits to Washington—and one to the President himself—to discuss his unconventional suggestions about the coming

Continued on page 2

"Gabe," Steinbeck's Mack. Photograph by Peter Stackpole.

Interview with photographer Peter Stackpole
Page 19

First page of an issue of the Steinbeck newsletter published by the Center for Steinbeck Studies at San Jose State University; the newsletter was renamed Steinbeck Studies *in 2001 (San Jose State University).*

cles for *The San Francisco News,* Steinbeck described the predicament of the migrants who would inspire his novel:

"They arrive in California usually having used up every resource to get here, even to the selling of the poor blankets and utensils and tools on the way to buy gasoline. They arrive bewildered and beaten and usu-

ally in a state of semi-starvation, with only one necessity to face immediately, and that is to find work at any wage in order that the family may eat."

In one camp, not far from Steinbeck's hometown of Salinas, he found about 2,000 people crammed into a pathetic shelter, many suffering from typhoid, flu, tuberculosis and pneumonia. There was little food to be had, and the drinking water was foul. Once, when a riot broke out, the police squashed it brutally. "You couldn't fight back if you didn't feel good," Steinbeck wrote. "That was the secret the bosses and police had, and they knew they'd win."

After publishing his articles on the migrants, Steinbeck correctly guessed that his material was substantial enough to form the basis of a novel, and the first glimmerings of *The Grapes of Wrath* came into his head. In his journal, he wrote: "If only I could do this book properly it would be one of the really fine books and a truly American book." With eight books under his belt already, including 1937's *Of Mice and Men,* which had been a huge success as both a novel and a play, Steinbeck felt well prepared for the task at hand; indeed, he set to work with a vengeance.

He planned to write the book on an epic scale and decided it should alternate chapters of exposition and narrative. To keep it focused, he would center the story on one family, the Joads, tracking them from their farm in Oklahoma, along Route 66, and into California, where they would be forced into a camp with thousands of other "Okies" like themselves. The book, Steinbeck noted in the journal that he kept alongside the novel, would be composed "in a musical technique." He would try "to use the forms and the mathematics of music rather than those of prose." It would be "symphonic," he said, "in composition, in movement, in tone and in scope."

Steinbeck struggled to keep his concentration and remain disciplined, and one can follow his ups and downs in his journal. The entry for June 13, 1938, is typical. Steinbeck had been drinking with his friend Martin Ray the night before, and he came into his study the next day with a hangover:

"Now a new week starts and unpropitiously for me. Last night up to Ray's and drank a great deal of champagne. I pulled my punches pretty well but I am not in the dead sober state I could wish. However, I will try to go to work. Don't have to because I have a day caught up. All sorts of things might happen in the course of this book, but I must not be weak. This must be done. The failure of will even for one day has a devastating effect on the whole, far more important than just the loss of time and wordage. The whole physical basis of the novel is discipline of the writer, of his material, of the language. And sadly enough, if any of the discipline is gone, all of it suffers. And this slight fuzziness of mine may be a break in the discipline. I don't know yet. But right now I intend to find out."

Despite the hangovers and self-doubts, the writing progressed with astonishing speed and fluency. Between May and October 1938, he produced a manuscript of 200,000 words, writing in longhand with

Tchaikovsky and Stravinsky playing on the gramophone behind his desk. On September 3, he christened the book *The Grapes of Wrath,* a title suggested by his wife and plucked from "The Battle Hymn of the Republic." The narrative was completed on October 26, when Steinbeck wrote in his journal: "Finished this day—and I hope to God it's good."

Published in April 1939, *The Grapes of Wrath* became an enormous bestseller, winning critical praise from many of the best reviewers in the country. It also earned the Pulitzer Prize and was made into a film by director John Ford. Not surprisingly, the novel helped to focus national attention on the migrant situation. Popular first lady Eleanor Roosevelt supported the book, and her strong views were widely reported in the press. Soon after, large sums of federal money were directed to California to aid the migrants, and Steinbeck's novel became a catalyst for the change in attitude of Californians themselves, many of whom had not understood the extent of the plight of the migrants.

Steinbeck had, in fact, managed to write his "big book." *The Grapes of Wrath* became an instant classic, and it has maintained its position over six decades, with a readership in the millions. There are precious few "great" American novels, and this is surely one of them.

—*Book,* no. 22 (May–June 2002): 24–26

* * *

Steinbeck's America
Vincent D. Balitas

Vincent D. Balitas wrote the following centennial tribute, focusing on the three Library of America volumes of Steinbeck's works, the last of which was published in 2002.

On the centennial of his birth—Feb. 27, 1902—it was obvious that the reputation of Nobelist John Steinbeck was secure. His books remain in print and continue to sell well. In fact, Viking-Penguin is releasing special commemorative paperback editions of six of them, including the often overlooked, always delightful *Travels With Charley in Search of America.* Viking also has recently published *John Steinbeck: America and Americans and Selected Nonfiction,* a splendid collection that deserves a place on the shelves of those who enjoy and respect his work.

This flurry of publication is complemented by celebrations in more than 30 states where writers, critics and professors will join fans to honor Steinbeck's contributions to American letters. Perhaps the largest of these events, and the most international in flavor, will be Hofstra University's "John Steinbeck's Americas," a three-day conference scheduled for March. Scholars

"Year-Long Salute"

In 2001 Library Journal *published an account of plans for Steinbeck centennial programs in the following year.*

A coalition of 26 nonprofit cultural organizations nationwide, led by the Center for Steinbeck Studies at San Jose State University, CA, and the Mercantile Library of New York, has received a $260,000 grant from the National Endowment for the Humanities to commemorate the centennial (February 27, 2002) of the birth of Nobel prize-winning author John Steinbeck. The grant will be used to sponsor a year-long salute featuring 120 exhibitions, performances, and lectures in 75 venues. As part of the celebration, Penguin Putnam, Steinbeck's publisher, will produce special centennial editions of his most famous works, and the Library of America will release the third volume in its Steinbeck series.

As a special feature, the project is seeking to recruit 50 additional libraries across the country to present public programs on Steinbeck, for which funding will be available. The project will be directed by Pedro Castillo (history, Univ. of California at Santa Cruz), Harold Augenbraum (Mercantile Library of New York, which will administer the grant), and Susan Shillinglaw (Center for Steinbeck Studies, San Jose State).

Most of the events will take place next year. "The main thing is going to be a tribute to Steinbeck that we're doing with the Library of America and the PEN American Center, March 19," Augenbraum told LJ. New York will host many Steinbeck events at libraries and colleges around the New York City area. "From March 21–23 there will be a scholarly conference at Hofstra University, Hempstead; the Mercantile Library will host a series of four lectures and four book discussions; the John Jermain Library in Sag Harbor, where Steinbeck lived for several years, is presenting an exhibition and several programs; the CUNY Graduate Center will be presenting an exhibition of movie posters from Steinbeck-related films; and Columbia University is doing an archival-related exhibition of materials in its collection," Augenbraum said. [. . .]

—Andrew Albanese and Michael Rogers, "Libraries To Honor Steinbeck's 100th," *Library Journal,* 126 (15 September 2001): 20

Just as it is difficult to believe that Steinbeck has been dead for 34 years (Dec. 20, 1968, of cardio-respiratory failure), so, too, is it startling to realize that the Library of America is 20 years old and has released more than 130 volumes in its ambitious and very successful cultural project. When the first volume *(Herman Melville: Typee, Omoo, Mardi)* appeared in 1982, it signaled the advent of a publishing venture that would provide the reading public with some of the best writing done by Americans.

Every volume remains in print in several formats, ranging from the slip-cased volumes subscribers receive to hardcover and softcover trade editions. Not only do these volumes make available, in reader-friendly editions, the works of Frederick Douglass, William Bartram, James Thurber, Henry James, Mark Twain and Edith Wharton, but they also afford collectors the opportunity to replace those musty, yellowing, heavily-annotated paperbacks used in college courses with sturdy books designed to retard time.

Each volume follows a similar pattern: first, the primary texts themselves; second, a lengthy "Chronology" that serves as an extensive biography focusing on the author's personal and professional life; third, a "Note on the Texts," which provides important information on the compositional history of each text; and fourth, "Notes," which seeks to clarify topical allusions, foreign quotations and obscure references. Readers are left free to form their own opinions of a writer's work because none of the cant the critical wars have generated is present. The Library of America's volumes are for readers who want to experience novels, plays, poems and political and journalistic writings directly.

To celebrate Steinbeck's centennial, the Library of America is releasing the last of three volumes devoted to his major work. The first volume appeared in 1994 and includes *The Pastures of Heaven, To a God Unknown, Tortilla Flat, In Dubious Battle* and *Of Mice and Men.* The second was published in 1996, with *The Long Valley, The Grapes of Wrath, The Log from the Sea of Cortez* and *The Harvest Gypsies.* The third volume *(John Steinbeck: Novels 1942–1952,* $35, 983 pp) gives us *The Moon Is Down, Cannery Row, The Pearl* and *East of Eden.*

All of Steinbeck's weaknesses and strengths are apparent in these volumes. For readers who expect an author to challenge universal themes with the innumerable difficulties language contains, his fiction is too accessible, too "easy" to read. Rarely do we find the nuances and complexities of style that, say, William Faulkner created to force readers to confront history, and themselves. Likewise, Ernest Hemingway explored the ironies and ambiguities of life in the face of a historical dehumanization with cold, clean minimalism, and F. Scott Fitzgerald exposed the failure of the mythic

from various countries will meet to present papers and engage in discussion on topics such as "Steinbeck and Musical Theater," with extracurricular events such as a tour of Sag Harbor, where the author lived, and a screening of the controversial *The Forgotten Village.* [. . .]

American Dream with his ebullient though controlled romanticism. Steinbeck, however, shaped characters that seem more contrived, more stereotypical than many of his peers, and in a rather simple prose. His work has been called "middlebrow," a label affixed to fiction that is too transparent, too, well, sentimental.

Some of his weaknesses also can be seen as strengths. He was, especially for readers with an eye for the historical or sociological, one of the great recorders of the proletariat, of ordinary people in a specific time caught up by forces they don't understand and are powerless to resist. They struggle simply to survive. It might be the Joads fleeing the Dust Bowl of Depression-era Oklahoma to find salvation in the false promise of California; or Kino, whose discovery of a large pearl initially offers hope but results in tragedy; or the Trasks, one of the most dysfunctional families in fiction, who only can try to bend in the storm of family and business horrors. Steinbeck's characters achieve a kind of nobility even as they are defeated.

Because of both his weaknesses and strengths, Steinbeck will remain a major voice in American literature. His wide, popular appeal ensures his place, if not in literature departments, then in his reader's hearts. What better way to celebrate his birthday than to read his books, and to suspect that in 2102, he will continue to be honored.

—Insight on the News, 18 (25 March 2002): 27

* * *

Recollecting Steinbeck
Bridget Kinsella

Many major newspapers and magazines reported on Steinbeck centennial celebrations in 2002. The following account is from Publishers Weekly.

What will the *Times* say this time? On February 27, the centennial of John Steinbeck's birth, his long-time publisher Penguin, along with booksellers, arts institutions, colleges and libraries, will be throwing the author—whom the *New York Times* editorialized as unworthy of the Nobel Prize when he won in 1962—one heck of a year-long celebration.

On the publishing front, Penguin has much planned for Steinbeck, whose works already sell about two million copies a year. The house has repackaged six of his paperback classics: *East of Eden, The Grapes of Wrath, Of Mice and Men, Cannery Row, The Pearl* and *Travels with Charley in Search for America,* now available individually and in a boxed set. In addition, this month Viking is releasing a new hardcover collection of Steinbeck's nonfiction, *America and Americans,* edited by Susan

Front cover of the 1986 publication of the 1976 paperback edition of Steinbeck's first novel, originally published in 1929 (Bruccoli Clark Layman Archives)

Shillinglaw and Jackson J. Benson. It includes essays, works of journalism and the original ending for *Travels with Charley.* From the Library of America comes a third volume of Steinbeck's work, *Steinbeck: Novels 1942–52,* edited by Robert DeMott.

On the actual birthday, soon to be declared John Steinbeck Day in New York City by mayoral proclamation, Penguin is throwing a party at the Barnes & Noble in Union Square. Actors from the Broadway production of *The Grapes of Wrath* will read, followed by a discussion led by Benson and DeMott. One of the biggest celebratory events takes place on March 19 at Alice Tully Hall in Lincoln Center, cosponsored by PEN and the Mercantile Library. Mercantile director Harold Augenbraum said that while plans for the Lincoln Center event are still being finalized, Arthur Miller, Studs Terkel, Bill Kennedy and Dorothy Allison are already on the bill.

Fittingly for a writer of the people, many of the Steinbeck centennial events are happening at the grass roots. Augenbraum and Shillinglaw (who is the head of the Center for Steinbeck Studies at San Jose State University) are codirectors of the national Steinbeck Centennial, which is distributing individual $500 National Endowment for the Humanities grants to 106 libraries in 39 states. "I think it is really the most widespread single author event in American history," said Augenbraum.

An admitted latecomer to the centennial, but certainly not an insignificant player, is the California Council for the Humanities, which is kicking off its first California Reads program by trying to get the entire state to read *The Grapes of Wrath.* Julie Levak, the organization's director of external affairs, told PW that when the organization picked Steinbeck as its first choice for the statewide program, it was unaware of the centennial. Still in the planning stages, the state program, called "California Is My Story," will occur in the fall. "We are looking for innovative ways of engaging people in humanities projects through story," said Levak. "*The Grapes of Wrath* is the quintessential California book and it provides a portal to discussion of immigration and displacement that so many Californians can relate to."

Judging from the national attention the centennial will get, however, Steinbeck is one writer who plays far beyond his hometown of Salinas, Calif. "He was a socially engaged and concerned man," said Shillinglaw. "People sensed his empathy, and that makes him very readable."

Steinbeck's social consciousness is a major reason why Judith Balk, director of the Chester Public Library in Chester, N.H., applied for an NEH grant for a week's worth of Steinbeck programs in February. "This is Robert Frost country," she said. "I think Steinbeck wrote about the same problems New England has," from migrant workers to keeping oceans clean to homelessness and poverty. "I wanted to bring back an awareness and appreciation for his writing and for the issues he writes about," she said.

Lorraine Borowski, the director of the public library in Decorah, Iowa, another of the 106 libraries planning to hold NEH grant-sponsored events for the centennial, said she thought Steinbeck had an "earthiness" that appeals to people. "It's a commonness," she explained. "He wrote about displaced people, people in strife and sociological issues that anyone can identify with personally, or through their ancestry."

—*Publishers Weekly,* 249 (28 January 2002): 142–143

* * *

Of Mice and Men and Novelists
Martin Arnold

Martin Arnold's centennial notice appeared in The New York Times.

John Steinbeck is making a comeback. Which is a strange thing to say about an author whose books still sell about two million copies a year, but it is true. The list of Nobel laureates in literature is filled with who's, as in "who is that?" Steinbeck is not one of them, but he has never been too popular among the higher academics of literature, his work considered too sentimental for great art, his writing simply not good enough.

Indeed, the interesting thing about the modest Steinbeck rally is that it is more about sociology and history than about literature. College departments of American and English literature still largely ignore the author of "The Grapes of Wrath" and "Of Mice and

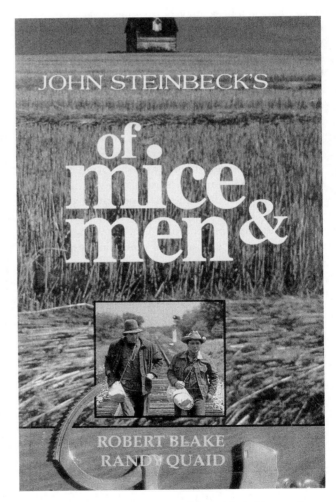

Cover for the 1985 video release of the 1981 television remake of Steinbeck's 1937 novel (Richland County Public Library)

Men," although high school syllabuses don't because, among other virtues, he's an easy read. The new evangelism comes from American studies programs and their examinations of history's disinherited.

Steinbeck was born on Feb. 27, 1902, so this is his centennial year, and there are close to 200 celebratory events planned in 38 states to honor the occasion, including the premiere in Steinbeck country by the Monterey County Symphony of a work by Allen Shaw, with an accompanying text by Jamaica Kincaid. It is also the 40th anniversary of his Nobel Prize in Literature. A lot of impetus.

Viking is publishing new trade paperback editions of six Steinbeck books, including the novels "Grapes of Wrath," "Of Mice and Men" and "East of Eden." It has recently published in hardcover a collection of his journalism, "America and Americans and Selected Nonfiction."

Steinbeck had perfect pitch for an era, the Depression. Alan Trachtenberg, who recently retired as professor of American studies at Yale, said that he had "a sense that Steinbeck may be making a bit of a comeback because a group of young scholars are trying to recover for study the radicalism of the 30's" and because "there's a new interest in the relationship between radical politics and some fiction."

So it's really Steinbeck's Great Depression resonance, and the mythology of the Dust Bowl, that accounts for the ready availability of his works in stores, when novels by, for instance, Theodore Dreiser, arguably a better novelist, aren't easily found.

In fact, Harold Bloom, who is a sort of chancellor of the Western literary canon, doesn't even include this Nobel winner in the canon's American division. He said that "The Grapes of Wrath" was "now a somewhat politically correct book" and that that perhaps accounted for the beginning of a new interest in Steinbeck. He doesn't even see many small excellences in Steinbeck's work and, in a reversal of the cliché, thinks that John Ford's 1940 movie of "The Grapes of Wrath" is better than the book.

"Sad to say, Steinbeck couldn't get Hemingway's music out of his head," Professor Bloom said. "You can't read three paragraphs of Steinbeck without thinking of a poorer Hemingway, with characterizations that are contrived." (Hemingway, the better writer, who won the Nobel Prize in 1954, seems to be making a bit of a comeback, too, partly because there is a re-examination of the "macho man" in today's social context and partly because he is to post–World War II America what Steinbeck is to the 30's.)

Michael Denning, a professor of American studies at Yale, said he had noticed an increase in Steinbeck interest over the last decade, but not because of this writer's influence in the chanceries of letters.

He said: "There is the whole mythology of the Dust Bowl, and the importance of that in American culture. Steinbeck, Woody Guthrie, Dorothea Lange are part of that. 'Grapes of Wrath' is studied as a way into thinking about that part of American history." Professor Denning said some of the Steinbeck revival has come about because the center of our culture "has shifted west, and he is seen by students as a California writer who thought about the West."

To make a comparison. There is also a Langston Hughes revival and centennial, but Professor Denning said he was coming back as a figure both in literature and in cultural history. "Hughes spanned a larger part of the century and spoke to a number of different moments," he said, "and I'm not sure Steinbeck did."

What about some of Steinbeck's contemporaries? Faulkner, for instance? There are professors who will say Faulkner is too difficult for many students to get into.

Laura Browder, associate professor of English at Virginia Commonwealth University and director of its creative writing program, makes an interesting point about the connection between novelists and political action. During the Civil War, our first great national crisis, "writers were read by everyone and were important figures," she said, adding, "By the 30's, the next great crisis, writers were supplanted by the movies and tabloid culture and had to find a way to make their books accessible to people who went to the movies and did not read serious literature."

It became a literary two-edged sword. Writing had to be sympathetic, not too edgy, and so Steinbeck's sentimentality, for instance, although criticized, made him popular. "Now for first-generation college students, and there are many, we need to find texts that they will sit through and connect to," Professor Browder said. "Steinbeck works on lots of levels. He's more to the left, which lots of students are, and he is accessible in dramatizing social issues, and wasn't afraid to use sentimental devices the way Stowe did in 'Uncle Tom's Cabin.'"

Giving the students books they like will perhaps lead them to other books, particularly when it comes to social history rather than literature. As Professor Browder said, "It's hard to find a radical text that's going to be comprehensible to students of this generation." Steinbeck, easy; Faulkner, difficult.

As for the Nobel Prize, and its measure of a writer's greatness, Professor Bloom sums it up this way: "The people in Stockholm often seem to have a dusty file on people no one ever heard of that they pull out when making the awards."

—New York Times, 7 February 2002, sec. E, p. 3

* * *

Sentimental for Steinbeck
Dagoberto Gilb

Dagoberto Gilb used the occasion of the centennial to recall his first encounter with Steinbeck's works.

Not being precocious in matters of literature—even to the end of my teenage years when I still thought of "book" as a verb, long before I read a poetic sentence—I knew of John Steinbeck, "The Grapes of Wrath" and "East of Eden." His name was bigger than these titles, than the movies that were made of the novels. He was up there with Marilyn Monroe, Sandy Koufax, John F. Kennedy.

Eventually, when books did become nouns for me, John Steinbeck was in my first stack of them, and it was not a good experience. That's because I'd been drawn to read "Tortilla Flat." If this had been all there was, I would have left it at that, groaning about Steinbeck as I did about this novel. I mean, what's with these sweet, mystically dumb and lazy Mexican "paisanos"? What nonmedieval writer creates lines like: "I swear, what I have is thine. While I have a house, thou hast a house. Give me a drink"? But this is how he had these "native" characters of the Monterey Peninsula speak to each other, even as, or especially when, they were drinking red wine by the gallon.

I'm easier on the novel now: it is simply another of those "exoticized" novels by a writer whose home was near—though on the good side of the tracks—an earlier culture that fascinates in its "strangeness." It's what young writers often begin with once they are stricken by the sense of mystery that is around and in them, that isolating awe that drives them to write. It's what bad writers never know how to transcend.

Steinbeck did. In "Tortilla Flat," Mexican-Americans were drawn as genetically predisposed to lazy innocence and drunken happiness. But when he matured to write about the people of the Dust Bowl and the Central Valley of California, Steinbeck began to portray people who were out of work more sympathetically. And that's when he became great; that's when what he wrote about was what I wanted to read, what I admired and was inspired by. When what he wrote wasn't just about poor Okies rattling across the Southwest into California, or about lonely people living on a ranch, but about how people are, how they should be and should be treated, and so about me, too, not to mention what I care about and what I believe in: that the West is not the East, that the West is a land unique and ruggedly beautiful, as are the people from it.

Steinbeck was the premier writer of the American West, but he didn't do cowboys and Indians. You see hitchhikers and waitresses, truck drivers speeding by cotton and corn fields. You feel wind, and it's dusty and the sun is hot and too bright. There are trains pounding railroad tracks, rivers and creeks and bridges and long stretches of highway. There are lone oak trees in dry, grassy fields, vistas with rolling hills and mountains. Men hunt for wood to burn at night in camps near gulleys with rocks and boulders. There are working ranches, but horseback riding and rifle shooting are not the story.

Steinbeck tells us stories of work, the dream of what work can do for people. Lenny [*sic*] and George, in "Of Mice and Men," are sent to the boss's ranch near Soledad for a job, expecting no more than to earn a living, hard as it comes. What they dream of is a house where they might listen to the rain outside, a couple of acres where they can raise rabbits in winter, have a chicken hutch, leave the thick cream on the milk, grow alfalfa, have a vegetable garden.

And stories not only about work, but about social cause. In "The Grapes of Wrath," Tom Joad, just released from prison, comes back to his Oklahoma home to find his parents, sharecroppers, displaced by the cigar-chewing bankers and anonymous corporations whose roaring tractors, rolling like tanks in a war, intend to pacify a land where families once were born and buried. The story of the Joads, traveling across the West to find work in the dreamland of California, is about disillusioned poor people who begin to organize against the meanest spirit of capitalism.

Steinbeck takes on the dangerous and divisive issue of fair and decent labor; he is unafraid to talk about lousy wages and the abuse of workers or to extol the virtues of unions and strikes. He allows Tom Joad, a man who can kill, to become inspired by a former preacher, to be the hero of his novel: "I been thinkin' a hell of a lot, thinkin' about our people livin' like pigs, an' the good lan' layin' fallow, or maybe one fella with a million acres, while a hunderd thousan' good farmers is starvin.' An I been wonderin' if all our folks got together an yelled."

Many have criticized Steinbeck—he's sentimental, he's melodramatic. I remember thinking this, too. But if that's so, even if it's only that, here at the centennial of Steinbeck's birth, I'm sentimental for him now. Because so many people, and so many writers, have left behind or never learned a respect for manual work, for people who carry and use tools for a living and get calluses and chapped hands and dirt under the nails, who bend and stoop, people who work by the hour or the basket, who build and fix things, who dig and plant and pick. The literary world is a powerful suit-and-tie business, and the well-dressed stories that editors look for are too much by writers whose game is played as professionally as a Harvard M.B.A.'s, whose marketing goals are not

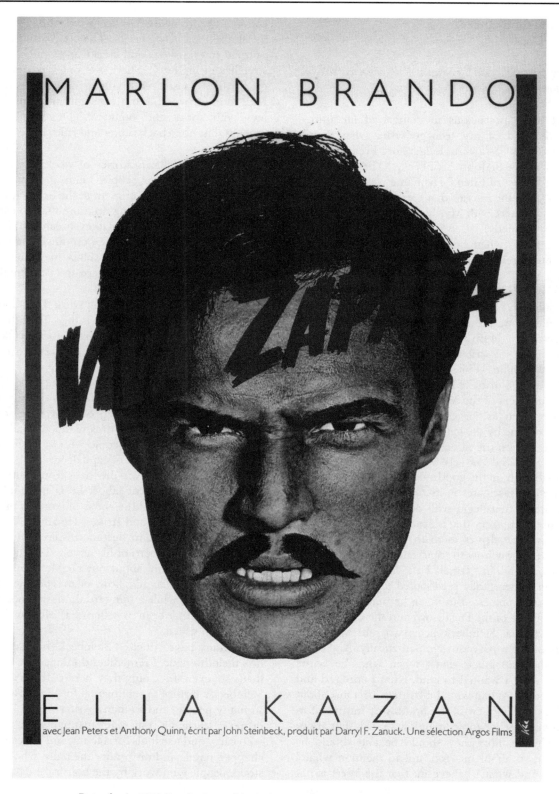

Poster for the 1970 French release of the 1952 movie for which Steinbeck wrote the screenplay
(Bruccoli Clark Layman Archives)

meant to cause readers to step outside the privileged cubicle to see who's sweeping the floor in the hours when they've gone home.

—*New York Times,* 18 March 2002, sec. A, p. 25

* * *

A Play to Be Played
Robert DeMott

Robert DeMott wrote the introductory essay for a booklet published in conjunction with the centennial exhibit "A Play to Be Played": John Steinbeck on Stage and Screen, 1935– 1960, presented at Columbia University's Butler Library from 29 July to 15 November 2002.

One hundred years after his birth, John Steinbeck (1902–1968) is best known as a novelist of America's Great Depression, whose enduring works such as *Tortilla Flat* (1935), *In Dubious Battle* (1936), *Of Mice and Men* (1937), and *The Grapes of Wrath* (1939) portrayed the bitter and often tragic experience of economic and social dispossession in 1930s America.

And yet despite the acclaim and widespread popularity, then and now, of those signature works, John Steinbeck's career had a much wider focus than that of proletarian fiction. In fact, it is much more accurate to consider Steinbeck a man of letters, which is to say that he was accomplished in a variety of genres. Steinbeck was primarily a populist writer—a bard of the people— who wanted to reach the largest audience possible; his ability to write in a number of forms allowed him to keep his avowed goal of making people understand each other in sight. A 1999 *Writers Digest* poll of "The 100 Best Writers of the Century" ranked Steinbeck Number 1. While John Steinbeck has never found the uniform academic acceptance that his fellow Nobel Prize winners William Faulkner and Ernest Hemingway have had, his high standing in a number of turn-of-the-century readers' and writers' polls suggests that his work remains broadly appealing and relevant.

The overwhelming commercial and critical success and subsequent public notoriety of his most famous novel, *The Grapes of Wrath*—a powerful naturalistic social epic that exposed deplorable conditions of migrant farm workers in Dust Bowl Oklahoma and depression California—nearly turned Steinbeck against fiction writing for good. *The Grapes of Wrath* not only sold over 500,000 copies in its first year, but was also publicly decried as communistic propaganda and banned (and even burned) as immoral trash in a number of locations across the United States, including his home town, Salinas, California. *The Grapes of Wrath* won a Pulitzer Prize for fiction in 1940, but by that time

Steinbeck, exhausted from the physical and emotional toll the novel's writing and subsequent notoriety had exacted, confided to a friend, Carlton Sheffield, that he had worked the "clumsy" novel form as far as he could and that he needed to move afield in his search for new subjects and new forms.

Steinbeck made good on his claim. In the years from 1940 to 1945 alone he turned his hand to various genres. Steinbeck produced film texts (*The Forgotten Village, Lifeboat, A Medal for Benny*), a collaborative ecological text with Edward F. Ricketts (*Sea of Cortez: A Leisurely Journal of Travel and Research*), a series of war reports from Europe and Africa for the *New York Herald Tribune* (later collected as *Once There Was a War*), a documentary text on the United States Army Air Corps (*Bombs Away*), and two short novels (*The Moon is Down* and *Cannery Row*). Although Steinbeck did not abandon fiction entirely, for the remainder of his writing career through 1966 he published more books of nonfiction, drama, or movie scripts (*A Russian Journal, Burning Bright, Viva Zapata!, Un Americain à New-York et à Paris, Once There Was a War, Travels with Charley, America and Americans*) than he did novels (*The Wayward Bus, The Pearl, East of Eden, Sweet Thursday, The Short Reign of Pippin IV, The Winter of Our Discontent*).

Add to that a considerable amount of both literary nonfiction for American and foreign commercial magazines and newspaper journalism on subjects as diverse as Joan of Arc, censorship, public morality, juvenile delinquency, undersea exploration, Democratic Party National Conventions, and the Viet Nam War, and a portrait of Steinbeck emerges as a versatile talent—a writer seriously engaged in exploring a multiplicity of themes, styles, genres, and forms. A restless experimenter as a writer, Steinbeck loved to change "pace," as he told film producer Darryl F. Zanuck in 1952, at a moment when he was writing *Bear Flag,* a musical comedy that later became his 1954 novel *Sweet Thursday.* In order to understand John Steinbeck's achievement as a writer and his contribution to American culture, it is necessary to see the entire arc of his career.

An especially significant part of that arc concerns Steinbeck's work for and adaptation by the theater community and movie industry. His work came to maturity at a time when myriad forms of popular culture and media, including jazz, cinema, drama, tabloid newspapers, and radio (and later television) were becoming widespread and ubiquitous. Steinbeck's writing incorporated some of those energies into his own prose. Jazz rhythms and cinematic jump cuts can be found in *The Grapes of Wrath* and *Cannery Row, Sweet Thursday* was partly indebted to Al Capp's comic *Li'l Abner* series, and his last novel, *The Winter of Our Discon-*

"A PLAY TO BE PLAYED"

John Steinbeck on Stage and Screen
1935–1960

A Centennial Exhibit featuring the Annie Laurie Williams Papers

July 29 – November 15, 2002

Alan & Margaret Kempner Exhibition Gallery
Rare Book & Manuscript Library
Butler Library, 6th Floor, East
Columbia University

Front cover of a Steinbeck centennial exhibition catalogue (Rare Book & Manuscript Library, Columbia University)

tent (1961), owes a great deal of its realistic punch to contemporary quiz show scandals then being covered by newspaper and television reporters. Like all writers Steinbeck could not escape the presences and forms of his own cultural milieu, nor did he wish to do so.

Steinbeck was a product of his times in another way too—because of their cinematic quality, his fiction was avidly sought for adaptation by Hollywood movie makers, and in this regard he was better served than his great contemporaries, Ernest Hemingway, William Faulkner, and F. Scott Fitzgerald. *Tortilla Flat, Of Mice*

and Men, The Grapes of Wrath, The Moon is Down, The Red Pony, The Pearl, The Wayward Bus, and *East of Eden* were all adapted during Steinbeck's lifetime, and of these versions, director Lewis Milestone's *Of Mice and Men* and director John Ford's *The Grapes of Wrath* are often considered among the best films ever made by Hollywood, with Elia Kazan's cult classic *East of Eden* not far behind.

Steinbeck refused "to go to Hollywood" (John Steinbeck to Elizabeth Otis and Annie Laurie Williams, December 1, 1937). At a time in the late Thirties when he was one of the hottest writers in America he resolutely resisted Hollywood's repeated offers to work under contract for the studios. He did, however, take an active interest in adaptations of his own work, and he produced important screenplays himself, including a documentary, *The Forgotten Village* (1941), *The Red Pony* (1949), *The Pearl* (1947, with Emilio Fernandez and Jack Wagner), and most notably *Viva Zapata!* (1951), directed by Elia Kazan and produced by Darryl Zanuck, which was nominated for five Academy Awards, including one each for Steinbeck's story and his screenplay.

Throughout Steinbeck's career some of the best directors and authors were drawn to his work. Unfortunately, the collaborations did not always go smoothly. In one instance, *Lifeboat* (1944), an Alfred Hitchcock film made from Steinbeck's unpublished 40,000-word novella about survivors of a torpedoed United States Merchant Marine ship, so deviated from Steinbeck's original text (which was quite politically charged) that he repudiated his involvement in the production (ironi-

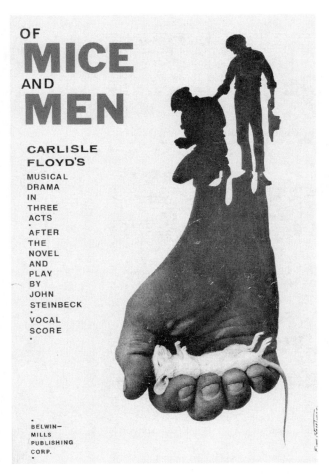

Front cover of the 1971 vocal-piano score for the 1970 opera adaptation of Steinbeck's 1937 novel (Music Library, University of South Carolina)

cally Steinbeck received an Academy Award nomination for best original story). Despite setbacks, Steinbeck seems never to have lost interest in writing for the screen. In later years, however, he worked on movie projects that remained unfinished: *The Witches of Salem* and *Christopher Columbus* never got beyond synopsis stage; a version of Henrik Ibsen's *The Vikings at Helgoland* became a completed screenplay, but was never produced.

Steinbeck's life in the American theater was a particularly rich one as well. Although he never comfortably thought of himself as a full-fledged playwright, he did have a naturally dramatic sense, both for characterization and for scene construction. In the mid-thirties he created a form all his own that he called the "play novelette." The first was *Of Mice and Men* (whose working title was *Something That Happened*), which he claimed "is neither a novel nor a play but it is a kind of playable novel. Written in novel form but so scened and set that it can be played as it stands." It will be unlike other plays, he continued, "since it does not follow the formal acts but uses chapters for curtains. Descriptions can be read for stage direction. . . . Plays are hard to read so this will make both a novel and a play as it stands" (John Steinbeck to Annie Laurie Williams, April 1936).

Steinbeck's hybrid experiment paid off in unprecedented ways. The novella version of *Of Mice and Men* was an enormous best seller and a Book of the Month Club selection in 1937. The play version, directed by George S. Kaufman, ran for 207 performances in 1938 at the Music Box Theater in Manhattan and won the prestigious New York Drama Critics Circle Award. That was followed by a successful cross-country tour in 1938 and 1939. In effect, with the artistic success of the 1939 film version of *Of Mice and Men* to boot, Steinbeck's little parable of human desire and loss proved remarkably durable in every genre (including an operatic version by Carlisle Floyd in 1970 and three other film versions, the most recent a 1993 production starring Gary Sinise and John Malkovich). In the ensuing years Steinbeck returned to the playable novel in *The Moon is Down* and *Burning Bright*. Although these were less spectacular successes than his initial venture, they were both true to his play-novel philosophy designed "to reach as many people as possible, even those people who do not read novels" (John Steinbeck, unpublished statement, ca. May 1942).

Reaching as many people as possible was not something John Steinbeck—or any writer, for that matter—could do alone. Publishing books is a collaborative effort, and from the outset Steinbeck was aided and abetted by his wives, Carol, Gwyn, and Elaine; by his early publisher and (from mid-1938 onward) senior editor at Viking Press, Pascal "Pat" Covici; and his agents

# of mice and men
act one
scene 1

based on the novel and play by

john steinbeck

libretto and music by

carlisle floyd

Scene: A clearing full of dense undergrowth in a woods.
At Rise:

(Police sirens are heard, whining in the distance, and searchlights from patrol cars probe the night sky in wide arcs. It is very dark, and the outlines of distant trees, bushes, and tall grass in the clearing are only gradually perceived.)

Precipitato ($\natural$ = 132)

(After a moment George runs onstage, stops for a moment breathing noisily, and then, quickly looking around him, plunges to his stomach in the undergrowth. He is a thin,

wiry man with strong, sharp features and everything about him suggests tension and alertness. He wears work clothes and a worn, shapeless hat, and, strapped across his back, he carries a bedroll, filled with his belongings.)

*First page of the vocal-piano score for the 1970 opera adaptation of Steinbeck's 1937 novel
(Music Library, University of South Carolina)*

at McIntosh and Otis, including Annie Laurie Williams, his drama agent, from whose correspondence and documents, housed in the Rare Book and Manuscript Library, this unparalleled archive of primary materials has been assembled. Steinbeck's career-long relationship with Mavis McIntosh, Elizabeth Otis, and Williams, which began in 1933, was truly exemplary, for they all came to think of themselves as family rather than as merely professional colleagues. Steinbeck was deeply appreciative of their efforts, which cannot be underestimated: "You don't know what you people do for me. It is a fine thing to know that everything is going to be done much better than I could do it myself" (John Steinbeck to Annie Laurie Williams, ca. November 27, 1937).

Steinbeck was something of an adopted younger brother or son, and all three older women were unstinting in securing his professional affairs and ministering when necessary to his personal life as well. Particularly noteworthy are Williams's letters to Steinbeck written between winter 1937 and spring 1938, which detail negotiations regarding film and drama versions of *Of Mice and Men,* and report on progress of George S. Kaufman's production. "As your motion picture and play representative I have been shining in your reflected glory. And everyone, thank goodness, has now stopped talking about *Gone With the Wind* [Williams had brokered its sale to Hollywood], and is talking about *Of Mice and Men*" (Annie Laurie Williams to John Steinbeck, March 10, 1937).

Moreover, Williams's correspondence reveals her genuine regard for Steinbeck as a person and as an artist. When Steinbeck destroyed a novel manuscript, *L'Affaire Lettuceberg,* because he thought it was too "vicious" and "mean" (John Steinbeck to Annie Laurie Williams, ca. April 20, 1938), Williams responded on behalf of his agents and his publisher: ". . . let me say how proud I am of you John for being yourself and not letting the new book out when you don't feel it does

you justice. I admire you for having the courage of your convictions and know you would feel better if you could have heard what Elizabeth and Pat both said when they read your letter. . . . [W]e all admire you more than ever for sticking by your instincts about your work. Bless you!" (Annie Laurie Williams to John Steinbeck, May 24, 1938). That Steinbeck went on immediately to write *The Grapes of Wrath* more than justified everyone's faith in his decision.

John Steinbeck was not only a productive author in a variety of genres, but he was a voluminous and obsessive letter writer as well. It was his habit to warm up for his day's main writing stint (usually 2,000 words per day) by penning as many as half a dozen letters to Elizabeth Otis and her staff, Pat Covici, and other close friends. Steinbeck disliked talking on the telephone, so his daily letters and journals were an indispensable way of explaining himself. This exhibit showcases his correspondence to and from Annie Laurie Williams, as well as the richness of his published and unpublished movie- and drama-related manuscripts. In its range and depth Columbia University's Steinbeck archive ranks with the very best Steinbeck collections in the world. Moreover, because these materials have so rarely been utilized in existing scholarship (in Elaine Steinbeck and Robert Wallsten's 1976 edition of *Steinbeck: A Life in Letters,* Robert DeMott's 1989 edition of Steinbeck's *Working Days: The Journals of The Grapes of Wrath, 1938–1941,* and Roy Simmond's 1996 critical biography *John Steinbeck: The War Years, 1939–1945*), they have an indisputable freshness and surprising, one-of-a-kind relevance. In this one hundredth anniversary of John Steinbeck's birth, the Annie Laurie Williams archive reveals a side of the Nobel Prize winner that should go a long way in creating a more comprehensive and accurate picture of his life and career.

– *"A Play To Be Played": John Steinbeck on Stage and Screen, 1935–1960* (New York: Rare Book & Manuscript Library, Columbia University, 2002), pp. 1–6

Checklist of Further Readings

Astro, Richard. *Edward F. Ricketts*. Boise, Idaho: Boise State University, 1976.

Astro. *John Steinbeck and Edward F. Ricketts: The Shaping of a Novelist*. Minneapolis: University of Minnesota Press, 1973.

Astro and Tetsumaro Hayashi, eds. *Steinbeck: The Man and His Work*. Corvallis: Oregon State University Press, 1971.

Astro and Joel W. Hedgpeth, eds. *Steinbeck and the Sea: Proceedings of a Conference Held at the Marine Science Center Auditorium, Newport, Oregon, May 4, 1974*. Corvallis: Oregon State University Press, 1975.

Beegel, Susan F., Susan Shillinglaw, and Wesley N. Tiffney Jr., eds. *Steinbeck and the Environment: Interdisciplinary Approaches*. Tuscaloosa: University of Alabama Press, 1997.

Benson, Jackson J. *Looking for Steinbeck's Ghost*. Norman: University of Oklahoma Press, 1988.

Benson. *Steinbeck's Cannery Row: A Reconsideration*. Muncie, Ind.: Steinbeck Research Institute, Ball State University, 1991.

Benson. *The True Adventures of John Steinbeck, Writer*. New York: Viking, 1984.

Benson, ed. *The Short Novels of John Steinbeck: Critical Essays with a Checklist to Steinbeck Criticism*. Durham, N.C.: Duke University Press, 1990.

Burrows, Michael. *John Steinbeck and His Films*. St. Austell, U.K.: Primestyle, 1971.

Coers, Donald V. *John Steinbeck as Propagandist: The Moon Is Down Goes to War*. Tuscaloosa: University of Alabama Press, 1991.

Coers, Paul D. Ruffin, and Robert J. DeMott, eds. *After The Grapes of Wrath: Essays on John Steinbeck in Honor of Tetsumaro Hayashi*. Athens: Ohio University Press, 1995.

Crouch, Steve. *Steinbeck Country*. Palo Alto, Cal.: American West, 1973.

Davis, Robert Con, ed. *The Grapes of Wrath: A Collection of Critical Essays*. Englewood Cliffs, N.J.: Prentice-Hall, 1982.

Davis, Robert Murray, ed. *Steinbeck: A Collection of Critical Essays*. Englewood Cliffs, N.J.: Prentice-Hall, 1972.

DeMott, Robert J. *Steinbeck's Reading: A Catalogue of Books Owned and Borrowed*. New York: Garland, 1984.

DeMott. *Steinbeck's Typewriter: Essays on His Art*. Troy, N.Y.: Whitston, 1996.

Ditsky, John. *Essays on East of Eden*. Muncie, Ind.: John Steinbeck Society of America, Ball State University, 1977.

Ditsky. *John Steinbeck and the Critics*. Rochester, N.Y.: Camden House, 2000.

Ditsky, ed. *Critical Essays on Steinbeck's The Grapes of Wrath*. Boston: G. K. Hall, 1989.

Donohue, Agnes McNeill, ed. *A Casebook on The Grapes of Wrath*. New York: Crowell, 1968.

Enea, Sparky, and Audry Lynch. *With Steinbeck in the Sea of Cortez*. Los Osos, Cal.: Sand River Press, 1991.

Fensch, Thomas. *Steinbeck and Covici: The Story of a Friendship*. Middleburry, Vt.: Paul S. Eriksson, 1979.

Fensch, ed. *Conversations with John Steinbeck*. Jackson: University Press of Mississippi, 1988.

Fontenrose, Joseph. *John Steinbeck: An Introduction and Interpretation*. New York: Holt, Rinehart & Winston, 1963.

Fontenrose. *Steinbeck's Unhappy Valley: A Study of The Pastures of Heaven*. Berkeley: Joseph Fontenrose, 1981.

French, Warren. *Filmguide to The Grapes of Wrath*. Bloomington: Indiana University Press, 1973.

French. *John Steinbeck*. New York: Twayne, 1961; revised, 1975.

French. *John Steinbeck's Fiction Revisited*. New York: Twayne, 1994.

French. *John Steinbeck's Nonfiction Revisited*. New York: Twayne, 1996.

French, ed. *A Companion to The Grapes of Wrath*. New York: Viking, 1963.

Gannett, Lewis. *John Steinbeck: Personal and Bibliographical Notes*. New York: Viking, 1939.

Garcia, Reloy. *Steinbeck and D. H. Lawrence: Fictive Voices and the Ethical Imperative*. Muncie, Ind.: John Steinbeck Society of America, 1972.

George, Stephen K., ed. *John Steinbeck: A Centennial Tribute*. Westport, Conn.: Praeger, 2002.

Gladstein, Mimi Reisel. *The Indestructible Woman in Faulkner, Hemingway, and Steinbeck*. Ann Arbor, Mich.: UMI Research Press, 1986.

Gray, James. *John Steinbeck*. Minneapolis: University of Minnesota Press, 1971.

Hadella, Charlotte Cook. *Of Mice and Men: A Kinship of Powerlessness*. New York: Twayne, 1995.

Hayashi, Tetsumaro. *John Steinbeck: A Concise Bibliography (1930–65)*. Metuchen, N.J.: Scarecrow Press, 1967.

Hayashi. *John Steinbeck: A Guide to the Doctoral Dissertations*. Muncie, Ind.: Ball State University, 1971.

Hayashi. *John Steinbeck and the Vietnam War*. Muncie, Ind.: Steinbeck Research Institute, Ball State University, 1986.

Hayashi. *A New Steinbeck Bibliography, 1929–1971*. Metuchen, N.J.: Scarecrow Press, 1973.

Hayashi. *A New Steinbeck Bibliography, 1971–1981*. Metuchen, N.J.: Scarecrow Press, 1983.

Hayashi. *Steinbeck's World War II Fiction, The Moon Is Down: Three Explications*. Muncie, Ind.: Steinbeck Research Institute, Ball State University, 1986.

Hayashi. *A Student's Guide to Steinbeck's Literature: Primary and Secondary Sources*. Muncie, Ind.: Steinbeck Research Institute, Ball State University, 1986.

Hayashi, ed. *A Handbook for Steinbeck Collectors, Librarians, and Scholars.* Muncie, Ind.: John Steinbeck Society of America, Ball State University, 1981.

Hayashi, ed. *John Steinbeck: The Years of Greatness, 1936–1939.* Tuscaloosa: University of Alabama Press, 1993.

Hayashi, ed. *John Steinbeck on Writing.* Muncie, Ind.: Steinbeck Research Institute, Ball State University, 1988.

Hayashi, ed. *A New Study Guide to Steinbeck's Major Works, with Critical Explications.* Metuchen, N.J.: Scarecrow Press, 1993.

Hayashi, ed. *Steinbeck and the Arthurian Theme.* Muncie, Ind.: John Steinbeck Society of America, Ball State University, 1975.

Hayashi, ed. *Steinbeck and Hemingway: Dissertation Abstracts and Research Opportunities.* Metuchen, N.J.: Scarecrow Press, 1980.

Hayashi, ed. *Steinbeck Criticism: A Review of Book-Length Studies, 1939–1973.* Muncie, Ind.: John Steinbeck Society of America, 1974.

Hayashi, ed. *Steinbeck's The Grapes of Wrath: Essays in Criticism.* Muncie, Ind.: Steinbeck Research Institute, Ball State University, 1990.

Hayashi, ed. *Steinbeck's Literary Dimension: A Guide to Comparative Studies,* 2 volumes. Metuchen, N.J.: Scarecrow Press, 1972, 1991.

Hayashi, ed. *Steinbeck's Short Stories in The Long Valley: Essays in Criticism.* Muncie, Ind.: Steinbeck Research Institute, Ball State University, 1991.

Hayashi, ed. *Steinbeck's Travel Literature: Essays in Criticism.* Muncie, Ind.: John Steinbeck Society of America, Ball State University, 1980.

Hayashi, ed. *Steinbeck's Women: Essays in Criticism.* Muncie, Ind.: John Steinbeck Society of America, Ball State University, 1979.

Hayashi, ed. *A Study Guide to Steinbeck: A Handbook to His Major Works,* 2 volumes. Metuchen, N.J.: Scarecrow Press, 1974, 1979.

Hayashi, ed. *A Study Guide to Steinbeck's The Long Valley.* Ann Arbor, Mich.: Pierian Press, 1976.

Hayashi and Thomas J. Moore, eds. *Steinbeck's Posthumous Work: Essays in Criticism.* Muncie, Ind.: Steinbeck Research Institute, Ball State University, 1989.

Hayashi and Kenneth D. Swan, eds. *Steinbeck's Prophetic Vision of America: Proceedings of the Taylor University–Ball State University Bicentennial Steinbeck Seminar Held at Taylor University, May 1, 1976.* Upland, Ind.: Taylor University / Muncie, Ind.: John Steinbeck Society of America, Ball State University, 1976.

Hayashi, Yasuo Hashiguchi, and Richard F. Peterson, eds. *John Steinbeck, East and West: Proceedings of the First International Steinbeck Congress Held at Kyushu University, Fukuoka City, Japan, in August 1976.* Muncie, Ind.: John Steinbeck Society of America, Ball State University, 1978.

Hedgpeth, Joel W., ed. *The Outer Shores,* 2 volumes. Eureka, Cal.: Mad River Press, 1978.

Hughes, R. S. *Beyond The Red Pony: A Reader's Companion to Steinbeck's Complete Short Stories.* Metuchen, N.J.: Scarecrow Press, 1987.

Hughes. *John Steinbeck: A Study of the Short Fiction*. Boston: Twayne, 1989.

Jones, Lawrence William. *John Steinbeck as Fabulist,* edited by Marston LaFrance. Muncie, Ind.: Ball State University, 1973.

Kiernan, Thomas. *The Intricate Music: A Biography of John Steinbeck*. Boston: Little, Brown, 1979.

Levant, Howard. *The Novels of John Steinbeck: A Critical Study*. Columbia: University of Missouri Press, 1974.

Lewis, Cliff, and Carroll Britch, eds. *Rediscovering Steinbeck: Revisionist Views of His Art, Politics, and Intellect*. Lewiston, N.Y.: Edwin Mellen Press, 1989.

Lisca, Peter. *John Steinbeck: Nature and Myth*. New York: Crowell, 1978.

Lisca. *The Wide World of John Steinbeck*. New Brunswick, N.J.: Rutgers University Press, 1958.

Lynch, Audry. *Steinbeck Remembered*. Santa Barbara: Fithian Press, 2000.

Marks, Lester Jay. *Thematic Design in the Novels of John Steinbeck*. The Hague: Mouton, 1969.

Martin, Stoddard. *California Writers: Jack London, John Steinbeck, The Tough Guys*. New York: St. Martin's Press, 1983.

McCarthy, Paul. *John Steinbeck*. New York: Ungar, 1980.

Meyer, Michael J. *The Hayashi Steinbeck Bibliography, 1982–1996*. Lanham, Md.: Scarecrow Press, 1998.

Millichap, Joseph R. *Steinbeck and Film*. New York: Ungar, 1983.

Moore, Harry Thornton. *The Novels of John Steinbeck: A First Critical Study*. Chicago: Normandie House, 1939.

Noble, Donald R., ed. *The Steinbeck Question: New Essays in Criticism*. Troy, N.Y.: Whitston, 1993.

O'Connor, Richard. *John Steinbeck*. New York: McGraw-Hill, 1970.

Owens, Louis. *The Grapes of Wrath: Trouble in the Promised Land*. Boston: Twayne, 1989.

Owens. *John Steinbeck's Re-Vision of America*. Athens: University of Georgia Press, 1985.

Parini, Jay. *John Steinbeck: A Biography*. New York: Holt, 1995.

Pratt, John Clark. *John Steinbeck: A Critical Essay*. Grand Rapids, Mich.: Eerdmanns, 1970.

Railsback, Brian E. *Parallel Expeditions: Charles Darwin and the Art of John Steinbeck*. Moscow: University of Idaho Press, 1995.

Schmitz, Anne-Marie. *In Search of Steinbeck*. Los Altos, Cal.: Hermes, 1978.

Simmonds, Roy S. *John Steinbeck: The War Years, 1939–1945*. Lewisburg, Pa.: Bucknell University Press, 1996.

Simmonds. *Steinbeck's Literary Achievement*. Muncie, Ind.: John Steinbeck Society of America, Ball State University, 1976.

Smith, Joel A., ed. *Steinbeck on Stage & Film*. Louisville, Ky.: Actors Theatre of Louisville, 1996.

St. Pierre, Brian. *John Steinbeck: The California Years*. San Francisco: Chronicle Books, 1983.

Steinbeck [Steinbeck Newsletter] (San Jose State University), 1987–2001. Continued by *Steinbeck Studies,* 2001– .

Steinbeck, John, IV, and Nancy Steinbeck. *The Other Side of Eden: Life with John Steinbeck*. Amherst, N.Y.: Prometheus Books, 2001.

Steinbeck Newsletter (Kent State University), 1968–1969. Continued by *Steinbeck Quarterly,* 1969–1993.

Tedlock, E. W., Jr., and C. V. Wicker, eds. *Steinbeck and His Critics: A Record of Twenty-Five Years*. Albuquerque: University of New Mexico Press, 1957.

Timmerman, John H. *The Dramatic Landscape of Steinbeck's Short Stories*. Norman: University of Oklahoma Press, 1990.

Timmerman. *John Steinbeck's Fiction: The Aesthetics of the Road Taken*. Norman: University of Oklahoma Press, 1986.

Valjean, Nelson. *John Steinbeck, the Errant Knight: An Intimate Biography of His California Years*. San Francisco: Chronicle Books, 1975.

Watt, F. W. *John Steinbeck*. New York: Grove, 1962.

Weber, Tom. *Cannery Row: A Time to Remember*. Kentfield, Cal.: Orenda Unity Press, 1983.

Whitebrook, Peter. *Staging Steinbeck: Dramatising The Grapes of Wrath*. London: Cassell, 1988.

Wyatt, David, ed. *New Essays on The Grapes of Wrath*. New York: Cambridge University Press, 1990.

Cumulative Index

Dictionary of Literary Biography, Volumes 1-309
Dictionary of Literary Biography Yearbook, 1980-2002
Dictionary of Literary Biography Documentary Series, Volumes 1-19
Concise Dictionary of American Literary Biography, Volumes 1-7
Concise Dictionary of British Literary Biography, Volumes 1-8
Concise Dictionary of World Literary Biography, Volumes 1-4

Cumulative Index

DLB before number: *Dictionary of Literary Biography,* Volumes 1-309
Y before number: *Dictionary of Literary Biography Yearbook,* 1980-2002
DS before number: *Dictionary of Literary Biography Documentary Series,* Volumes 1-19
CDALB before number: *Concise Dictionary of American Literary Biography,* Volumes 1-7
CDBLB before number: *Concise Dictionary of British Literary Biography,* Volumes 1-8
CDWLB before number: *Concise Dictionary of World Literary Biography,* Volumes 1-4

J

L

W

ISBN 0-7876-8127-X

90000

9 780787 681272